D0583980

DATE DUE

DEMCO 38-296

THE CAMBRIDGE HISTORY OF LATIN AMERICA

VOLUME VII

Latin America since 1930:
Mexico, Central America and the Caribbean

THE CAMBRIDGE HISTORY OF
LATIN AMERICA

THE CAMBRIDGE
HISTORY OF
LATIN AMERICA

VOLUME VII

Latin America since 1930
Mexico, Central America and the Caribbean

edited by

LESLIE BETHELL

Professor of Latin American History
University of London

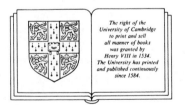

The right of the
University of Cambridge
to print and sell
all manner of books
was granted by
Henry VIII in 1534.
The University has printed
and published continuously
since 1584.

CAMBRIDGE UNIVERSITY PRESS

Cambridge

New York   Port Chester   Melbourne   Sydney

Published by the Press Syndicate of the University of Cambridge
The Pitt Building, Trumpington Street, Cambridge, CB2 1RP
40 West 20th Street, New York, NY 10011, USA
10 Stamford Road, Oakleigh, Melbourne 3166, Australia

First published 1990

Printed in the United States of America

Library of Congress Cataloging-in-Publication Data

Mexico, Central America, and the Caribbean since 1930 / edited by
Leslie Bethell.

p.   cm. – (The Cambridge history of Latin America ; v. 7)

Includes bibliographical references (p.

ISBN 0–521–24518–4

1. Caribbean Area – History – 1810–1945.   2. Caribbean Area –
History – 1945–   3. Central America – History – 1821–1951.   4. Central
America – History – 1951–   5. Mexico – History – 20th century.
I. Bethell, Leslie.   II. Series.
F1410.C1834   1990 vol. 7
[F2183]
980 s–dc20
[972.9]   90–31440
                                                                      CIP

British Library Cataloguing in Publication Data

Latin America since 1930: Mexico, Central America and the Caribbean
(The Cambridge history of Latin America vol. 7)

1. Latin America. History
I. Bethell, Leslie
980

ISBN 0–521–24518–4 hardback

CONTENTS

v

PART THREE. THE CARIBBEAN

PART FOUR. PANAMA

MAPS

GENERAL PREFACE

In the English-speaking and English-reading world the multi-volume Cambridge Histories planned and edited by historians of established reputation, with individual chapters written by leading specialists in their fields, have since the beginning of the century set the highest standards of collaborative international scholarship. *The Cambridge Modern History,* edited by Lord Acton, appeared in sixteen volumes between 1902 and 1912. It was followed by *The Cambridge Ancient History, The Cambridge Medieval History* and others. The *Modern History* has now been replaced by *The New Cambridge Modern History* in fourteen volumes, and *The Cambridge Economic History of Europe* has recently been completed. Cambridge Histories of Islam, of Iran and of Africa are published or near completion; in progress are Histories of China, of Judaism and of Japan.

In the early 1970s Cambridge University Press decided the time was ripe to embark on a Cambridge History of Latin America. Since the Second World War and particularly since 1960 research and writing on Latin American history had been developing, and have continued to develop, at an unprecedented rate – in the United States (by American historians in particular, but also by British, European and Latin American historians resident in the United States), in Europe (especially in Britain and France) and increasingly in Latin America itself (where a new generation of young professional historians, many of them trained in the United States, Britain or continental Europe, had begun to emerge). Perspectives had changed as political, economic and social realities in Latin America – and Latin America's role in the world – had changed. Methodological innovations and new conceptual models drawn from the social sciences (economics, political science, historical demography, sociology, anthropology) as well as from other fields of historical research were increasingly being adopted by historians of Latin America. The Latin American Studies monograph series and the *Journal of Latin American Studies* had already been established by the Press and were beginning to publish the results of this new historical thinking and research.

Dr Leslie Bethell, then Reader in Hispanic American and Brazilian History at University College London, accepted an invitation to edit *The Cambridge History of Latin America,* and began work on the project in 1976. For the first time a single editor was given responsibility for the planning, co-ordination and editing of an entire *History.*

The Cambridge History of Latin America, to be published in ten volumes, is the first large-scale, authoritative survey of Latin America's unique historical experience during the five centuries since the first contacts between the native American Indians and Europeans (and the beginnings of the African slave trade) in the late fifteenth and early sixteenth centuries. (The Press will publish separately a Cambridge History of the Native Peoples of the Americas – North, Middle and South – which will give proper consideration to the evolution of the region's peoples, societies and civilizations, in isolation from the rest of the world, during the several millenia before the arrival of the Europeans, as well as a fuller treatment than will be found here of the history of the indigenous peoples of Latin America under European colonial rule and during the national period to the present day.) Latin America is taken to comprise the predominantly Spanish- and Portuguese-speaking areas of continental America south of the United States – Mexico, Central America and South America – together with the Spanish-speaking Caribbean – Cuba, Puerto Rico, the Dominican Republic – and, by convention, Haiti. (The vast territories in North America lost to the United States by treaty and by war, first by Spain, then by Mexico, during the first half of the nineteenth century are for the most part excluded. Neither the British, French and Dutch Caribbean islands nor the Guianas are included even though Jamaica and Trinidad, for example, have early Hispanic antecedents and are now members of the Organisation of American States.) The aim is to produce a high-level synthesis of existing knowledge which will provide historians of Latin America with a solid base for future research, which students of Latin American history will find useful and which will be of interest to historians of other areas of the world. It is also hoped that the *History* will contribute more generally to a deeper understanding of Latin America through its history in the United States, Europe, and elsewhere and, not least, to a greater awareness of its own history in Latin America.

For the first time the volumes of a Cambridge History have been published in chronological order: Volumes I and II (Colonial Latin America – with an introductory section on the native American peoples and civilizations on the eve of the European invasion) were published in 1984; Volume III (From Independence to *c.* 1870) in 1985; Volumes IV and V (*c.* 1870 to 1930) in 1986. Volumes VI–IX (1930 to the present) will be published between 1990 and 1992. Each volume or set of volumes examines a period in the economic, social, political, intellectual and cultural history of Latin America. While recognizing the decisive impact on Latin America of external forces, of developments within what is now called the capitalist world system, and the fundamental importance of its economic, political and cultural ties first with Spain and Portugal, then with Britain, France and Germany, and finally with the United States, the *History* emphasises the evolution of internal structures. Furthermore, the emphasis is clearly on the period since the establishment of all the independent Latin American states except Cuba at the beginning of the nineteenth century. Seven volumes are devoted to the nineteenth and twentieth centuries and consist of a mixture of general, comparative chapters built around major themes in Latin American history and chapters on the individual histories of the twenty independent Latin American countries (plus Puerto Rico), and especially the three major countries – Brazil, Mexico and Argentina.

An important feature of *The Cambridge History of Latin America* are the bibliographical essays which accompany each chapter. These give special emphasis to books and articles published during the past 20 years or so, that is to say, since the publication of Charles C. Griffin (ed.), *Latin America: a guide to the historical literature* (published for the Conference on Latin American History by the University of Texas Press, Austin, Texas, 1971), which was prepared during 1966–9 and included few works published after 1966. The essays from Volumes I–IX of the *History,* revised and updated, will be brought together in a single bibliographical Volume X, to be published in 1992.

PREFACE TO VOLUME VII

Volumes I and II of *The Cambridge History of Latin America*, published in 1984, were largely devoted to the economic, social, political, intellectual and cultural history of Latin America during the three centuries of Spanish and (in the case of Brazil) Portuguese colonial rule from the European 'discovery', conquest and settlement of the 'New World' in the late fifteenth and early sixteenth centuries to the late eighteenth and early nineteenth centuries, the eve of Latin American independence. Volume III, published in 1985, examined the breakdown and overthrow of colonial rule throughout Latin America (except Cuba and Puerto Rico) during the first quarter of the nineteenth century and – the main focus of the volume – the economic, social and political history of the independent Spanish American republics and the independent Empire of Brazil during the half-century from independence to *c*. 1870, which was, for most of Spanish America at least, a period of relative economic stagnation and violent political and ideological conflict. Volumes IV and V, published in 1986, concentrated on the half century from *c*. 1870 to 1930, which was for most Latin American countries a 'Golden Age' of predominantly export-led economic growth as the region became more fully incorporated into the expanding international economy; material prosperity (at least for the dominant classes); political stability (with some notable exceptions like Mexico during the Revolution) despite rapid social change, both rural and urban; ideological consensus (at least until the 1920s); and, not least, notable achievements in intellectual and cultural life.

Latin America since 1930 is the subject of Volumes VI to IX of the *History*. Volume VI will bring together general essays on major themes in the economic, social and political history of Latin America from the crisis of the 1930s to the crisis of the 1980s. Volume VII is a history of Mexico, Central America and the Caribbean, Volume VIII a history of the nine republics of Spanish South America (from Argentina to Venezuela). Volume IX will have two distinct parts: a history of Brazil since 1930, and general essays on the intellectual and cultural history of Latin America in the twentieth century.

Volume VII is the first to appear of the four volumes on Latin America since 1930. Part One consists of two chapters on Mexico: the first examines the course of the Revolution during the 1930s, and especially during the administration of Lázaro Cárdenas (1934–40), the impact on Mexico of the Second World War, and the nature of the immediate postwar conjuncture; the second examines the period since 1946, with emphasis on economic growth (until the 1980s), social change and political stability. Part Two has a general overview of economic and political developments in Central America from the 1930s to the 1980s and separate chapters on the histories of Guatemala, El Salvador, Honduras, Nicaragua and Costa Rica. Part Three has two chapters on Cuba – the first on the period from the dictatorship of Machado to the dictatorship of Batista, the second on the Revolution – and chapters on the Dominican Republic, on Haiti and on Puerto Rico. Part Four is devoted to Panama, with chapters on the history of the republic since its creation in 1903 and on the history of the Panama Canal Zone.

Many of the contributors to this volume – five British (one resident in the United States), five North American and three Latin American – commented on the chapters of their colleagues. I am especially grateful in this respect to Victor Bulmer-Thomas, James Dunkerley, Alan Knight and John Major.

James Dunkerley also agreed to serve as an associate editor on Volume VII of the *History*. His advice and encouragement as well as his skills as an editor proved invaluable in the final preparation of this volume for publication.

The New York office of the Cambridge University Press has responsibility for the production of the final volumes of *The Cambridge History of Latin America*. Katharita Lamoza was production editor and Nancy Landau copy editor on Volume VII. The index was prepared by Michael Gnat. Secretarial assistance was provided by the staff of the Institute of Latin American Studies, University of London.

Part One

MEXICO

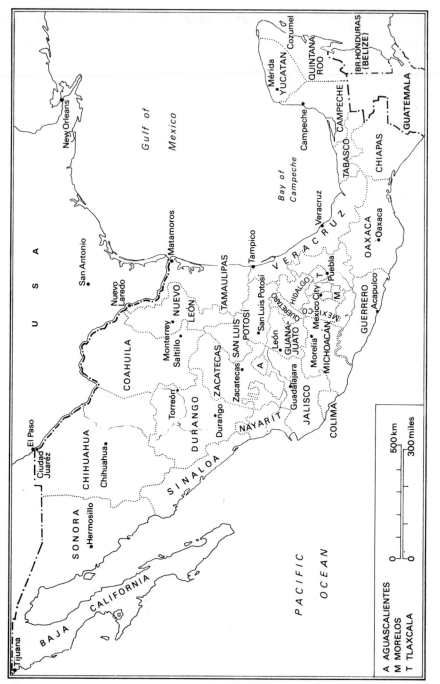

Mexico

1

MEXICO, *c.* 1930−46

After the outbreak of Revolution in 1910, Mexico experienced a decade of armed upheaval followed by a decade of political and economic reconstruction. The revolutionary campaign destroyed the old regime of Porfirio Díaz, liquidated the Porfirian army, and brought to power a coalition that was heterogeneous yet strongly influenced by forces from the north and broadly committed to a project of state-building and capitalist development. If, in regard to these broad *ends,* the revolutionary leadership pursued Porfirian precedents, the *means* they employed were markedly different, as was the socio-political milieu in which they operated. It is true that Mexico's economy had not been revolutionized by the Revolution. The old pattern of export-led capitalist growth − *desarrollo hacia afuera* − had not fundamentally changed. The economic nationalist leanings of the regime, expressed in the Constitution of 1917, led to wrangles with the United States, but there was no complete rupture, and U.S. direct investment in Mexico was higher in 1929 than it had been in 1910. Furthermore, despite the decline in petroleum production after 1921, the economy recovered and grew, at least until 1927. In contrast, Mexico's social and political life was dramatically changed by the Revolution, albeit in an often unplanned and unforeseen manner. The armed mobilization of 1910−20 gave way to new forms of institutional mobilization: peasant leagues, trade unions and a mass of political parties, left and right, great and small. The result was not a decorous liberal politics, such as Francisco Madero had advocated in 1910; but neither was it a closed, personalist, autocratic system of the kind Díaz had maintained to the end. The political nation had expanded to become perhaps the largest in Latin America; a form of mass politics − restless, sometimes radical, often violent and corrupt − was gestating. Such a politics defies neat generalization. It embraced local *caciques* and regional *caudillos* (many, but not all, of them of new, revolutionary provenance);

3

radical agrarianism, as in Morelos, and conservative landlordism, as in Chiapas; revolutionary anti-clericalism and Catholic social action (not to mention Catholic conservative clericalism); an aggressive, ambitious praetorianism and an emergent civilian technocracy.

A major concern of the central government, especially during the presidency of Plutarco Elías Calles (1924–8), was the control and co-optation of these jostling, fissiparous factions. To this end, Calles warred with the Church, on the battlefield and in the schoolroom; he cut down and professionalized the bloated army; he cultivated organized labour, notably the official Confederación Regional Obrera Mexicana (CROM) led by Luis N. Morones; and he tolerated – sometimes tactically encouraged – peasant mobilization. Although state control over civil society thus increased – given the quasi-anarchy of 1910–20, it could hardly deteriorate – the state built by the leaders from Sonora (1920–34) was not an authoritarian leviathan. The rumbustious civil society of the 1920s defied such control. The Cristeros fought Calles to a bloody stalemate; local *caciques* and *caudillos* contested the expansion of state power; and the army rebelled twice. Regional elites, such as the powerful Yucateco planter class, resisted the reforms of self-styled Callistas. Organized workers and peasants often elected to ally with the state, but they usually did so conditionally and tactically, and there were many examples of popular dissidence.

This was a political panorama very different from that of the Porfiriato, with its personalist, centralized control, its narrow *camarilla* politics and outright denial of mass political participation. Under Díaz popular dissidence and protest occurred, but they were usually swiftly put down; they did not achieve institutional form and they certainly did not colonize the Porfirian state itself. What is more, by the 1920s the demands and rhetoric of popular movements – and of *políticos* who sought to capitalize on them – displayed a new radicalism, a new self-confidence. The Revolution had sapped old social certitudes and the deference which accompanied them. The CROM, the dominant official labour confederation, was not simply a cipher of the Callista state: it forced employers to reckon with labour as never before. Independent *sindicatos,* such as the railwaymen and oil-workers, stood further to the left, resisted the embrace of the CROM and relied on their own industrial muscle. Equally, the peasantry, which still constituted the bulk of the population, displayed a different temper compared with pre-revolutionary days. They, after all, had been the shock-troops of the revolution. It is true that the official agrarian reform came only slowly and gradually: by 1930, a mere 9 per cent of Mexico's land – by value – had been transferred to *ejidal* (communal) farms. But such figures are misleading and could arguably underestimate the scale of land distribution; certainly they fail to convey the changes in social relations and *mentalité* which the Revolution ushered in. Landlords retained the bulk of their land, but they did so on different terms, at greater cost. Their resident peons might – on the whole – remain docile; but neighbouring villagers, entitled to petition for land, presented a constant, enervating threat. Landlords thus had to contend with an increasingly organized peasantry and a state which, in its regional and national manifestations, was by no means as congenial or as reliable as its Porfirian predecessor. Some landlords had already gone bust during the upheaval of 1910–20; many now had to contend with heavier taxes, uncertain markets and higher labour costs. The landlord class yearned for the belle époque of the Porfiriato and lamented the rise of troublesome *agraristas* and the rabble-rousing parvenu politicians who abetted them. Some landlords prudently shifted their capital into urban industry and commerce, accelerating the demise of the traditional land-hungry, labour-intensive hacienda. The landlord class (which, of course, varied from region to region) was not eliminated by the armed revolution, but it was severely weakened – in some states, like Morelos, grievously so. Thus, well before the radical surgery of the 1930s, the hacienda system was displaying the symptoms of a progressive debilitating anaemia, and its prospective legatees were already gathering around the sickbed.

Meanwhile, although the extreme nationwide violence of 1910–20 had abated, local and regional violence remained endemic. The massive peasant mobilization engendered by the Cristero revolt of 1926–9 racked centre-west Mexico. In the localities, landlord fought with villager, *agrarista* with Cristero. *Caciques* battled for power; communities, for land or corporate independence. The Sonoran ship of state bobbed on the waves of an agitated society. At times – we may suggest with the benefit of hindsight – Mexico threatened to go the way of Colombia after 1949: that is, towards endemic, self-sustaining, factionalized conflict on the lines of the *Violencia*. That it did not was in some measure due to the statecraft of the victorious faction: of Venustiano Carranza, Alvaro Obregón and, above all, Calles, who never lost sight of the need for national integration and reconstruction. More importantly, Mexico's endemic violence was the outcome of – not the surrogate for – a genuine social revolution. It was not simply the aimless, stultifying violence of entrenched factions, nor the violence recurrently perpetrated by the

Porfirian old regime. And it was accompanied by a range of phenomena, important by-products of revolution: enhanced social and spatial mobility; migration, both national and international; the rise of new entrepreneurial groups and families; expanded educational programmes; *indigenismo* and 'revolutionary' art.

At the close of the 1920s, therefore, the Revolution had already changed Mexican society and politics in important ways. Yet the outcome of the Revolution remained unclear. Its course was still being run, and there were very different views as to where that course should lead. Classes, factions and regions contested with each other; the state's control of civil society grew, but even with Calles' sponsorship of the new official party, the Partido Nacional Revolucionario (PNR) in 1929, that control remained patchy and sometimes tenuous. The broad revolutionary ends of state-building and capitalist development were being advanced, but slowly and in the face of repeated challenges. And there were major disagreements – even among the ruling elite – as to the best means to be adopted.

For a time, during the favorable fiscal and economic conjuncture of 1924–6, the new Calles administration seemed imbued with a certain confidence. Banking reform and public works testified to the state's burgeoning powers. Seeking to implement the constitutional controls which had been placed upon the Church and the petroleum industry, Calles boldly challenged both the Catholics and the gringos. Soon, however, he faced the Cristiada uprising, conflict with the United States and a deteriorating economic situation. The Callista project began to falter; and the President shifted to the right. The assassination of former president (1920–4) and president-elect Alvaro Obregón in July 1928 added political crisis to economic recession, which, in Mexico, antedated the world slump of 1929. Calles now responded with ingenuity and statesmanship. He declined to prolong his own term of office, preferring to exercise power from the wings. Thus, three successive presidents – Emilio Portes Gil, Pascual Ortiz Rubio and Abelardo Rodríguez – governed during the following *sexenio*, with Calles, the *jefe máximo*, acting as the power behind the throne; hence the conventional title of this transitional period, the *maximato*.

The *maximato* was transitional in two senses. First, it witnessed a distinct shift from personalist to institutional rule. Having proclaimed the end of *caudillo* politics, Calles convened an assembly of a new official revolutionary party, the PNR, early in 1929. In the course of that hectic year an Obregonista military revolt was crushed; the Cristero rebellion was brought to a negotiated conclusion; and Ortiz Rubio, the lacklustre PNR candidate, overwhelmed the liberal, anti-reelectionist opposition of José Vasconcelos in the November presidential election. We can, then, date the unbroken hegemony of the official party back to 1929.

Nonetheless, the political institutionalization of the *maximato* was accompanied by growing social conflict and ideological polarization. Herein lay the genesis of Cardenismo, the political movement associated with President Lázaro Cárdenas (1934–40). Like all 'great men', Cárdenas was a product of his times: he lent his name to a period which – Mexican presidential supremacy notwithstanding – moulded him more than he moulded it. It is, however, valid to see the history of Mexico in the 1930s as the story of the rise and rule of Cardenismo: a radical, nationalist project which fundamentally affected Mexican society, and which represented the last, great reforming phase of the Mexican Revolution. The 1940s no less surely witnessed the decline of Cardenismo: the attenuation of its policies, the elimination of its political cadres, the rise of new leaders committed to an alternative project.

No historian questions the importance of Cardenismo, but many disagree as to its character. Traditionally, Cardenismo has been seen by both supporters and opponents of revolutionary orthodoxy as the culmination of the social revolution. Alternatively, Cardenismo has been depicted as a dramatic, radical interlude within the revolutionary process, for some a quasi-Bolshevist deviation. Recent scholarship has once again stressed continuities, though of a different kind: those of state-building, corporatism and capitalist development. Here, Cardenismo fits snugly within the revolution – the revolution, however, as a vehicle not of national redemption and popular radicalism but of statism and capital accumulation.

Any evaluation of Cardenismo must transcend the Cárdenas presidency. Its history is not the history of one man or even of one *sexenio*. Its origins derived from two broad socio-economic trends that intersected with two more specific political crises. In terms of ideology, personnel and class alignments, Cardenismo did indeed hark back to the Revolution of 1910. But it was also prompted by the experience of the depression and the social conflicts and ideological reassessments the depression provoked. If the first was an autochthonous influence, the second bears comparison with the wider Latin American experience. Cardenismo also sprang from successive political crises: that associated with the assassination of Obregón in 1928, which led to the formation of the PNR; and, more important, the battle for control of party and government which culminated in the struggle between Calles, the *jefe máximo,* and Cárdenas, the President, in 1935–6.

This struggle must be seen in terms of its immediate political background: the creation of the official party, the PNR, in 1929; the defeat of the rebellious Obregonista military in the same year; and the manipulation, humiliation and eventual ouster of the effete president Ortiz Rubio in 1932. This sequence of events demonstrated both the gradual solidification of the national regime and the pervasive personal power of Calles, whose control of the succeeding president, Abelardo Rodríguez (1932–4), was less blatant but no less real. Calles' achievement – the maintenance of personal power behind and despite the formal institutionalization of politics he had himself pioneered – was more precarious than many realized. It had earned him numerous and cordial political enemies; and it meant that any incoming president (especially the proud and obstinate Cárdenas, who had witnessed the destruction of Ortiz Rubio at close quarters) would be acutely aware of the dilemma he faced in his relations with the *jefe máximo:* to defer or to defy?

Enemies and critics of Calles and Callismo were the more numerous as a result of the impact of the Depression. Its effect in Mexico was cumulative rather than instantaneous, and it was less serious and protracted than in monoculture economies like those of Chile or Cuba. The country had already suffered falling export prices, deflation and economic contraction since 1926. Between 1929 and 1932 foreign trade fell by around two-thirds; the capacity to import halved; unemployment rose, swollen by the repatriation of some three hundred thousand migrants from the United States. Within the great 'commodity lottery' of the depression, however, Mexico was relatively fortunate. Gold, silver and petroleum, which together made up three-quarters of Mexico's exports, did not suffer so extreme a fall in demand and price as other raw materials; furthermore, employment in the export sector was small (a mere 3 per cent of the non-rural labour force generated two-thirds of Mexico's export earnings), hence the impact on wages, employment and living standards was less marked than in labour-intensive agrarian export economies like Brazil's. Meanwhile, Mexico's large subsistence agricultural sector recovered from the poor harvests of 1929–30 (the climate proved benignly counter-cyclical), while manufacturing industry – catering to domestic demand – was less severely affected than extractive industry and proved capable of benefiting from the country's incapacity to import. A process of import substitution industrialization was thus stimulated by the depression.

Between 1929 and 1932, therefore, Mexican gross domestic product (GDP) may have fallen some 16 per cent. The effect of this recession on the mass of the people is hard to evaluate. Real wages certainly fell (again, the trend may be discerned as early as 1927) and some historians identify a phase of 'frequent but fragmented mobilization' – characterized by strikes, land seizures and hunger marches – coinciding with the economic slump. It is clearer that popular militancy, following the familiar pattern, became more marked as the economy revived, which it did with some rapidity, thanks in part to the reflationary Keynesian policies pursued by Alberto Pani as Secretary of the Treasury (1932–3). Pani boosted the money supply (31 per cent in 1932, 15 per cent in 1933), and sacrificed the peso in the interests of growth. Exports, employment and real wages all revived. By 1934, GDP was back to 1929 levels, the peso was stabilized, and the economic outlook was encouraging. Cárdenas thus came to power as the effects of the depression receded, even though its political impact remained. For many, the *maximato* (1928–34) had meant hard times, and now the presidential succession offered a political *apertura* through which pent-up popular grievances might be channeled.

The political elite's response to the depression was mixed, producing polarization within the nascent PNR. For Calles and his supporters – the 'veterans' – recent events in no way invalidated the existing model of capitalist development based on private enterprise, exports, foreign investment, tight control of labour and a generally 'passive' state. Rather, the model should be refined, not least by curtailing anomalies like *ejidal* agriculture. In 1930 Calles pronounced the agrarian reform a failure: the *ejido* encouraged sloth; the future lay with private, capitalist farming. Efforts were made to bring the reform to a swift conclusion and *ejidal* grants became less frequent after the 1929 peak. Calles was also alarmed by labour agitation: capital needed security if it was to pull the country out of recession, and strikes should be severely discouraged. Calles continued to harp on the old anti-clerical theme, the leitmotiv of 1920s politics, and on the role of education as a means of revolutionary transformation. Minds, not means of production, were the appropriate objects of Sonoran social engineering. The anti-clerical issue was revived and the new Minister of Education, Narciso Bassols, gave fresh stimulus to the policy of laicization (1931). Three years later, in his celebrated Grito de Guadalajara, Calles called for a 'psychological' revolution, a 'new spiritual conquest' to win the hearts and minds of youth for the Revolution. Calles and his 'veterans' clung to the norms and nostrums of the 1920s and, amid the political and social flux of the early 1930s, seemed increasingly a force for conservatism, admired by the right. Fascist examples were indeed uppermost in Calles' mind, and he cited Italy and Germany (as well as the Soviet Union) as cases of successful political education.

Calles appreciated that a new generation, for which the heroics of 1910 were myth or history, and which was increasingly disillusioned with the Sonoran-style revolution, was reaching political maturity. It rejected the ideology of the 1920s – anti-clerical, economically liberal, socially conservative – and advocated radical socio-economic change. It participated in the global shift from cosmopolitan laisser-faire to nationalist *dirigisme*. If, like Calles, it drew on foreign models, it was the New Deal or the economic planning of the Soviet Union (misconstrued, no doubt) which carried weight. Even while Calles and the Callistas still ruled, new men and ideas could not be ignored. After 1930 reformist and interventionist policies were tentatively introduced. A Federal Labour Law (1931) offered concessions with regard to hours, holidays and collective bargaining, in return for closer state regulation of industrial relations. Seen as dangerously radical by the right, it was castigated by the left as fascist, while the more percipient saw that minimum wages could boost internal demand to the advantage of industry. In 1934 an autonomous Agrarian Department was established and a new Agrarian Code for the first time allowed hacienda peons to petition for land grants. The Code also extended guarantees to private farms, this ambivalence reflecting profound divisions within the PNR. From the 1933 party congress emerged a Six Year Plan which, for all its lack of policy detail, embodied elements of the new philosophy demanded by the rising generation of technocrats, *políticos* and intellectuals. Implicitly critical of the Sonoran model, the plan stressed the role of the interventionist state and the need for Mexican resources to be developed by Mexicans; it promised labour minimum wages and collective-bargaining rights; and it underlined the paramount importance of the agrarian question, which required radical solutions including the division of the great estates.

On the eve of the Cárdenas presidency, therefore, the ideological climate was fast changing. But the new ideas coexisted with the old political cadres, who inhibited radical démarches in practice while tolerating rhetorical radicalism which left the substance of their power intact. Nor did the Cárdenas candidacy appear to challenge their position. In choosing Lázaro Cárdenas as the official candidate for the 1934 election the PNR inclined left; but, so the old guard consoled themselves, thereby the better to control the left. Cárdenas had proved himself a radical – within orthodox, institutional terms – while governor of Michoacán (1928–32); but in most respects he was a model *político* whose career had taken him through the ranks of the revolutionary army (where he first served under Calles), through major commands in the 1920s, to the presidency of the party and the Ministry of Defence. A loyal lieutenant – though not an intimate crony – of Calles, he was a key general in the politico-military hierarchy. He had helped crush *cuartelazos* and had seen to the disarming of the *agraristas* in Veracruz in 1932. If he was not Calles' first choice, he was safe: in part, because he lacked a local base (his successor in Michoacán had dismantled what Cardenista machine there was) and in part because he seemed loyal – even dull and obtuse (a reputation reinforced by his austere, honest and puritanical personal life). Although the institutional left within the PNR backed his candidacy, his record did not inspire support among labour or the independent left; the Communists ran a rival candidate, declaring themselves to be 'with neither Calles nor Cárdenas; with the Cardenista masses'.

Once chosen as party candidate, however, Cárdenas began to display a wayward heterodoxy. His 1934 electoral campaign outdid all previous campaigns (save, perhaps, Madero's in 1909–10) in its scope and activity. Travelling some eighteen thousand miles, visiting towns, factories and villages, Cárdenas set a peripatetic style which was to be continued in office, taking him repeatedly into the provinces (over a year of the *sexenio* was spent outside Mexico City), sometimes to remote communities and 'well-nigh inaccessible places' which, to the consternation of the presidential entourage, had to be reached on horseback or even, it was said, by swimming ashore from the presidential ship.[1] The election campaign and the subsequent itineraries gave the president first-hand knowledge of conditions and, it is plausibly argued, served to radicalize him. Coupled with his reformist, especially *agrarista,* rhetoric, these trips raised popular expectations and demands; and they brought home to remote communities the realities of presidential power. No doubt Calles and the conservatives reasoned that this initial bravura would burn itself out; that once

---

[1] Rees, Mexico City, 19 December 1939, FO (Foreign Office) 371/24217, A359, Public Records Office, London.

Cárdenas was ensconced in the presidential palace, the old song would still apply and:

> 'el que vive en esta casa / es el señor presidente
> pero el señor que aquí manda / vive en la casa de enfrente'.[2]

After the rousing electoral campaign the election itself was a dull affair, quite unlike the battles of 1929 or 1940, and the new president, overwhelmingly elected, took power in December 1934 'in the greatest possible calm'.[3] Stability and continuity also seemed served by the composition of the new cabinet, which included Callistas in key positions, outweighing Cárdenas' partisans. Calles' hopes of a continued *maximato* were reflected in a disgruntled public opinion, which saw Cárdenas as another puppet, and in Cárdenas' own fears that he would go the way of Ortiz Rubio. As Cárdenas became acquainted with the apparatus of power, diehard Callistas like Tabasco's governor, Tomás Garrido Canabal – whose anti-clerical excesses now gathered pace – were at pains to embarrass and weaken the new executive.

Callista control was not, however, all it seemed; maybe it never had been. In the provinces, the Callismo of many local *caciques* was necessarily provisional. So long as a Callista allegiance shored up local power, they were for Calles, but a national crisis could induce a rash of defections. This happened in 1935–6. Nationally, where politics were more volatile, Callismo was on the wane. Callistas still controlled key ministries, army commands and labour unions, but a new generation was jostling at the door, nudging aside the 'veteran' generation which had been born in the 1880s and which had won power during the armed revolution. (It should, though, be noted that the newcomers' advancement also required tactical alliances with veterans - Saturnino Cedillo, Juan Andreu Almazán, Cándido Aguilar – who were strong respectively in San Luis, Nuevo León and Veracruz and who were ready to renege on Calles.) This new generation implied a change of character and political emphasis. Its members tended to be more urban and educated, and less conspicuously northern than their predecessors; and, like any rising generation, they fastened on the failings of their forebears (their sins of commission: anti-clericalism, militarism, graft; their sins of omission: agrarian and labour reform), stressing instead

---

[2] Loosely translated as 'the house you see before you / is the president's abode / but the man who calls the tune / lives in the house across the road'; Luis González, *Historia de la revolución mexicana, 1934– 1940: Los días del presidente Cárdenas* (Mexico, 1981), p. 44.

[3] Farquhar, Mexico City, 6 December 1934, FO 371/18705, A706.

the new policies outlined in the Six Year Plan. All this they were free to do, being less bound by the prior commitments of middle age and established careers. The old revolutionaries had fulfilled their 'historic mission', Cárdenas later declared; it was time for a new generation to come forward, 'so that the masses can benefit from different political perspectives, produced by men who are fresh'.[4]

Intra-elite struggles were all the more significant because they coincided with demands and pressures evident in the country at large, which the incoming administration had at once to confront. Rival elites manipulated the masses, but the masses could, to an extent, manipulate the rival elites too. Thus, any president who bucked the control of the *jefe máximo,* and who sought mass support in opposition to Callista conservatism, had to move left towards the increasingly militant unions and restless peasantry. For now, as the economy revived, strikes proliferated. Official figures, which show a prodigious increase (13 strikes in 1933; 202 in 1934; 642 in 1935), are significant but misleading: they reflect a shift in government policy as more strikes were recognized as legal. Though figures of de facto strikes are hard to obtain, the impressionistic evidence is overwhelming as stoppages affecting the railways (long a focus of labour militancy), the mines and smelters, the oil camps and textile factories. The year 1934 witnessed an unprecedented spate of strikes in these and other, less crucial sectors. Sixty were pending in Mexico City alone as Cárdenas took power in December; and the early months of 1935 witnessed major strikes against the Aguila Oil Co., on the trams and railways, and on commercial haciendas, as well as attempted general strikes in Puebla and Veracruz. Cárdenas, it has been said, inherited a 'syndical explosion'.[5] Grievances were basically economic (some strikers sought to claw back what they had lost in the pay cuts of recent years), but they were aired with a new-found militancy. A high proportion of strikes was classified as sympathetic: the electricians of Tampico, striking in support of the workers' claim against the Huasteca Oil Co., received support as far afield as San Luis Potosí, Guanajuato, Yucatán, Michoacán, and Jalisco.

This state of affairs reflected both the radicalization of national politics and the growing sophistication of working-class organization. Since its heyday in the 1920s, the CROM had suffered a hemorrhage of support. In 1929 Fidel Velázquez and the *cinco lobitos* split away, taking with them

[4] González, *Los días del presidente Cárdenas*, p. 57.
[5] Alicia Hernández Chávez, *Historia de la revolución mexicana Periodo 1934–1940: La mecánica cardenista* (Mexico, 1979), p. 140.

thirty-seven unions, including the bulk of the capital's organized labour; they were followed by the electricians and railwaymen – traditionally well organized and militant – who formed the Cámara de Trabajo. In 1933 the CROM divided again as Vicente Lombardo Toledano's radical wing broke with the Morones leadership. The CROM – politically weakened since Obregón's assassination – found its numbers much reduced and its monopoly of labour representation within the PNR and on labour arbitration boards lost beyond recall. Meanwhile, the dissidents – Velásquez's Federación Sindical del Distrito Federal (FSTDF), the Lombardista CROM, and other anti-CROM groups, including the electricians – came together in October 1933 in the Confederación General de Obreros y Campesinos de México (CGOCM) which espoused a form of more militant, nationalist syndicalism. The Communists, too, driven into clandestinity after 1929, formed a new labour front, the Confederación Sindical Unitaria de México, (CSUM), which recruited with success among teachers and rural workers (notably in the Laguna and Michoacán), in the capital, and in the conservative bastion of Nuevo León. The diatribes of Calles and the CROM against communism were not entirely paranoid; by 1935 the party line was impelling the CSUM and the Partido Comunista Mexicano (PCM) towards a common front with progressive forces, which would include Lombardo's CGOCM and, eventually, Cárdenas' administration.

Meanwhile, the spectre of *agrarismo* revived. After the great upheaval of 1910–15, agrarian protest had ebbed or been channeled into the official and often manipulative reform, which peaked in 1929. The CROM had swollen its paper strength with *campesinos,* and *agraristas* had been recruited to fight the Cristeros. Old agrarian trouble spots, such as Zapata's Morelos, Cedillo's Valle del Maíz, had experienced the sedative of controlled reform; others – the Laguna, Michoacán – the concerted repression, physical and ideological, of governors, generals, landlords and not a few clerics. By the 1930s, however, the dammed streams of *agrarismo* again swelled and threatened to burst their banks. Already, some state governors had given a lead: Adalberto Tejeda in Veracruz, Portes Gil in Tamaulipas, Cárdenas himself in Michoacán. Although this was often for their own political advantage, it still required mobilization, which in turn offered experience and opportunity. But local mobilization was precarious and – in both Veracruz and Michoacán – it soon collapsed. The election and the new presidency, however, raised agrarian expectations – and revived landlords' fears. The anonymous struggle going on in much of the countryside now became vocal, noticeable and directly relevant to the struggle for national power. The early thirties witnessed sporadic land seizures, recurrent rural strikes and renewed agitation, local and national, for land distribution. The Rodríguez administration was pushed reluctantly towards reform; that of Cárdenas enthusiastically embraced it.

The radicalization of the regime was closely bound up with the struggle for power which dominated 1934–6 and in which Calles' conduct was no less important than that of Cárdenas. Known as a clerophobe, hostile to *agrarismo* and labour agitation, Calles proved unable to adjust to the changing climate of politics. When obsequious *políticos* came to pay court at Cuernavaca, Calles expounded on the industrial subversion jeopardizing the economy, and although reserving kind words for Cárdenas, he lambasted Lombardo and the radical labour leaders, denouncing such 'bastard interests' and hinting that a repeat of the presidential ouster of 1930 was on the cards. These 'patriotic declarations', as the Callista press called them, were promptly and widely published. As the confrontation built up, Calles drew attention to Cárdenas' weaknesses, denounced the 'Communist tendencies' he discerned at work and pointed to the wholesome example set by the fascist states of Europe.[6] Given both his character and the political pressures acting upon him, Cárdenas could not but respond; he would be no Ortiz Rubio. Anti-Callista leaders – radicals like Tejeda, opportunists like Almazán – were keen for the *jefe máximo* to get his comeuppance. So, too, were public opinion and organized labour. On the left, the threat of a renewed *maximato*, of repression, even a drift towards fascism, engendered an urge for solidarity, which complemented the official line now emanating from Moscow. Mexico in 1934–5 was fertile soil for popular frontism.

As Cárdenas and his allies moved to the attack, they faced a still formidable opponent. Calles might graciously proclaim his retirement from politics (as he did in June 1935, following the furor of the Cuernavaca interview) and he might roguishly confess his preference for golf over politics as he did in December, returning from the United States. Yet his continued ambition and antipathy to the new regime's course could not be disguised, and powerful groups were pushing him towards confrontation. Business feared the militancy of labour and looked to Calles for reassurance, while the urban middle class resented the rash of strikes disrupting city life. Plenty of Callista *políticos* survived in the Congress,

[6] John W. F. Dulles, *Yesterday in Mexico: A Chronicle of the Revolution, 1919–1936* (Austin, Tex., 1961), pp. 636–9; González, *Los días del presidente Cárdenas*, p. 78.

party, CROM and state governments, their political futures mortgaged to that of the *jefe máximo*. The army, too, had its restless elements, while the United States had misgivings about the drift of policy and hoped – maybe worked – for accommodation rather than confrontation between the two. Experienced *políticos*, like the Callista Juan de Dios Bojórquez, now Secretary of Gobernación, similarly advised compromise, arguing that confrontation could lead to civil war and shatter the precious political stability achieved by the Sonorans. As this scenario suggests, elements of bluff entered political calculations. Calles could destabilize the new administration, but at great risk to his life's work. Cárdenas, if he rejected compromise, would have to call on the support of the left, which implied new, radical commitments.

As it was, Cárdenas called Calles' bluff. He checked out the loyalty of key *políticos* and generals and, in the wake of the Cuernavaca interview, sacked several Callista cabinet ministers, promoting his own men including some anti-Callista veterans (in this crisis, the support of such figures as Cedillo, Almazán and Portes Gil was crucial). As the great electors were seen to shift, the Callista bloc in Congress crumbled. The PNR now experienced a gentle purge; obstreperous state governors, like the notorious Garrido Canabal of Tabasco, were ousted; and local *caciques* readily changed their colours. The army was a tougher proposition, but here Cárdenas was helped by his long years of service in and solicitude for the military, as well as by the loyalty of Manuel Avila Camacho who, as Subsecretary of War, had assiduously promoted the Cardenista cause. Army commands were shuffled, safe men were seeded throughout the country and the police were similarly renovated. This political house-cleaning, well under way by mid-1935, enabled Cárdenas to achieve a stalemate; next year, the President could go on the offensive, confident of victory. In the meantime, one consequence of this battle was the rapid turnover of generals and *políticos*. By 1938, of the 350 generals Cárdenas had inherited, 91 had been removed. Casualties now included old allies like Saturnino Cedillo, state boss of San Luis, and Joaquín Amaro, the chief architect of the professional post-revolutionary army. Even as it entered its radical, institutional phase, the Revolution retained a Darwinian character.

The struggle within the elite affected the temper of national politics to an unusual degree. Cárdenas, for example, set out to rein in the extreme anti-clericalism which had been the hallmark – and probably the most hated feature – of Callismo. After the brief truce between Church and state in 1929, official anti-clericalism revived in 1931; when Cárdenas took office, Garrido's anti-clerical excesses continued unabated, while some seven thousand Cristeros were still active in a hopeless cause in the north and west. Cárdenas played a careful hand. Though he had treated the Cristeros more decently than most army commanders, he was tarred with the anti-clerical brush. He still rehearsed the old theme of clerical oppression; and his educational policy, with its stress on socialist education, was calculated to inflame Catholic sensibilities. But political wisdom conspired with personal moderation in dictating a degree of détente. The anti-clerical issue conveniently distanced the new regime from the old; Calles continued to plant anti-clerical barbs, but Cárdenas was more circumspect; and Garrido, importing his red-shirt thugs from Tabasco to Mexico City (where he briefly served as Minister of Agriculture), incurred both Catholic protests and presidential displeasure, which led to his fall. Catholics, it was said, were heard crying, 'Viva Cárdenas' in the streets of the capital. Thereafter, the stricter anti-clerical regulations (limiting the number of priests and churches, and the dissemination of religious literature) were progressively relaxed, to the delight of the faithful and to the relief of the devout U.S. ambassador Josephus Daniels. Socialist education, the President was at pains to point out, combated fanaticism, not religion per se; he was even seen to hug a priest in public. While a few *enragés* continued to pen their anti-clerical tracts and vandalize churches, they were a dwindling minority. By the time they were written, Graham Greene's famous jeremiads were already out of date.

The counterpoint to this cessation of hostilities between Church and state was mounting class conflict. The President's cultivation of mass support and pugnacious rhetoric appeared to encourage this, but the Cárdenas government responded to demands as much as it initiated them. The break-up of the CROM heralded a more militant working-class politics, involving competitive recruitment by rival unions and *políticos*. The unions rallied behind Cárdenas, demonstrating against Calles' anti-labour declarations, and fighting street battles with Callista and conservative opponents (like the fascist Gold-shirts). And if the urban working class was in the forefront of such semi-official mobilization, the peasantry did not remain inert. Again, spontaneous movements meshed with the intra-elite struggle to help form a new radical coalition. Nationally, *agrarista* organizations, like the Confederación de Campesinos Mexicanos (CCM), had backed Cárdenas for the presidency. Locally, embattled *agraristas,* like those of Chiapas facing a hostile governor, now found they could look to a sympathetic 'centre', which could, in turn, mobilize *agraristas* against

Callismo. As the pace of agrarian reform quickened, revolutionary 'veterans' soon figured as victims: Calles and his family; the Riva Palacio brothers, bosses of Mexico state, who faced expropriation and expulsion from the official party; governors Villareal of Tamaulipas and Osornio of Querétaro, undermined by *agrarista* opposition; Manuel Pérez Treviño, *cacique* of Coahuila and Cárdenas' right-wing rival for the presidential candidacy in 1934, who suffered with others from the great Laguna *reparto* of 1936. Official *agrarismo* was already a proven weapon when it was deployed, perhaps most blatantly, in the ouster of Cedillo in 1938.

By then, the national schism had been long resolved. Cárdenas' deft combination of tactical alliance and popular mobilization had toppled the *maximato* and brought the era of Sonoran rule to an end. Following a six-month absence in the United States, Calles had returned – to a chorus of condemnation – late in 1935. As the polemics and street violence resumed, the administration took advantage of a terrorist attack on a Veracruz train to crack down. Police swooped on the leading Callistas: Morones, Luis León, and Calles himself, who was found in bed at his ranch near the capital, recovering from influenza and reading *Mein Kampf.* Still immersed in Hitler's rant – the story went – he was bundled onto a plane for the United States. By the spring of 1936, therefore, Cárdenas had rid himself of Calles' tutelage, affirmed his presidential power, and demonstrated an unexpected combination of steel and acumen. All this had been achieved without significant violence. Institutional conflict was pushing the *ultima ratio* of force into the background, at least at the upper level of politics, where 'sordid killing, as a way of enforcing the official will . . . well-nigh disappeared' during the *sexenio.*[7] In the process, popular demands and mobilization had necessarily been stimulated, the administration 'charting a course with an unknown destination', which would only become clear as the radical reforms of 1936–8 unfolded.[8]

Agrarian reform was the regime's key policy in 1936–7. It served both as a political weapon to cut down opponents and as an instrument to promote national integration and economic development. But its instrumentality – stressed by recent scholarship – should not be exaggerated. Reform was also a response to popular demands, often sustained in the face of official

---

[7] Frank L. Kluckhohn, *The Mexican Challenge* (New York, 1939), p. 3. At local level the decline of political violence was slower and more patchy.

[8] Nora Hamilton, *The Limits of State Autonomy: Post-revolutionary Mexico* (Princeton, 1982), pp. 144–5.

opposition in states where *agrarismo* was politically suspect: Sonora, Chiapas, Veracruz. None of this was new, but the agrarian reform was now carried farther and faster, in pursuit of grander national objectives. Where Calles had pronounced the reform finished, Cárdenas – backed by the vocal *agrarista* lobby – saw it as a means to transform rural society, and with it the nation. With his provincial Michoacano background, Cárdenas entertained a genuine sympathy for the *campesino,* a taste for the rustic life and a certain puritanical antipathy to the city (which made him the butt of cosmopolitan wits). Unlike his Sonoran predecessors, he conceived of the *ejido* not as a temporary way station on the road to agrarian capitalism nor as a mere political palliative, but as the key institution which would regenerate the countryside, liberate the *campesino* from exploitation and, given appropriate back-up, promote the development of the nation. In this respect, the new device of the collective *ejido,* which for the first time made feasible the wholesale expropriation of large capitalist farms, was to be crucial. Finally, the *ejido* would be the political training-ground of an educated, class-conscious peasantry. At the height of the *agrarista* campaign, no bounds were set to the *ejido*'s potential: 'If the *ejido* is nurtured, as has been so far planned', Cárdenas declared, 'it is possible that the *ejidatarios* may be able to absorb all the land which today remains outside their jurisdiction'.[9]

Such a project might be termed Utopian, naive and populist, but it certainly cannot be seen as a strategy for industrial development, favouring capital accumulation. Nor, of course, was it seen in those terms at the time; on the contrary, it incurred the hostility of landlords and bourgeoisie alike.

This *agrarista* ascendancy – brief and anomalous within the history of the Revolution – must be seen within the contemporary context. The old project of export-led growth (with agriculture an important source of foreign exchange) had palpably failed, leaving once dynamic, commercial regions like Yucatán and the Laguna depressed and undercultivated. The social tensions first released by the Revolution, and subsequently compounded by the economic slump and the Calles–Cárdenas conflict, demanded resolution. A new generation, impressed with foreign, *dirigiste* examples and concerned to distance itself from its politically bankrupt predecessor, now sought power. This generation was more urban and less plebeian in origin than the revolutionary veterans, but it hailed from

[9] González, *Los días del presidente Cárdenas,* p. 114.

central rather than northern Mexico – hence, it showed greater sympathy to peasant interests – and it was convinced of the need for radical measures. Thus, while other Latin American regimes responded to the pressures of the 1930s through political reform, proletarian mobilization and economic nationalism, the Mexican government was unique in adding to these responses a sweeping agrarian reform – proof of the *agrarista* tradition which lay at the heart of the popular revolution and which now infused official thinking. *Agrarismo,* once equated by many with Bolshevism, was now politically respectable – even politically required. The jargon of *agrarismo* permeated political discourse; it inspired art, literature and cinema (not always to great aesthetic effect); it won both devotees and time-servers – not least within the burgeoning agrarian bureaucracy and among local *caciques*. Such sudden, superficial conversions did not, of course, augur well for the longevity or purity of the *agrarista* campaign.

Meanwhile, the achievements were impressive. By 1940, Cárdenas had distributed some 18 million hectares of land to some 800,000 recipients; *ejidos* now held 47 per cent of cultivated land, compared with 15 per cent in 1930; the *ejidal* population had more than doubled (from 668,000 to 1.6 million), and the landless population had fallen from 2.5 million to 1.9 million. As government revenue swelled with economic recovery, resources were channeled into agriculture. Compared with others, this administration 'worked miracles' in the provision of agricultural credit, which took a massive 9.5 per cent of total expenditures in 1936, the new National Bank of Ejidal Credit receiving the lion's share.[10] Additional resources went to irrigation, roads and rural electrification although these infrastructural investments probably benefited private agriculture more than the reform sector. Meanwhile, the *campesinos,* like the urban workers, were urged to organize, and their organizations – numerous, disparate, but growing in size and militancy – were increasingly linked to the state apparatus. In 1933, the CCM had backed the Cárdenas candidacy; two years later, Portes Gil assumed the task of forming a central peasant confederation, under the aegis of the PNR; thus, the nucleus of the future Confederación Nacional Campesina (CNC) (1938) was created.

The Cardenista agrarian reform, however, was not conducted in gradual, bureaucratic style, as reforms before and (usually) since have been.

[10] James W. Wilkie, *The Mexican Revolution: Federal Expenditure and Social Change Since 1910* (Berkeley, 1970), pp. 136–40.

Rather, it was launched with 'terrific fervour' and punctuated with dramatic presidential initiatives.[11] In regions of long-standing agrarian conflict the climate changed overnight; beleaguered *agraristas* suddenly found the weight of the 'centre' behind them. A classic case was the Laguna. A major centre of agrarian conflict and rebellion during the revolution, the region had known 'constant peasant agitation' during the 1920s, despite the hostile political climate.[12] Though the bulk of the Laguna workers were proletarians, wholly or partly employed on the cotton estates, they were by no means immune to the appeal of land reform, especially given high seasonal unemployment. Thus, classic 'proletarian' demands – for better pay and hours – coexisted with repeated petitions for land grants. The bad conditions (such that 'no self-respecting urang-outang would tolerate')[13] were exacerbated by the slump in cotton production in 1931–2. As the Communist Dionisio Encina took the lead organizing the peons, landlords responded with their habitual methods: violence, strike-breaking and company unions. They also thought it prudent to initiate a cosmetic reform, and two small land grants were made late in 1934, but the next year, labour troubles multiplied, and in May 1936 a general strike was called. As in the case of the later railway and oil expropriations, the government now stepped in to settle the dispute in radical fashion; labour disputes thus led to major restructuring of property relations. In October 1936, Cárdenas personally intervened and decreed a sweeping reform whereby three-quarters of the valuable irrigated land and a quarter of the non-irrigated were turned over to some thirty thousand *campesinos*, grouped in three hundred *ejidos*. Among the victims were several foreign companies and at least five revolutionary generals: 'The Revolution gave me the land', one observed philosophically, 'and the Revolution is taking it away'.[14]

The Laguna expropriation was unprecedented in scope and character. The 1936 expropriation law was invoked for the first time, and large commercial estates were handed over, in bulk, to their employees – to peons, not villagers. This novel expropriation demanded a novel approach. The regime opposed the fragmentation of large, productive units, and the beneficiaries followed official guidance in voting four to one in favour of collective *ejidos* rather than individual plots. Each collective would share

[11] R. H. K. Marett, *An Eye-witness of Mexico* (London, 1939), p. 142.

[12] Clarence Senior, *Land Reform and Democracy* (Gainesville, Fla., 1958), p. 52.

[13] Pegram, in Murray, Mexico City, 21 April 1936, FO 371/19792, A3895.

[14] González, *Los días del presidente Cárdenas*, p. 103.

land, machinery and credit and would be run by elected committees; the harvest would be shared among workers in proportion to their inputs of labour ('from each according to his labour': this was, at best, socialism; not, as critics alleged, communism). The Ejidal Bank would supply credit, technical advice and general supervision; the *ejido* itself would provide a range of educational, medical and recreational services. The performance of the Laguna collectives – key items of the Cardenista project – merits analysis, which must logically extend beyond 1940. Initially, landlords and businessmen confidently predicted failure: 'Give them two years and they'll crawl back on their hands and knees begging to be put back to work for their old employers'.[15] This did not happen. Cotton production (which was 70 per cent *ejidal* in 1940 compared with 1 per cent in 1930) rose immediately after expropriation, stabilized in the late 1930s, fell with the onset of the war and then boomed after 1941. Other crops, such as wheat, displayed an even more rapid increase. Collective farming thus proved capable of delivering the goods, in a material sense. Productivity, it is true, was reckoned to be lower on the collectives than on private farms; but the latter, representing the better irrigated land which landlords had conserved, enjoyed higher levels of capital investment. Indeed, here, as elsewhere in Mexico and Latin America, one major effect of the agrarian reform was to stimulate more efficient farming in the private sector. Meanwhile, with the active support of the Ejidal Bank, the standard of living of the Laguna *campesinos* rose, both absolutely and relatively, at least until 1939. Rural minimum wages, equal to the national average in 1934–5, were a third higher in 1939. There was, too, a perceptible increase in consumer spending, in literacy (hence a 'tremendous increase' in newspaper circulation) and in levels of health: on this, observers, both sympathetic and critical, agreed. And such quantifiable improvements were not all. With literacy and self-management the *campesinos* were thought to display new skills, responsibility and dignity. 'Before we lived like beasts. Now, at least, we are men and as we increase the crop, we earn more', one traveller was told.[16] Enhanced material and physical security went together: political unrest subsided and it was no longer de rigueur to carry pistols in the Laguna.

Nevertheless, the success of the experiment depended on favourable circumstances, on demand for cotton (which dipped in 1939–41 and

---

[15] Senior, *Land Reform and Democracy*, p. 97.
[16] Dutton, Torreón, 4 January 1939, FO 371/22780, A1015; Fernando Benítez, *Lázaro Cárdenas y la revolución mexicana, Vol. 3: El cardenismo* (Mexico, 1978), p. 66.

again in 1945–7); on adequate supplies of water (which even the new Lázaro Cárdenas dam, completed in 1946, could not guarantee); and, above all, on political back-up. Although Cárdenas was alert to the Laguna's problems, and the Ejidal Bank was generous, 1941 saw a new administration and an immediate change in priorities. The Ejidal Bank now imposed a more rigorous 'economic' policy, 'non-economic' projects were stringently cut back, credit was allocated more parsimoniously and the bank and its creditors had to resort to private sources, such as the Anderson Clayton Co. Parcellized *ejidos* now began to replace collectives, and within the collectives a payment system geared to incentives was introduced. The Central Union, the combative *ejidatarios'* association, found itself both losing control of economic resources (such as the machinery centres, which were transferred to the Ejidal Bank in 1942) and facing direct political competition as the government cut back its funds, alleged Communist influence (which had certainly grown during the early 1940s) and promoted the rival CNC. *Campesino* unity, which Cárdenas had tirelessly advocated and actively fostered, was shattered. The old leadership of the 1930s lost ground, and the Laguna became a site of factional squabbles. Thus was lost the best defence against bureaucratic sclerosis and corruption – which, already incipient in the thirties, reached grand proportions in the following decade.

In these new circumstances, the defects of the experiment were cruelly exposed. Like many Cardenista reforms, it was the result of hasty improvization; it needed time and solicitude to succeed. The original *reparto,* like others of the time, had been accomplished in six weeks, retaining the original 'crazy quilt' pattern of cultivation. It had left the landlords in control of the choice land and, above all, it had distributed the available land among too many recipients – including many non-resident migrants. These defects, of course, contained their virtues – speed, continuity of production, generosity of allocation – and, given will and time, might have been corrected. But after 1940 the will was lacking, and as population grew, the Laguna *ejidos* could no longer support the families crowded upon them. Here, as elsewhere, collectives underwent marked stratification between full *ejidatarios* and de facto proletarians. This the market encouraged and the government allowed. Egalitarian alternatives – involving the movement of population and drastic official intervention – were mooted; some argued that instead of 'distributing land among men' according to the classic *reparto* principle, the regime should 'distribute men among land', that is, 'place, in each unit of production, the number of men necessary to

carry out that production without destroying the unity [of the enter-
prise]'.[17] Though entirely rational, such a solution would scarcely have been
popular – as, indeed, the advocates' slogan 'haciendas without hacendados'
tends to confirm. Cardenismo was not Stalinism. If reform was to be swift,
ample and popular, defects were inevitable, which only later administrations could correct. This they chose not to do.

In terms of origins, scope, speed and outcome, the Laguna reform set
precedents which were followed elsewhere: in the Mexicali Valley, where
the Colorado Land Co. was expropriated in favour of *ejidadarios,* individual
and collective, of smallholders and colonists; in Sonora, where the Yaqui
and Mayo Indians won partial restitution of their lands; in Michoacán,
where the properties of the Cusi family – progressive, socially conscious
Italian entrepreneurs – were handed over, intact, to some two thousand
campesinos grouped in nine *ejidos.* The south, too, long the preserve of
the plantocracy, now experienced sweeping collectivist reform. Most
dramatic – and least successful – was the great Yucatán reform, which
closely followed the Laguna precedent. Because the *henequen* industry had
declined steadily since the First World War boom, the opportunity cost of
the reform was low and the demands of social justice all the more compelling. Moreover, reform offered a lever whereby the central government
could insert itself into the traditionally intraverted politics of the south-
east. Thus, in August 1937, the President arrived in the peninsula along
with a boatload of generals, engineers, bureaucrats, journalists and curious
foreigners. Eighty per cent of the *henequen* estates were at once given over to
thirty-four thousand Maya peons, grouped in more than two hundred
ejidos: it was the 'largest single episode of agrarian reform ever carried out
in Mexico'. Yucatán would join the Laguna as a 'showpiece' of the collective *ejido.*[18] But the problems inherent in this precipitate reform were also
soon apparent. Old productive networks were broken up, leaving some
ejidos without access to the vital rasping machinery, many possessing
henequen plants that were either too old or too young. Recipients, it was
said, included many non-peasants, and the familiar complaints of graft and
bureaucratic oppression were soon aired. But the chief problem – more
acute in Yucatán than in the Laguna or even neighbouring Chiapas – was
the state of the external market. Yucatán, which had cornered 88 per cent

[17] Iván Restrepo and Salomón Eckstein, *La agricultura colectiva en México: La experiencia de La Laguna*
(Mexico, 1975), p. 35.
[18] See G. M. Joseph, *Revolution from Without: Yucatán, Mexico and the United States, 1880–1924*
(Cambridge, 1982), pp. 288–9.

of world sisal trade in 1915, enjoyed only 39 per cent in 1933 and 17 per cent in 1949. From the outset, the socialization of a dependent, declining industry offered a poor showpiece for collectivization.

Even when demand remained buoyant – as it did for coffee – the internal obstacles to successful collectivization were formidable. The last major reform of the Cárdenas years was directed against the Chiapas planters, who had also beaten off peasant and proletarian challenges since the revolution and who, faced with the resurgent *agrarismo* of the thirties, redeployed their old weapons: pre-emptive division of properties, use of *prestanombres,* cosmetic reform, the co-option or elimination of opponents. Even as the reform got under way in 1939, the planters sought to use their processing and marketing facilities to bankrupt the new *ejidos.* Although an extension of the reform to include processing plants helped avert this threat, the change of administration in 1940 had an immediately unfavourable effect. The reform was halted; the large collectives were broken up; the Ejidal Bank and its allied *caciques* came to exercise a corrupt control over the reform sector: 'The Bank became a bureaucratic hacendado, the *ejidatario* a peon of the Bank'.[19] In the 1940 election the *ejidatarios* were reckoned to be the only local supporters of the official candidate. Thus, institutions developed during a phase of genuine peasant mobilization (*c.* 1930–40) soon began to serve as instruments to control – even to 'demobilize' – that same peasantry. When the post-war boom got under way (Chiapas' coffee production grew by two-thirds between 1945 and 1950) it was private agriculture – now basking in a newly benign climate – which benefited.

These spectacular, if problematic, reforms were paralleled by many lesser examples, some following the new, collective pattern (Atencingo, Zacatepec, El Mante), some cleaving to the old principle of individual usufruct. Over time, the first often gave way to the second, and by the 1940s, demands for the individual parcellization of communal lands had become strident and, in places, the source of violent conflict. Furthermore, even where the collective mode survived (as in the Laguna, Chiapas, Atencingo) it tended to produce internal stratification between full beneficiaries on the one hand and whole or semi-proletarians on the other. The result of brief, forced growth, the Cardenista collectives soon wilted in the uncongenial climate of the 1940s. Conventional *ejidos* survived more dog-

[19] Thomas Louis Benjamin, 'Passages to Leviathan: Chiapas and the Mexican State, 1891–1947', unpublished Ph.D. dissertation, Michigan State University, 1981, pp. 247–50.

gedly. They were often the fruits of long-standing agrarian struggles, and the Cardenista *dotación* was the culmination of years of petitioning, politicking and armed protest. Sometimes, as recent scholarship stresses, reform served the interests of opportunistic local elites or was imposed, alien and resented, from above; but even initially reluctant *ejidatarios* showed no desire to revert to peon status. Whatever the motives, the result was a massive transfer of resources that profoundly changed the socio-political map of Mexico. In the short term, it not only enhanced peasant living standards and peasant self-esteem but also shifted the political balance, conferring on peasant organizations a brief moment of conditional power. Conditional because the regime ensured that peasant mobilization was closely tied to the official party; brief because by the 1940s this tie, far from strengthening peasant organization and militancy, now served to bind the peasants to a political structure whose character was fast changing. The demise of the Cardenista project thus involved 'a demobilisation of class solidarity and independent struggle, rather than a disbanding of formal organizations'.[20] The Cardenista organizations lived on, but serving new ends.

Agrarian reform and peasant mobilization were inextricably bound up with the educational policy of the Cárdenas years, and with the commitment to 'socialist' education. Here, however, the administration displayed more continuity. The Sonorans, boosting the educational budget from 4 per cent to 14 per cent of government spending (1921–31), building six thousand rural schools and casting the *maestro* as the carrier of national, secular values, had shown more active commitment in this area than in that of agrarian reform. In education, therefore, the 'active state' was already in being. But with the 1930s came new initiatives which, antedating the Cárdenas presidency, were signalled by the appointment of Narciso Bassols to the Ministry of Education (1931). Young, high-powered and impatient, Bassols was the first Marxist to hold ministerial office. He rescued the ministry from a period of drift (1928–31) and began a phase of aggressive reform, seen by some as the state's response to the Cristiada. Under the guise of 'socialist' education, Bassols promoted the laicization of education through the enforcement of Article 3 of the Constitution: Catholic schools which failed to comply with lay principles were fined and sometimes closed, and Catholic hostility was compounded by Bassols' bold commitment to Mexico's first systematic sex-education programme.

[20] Ibid., p. 251.

These were not individual whims. Behind Bassols stood a phalanx of progressive groups, evidence of the changing ideological climate of the early 1930s. Teachers' associations now advocated a 'frankly collectivist' syllabus,[21] the largest (and not the most radical) teaching union calling for the socialization of primary and secondary education. Similar currents agitated the National University. More broadly, socialist realism became culturally fashionable. And the Six Year Plan included a deliberately ambiguous but significant commitment to education based on 'the socialist doctrine sustained by the Mexican Revolution'. More practically, the plan envisaged a 1 per cent annual increase in the educational budget, which would rise from 15 per cent to 20 per cent of total spending between 1934 and 1940. Finally, Congress bowed to the PNR's recommendation and approved a form of socialist state education that would combat prejudice and fanaticism (read 'clericalism') and instil a 'rational, exact concept of the Universe and of social life'.[22] The commitment to 'socialist' education was therefore inherited by the Cárdenas administration.

'Socialism', of course, meant all things to all men. It had dignified the *étatiste* social Darwinism of Sonorans like Salvador Alvarado; the rampant anti-clericalism of Garrido; the pseudo-radicalism of the CROM. The educational debates of the 1930s revealed (one careful student has calculated) thirty-three different interpretations.[23] Even more than agrarian reform, education was susceptible to rhetorical camouflage. Callistas who by 1930 had turned their back on agrarian reform could still put on a show in the educational arena, the ideal place for displays of middle-aged radicalism. With fascist examples in mind, they hoped to capture the mind of youth and perhaps to divert attention from the miseries of recession. Thus, in his Grito de Guadalajara, Calles could sound like a young radical and an old Jesuit at the same time.

For many, 'socialism' was simply a new label for anti-clericalism, the old staple of Sonoran policy. 'Socialism' and 'rationalism' were used interchangeably. Others took the semantic shift seriously. Bassols stressed the practical role of education, which would stimulate a collectivist ethic; teachers would not only teach but would also 'modify systems of production, distribution and consumption', stimulating economic activity to the

[21] David L. Raby, *Educación y revolución social en México, 1921–1940* (Mexico, 1974), p. 39.
[22] Ibid., pp. 40–1.
[23] Victoria Lerner, *Historia de la revolución mexicana Periodo 1934–1940: La educación socialista* (Mexico, 1979), p. 83.

advantage of the poor.[24] Others went further, making education the central plank in a broad platform of radical reform. It would, the Secretary of
Education asserted, combat capitalist and individualist values and inculcate, especially in youth, 'the revolutionary spirit, with a view to their
fighting against the capitalist regime'.[25] Contemporary literature and
rhetoric suggest that 'many teachers believed it was possible to overthrow
capitalism solely by means of education'; a method which had the merit of
being peaceful and exhortatory rather than violent.[26] Art and poetry – of a
suitably committed kind – would work to the same end.

It was an old Mexican dream, entertained by nineteenth-century liberals and twentieth-century revolutionaries alike: education to change the
social world. As the educational radicals of the 1930s harped on the
familiar themes of Catholic obscurantism, and the liberating alliance of
literacy, hygiene, temperance and productivity, so old, even positivistic,
emphases reappeared in 'socialist' guise. Indeed, some socialist radicals
boasted of their Comtean pedigree. 'Socialism' thus absorbed many of the
developmental obsessions of an earlier generation (the most urgent necessity, an educational bureaucrat argued in 1932, was to 'teach the people to
produce more'; Bassols' 'socialism' has been seen as a surrogate ideology of
modernization).[27] It also embodied the traditional quest for cultural cohe-
sion and national integration. Such continuities helped to explain the
facile conversion to 'socialist' education even of those on the official right.
But there were genuine radicals, too, who saw education as a means to
subvert, not to sustain, old ways. The Soviet model again exerted influence. To old revolutionaries like Luis G. Monzón it offered the only
alternative to a bankrupt capitalism. Soviet methods were imported –
unsystematically and largely unsuccessfully – and Marxist texts circulated, even in the Colegio Militar. Although on the face of it, this
mimetism accorded with the regime's stress on class consciousness and
struggle, the Soviet example was more logically invoked by proponents of
development and productivity. The Soviets were seen less as carriers of
class war than successful exponents of large-scale modern industrialization:
more Fordist than Ford. This appeal depended on the economic circumstances of the time and the radicalization they encouraged, both of which

[24] John A. Britton, *Educación y radicalismo en México. I: Los años de Bassols (1931–1934)* (Mexico, 1976), p. 52.
[25] Farquhar, Mexico City, 24 January 1935, FO 371/18705, A1338.
[26] Raby, *Educación y revolución social*, p. 60.
[27] Ibid., p. 38; Britton, *Los años de Bassols*, p. 17.

had direct impact on education. The resurgent left brandished its educational proposals; a more militant teaching profession (many though by no means all of them, on the left, and a significant minority of them Communist activists) pressed their political, pedagogical and syndical interests. Teachers had been hard hit by the recession and consequent government cuts, and Bassols, for all his radicalism, had been a parsimonious paymaster. Although teachers' numbers swelled through the 1930s, unemployment persisted; teachers' groups often figured in the forefront of local politics (they mounted the only serious challenge to Cedillo in his San Luis fief); and teachers' unions aligned with others out of material interest as well as ideological solidarity.

These factors assisted the official commitment to socialist education, which owed little to popular demand. Fifty thousand marched in the streets of Mexico City to applaud the new programme (October 1934) but the demonstration was one of the last flings of the CROM apparatus. Generally (but particularly in the countryside, for which the reform was especially destined) the popular response was tepid or downright hostile. If, as has been suggested, socialist education was a key device 'to recover the lost sympathy and support of the masses',[28] it was a failure; in fact, however, it was less opportunist populism than grand, somewhat naive social engineering. To a greater extent than the agrarian reform, socialist education came as a revolution from above, and often as an unwanted, blasphemous imposition.

Educational projects proliferated: the important programme for rural schools was greatly extended along with ancillary schemes – the Cultural Missions, the Escuela Normal Rural, the special army schools (a project close to the President's heart) and the 'Article 123' (company) schools. Special efforts were made – again, building on Sonoran precedent – to reach the Indian population, which, defined in terms of those who spoke an Indian language, constituted perhaps one-seventh of Mexico's total population. In this the President, the grandson of a Tarascan Indian, who had made much of the Indian question during his 1934 campaign, lent his personal energy and authority. But the emphases now shifted. *Indigenismo* figured less as an autonomous policy, geared to national integration, than as part of the broad Cardenista offensive against poverty, and inequality. Although the Department of Indian Affairs ran special educational and research programmes (in Chiapas, these were of grand

[28] Arturo Anguiano, *El estado y la política obrera del cardenismo* (Mexico, 1975), p. 45.

proportions), its budget was too small to bear the full burden of *indigenista* policy. Instead, the regime sought to subsume the Indian to the mass of workers and peasants, stressing class over ethnicity: 'the programme of the emancipation of the Indian is, in essence, that of the emancipation of the proleteriat of any country', although particular historical and cultural traits might have to be taken into account.[29] The aim – optimistic if not downright Utopian – was to achieve social and economic emancipation without destroying the fundamentals of Indian culture. The chief impact of government on the Indian was less through specifically *indigenista* programmes than through more general measures that affected Indians as *campesinos:* the rural education programme, and above all the agrarian reform in Yucatán, Chiapas and the Yaqui region (where Cárdenas was well remembered long after). *Indigenismo* itself achieved only limited, often transient, effects. One permanent consequence, however, was the growth of federal power as the Indian question became the preserve of national government, and could even be used to prise open hostile local *cacicazgos.* Even under Cárdenas it became clear that the federalization of the Indian question often meant the substitution of local *patrones* – landlord, *cacique,* priest, labour contractor – by new, bureaucratic bosses, agents of *indigenista* or agrarian programmes, some of them Indians themselves. After 1940 these trends accelerated. The Cardenista hope of achieving integration with equality and cultural survival was bound to fail; the Indians were integrated, but as proletarians and peasants, official clients and (occasionally) official *caciques.*

At the other end of the spectrum, higher education now faced the challenge of 'socialism', which exposed the position of the universities (especially the traditionally conservative, elitist and, since 1929, formally autonomous National University) as bastions of middle-class privilege. Like others in the educational field, this conflict antedated the Cárdenas presidency. In 1933 there had been a polemic between University factions, in which Lombardo Toledano – opposed by Antonio Caso – argued that the university align itself with the new, materialist ideology. Despite student fights and strikes, the liberals retained a precarious control; but, in response, the government cut the university's grant by half. Provincial universities, too, fearful of ideological browbeating, demanded similar autonomous status and at Guadalajara the state governor evicted the defiant university authorities from the premises by force. Many on the left

[29] González, *Los días del presidente Cárdenas,* p. 120.

applauded such humbling of the academic high-and-mighty (Cárdenas himself was said to entertain a healthy dislike of *hombres cultos,* which was often reciprocated).

Meanwhile, the political alarums of 1935 echoed through the halls of academe. In September 1935 a leftist faction of staff and students launched an internal coup and aligned the National University with official, 'socialist' policy. The government could now regularize its relations with the university, reaffirming its autonomy and restoring its subsidy; the university, in return, undertook some new, seemingly radical, initiatives (workers' legal services, 'relevant' social research) which probably represented outward conformity rather than genuine conversion. In addition, the regime created new higher education institutions more to its liking. Some of these, like the National Polytechnic Institute, survived and prospered; others, like the Workers' University, proved ephemeral.

Much more important were efforts and conflicts in the sphere of rural education. Here lay the chief innovation of the Cárdenas years; not in the formal content or organizational structure of education (for which there were ample precedents) but rather in the social and political context within which rural education was undertaken. The administration's commitment was unequivocal. Although the ambitious targets of the Six Year Plan could not be met, between 1935 and 1940 educational expenditure hovered at 12 per cent to 14 per cent of total government spending – levels unattained before or since. In real terms, this doubled Callista spending. Thus, the growth in rural schools, notable under Bassols, continued, and these schools were expected to do much more than inculcate basic literacy and numeracy. The teacher, Cárdenas explained, had a social, revolutionary role, 'the rural teacher is the guide of peasant and child, and must be concerned for the improvement of the village. The teacher must help the peasant in the struggle for land and the worker in his quest for the wages fixed by law'.[30] Nor was this empty rhetoric; just as teachers can impart literacy only where a demand for literacy exists, so teachers can engage in social engineering only when the appropriate parts lie to hand, as they did in Mexico in the 1930s. The *maestro rural* could fulfill his alotted function not because the peasants were an inert, malleable mass, but rather because he responded to actual – or, sometimes, realized latent – demands, especially in the field of agrarian reform. In the classic case of the Laguna collectives rural teachers played a key role in a set of

[30] Lerner, *La educación socialista,* pp. 114–5.

integrated reforms – educational, agrarian, technical, medical. In other cases, the *maestro* was pitched into existing local conflicts and his work necessarily became highly political, contentious and risky. *Maestros* were applauded (or condemned) for agrarian agitation in Chiapas, Michoacán, Jalisco, Colima, Sinaloa and elsewhere. They helped organize the Mixtec pueblos of Oaxaca, demanding 'Tierra y libertad' and a school in every village; in Mexico state they were held responsible for inciting land invasions; in Michoacán they were to be found explaining agrarian legislation, drawing up petitions and pursuing them through the relevant agencies. Critics alleged that hitherto tranquil Arcadias were disrupted by rabble-rousing socialist *maestros;* radicals, though putting the point differently, often liked to think the same. True, *maestros* sometimes stimulated a latent *agrarismo,* occasionally helping to foist *agrarismo* on reluctant communities; but there were also cases where teachers were won over to the agrarian cause by the *campesinos* themselves. Those who 'went to the people' like naive *Narodniki* got short shrift. Conversely, those who succeeded did so not by virtue of shrill agitation, but because they supplied practical help and, by their very presence, living proof of the regime's commitment. They engaged in agriculture, introducing new crops and methods; they placed their literate skills at the community's benefit; and above all, they facilitated that supra-communal organization which has often proved the key to success for peasant movements.

For this they paid a price. There is no surer proof of the real impact of the *maestro rural* than the record of violence which spans the 1930s. This must be seen in terms of the stark polarization which the socialist education programme provoked. If initially some on the left were critical, pointing out that it was illusory to attempt a transition to socialism by means of the superstructural machinery of education, most came round. This was especially the case with the Communists, who soon relinquished this position, which accorded well enough with the Comintern's 'third period', and espoused the programme as eagerly as they did popular frontism. At most a sixth of Mexico's teachers were Communists, but this activist minority was enough to feed the suspicions and assist the propaganda of critics. These were numerous, strenuous and often violent. The growing organization and militancy of the left were paralleled on the Catholic and conservative right – among the hierarchy, the Catholic student movement and lay associations such as the National Union of Parents. Socialist and sex education were their chief targets. Catholic students protested, struck and rioted. Parents voted with their children's feet and absenteeism grew, in both city and countryside; the private (Catholic) schools of San Luis, protected by Cedillo, bulged at the seams. To the extent that 'socialism' meant 'anti-clericalism', and anti-clerical excesses continued under 'socialist' auspices, this Catholic reaction was defensive, even legitimate. But in general the anti-clerical thrust was weakening, and Catholic opposition now focussed on wider issues, like medical services and mixed and sex education, which was denounced as a Communist plot, bringing pornography into the classroom. The Catholic press was appalled that country children – familiar enough with rutting pigs – should be shown pictures of flowers' sex organs.

Catholics also took a stand against *agrarismo* both in the abstract, by defending private property rights, and specifically, by aligning with landlords against *agraristas*. Priests were said to inveigh against the reform and incite mobs to violence (Contepec, Michoacán); they said mass for thugs who had murdered a teacher (Huiscolo, Zacatecas). Clerical influence was blamed for recurrent attacks in the Colotlán region of Jalisco, where in one year forty schools were allegedly put to the torch. Such allegations, of course, were sometimes exaggerated. Furthermore, like the teacher, the priest, was not a free agent. He figured in local conflicts not of his own making. Plenty of rural violence occurred without clerical intromission; it was 'spontaneous' or derived from the incitement of landlords, *caciques,* even state governors. The victims – *maestros* like López Huitrón of San Andrés Tuxtla, murdered in 1939, or the twenty-five *maestros* murdered in Michoacán up to 1943 – stand as a reminder that although the powers of the central government was expanding, they were still limited and liable to falter; they could not guarantee the safety, let alone the success, of their forward agents in hostile territory.

Thus, *maestros* often faced a lonely, dangerous task. Many were ill-prepared, certainly for the 'socialism' (sometimes even for the tuition) they were meant to impart; one critic sneered at them for being former 'motor lorry assistants, breadsellers off the streets, [and] overseers from coffee plantations'.[31] They were ill-paid and, save in cases of integrated reform like the Laguna, they usually lacked local, institutional allies. They often faced popular indifference and hostility. Their syndical organizations were plagued with conflict. With the expansion of education in the early 1930s, large-scale unionization became feasible; the pay-cuts of those years providing the teachers with plenty of grievances. They repeatedly

[31] Murray, Mexico City, 31 October 1935, FO 371/18707, A9693.

demanded better wages (which, in part, they got) and the federalization of education, which would concentrate decision-making with the sympathetic central government at the expense of capricious, state administrations. Although in this field, as in others, federalization accelerated through the decade, it was not wholly achieved. Meanwhile, the Ministry of Education pressed for the formation of a single teachers' union in the face of serious internal divisions (as many as 60 per cent of teachers were said to be Catholics and, despite purges and recruitment drives, the profession was never thoroughly radicalized). Since the left, too, was split between Communists and Lombardistas, unity proved chimerical and internal conflict endemic, to the detriment of morale.

There were permanent gains in the race between population growth and educational provision: literacy rates improved and the school's nationalist, integrating role was enhanced. As a system of socialist proselytization and social engineering, however, the project failed. No matter how congenial or appropriate in zones of *agrarismo* and class conflict, socialist education could not revolutionize capitalist society as a whole. Like many Cardenista reforms, it proved a fair-weather phenomenon, dependent on the briefly benign official climate. Even before Cárdenas left office, the climate began to change. By 1938 financial stringency and renewed opposition (now mobilized against the proposed 'regulation' of Article 3) forced a retreat. The *reglamento* ended as a compromise, the more radical textbooks were withdrawn, the Cultural Missions wound up; private education revived and ambitious educational projects, like those of the Laguna, were phased out. Cárdenas' last New Year message (January 1940) was decidedly conciliatory, as were the speeches of the official presidential candidate, Avila Camacho. And once the latter came to power, these changes gathered pace. 'Socialism' remained, for a time, the official line; but then – given the almost infinite flexibility of the term – it became synonymous with social conciliation and class equilibrium. The discourse of the Sonorans was revived. Educational socialism, like much of the Cardenista project, proved to be an interlude, not a millennium.

The battle against Calles in 1935 had involved a spate of strikes and a significant mobilization of the labour movement. Both continued after the fall of *jefe máximo*: 1935–6 were years when, unusually, Mexican strike action exceeded that in the United States; and 1937 (a year of growing inflation) saw a peak, at least in terms of official strikes. During this period, strikes affected all of Mexico's basic industries – mines, oil companies, railways, textile factories – as well as government services, and commercial agriculture. As in the Laguna, labour protest against foreign companies could presage government intervention and expropriation, in accordance with the doctrine boldly proclaimed in February 1936 by the President on his celebrated trip to the free-enterprise citadel of Monterrey, then hit by strikes and a lockout: if entrepreneurs could not avert industrial paralysis, the state would step in. Labour disputes thus afforded a lever against foreign enclaves. Meanwhile, union organization progressed, culminating in the formation of the new *central,* the Confederación de Trabajadores de México (CTM); and the militancy of labour contributed to the upward trend of real wages. This would not have happened without official backing, which, first evident during the political crisis of 1935, was maintained thereafter, albeit neither uniformly nor uncritically. The administration certainly adopted an interventionist approach to labour relations ('the government', Cárdenas declared at Monterrey, 'is arbiter and regulator of social problems'); arbitration became systematic (though not automatic) and generally favoured the workers' side. There were, however, cases of major strikes being opposed (notably that of the railwaymen in May 1936), and, especially after 1938, the government bent its efforts to pre-empt strikes, in the interests of the economy. Nonetheless, it would be wrong to seize upon these cases and assert the paramountcy of production and class conciliation, hence the continuity of a manipulative *política de masas,* as between Calles and Cárdenas. Intervention, arbitration and *política de masas* meant different things at different times. And under Cárdenas, especially before 1938, they involved active support for unions against business, encouragement as much as mollification of industrial conflict, and radical new departures in the field of workers' control. Again, therefore, Cardenista 'populism' differs in important respects from some of its presumed political kin.

The regime never lost sight of economic realities. It combated what it saw as irresponsible syndicalism (e.g., on the part of the oil-workers). It appreciated that raising wages would deepen the domestic market to the advantage of some sectors of industry. Yet this Keynesian approach cannot be seen as the raison d'être of Cardenista labour policy. A few enlightened businessmen and bankers shared this appreciation, but private enterprise – above all, the nucleus of the national bourgeoisie based at Monterrey – was overwhelmingly hostile and consistently critical of Cardenismo. Nor did this change after 1938. In 1940 business spokesmen were still denouncing the government's 'fantastic policy of unilateral betterment in compliance with promises made to the proletariat'. The new excess profits tax was an example of 'Hitlerite totalitarianism'.[32] If Cárdenas saved the Mexican bourgeoisie from revolution or collapse (which seems doubtful), the bourgeoisie did not show much gratitude.

It is also true that Cardenista labour policy, like Cardenista *agrarismo,* involved an educative or tutelary aspect; a facet of the *estado papá.* The President looked to the gradual maturation of the working class as an organized, unified, responsible entity; organized, so that its numbers would count; unified, so that its strength was not dissipated in fratricidal struggles; and responsible, so that it would not place excessive demands upon an underdeveloped economy recently emerged from recession (for, if it did, the workers themselves would be the main sufferers). From the 1934 election campaign to the 1940 farewell address, therefore, Cárdenas' constant theme was, like Lenin's, 'organize'. Organization required the active support of the state, but it would be wrong to see this as cynical manipulation, evidence of unbroken continuity from Calles and the CROM to Miguel Alemán and the *charrazos* of the 1940s. Nowadays labelled an ardent *étatiste,* Cárdenas in fact conceived of organized economic blocs and classes as the bases of politics. Thus, the surest guarantee of the continuation of his radical project was a powerful, organized working class. The formation of the CTM, the experiments in workers' control and socialist education, and the constant exhortation all served a distant, optimistic vision: a workers' democracy embodying the Cardenista virtues of hard work, egalitarianism, sobriety, responsibility and patriotism. This, roughly, was Cárdenas' long-term 'socialist' goal.

A degree of state tutelage was necessary because the creation of a united labour confederation was a formidable task, unlikely to occur spontaneously. The decline of the CROM had left labour militant but fragmented. But the coincidence of the campaign against Calles with rapid economic recovery afforded an opportunity for regrouping. The National Committee for the Defence of the Proletariat, marshalled by Lombardo against Calles and the CROM, served as nucleus for the emergent CTM, which, at its foundation in February 1936, rallied several key industrial unions prominent in the recent strikes (railwaymen, miners and metal-workers, electricians, printers and tram-workers) as well as the old anti-CROM confederations, Lombardo's CGOCM and the Communist CSUM. Claiming 3,594

---

[32] Rees, Mexico City, 3 January 1940, FO 371/24217, A547; Hamilton, *Limits of State Autonomy,* p. 192.

affiliates and 946,000 members, the CTM dwarfed both the rump anarcho-syndicalist Confederación General de Trabajadores (CGT) and the CROM, although the latter survived (some of its affiliates as company unions) and could still contest CTM hegemony, occasionally by violence, in certain regions and industries (e.g., textiles). Two additional barriers to CTM hegemony were erected by the state: the civil servants' union, the Federación de Sindicatos de Trabajadores en el Servicio del Estado (FSTSE), was prevented from affiliating (the whole question of civil servants' union rights was the subject of intense debate, culminating in special legislation); and, more important, the peasantry was preserved from the CTM embrace, notwithstanding the significant recruitment which had already taken place, chiefly in regions of commercial farming. Peasant organization remained the prerogative of the PNR. Though some residual CTM influence remained in the countryside, the leadership could not challenge the official ruling.

The ideology of the CTM mutated rapidly. During the struggle against Calles its constituent parts had stressed their independence from parties or factions. This commitment – radical, nationalist, autonomous – was carried over into the new CTM, which began life with lusty cries redolent of revolutionary syndicalism. But just as Calles had quietened the CROM, whose infantile noises had been similar, so Cárdenas won over the CTM. In this he was helped by the presence within the CTM of ex-CROMistas like Fidel Velázquez and the *cinco lobitos,* schooled in the Mexico City labour politics of the 1920s. As the CTM gained official subsidies, premises, and places on the arbitration boards, its leaders came to see the virtues of collaboration. For this, three reasons were adduced; the need to defeat the remnants of Callismo, to mount a united front against imperialism (soon to be identified with the Anglo-American oil companies), and to construct a popular front against fascism both international and, some said, domestic ('creole fascism', in Lombardo's phrase).

Indeed Lombardo Toledano now emerged as a pivotal figure in the politics of the period, second only to Cárdenas himself. Born of a once rich but ruined business family, Lombardo had progressed from the philosophical idealism of the Ateneo de la Juventud to Marxism (though he never joined the PCM). By the early 1930s he was a leading figure in the Mexico City intelligentsia – '*the* Mexican Marxist'[33] – active in labour and university politics; and with his secession from the CROM and creation of the

[33] Enrique Krauze, *Caudillos culturales en la revolución mexicana* (Mexico, 1976), p. 328.

CGOCM, he laid the foundation for his subsequent leadership of the CTM. Articulate, autocratic and narcissistic, Lombardo lacked an institutional base, regional or syndical. His power depended on the CTM bureaucracy, and government support (hence, in the 1940s, his ideological contortions to retain both). Having tactically backed Cárdenas in 1935, he now sought to cement the alliance, stressing first an old theme – the national responsibility of the working class – and second, a new one – the threat of fascism. In this context, Communist policy was crucial. Driven into clandestinity in 1929, the Communists remained active in local agrarian struggles as well as key unions, such as the railwaymen, printers and teachers. Although they had opposed Cárdenas' presidential candidacy, they were drawn into the anti-Calles coalition, and backed the CTM; and, providentially, 1935 saw a Comintern volte-face which legitimized – required – full collaboration with progressive, anti-fascist forces. The Mexican delegation returned from the Seventh Comintern Congress pledged to popular frontism, and thus to support for the PNR, the Six Year Plan and the Cárdenas government, now deemed to be a nationalist–reformist regime, quite different from its Callista predecessor. The CSUM therefore merged with the CTM and workers were enjoined to participate in elections. In 1937 the PCM and CTM joined in a common electoral front, in the following year the Communists supported the CTM's assumption of a central role in the new, official corporate party, the PRM. CTM collaboration had proceeded to the extent that CTMistas now held political office at local and national level, including thirty seats in the Chamber.

Within so large a conglomerate, divisions were inevitable. Lombardo and his lieutenants had no love for the Communists. Historical and ideological differences were compounded by their rival institutional bases: the Lombardistas depended on numerous small unions and federations, especially in the capital, and their lack of industrial muscle made collaboration with government attractive; the Communists' strength lay in the big industrial unions – railwaymen, printers, electricians – who leaned towards apolitical syndicalism. Each side battled for control of individual unions, such as the teachers', and of the CTM itself, where the Lombardistas relied on their superior numbers – even if they were paper numbers, dispersed among a legion of affiliates – to offset the Communists' industrial clout. In April 1937 a major schism opened up and the Communists, finding themselves frozen out of key jobs, quit the CTM, taking with them between a half and one-quarter of the membership, including such major unions as the railwaymen and electricians. Cardenista hopes of a united workers' front, apparently dashed, were resurrected as the Comintern came to the rescue. Earl Browder hurried down from the United States, Moscow exerted pressure, and after two months the errant Communists returned to the CTM fold. Some would not go to Canossa: the traditionally independent miners and railwaymen stayed out. But the bulk of the Communists complied, returning to a CTM yet further in fief to Lombardo; they agreed, furthermore, to support PNR candidates in internal party elections and to mute their already temperate criticism of the regime. It was the first of several 'necessary sacrifices' which the PCM, wedded to popular frontism and prodded by Moscow, was to make between 1935 and 1946, and which were to be instrumental in the assembly and maintenance of the Cardenista coalition.

Cárdenas' encouragement of working-class organization under the aegis of the state involved two key cases – railways and oil – in which wholly or partly foreign-owned enterprises, racked by labour disputes, were expropriated and fundamentally reorganized. In a manner analogous to the Laguna collectivization, therefore, labour disputes led to government intervention and experiments in new forms of economic organization (and, in the case of oil, to a major international wrangle). Interpretations differ: were these bold, generous and radical démarches, perhaps indicative of a residual syndicalism in official thinking? Or were they further examples of Realpolitik masked as radicalism, whereby a Machiavellian regime, flaunting its nationalism, off-loaded stricken industries upon workers who had then to subject themselves to the harsh discipline of the market?

The two industries were not directly comparable. While oil production showed a modest increase during the 1930s, the railways were in a parlous state: under-capitalised, over-manned, hit by road competition (which the government's vigorous road-building programme exacerbated) and heavily indebted to foreign bondholders. Indeed, there was a general recognition that some radical reorganization, possibly involving nationalization, was necessary. The traditionally militant railwaymen, organized in 1933 in the new Sindicato de Trabajadores Ferrocarrileros de la República (STFRM), strenuously resisted job losses, with which they were all too familiar (10,000 jobs had been shed in 1930–1). Strikes were called in 1935 and again in May 1936, when, to the disgust of the work force, the government refused to recognize a national strike in support of a new collective contract. The railwaymen's demands were met, but the basic economic problems remained. A year later the administration resolved to tackle than, Laguna-style, by means of a dramatic structural reform. In June

1937 the railways were nationalized, the bonded debt being consolidated with the national debt. After a year of direct government management and prolonged negotiations with the union, the enterprise was placed under workers' control on 1 May 1938. This was not a unique case. Other enterprises – mines, foundries, factories – had been turned over to the work force when labour disputes proved insurmountable, as Cárdenas had promised they would. But the railways, which still carried 95 per cent of Mexico's freight, were by far the most important instance.

The initial expropriation, exhibiting patriotism and political *machismo*, was welcomed even by right-wing middle-class groups more accustomed to carp at Cardenista policy. After all, José Yves Limantour, doyen of the Científicos, had begun the nationalization process thirty years before; and in creating a state-owned railway system, Mexico was doing nothing that had not already been done in several Latin American countries. Better this than socialist education or the confiscation of Mexican private assets via the agrarian reform. Even the foreign bondholders were glad to be relieved of a wasting asset. One group with misgivings was the railwaymen themselves. Although sympathetic to nationalization in the abstract (for some, like their militant leader, Juan Gutiérrez, it was a step towards a socialized economy), they feared that a sudden switch to federal employment would jeopardize their union rights and recently won contract. Thus, the union's decision to undertake the management of the railways was strongly influenced by the desire to preserve hard-won gains, even though, during the long union–government talks of 1937–8 it was made clear that the workers' control would operate under stringent financial conditions (including a government veto on increases in freight charges) and that a workers' administration would be no soft option.

Assuming control on these terms, the union grappled manfully with massive problems. It overhauled the administration, repaired old track and rolling stock, cut costs and met its initial financial obligations; even the U.S. commercial attaché was favourably impressed. However, starved of capital investment and operating at levels of demand and price the union could not influence, the railways soon ran into deficit. In addition, the new administration, in its anomalous role as both trade union and employer, faced major problems over pay differentials and work discipline. A series of crashes indicated the severity of these problems, which the administration frankly admitted; it also gave the conservative press (which, however sympathetic to nationalization, disliked workers' control) ample ammunition to snipe at this exercise in irresponsible, 'unpatriotic' behaviour. In his final year, Cárdenas devoted close attention to the railway question, and in accord with the prevailing trend towards 'moderation', both the payroll and the union's autonomy were cut back, leaving the railway administration 'a simple appendix of the state apparatus'.[34] These measures foreshadowed the complete termination of workers' control and imposition of full state management under Avila Camacho. The railway workers, now 'thoroughly disillusioned', figured prominently in the Almazanista opposition of 1940.[35]

Compared to the railways, the oil industry was wholly (98 per cent) foreign-owned; smaller (it employed some 14,000 to the railway's 47,000); and profitable. Since the peak production of 1921 (193 million barrels) output had declined to 33 million in 1932, reviving to 47 million in 1937, thanks partly to the big Poza Rica strike. By then, the industry had undergone a major intraversion since the halcyon days of export boom. It now played a major role in the domestic economy (nearly half the 1937 production was domestically consumed) and it logically figured in government development strategy. The Six Year Plan envisaged the creation of a state oil company, Petróleos Mexicanos (PEMEX) and the exploitation of new fields, which the oil companies – more interested in the Venezuelan bonanza – seemed reluctant to undertake. Such moderately *dirigiste* intentions were entirely consonant with post-revolutionary policy, which had generated successive confrontations – and compromises – between the government and the oil companies. The most recent, culminating in the Calles–Morrow accord of 1928, effectively preserved the companies' position; but by 1934, with the challenge of the Six Year Plan and PEMEX, this showed signs of breaking down. Cárdenas himself took a typically tough line. As military commander in the Huasteca (1925–8) he had gained first-hand experience of the oil industry, its enclave character, its penchant for bribery and *pistolerismo*. He had disdained the offer of a 'beautiful Packard sedan' made by a company as 'proof of its high esteem and respect'; ten years later he showed the same resistance to graft, which the oil companies and their friends, conditioned to Callista political mores, found incredible. The new President, they complained, was 'curiously naive in these matters and did not appreciate business convention as understood in Mexico'.[36]

[34] González, *Los días del presidente Cárdenas,* p. 289.
[35] Davidson, Mexico City, 15 August 1940, FO 371/24217, 3818.
[36] William Cameron Townsend, *Lázaro Cárdenas, Mexican Democrat* (Ann Arbor, Mich., 1952), pp. 43–51; Murray, Mexico CIty, 15 July 1935, FO 371/18707, A6865.

Cárdenas, therefore, had no love for the oil companies. He made clear his intention of making them conform to national needs as laid down in the Six Year Plan, and he later undertook to raise royalties. But none of this heralded expropriation. Foreign investment – in oil and other sectors – still figured in government plans; expropriation per se was not sought. The foreign-owned mines (collectively more important than the oil industry) were never considered ripe for nationalization despite some pressure from the miners' union; foreign investment in the electricity and other industries was actively encouraged. Thus, while Cardenista policy towards foreign investment in general was pragmatic, oil was something of a special case. It was a 'sacred symbol' of national identity and independence; conversely, the oil companies represented a perverse, parasitic imperialism. So the eventual expropriation was less a typical example of consistent economic nationalist policy than a spectacular exception, brought about by the intransigence of the companies (some of whom persisted in 'conceiving of Mexico as . . . a colonial government to which you simply dictated orders').[37] Furthermore, it transpired after years of mounting industrial conflict in which the struggle between capital and labour constituted a crucial autonomous factor, making for unforeseen results.

Like the railwaymen, the oil-workers had a reputation for independence and militancy, which was enhanced with the foundation of the unified Sindicato de Trabajadores Petroleros de la République Mexicana (STPRM) in August 1935. In the recurrent strikes of 1934–35 the companies faced demands they considered 'preposterous'; in November 1936 they were threatened with strike action if a new national collective contract was not conceded. The worker's claims – running to 240 clauses – included rapid Mexicanization of the work force, the replacement of 'confidential' (non-union) employees by union members in all but a handful of posts, greatly improved wages and social benefits, and a forty-hour week. According to the companies such demands threatened both managerial prerogatives and economic viability; they costed the claim at 500 per cent of the current wage bill (the union preferred 130 per cent, which it maintained was justified by profit levels; throughout the dispute, figures were traded like blows in a prize fight). The companies' counter-proposals served only to reveal the huge gulf between the parties, which lavish company propaganda (denouncing the greed of the oil-workers – the 'spoiled darlings' of

---

[37] The attitude of Sir Henry Deterding, of Royal Dutch Shell, described by the managing director of Shell's Mexican subsidiary, El Aguila, in Murray, Mexico City, 17 September 1935, FO 371/18708, 8586.

Mexican industry) did nothing to narrow. After protracted talks failed, the workers struck (May 1937), alleging an 'economic conflict' before the Federal Arbitration Board.[38] Arbitration was clearly favoured by both the CTM and the government, which exerted pressure to achieve a settlement and avert further economic disruption (the notion that the government incited the dispute in order to justify a planned expropriation is unconvincing). By August, a massive federal commission had reported, recommending a modest increase on the companies' offer, and similarly modifying the 'social' demands; but it also lambasted the companies for their monopolistic, enclave status, their record of political meddling, their devious bookkeeping, tax privileges and excessive profits. The initial labour dispute thus opened up much wider economic questions.

The companies remained intransigent, impugning the report's accuracy and refusing to increase their offer. When the Arbitration Board accepted 'almost in their entirety' the commission's recommendations, the companies took the case to the Supreme Court; and when the latter found against them, they again ignored the finding. Meanwhile, they propagandized and lobbied in both Mexico and the United States. They had, however, painted themselves into a corner. Confident of their essential economic role – and thus convinced that both union and government would have to compromise as in 1923 and 1928 – the companies held out to the last, rejecting a financially feasible settlement (the difference in cash terms was not so great), fearful of the impact this might have in other oil-producing nations. Initially a labour dispute, the conflict now centred on grand questions of prestige and principle. For by early 1938, the government also faced limited options: a humiliating surrender, a temporary take-over of the companies' properties, or outright expropriation. Although the third alternative was the final outcome, it was not the government's persistent aim, as the companies alleged in the face of official denials. Nationalization of this basic resource was, for some, a long-term objective, but there is no evidence that 1938 was pre-selected as the *annus mirabilis*. On the contrary, official pragmatism was evident in the grant of new oil leases in 1937, and in the discussions held, after expropriation, with a view to possible foreign investment in the oil industry. What is more, the cabinet was divided during the critical early weeks of 1938, and few doubted the risks – economic, financial, political – which expropria-

---

[38] See Joe C. Ashby, *Organized Labor and the Mexican Revolution Under Lázaro Cárdenas* (Chapel Hill, N.C., 1963), pp. 197–212.

tion would involve. But even these risks could not justify a humiliating climb-down. 'We would burn the oil-fields to the ground', as Cárdenas put it, 'rather than sacrifice our honour'.[39] When, at the last, it became clear that their bluff was being called, the companies sought a compromise. It was now too late. The government was resolved, the public mood exalted. On 18 March 1938, Cárdenas broadcast to the nation, rehearsing the sins of the companies and announcing their outright expropriation. Workers were already moving in to take physical control of the plants. As one declared, barring the entry of British employees to the Minatitlán refinery: 'The ambition of the foreigner is at an end'.[40]

In terms of political drama and presidential prestige, the oil expropriation was the high point of the Cárdenas years. The companies were 'stunned'.[41] From the bishops to the students of the National University, Mexicans rallied to the national cause, endorsing the president's patriotic stance and admiring, probably for the first time, his personal *machismo*. Massive demonstrations were held: perhaps a quarter of a million paraded through the streets of the capital carrying mock coffins inscribed with the names of the fallen giants: Standard, Huasteca, Aguila. Government bonds, issued to cover the future indemnity, were snapped up in a spirit of patriotic euphoria, and women of all classes stood in line to donate cash, jewellery, sewing machines, even wedding rings. Never before, or after, did the nation display such solidarity. Briefly, the popular frontism of the CTM seemed to encompass the entire population. In this congenial atmosphere, the PNR gathered for its third national assembly and turned itself into the new, corporately structured Partido de la Revolución Mexicana (PRM).

Popular euphoria could not pump oil, but it helped: the oil-workers – armchair experts collaborating with veteran drillers – displayed great energy and ingenuity in taking control of an under-capitalized industry. A twenty-eight-year-old found himself in charge of the Aguila Company's prize Poza Rica field. As the distant precedent of 1914 suggested, Mexicans were entirely capable of running the industry. The companies who, like the Laguna landlords, predicted that their departure would signal chaos, were proved wrong. However, the companies had more power than the landlords to realize their prediction. As the American and British governments made their official protests – the Americans circumspectly,

[39] Ibid., p. 180.
[40] Marett, *An Eye-witness of Mexico*, p. 227, where the author stresses the spontaneity of the comment.
[41] Ashby, *Organized Labor*, p. 237.

the British rudely – the companies at once went on the attack, shipping funds out of Mexico, boycotting Mexican sales, pressuring third parties to enforce the boycott and refusing to sell equipment. Coinciding with other economic troubles (inflation, growing government deficit, falling trade surplus), this action had serious consequences. Business confidence wavered, credit dried up and – with the United States temporarily suspending its purchases of Mexican silver – the peso slipped. For once, it was said, even the phlegmatic President had a sleepless night. Regarding the oil industry itself, export sales halved and production fell by about a third. The outbreak of the Second World War compounded the industry's problems and by the end of 1939 it was running a marked deficit. Again, therefore, a Cardenista economic reform was conducted under extreme conditions. Parallels with the railways became evident. The oil workers – traditionally syndicalist and confident of the industry's viability – favoured a workers' administration although they, too, were leery about assuming 'federal' status. However, the government would not relinquish control of so valuable an asset, and PEMEX was constituted on the basis of joint government–union collaboration. This gave local sections of the union considerable power and autonomy, while the government retained ultimate control of policy and finance. The union leaders – the meat in the sandwich – faced a recurrent dilemma: traitors to their country if they obstructed the running of this new national asset, they were traitors to their class if they scrupulously followed government direction. And there were ample grounds for conflict: over the size of the payroll, the organization of the union, promotion policy and managerial prerogatives. In this, the expropriation settled nothing and exacerbated a good deal. The industry was potentially healthy, but the boycott and war invalidated previously optimistic prognoses. Furthermore, as the labour force grew (from some 15,000 to 20,000) and wages rose, so the industry's wage bill shot up (around 89 per cent by late 1939). With PEMEX now in deficit, the government faced a difficult problem. Cárdenas and the CTM called for reorganization and cut-backs. Work discipline, it was said, had suffered; the workers had arrogated to themselves excessive rights, to the detriment of management; payrolls were too long, wages too high, perks too generous. Indeed, with expropriation, the fundamental status of the industry had changed, invalidating the 1937 award; like the railwaymen, the oil-workers were now enjoined to tighten their belts in the national and – the CTM stressed – their own class interest. For their part, the workers blamed inherited problems and poor management, and they argued for more, not less, workers' autonomy. By 1940, strikes were occurring and a rift opened between the union leadership and the more militant sections. As with the railways, Cárdenas spent much of his last year grappling with the reorganization of this newly nationalized enterprise (he was often to be found working in the old Aguila Co. offices). He backed the management's retrenchment plan, urging wage and job cuts, greater effort and discipline – in all of which he was faithfully seconded by the CTM. There was a modest improvement in PEMEX's trading position in 1940, but basic problems remained, raising hopes in some quarters that the properties might be returned to their previous owners. The next administration, which faced a serious strike threat in 1943, prevaricated; the showdown between government and union was postponed until the aftermath of the war.

With the oil expropriation, the diplomatic furor and economic repercussions it provoked, and the onset of the war, foreign relations for the first time assumed central importance for the regime, Hitherto its foreign policy – if conducted with unusual moral fervour and consistency – followed familiar 'revolutionary' traditions: respect for national sovereignty, non-intervention, self-determination. These principles were vigorously sustained in the League of Nations and in successive Pan-American conferences, where Mexican spokesmen advocated the peaceful settlement of international disputes and, in even-handed fashion, denounced aggression, be it American support for Somoza's coup; the Italian invasion of Abyssinia; Japanese imperialism in China; the Anschluss and Nazi attack on Poland; and – to the chagrin of the PCM – the Soviet campaign against Finland, which, given the geopolitical parallels, excited genuine condemnation. But it was the Spanish Civil War which drew greatest attention, official and popular. At the outset Cárdenas acceded to a Republican request for arms, and supplies continued – at a modest rate – as the war went on. Official condemnation of the Nationalists was seconded by the CTM; and, as the Republican cause failed, Mexico became a haven for Spanish refugees (ultimately some thirty thousand), who included a clutch of distinguished intellectuals as well as the Basque football team, both of whom left their mark on their host country.[42] Like the coincidental arrival in Mexico of Leon

---

[42] The Casa de Espanã, composed of refugee intellectuals, later metamorphosed into the illustrious Colegio de México; the Basque footballers helped convert Mexico from the 'rough, graceless style' originally imparted by the English to one more attuned to the 'Mexican personality': González, *Los días del presidente Cárdenas*, pp. 229–35, 276.

Trotsky (another example of Cárdenas' even-handedness), the war impinged directly on domestic politics. Given the obvious parallels, it was not surprising that Mexican opinion polarized, and that right-wing, Catholic and fascist groups endorsed Franco. Some, indeed, hoped wistfully for a Mexican Generalísimo; they condemned the government's support for atheistic communism, and they deplored the arrival in Mexico of its defeated agents. In 1938 jubilant posters proclaimed Cárdenas vanquished at Teruel. The Spanish Civil War thus helped define domestic alignments during the approach to the 1940 election.

Meanwhile, with the oil expropriation, Mexican relations with the United States – always the cardinal point of the diplomatic compass – deteriorated. Hitherto they had seemed to prosper, the Calles–Morrow détente being reinforced by the supposed (though easily exaggerated) congruence between Cardenismo and the New Deal, by Roosevelt's Good Neighbor Policy, and by the happy choice of Josephus Daniels as American ambassador. If during the Calles–Cárdenas struggle American sympathies, both private and official, had been divided, and American influence had been exerted in favour of compromise, it was clear that the United States would have no truck with rebellion – which decision, of course, favoured the legal incumbent. Daniels gave staunch support to the regime in defiance of State Department and American Catholic opinion, and his puritan progressivism and boyish enthusiasm endeared him to Cárdenas as much as they appalled European career diplomats. With the formulation of the Good Neighbor Policy, Mexican and American delegates to successive Pan-American conferences found themselves in unusual accord.

Domestic developments soon began to chill this warmer relationship. The expropriation of American landholdings elicited stern protests; and if the railway nationalization relieved more headaches than it caused, that of the oil industry was immediately contested. The U.S. government backed the companies' boycott, demanded an indemnity (if not the return of the properties), halted talks on a commercial treaty, and suspended silver purchases. Britain's response – less efficacious and more offensive – provoked a diplomatic rupture. American official opinion was divided, rival economic interests (silver miners, manufacturers whose Mexican investments had recently grown, and exporters who now looked to oust the Germans from Mexican markets) favouring conciliation over confrontation. Roosevelt, encouraged by Daniels, was prepared to ignore the hawkish advice of the oil companies, State Department and financial press. He conceded Mexico's right to expropriate, ruled out the use of force and tried to mitigate the damage done to U.S.–Mexican relations. Silver purchases were resumed and talks began on the question of companies' indemnity (the principle of which the Mexican government did not contest). The companies, however, busy lobbying in Europe and the United States, held out for the full restitution of their properties, which, as the boycott bit and the fortunes of Mexico's oil industry and economy sank, they anticipated with unswerving confidence.

Crucial in the formulation of U.S. policy were perceptions of the growing Axis threat. These – already evident in the cultivation of Pan-Americanism – now dominated policy, as the Cárdenas government had anticipated. Furthermore, the boycott obliged Mexico to conclude sales agreements with the Axis powers, which (although they were neither economically favourable nor ideologically congenial to Mexico, nor even strategically vital to the Axis) exacerbated U.S. fears of German political and economic penetration of Mexico. As the spectre of Nazi fifth columnism grew apace, the U.S. government decided that détente with Mexico was as essential as it had been twenty-five years before. Even the hawkish Secretary of State, Cordell Hull, grew impatient with the oil companies' intransigence and eager for a settlement, even at their expense. Intransigence appeared all the more anomalous as the Sinclair Co. broke ranks and reached a unilateral settlement (May 1940) and as other outstanding U.S.–Mexican differences were resolved under the pressure of war. In November 1941 a general settlement of American property losses arising from the Revolution was concluded; in return, the United States agreed to increase silver purchases, to furnish credit in support of the peso and to begin talks on a commercial treaty. Finally, in April 1942, the oil companies settled for compensation of $23.8 million – 4 per cent of their original claim.

The U.S.–Mexican détente covered wider issues and had a notable impact on domestic politics. As war approached, the United States tightened its relations with Latin America and, at successive Pan-American conferences (Panama, 1939; Havana, 1940), concluded agreements pledging hemispheric security and warning off belligerent powers from the New World. Brazil and Mexico emerged as the key actors in this hemispheric alignment and during 1940–1, as American fears of Japan were quickened and finally justified, Mexico came to figure as the political and strategic pivot of American policy in the continent. Cárdenas' staunch anti-fascism now afforded grounds for a rapprochement with the United States which his successor would further develop and which, in turn, favoured the moderation of the 'Cardenista project' in the years after 1938. The President was forthright in his condemnation of Nazi aggression and his support for the democracies; he promised full cooperation against any Axis attack on the American continent, and to underwrite this commitment, he authorized U.S.–Mexican military talks. German propaganda in Mexico was curbed. In addition, a reorganization of the armed services was begun; military expenditure, which had dropped to a post-revolutionary low of 15.8 per cent of total spending in 1939, jumped to 19.7 per cent in 1940. A new Military Service Law established a year's service for all eighteen-year-olds which, it was hoped, would not only prepare Mexicans 'to cooperate in the defence of our Continent' (Ezequiel Padilla's words), but also inculcate 'a disciplined education which would benefit the youth of our country in all works of life' (Avila Camacho's).[43] Symptomatic of the times, and of the new priority of national over class rhetoric, the rural school (now under threat) was supplanted by that other, classic instrument of national integration, the barracks.

Here, however, official action outran public opinion. The CTM, foghorn of the official left, blared its support for the democratic crusade against fascism, anticipating eventual Mexican participation, which would combine ideological correctness with economic advantage. But Lombardista belligerence cooled with the onset of the phony war, and the CTM line echoed that of the PCM: the war was an imperialist 'war for markets', and Mexico should remain strictly neutral. Yet later in 1940 the CTM veered back to its pro-war, anti-fascist line, which more comfortably fitted its domestic stance, and by early 1941 Lombardo was pledging 'all . . . material and moral help' against fascism and hoping for American participation.[44] With the Nazi attack on the Soviet Union, the PCM joined the patriotic democratic front, whose membership was completed thanks to Pearl Harbor. If the left, official and Communist, first leaned, then lurched, to the Allied side, the right naturally, dissented. Conservative and fascist groups, such as Acción Nacional and the Unión Nacional Sinarquista (UNS), inclined to the Axis cause and criticized military collaboration with the United States, at least at the outset. In this, they espoused a popular cause. For most Mexicans the war was an irrelevant conflict in remote lands, and very few people took a real interest in its progress. There was little incentive to fight, and the new

---

[43] Ibid., p. 308; *Hoy*, 20 September 1940.
[44] Blanca Torres Ramírez, *Historia de la revolución mexicana Periodo 1940–1952: México en la segunda guerra mundial* (Mexico, 1979), pp. 66–7.

military service raised memories of the hated *leva* (the pressgang of Porfirian and revolutionary times) and provoked violent protest when implemented after 1941. To the extent that popular sympathies were engaged in the war, they inclined towards Germany: an international victim in 1918, some felt; the 'antithesis of Communism' for others; or the fount of anti-Semitism, then on the rise in Mexico.[45] If Mexico was to be committed to the Allied cause, it would require active government encouragement.

As foreign affairs absorbed growing attention, domestic politics underwent important realignments. Amid the euphoria of the oil expropriation, a staple Cardenista objective was achieved: the restructuring of the official party (now the PRM) along corporate lines. This, Cárdenas hoped, would guarantee the continuation of reform and overcome the factionalism which still gnawed at the vitals of the PNR, especially as the left (Francisco Múgica, Gonzalo Vázquez Vela, Ernesto Soto Reyes) feuded with the 'centre', unofficially captained by that great fixer and survivor, Portes Gil. The latter, installed as party president for his help in the ouster of Calles (July 1935) set out to 'purify' the PNR (that is, to eliminate the vestiges of Callismo) and to broaden its appeal by extensive use of film, radio, newspapers and conferences. State committees were urged to recruit and involve working-class members; the PNR (not the CTM) undertook the national organization of the peasantry. Like some medieval inquisitor, however, Portes Gil fell foul of his own 'purification' campaign and was replaced by the radical Cardenista Barba González (August 1936). Meanwhile, the process of party organization and sectoral integration went on: with the union of the PNR, CTM, CCM and PCM in an electoral pact (February 1937); with the genesis, a year later, of the PRM, which grouped the military, the workers (CTM), the peasants (initially represented by the CCM, soon to be supplanted by the all-encompassing CNC), and the 'popular' sector, a catch-all of cooperatives, officials and unorganized (largely middle-class) elements, which would not achieve formal corporate existence until 1943. Again, this new mass organization combined a tutelary aspect with a long-term commitment to radical change: the party would undertake 'the preparation of the people for the creation of a workers' democracy and to achieve a socialist regime'.[46]

---

[45] González, *Los días del presidente Cárdenas*, p. 256; Davidson, Mexico City, 4 January 1940, FO 371/ 24217, A813.

[46] González, *Los días del presidente Cárdenas*, p. 183.

Ironically, the creation of the PRM, pledged to these grand objectives, came just when the regime began to falter; when, under the joint pressure of internal and external forces, the President chose to consolidate, to avoid further radical commitments and to prepare for a peaceful, democratic and politically congenial succession. The year 1938, which began in patriotic exaltation, ended with the radicals in retreat; if there was a Cardenista Thermidor – when the forward march of the revolution was halted and reversed – it came in 1938, not 1940. Of course, leftist critics see Cardenismo as a protracted Thermidor; while for loyal partisans there was no retreat, only tactical withdrawals. But the evidence such partisans cite as proof of sustained radicalism after 1938 (continued socialist education, excess profits tax, legislation covering the electricity industry) hardly compares with the sweeping reforms of earlier years. If there was not a full-scale retreat, there was certainly a 'notable change of direction',[47] which, however, was the product of circumstances rather than autonomous decision. There was a dramatic decline in presidential power in 1938–40, the result of new political pressures, the ending of the sexenio and Cárdenas' unprecedented refusal to cultivate a successor. Squabbles within the PRM, and the final electoral debacle of 1940, revealed this erosion of power, which in turn undermined the entire Cardenista coalition, with the CTM chiefly affected. As in the early 1930s, the ideological climate brusquely changed; by 1940, conservatives were confidently reporting that 'the great majority of thinking people . . . are now sick of socialism'; and that 'the trend over the next few years will be to the right'.[48]

Both the war and internal pressures encouraged caution and consolidation. Foremost among these pressures was the state of the economy. Cárdenas had inherited an economy recovering from the depression in which manufacturing industry and certain exports (e.g., silver) were buoyant. Even without radical changes in the tax structure, government income rose (almost twofold between 1932 and 1936). But so, too, did government expenditure: modestly in 1934–5, when the battle with Calles enjoyed priority, rapidly after 1936 as the major reforms got under way. Thus, expenditure rose, in real terms, from 265 million pesos (1934) to 406 million (1936), 504 million (1938), and 604 million (1940), with 'social' and 'economic' spending in the van. Exports, however, peaked in

[47] Ibid., p. 272; cf. Tzvi Medin, *Ideología y praxis política de Lázaro Cárdenas* (Mexico, 1972), pp. 204–6.
[48] Davidson, Mexico City, 4 January 1940, FO 371/24217, A813.

1937, and the government ran budget deficits that grew from 5.5 per cent of income in 1936 to 15.1 per cent in 1938. By then, deficit financing had become an effective tool whereby the government – possessed of political will and powers of monetary intervention that were alike unprecedented – countered the effects of renewed recession, transmitted from the United States in 1937–8. Compared with a decade before, Mexico was now better placed to withstand such external shocks.

But the inflationary pressures thus engendered were now aggravated by the rising costs of both imports and domestic foodstuffs. *Ejidal* inefficiency was readily, but usually wrongly, blamed for the cost of food. In fact, though agricultural production was hit by the upheaval of the agrarian reform and the landlords' consequent reluctance to invest, total output of maize in 1935–9 was about the same as it had been ten years before; given both a larger population and cultivated area, these (official) figures suggest a 17 per cent drop in per capita consumption and a 6 per cent fall in yields per hectare. It is very probable, however, that these figures (which are contradicted by alternative evidence) under-estimate both peasant production and peasant consumption, which were, of course, more decentralized and elusive than previous hacienda equivalents.[49] All the same, if the *ejidatarios* ate better, the supply of food to the cities was constricted and prices began to edge up. Like Germany, Mexico had had recent experience of hyper-inflation and opinion was sensitive to this ominous – albeit modest – rise in prices. Adverse comment was heard as early as 1936; even Lombardo admitted there were problems. Between 1934 and 1940 the retail price index rose 38 per cent, but between 1936 and 1938 – the years of dramatic social reform – it jumped 26 per cent, with foodstuffs worst affected. However, apocalyptic analyses positing a sustained fall in real wages through the depression, the inflationary later 1930s and the yet more inflationary 1940s, are unconvincing. Under Cárdenas the minimum wage outstripped inflation, and the aggregate purchasing power of wages rose, to the advantage of the domestic market. The chief beneficiaries were the *ejidatarios,* organized labour and workers – like the *gente decente* employed by General Motors – who took advantage of the changing occupational structure as agricultural jobs gave way to industrial. Rural proletarians (especially those employed by haciendas facing expropriation) did less

[49] E. Alanis Patiño and E. Vargas Torres, 'Observaciones sobre algunas estadísticas agrícolas', *Trimestre Económico* 12 (1945–6): 578–615.

well, while it was the urban middle class – Cárdenas' loudest critics – who were relatively worst hit by inflation.

Nevertheless, inflation jeopardized recent working-class gains, and thus working-class support for the regime. It also deterred private investment and encouraged capital flight. The government's response was contradictory – further evidence, perhaps, of the structural constraints under which Cardenismo operated. A serious attempt was made to regulate food prices: as the hostile reaction of private enterprise suggested, this was no mere palliative, and during the last quarter of 1938 the general price index fell modestly (4 per cent), the index for foodstuffs significantly (8 per cent). In pursuit of more fundamental solutions, the government raised tariffs (December 1937) and, following the 1938 devaluation, imposed new export taxes and cut capital projects (per capita spending on public works fell 38 per cent between 1937 and 1938; road-building was 'practically halted'). Workers in the public sector – such as railways and oil – had to tighten their belts. With government agricultural credit also falling, *ejidatarios* went short or, like the Laguneros, looked to private sources. And after the heady days of 1936–7, the pace of agrarian reform slowed – some said out of deference to U.S. interests. Certainly the government entertained hopes of an American loan and the U.S. government, although favouring a broader 'programme of economic assistance', was not entirely averse. But the oil expropriation ruled out any deal.[50]

As economic problems built up, the administration lost momentum and political opposition mounted. On the one hand, as the Cardenista coalition fissured, erstwhile supporters (chiefly working-class groups) defected; on the other, conservative and Catholic opponents, in retreat since the fall of Calles if not the defeat of the Cristiada, made a decisive recovery. Although official strike figures fell after 1937 (reflecting official reluctance to recognize strikes as legal), de facto industrial action grew, with major strikes by bakers, teachers, electricians, miners and sugar, textile and tram workers, as well as conflicts on the railways and in the oil industry. By 1940 there was ample evidence of working-class support for the opposition presidential candidate; even the May Day rally in Mexico City was marred by anti-government catcalls. Nor did business love the regime any the more for its new-found moderation. Price regulation and tax increases were denounced; attacks on militant unions became more vociferous, and as the export of capital weakened the economy, so the

[50] Hamilton, *Limits of State Autonomy*, p. 224.

political opposition reorganized and acquired fresh funding. Following the regime's example, business itself now displayed greater corporate organization, as did the conservative and fascist opposition. The year 1937 saw the birth of the Unión Nacional Sinarquista (UNS), a mass-based Catholic integralist movement (it rejected the concept of 'party'), which roundly rejected the Revolution, liberalism, socialism, class struggle and gringo materialism, offering instead the values of religion, family, private property, hierarchy and social solidarity. Possibly helped by business subsidies but primarily dependent on genuine peasant support, especially in the old Cristero regions of west–central Mexico, the Sinarquistas fast grew in numbers (they claimed half a million by 1943), mounting massive revivalist rallies in the towns of the Bajío. Initially sharing a similar ideology, but recruiting urban-middle-class support along more conventional lines, was Acción Nacional, founded in 1939 under the leadership of Manuel Gómez Morín, with the support of lay Catholics and the financial backing of the Monterrey bourgeoisie.

The 'secular' right was less numerous but just as strident.[51] As 1940 approached, a crop of lesser parties sprouted, some clinging to individual revolutionary veterans who, as they aged, grew rich, and fell to lamenting the revolution's decline, became converts to conservatism or downright fascism (Marcelo Caraveo, Ramón F. Iturbe, Cedillo, Joaquín Amaro). Some, like Jorge Prieto Laurens' Partido Social Demócrata (PSD), appealed to the anti-Cardenista middle class, tapping the liberal tradition which had manifested itself in 1929; but most, with their denunciations of communism, the influx of Spanish subversives and the pervasive influence of the Jews, revealed how a large slice of the middle class had been pushed to the far right by the political polarization of the 1930s. The shift was typified by José Vasconcelos, paragon of the anti-reelectionist opposition in 1929, who now flirted with fascism in the pages of *Timón,* arguing that the Axis would win the war, that Hitler constituted an Hegelian world-historical figure (it took one to know one) and that Mexico would have to conform to such historicist imperatives and submit to authoritarian rule. Both anti-communism and anti-Semitism were now the vogue. Bernardino Mena Brito regaled fellow-veterans with exposés of the role of 'universal Jewry', which the Sinarquistas also propagated. The Partido Revolucionario Anti-Comunista (PRAC), founded in 1938 by the old PNR boss and landlord Manuel Pérez Treviño, proclaimed in its title its

---

[51] Hugh G. Campbell, *La derecha radical en México, 1929–1949* (Mexico, 1976), p. 47 ff.

raison d'être. Many organizations like this were set up in 1938–40; feeble, fly-by-night, often dependent on the whims and ambition of an ageing *caudillo*. But they indicated a real shift in the ideological climate: a resurgence of the right (a shrinking liberal right, and a growing aggressive, authoritarian right, attuned to foreign examples); a new nostalgia for the Porfiriato, evident in the cinemas's loving evocation of *ranchero* life; and a corresponding loss of political initiative by the left.

The right increasingly aped the methods of the left. It formed mass organizations or even filched those of its opponents (as Almazán did with the dissident unions in 1940), thus participating in the gradual institutionalization and 'massification' of politics which characterized the 1930s. Even in regions of Sinarquista activity, the politics of the later thirties were relatively peaceful compared to the gross violence of the Cristiada; the more so since the Catholic hierarchy strove to contain the movement's radical fanatics. In this, the leader of Partido Acción Nacional (PAN) – the smart, articulate intellectual Gómez Morín, the right's answer to Lombardo – was more typical and effective than old veterans like Amaro, whose bloody record and autodidact mentality disqualified him from the presidential office he coveted. Amaro may have itched to take power by *cuartelazo,* but the times were no longer propitious; Almazán talked rebellion in 1940, but went no further. One veteran, however, clung to the old ways, unable to fathom the new. For years Saturnino Cedillo had run the state of San Luis Potosí more as a grand 'village patriarch' than the machine politician who was fast becoming the norm.[52] He counted on the support of his agrarian colonists (who had fought for him in the Revolution and Cristero wars), on the sympathy of the Catholics, whom he protected, and on a network of petty municipal *caciques.* Sponsor of an extensive personal and popular agrarian reform, Cedillo now tolerated landlords and businessmen who sought refuge from Cardenista radicalism. His relations with the labour movement were generally hostile, and as Minister of Agriculture (which Cárdenas had made him by way of reward after Cedillo had backed him against Calles) he dispensed patronage, promoted colonization over collectivization and earned the hatred of radicals like Múgica. In San Luis, where his power endured, independent unions gathered strength with the support of the CTM, which took advantage of strikes at the Atlas and Asarco plants to weaken Cedillo's local

[52] Dudley Ankerson, *Agrarian Warlord: Saturnino Cedillo and the Mexican Revolution in San Luis Potosí* (De Kalb, Ill., 1984), chap. 6.

control, alleging that he was a friend of international fascism (doubtful) and an enemy of organized labour (true). In 1937, the PNR joined the game, contesting Cedillo's control of congressional elections, and his removal from the Ministry of Agriculture was contrived, according to the Cedillistas, by Múgica, Lombardo and the left. By late 1937, Cedillo was sulking in San Luis, thinking rebellious thoughts, encouraged by ambitious advisers and by the palpable growth of conservative discontent.

The conversion of general discontent into effective opposition was not easy, especially since Cedillo's ideas were primitive and his potential allies so disparate. Although he planned a political, possibly presidential, campaign, he also anticipated and probably relished the prospect of armed revolt. Overtures to prospective allies, however, were largely unsuccessful: Monterrey business chipped in some cash; the oil companies were approached but no deal was struck (the notion that Cedillo's revolt was not only financed but also concocted by the oil companies is ubiquitous but false); and prominent conservatives like General Almazán, who commanded in the north-east, or Román Yocupicio, the governor of Sonora, preferred political obstructionism to outright rebellion. Cedillo had to rely on his local resources, notably his fifteen thousand agrarian veterans. But here, too, he was thrown on to the defensive. Apprised of Cedillo's intentions, the government shuffled military commands, encouraged CTM recruitment in San Luis, and, most dramatically, launched a major agrarian reform which, by distributing up to a million hectares of Potosino land, created a rival *agrarista* clientele in Cedillo's back yard. The Cedillo *cacicazgo,* it was clear, was going the way of Garrido's in Tabasco or Saturnino Osornio's in Querétaro. But Cárdenas offered his old ally an honourable exit by appointing him military commander in Michoacán. Through the spring of 1938, Cedillo debated, planned and negotiated. Ultimately he refused to leave San Luis, and Cárdenas, fearful lest this defiance prove contagious, came to get him. In another dramatic presidential initiative, Cárdenas arrived in San Luis (May 1938), addressed the populace and called on Cedillo to retire. Instead, Cedillo rebelled; or, as a supporter put it, 'No se levantó, lo levantaron' ('He didn't rebel, they made him'). It was a half-hearted affair, more a display of pique than a serious *pronunciamiento.* Indeed, Cedillo humanely advised most of his followers to stay at home, preferring to take to the hills in the hope of some favourable *apertura* in 1940 (exactly as he had done in 1915). But by 1938 times had changed. There were only the merest echoes of sympathetic revolts in Jalisco, Puebla and Oaxaca; even in San Luis itself the

Cedillistas were split, and many rallied to Cárdenas, who remained in the state, travelling, propagandizing and revealing to all the hollowness of Cedillo's pretentions. Of those who rebelled, many were amnestied; a few, including Cedillo himself, were hunted down and killed. Cárdenas, it was said, genuinely mourned.

Thus ended the last old-style military rebellion of the long revolutionary cycle. Even as Cedillo was being pursued through the hills of San Luis, the conservative opposition was marshalling its forces to contest the 1940 election in peaceful fashion. The government, alarmed by Cedillo's revolt and the deteriotating economic situation, set out to conciliate. Reform was curtailed and rhetoric softened. On his extensive 1939 tour through Almazán's territory in the north, Cárdenas was at pains to deny the 'Communist' taint; at Saltillo he praised north-eastern business, which formed 'a constituent part of the respectable, vibrant forces of the country' (terms which contrasted with the reproof delivered three years earlier at Monterrey). By now, this denial of 'Communism' and stress on constitutional consensus was standard fare.[53] Congress was busy watering down the socialist education programme; the CTM showed its concern for national unity and social equilibrium by pressing unions to avoid strikes (many of which were pending), while denying that it sought the abolition of property or the dictatorship of the proletariat. That such denials were felt necessary was comment enough on conservative scare-mongering. But there was sound logic behind Cardenista conciliation – which the right, in a sense, accepted. Instead of compromising and deploying its ample resources within the capacious arena of official politics, the right preferred to remain outside, grouped in a congeries of conservative and fascist-like parties, hopeful that continued radicalism would lead to the complete collapse of Cardenismo, from which the right would benefit hugely and permanently. Accordingly, the right 'prefer[red] to see [an] acceleration of [the] radical programme, on the grounds that some reaction would be all the more likely under the new administration'.[54] Indeed, were Cárdenas to impose a radical successor espousing a radical programme, a conservative coup, possibly linking army and Sinarquistas, could not be ruled out. In such a climate – ignored by armchair critics – conciliation had a definite logic.

[53] Ariel José Contreras, *México 1940: industrialización y crisis política: Estado y sociedad civil en las elecciones presidenciales* (Mexico, 1977), pp. 154–5; Luis Medina, *Historia de la revolución mexicana Periodo 1940–1952: Del Cardenismo al Avilacamachismo* (Mexico, 1978), p. 93.
[54] Davidson, Mexico City, 9 January 1940, FO 371/24217, A1301.

It was in this climate that the succession question was broached in the
summer of 1938. Rival groups inside and outside the PRM began to shape
up, aware that the 1940 election would be politically crucial. Here was a
chance to halt Cardenismo (already a decelerating vehicle) in its tracks; to
install a moderate or downright conservative regime; or, alternatively, to
continue the pace of reform. Cárdenas' own role, often debated, was
important but not decisive. His personal power was waning and he was
unable to stop speculation about the succession. Even had he wanted, he
alone could not determine the outcome; neither could the PRM, which, if
it constituted a leviathan, was a gross, uncoordinated beast lacking a
directing brain commensurate with its corporate bulk. Internally divided,
the party could not guarantee a smooth succession; indeed, the emergent
heir-apparent, Avila Camacho, built his nomination campaign on parallel
organizations outside the party, and the PRM endorsed his candidacy once
it was a fait accompli. Conflict was aggravated by Cárdenas' political self-
abnegation. He ruled out his own re-election and advocated a genuinely
free choice within the PRM. The succession would be determined by the
new mass organizations established during the 1930s. However bold or
enlightened, this novel refusal of an outgoing president to pick – or at
least to influence strongly – the succession constituted an invitation to
factionalism, a self-mutilation of presidential power and a death sentence
for the official left. The latter, backing Cárdenas' close friend and adviser
Francisco Múgica, were disappointed not to receive presidential backing.
Their centre-right rivals, supporting Secretary of Defence Avila Camacho,
stole a march on them by defying presidential wishes and getting their
campaign under way in 1938, after which the left was on the defensive.
Furthermore, Avila Camacho had prepared the ground well. A member of
a powerful political family from Puebla, a shrewd ally of Cárdenas through
the 1930s, he was – despite his general's pips – more career politician
than *caudillo*. Yet as Secretary of Defence (and Defence was still the presidential anteroom that Gobernación would later become), he had won the
ample, if not overwhelming, support of the military – a crucial consideration in view of current fears of *cuartelazo,* which, for the last time,
seriously affected the succession question. He also counted on the majority
of the state governors, who had been lined up by his adroit campaign
manager, the governor of Veracruz, Miguel Alemán; and with them came
many local *caciques* who, in order to maintain their fiefs in the face of
burgeoning federal power, converted an opportunistic Cardenismo into an

opportunistic Avilacamachismo. Congress, especially the Senate, became a nest of Avilacamachistas.

The organized sectors of the party, discerning the drift of events and directed by their leaders, soon acquiesced. The CNC, left by Cárdenas to reach its own decision, fell prey to lesser manipulators and its overwhelming vote for Avila Camacho was at once denounced by the Mugiquistas as a travesty of peasant opinion, evidence that the CNC had rapidly become a mere 'ghost' controlled by unrepresentative bureaucrats.[55] More important, the CTM declared for Avila Camacho, its leaders arguing a now familiar case: that unity was vital, that in the face of fascist threats, internal and external, 1940 was a time for consolidation, not advance (the PCM, rebuffing Mugiquista overtures, took the same line). The CTM sublimated its radicalism by compiling a massive second Six Year Plan which envisaged further economic *dirigisme,* workers' participation in decision-making, and a form of 'functional' democracy. Reviled by the right as both communist and fascist, the plan displayed a naive faith in paper proposals and in the CTM's ability to realize them. As for the candidate whom the CTM thus hoped to bind, Avila Camacho obligingly endorsed the proposals. In the event, the final PRM programme was a predictably moderate document.

Favoured by circumstances, Avila Camacho could garner the support of both centre and left. He also pitched an appeal to the right: as candidate and president-elect he cultivated the 'moderate' rhetoric of the time, echoing Cárdenas' denials of Communism and contriving to align himself – PCM support for his candidacy notwithstanding – with the growing anti-communist sentiment. Workers were warned against militancy and advised to protect existing gains; small property-owners were reassured; Monterrey's businessmen were praised as those 'who dream and plan for the prosperity and greatness of Mexico'.[56] Regarding education (still a live issue), Avila Camacho was again for moderation and conciliation, rejecting doctrinaire theory and advocating respect for family, religion and national culture; it was noted that he was 'cordially welcomed' in the old Cristero heartland of Los Altos.[57] And in September 1940, now elected, he ringingly declared his faith: 'Yo soy creyente'. Throughout, his campaign rhetoric – stressing liberty, democracy (now often counterposed to Communism) and, above

[55] Contreras, *Mexico 1940,* pp. 55–6.
[56] Ibid., pp. 155–6.
[57] Rees, Mexico City, 9 February 1940, FO 371/24217, A1654.

all, *unity* – contrasted with the pugnacious radicalism of Cárdenas six years before. It soon became clear that Avila Camacho was 'little by little denying the continuity with Cardenismo expressed in the Six Year Plan'.[58] Nevertheless the CTM, the first begetter of that plan, continued to back the candidate and even to echo his soporific sophisms.

Avila Camacho thus offered all things to all men, cultivating CTMistas and Cristeros, workers and capitalists; here – rather than with Cárdenas six years before – was a thoroughly populist appeal in which differences of creed and class were submerged in a glutinous national unity. The circumstances of 1940 were propitious and the strategy worked, to an extent. The Monterrey bourgeoisie hedged their bets in the classic fashion of big business: responding positively to Avila Camacho's overtures, they established some purchase within the official party; but they also sponsored its main Catholic rival, the PAN (and perhaps the UNS too). The PAN agonized whether to back the opposition or – as their Monterrey paymasters probably preferred – to take the more prudent line of abstention. Finally, the party resolved to support the opposition 'in a very conditional form', which represented the worst of both worlds. The Sinarquista leaders, too, trimmed their sails, spurned Almazán and, coaxed by Alemán, urged abstention: further evidence of the growing division between them and their radical rank and file, which the ouster of the populist leader Salvador Abascal in 1941 accentuated.

The hesitations of the PAN and UNS further divided an already divided opposition. The plethora of conservative parties, groups and would-be candidates attested to the breadth of anti-government sentiment but also made co-operation against the common enemy difficult. The PAN and UNS – the intellectual brain and popular muscle of the Catholic right – were manipulated and marginalized. Other groups served the personalist interests of ageing *caudillos:* the Frente Constitucional Democrático Mexicano (FCDM) supported the perennially opportunist and optimistic General Rafael Sánchez Tapia; the PRAC, captained by old Callista bosses like Manuel Pérez Treviño, backed Amaro, but when Amaro's candidacy floundered (his image as a violent throwback to a former praetorian age did not help, and was enhanced by the belligerent manifesto with which he opened his campaign), the PRAC peevishly refused to switch its support to the main contender, Almazán.[59] For it was Almazán, backed by a

---

[58] Medina, *Del Cardenismo al Avilacamachismo*, pp. 92–3.

[59] Ibid., pp. 100–5; Virginia Prewett, *Reportage on Mexico* (New York, 1941), pp. 184–8.

diverse coalition, who now emerged as the chief challenge to Avila Camacho. Politically experienced, rich (he was reckoned to be worth $5 million), and smarter than Amaro (he had dispayed 'an impressive talent for hoax and skulduggery' during his chequered revolutionary career, and was 'too astute' to back Cedillo in 1938), Almazán had extensive interests in Nuevo León, where his military command was based and where he enjoyed warm relations with the Monterrey group.[60] Denied the chance to channel his known ambitions through the PRM – as Cárdenas hoped he would – Almazán benefited from the errors and failings of his fellow-oppositionists; and, denied the full support of organized right-wing groups (PRAC, PAN, UNS), he depended more on large, diffuse constituencies – Catholics, the middle class, smallholders – which were only loosely integrated into the Almazanista party, the Partido Revolucionario de Unificación Nacional (PRUN). If it was organizationally weak, Almazanismo was potentially powerful, especially because the candidate exercised a broader appeal than a spurred and booted *caudillo* like Amaro. He mobilized middle-class liberals, who relived the constitutional protest of 1929; peasants, disenchanted with the chicanery of the CNC and the slow pace or downright corruption of the agrarian reform; junior army officers (their commanders were sewn up by the PRM); and many working-class groups – notably the big industrial unions, the railwaymen and oil-workers, who resisted Lombardista log-rolling and Cardenista coercion, as well as the electricians and tram-workers, sections of the miners and the fissiparous teachers' union, the *sindicatos* of Guadalajara and the sugar-workers of Los Mochis, recent victims of a CTM-engineered internal coup. The capacious bosom of Almazanismo embraced the Trotskyist Partido Revolucionario Obrero Campesino (PROC), led by Diego Rivera, whose illicit liaison with the right was the logical result of the PCM's scarcely more licit liaison with the centre.

Almazanismo thus constituted a cave of Adullam in which gathered all groups hostile to official manipulation and critical of a regime which, in their candidate's words, 'far from realizing the promises of the Revolution has disorganized the economy . . . and brought dearth and poverty to the people'.[61] Almazán pitched his appeal at this level: broad, eclectic, critical of the regime but neither too specific nor too radical in its proposed alternatives. He harped on economic failure, official corruption, and nox-

[60] John Womack, Jr., *Zapata and the Mexican Revolution* (New York, 1969), p. 80; Davidson, Mexico City, 9 January 1940, FO 371/24217, A1301.
[61] González, *Los días del presidente Cárdenas*, p. 227.

ious foreign influence, Nazi or Communist; he lambasted the left (notably Lombardo) and resorted to an alternative populism, concluding speeches with cries of 'Viva la Virgen de Guadalupe' and 'Mueran los Gachupines' (these Gachupines being no longer the spurred Spaniards of the colony but the hated Republican refugees). Given Avila Camacho's own stress on national values and repudiation of communism, there was a distinct sameness about the candidates' rhetoric; Luis González exaggerates only slightly when he observes that 'Almazán could have been the candidate of the PRM and Avila Camacho of the PRUN'.[62]

Cárdenas hoped for an open debate and free election. He would not impose a successor on party or country. 'If the people want Almazán', he told a colleague, 'they shall have him'.[63] This approach, if characteristic, was novel and risky. The President himself might remain unperturbed as Almazán's candidacy – backed by monster rallies unseen since the days of Madero – began to boom; he might even concede, on election night, that the opposition had won and Almazán should take office. But others, seeing their positions and policies jeopardized, displayed less democratic equanimity; *la révolution en danger* justified tough measures. The CTM swung into action, pressuring constituent unions, mounting demonstrations, physically attacking opposition headquarters, engineering internal coups in recalcitrant organizations (such as the CGT and STFRM). Almazanistas complained of sackings and beatings; trains and meetings were attacked, sometimes with fatal consequences. The administration also delayed legislation on female suffrage, rightly apprehensive that the women's vote would go to the opposition. A dirty campaign culminated in a dirty election (July 1940), conducted under electoral rules that were an invitation to rigging and violence. Throughout the country, PRM and PRUN factions fought for control of polling booths, the CTM seizing many by force. Ballot boxes were stolen, there were numerous injuries (and thirty fatalities in the capital alone) and widespread complaints of official abuse. At Monterrey, the capital of Almazán's fief, post-office workers and even prisoners were reported as being dragooned into voting for the official ticket, which triumphed by 53,000 votes to 13,000 (the PRUN claimed to have polled 63,000). All this was fresh evidence, the press commented, of the 'democratic incapacity' of the Mexican people. Cárdenas possibly agreed. But if force and fraud were evident, so, too, was

[62] Ibid., p. 259.
[63] According to Luis Montes de Oca, in a memorandum of E. D. Ruiz, 5 August 1940, FO 371/ 24217, A3818.

widespread participation. Towns like Tampico recorded the biggest turnout ever.[64]

The final result gave Avila Camacho 2.26 million votes to Almazán's 129,000. The PRUN claimed 2.5 million, and its claim did not lack foundation. Certainly Almazán carried the major cities, where official control was more difficult and CTM mobilization proved indifferent; but, here as elsewhere in Latin America, the *voto cabreste* went the way of the government, thus justifying the Secretary of the Interior's reassuring election-night report to the President: 'The peasants' vote had . . . turned the election result in favour of Avila Camacho'.[65] Like Madero in 1910, Almazán retired to the United States, crying foul and breathing defiance. The parallel was noted: the Almazanista martyr General Zarzosa, killed when police attempted his arrest, was cast as the Aquiles Serdán of 1940. But the parallel did not hold. Times had changed and Almazán was too shrewd – also too 'fat, sick and rich' – to chance rebellion.[66] The United States (as Alemán confirmed on a flying visit) would lend Almazán no aid or comfort. And Almazán's coalition, though broad, was too disparate to present a concerted challenge (Lombardo feared the military, but Avila Camacho and his backers had done their homework, and Cárdenas took the precaution of switching key commands and paying a personal visit to the Almazanista north; by now, Lombardo's fears of militarism and fascism were acquiring a certain theatrical contrivance). In a *país organizado,* rebellion had to be a professional business, not a Quixotic re-run of 1910; the regime of the PRM was not the regime of Porfirio. Above all, political discontent did not imply revolutionary commitment. Many on the right (above all, the Monterrey group) were content to give the regime a bloody nose, which would encourage caution in future. Equally, the industrial unions, by flirting with Almazán, no more committed themselves to revolution than to conservative populism, although they did set themselves up as targets for the incoming administration, which did not forget their defection. Therefore, 1940 was less a revolution *manqué* than a requiem for Cardenismo: it revealed that hopes of a democratic succession were illusory; that electoral endorsement of the regime had to be manufactured; and that the Cardenista reforms, while creating certain loyal clien-

---

[64] González, *Los días del presidente Cárdenas,* pp. 302–3; *El Universal,* 8 July 1940; Rees, Mexico City, 12 July 1940, FO 371/24217, A2619, and enclosures.

[65] Medin *Ideología y praxis política,* p. 222.

[66] Rees, Mexico City, 9 February 1940, FO 371/24217, A1654.

teles (some loyal from conviction, some by virtue of co-option) had also raised up formidable opponents who now looked to take the offensive.

Avila Camacho ran for office stressing conciliation and national unity, rejecting communism and class struggle.[67] So he continued after 1940, the rhetoric reinforced by the electoral trauma of that year, by Mexico's growing involvement in the war and by the economic and military dependence on the United States which the war encouraged. Systematically, the *presidente caballero* appealed for unity in order to produce, export and industrialize, and to resist fascism, inflation and communism. In the process, much of the dissident right of 1940 was incorporated into official politics (if it did not colonize the PRM, it nevertheless conformed to the rules of the game, as did the PAN and even the UNS leaders). The left, meanwhile, found itself acting more as instrument – or victim – than as maker of policy. It was unable or unwilling to halt the rightward drift which the rhetoric of consensus concealed: the decline of agrarian reform, the curtailment of workers' control, renewed stress on private enterprise and commercial agriculture, the dynamic growth of private and foreign investment (and of profits at the expense of wages), accommodation with the Church and the elimination of socialist education.

Détente with the United States was already under way as Avila Camacho took power. The events of 1941–2, which brought both the United States and Mexico into the war, served to accelerate this trend. In the wake of Pearl Harbor, Mexico broke relations with the Axis powers, extended special rights to the U.S. Navy and from January 1942 collaborated in a Joint Defense Commission. Mexico's chief contribution was still economic: the 'battle for production', which the President announced in his 1942 New Year message. In May of that year, the sinking of Mexican ships by 'totalitarian' (German) submarines in the Gulf provoked protests and – when these were ignored – a statement to the effect that a 'state of war' existed between Mexico and the Axis. By this novel diplomatic concept (no formal declaration of war was issued) the government implied that the war was a defensive struggle, thrust upon a reluctant people. During 1942–3, defence of the continent, especially the west coast, dominated Mexican and U.S. strategic thinking. Military co-operation soon began, but it encountered serious obstacles, monuments to the two countries'

---

[67] Davidson, Mexico City, 9 January 1940, FO 371/24217, A1301; Prewett, *Reportage on Mexico*, pp. 191, 221.

historically antagonistic, unequal relationship. On the Mexican side, reorganization and modernization of the armed forces were high priorities. By 1942, national military service and civil defence were instituted, the Supreme Defence Council was set up, and Cárdenas – already commanding in the crucial Pacific zone – was appointed Minister of Defence (a measure which calmed nationalist fears that collaboration was proceeding too far and too fast, and which further reinforced both the left's commitment to the war and its confidence in the future). During the long, ticklish talks concerning American military rights in Mexico (radar surveillance, landing rights, naval patrols, chains of command) the ex-president proved an obdurate negotiator. Meanwhile, the United States furnished credit for the modernization of Mexico's armed forces, and during 1940–3 the secular decline in military expenditure was briefly reversed. The new *matériel* was put on display at the annual military parade of 16 September 1942 in the hope that it would quicken the enthusiasm of the pacific masses and, more certainly, of the recipient generals, whose itch to participate in the war grew as re-equipment proceeded and the fortunes of war changed. For by early 1943, with the battles of Stalingrad and (more important) Midway won, Mexico's defensive posture lost its rationale. The ancient fear of a Japanese descent on Baja California and points south was finally laid to rest. Now the question of active participation arose, encouraged by generals who wanted to fight, by politicians who sought a place at the post-war peace conference, and by the United States, which saw Mexican participation as advantageous in respect of the rest of Latin America and of future Mexican–American relations. Accordingly, an air force squadron – the famous no. 201 – was selected, trained and sent to the Pacific front, where it arrived for combat in spring 1945.

This was an important and – from the government's point of view a successful – symbolic action, although it involved only forty-eight air crews, all of them professionals. More delicate was the question of national conscription, which revealed the gulf between official commitment to the war and popular indifference or hostility. Conscripts were not sent to the front, but this fact did not overcome the old antipathy to military service, and the problem was compounded by the drafting into the U.S. Army of Mexican citizens resident north of the border. (Condoned by government agreement, this practice resulted in the recruitment of some 15,000 Mexicans, 10 per cent of whom became casualties.) Within Mexico military service provoked wide-spread, sometimes violent, protest in which the old anti-revolutionary Catholic cause blended with a new, genuine grievance

(Cárdenas' presence at the Ministry of Defence encouraged this amalgam). Telegraph lines were cut, army trucks and barracks attacked, to cries of 'death to Cárdenas and conscription', 'Long live Sinarquismo', and 'Long live the Virgin of Guadalupe'. In the biggest incident, three hundred rebels fought with the army in Puebla. But with official assurances that conscription would not involve service outside Mexico, the protest ebbed; the UNS – already weakened by internal divisions and by its moderate leaders' desire for accommodation with the regime – lost its last, best cause and went into decline. In 1944 it was dissolved by government decree.

Violent protest was only the most extreme example of the gap separating official and popular attitudes to the war. Mexico's participation had been endorsed by the left (CTM, PCM) and, surprisingly and significantly, by the Catholic hierarchy, by most of the right-wing press, by the PAN and other conservative groups. Something of the bipartisan nationalism of 1938 was thus revived. Yet, as polls revealed, even party members and officials were divided over the issue; the man in the street did not share the belligerence of the regime unless he happened to be a committed leftist. As *El Tiempo* neatly summarized the situation, it was the *pueblo no organizado* who were least belligerent and most suspicious.[68] Like previous official causes – anti-clericalism, socialist education – belligerence was foisted upon a skeptical population by an organized minority. Facing such indifference, and fearful of fifth-column activity (none of which occurred), the government resorted to controls and exhortation. Constitutional guarantees were lifted, internal surveillance was increased, the executive was voted extraordinary powers. In general, these were used with sufficient moderation to deflect criticism. The administration also mounted a sustained propaganda campaign designed to win popular support: the war thus offered superb terrain on which to build the national consensus to which the regime was committed and to which the United States now also contributed – not, as in 1938, as the external enemy but as a fellow-democracy and military ally. Leading *políticos* joined in a chorus of patriotic union which, beginning with the solemn burial of a victim of the torpedoed tanker *Potrero de Llano,* culminated in the military parade of 16 September 1943, which six ex-presidents reviewed, Cárdenas standing shoulder-to-shoulder with Calles and, of course, Avila Camacho. The press, curbed by law but positively encouraged by a generous supply of

[68] Torres, *México en la segunda guerra mundial,* pp. 85–6.

American newsprint, readily collaborated; street posters and cinemas (the latter also favoured by American largesse) rammed home the message of patriotism, hemispheric unity and productive effort. Propaganda, both Mexican and American, drenched the population, 'diluting anti-American- ism and encouraging, first, conformity and, second, adherence to the Allied cause'.[69] The penetration of American mores – the *pochismo* which Vasconcelos had been denouncing for years and which had grown with the roads, tourism and manufacturing of the 1930s – thus accelerated during the war, in Mexico as in Europe. Coke, Garbo, Palmolive and Protestant- ism seemed ubiquitous; and Protestants (by no means the most effective agents of *pochismo*) began to experience a fierce Catholic backlash.

The specific impact of wartime propaganda is hard to evaluate, easy to exaggerate. Economic collaboration was more effective in changing Mexi- can ways and linking the destinies of the two neighbours. The trends may be statistically summarized: in 1937–8 a third of Mexico's trade was with Europe; by 1946 this had fallen to 5 per cent (of imports) and 2 per cent (of exports); the United States took 90 per cent of Mexican exports in 1940 and supplied 90 per cent of imports in 1944. Furthermore, Mexico's foreign trade had grown appreciably: exports from 6.9 million pesos (1939–41 average, in 1960 pesos) to 9.1 million (1943–5), 1.1 million of which derived from migrants' remittances; imports grew from 6.1 million to 9.1 million. In the process, Mexico passed from a surplus on visible trade in 1942–3 to a modest deficit in 1944 (1.6 million pesos) and yet larger deficits in 1945 (2.8 million) and 1948 (5.4 million), as U.S. controls were relaxed and imports flooded in. With increased trade came increased U.S. investment, especially in manufacturing industry. The tran- sition from an economy based on the export of primary goods to one in which a sizeable manufacturing industry catered to domestic demand was accelerated during the war, though with the consequence of enhanced U.S. participation and an unprecedented degree of external dependency (for once the term is entirely appropriate).

In the economic as in the military field Mexico and the United States did not establish their new intimacy easily. Industrialization was now the key item of government policy, stressed by Avila Camacho, Lombardo and others as a means to enlarge the social product, escape agrarian backward- ness and mitigate – if not escape – the vicissitudes of the trade cycle. Co- operation with the United States offered a fast route to industrialization,

[69] Ibid., p. 104.

but if it was to confer the desired economic autonomy it had to be co-operation on the right terms. The oil companies' attempt to exploit war-time collaboration and PEMEX's shortage of funds in order to reclaim their properties was resisted, even if foreign credit was thereby restricted. For similar reasons, negotiations for a bilateral trade treaty (a long-term Mexican objective) proved arduous, although they were ultimately success-ful. Throughout, Mexico sought to protect domestic industry while nego-tiating a lowering of American tariffs, access to American credit, and easier import of capital goods and certain raw materials (which were in short supply and subject to American wartime controls). The United States sought short-term, guaranteed access to key Mexican resources (minerals, oil and, no less, manpower) and perhaps the long-term subordi-nation of the Mexican to the American economy. A general commercial treaty concluded in December 1942 was supplemented by a range of specific agreements, covering particular products; between 1943 and 1945 the Mexican–American Commission for Economic Cooperation channeled U.S. credit into a variety of projects: steel, paper, dams, hydro-electric power, cement and chemicals. Thus, the earlier plans for co-operation favoured by Cárdenas and Roosevelt but shelved in 1938 came to fruition. The provision of credit, however, was of limited duration and quantity: by 1946 the United States had switched its priorities to Europe, asserting the obligation of private institutions to meet Mexico's requirements.

The Second World War, like the First, produced a dramatic turn in the recurrent ebb and flow of Mexican migration to the United States (it also had the less publicized effect of sucking Guatemalan migrants into south-ern Mexico, with dire consequences for local labour). Some ten years after the hordes of migrants had headed south, they began to return north again – at the rate of some 6,000 a month by the summer of 1942. They came from all parts of Mexico and embraced a wide range of trades and backgrounds; most were young and unmarried, while many were em-ployed, skilled, even educationally qualified. Both governments sought to control this spontaneous tide: the American, in order to guarantee suffi-cient labour for a voracious war economy; the Mexican, to avert labour shortages at home and abuses of migrant workers abroad, which the half-hearted efforts of the American authorities could not prevent. By 1942, numbers and terms of employment had been fixed by governmental agree-ment. But so great was the demand for jobs that when official labour recruitment began in Mexico, the offices were besieged by supplicants; in March 1944, 3,000 gathered in Mexico City's national stadium for precious *bracero* permits. A year later the official programme covered more than 120,000 workers, whose remittances constituted 13 per cent of total foreign exchange earnings. Illegal migration, however, was running at the same rate (and with it recurrent deportations which, as American demand began to drop after 1944, were running at 7,000 a month). During 1945–6 the official quota was progressively cut; *braceros* joined the deportees being herded south, where they joined the jams at the border or lodged in the shanty-towns of San Diego and the Imperial Valley. For many, the return south proved temporary because a renewed boom soon pulled migrants – legal and illegal – back to the fields and factories of the north.

Economic collaboration with the United States thus favoured the Avilacamachista project of industrialization, social conciliation and national consensus. These, in turn, demanded of the President an ostensibly even-handed approach to the distribution of power and determination of policy. He had to appear a 'trimmer', not a 'partisan'.[70] The initial cabinet neatly balanced left and right; in Congress the leftist Chamber countered the conservative Senate. But just as Cárdenas was pushed left, so his successor was moved by circumstances as well as inclination to the right. In the field of education there was a retreat from 'socialism', first in spirit, then in name. Under the new minister Vejar Vázquez (1941–3), the so-called *escuela de amor* (which had nothing to do with Bassols' sex education) officially replaced the socialist schools; education now served to endorse the anodyne slogans of the regime, and Communist *maestros* were weeded out. Conservative and Catholic groups, delighted at this development, also welcomed the warmer relations between Church and State. The official right, in the shape of the President's brother Maximino, also controlled the Ministry of Communications, where the incumbent fostered his own presidential ambitions, feuded with Lombardo and other surviving radicals, and (it was said) entertained grand plans for the emasculation of the CTM. In the states, too, gubernatorial elections brought a shift to the right (by 1945 only eight out of thirty-one governors were reckoned to be Cardenistas); in Congress, debates, votes and appointments revealed a degree of conservative self-confidence and aggression not seen since the days of the *maximato*. The official right – with Maximino Avila Camacho and Abelardo Rodríguez prominent – now constructed a new rhetoric, allied to the administration's line in its concern for unity, democracy, and

[70] Bateman, Mexico City, 14 February 1944, FO 371/38312, AN798.

the defeat of fascism, but also stridently anti-communist, critical of the CTM and designed to depict Cardenismo in the same crude red colours. Indeed, there were underhanded attempts to embarrass Cárdenas himself, and a dirty press campaign against Lombardo. Leftists even found the hand of the executive working against them, in murky circumstances.[71] The left was not powerless in the face of such provocation: the President had to make them concessions (for example, throwing the Secretary of Economy to the CTM wolves in 1944); and it had its own repertoire of dirty tricks (such as, the contrived court-martial of Macías Valenzuela, the ex-governor of Sinaloa). The National University, too, was the scene of a careful political balancing act. The tight embrace of national consensus, to which most political actors had surrendered, made outright ideological pugilism difficult; the result was dirty in-fighting in which the executive, with its control of the courts, electoral machinery and parastatal agencies, was at a decisive advantage over mass organizations like the CTM. Both the climate, and the modus operandi of politics were changing.

Despite judicious displays of presidential balance, the trend – revealed in the 1943 congressional elections – was inexorably right. In part this responded to the President's desire to build up a solid, centre-right clientele in the legislature. A convenient instrument was at hand: the Confederación Nacional de Organizaciones Populares (CNOP), hitherto a diffuse conglomerate, which now became the institutional representative of the political class in particular, and of the middle class in general (a class increasingly flattered by official rhetoric). It also proved a loyal creature of the executive and a counter-weight to both the official left (chiefly the CTM) and also the middle-class opposition which had upset PRM calculations in 1940. This became clear in the 1943 congressional elections, conducted in indecent haste and with the usual fixing. The CNOP was rewarded with 56 of the 144 PRM candidacies (the CTM got 21) and the extra-official extremes were shut out. Both the Communists and Bassols' Liga de Acción Política were denied seats; the PCM stoically accepting another reverse in the name of wartime consensus, protested less shrilly than Bassols. The PAN, running a clutch of middle-class candidates on a conservative Christian Democratic ticket (leftist allegations of fascism were now rather dated), was also disappointed. Indeed, the radical right found its popular appeal fast diminishing as the regime itself 'moderated' and the provocations of Cardenismo faded into the past.

[71] Medina, *Del cardenismo al avilacamachismo*, pp. 163–72, 222–4.

The official left was also changing. In 1943 the Cardenista stalwart Graciano Sánchez quit the CNC leadership in favour of Gabriel Leyva Velázquez, son of a revolutionary martyr but a dedicated Avilacamachista and an implacable enemy of the Communists. The CTM bent its efforts to curb strikes and sustain economic production (arguably it made a virtue of necessity: the government had powers to compel if collaboration was not forthcoming); and in June 1942 it joined with rival confederations in the Pacto Obrero, which abjured strikes and provided for rapid arbitration of disputes. In return, the government established a social security law which became operative – albeit in controversial fashion – in 1943. By now Lombardo had, with typical rhetorical flourish, quit the leadership of the CTM and was busy rallying to the Allied cause the Confederación de Trabajadores de América Latina (CTAL), of which he had been president since its birth in 1938. His influence endured, though less tenaciously than he himself imagined; and it was used to bolster his successor, Velázquez, against the attacks of Communists and dissident Lombardistas. The official left thus tolerated the growing conservative presence in government, and the frequent barbs of the resurgent right. Unity remained the watchword.

With the left quiescent and his own authority enhanced, Avila Camacho could pursue his chosen policy of industrialization via co-operation with the United States. Industrialization had, of course, been espoused by Lucas Alamán in the aftermath of independence, by Porfirio Díaz, by Calles and by Cárdenas; it had prospered during the 1930s despite the Cárdenas reforms, but the unique circumstances of the war seemed unusually propitious. The social truce and Pacto Obrero conferred industrial tranquillity while the United States, newly complaisant of Mexico's needs, provided both a market and, with qualifications, a source of capital goods and investment. The promises made to private enterprise in 1940 were honoured in continued rhetorical reassurance and numerous practical measures: the elimination of the superprofit tax, the development of Nacional Financiera as a major source of industrial finance, the maintenance of a regressive fiscal system, generous tax concessions and tariff protection, and a Supreme Court hostile to labour. Between 1940 and 1946 manufacturing output grew 43 per cent in constant pesos (59 per cent if construction is included: Mexico City especially enjoyed a prodigious building boom). Food, textiles, chemicals and metals were prominent. Manufacturing investment quintupled, and manufacturers' profits were bountiful, reaching 18 per cent on invested capital in 1941–2. Thus, the ratio of returns to labour and capital shifted from 52:48 in 1939 to 39:61 in 1946. In 1942 the Monterrey group expressed their confidence that the President 'would not follow the labour policies of his predecessor'; which confidence (as arbitration rulings showed) was not misplaced.[72] The PAN's assumption of the role of a loyal Christian Democratic opposition was, then, not entirely due to its enthusiasm for the Allied cause.

As the *sexenio* drew to a close, however, the economic climate worsened. Inflation grew, generating enhanced profits (1945–6 were boom years for industry) but also bringing renewed labour unrest, which could less easily be checked by patriotic appeals. The surge of American imports helped the supply of capital goods, but it also jeopardized the balance of payments and Mexico's infant industries. The industrial bourgeoisie – now organized to an unprecedented degree - exhibited two responses. Representatives of the nascent manufacturing industry, grouped in the Confederación Nacional de la Industria de Transformación (CNIT), favoured corporate agreements with labour, mixed arbitration of labour disputes, a degree of state intervention in industrial relations, tariff protection, and close regulation of foreign investment. On this basis, the CNIT could reach agreement with the CTM (March 1945) reaffirming in vague terms the old wartime alliance for production. But the senior business organizations – especially the Confederación Patronal de la República Mexicana (COPARMEX), which the Monterrey group dominated – disapproved of the liaison with labour (they had never espoused the Pacto Obrero), favoured tougher laws to deter strikes, and adhered to traditional laisser-faire notions of the role of government. Business emerged from the war politically and economically stronger but also divided, and with a major sector advocating policies of red-blooded, free-enterprise conservatism.

Labour chafed at the restraints placed upon it – by government and unions alike – at a time of mounting inflation. By 1942 the U.S. connection, compounded by domestic factors (population growth, government deficits, and poor harvests in 1943–5) began to generate inflation rates far higher than those which had caused concern in the later 1930s. The cost-of-living index (1939=100) rose to 121 in 1942, 198 in 1944 and 265 in 1946, with food and basic consumer goods making the running (while the retail price index rose by two and two-thirds between 1940 and 1946, the price of maize tripled, that of beans and meat quadrupled). Moreover, official counter-measures were less effective than in 1938–9. Attempts to

[72] Ibid., p. 300.

limit the money supply, avert speculation and hoarding, and curtail price rises began in 1941; their failure was evident in the accelerating inflation and the booming black market, and in the further controls, measures and penalties which proliferated after Mexico's entry into the war. Private enterprise, earning handsome profits, cavilled at the constraints, whereas the CTM called for tougher measures to curb inflation and/or raise wages. The squeeze on wages was acute; between 1940 and 1946 prices almost tripled but the minimum wage barely doubled; 1946–7 marked a historic low for real wages, which had fallen by as much as a quarter in industry, and more in other sectors. Popular hardship contrasted with the conspicuous consumption of the wartime nouveaux riches – 'the privileged classes whose one idea was to get rich quick before the war ended'.[73] Both the president and his heir-apparent had to take note. By 1942–3 the reasoned complaints of the CTM were seconded by Sinarquistas, by demonstrators on the streets, and by increased – often wildcat – strikes. Buses were burned in Monterrey as a protest against fare increases; by 1944 food lines and hunger marches had become familiar. Even the new social security system, introduced to appease labour, had the opposite effect, the deduction of contributions from slim wage-packets generating a series of riots, the most serious in Mexico City in July 1944. Strikes, both official and unofficial, increased during 1943–4, as did pre-emptive wage rises designed to buy off the industrially powerful. Members of the big unions were therefore better protected against inflation than most rural or white-collar workers, the hardships of whom were compounded by wartime shortages (e.g., oil and rubber) and cuts in urban services (transport, electricity). Some – to the detriment of public ethics – sought compensation in the *mordida,* the back-hander.[74]

Labour, too, began to question the purpose of the 'social truce', which now seemed chiefly a means of boosting profits at the expense of wages. In facing renewed militancy, the government found an ally in Lombardo, whose commitment to consensus had evolved from a tactic into an article of faith. Because the much flourished fascist menace was fading, Lombardo now argued for a national alliance of workers and bourgeoisie against foreign imperialism. The CTM–CNIT agreement of March 1945 seemed to foreshadow this, but the CNIT did not speak for all Mexican business. The Monterrey group had no time for pacts and no taste for

---

[73] Cheetham, Mexico City, 10 January 1944, FO 371/38312, AN293.
[74] Ibid.; Lesley Byrd Simpson, *Many Mexicos,* 4th ed. (Berkeley, 1971), pp. 342–4.

labour militancy. It crossed swords with the CTM in a major dispute at the Cristalería Monterrey (summer 1946), during which the city was briefly paralysed and a general strike narrowly averted. Presidential intervention calmed but could not settle a conflict that remained unresolved as Avila Camacho left office, bequeathing his successor a legacy of high inflation, falling real wages and renewed industrial conflict.

In agriculture, as in industry, the administration claimed to stand on the middle ground, guaranteeing *ejidal* and private property alike. In practice, however, the *ejido,* the central item of the Cardenista project, was relegated to a secondary role and its internal workings changed. The new emphasis was in part a reaction against Cardenismo; in part a response to Sinarquismo and Almazanismo; and in part a recognition of the need to boost agricultural production, for both consumption and export (a need reinforced by the dearth and inflation of the war). More private land was protected and the new concessions to private farmers embodied in the Agrarian Code of 1942 also figured as incentives in the administration's plans for coastal colonization: the 'march to the sea'. The guarantees against expropriation offered to small proprietors by Cárdenas were extended, and private landowners benefited disproportionately from the administration's major investments in irrigation, from available public credit and from inflation. Although the distribution of land did not cease, it slowed to one-third the rate of the Cárdenas years. The land was now of inferior quality (some recipients declined to accept it), and the administrative delays lengthened. The days of grand presidential initiatives, of drastic dismemberments of ancient latifundia, were over. Landlords appreciated they could now count on the neutrality if not the positive support of the central government − historically the crucial agent in determining the pace of reform. Litigation again became prolonged, expensive and corrupt, as the old stratagems of the *maximato* were revived: *prestanombres,* pseudo-division of estates, white guards and violence. The restoration of the agrarian *amparo* (a key weapon of landlord legal defence) was considered, and finally implemented under the next administration. As the CNC moved towards boss rule and co-optation, *ejidatarios* increasingly provided the loyal clienteles of president or governor, and private landlords organized themselves to an unprecedented degree.

Ejidatarios now faced mounting insecurity which reinforced such clientalistic dependence: shortages of credit, political sniping (the collective *ejidos* were favourite targets), even the outright loss of *ejidal* land, especially in zones where land values were boosted by tourism (e.g., Guerrero) or urbanization. The relative, though not the absolute, size of the *ejidal* sector began gradually to decline. Internal structures changed as the government encouraged the parcellization of collectives (a policy for which there was general demand and broad political support from the UNS to the PCM). The collective form was retained where it was deemed economic (that is, profitable: some collective *ejidos* were highly productive and made a contribution to exports); but it was now subject to the imperatives of a global market, of an administration keen to promote exports and of an increasingly corrupt officialdom. Sugar co-operatives had to obey rules favouring the private *ingenios;* in Yucatán the demands of war production justified the *hacendados'* recovery of their rasping machines (as one landlord put it, robbing *ejidatarios* was no crime as *ejidatarios* were themselves *ladrones*). Internal stratification accelerated as *ejidal caciques* gained control and the *ejidatarios* polarized into a relatively affluent elite and a semi-proletarian majority, whose numbers were swollen by rapid population growth.

Campesino resistance to these changes was inhibited by the wartime social truce, by the landlords' political recovery and by the flaccidity of the CNC. *Bracerismo* and internal migration, too, offered palliatives. Hence land seizures, notable in 1941–2, declined thereafter. Protest continued in areas of traditional militancy: the Laguna, and Morelos, where Rubén Jaramillo's guerrillas became active after 1943, demanding continued reform and guarantees for existing *ejidos*. But these struggles went against the political grain. The stress laid by the president himself and the new technocrats of the 1940s on productivity and profit, the assumption that private farming was superior to the *ejido* – and for that matter, industry to agriculture – indicated a profound ideological shift since the 1930s. And their objectives seemed to be attained. During the *sexenio* agricultural output grew some 3.5 per cent a year in real terms (about the same rate as industry), with gains accruing from higher productivity rather than expanded cultivation; exports, too, rose even faster. Private and *ejidal* farmers alike contributed to this growth: the former including both 'neo-latifundista' agrarian capitalists and *rancheros* who reaped the benefit of secure tenure, mounting demand and better road links. No longer a social and economic project in its own right, the linch-pin of Cardenista policy, the *ejido* was fast becoming a productive adjunct of the booming urban, industrial economy, and the *ejidatarios* the most docile clients of the official party.

Avila Camacho's presidency ended amid inflation, *ejidal* decline, industrial boom, and unprecedented dependence on the United States. The left, not least Lombardo Toledano, entertained hopes of a major recovery in its fortunes. The right for its part including the burgeoning industrial bourgeoisie, looked askance at growing labour militancy and sought to contain the unions and the left, thus guaranteeing continued industrial advance and ensuring that Avilacamachismo would prove not a hiatus between bouts of radicalism, but a bridge linking the dangerous Cardenismo of the past to the secure conservatism of the future. For both sides it seemed there was all to play for; and the outcome of their conflict in 1946–9 would determine Mexico's future for over a generation.

The presidential succession – which quickened ambitions as early as 1942 – focused on two aspirants: Miguel Alemán, ex-governor of Veracruz, Avila Camacho's campaign manager in 1940 and then Secretary of Gobernación (which ministry now began to take on its role as the nursery of presidents); and Ezequiel Padilla, an old Callista, Mexican ambassador to the United States and major architect of the new Mexican-American detente. Both were civilians; the wartime professionalization of the army had delivered the *coup de grâce* to *caudillismo*. Leftist candidates – Javier Rojo Gómez, Miguel Henríquez Guzmán – played brief, inglorious roles, before it was made clear that Avila Camacho favoured Alemán, that Cárdenas and most state governors acceded to the presidential choice and that the left had better bow to the inevitable, which it did, with Lombardo supplying the appropriate sophisms. By autumn 1945 the CTM, CNC, CNOP and even the PCM had endorsed Alemán, and Padilla was obliged to play the part of an independent candidate, backed by a makeshift party.

In retrospect, the left's endorsement appears a costly error. Perhaps resistance was futile since the CTM leaders, scarcely popular, wielded power by following the rules of the game, not by bucking them. But contemporary estimations of Alemán differed from those of posterity. He was the candidate of the centre, Padilla, the candidate of the right; and, like Avila Camacho, he preached a bland populism; he also promised some democratization of the party. To private enterprise he offered reassurance and an end to wartime controls, but he also affirmed the state's concern for the working class and responsibility for the problems of dearth and inflation. Although his reassurances covered foreign investment, Alemán was seen as the nationalist candidate who would resist the economic hegemony of the United States (even the Americans took this view). Misconceived though this was, it was music to the ears of Lombardo, who was persuaded by the outgoing President to postpone plans for the launch of a new Lombardista party of the left until the election was over. Alemán's presumed nationalism gave the left's ultimately bitter liaison with him an initial ideological savour.

Although Alemán was assured of victory, it was felt necessary to impart greater democratic legitimacy to the electoral process and to avert a repeat of 1940. A new electoral law required stricter national organization of parties and closer federal supervision of elections: this inhibited the kind of decentralized chaos and conflict seen in 1940, and enhanced both official control of the opposition and the President's role as the Great Elector. The official party, conforming to the new order, underwent its final metamorphosis from PRM to the Partido Revolucionario Institucional (PRI): a change more cosmetic than real, in which the promise of internal democratization chiefly involved a demotion of the power of the CTM. Under this new dispensation the 1946 elections were almost free of violent incident despite the usual abuses and opposition complaints. Neither Padilla nor the fragmented, independent left, nor the right – the PAN and the Sinarquista successor party, Fuerza Popular – could mount a challenge comparable to Almazán's six years before. Alemán with 78 per cent of the vote won the presidency by a huge margin.

Thus mandated, the new President had less need than his predecessor to trim. His cabinet was packed with young men – most, like the President himself, too young to be revolutionary veterans. Four industrialists now figured, evidence of the new bourgeois power within the bosom of the party, and only two ministers were military. With the continued elimination of Cardenista governors (sometimes by constitutional strong-arming) it became clear that power had shifted to a new, technocratic generation for whom the revolution was less a personal experience than a convenient myth. Their rise paralleled the rise of the CNOP, which, as the CTM declined, assumed the political direction of the party, supplied the *políticos* of the day (much as the army had in the past) and served as a firm basis for presidential power. It paralleled, too, the growth of graft on a grand scale. It was now – rather than in the 1920s or 1930s – that the regime acquired its distinctive contemporary characteristics: presidential preeminence, the political monopoly of the official party, the deft manipulation of mass organizations, the dilution of class and ideological differences in the solvent of nationalism.

The ideas and mechanisms of Cardenismo were now put to new pur-

poses. Alemán's succession came at a time when U.S. influence –
economic, political, cultural–was pervasive and unprecedented, above all
because of the new purchase it acquired in domestic circles. In the past,
revolutionary Mexico had had to contend with White House liberals who
were vaguely sympathetic if sometimes meddlesome (Wilson, FDR); or
conservative pragmatists (Taft, Coolidge) whose antipathy was tempered
by businesslike caution. Now, Mexico faced the America of Truman, the
Truman Doctrine, 'containment' and National Security Council resolution
248; ideology and geopolitics underpinned systematic policies of intervention, pressure and co-option. Already, under Roosevelt, the United States
had shown itself eager to sustain the close military co-operation of the war
into peace time; and at the 1945 Chapultepec Conference, it pressed its
obsessive case for an open, free-trading system–thus, for continued American hegemony in Latin America. Alemán, seen as a prickly nationalist,
was at pains to reassure the United States, promising continued economic
collaboration, and pandering to the new prejudices of the Cold War. In
this, he set the tone of the *sexenio*, when anti-communism, incorporated
into traditional, nationalist discourse and presented in terms of the new
polarization of democracy and communism, became a staple of Mexican
politics, 'elevated to the rank of an official doctrine'.[75] The revolutionary
tradition ruled out the cruder forms of McCarthyism; but it also provided
the best ideological defence against communism, which, like fascism in
previous years, could be depicted as a dangerous alien import. Thus, in
Mexico as in Europe, the democratic crusade against fascism transmuted
imperceptibly into the democratic crusade against communism and, as in
the early 1930s, the ideological temper of politics rapidly changed, leaving the left weakened and defensive, the right in brazen possession of a
new, democratically justified, nationalist cause. Alemán's anti-communism was soon echoed by the party president, by leaders like Fernando
Amilpa, the CTM veteran and crony of Fidel Velázquez, and by business
mouthpieces like the Confederación Patronal de la República Mexicana
(COPARMEX), which alleged the subversive role of Communist cells in
the big industrial unions. Anti-communism was particularly effective at a
time when Lombardo was cobbling together his new party of the left,
when the major unions were displaying renewed militancy, and when, of
course, the climate of international politics was rapidly, propitiously freez-

[75] Luis Medina, *Historia de la revolución mexicana Periodo* 1940–1952: *Civilismo y modernización del
autoritarismo* (Mexico, 1979), p. 110.

ing. The most decisive achievement of the Alemán administration was thus a negative one: its isolation and emasculation of the left, and its concerted campaign against organized labour.

Lombardo, having obligingly deferred the launch of his new party, now sought the continuation of the old Lombardista project – a broad, nationalist, anti-imperialist alliance of progressive groups – outside, but not in opposition to, the official party. But the PRI did not appreciate this comradely rivalry; nor were the Communists entirely sympathetic. Eventually founded in June 1948, the Partido Popular (PP) grouped disaffected members of the official left (Lombardo, Bassols, Rivera) and certain worker and peasant groups behind a moderate, nationalist programme. But, as state elections revealed in 1949, the PRI would have no truck with the PP and Lombardo (whose own presidential candidacy was to flounder in 1952) was now widely depicted as a fellow-traveller or downright instrument of Stalin, 'bought by Moscow gold'. The CTM, which initially gave Lombardo tepid support in return for his co-operation against the independent unions, now came out in opposition, casting similar aspersions, which wholly accorded with their present, systematic, anticommunist line.

Times had changed since 1933, when Lombardo had successfully launched his breakaway CGOCM, and the fast-maturing official party was now keen and able to stifle such challenges. Crucial to the outcome was the regime's confrontation with organized labour. The prolonged wartime collaboration and inflation had left a legacy of division, dissent and accumulated demands, on which Lombardo hoped to capitalize. In particular, the major industrial unions (foremost among them the STFRM) resented continued CTM docility, and by 1947 were ready to challenge its leaders – who, in turn, could count on the support of a host of minor unions and federations. The old division of 1937 thus resurfaced, aggravated by wartime trends and now posed in terms of 'purification' (i.e., change and militancy) against *continuismo.* The government, dedicated to industrialization, could not accommodate union militancy; and the erosion of Lombardo's influence ruled out his familiar arbitral role, ensuring that the confrontation with organized labour would be all the sharper. The indecisive skirmishing of 1938–46 thus gave way to the outright conflict of 1947–9.

The challenge to the CTM leaders was parried by the usual methods of electoral manipulation; the CTM thus opted for *continuismo, charrismo,* and generally uncritical support of a government of the right, which was justified in terms of nationalism and moderation ('no to extremism; rejection of the left and imperialism alike'). Those militants who stayed with the CTM (including some self-sacrificing Communists) lost all power. The vestigial remnants of syndicalism and socialism were swept away. The tactic of the general strike was repudiated and the old CTM slogan – 'for a classless society' – was replaced by nationalist flummery: 'for the emancipation of Mexico'.[76] In response, the railwaymen led a secession from the CTM which involved electricians, tram-workers and lesser unions (March 1947). Their new organization, the Confederación Unica de Trabajadores (CUT), was soon backed by the other, major dissidents, the oil-workers and miners, with whom a solidarity pact was concluded, forming a Mexican triple alliance openly defiant of the CTM and its 'tattered banner of anti-communism'. Fragmentation of the CTM went further, with internal dissent, expulsions and in 1948 the creation of a rival *central,* the Alianza Obrera Campesina Mexicana (AOCM), in which peasant elements, especially the *ejidatarios* of the Laguna, were prominent. Opposed and probably outnumbered by these rivals, the CTM faced its biggest test since 1937; and now neither Lombardo nor Moscow, nor even the regime (which wanted victories rather than compromises) would urge conciliation.

The key to the conflict lay with the main independent unions, the oil-workers and railwaymen. The former had struck in the first month of the *sexenio* (it was the culmination of sporadic wartime conflict in the industry). The government declared the strike illegal, deployed troops and imposed an arbitrated settlement. Divided in its response, the union accepted the new agreement, under which PEMEX was able to stabilize the payroll and increase managerial control (both objectives which the administration, keen to boost production and secure American credit, fully endorsed). In the subsequent battle for power within the union, the government bent its efforts to ensure a victory for collaboration and *charrismo.* It also looked to a similar rationalization of the railways, which had been the subject of a major inquiry in 1948. Again the union was split, and the government intervened on behalf of the fervently anti-communist faction of Jesús Díaz de León (*el charro*). His main rival was gaoled following plausible charges of corruption; independent union branches were seized; Communists were systematically removed. With the union's independence broken and the *charro* faction installed in power, the government could proceed to reorganize the railways, under threat of mass

[76] Ibid., p. 132.

sackings and wage cuts. But the new union leadership faced the classic dilemma of the official labour bureaucracy (with which Fidel Velázquez was to live for over a generation): although Díaz de León's 'moralization' campaign won him some genuine support, he was ultimately a creature of the government; but both he and the government had to maintain a semblance of workers' representation and co-operation. Coercion alone could not run the railways. *Charrazo* was therefore followed by negotiation and a new collective contract (1949), which combined cost-cutting with judicious job protection. Thus, even *charrismo* could be seen to deliver some of the goods; and to many it seemed preferable to a perilous, quixotic militancy. As one labour leader put it in 1947: 'better a bad collective contract (bad in that it curtails our rights) but which is at least honoured, than a good one which remains a dead letter'.[77] In this lay the secret of the CTM's success in the decades to come. To put it differently, Alemán's counter-revolution – the defeat of those radical, syndical and Cardenista elements which resisted the Alemanista project – had to be a good deal more subtle and moderate than those later implemented elsewhere in Latin America, following a comparable rationale but requiring outright military repression.

With the independence of the STFRM broken, the cause of the other industrial unions – miners, oil-workers, electricians – wilted. They had greeted the *charrazo* with protests but no strikes. Only the miners and the divided oil-workers affiliated to the new Lombardista central federation, the Unión General de Obreros y Campesinos de México (UGOCM); and the latter, like its political cousin the PP, soon proved a vulnerable target of government hostility. It was denied recognition; strikes it espoused were declared illegal; its affiliates suffered internal intervention and coup; its peasant members were subjected to the various persuasions of the CNC and the *ejidal* bureaucracy. The oil-workers' union, once it was securely in the hands of the *charro* faction, returned to the CTM fold (1951), setting a precedent other affiliates would follow. CTM control was thus reasserted, at a price. With the independent left emasculated, and the radical right either disappearing or fast mutating into a loyal Christian Democratic opposition, the peace of the PRI prevailed. The regime could pursue its chosen model of industrial development and capital accumulation without fear of major social mobilization. Nationally, 1949 revealed 'a panorama

---

[77] Hernández Abrego, of the oil-workers' unions, quoted in Rosalia Pérez Linares, 'El charrismo sindical en la decada de los setenta. El sindicato petrolero', in *Historia y crónicas de la clase obrera en México* (Mexico, 1981), p. 172.

totally distinct from that . . . of 1946'; locally, too, the late 1940s saw the crystallization of 'a political structure and pattern of political behaviour that has continued to this day.'[78] If the revolution experienced a decisive Thermidor, it was then. The Cardenista experiment, increasingly controlled after 1938, was now terminally halted, by new men who, ingeniously, found new uses for the old laboratory equipment. Or, changing the metaphor, the civilians and *técnicos* of the Alemán *sexenio,* imbued with a modernizing, Cold War ideology, and a get-rich-quick ethic, quarried the rubble of Cardenismo and utilized the material – the corporate party, the mass institutions, the powerful executive, the tamed army and subordinated peasantry – to build a new Mexico. The material was Cardenista, but the ground-plan was their own. It was build to last.

[78] Ibid., p. 94; Benjamin, 'Passages to Leviathan', p. 268.

2

MEXICO SINCE 1946

Mexico stands out as a paragon of political stability within contemporary
Latin America. There have been no successful military coups since the
nineteenth century and hardly any serious attempts since the Revolution
of 1910–20. Presidential successions have become genteel negotiations
within the semi-official party, the Partido Revolucionario Institucional
(PRI), which has dominated the electoral arena for more than half a
century. Civilians have gained control of the ruling apparatus. Consensus
appears to prevail on most policy questions, and the Constitution of
1917 – forged in the heat of armed conflict – has continued to provide
the regime an aura of legitimacy. Claiming a revolutionary heritage and
wielding a practical monopoly over the instruments of power, the Mexican
state has appeared to function smoothly, steadily and (in its own way)
efficiently. The consequent achievement of stability has thus come to be
hailed as the political component of the post-war 'Mexican miracle'.

Indeed, the perception of Mexico's political stability has imbued much
of the scholarly literature on contemporary Mexico with a tacit presump-
tion of continuity, a sense almost of timelessness. There tends to be an
unspoken assumption that nothing much has changed in Mexican politics
since the late 1930s, much more attention being given to the workings of
the system and the mechanisms of authority than to historical events or
discrete occurrences; most existing literature reveals a general, abstract
quality. This may illustrate one of the implicit biases of what has come to
be called 'systems analysis' in political science: preoccupation with the
maintenance of the political system rather than with patterns of transformation. Viewed in this perspective, post-war Mexico often looks flat and
one-dimensional.

In an effort to redress this imbalance this chapter will consider the
experience and socio-economic context of political change in Mexico since

the Second World War. In these years three separate historical phases can be identified: first, a period of definition and consolidation of the contemporary system, from the mid-1940s to the late 1950s; second, an era of domination and hegemony, from the late 1950s to perhaps the early 1970s; and third, a time of system stress and declining power, from the mid-1970s to the late 1980s. Since precise dates are difficult to fix, such a periodization provides only a general guideline for the analysis of political change, which, it should be stressed, is itself a very amorphous concept. At one end of the spectrum, it can refer to an alteration of political regime, as from democracy to authoritarianism. At the other end, it can refer to the kind of self-regulating adjustments which often help perpetuate a regime. Here, however, attention will be focussed on an intermediate level, on qualitative and quantitative transformations *of* and *within* the authoritarian regime which Mexico has maintained throughout the contemporary era. For this, it is necessary to assess the system's ability to satisfy the preconditions for stability – political balance, economic growth and rapprochement with the United States. These preconditions depend, in turn, on a number of salient factors: (1) the composition of the ruling coalition; (2) the coherence of the ruling coalition; (3) the power and legitimacy of the ruling coalition; (4) the policy orientations; and (5) the actions, responses and reactions of the system's constituent groups.

POSTWAR ECONOMY, SOCIETY AND POLITICS: AN OVERVIEW

The accomplishment of political stability is all the more remarkable in light of the dynamic transformations that have taken place in Mexican society. Over the past century the Mexican economy has undergone two fundamental transitions, one based on the export of primary products and the other characterized by import substitution industrialization (ISI). The first phase followed the consolidation of political power under Porfirio Díaz (1876–1911). A liberal in economic matters, Díaz opened the country to foreign investment and strengthened Mexico's commercial links to the outside world. Stimulated by the construction of a railway system, the volume of foreign trade increased nine times between 1877 and 1910. As well as silver and gold, Mexico began to export such industrial minerals as copper and zinc, mainly from the north; goods produced from cattle- and sheep-herding, also from the north; sugar, from the centre-south; and fibre, especially *henequen* from Yucatán. Oil production started just after 1900, and by the 1920s Mexico was one of the world's leading sources of petroleum. Like many other Latin American countries, Mexico pursued the classical strategy of 'comparative advantage', exporting raw materials and importing manufactured goods. The United States became the nation's leading source of investment and trade, and by 1910, at the centennial celebration of national independence, it seemed to many observers that Mexico was heading for prolonged prosperity. However, that year witnessed the outbreak of the Revolution, which took a massive human and economic toll, and then, just as an economic recovery was starting to pick up in the 1920s, the world depression struck. Investment stopped and commerce plummeted. In 1930, Mexico's gross domestic product (GDP) fell to 12.5 per cent below its 1925 level. The Mexican economy followed that of the United States, and the 1930s proved to be an arduous decade.

Mexican leaders now took a new tack. Instead of relying on international trade, which made the country vulnerable to economic trends elsewhere (especially in the United States), they began to favour industrialization. Instead of importing finished goods from abroad, Mexico proceeded to manufacture its own products for domestic consumption. The state, moreover, assumed an active role in the economy. President Lázaro Cárdenas (1934–40) expropriated foreign-owned oil companies in 1938 and placed them under the control of Petróleos Mexicanos (PEMEX), a state-run enterprise which would eventually become one of the most important institutions in the country. The Second World War provided substantial impetus for Mexico's nascent industrial development by cutting back the flow of imports from the United States. The government took advantage of these conditions by implementing a variety of protectionist measures. Import quotas and tariffs kept foreign competition within acceptable bounds, and the devaluation of the peso in 1948–49 (and later in 1954) discouraged Mexican consumers from purchasing imported goods. (The exchange rate soared from 4.85 pesos per U.S. dollar to 12.50.) The result was to stimulate local manufacturing and to create a new cadre of prominent industrialists.

By some standards Mexico's import substitution policies met with resounding success. Between 1940 and 1960 the GDP grew from 21.7 billion pesos to 74.3 billion pesos (in constant 1950 prices, thus adjusting for inflation), an average annual increase of 6.4 per cent. During the 1960s Mexico managed to sustain this level of growth, achieving – despite one of the most rapidly swelling populations in the world – a solid per capita growth rate of 3.3 per cent per year. By the late 1970s

Table 2.1. *The structure of production: 1960 and 1979*
(percentage of gross domestic product)

	1960	1979
Agriculture	16.2	9.0
Industry:		
manufacturing	19.3	24.9
mining	4.2	5.2
construction	4.8	6.6
utilities	0.8	1.8
(subtotal, industry)	(29.1)	(38.5)
Services and other:		
transport and communication	2.7	3.6
commerce	28.6	26.7
housing and other	24.1	22.3
Size of GDP (billions of 1970 dollars)	16.2	51.2

Source: Statistical Abstract of Latin American 21 (Los Angeles: UCLA Latin American Center, 1983).

manufacturing represented nearly one-quarter of the GDP and, as shown in Table 2.1, the industrial sector as a whole accounted for 38.5 per cent of national output. It was this performance that came to be known as the 'Mexican miracle', an exemplary combination of economic progress and political stability in an area of the developing world.

Yet Mexico encountered limits in the process of import substitution industrialization. Protectionist policies helped local industry to displace foreign competition from the consumer market, and by 1950 only 7 per cent of the final value of non-durable *consumer goods* was imported from abroad. Mexico also made some headway with regard to *intermediate goods* such as fuel and fabric. But there was conspicuously less progress in the *capital goods* sector (technology and heavy machinery) which from 1950 to 1969 declined from 74 per cent to 51 per cent of the total, remaining thereafter in this general range. As a consequence, Mexico's industrial expansion continued to call for substantial amounts of imports – which could only be paid for by exports. Despite the quest for self-sufficiency, Mexico continued to rely on international trade.

A second weakness derived from a long-term shortage of capital. Industrialization is expensive. Some local entrepreneurs, as in the city of

Monterrey, managed to finance a fair share of industrial development. The Mexican state likewise assumed a *dirigiste* role, extending credit through such lending institutions as the Nacional Financiera (NAFINSA) and creating an impressive array of government-run companies. Foreign capital provided yet another source of funds. By 1970 direct foreign investment amounted to nearly $3 billion, 80 per cent of which came from the United States. In contrast to previous eras, when mining, communications and transport were the dominant activities for foreigners, nearly three-quarters (73.8 per cent) of this investment was in the manufacturing sector, mostly in critical industries: chemicals, petrochemicals, rubber, machinery and industrial equipment. Yet another solution was to obtain funding from the international credit market. During the 1960s Mexico cautiously began to borrow capital abroad, and by 1970 the country had a cumulative debt (both public and private) of about $3.2 billion. Subsequent governments were more extravagant, and by the mid-1970s the figure was close to $17 billion. The impact of this burden would depend on Mexico's capacity to repay. As the debt continued to mount – passing $80 billion by 1982 and topping $100 billion by 1987 – the costs would become painfully clear.

A third, and paradoxical, consequence of Mexico's ISI strategy was widespread unemployment. The nation's industrial sector was more capital-intensive than labour-intensive; increases in production tended to come from investments in machines and technology rather than from hiring more workers. (The agricultural sector, by contrast, has been more labour-intensive, with about 40 per cent of the work force producing about 10 per cent of the GDP.) As a result of this tendency Mexico experienced a remarkable rate of joblessness: by the mid-1970s open unemployment was around 10 per cent but under-employment may have been as high as 40 per cent, creating a functional unemployment rate equivalent to around 20 per cent. Yet by the mid-1980s between nine hundred thousand and one million young people were entering the labour force each year in search of jobs.

Partly for these reasons, the policies of ISI led to the increasingly uneven distribution of national income. As revealed in Table 2.2, the percentage share of income going to the poorest 20 per cent of Mexican households dropped from 5.0 per cent in 1958 to only 2.9 per cent in 1977. The proportional income of the highest stratum also decreased; for the top 10 per cent it declined from nearly 50 per cent to just over 40 per cent. The biggest relative gain was made by the so-called fourth quintile,

Table 2.2. *Patterns of income distribution: 1958 and 1977 (percentage shares for household groups)*

	1958	1977
Lowest 20 per cent	5.0	2.9
Second quintile	7.2	7.0
Third quintile	10.0	12.0
Fourth quintile	14.9	20.4
Highest 20 per cent	62.9	57.7
(Top 10 per cent)	(49.3)	(40.6)

Sources: Ifigenia M. de Navarrete, 'La distribución del ingreso en México: tendencias y perspectivas', in *El perfil de México en 1980* I (Mexico, 1970), p. 37; and World Bank, *World Development Report 1987* (New York, 1987), p. 253.

whose share of income went from 14.9 per cent in 1958 to 20.4 per cent in 1977, and by those in the 11–20 per cent bracket (the ninth decile). These figures clearly illustrate the economic conquests of the Mexican middle class as well as demonstrating a fact evident throughout the developing world: ISI tends to exacerbate, rather than alleviate, inequalities of income distribution.

A final result of Mexico's import substitution strategy was that the nation's industrial sector came to be inefficient and, by international standards, uncompetitive. Assured of domestic markets and protected from foreign challenges, manufacturers kept costs down – and profits up – by making only minimal investments in plant renewal and modernization. Hardly any national firms made significant budgetary allocations to research and development. Reliance on imported technology tended to elevate production costs and to ensure built-in obsolescence. Consequently the Mexican private sector became highly dependent on its near monopoly of the domestic market and on protection by the state. The socioeconomic costs inherent in ISI began to take their toll in the early 1970s. Production declined and conflict mounted. National leaders attempted to forge a new consensus around a vision of 'shared development' (in contrast to 'stabilizing development'), but their entreaties were in vain. Mexico seemed to be heading for trouble.

Then the country struck oil. As the international price of petroleum continued to climb, Mexico discovered massive new reserves and quickly regained its status as a major producer. This not only enhanced the country's international position but also provided state authorities with a huge windfall of foreign exchange, enabling the government to embark on a large-scale program of public spending designed to alleviate the shortcomings of ISI development. The petroleum bonanza thus temporarily postponed any thoughts of implementing structural change in the economy. However, when the oil boom collapsed in the early 1980s, the government sought to confront the deepening crisis by adopting a policy designed to 'liberalize' the national economy and to promote the exportation of manufactured goods. This would require the abandonment of long-standing assumptions, the rearrangement of relations between the state and the private sector, and the renovation of the nation's industrial plant. The challenges were formidable.

Mexico's economic transformation since the 1940s greatly affected – and was affected by – changes in its agricultural sector. Official policies for the most part kept agricultural prices artificially low, and the consequently modest cost of food to urban consumers amounted to a large-scale transfer of resources from the countryside to the city, this subsidy playing an essential part in maintaining social peace there. At times agricultural exports earned significant amounts of foreign exchange, and these profits helped provide capital for industrial development.

From the mid-1930s to the mid-1960s, Mexico achieved a remarkably well-balanced pattern of overall growth. As industrialization took place via import substitution, agricultural production was steadily increasing at an average annual rate of 4.4 per cent. By the early 1960s Mexico was exporting basic grains (including wheat) as well as 'luxury' crops (such as avocados and tomatoes). To the degree there was a 'Mexican miracle', some analysts have said, it may have taken place in the agricultural sector. Within ten years this situation suffered a drastic reversal. By 1975 Mexico was importing 10 per cent of the grain it consumed; by 1979 it was importing 36 per cent of its grains, and in 1983 it imported roughly half the grain it needed. Food became a scarcity for some, and malnutrition may have come to afflict nearly forty million Mexicans. This not only revealed a national crisis in agriculture. It also meant that Mexico had to divert capital which could be used for other purposes, such as job-producing investments.

Mexican agriculture lost its internal balance. Growth continued in the commercialized sectors, especially in high-value crops (fruits and vegetables) and livestock feeds (sorghum and forage for poultry and pigs; beef cattle are grass-fed in Mexico). Government policies sustained relatively high levels of production for export, mainly to the United States, and for consumption in the cities, mainly by the middle class. This emphasis was reinforced by the entry of large-scale agribusiness – transnational corporations which acquired major interests in the agricultural arena, particularly in the animal-feed industry. Small farmers and peasants did not, however, share in the benefits. From the 1960s onward Mexican governments permitted the real prices of staple goods (especially corn) to undergo long-term decline, a policy which favoured working-class consumers in the short run but discouraged agricultural output in the long run. Credit went to large-scale operators and agribusiness took control of large parcels of land. By the mid-1980s approximately four million Mexican peasants had no land. From time to time their frustration boiled over and bands of *campesinos* seized and occupied lands for their own use.

These developments have produced considerable controversy over the legacy of agrarian reform in Mexico and, in particular, of the collective *ejidos*. Production on the *ejidos* has not grown as rapidly as on large-scale private farms (whose per-acre output increased by 147 per cent between 1950 and 1970, compared to 113 per cent for the *ejidos*). This has prompted some observers to conclude that agrarian reform and collective ownership have reduced agricultural productivity and exacerbated economic difficulties. But other factors have also been at work: *ejidos* generally had lower-quality land and less access to credit and technology; they also tended to concentrate less on luxury crops for export than on staple foodstuffs for the domestic market. In what may be a revealing comparison, *ejido* productivity increased more rapidly than that of small-scale farmers (113 per cent to 73 per cent for 1950–70). The problem may lie not in *ejidos* themselves but in their resources and incentives.

Economic growth and industrial development in the post-war period exerted a profound impact on Mexico's social structure. One of the most conspicuous features of this change, both cause and effect of the country's economic transformation, was a secular trend towards urbanization. As land and jobs in the countryside grew scare, peasants left their villages in search of sustenance or work in the cities. Sometimes they would move alone, sometimes as family units; sometimes whole villages would set out on a hegira. As often as not they would find their way into the slums or, more commonly, they would establish entire communities on the outskirts of the country's major cities. Some of these shanty-towns would become mini-cities in their own right. In 1900 only 9.2 per cent of the Mexican population lived in cities (defined as communities with 20,000 inhabitants or more). By 1940 the figure had climbed to 18 per cent, and by 1970 it stood around 35 per cent. In the meantime Mexico City became one of the largest metropolises on earth, its population in the late 1980s being estimated at between 14 and 16 million. Contrary to widespread assumption, Mexico was no longer a rural society of sedentary *campesinos*. The proportion of the economically active population engaged in agriculture had fallen from approximately 70 per cent at the beginning of the century to 40 per cent. Concurrently, the percentage of workers employed in industry rose steadily, from roughly 10 per cent in 1900 to 30 per cent in 1980.

Notwithstanding questionable statistics and scholarly disputes over the precise meaning of 'class', it is evident that economic transformation had a major impact on Mexico's social structure. The census of 1960 suggests that Mexico's 'upper' class had remained very small, about half of 1 per cent of the population, and that it had shifted its social location from the countryside to the city – as traditional *hacendados* gave way to bankers and industrialists. The 'middle' class had grown to approximately 17 per cent of the total, with urban and rural components becoming nearly equal in magnitude. (By the mid-1980s the middle class represented as much as 25 or 30 per cent of the total population.) In fact, the distinction between upper- and middle-class occupational strata is extremely tenuous because many people in middle-class jobs had upper-class incomes (and vice versa), and it might well be preferable to combine the two into a single social class: the non-manual class, consisting of those who do not work with their hands. In all events, one fundamental point comes through: relatively speaking, the middle class has been a privileged class, people with middle-class incomes falling into the upper third of the country's income distribution.[1] The 'lower' class consists of those who perform manual labour. This stratum appears to have declined from over 90 per cent in 1900 to around 82 per cent in 1960 and, perhaps, to 65–75 per cent by 1980. But this should not obscure the constant increase in absolute size as a result of population expansion. The lower class has also become increasingly industrialized and, within limits, proletarianized.

Population growth sharply accelerated from the 1940s. From the late

---

[1] See Arturo González Cosío, 'Clases y estratos sociales', in Julio Durán Ochoa et al., *México: cincuenta años de revolución,* vol. 2: *La vida social* (Mexico, 1961), p. 55. For a subsequent discussion and some alternative estimates, see James W. Wilkie and Paul D. Wilkens, 'Quantifying the Class Structure of Mexico, 1895–1970', in *Statistical Abstract of Latin America,* vol. 21 (Los Angeles, 1983).

colonial period until the 1930s the Mexican population grew at a relatively modest rate, partly because of periodic devastation – once during
the wars of independence (1810–21) and again during the Mexican Revolution (1910–20). Thereafter the population started a steady climb, from
20 million in 1940 to 36 million in 1960 and 70 million in 1980. By the
late 1960s, Mexico had one of the highest population growth rates in the
world, around 3.6 per cent per year. Since then, partly in response to
governmental policies, the growth rate has subsided, hovering around 2.5
per cent in the mid–1980s. Nonetheless a basic fact persisted: nearly half
the nation's population was under the age of sixteen. One of the political
ramifications of this demographic growth has been a weakening of links to
the past. Of the 70 million Mexicans alive in 1980 only 13.3 per cent
were aged fifteen or over in 1950 and could have direct memories from
that period. Nearly half the 1980 population (45 per cent) had still not
reached the age of fifteen – so their adulthood lay in the future. Demography discouraged the maintenance of inter-generational continuity.

These social and demographic developments manifested important regional variations. Although Mexico City exercised political dominance, it
was somewhat less commanding than the capital cities of some other major
Latin American nations. The vast majority of Mexicans – at least three-
quarters – lived in some other part of the nation, and the socioeconomic
contours of daily life provided each region with a distinct flavour. The
central zone of the country was in itself richly varied. Although some of its
cities (Toluca, Puebla, Querétaro) fell within the cultural and political
orbit of Mexico City, parts of the central zone maintained strong re-
gionalist traditions. Guadalajara, the nation's second largest city, with 3.6
million inhabitants by the 1980s, had a conservative and Catholic tone;
paradoxically, as the home of mariachi music and tequila, it was also a
nationalist symbol. Veracruz, a languid port on the Caribbean, had the
dubious historical distinction of having been the launching point for
various foreign invasions from the arrival of Hernán Cortes to the incursion of U.S. marines. Neither Guadalajara nor Veracruz possessed an industrial elite which might challenge Mexico City's business giants, and both
cities collaborated with social forces in the capital.

The south had been much less privileged and less developed. The states
of Oaxaca and Chiapas maintained relatively large indigenous populations, often living in traditional subsistence communities on the margins
of national society. The south played precious little part in the rush toward
industrialization, and as a result it remained rural and impoverished.

Tourism gave a boost to Guerrero and Quintana Roo through such lavish international resorts as Acapulco and Ixtapa and Cozumel, and Yucatán recovered from the collapse of the international market for *henequen*. Parts of southern Mexico, as well as the Gulf, became centers for the petroleum boom. But for the most part, southern states received relatively modest attention (and funding) from the national government, and – perhaps as a result – they nourished opposition parties, radical politics and secessionist movements.

The north stood at the other end of the economic spectrum. A cradle of private entrepreneurship, the city of Monterrey became the nation's second largest industrial center and third largest metropolis (with more than 2.2 million residents). The driving force behind this development was provided by two families, the Garza and the Sada clans, who started with a brewery around the turn of the century and eventually built a huge conglomerate which included steel, glass, chemicals and finance. The northern states of Sonora and Chihuahua witnessed the pre-eminence of wealthy conservative farmers and ranchers while the border regions, with such thriving cities as Ciudad Juárez and a refurbished Tijuana, came to benefit from economic links with the United States. In general the north was prosperous, conservative, pro-American – and distant from Mexico City. However, all sectors of Mexican society – not only in the north – came to feel the impact of American popular culture. Through movies, television, language and the marketplace, Mexico underwent a steady and accelerating process of 'Americanization' – a trend which gave added urgency to the protection of national identity.

The complexity of Mexico's political system has long defied straightforward classification. In the optimistic spirit of the 1950s some analysts depicted the regime as a one-party structure in the process of modernization and democratization. With the disenchantment of the 1970s, most observers stressed the 'authoritarian' qualities of the regime, but even this characterization would be subject to qualification. Mexico has had a pragmatic and *moderate* authoritarian regime, not the zealously repressive kind that emerged in the Southern Cone during the 1960s and 1970s; an *inclusionary* system, given to co-optation and incorporation rather than exclusion or annihilation; an *institutional* system, not a personalistic instrument; and a *civilian* leadership, not a military government. Whatever else might be said, the Mexican regime has confronted and apparently resolved one of the most intractable problems for non-democratic systems, the issue of elite renewal and executive succession. It is an authoritarian system, but one with many differences.

Political power resides at the top. Mexican presidents rule for non-renewable six-year terms, during which time they command supreme authority: they possess the final word on all major policy questions, they control vast amounts of patronage, and, given the importance of the state, they have enduring influence on the path of national development. But once their terms are up, they are out. The constitutional prohibition on re-election (a legacy of the Mexican Revolution) has become a sacrosanct principle of politics – in part, one suspects, because it signifies the regular renovation of opportunities for public office. For these reasons the para-mount event in Mexican politics has been the presidential succession. Selection of the president is the pre-eminent decision in national life, the process which sets and controls the sexennial rhythm of public and politi-cal activity. The precise mechanisms behind the succession have been withheld from public view, but it appears that they have undergone some meaningful change. Two assertions seem to be beyond dispute: first, the outgoing president plays a central (usually dominant) role in the selection of his successor; and second, the unveiling (or *destapamiento*) of the president-to-be prompts an immediate and virtually unanimous declara-tion of support from members of the political establishment. Competition comes to an end with the *destape*.

Elections have been regularly dominated by the Partido Revolucionario Institucional (PRI). Opposition parties have been fragmented and weak, although their potential has grown over time. Until the late 1970s a handful of political parties – principally the Partido de Acción Nacional (PAN), the Partido Popular Socialista (PPS), and the Partido Auténtico de la Revolución Mexicana (PARM) – provided the regime with loyal parlia-mentary dissent. With low-to-minuscule electoral support, their leaders accepted seats in the Congress, criticized occasional decisions (but never the system itself), made frequent deals with the PRI and, by their mere existence, strengthened the government's claim to popular support and legitimate authority. In the 1970s less collaborationist parties appeared – on both the left and the right – but in the mid-1980s they did not yet pose a serious electoral threat to the regime on a national scale. Outside the party structure there were terrorist movements, both urban and rural, to which the government offered no quarter. Crackdowns and anti-guerrilla campaigns by army and police units crushed armed rebellions ruthlessly. The regime took political prisoners, a fact authorities often denied, and there were moments of outright repression. Activists and agitators mysteriously disappeared from time to time.

One of the most pervasive aspects of popular feeling was apathy. Voter turn-out in presidential elections ranged from 43 per cent to 76 per cent, though the ballot was obligatory, and as a whole the Mexican people tended to perceive their government as distant, elitist and self-serving. A sizeable share of the populace, perhaps as much as one-third, was underfed, underschooled, underclothed, and so marginal to the political process that it came to represent, in Pablo González Casanova's phrase, an 'internal colony'. Although indicative of potential discord, apathy and marginalization did not necessarily constitute dangers for the regime since they often permitted it freedom of action; if the Mexican political system exhibited authoritarian features, it possessed flexibility too. Top-heavy as it was, the PRI was organized around three distinct sectors: one for peasants, one for workers and one, quixotically called 'the popular sector', for almost everyone else. The structure provided at least token representation for broad strata of Mexican society and helps explain the passive acceptance, if not enthusiastic endorsement, the regime enjoyed among the mass of the population. A steady rotation of political personnel meant that new people, some with new ideas, were able to gain access to high office. When signs of discontent appeared, Mexico's rulers usually co-opted mass leaders by providing them with public positions, further broadening the base of support for the system. And every decade or so the system underwent a period of self-examination that often led to some kind of reform. The results were normally less than dramatic, but they affirmed the system's basic code, which one close observer succinctly summarized: two carrots, even three or four, but then a stick if necessary.

The Mexican power structure in this period can perhaps best be viewed as an interlocking series of alliances or pacts – *acuerdos,* in the expressive Spanish term. In the broadest sense, the country's ruling coalition contained three separate segments: the state, the local private sector and the foreign sector (transnational banks and corporations and their governments). Relationships between these partners were sometimes uneasy and tense, and it was not uncommon for two to join together against a third. Yet beneath these struggles there existed a deep-seated consensus, a set of understandings which kept the power structure intact: (1) Mexico would pursue a capitalist path to economic growth, a premise requiring that (2) the popular masses would be kept under control, which meant that (3) the state must play a dominant role in this arrangement, while (4) the state and entrepreneurs could still compete for relative superiority. In such a 'mixed economy' the state assumed multiple tasks: it protected the capitalist system, it established the rules for development and it took part as the largest single entrepreneur.

The state was led by a political elite which contained in turn, three identifiable groups. One consisted of *técnicos*, a highly trained corps of bureaucrats whose main resource was technical expertise; they played critical roles in policy planning, especially in the economy. The second group was the *políticos*, seasoned politicians who made their way up through the PRI hierarchy and whose institutional base came from electoral posts (in town councils, state assemblies, state governorships and the national Congress). Rivalry between *políticos* and *técnicos* was a recurrent theme in Mexican politics from the 1950s, and it very much affected the balance of power within the national elite.[2] A third group, often unnoticed by observers, consisted of the professional army. The Mexican military maintained a low profile in the period after the Second World War, but it consistently performed a number of crucial duties – hunting down guerrillas, supervising tense elections, repressing vocal opponents and generally upholding law and order. In effect, the army operated as a 'silent partner' within the political class and its collaboration was essential.

Mexico's political regime relied on popular support from three main social-class groups. Particularly prominent was the middle class, the relatively privileged and largely urbanized stratum which received many of the benefits of economic growth. Special symbolic significance was given to the rural masses, especially the peasantry, although its share of material rewards was disproportionately small. Equally, the maintenance of the regime depended upon the urban workers, whose unions collaborated under the centralized leadership of the Confederación de Trabajadores de México (CTM). Each group was a separate unit within the PRI, which simultaneously provided an institutional outlet for the expression of sectoral interests and kept them under control. For this purpose it was especially important to keep workers and peasants apart from each other, thereby preventing the formation of a lower-class coalition that could threaten the system as a whole. As former president Miguel Alemán once recalled, in the late 1930s and early 1940s 'there was an effort to merge the peasant organizations with those of the workers. . . . With that',

---

[2] See Peter H. Smith, 'Leadership and Change: Intellectuals and Technocrats in Mexico', in Roderic A. Camp (ed.), *Mexico's Political Stability: The Next Five Years* (Boulder, Colo. 1986), pp. 101–17, esp. 102–4.

insisted Alemán, 'the political stability of Mexico would have disappeared. Who would have appeased this group? . . . Would we have been able to preserve stability in such a situation'?[3] To forestall this outcome Mexico instead constructed a corporate state, and the PRI and its sectors constituted its fundamental pillars of support.

Over time it became apparent that Mexico's political stability depended upon three major conditions. First, there was the maintenance of an *equilibrium* among the constituent groups. Although there might be inequalities, it proved essential to retain the notion of access for all and supremacy for none. Legitimacy rested on the acceptance and participation of sectoral leaders, and this entailed the belief – or the myth – that redress of particular grievances and advancement of general interests would always be possible; the watchword of this system was 'balance'. The second condition was the continuing *distribution* of material rewards – made possible, in turn, by long-run patterns of economic growth. These benefits could take a variety of forms, usually under the sponsorship of the state (subsidies, price controls, wage agreements), permitting the regime to retain support from its heterodox and contradictory social-class constituencies. This kind of populist coalition required a steady stream of pay-offs, the state's ability to deliver depending upon the performance of the national economy. The Mexican regime therefore needed economic growth: the post-war 'economic miracle' and the maintenance of political stability possessed a symbiotic and dialectical relationship to each other.

The third broad condition for stability was the cultivation of a mutually acceptable relationship with the United States, a kind of *bilateral détente*. While upholding the sacrosanct notions of national sovereignty and self-determination, the Mexican regime assiduously sought to avoid direct confrontations with its neighbour to the north. Relations with the United States were a constant preoccupation of policy-makers, whose memories included not only the humiliating wars of the nineteenth century but also the military interventions of the early twentieth century and virulent hostility toward the oil nationalization of 1938. Keeping the lion at political bay while cultivating productive economic connections proved to be a precarious exercise that often took the form of legalistic evasion and practical ambiguity.

In the period from the 1940s Mexico's relations with the United States exhibited three enduring features. First, asymmetry: the United States was

[3] Miguel Alemán, *Miguel Alemán contesta* (Austin, Tex., 1975), pp. 32–3.

bigger, stronger and richer than Mexico, and had been ever since the early nineteenth century. There could be ńo bargaining here between equals: the United States would always have a much larger influence on Mexico than Mexico would have on the United States. Second, conflict: despite some common outlooks and goals, there could be disagreement on specific issues. What was good for Mexico was not always good for the United States and vice versa (or, more precisely, what was good for certain interests in Mexico might not be good for certain interests in the United States). The task of Mexican authorities was to represent national interests without incurring an excessively negative response from the United States. Third, diplomatic limitations: government-to-government negotiations lacked the capacity to resolve all key bilateral issues in a definitive manner. This was partly due to the nature of important issues at stake, such as labour migration, which responded mainly to socio-economic stimuli and stoutly resisted official regulation. It also reflected diversity and contradictions in policy-making, multitudinous agencies taking part in the U.S. policy process, whereas in Mexico presidential will tended to prevail.[4]

For the most part, Mexican leaders from the mid-1940s to the mid-1980s managed to fulfill these three conditions. They nurtured the idea of balance among constituent groups; they supported the drive towards economic growth; and they maintained an appropriately ambiguous – but essentially supportive – relationship with the United States. The result of these efforts proved to be as remarkable as it was rare: a stable political regime under the aegis of civilian leaders.

1946–58

At the end of the Second World War, Mexico was on exceptionally good terms with the United States. In 1941, as the conflict approached, President Franklin Delano Roosevelt had urged the petroleum companies to accept a negotiated settlement to the 1938 nationalization. In 1942, after Germany torpedoed two oil tankers bound for the United States, Mexico declared war on the Axis, and that same year the government signed accords with Washington on trade, opening American markets to Mexican goods, and on migrant labour, providing for Mexican *braceros* to work on American railroads and farms and later in other sectors. The tone of these

---

[4] On these and other matters, see Peter H. Smith, 'U.S.–Mexican Relations: The 1980s and Beyond', *Journal of Interamerican Studies and World Affairs* 27, no. 1 (February 1985): 91–101; and Josefina Zoraida Vazquez and Lorenzo Meyer, *The United States and Mexico* (Chicago, 1986), passim.

agreements stressed harmony and collaboration. Indeed, some influential Mexicans believed that they heralded the beginning of a 'special relationship' between the two countries. Wartime conditions had also encouraged industrial development. There appeared a nascent business class, nurtured and protected by the state, along with the outlines of a modern middle class (accounting for perhaps 15 per cent of the population as a whole at the time). Yet much of Mexican society retained its traditional rural and immobile character; with some 2 million residents, Mexico City was far from the megalopolis it would later become.

Within this setting, the inauguration of Miguel Alemán in 1946 marked a decisive change in Mexico's politics. Only forty-six years old, a civilian, he was the first post-revolutionary president not to have played a conspicuous role in the armed conflict of 1910–20; educated as a lawyer, he represented a generation of ambitious *universitarios;* articulate in Spanish (and fluent in English), he brought a new combination of skills into the nation's executive office. He had, however, diligently worked his way up through the system, entering the Senate in 1934, becoming governor of Veracruz in 1936, and directing the presidential campaign of Manuel Avila Camacho in 1939–40. For his efforts Alemán was rewarded with the Ministry of the Interior (Gobernación), a post where he showed both toughness and skill.

By late 1944 there were numerous credible contenders for the succession. Five were civilians: Javier Rojo Gómez, regent (appointed head) of the Federal District; Marte R. Gómez, Secretary of Agriculture; Dr. Gustavo Baz, Secretary of Health; Ezequiel Padilla, Secretary of Foreign Relations; and Alemán himself. Four were from the military: Miguel Henríquez Guzmán, Enrique Calderón, Jesús Agustín Castro and Francisco Castillo Nájera. Early speculation tended to favour Gómez and Padilla, both seasoned and prominent *políticos,* but Alemán employed his portfolio to build up a personal following – especially among the state governors and also among key leaders of worker and peasant organizations. The groundwork had been well prepared when in May 1945, Alemán resigned from the cabinet. The Workers' Federation of Veracruz publicly supported its favourite son. The national leadership of the CTM met in special session and backed Alemán. Other groups, from the middle class to the Communists, then joined the bandwagon. Meanwhile Avila Camacho extolled the virtues of military professionalism in a speech to the Higher War College. (His meaning was not lost on the assembled officers: get ready for a civilian president). Rojo Gómez and Henríquez Guzmán withdrew from the race, and early in 1946 a pliant congress of the ruling party, which changed its name from the Partido de la Revolución Mexicana (PRM) to the Partido Revolucionario Institucional (PRI), nominated Alemán unanimously. A campaign nonetheless ensued. Two of the disgruntled generals, García Castro and Calderón, headed tickets for short-lived parties while Ezequiel Padilla, who had guided foreign policy through the Second World War and gained great favour in the United States, launched an independent candidacy with the creation of the conservative Partido Demócrata Mexicano (PDM). Energetic but quixotic, Padilla may have suffered from his pro-American label. In all events, the outcome of the election was clear: 78 per cent for Alemán, 19.3 per cent for Padilla, only token returns for García Castro and Calderón. There were neither protests nor violence, and Alemán took office in December 1946 amid tranquillity.

The country's new leader had a clear national project. Alemán was determined to continue and extend the process of import substitution industrialization that had started during the war. To achieve this goal he would forge an alliance between the state and private capital, both national and foreign. As he explained in a speech to the CTM:

Private enterprise should have complete freedom and be able to count on support from the state, so long as it acts on behalf of the general interest. Property ownership should preferably be in the hands of Mexican citizens, in accord with the lines already established by our legislation; but foreign capital that comes to unite its destiny with that of Mexico will be able to freely enjoy its legitimate profits.

'The role of the state', he went on to say,

is to guarantee for workers the right to organize, to reach collective contracts and to defend themselves as necessary through fair and legal means, not through procedures outside the law. At the same time, the state should guarantee the rights of businessmen to open centers of production and to multiply the country's industries, confident that their investments will be safe from the vagaries of injustice.[5]

His vision called for a conciliation of classes, not the promotion of struggle, with the state as ultimate arbiter.

To implement this strategy the Alemán administration poured considerable state investment into public works. Large-scale dams on the Colorado River, the lower Rio Grande and the Papaloapán River controlled flooding, increased arable land acreage and generated much-needed electric

[5] Quoted in Luis Medina, *Historia de la Revolución Mexicana*, vol. 20: *1940–1952: Civilismo y modernización del autoritarismo* (Mexico, 1979), pp. 37–8.

power. Roads, highways and an international airport in Mexico City strengthened communications and transportation networks. A new campus for the National University not only boasted major architectural and artistic achievements but also bespoke the government's commitment to the formation of highly educated cadres of public servants and private entrepreneurs. At the same time as he opened the doors to foreign enterprise, Alemán sought to strengthen Mexico's own business class through a variety of protectionist measures. Import quotas and tariffs kept competition within acceptable bounds, and the devaluation of 1948, from 4.85 pesos per dollar to 8.65 pesos per dollar, discouraged Mexican consumers from purchasing imported goods (and raised the cost of living). Thus began the 'Mexican miracle'.

The agricultural component of this strategy promoted a programme of modernization that quickly came to be known as 'the green revolution'. Concentrating on the improvement of crop yields and productivity, the programme employed a variety of instruments: the development and use of new plant varieties, many resulting from the efforts of an Office of Special Studies established in 1943 in the Secretariat of Agriculture with the support of the Rockefeller Foundation; government restrictions on the costs of inputs (such as energy, seeds and fertilizers); and state-sponsored subsidies for credit and commercialization. But the most conspicuous contribution, especially during the Alemán era, was the extension of irrigation, the Secretariat of Water Resources, established in 1946, playing a central role in the development of infrastructure. The green revolution emphasized productivity and profit, not land distribution. Much of the government's investment, especially irrigation, was directed towards the large haciendas and ranches of the north rather than towards the peasant states of the center and the south. And, as if in defiance of land reform itself, the Alemán group supported a constitutional amendment raising the allowable size of 'small properties' to 100 hectares. As a result there was an improvement in efficiency and productivity: corn yields increased from 300 to 1300 kilos per hectare; wheat, from 750 to 3200 kilos per hectare.[6] However, these policies also deepened fissures within the Mexican countryside. Alemán and his successors clearly favored the large-scale, mechanized, commercialized producers of the north who sold their goods either in Mexico City or in the United States; small-scale and traditional

[6] 'Wheat, not corn, was the principal protagonist of the green revolution, above all during the early years', Gustavo Esteva has argued in *La batalla en el México rural* (Mexico, 1980), p. 21.

farmers of the center and south were mostly left behind. The green revolution not only exacerbated these differences but also tended to fragment the array of interests in the rural sector. As a consequences, the major agrarian organization, the Confederación Nacional Campesina (CNC), came to represent a multiplicity of often conflicting groups: small farmers (*ejidatarios*), landless wage-labourers (*jornaleros*) and commercial owners (so-called *pequeños proprietarios*). The social effects of the green revolution – plus the tenacity of rural bosses, the *caciques* – thus lie behind the continuing weakness of the post-war peasant movement and the CNC.

Alemán's political record was mixed. Allegiance to the Allies in the Second World War had stirred hopes for democratization, and in 1945 Avila Camacho took a step in this direction by proposing to centralize and reform the system of electoral practice which had long favoured local bosses and *caciques*. The CTM predictably expressed disapproval, but the legislature nonetheless endorsed the plan after a timely intervention by a young deputy from Puebla named Gustavo Díaz Ordaz. Within the PRM/PRI party, leaders agreed to base nominations on internal elections while attempting to avoid internecine conflict by respecting 'the principle of majority rights within each of the sectors'.[7] It was not self-evident what this would mean, except that the national state was taking over from regional *caciques* in the name of democratization. Indeed, the Alemán administration gave a consistency and shape to the Mexican political system which would endure for many years. As it developed, the overall project revealed several interrelated features: the imposition of a single ruling group; the elimination of the left from the official coalition; the state domination of the labour movement; and the cultivation and co-optation of sectoral leaders.

The insistence on homogeneity was most apparent in Alemán's cabinet. Almost to a man, the new ministers resembled the President himself: they were young (average age: forty-four), articulate and highly educated. Most important, they had close personal ties to the President (around 20 per cent of Alemán's own law-school class would reach high positions in national politics). This was not a coalition government, a tactfully constructed consensus of rival factions, as under Avila Camacho. This was Alemán's personal instrument. In keeping with this outlook, Alemán ousted governors who represented other groups – most conspicuously Marcelino García Barragán, the Cardenista (and later Henriquista) governor of

[7] Medina, *Historia*, p. 79.

Jalisco, and the Emilio Portes Gil supporter J. Jesús González Gallo in the state of Tamaulipas.

The isolation and exclusion of the left coincided with the Cold War era. It began in 1946 with the proclamation of stringent registration require-ments for political parties, which made it impossible for the Communists to maintain their legal status, and it picked up in 1947 when Teófilo Borunda, secretary-general of the PRI, announced that the party would steer a middle course 'neither extreme left nor extreme right'. Rodolfo Sánchez Taboada, the party president, issued a ringing denunciation of Marxist influence:

> We declare with firmness and clarity that we are not Communists and we will not be Communists; that we love above all else liberty and we do not accept any imperialism; that we affirm our belief in and our commitment to democracy, and that we are ready to fight at the side of the people, including against those who, with pretentious displays of verbal gymnastics, tend to expound ideas which do not accord with Mexican realities.[8]

Anti-communism thus became identified with anti-imperialism and, at bottom, with the affirmation of Mexican nationalism.

Perhaps the most important development in the containment of the left was the decision by Vicente Lombardo Toledano, intellectual leader of the Mexican labour movement and a former secretary-general of the CTM, to create a new political party. Its platform was twofold: to promote industri-alization, thus creating the material base for social progress; and to foster anti-imperialism, thus defending national sovereignty from the post-war hegemony of the United States. At Avila Camacho's request Lombardo Toledano had agreed to postpone plans for the new party until after the succession of 1946. Attention then shifted to the CTM, where a radical contingent sought to challenge the dominant Fidel Velázquez faction in a battle over the secretary-generalship in 1947. Lombardo attempted to mediate the dispute, the Velázquez group artfully agreeing to support the formation of a new party in exchange for Lombardo's backing. In the face of such manoeuvres the radical unionists, led by railway leader Luis Gómez Z., founded a dissident anti-CTM organization, the Confederación Unica de Trabajadores (CUT). The Velázquez group consequently won a resounding victory within the CTM, installing Fernando Amilpa as secretary-general while formally agreeing to contribute to the creation of a new party for the masses.

[8] *Excélsior*, 1 September 1947.

This was hardly Amilpa's intent. An enthusiastic supporter of Alemán, he was eager to consolidate labour's position within the PRI and to expunge it of communist elements. On one occasion he sought to expel Lombardo Toledano from the CTM; on another, he withdrew his union from the Confederación de Trabajadores de América Latina (CTAL), which Lombardo had created in 1938. By the time Lombardo finally founded his new Partido Popular, in 1948, he had become almost entirely isolated from the CTM, which he once headed. The left had gained its party but lost its position within the constellation of ruling forces. From now on it would have to work from the outside.

In addition to excluding the left, the Alemanista regime sought to gain direct control of the mainstream labour movement. The tensions of the mid-1940s led to a profound division within the organized working class, pro-government forces claiming about 500,000 members and the dissidents having around 330,000. While many in the rank and file accepted the injunctions of Alemán and the CTM leaders to reject radical views as alien and unpatriotic, this was challenged by unions in the public sector, especially in nationalized industries, whose workers tended to identify national sovereignty with an anti-imperialist opposition to foreign investment. There was a minor revolt in 1946 among oil workers, which was quickly snuffed out after soldiers took command of PEMEX installations.

A larger crisis came in 1948 when rail-workers protested against real-wage cuts deriving from the devaluation of the peso. Dissident labor leader Luis Gómez Z. had just turned over the secretary-generalship of the union to Jesús Díaz de León, an opportunistic operator nicknamed *el charro* because of his devotion to rodeo-type fiestas of the Mexican cowboy (*charro*). The government immediately began to support Díaz de León in his struggle against the popular Gómez, who insisted both on compiling a report about the impact of the devaluation and on presenting it to the board of his newly founded CUT, not to the railway union. An angry Díaz de León responded by accusing Gómez of fraud, a charge the government surprisingly – and inappropriately – agreed to investigate. In exchange for the President's backing Díaz de León accepted a new contract granting management the right to fire as many as two thousand workers whose jobs had formerly been secure. This established a pattern since known by the opprobrious epithet of *charrismo:* docile labour leadership would sell out the interests of its membership and receive, in return, political backing (and financial benefits) from the state and/or management. Labour would thus be controlled through the co-optation of its leadership, and the consequent arrangements would permit and facilitate the pursuit of capitalist growth via industrialization.

Independent unionists continued to search for a new vehicle, and in mid-1949 dissident mining and petroleum leaders joined with Lombardo Toledano to form the Unión General de Obreros y Campesinos de México (UGOCM). The government responded with hostility – refusing to recognize a strike against Ford Motors, negating UGOCM registration on a technicality and supporting a breakaway group within the union. Some miners withdrew from the UGOCM and in 1951 the oil-workers decided to return to the CTM. The UGOCM continued in existence but without posing a significant challenge. The political lesson was clear: with the emasculation of the UGOCM, Lombardo Toledano and the Partido Popular would not have any institutional base. At the same time, the government placed constrictions on the CTM, supporting the formation in 1952 of the Confederación Regional de Obreros y Campesinos (CROC), a nationwide labour organization within the PRI, as a counter-weight. By this divide-and-rule tactic, the Mexican state once again demonstrated its determination to maintain tight control over organized labour.

Alemán and his collaborators also sought to discipline the PRI. After tentative experiments with internal primaries, the President turned against the idea after the midterm congressional elections of 1949, and sent congress a law to prohibit parties from holding their own public elections. In 1950, Sánchez Taboada managed to gain re-election as PRI president against some opposition from old-time *políticos,* but he surrendered his commitment to primaries (candidates would henceforth be selected by party assemblies) and agreed to changes in the leadership structure. The party's dinosaurs returned to the fold, the Young Turks lost their advantage and PRI negotiations went back behind closed doors.

As a result, speculation about the 1952 succession was muted. Asked what to do about the transition in June 1951, Alemán uttered a classic response: 'Just wait'.[9] Perhaps because there was no obvious front-runner within the cabinet, some observers began to gossip about a constitutional amendment which would either permit Alemán's re-election or extend his term (an idea Lázaro Cárdenas strenuously opposed). Others focussed on the able Secretary of the Treasury, Ramón Beteta, but he suffered the

---

[9] Daniel Cosío Villegas, *La sucesión presidencial* (Mexico, 1975), p. 112.

political misfortune of having an American wife. Others discussed Fernando Casas Alemán, the regent of the Federal District, who was the President's cousin and said to be his favorite despite having a reputation for corruption.

It was in this context that Miguel Henríquez Guzmán, the career military officer and pre-candidate in 1946, decided to launch his own campaign. He garnered early support from three principal elements: Cardenistas, including members of the Cárdenas family, opposed to the conservative policies of the 1940s; alienated factions of the elite who resented their exclusion from power; and dissident leaders of the popular movement. Leaders of the Henriquista movement included such prominent figures as Antonio Espinosa de los Monteros, Mexican ambassador to Washington; Pedro Martínez Tornell, ex-Secretary of Public Works; Ernesto Soto Reyes, former leader of the Senate; Wenceslao Labra, ex-governor of the state of Mexico; and, among other military officers, the ubiquitous Marcelino García Barragán. This was not, at first, an opposition movement. Henriquista strategists sought to work within the system, not against it. They wanted to stop the candidacy of Casas Alemán, to have the PRI give serious consideration to Henríquez Guzmán, to incorporate democratic practices in the nominating procedure and to halt the excessive corruption taking place under Alemán. The ideological standard of the movement was vacuous and brief; 'not to depart to the slightest degree from the ideals of the Mexican Revolution', and, of course, to uphold the Constitution of 1917.[10] A change of leaders, not of national purpose, would be sufficient to rectify the course of public life. The iconoclastic ex-general eventually adopted some tacitly radical positions, such as support for small rural producers and independent labour unions, but he took care not to develop their implications.

Predictably enough, the docile PRI expressed adamant opposition to the upstart Henriquistas and attempted to throw them out of the party. Seeing no alternative, the dissidents created a new vehicle – the Federación de Partidos del Pueblo (FPP) – in March 1951, well in advance of the PRI's nominating convention. Henríquez Guzmán began waging an intense campaign, gaining support among such disparate constituencies as idealistic students, pro-democratic elements of the middle class, independent *campesino* groups and disenchanted workers. It is said that Alemán took this challenge seriously enough to dispatch an emissary to Cárdenas

---

[10] *Excélsior*, 30 July 1951.

in order to explain the dangers it posed to the system – including the possibility of a military coup.[11]

Early in October the word came down that the establishment's choice would be Adolfo Ruiz Cortines, the fifty-five-year-old Secretary of Gobernación from the state of Veracruz. Colorless but honest, he was clearly a compromise candidate, someone who might be able to heal the rifts within the country's political class. The machinery promptly went to work. Fidel Velázquez had already announced that labour would support the PRI instead of the Communists or, more pointedly, Lombardo Toledano's Partido Popular. 'The Mexican proletariat has today taken the most transcendental decision of its life', he intoned before the crowd on May Day: 'to identify itself definitively with the Revolution, with the fatherland, and to discard as incompatible all alien doctrines and ideologies'.[12] Or in translation: Marxists need not apply. At the same time, Sánchez Taboada offered Catholics a place within the PRI in order to weaken conservative support for Efraín González Luna of the PAN. The ruling elite spared no effort to create a ground-swell of public acceptance for Ruiz Cortines.

In the end they could claim success: official results of the 1952 election gave 74.3 per cent of the vote to Ruiz Cortines, 15.9 per cent to Henríquez Guzmán, 7.8 per cent to González Luna and 1.9 per cent to Lombardo Toledano. This was, however, the highest opposition vote recognized since 1929, and it proved to be the last of the open campaigns. Some Henriquistas protested against the result, a few went to prison, some pursued dreams of a military coup and some found their way back into the regime (the most spectacular case of co-optation being García Barragán, who eventually became Secretary of Defence in 1964–70). In 1954 the FPP dissolved and Henriquismo disappeared. After that, as Daniel Cosío Villegas has written, 'the true era of the *tapado* begins'.[13]

Despite his modest political credentials, Ruiz Cortines managed to maintain the PRI's subordination to the President. An opening statement at a party assembly in early 1953 identified its guiding lights: 'The people is its guide, the Constitution is its slogan, and Adolfo Ruiz Cortines is its standard-bearer'. And in keeping with rhetorical imperative, party leaders dedicated themselves to historical tradition and personalistic solidarity:

[11] Cosío Villegas, *La sucesión*, p. 131.
[12] Ibid., p. 115.
[13] Ibid., p. 139.

'the PRI will follow the revolutionary path shown by President Ruiz Cortines', who might have been surprised by this characterization of his political performance.[14] Notwithstanding such support, the new President faced several challenges. Perhaps the most pervasive problem was the unpopularity of the ruling elite, the widespread disenchantment with the greed of Alemán and his collaborators. The necessary response was simple but formidable: to strengthen and restore the political legitimacy of the regime – but without imposing any major change in policy. Ruiz Cortines went about this task in several ways. One was to stress the austerity of his own personal example, to promote the image of a hard-working and solid civil servant. Another was to distance himself and his team from the Alemán group, quietly punishing selected members of the previous administration (including Agustín García López, the former Secretary of Transportation, who lost millions in speculative ventures).[15] A third measure was to grant political rights to women, thus invoking the time-honored notion of the female as moral guardian while also broadening the government's popular base. Finally, the president announced impressive-sounding reforms in laws on corruption and public responsibility; although never strictly applied during his *sexenio,* these had a temporarily cathartic effect.

The Ruiz Cortines administration faced a second major challenge in the rising cost of living. The purchasing power of the mass of the population had been declining for several years, partly because of Alemán's economic strategy, and more recently because of international inflation resulting from the Korean War. To attack this problem – and to emphasize his administration's anti-corruption drive – Ruiz Cortines promoted a measure which would impose strict fines on monopolies and on the hoarding of goods. As the new President declared soon after taking office, 'One of the most basic objectives of my government will be to find adequate legal means to prevent an increase in the cost of living'.[16] One of his first economic measures was to lower the retail price of corn and beans, the government declaring its solidarity with the workers and the dispossessed. This stance appeared to jeopardize the close alliance between the state and private capital forged by Alemán. Cautious at first, business leaders refrained from opposing pro-consumer measures, but as time went on they

[14] *El Nacional,* 7 February 1953.
[15] Peter H. Smith, *Labyrinths of Power: Political Recruitment in Twentieth-Century Mexico* (Princeton, 1979), pp. 273–4.
[16] *Excélsior,* 24 December 1953.

expressed serious misgivings about any alteration of the basic economic model. Spokesmen for the Confederación de Cámaras Nacionales de Comercio (CONCANACO) insisted that government intervention would distort the marketplace and create inefficient monopolies. In other words, the state should sustain and protect the market but not participate directly in it.[17] In 1953, the business sector resorted to its ultimate weapon: reduced investment and capital flight. The result was a slow-down in economic growth and a consequent threat to the viability of the overall import substitution strategy. Here was an obvious challenge: in effect, the capitalists went on strike.

It was not long before the government caved in. By early 1954 the Ruiz Cortines administration began to favour the business sector with incentives and resources for increased production, including tax relief and easy credit. In mid-April the government took a decisive step by devaluing the peso from 8.65 per dollar to 12.50 (where it would remain for many years). As in 1948, the idea was to provide across-the-board protection for local industrialists and to entice them to reinvest in Mexico. By the end of the year production had picked up and growth resumed. The recovery of the U.S. economy from the high-inflation years of the Korean War further improved the general outlook. Mexico was back on the road to its miracle.

Confirmation of the business–government alliance made it all the more necessary for the state to assert its control over organized labour. Perhaps sensing the change in policy, prominent labour leaders came out in support of the April 1954 devaluation and pledged that the working class would make the necessary sacrifice. When Ruiz Cortines offered public employees a modest 10 per cent compensatory rise, exhorting the private sector to do the same, Fidel Velázquez proclaimed 'the strongest support' from the working class. However, UGOCM rivals and grass-roots spokesmen denounced the increase as insufficient, and the ever-alert Velázquez quickly persuaded the CTM to demand a 24 per cent increase – or threaten a general strike in mid-July. Into this breach stepped Adolfo López Mateos, the dashing young Secretary of Labour, who proceeded to head off a potential crisis through persuasion and negotiation. Some stoppages occurred, most notably in textiles and the movies, but López Mateos managed to avoid large-scale confrontations. The average raise came out to

---

[17] Olga Pellicer de Brody and José Luis Reyna, *Historia de la Revolución Mexicana*, vol. 22: *1952–1960: El afianzamiento de la estabilidad política* (Mexico, 1978), p. 25.

be around 20 per cent: somewhat less than labour wanted and far less than labour's loss in purchasing power, but enough to silence criticism and keep Velázquez in charge. Once again, the velvet glove was shown to sheathe an iron fist. In order to institutionalize this outcome the Ruiz Cortines administration backed the formation in 1955 of the Bloque de Unidad Obrera (BUO), an umbrella organization designed to centralize the labour movement under Velázquez and his cronies. The impetus for the Bloque came mainly from the CTM, although it was supported by numerous other unions, including the CTM's arch-rival, CROC. Notwithstanding governmental benevolence, however, the BUO never became a major force in itself; as Luis Araiza has observed, it was 'a giant blindman without any guide' (*'un gigante ciego sin lazarillo'*).[18] Industrial relations were generally subdued in the mid-1950s, workers winning minor victories in the electrical and textile industries. Turmoil beset the teachers' union from 1956 to 1958, when independent leadership under Othón Salázar Ramírez provoked resistance among the rank and file in Mexico City. A demonstration in August 1958 was repressed by the police, but the government later permitted one of Salázar Ramírez' allies to win a union election. Coercion and co-operation appeared to work.

This relative tranquility on the labour scene was disturbed by the railway strikes of 1958–9. The railway-workers' union, the Sindicato de Trabajadores Ferrocarrileros de la República (STFRM), had a long tradition of radical nationalism, and their strategic location in the country's transportation network gave them considerable leverage. Under the forceful leadership of Luis Gómez Z. and Valentín Campa, founders of the dissident CUT, they had energetically protested the devaluation of 1948; and ever since the imposition of Díaz de León in the *charrazo* the workers had steadily lost ground. Between 1952 and 1957 their real wages declined by -0.3 per cent a year – while the electricians, for instance, steadily improved their lot.[19] In February 1958 anti-*charro* forces within the STFRM sought an open confrontation by demanding an increase in wages. Union leaders eventually agreed to create a committee to study the real-wage problem. The report, issued in May, estimated a 40 per cent loss in purchasing power since 1948 and recommended an immediate wage increase of 350 pesos a month (around U.S.$28). Díaz de León instead called for a raise of 200 pesos, and the management ostentatiously under-

[18] Luis Araiza, *Historia del movimiento obrero mexicano* (Mexico, 1965), p. 281.
[19] Kevin Jay Middlebrook, 'The Political Economy of Mexican Organized Labor', unpublished Ph.D. dissertation, Harvard University, 1982.

took to study this proposal during a sixty-day period – and, conveniently, to render its decisions after the presidential elections of July 1958.

Resistance consolidated behind Demetrio Vallejo, a rank-and-file dissident who had served on the wage–price commission. As head of a new general action committee he declared a series of 'escalating stoppages' *(paros escalonados)*, starting with a two-hour stoppage and gradually working up to an eight-hour stoppage and then a general strike. The Ruiz Cortines government responded by jettisoning one of the *charro* leaders, installing another and decreeing a wage increase of 215 pesos in July. But co-optation failed to work this time: in August union members voiced their protest by electing the obstreperous Vallejo to head the STFRM. Within months Vallejo began threatening strikes over further demands, including calculation of the 215-peso increase on the basis of a six-day (not seven-day) work week. After achieving satisfaction from Ferrocarriles Nacionales, the most important line, he brought these same concerns before three other companies in March 1959, just before the Holy Week vacation. The pro-establishment BUO denounced Vallejo's audacity, while labour dissidents – some teachers, telephone operators, oil-workers – rallied behind the STFRM. A frightened government declared the strike to be illegal, the army commandeered the railroads, the police imprisoned Vallejo and thousands of his followers. Within weeks the strike was broken and the leadership replaced. Vallejo finally came to trial in 1963 and, convicted of conspiracy and sabotage under the law of 'social dissolution', he went back to jail for sixteen years.

The railway strikes proved to be a momentous episode. As José Luis Reyna and Olga Pellicer observed, 'this was the first important proletarian social movement that, for a moment, put the political system into a crisis. . . . It [was], without doubt, the most important movement to occur since 1935.'[20] But if it posed a challenge to the system, it also conveyed a sobering lesson: there would be little tolerance of independent unionism. As it showed in the case of Vallejo, the Mexican state demanded obsequious compliance from the leaders of organized labour.

So, too, in regard to the peasants, although there was not much provocation from this quarter. Mexican agriculture underwent a major transformation in the 1940s, as rising international prices encouraged production for export and capital investment (especially in irrigation) led to increasing yields on medium- and large-scale commercial farms. Although most

[20] Pellicer and Reyna, *Historia* 22:157.

campesinos did not share these benefits, the leaders of the peasant federation, the CNC, offered unwavering allegiance to the system. When Secretary of Agriculture Gilberto Flores Muñoz unveiled a plan for increased food production which favored large-scale proprietors at the expense of medium- and small-scale farmers, the secretary-general of the CNC expressed his support for the project in disarming style. 'Given this example of unquestionable and positive activity, peasants affiliated to the CNC have only to fulfill once again their patriotic duty'.[21]

Peasants mounted some successful local movements in Nayarit and other places, and the UGOCM made some sporadic attempts to mobilize *campesinos* in the north. The sharpest challenges occurred in 1958, when land invasions in Sinaloa spread to Sonora, Colima and Baja California, Flores Muñoz assuaging some of the agitation with modest schemes for land distribution. By far his most inventive response was the expropriation 'for the public interest' of a latifundio in Sonora leased to the U.S.-owned Cananea Cattle Company: billed as a nationalistic and populistic measure, the decision included a provision to repay the owners for the land's commercial value in hard cash. The proprietors were content, the UGOCM leaders went to jail, the peasants returned to work and the system survived intact. This was not an untypical solution.

Throughout their *sexenios* both Alemán and Ruiz Cortines cultivated close relations with the United States to the end of establishing a 'special relationship'. This entailed a low profile in the international arena and general support for the United States. The main exception to this rule came in 1954, as Washington prepared to launch a move to overthrow the reformist government of Jacobo Arbenz in Guatemala – partly because of the spectre of international communism, partly because land-reform measures threatened the interests of the United Fruit Company. At an inter-American conference in Caracas, the U.S. Secretary of State, John Foster Dulles, sought a condemnation of the Arbenz regime. Invoking the principle of non-intervention, Mexico joined with only two other nations – beleaguered Guatemala and Peronist Argentina – in opposing the U.S. proposal. When the CIA-sponsored movement overthrew the Arbenz regime in June 1954, Mexico's leftist and nationalist groups protested, but in vain. The Mexican government's stance was most revealing: having upheld the principle of non-intervention, it thereafter remained silent.

[21] *El Nacional*, 26 January 1953.

The episode thus revealed the limits of, as well as the capacity for, independent action by Mexico.

1958-70

The suppression of the railway strikes in 1958–9 inaugurated a period of relative political tranquillity in Mexico. Continuation of the economic 'miracle' provided the material foundation for consensus and co-optation, and the ruling elite displayed a clear capacity for both coercion and persuasion. The state directed economic growth through a delicate alliance with private capital, domestic and foreign. There was effective political co-operation at the top between *políticos, técnicos* and military officers. The verticalist organization of workers and peasants secured a popular base for the regime, while prospering urban middle classes – inchoate, opportunistic and politically volatile – offered substantial support for a system that served them well. There would be protests and disturbances, but throughout this period the State exercised a generally impressive degree of hegemony.

The presidential succession of 1958 both symbolized and strengthened the centralization of authority. All the leading candidates came from the cabinet: Angel Carvajal, the Secretary of Gobernación; Ernesto P. Uruchurtu, regent of the Federal District; Antonio Carrillo Flores, Secretary of the Treasury and a consummate bureaucrat; Ignacio Morones Prieto, Secretary of Health, a *político* of long-standing prominence; Gilberto Flores Muñoz, the Secretary of Agriculture and political boss from the rural state of Nayarit; and Adolfo López Mateos, the accomplished Secretary of Labour. Virtually every major faction within the system had a pre-candidate: Carrillo Flores was seen as an Alemanista, Flores Muñoz as a Cardenista; labour and the peasantry, *políticos* and *técnicos,* all had their representatives. It would seem that López Mateos won because of his performance in containing the labour movement, because of his ties to Ruiz Cortines (whose campaign he had managed in 1952) and because of his acceptability to both Cardenistas and Alemanistas. The selection process was discreetly dominated by Ruiz Cortines: as Alfonso Corona del Rosal would later say, the outgoing president 'selects his successor, supports him, and sets him on his course'[22] – and by this time there would be no visible internal opposition. Energetic and charming, López Mateos ran a whirlwind campaign, obtaining endorse-

[22] *Excélsior,* 14 September 1975.

ments from the PPS and the PARM as well as from the PRI; even opposition parties joined the juggernaut. Token resistance came only from the *panista* candidacy of Luis H. Alvarez. With women voting in their first presidential election, 7.5 million people went to the polls in July 1958, and more than 90 per cent cast their ballots for López Mateos. The PRI and its machinery looked invincible.

Once in office López Mateos startled some observers, especially the Eisenhower administration in the United States, by declaring himself to be 'on the extreme left within the Constitution'. The statement was shrewd and significant. It pre-empted any move on the radical wing of the PRI and isolated the anti-establishment left, specifically the PPS and other Marxists who were presumed to be 'outside' the Constitution. It signalled an ideological solidarity with Zapata, Villa and other major figures of the Revolution, and it asserted Mexico's sovereignty from the United States, still in the grip of the Cold War. Moreover, it reaffirmed the incontestable fact of presidential power.

In keeping with this stance, López Mateos increased the role of the state in the national economy. The government gained control of the electric-power sector by buying out the American and Foreign Power Company, and it also purchased controlling shares in the motion-picture industry from long-resident U.S. millionaire William Jenkins. Government spending as a ratio of GNP rose from 10.4 per cent under Ruiz Cortines to 11.4 per cent. López Mateos also took an outspoken stand on land reform. In order to consolidate loyalty among the peasantry, he ordered the distribution of approximately 11.4 million hectares of land to more than 300,000 *campesinos,* an activist record that placed him second only to Cárdenas.[23] In 1963 he raised the basic price for staple commodities, later likening the measure to 'a minimum wage for workers in the countryside'.[24] Credit and basic services were harder to provide, but the political message was clear: at least symbolically, the government was siding with the masses.

The President adopted a similarly populist posture toward labour, proposing in 1961 a measure to institute profit-sharing between workers and proprietors. In belated fulfilment of a key clause in the Constitution of 1917 (with which López Mateos so closely identified himself), the new law seemed to represent a major victory for labour. However, the amount of profit to be shared was so small as to be acceptable to employers, and

[23] In actual practice, however, only 3.2 million hectares were distributed: Esteva, *Batalla,* pp. 230–1.
[24] Esteva, *Batalla,* p. 85.

the final law – adopted in 1963 – was never strictly enforced. Labour had achieved only a paper triumph, and business had successfully defended its own interests. Yet, by proposing the legislation without consulting business leaders, the politicians displayed their willingness and ability to take autonomous action. And the state acquired yet another weapon with which it could, in the future, threaten or challenge private capital.

Despite these populist gestures (and perhaps in deliberate combination with them) López Mateos continued to engage in selective crackdowns and repression. In 1959 David Alfaro Siqueiros, the internationally renowned painter, was put in jail (and not released until 1964). In 1963, as we have seen, Demetrio Vallejo was convicted of sedition and jailed for sixteen years. Peasant leaders fared no better, the most infamous case bring that of Rubén Jaramillo, an old Zapatista from Morelos who had brought his guerrilla band down from the hills in order to accept an amnesty and truce from López Mateos himself. When presidential blandishments failed to result in land for his people, Jaramillo ordered the occupation of fields owned by prominent politicians. Fruitless negotiations followed, and as a stalemate developed, Jaramillo and his family were found dead in the spring of 1962. No one doubted that orders for the murder had come from Mexico City.

The López Mateos administration continued to support the business sector and to court foreign capital. Investment was high and Mexico began raising capital abroad, especially in the New York bond market. The government managed to control inflation so strictly that López Mateos could retain the fixed exchange rate of 12.50 pesos to the dollar; there was no devaluation during this *sexenio*. Nor were there any statutory limits on profit remittances, allowing foreign investors to repatriate their earnings at a predictable (and favourable) rate of exchange, a factor which greatly encouraged foreign investment. The economy continued its path of high growth.

López Mateos attempted to establish diplomatic independence from the United States as Washington's relations with Cuba deteriorated and the Eisenhower administration began to pressure the Mexicans for support. López Mateos sought to walk a thin line: Mexico wanted to sustain the principles of non-intervention and self-determination, but it also wanted to avoid direct confrontation with the United States. Throughout 1960, therefore, Mexican representatives attempted to achieve these goals by upholding non-intervention without defending either communism or the Soviet Union. At the same time Mexico did not come out in favour of the

United States because this would have meant accepting the leadership of the Organization of American States (OAS), which (at Washington's insistence) had turned its back on Cuba and urged Mexico to follow suit: this itself would have compromised Mexico's own sovereignty. In the midst of these delicate negotiations López Mateos invited Cuban president Osvaldo Dorticós for a state visit in June 1960. The ceremonies led to a ritual identification of the Cuban Revolution of 1959 with the Mexican Revolution of 1910. A Mexican legislator condemned U.S. actions against Cuba, especially the closing of the sugar market. U.S. officials expressed their disapproval. The situation was tense but ambiguous.

After the Bay of Pigs invasion, and especially after Fidel Castro's profession of Marxist-Leninism, the Mexican government began to view the issue as an East–West problem, but they still rejected the idea of intervention. The Bay of Pigs fiasco prompted anti-U.S. demonstrations, Mexican spokesmen condemning the U.S. action as a violation of self-determination and maintaining that the problem should be discussed within the United Nations (where Cuba would get substantial support) and not in the OAS (where the U.S. would easily prevail). This position changed in 1962. Early in the year Mexican foreign minister Manuel Tello stated that 'there is an incompatibility between belonging to the OAS and to a Marxist-Leninist profession', but he simultaneously rejected the idea of expelling Cuba since the OAS charter made no provision for such a possibility.[25] Then came the missile crisis of October. Subjected to an extraordinary barrage of pressures, López Mateos finally came out in public support of the U.S. blockade of Cuba and instructed his representative at the OAS to vote in favour of a resolution demanding the withdrawal of the missiles. Mexico still imposed a face-saving condition – the vote was not to be used as justification for another invasion of Cuba. But even this stance had its limits: Mexican authorities systematically put passengers to Cuba on a black list, confiscated political material and maintained a silent blockade in disguise. Once again, the limits of autonomy became apparent.

The overall emphasis in foreign policy was on moderation and pragmatism. López Mateos held personal meetings with three successive U.S. presidents – Eisenhower, Kennedy and Johnson – and in 1964 he succeeded in regaining Mexican sovereignty over the Chamizal, a disputed section of land which had become part of U.S. territory after the Rio Grande changed its course. U.S. and Mexican leaders continued to pro-

[25] Vázquez and Meyer, *United States*, p. 178.

mote an atmosphere of harmony, and Washington even came to accept some measure of independence for Mexican foreign policy. Although direct U.S. investment in Mexico increased from $922 million in 1959 to nearly $1.3 billion in 1964, there was not much governmental aid, even under the Alliance for Progress. On the other hand, no restrictions were imposed on Mexico's access to international capital markets. Even under a self-declared leftist, Mexico's bilateral connection to the United States retained the appearance of a 'special relationship'.

In 1963, López Mateos promulgated an electoral reform that guaranteed a minimum number of five seats in the Chamber of Deputies to any party winning more than 2.5 per cent of the total vote (with an additional seat for each 0.5 per cent of the vote, up to a maximum of twenty). This way opposition parties could obtain representation in the national legislature without actually winning any electoral races. The point was to co-opt the challengers – the PPS, the PARM, and above all the PAN – and to create a loyal opposition. This would strengthen the legitimacy of the regime, especially in the aftermath of the repression of 1958–9 and in the light of the Cuban Revolution, further isolating the anti-establishment left and defining the Mexican regime as representative of a national consensus. López Mateos thereby finished out his term with a characteristic flourish.

The presidential succession of 1964 went smoothly. As usual, top contenders all came from the cabinet: Javier Barros Sierra of public works, Donato Miranda Fonseca of *presidencia,* Antonio Ortiz Mena of the treasury and Gustavo Díaz Ordaz from Gobernación. There were rumors that López Mateos favoured Miranda Fonseca, his erstwhile companion in Vasconcelos' movement of 1929 and a seasoned politician from Guerrero, but he ultimately settled on Díaz Ordaz – the competent but unglamorous ex-legislator from the state of Puebla. His selection appeared to confirm a tradition that, everything else being equal, the Secretary of Gobernación would become the next president (as had happened with Alemán and Ruiz Cortines). A mestizo by origin, much darker in appearance and less handsome than his predecessors, Díaz Ordaz instantly became the butt of savage jokes, including perhaps the most sardonic line of all: 'Anyone can become president'.

Once in office, Díaz Ordaz ruled with an iron hand. Without hesitation he dismissed office-holders with either too much political power, in which case they threatened him, or with too little political power, in which case they embarrassed him. In August 1965 he dismissed Amador Hernández, the head of the CNC, after an armed clash broke out between rival peasant groups. In late 1966, Díaz Ordaz fired Ernesto Uruchurtu, long-time mayor of Mexico City (and erstwhile presidential pre-candidate), after the much-criticized bull-dozing of a squatter settlement. He ousted Enrique Ceniceros from the governorship of Durango for failing to suppress a popular protest against foreign mining companies, and Ignacio Chávez from the rectorship of UNAM, the National University, for failing to crush a student strike. Unlike López Mateos, who managed to blend coercion with an artful dose of co-optation, Díaz Ordaz tended to rely on force and discipline alone.

Perhaps the most telling instance of this concerned the internal organization of the PRI. In 1964 the party presidency passed to Carlos Madrazo, forty-nine-year-old ex-governor of Tabasco and the first civilian in nearly twenty years to lead the PRI (thus marking yet another retreat by the military from the public eye). Himself a controversial figure, Madrazo sought to reinvigorate the party through the series of reforms, the most important being a plan for primary elections at the local level. Old-line *políticos* resisted, just as they had in the late 1940s, and Díaz Ordaz eventually decided to throw his weight behind the anti-democratic forces. Madrazo lost his post in 1966 and, in what many see as a suspicious airplane crash, lost his life in 1969. So ended the impulse for reform. Reinforced, if not rejuvenated, the traditional machinery asserted its dominance. The PAN was allowed to capture a municipality near Monterrey in Nuevo León in 1965, but the PRI reimposed its own mayor in 1969. In Sonora the PAN took Hermosillo in 1967, but Mexico City insisted on the triumph of the official candidate for governor. A year later hotly contested elections in Baja California were annulled because of 'irregularities' and the PRI claimed total victory. In 1969 the Díaz Ordaz government refused to accept what many thought was a PAN victory in the race for governor of Yucatán, dispatching the army to assure law and order (and a PRI victory).

Díaz Ordaz continued the policy of cultivating close links to the United States, although there was some tension in 1965 when Mexico – along with four other Latin American countries – refused to support the U.S. occupation of the Dominican Republic. Late in 1969, too, Díaz Ordaz protested when the Nixon administration's Operation Intercept, a blunt instrument against narcotics, led to the interruption of social and commercial traffic in the border area. But both sides saw these as fairly minor incidents, and the U.S.–Mexican relationship was generally smooth.

Perhaps more than any government since Alemán, the Díaz Ordaz team established intimate working connections with the nation's private sector. This alliance was clearly manifested in the question of tax reform, the government proposing to close two of the most egregious loopholes in Mexico's income-tax code: one permitting the fragmentation of total income into separate categories (so lower rates would apply on each); another allowing for the anonymous ownership of stocks and bonds (*al portador*). The President appeared at first to support the measure but soon withdrew the key provisions. As Secretary of the Treasury Antonio Ortiz Mena explained, tax reform should come from consultation not by fiat:

In the process of the tax reform initiated but not concluded . . . we gave top priority to acquiescence of the different sectors of the population, because little can be done in any system without a general conviction of the various sectors as to the necessity of the measures and the justice and timeliness of their implementation. . . . The income tax law . . . was made listening to the viewpoints of the affected sectors.[26]

In other words, the government would not incur the opposition of the private sector. The law that finally passed resulted in a highly regressive tax: revenue from labour income as a proportion of total governmental receipts from the individual income tax went up from 58.1 per cent in 1960 to 77.9 per cent in 1966.

To help domestic industry the government imposed an additional 6 per cent increase in tariffs in 1965, and broadened the effect of quotas by creating about a thousand new import categories per year, so that by the end of the *sexenio* the total number was nearly 13,000. In Clark Reynolds' memorable phrase, the state and local entrepreneurs happily formed an 'alliance for profits'.[27]

Such overtures to business required Díaz Ordaz to reassert governmental control over organized labour. The ties between labour and the state had never fully recovered from the traumas of 1958–9, and the Bloque de Unidad Obrera – Ruiz Cortines' attempt to centralize and consolidate those links – had become little more than a phantom. Hence, early in 1966 the Díaz Ordaz regime supervised the formation of the Congreso del Trabajo (CT) as a new vehicle that would ratify the supremacy of Fidel Velázquez and reaffirm close state–labour linkages. The CT granted lead-

---

[26] Leopoldo Solís, *Economic Policy Reform in Mexico: A Case Study for Developing Countries* (New York, 1981), pp. 24–5.

[27] See Reynolds, *The Mexican Economy: Twentieth-Century Structure and Growth* (New Haven, 1970), esp. pp. 185–90.

ing roles to Velázquez's CTM and to the government-workers' union, the Federación de Sindicatos Trabajadores en el Servicio del Estado (FSTSE), thereby developing strong links with both the worker and the popular sectors of the PRI. The traditional structures continued to reign supreme.

Cultivation of the urban sectors, including labor, was undertaken at the expense of the countryside. The Díaz Ordaz government never once raised the minimum price for the purchase of basic grains from the level established by López Mateos in 1963, and reduced the relative share of agricultural credit from 15 per cent of the total in 1960 to only 9 per cent in 1970. In 1966 the administration initiated a program of agrarian warehouses, the so-called *graneros del pueblo,* ostensibly designed to assure the poorest farmers and *ejidatarios* a timely and effective support price for basic commodities (especially corn, beans and wheat). But the network of storage facilities suffered from hasty construction, poor location and incompetent administration; by 1971 only 15 per cent of the *graneros* were in use. Peasants erupted in isolated protest against their mistreatment – in land seizures, hunger marches, occasional outbursts of violence – but the voice of the *campesino* fell on deaf ears.

It was the middle classes, not the poor, that staged the most visible disturbances. Near the end of 1964 medical interns in Mexico City went on strike, initially over the withholding of their traditional Christmas bonus (the *aguinaldo)* and eventually over workplace conditions. Early in 1965, Díaz Ordaz, only months into his presidency, met with the strikers and their moderate supporters and issued a decree addressing some but not all of the demands. When a dissident faction of young doctors launched another strike in April 1965, the government took a tough stance and the interns went back on the job. And when they proclaimed yet another strike, this time in August, the regime responded with brute force. Riot police took possession of the Veinte de Noviembre hospital in Mexico City, prominent sympathizers were jailed, and after Díaz Ordaz had issued a stern warning in his state-of-the-nation address of 1 September, more than two hundred strikers were fired. The rest returned to work.

By contrast, the student movement of 1968 shook the system to its foundations. There had been a long and venerable tradition of student activism in Mexico, with disturbances customarily put down either by limited force (as in Guerrero, Morelia and Sonora) or by the dismissal of the rector (as at UNAM in 1966). In such instances authorities and students recognized and accepted rules of the game, a set of boundaries and codes that neither side would transgress. This time would be different.

The tortuous path of events commenced in July 1968, when police broke up a series of demonstrations by pro-Castro student groups. On 26 July (the anniversary of the Cuban Revolution) a loose federation of student organizations from the Polytechnic Institute, the agriculture school at Chapingo and the UNAM issued a set of demands: indemnization for families of students injured or killed in the disturbances, release of those in jail, abolition of the anti-subversion law on 'social dissolution', and elimination of special shock-troop police squads. Otherwise, the youths announced, there would be a general student strike. The authorities answered with a lock-out, closing all university-related institutions in the Federal District. Police forces shelled the San Ildefonso preparatory school (in what came to be known as the *bazukazo*) and stormed the premises. Another squadron invaded the Instituto Nacional de Bellas Artes and arrested seventy-three student demonstrators. In a major speech on 1 August Díaz Ordaz offered 'an outstretched hand', but by this time the students were beyond reconciliation.

Popular mobilization set the stage for confrontation. With remarkable boldness UNAM rector Javier Barros Sierra led a public march of 80,000 to mourn police invasions of the campuses in violation of longstanding traditions of university autonomy. A 13 August demonstration drew about 150,000 participants, and on 27 August, in an event of unprecedented magnitude, approximately 300,000 protestors took part in a march from Chapultepec Park down the Paseo de la Reforma to the central square or *zócalo*. In the meantime students organized a Comisión Nacional de Huelga (CNH) to coordinate actions and to promote the demands first set forth in July. Tension mounted. With Mexico about to host the Olympic Games in October, Díaz Ordaz used his address of 1 September to accuse the protestors of anti-patriotic conspiracy. The CNH proposed a dialogue but nothing happened. On 10 September an ever-pliant Senate authorized the President to call out the armed forces 'in defense of the internal and external security of Mexico'.[28]

Matters came to a head on 2 October, when students and supporters came together for another round of speeches and proclamations in the open plaza of the Tlatelolco apartment complex in downtown Mexico City. Without advance warning, white-gloved security agents waved in security forces that opened fire on the helpless crowd. At least two thousand demonstrators were placed under arrest. An official report admitted that

---

[28] Evelyn P. Stevens, *Protest and Response in Mexico* (Cambridge, 1974), p. 228.

forty-nine people were killed; a *New York Times* correspondent placed the death toll at more like two hundred, with hundreds of others wounded. It was a brutal massacre, since remembered as Mexico's contemporary *noche triste* ('sad night'), a primitive occasion when the system inexplicably chose to devour its own young. Schools reopened and the CNH dissolved, but Tlatelolco cast a long shadow over Mexican society and politics. Some high-level officials resigned in disgust. A wary public speculated about who bore primary responsibility – Luis Echeverría, the Secretary of Gobernación; Alfonso Corona del Rosal, regent of the Federal District; Marcelino García Barragán, the Secretary of Defence; or the President himself. Beneath the palpable anguish there lurked unsettling questions: Was this the product of Mexico's miracle? Was it the price of political stability? What kind of nation was Mexico?

While many engaged in painful soul-searching, others turned to violence. Terrorist groups began to appear in the cities, the most prominent being the September 23rd League, and rebellious peasants took to the hills. The best-known agrarian revolutionary of this era was Lucio Cabañas, who began forming a guerilla movement in the mountains of Guerrero in 1968; he and his band subsequently won considerable renown, at one point kidnapping the state governor, but he would meet his death at the hands of the military in 1974. Violence only begat more violence.

The Tlatelolco massacre had a more enduring effect in engendering the progressive alienation of the intelligentsia from the regime. For decades after the Revolution the nation's intellectuals had tended to collaborate with state authorities. The promotion of education was a primary goal of revolutionary leaders, and universities developed into crucial training grounds for national leaders. Artists and writers dedicated themselves to the articulation and elaboration of a political ideology which came to form the basis of a national consensus, a set of assumptions which endowed the state with the legacy of the Revolution itself. In tacit recognition of this service the Mexican government constantly cultivated contact with intellectual figures and supported their endeavours, frequently enticing them into semi-honorific public offices. The state and the intelligentsia both needed and supported each other. Tlatelolco shattered this long-standing pact. Such leading writers as Octavio Paz and Carlos Fuentes strongly denounced the repression – the memory of which inspired a whole genre of Tlatelolco literature – and essayists began to question the basic legitimacy of a regime that would wage such brutal war on its youth.[29] The increasingly radicalized universities became hotbeds of opposition. The relationship between students and the state, historically enriching for both, degenerated into mutual resentment and open hostility. Tlatelolco would by no means spell the end of the regime; but it opened a delicate fissure in the edifice of state.

The close of the Díaz Ordaz *sexenio* also brought an end to the postwar era of the Mexican economic miracle, the epoch of *desarrollo estabilizador* marked by continuous economic growth, price stability and balance-of-payments stability. Under the skilful orchestration of Antonio Ortiz Mena, Secretary of the Treasury under both López Mateos and Díaz Ordaz, and Rodrigo Gómez, long-time director of the central bank, economic policy employed a variety of fiscal and monetary instruments: tax incentives to favour reinvestment, public-sector spending and foreign borrowing, and control of credit and the money supply. Interest rates were pegged at attractive levels (above prevailing U.S. rates) to encourage domestic savings and foreign investment. By conventional standards Mexico's post-war industrialization policies had been a resounding success: during the decade of the 1960s Mexico sustained high levels of growth, around 7 per cent a year, and – with one of the most rapidly swelling populations in the world – achieved a solid per capita average growth rate of 3.3 per cent. Inflation was negligible, around 3.5 per cent a year, and the peso maintained its rate of 12.50 per dollar.

Yet the strategy of 'stabilizing development' was beginning to reveal its weaknesses. If the hard-money policy had become a symbol for the stability and strength of the political regime, it also imposed economic burdens, not the least of which was to discourage exports because Mexico's rate of inflation was generally higher than in the United States. (In fact the peso became overvalued by the mid-1960s, after a burst of high-growth inflation in 1964, but this was largely camouflaged by U.S. inflation resulting from Vietnam.) Gradually, the effects of overvaluation showed up in the trade deficit, which increased from $367 million in 1965 to $946 million by 1970. During this period Mexico accordingly began to borrow capital abroad, and by 1970 the country had a cumulative debt (both public and private) of about $4.2 billion. Unemployment (and

---

[29] See Dolly J. Young, 'Mexican Literary Reactions to Tlatelolco 1968', *Latin American Research Review* 20, no. 2 (1985): 71–85.

under-employment) continued at high levels.[30] And by the mid-1960s the depletion of agriculture had started to require the large-scale importation of foodstuffs.[31] Even as the performance of Mexico's political economy approached its zenith, there were signs of trouble on the horizon. The party was far from over, but the lights were beginning to dim.

1970–88

Mexico's political system had demonstrated extraordinary effectiveness in resolving the crises and challenges that beset the country through the 1960s. A variety of state-directed programs – subsidies, price controls, wage agreements – provided the mass of the population with sufficient tangible benefits to prevent any serious radical challenge to the system as a whole. Such policies may not have complied with orthodox economic doctrine, but they met a crucial political goal; labour and the peasantry both continued to be essential pillars of the system. Discontent appeared mainly among the middle classes, among doctors and students, and although Tlatelolco had bequeathed a painful legacy, the regime had shown the resilience to overcome even this episode.

Mexico continued to experience rapid social change in the 1970s. Although rates of growth declined, the population increased from fewer than 50 million in 1970 to 70 million in 1980 and nearly 80 million by 1985. Almost a million new people entered the labour force every year, posing enormous pressure for the creation of jobs. As a result, Mexicans were on the move: migrants set out constantly in search of work, either going to the cities or crossing the border into the United States (where they would be declared 'illegal aliens', the *bracero* agreement having expired in 1964). Alarmists and politicians in the United States rabidly denounced what they viewed as a 'silent invasion,' proclaiming that there were 8 to 12 million 'illegals' in the United States. Although detailed research revealed that most 'undocumented workers' returned to Mexico and that the accumulated stock may have been in the range of 1.5 to 3.5 million, this did not prevent the surge of anti-Mexican nativism.[32]

[30] See Clark W. Reynolds, 'Why Mexico's "Stabilizing Development" Was Actually Destabilizing (With Some Implications for the Future)', *World Development* 6, nos. 7–8 (July-August 1978): 1005–18.

[31] Esteva clearly sees 1965 as the turning-point: *Batalla,* pp. 17, 71.

[32] Kenneth Hill, 'Illegal Aliens: An Assessment', in Daniel B. Levine, Kenneth Hill, and Robert Warren (eds.), *Immigration Statistics: A Story of Neglect* (Washington, D.C., 1985), pp. 225–50.

Population growth and social mobility also propelled the expansion of Mexico City, which swelled to a megalopolis with 14 to 16 million inhabitants by the mid-1980s. About half of this growth came from internal migration (indeed, about half the country's migrants headed for the capital). By official estimates there were at least 5 million poor people in Mexico City and its environs, as in Netzahuálcoyotl, a burgeoning community outside the Federal District that began as a squatter settlement in the 1960s and claimed more than 2 million residents by the 1980s. Notwithstanding this spread of poverty, the middle classes increased in magnitude and prominence, embracing perhaps one-third of the nation's population by the early 1980s. Unequal distribution of the benefits from 'stabilizing development' also enriched an upper layer, a wealthy and well-connected cadre that may have accounted for another 1 or 2 per cent of the total. The expansion of these middle- and upper-class sectors became clearly evident in consumption patterns: weekend shopping trips to Los Angeles and Houston became a matter of course, while the number of registered automobiles increased from 1.2 million in 1970 to 4.3 million by 1980. (It would seem, at times, as though each and every one of them was jammed into a single intersection in downtown Mexico City.)

This period also witnessed the development of the Mexican north, which became increasingly distant – economically, politically and culturally – from the center of the nation. By 1980 there were over 3.4 million residents in such border towns as Tijuana, Ciudad Juárez and Matamoros. The cities of Chihuahua, Torreón, Tampico and Monterrey continued to grow in importance and size. As many as 250,000 people worked in special 'in-bond' factories (*maquiladoras*) that produced goods for export to the United States (the number would fluctuate according to demand in the United States). Always fiercely independent, many *norteños* would come to see themselves as having little in common with the *chilangos* of Mexico City. Such perceptions would sometimes stimulate opposition to the regime and the PRI. In fact, this may have reflected an even more fundamental process – the appearance (however skeletal the form) of 'civil society' in Mexico. Independent citizens' organizations emerged in a variety of fields, no longer necessarily seeking tutelage or support from the state. Professionals, businessmen, academics and others came to adopt a somewhat more independent and less pliant attitude toward the regime; from outward impressions it seemed that political culture was becoming more activist and participatory, less passive and submissive.[33] It was also taking new forms, especially through the expression of growing concern about the authenticity of the electoral process. Further evidence, ominous to some, lay in the partial re-emergence of the Catholic Church as a public social force. For decades there had prevailed a tacit *modus vivendi*, a silent agreement for the Church and state to leave each other alone – so long as priests would refrain from politics. This began to change. In 1983, for instance, the Church managed to block a move to legalize abortion, and in 1986 an archbishop spoke out against electoral fraud. Conversations throughout informed circles often prompted intense speculation about the mysterious power of Opus Dei.

As the breach between the government and intellectuals widened, an independent press began to appear. Julio Scherer García, the displaced editor of the prominent newspaper *Excélsior*, took many of his top writers and created a weekly news magazine, *Proceso*. A new daily, *Unomásuno*, challenged *Excélsior's* position as the foremost paper in Mexico City. In 1984 it was followed by *La Jornada*, led by some of the most prominent young intellectuals in the country. Reviews like *Nexos*, modeled after *The New York Review of Books*, provided still other outlets. In effect, radical critics of the regime found new means of expression. They would still be dependent upon official toleration, and they would pay heavy prices for transgressions. (Journalists became common targets of attack, and some – like the well-known Manuel Buendía – were even murdered.) Dissidents were mostly confined to the Mexico City print media; television remained firmly in pro-establishment hands, while radio occupied a kind of middle ground. But the bounds of permissibility had nonetheless been stretched – and the range of possibilities increased.

In 1970 Luis Echeverría became Mexico's fifth post-war president. He appeared to be the embodiment of Mexico's political elite; born in Mexico City in 1922, he had studied at UNAM, taken a degree in law and taught courses there as well. He married into a prominent political family from the state of Jalisco, promptly entering the PRI and, more importantly, joining the *camarilla* of party president Rodolfo Sánchez Taboada. After the *cacique's* death Echeverria became *oficial mayor* of the PRI, and acquired prominence through his work during the López Mateos campaign; in 1958

---

[33] Solid evidence for this point simply does not exist; for a recent review of the literature, see Ann L. Craig and Wayne A. Cornelius, 'Political Culture in Mexico: Continuities and Revisionist Interpretations', in Gabriel A. Almond and Sidney Verba (eds.), *The Civic Culture Revisited* (Boston, 1980), pp. 325–93.

he landed the crucial position of Subsecretary of Gobernación under Díaz Ordaz. When in 1964 Díaz Ordaz assumed the presidency, Echeverría received the post of secretary. Six years later Echeverria repeated the move that Alemán, Ruiz Cortines, and Díaz Ordaz all had made before, from Gobernación to the presidency.

Throughout his career, Echeverría had labored intensively behind the scenes. He was the first constitutional president since the end of the Mexican Revolution who had never held a single elective position. He had become, over the years, a master of bureaucratic manoeuvring. Only one event – the massacre of students in 1968 – had brought him into the limelight, and though many held him responsible for that wanton display of naked force, his role was not at all clear. In spite, or possibly because, of that episode he managed to edge out several strong rivals for the presidency, including Alfonso Corona del Rosal, the head of the Federal District; Juan Gil Preciado, the Secretary of Agriculture; Emilio Martínez Manautou, Secretary of the Presidency; and Antonio Ortiz Mena, the Secretary of the Treasury widely regarded as the architect of Mexico's economic miracle. An austere, ambitious man, balding, bespectacled, non-smoking, teetotalling and trim, Luis Echeverría was the consummate expression of Mexico's new breed: the bureaucrat-turned-president.

Reflecting his experience in Gobernación, Echeverría moved quickly to strengthen and consolidate his own political power. From the outset, he strove to isolate and dismantle some rival *camarillas,* pointedly failing to give a cabinet appointment to one of his leading pre-presidential rivals, Alfonso Corona del Rosal. In June 1971, a bloody assault on students by paramilitary thugs gave him an opportunity to expel Alfonso Martínez Domínguez, then head of the Federal District. Echeverría ousted no fewer than five state governors from office (in Guerrero, Nuevo León, Puebla, Hidalgo, Sonora) and he made frequent changes in his cabinet: by November 1976 only six out of the seventeen secretaries still occupied their original positions. Echeverría cultivated his own political base from a cadre of young men, mostly in their early thirties, to whom he gave top-level, sensitive posts: Francisco Javier Alejo, Juan José Bremer, Ignacio Ovalle, Fausto Zapata, figureheads for what came to be known, with derision at the end, as a 'youthocracy' (*efebrocracia*). Here was a new generation, defined by both outlook and age, nurtured and brought to power by the President, a group who would presumably remain in his debt for many years to come. It also bespoke his desire, perhaps in the wake of Tlatelolco, to re-establish links with the country's intelligentsia.

Once in office, Echeverría revealed the power of his personality. Impatient and energetic, he took to his work with passion to re-establish official legitimacy in the aftermath of Tlatelolco, attempting to create a means for dialogue, a so-called *apertura democrática* in which he would himself play the central role (rather than impose an institutional reform). Exhorting his countrymen to labour with 'creative anguish' and apparently hoping to become a latter-day Cárdenas, he went everywhere, saw everyone, gave speeches, made pronouncements, talked and talked some more; as Daniel Cosío Villegas wryly observed, talking seemed to be a 'physiological necessity' for the new president. Echeverría's style of rule was neither institutionalized nor bureaucratized. It was extremely, urgently and intensively personal, and his style and rhetoric took on a highly populist tinge.[34]

As the United States accepted its defeat in Vietnam and moved toward détente with the Soviet Union, Echeverría sought to take advantage of the opportunity by establishing Mexico as a leader of the Third World countries, with himself as major spokesman. He was frequently critical of the United States, and traveled widely, reaching China in 1973. He exchanged visits with Salvador Allende, welcoming hundreds of Chilean exiles after the coup of 1973 (including Allende's widow) and eventually withdrawing recognition of the military junta. At the United Nations, he promoted a Charter of Economic Rights and Obligations and, in 1975, he instructed the Mexican ambassador to support an anti-Israeli denunciation of Zionism as a form of 'racism' (thus precipitating a tourist boycott by Jewish leaders in the United States; the next time around, Mexico would quietly abstain). Greatly over-estimating his prestige, Echeverría also presented himself as a candidate for the secretary-generalship of the UN near the conclusion of his presidential term.

On the domestic front, economic down-turns posed an immediate challenge for the government. Echeverría's initial reaction was to adjust and modify longstanding policies rather than to undertake any major innovations. To counter deficits his treasury secretary tried to hold down government spending, but the resulting decline in public investment led to sharp recessions in 1971–2 (with growth rates under 4 per cent). An opportunity to revise foreign-exchange policy came in August 1971, when President Nixon took the dramatic steps of imposing a 10 per cent tax on imports (including those on Mexico, thus bringing an end to the idea of a

---

[34] Daniel Cosío Villegas, *El estilo personal de gobernar* (Mexico, 1975), p. 31.

'special relationship' between the two countries) and taking the dollar off the gold standard to float on the international market. Some of Echeverría's advisers argued that this would be the time to float or devalue the peso as well, rather than keep it pegged to the dollar. But Secretary of the Treasury Hugo Margáin voiced quick disapproval: devaluation, he remarked, 'is a word that does not exist in my dictionary'.[35]

Echeverría also took a cautious approach toward the long-standing issue of tax policy. By late 1972 his economic advisers had put together a tax bill based on the one that Díaz Ordaz had scuttled in 1964–5, a proposal that would face the problems of fragmented income and anonymous holdings. Impressed by the logic of the proposal, the President instructed his finance minister to explain the bill to private-sector representatives. Margáin hosted two meetings at his private residence with leading industrialists from CONCAMIN and CANACINTRA, bankers and merchants. The businessmen offered strenuous objections, but according to one top adviser, the treasury secretary (and ex-ambassador to the United States) 'showed all his diplomatic skill in overlooking the carping tone' of his guests and countered their every argument. Without a word of explanation, however, the government suddenly dropped the whole plan.[36] Apparently the Ortiz Mena dictum of the 1960s still held true: tax reform cannot be achieved against the wishes of the private sector.

At the same time, Echeverría was preparing to cast aside the old formulas of 'stabilizing development' in favor of what he would come to call *desarrollo compartido* or 'shared development'. The year 1973 marked the final end of the financial boom of the late 1950s and 1960s. As inflation mounted, Echeverría appointed a new treasury minister, José López Portillo, who immediately began to take decisive steps. Price hikes in energy (gas and electricity) were followed by a wage and salary increase in September 1973, together with price controls on basic consumer products. As businessmen complained about these measures – and quietly threatened capital flight – Echeverría responded in tones of exasperation and anger. In his state-of-the-nation address in 1973 the President complained about idle industrial capacity and attacked criticism of the government as 'a lie that only benefits the interest of reactionary groups'. A year later he departed from his prepared text to launch a diatribe against speculators, the *'little rich ones'* who 'are despised by the people, by their own sons,

---

[35] Solís, *Economic Policy*, p. 61.
[36] Ibid., pp. 75–6.

because they are not strengthening the fatherland for their sons'.[37] The pact between the state and the private sector was suffering from strain.

As Echeverría's strategy for 'shared development' took shape, it came to stress the importance of distribution as well as production: for ethical and social reasons, it was held, the masses would need to share significantly in the benefits of growth. To achieve this goal and impose the necessary policies, the state would be a strong and autonomous force; private capital could play a constructive role, but profit would be less important than social equity. Whereas 'stabilizing development' relied on a close alliance between the state and the private sector, the political logic of the 'shared development' model called for a populist coalition of workers and peasants under the tutelage of a powerful state.

Desarrollo compartido placed special emphasis on the agrarian sector and on the long-suffering *campesinos*. The institutional cornerstone of this orientation would be Compañía Nacional de Subsistencias Populares (CONASUPO), an established organization with three major objectives: to regulate the market for basic commodities, to increase income for poor farmers and to ensure the availability of basic goods to low-income consumers. These goals could be contradictory, of course, and from Alemán to Díaz Ordaz, CONASUPO and its predecessors tended to protect the interests of urban consumers at the expense of rural producers. As one Echeverría official flatly observed, 'the traditional role of CONASUPO . . . has been to protect consumers. The government's economic policy was to keep prices stable, especially in urban areas, keeping salaries low and stimulating industry. That is why DICONSA [the chain of retail stores] has grown so greatly in urban areas and why corn was bought in the areas of highest production with little thought to the protection of producers'.[38]

Under Echeverría this was to change. In 1970, Mexico had to import more than 760,000 tons of corn, a symbolic and economic set-back that apparently stunned the President. He placed CONASUPO under the directorship of Jorge de la Vega Domínguez, an able and experienced political administrator, whose staff worked for nearly two years on a diagnosis of the country's agrarian problem. Presenting their results in mid-1972, the research team argued that previous agriculture policies had placed too much stress on the modern, mechanized commercial sector

---

[37] Quoted in ibid., pp. 81–2.
[38] Merrilee Serrill Grindle, *Bureaucrats, Politicians, and Peasants in Mexico: A Case Study in Public Policy* (Berkeley and Los Angeles, 1977), p. 75.

(mainly in the north). The key to self-sufficiency and income redistribution lay in the traditional corn-producing sector (mainly in the centre and south). A crucial obstacle was not just market forces but the role of middlemen, often powerful *caciques* who dominated villages or regions with the approval and support of superior authorities. According to the team, the answer to this lay in a programme of 'integrated' development, one that would by-pass the power of local *caciques* and reach directly to the peasants. The state should therefore intervene to help the poor, CONASUPO offering an integrated package of services (fair prices for inputs, reasonable price supports for harvests, adequate credit and storage facilities, assistance with marketing and advice for reinvestment).

The integrated programme for rural development soon became national policy and one of Echeverría's highest personal priorities. By the end of his *sexenio,* agriculture accounted for 20 per cent of the federal budget, by far the highest figure since the 1940s (when Miguel Alemán was pouring funds into large-scale irrigation projects). As its own budget quintupled, CONASUPO grew into a massive agency with as many as 15,000 employees (including subsidiary companies). Its purchasing agents focussed their attention on low-income *campesinos;* retail stores mushroomed in the countryside as well as in the cities, the total number increasing from around 1,500 in 1970 to 2,700 in 1976. But the agrarian programme could claim only limited success. The challenge, of course, was enormous. The resistance of unenthusiastic bureaucrats in rival organizations, such as the Secretariat of Agriculture, was considerable. And the tenacity of the *caciques* proved to be ferocious. In the end, the much-touted plan for integrated development fell victim to bureaucratic inertia and to the politics of presidential succession, already under way by late 1974.

The commitment to 'shared development' also entailed a rapprochement with organized labour. In the first few years Echeverría and Secretary of Labour Porfirio Muñoz Ledo tried to curtail the power of CTM boss Fidel Velázquez and even flirted with the idea of ousting him from his position. One government tactic was to grant tacit encouragement to an insurgent 'independent' worker movement, which became especially strong among auto-workers, railway-workers, and electricians – in the most modern and mechanized sectors, where traditional patron–client ties were weaker. In this vein, Echeverría extended legal recognition to the Unidad Obrera Independiente (UOI), an organization that explicitly defied the CTM. However, when inflation began to accelerate in 1973, Echeverría came to recognize his need for Velázquez's control of rank-and-file demands for compensatory wage increases. The President thus made amends, Velázquez continuing his prolonged supremacy as the state threw its weight behind his leadership and the independent movement withered away (by 1978 it accounted for merely 7 per cent of Labour Congress membership).[39] Labour was back in safe hands.

Echeverría nonetheless continued to pursue an activist, growth-oriented economic policy. In keeping with his nationalistic and *tercermundista* pronouncements, Mexico passed new laws in 1973 to regulate – but by no means eliminate – the actions of foreign enterprise, especially the multinational corporations. The role of the state, already large, expanded sharply; total government revenue rose from around 8 per cent of the gross domestic product in 1970 to roughly 12.5 per cent in 1975. Public spending poured into housing, schooling and other development programmes. Agriculture credit increased. The nation doubled its capacity to produce crude oil, electricity, and iron and steel. As a result, Echeverría proudly pointed out, the GDP grew at an annual average rate of 5.6 per cent. Nonetheless, this expansion of state activity brought Echeverría into constant conflict with the domestic private sector, caught in a squeeze between multinational corporations and the Mexican state. Only the strongest local firms could survive, and the government bought out many of the weaker ones (the number of state-owned corporations swelled remarkably, from 86 to 740 during Echeverría's regime). Between 1970 and 1976 the money supply grew about 18 per cent a year, compared to previous rates around 12 per cent, and the federal deficit increased sixfold. This contributed to an inflationary spiral – prices rose by about 22 per cent a year – which, in turn, priced Mexican goods out of international markets. As a result, the deficit in the balance of payments tripled between 1973 and 1975 – thus placing great, ultimately overbearing pressure on the value of the peso.

As the *sexenio* wore on there were signs that the still young Echeverría intended to broaden and perpetuate his influence. Five of his cabinet secretaries left office in order to assume state governorships, and a sixth started running for another just after the conclusion of the presidential term. Several members of the sub-cabinet became governors of states as well. Most observers noted that these politicians, Echeverrista to a man, would be solidly ensconced in state capitals well after the President stepped down. It was in this context that Echeverría broke all precedent by publicly calling attention to the forthcoming presidential succession.

[39] See Middlebrook, 'Political Economy', p. 316.

'It is useful', he stated in late 1974, 'for public opinion to analyze and evaluate men in relation to the presidential succession, and it is good for it to be that way. . . . I should think that public opinion will start to define its preferences sometime in the latter part of next year; but in the meantime, everyone should be the object of study, observation, and judgement. That is democratically healthy.'[40] He returned to the subject on subsequent occasions, and in April 1975, Leandro Rovirosa Wade, the Secretary of Hydraulic Resources, startled the press by announcing the names of plausible contenders. The move was so novel that it could only have been prompted by Echeverría, perhaps to demonstrate his own control of the selection process.

Thus revealed before 'public opinion', the so-called *tapados* were seven: Mario Moya Palencia, forty-two, Echeverría's successor at Gobernación and for that reason widely regarded as the front-runner; Hugo Cervantes del Río, forty-nine, Secretary of the Presidency; José López Portillo, fifty-four, Secretary of the Treasury and a boyhood friend of the President; Porfirio Muñoz Ledo, forty-one, Secretary of Labour and a well-known intellectual; Carlos Gálvez Betancourt, fifty-four, director of the Social-Security Institute; Augusto Gómez Villanueva, forty-four, Secretary of Agrarian Reform; and Luis Enrique Bracamontes, fifty-one, Secretary of Public Works. 'Any one of them is excellent', concluded Rovirosa Wade. 'Each one has managed admirably to perform the tasks with which President Echeverría has entrusted him'.[41]

At the time of this announcement, Jesús Reyes Heroles, president of the PRI, proclaimed the party's intention to draft a 'basic plan of government' for the 1976–82 administration. The idea would be to forge a platform, a series of policy commitments by the government. With Echeverría's evident approval, Reyes Heroles revealed that the plan would be ready by late September and submitted to the party leadership for ratification. The candidate would be selected in October, presumably as the person most capable of carrying out the plan. The slogan went forth: 'First the programme, then the man'! It seemed, to some, that Echeverría had found a novel way to tie the hands of his successor. On the morning of 22 September, right on schedule, Reyes Heroles was chairing a meeting about the 'basic plan' when he received a call from the presidential residence. He returned to the session, disconcerted and surprised, and hurried

[40] Andrés Montemayor H., *Los pridestinados* (Monterrey, 1975), p. 8.
[41] *Hispano Americano*, 21 April 1975.

out to Los Pinos for a brief visit at midday. In the afternoon, three of the presidential hopefuls – Moya Palencia, Cervantes del Río and Gálvez Betancourt – were together with Echeverría at a ceremonial lunch. When interrupted by an aide, Moya Palencia reportedly turned pale and left the table. The choice was López Portillo. Meanwhile, Fidel Velázquez was publicly proclaiming labour's support for the Secretary of the Treasury, and others were rapidly joining the ranks. For some the *destapamiento* was a surprise, for others it was a shock. A leader of the CNC was asked if the peasant sector would add its backing: "To whom?" he enquired. Shown a copy of the afternoon paper, with López Portillo's name in the headline, he merely nodded and said: 'Of course'. Velázquez and other party leaders went to the treasury building to offer their congratulations, and early in the evening a crestfallen Moya Palencia came to express his own capitulation: 'José López Portillo is the best man the Mexican Revolution has. Let us believe in him'.[42]

Even as they climbed upon the bandwagon, people in the political world mused over the choice of López Portillo. Although a lifelong friend of the President, he had never been able to curry the favor of labour or the peasant sector in the course of his relatively brief public career. In mid-November, Echeverría himself offered a clue when he made the remarkable declaration – breaking all precedent again – that López Portillo won out 'because he was the one with the fewest political attachments, the one who had not reached any secret or discreet agreement, the one who dedicated himself to the service of the country without engaging in cheap politics (*política barata*)'.[43] The denunciation of *política barata* was widely interpreted as a rebuke to Moya Palencia, generally regarded as the *tapado* with the widest political support. But López Portillo's greatest asset was also his greatest liability: he did not have a team of his own. From Echeverría's point of view, this might be the easiest person to control from behind the scenes.

In the following months Echeverría held the spotlight while López Portillo, true to form, remained in the shadows. The July 1976 election was itself a desultory affair, partly because an internal schism had prevented the PAN from fielding any candidate at all. This made the campaign a race between López Portillo and abstentionism, and if it is true that 69 per cent of the eligible population went to the polls, with 94 per cent casting ballots in favor of the PRI candidate, this would have to go

[42] *Excélsior,* 23 September 1975.
[43] Ibid., 13 November 1975.

down as a triumph for López Portillo, who had shown himself to be easy-going and friendly – *simpático.*

But a sense of malaise began to spread. Early in July a rebellion had erupted within the staff of *Excélsior,* then Mexico City's leading newspaper, owned collectively as a co-operative venture. The insurgents resorted to numerous illegal tactics, but governmental authorities – from Echeverría on down – refused to take any action. The uprising succeeded, the direc-torship changed hands, and what had become a proud and critical voice was now stilled. (The departed staff would go on to found the magazine *Proceso.*) And when it was reported that Echeverría had become a major shareholder in a new newspaper group controlling thirty-seven dailies, the implications became ominous. On 11 August an unidentified terrorist organization, possibly the leftist September 23rd League, attacked a car that was carrying Margarita López Portillo, a sister of the President-elect. She was unhurt but one of her bodyguards was killed, three others were wounded and the leader of the gang was shot to death. Viewed in isola-tion, the incident was unsettling enough, but the unanswered questions were deeply disturbing: Who was really behind the attack? What if López Portillo had been the real target? How could this happen in broad daylight in Mexico City?

There followed a crushing blow. On 31 August, after months of official denial, the government devalued the peso for the first time since 1954. The drain on the country's foreign reserves had reached intolerable limits, there had been large-scale capital flight since the previous April, and exports remained overpriced. As a result the government finally decided to 'float' the peso, letting it find its new level – which the Bank of Mexico pegged at 19.90 on 12 September, a 37 per cent drop in value from the long-standing rate of 12.50. As if this were not enough, the government refloated the peso a second time, on 26 October, and the exchange rate quickly jumped to 26.50 to the dollar. Within two months, the interna-tional value of the peso had been cut in half. For those who viewed the currency's position as a sign of strength and stability, a manifestation of the 'Mexican miracle' and a hallmark of national pride, this was bitter medicine indeed.

Rumours started to intensify. Somewhat cryptically, Echeverría de-nounced 'insidious attacks' against Mexico in his final state-of-the-nation address,[44] and gossip spread throughout the capital. There would be an

[44] Ibid., 2 September 1976.

assault on Echeverría's wife. There would be an attempt on López Portillo's wife. Someone would try to murder Hermenegildo Cuenca Díaz, Echeverría's Secretary of Defence. A local boss in Jalisco had put out a contract on the life of the redoubtable Marcelino García Barragán. But the chief rumour, the one that captured the popular imagination, was the most implausible of all: there would be a military coup. The first time around, the coup was to occur on 16 September, the anniversary of Mexico's independence. After that, attention focussed on another date: 20 November, the anniversary of the Revolution, only ten days before the end of Echeverría's term. On 29 November a series of explosions took place in the capital, causing extensive damage but provoking no outward challenge to the regime.

Especially during November, events in the north created further tension and exacerbated popular gullibility. Around the middle of the month peasant groups seized extensions of land in Sonora, Sinaloa and Durango. The actions reflected long-standing grievances, and agrarian resentment had been smouldering for years; what was novel about these confrontations was the timing, only days before the end of a regime. On 20 November Echeverría, not about to give up power till the final minute, suddenly expropriated nearly 100,000 hectares of rich privately owned land in Sonora for collective *ejidos*. Outraged by this action, land-owners protested, and in Sinaloa some 28,000 announced a stoppage in the fields. In a demonstration of solidarity, businessmen and merchants in Puebla, Chihuahua and Nuevo León joined in brief work stoppages. Encouraged by the outcome in Sonora, peasants invaded other lands in Durango and Jalisco.

At the inauguration López Portillo delivered an eloquent call for collaboration instead of conflict, and then he installed his new team. One source of cabinet leaders came from the president's own political background, people with whom he had worked in the course of his career – *técnicos* in charge of economic policy, men such as Rodolfo Moctezuma Cid, Carlos Tello, and the youthful Andrés Oteyza. López Portillo also drew on personal friends (Antonio Farell Cubillas at IMSS, Pedro Ojeda Paullada in labour, Jorge Díaz Serrano at PEMEX) and family relations (sister Margarita, for example, became a departmental director within Gobernación), the administration eventually coming under withering criticism for nepotism. In all these ways, López Portillo managed to construct a *camarilla* that had as its common denominator personal loyalty to himself.

To extend and strengthen popular support for the regime, López Portillo adopted a time-tested strategy: electoral reform. The legacy of Tlatelolco still cast a pall over the nation's politics, especially among the young, and the tumult of the Echeverría years had created a widespread sense of apprehension. Electoral abstention caused considerable concern, and it became apparent that the system would have to open up in order to provide orderly channels for the opposition, especially since the the PPS and the PARM had long lost their relevance and followings. Moreover new parties were starting to appear, at least one on the right (the Partido Demócrata Mexicano, founded 1971) but most on the left: the Partido Socialista de los Trabajadores, or PST (1973); the Unidad de Izquierda Comunista or UIC (1973); the Movimiento de Acción y Unidad Socialista, or MAUS (1973); the Partido Mexicano de los Trabajadores (1974); the Partido Popular Mexicano, or PPM (1975); the Partido Socialista Revolucionario, or PSR (1976); and the Partido Revolucionario de los Trabajadores, or PRT (1976).

In response to these developments the reform measure of December 1977 contained three basic elements: first, a liberalization of the procedures for party registration (which could now be achieved either by getting 1.5 per cent of total vote in any national election or by enrolling 65,000 members); secondly, an expansion of the Chamber of Deputies to four hundred members, with three hundred elected by simple majority in single-member districts and one hundred by proportional representation (in other words, these seats were reserved for opposition parties); and, finally, extension of access to mass media for opposition parties and opposition candidates. Initially, the left appeared to benefit most. Under the new registration laws the Partido Comunista Mexicano was in 1979 able to take part in its first election since 1946, and in 1981 the PCM joined with several other leftist parties to form the Partido Socialista Unificado de México (PSUM). Not all radical parties joined this coalition, which would soon be rent by internal divisions, but the mere prospect of a unified electoral left signified a profound change in the tenor and tone of national politics.

It was, however, the economy, more than the political opposition, that posed the most crucial challenge. By the mid-1970s import substitution industrialization had lost much of its dynamism, unemployment was rampant, and inflation was starting to rise. Echeverría seemed only to aggravate social tension through his incendiary rhetoric, his permissive stance toward land seizures in the countryside, and his continuing conflict with the entrepreneurial sector. As José López Portillo assumed the presidency in December 1976, many Mexicans were anticipating difficult times. Then the country struck oil.

Here, it seemed, was the solution to Mexico's problems. For decades after the expropriation of foreign-owned companies in 1938, Mexico had kept a low profile in the international world of petroleum. PEMEX functioned efficiently enough, producing steady supplies of oil at very low prices for the nation's growing but relatively modest needs. Exports were negligible and imports occasionally significant. By 1976 successive oil discoveries had raised Mexico's proven oil reserves to approximately 6.3 billion barrels, suggesting that PEMEX would be able to satisfy domestic requirements for the foreseeable future. Talk of bonanza began. Announcements of new discoveries, especially in the south, doubled and redoubled official estimates of Mexican oil reserves. By September 1979, López Portillo could confirm that the country's oil and natural gas deposits contained the energy equivalent of 45.8 billion barrels of 'proven' reserves, 45 billion barrels of 'probable' reserves and 110 billion barrels of 'potential' reserves – a grand total of 200 billion barrels in all. (According to these estimates, Mexico possessed about 5 per cent of world proven reserves of crude oil and 3 per cent of world proven reserves of natural gas.)

The oil discoveries prompted intense debate within Mexican political circles. What was to be done with the deposits? The left, led by students and intellectuals, called for limitations on petroleum production that would preserve the nation's patrimony, avert over-dependence on buyers and prevent the social dislocations – inflation, frustration and inequality – seen in such countries as Iran. The right, mainly industrialists, clamoured for a rapid-development policy in order to pay off the national debt, acquire reserves of foreign exchange and ward off potential commercial threats from alternative energy sources. After some hesitation the López Portillo administration took an intermediate course, seeking to satisfy domestic needs and to export 1.25 million barrels per day (bpd). The aim was to stimulate growth, promote employment and pay for imports – without creating inflation or excessive dependence on oil sales. Under no circumstances, government officials vowed, would Mexico become beholden to its bounty.[45] Yet, to meet the need for foreign exchange, both to stimulate growth and to deal with the debt, the López Portillo administration pushed ahead with petroleum exports, increasing the daily ceiling to 1.50 million bpd. And as the international price of oil kept

[45] See Gabriel Székely, *La economía política del petróleo en México, 1976–1982* (Mexico, 1983).

rising, owing largely to the efforts of the Organization of Petroleum Exporting Countries (OPEC), so did Mexico's receipts. Oil earnings soared from $311 million in 1976 to nearly $14 billion by 1981, by that time accounting for nearly three-quarters of Mexican exports. At the same time, there was a relative decline in the role of non-oil exports, especially agricultural commodities. Almost in spite of itself, the Mexican economy was undergoing a process of 'petrolization'.

In a sense the strategy appeared to work. In real terms (that is, allowing for inflation) the GDP grew by the highest rates in recent memory: 8.2 per cent in 1978, 9.2 per cent in 1979, 8.3 per cent in 1980 and 8.1 per cent in 1981. This was an extraordinary achievement, especially during a period when the United States and the industrial world were floundering through stagflation and recession, and it seemed to justify the government's headlong pursuit of petroleum-led growth. This expansion resulted in the creation of all-important new jobs – nearly a million of them in the spectacular year of 1979 – and it also increased the magnitude of the economic role of the state.

The López Portillo government attempted to use this expanded influence to develop a new and coherent policy for the long-beleaguered agrarian sector. As Mexico continued to import basic grains and the dimensions of the country's agricultural crisis became apparent, López Portillo and his advisers designed and in 1980 launched the Mexican Food System programme (Sistema Alimentario Mexicano, or SAM). The goal was to achieve self-sufficiency in food production, thus eradicating malnutrition and asserting national autonomy with a single stroke. The strategy was to channel income from oil exports into the countryside for both the production and the consumption of basic grains – 'sowing the petroleum', as the catchy slogan stated. SAM was an ambitious and expensive plan, costing nearly $4 billion in 1980 alone. Exceptional weather yielded a bumper crop in 1981, and grain production was nearly 30 per cent higher than in the drought year of 1979. Officials claimed instant success for SAM. Others kept an eye on the weather, and greeted dry spells in 1982 and 1983 with a sense of deep foreboding.

Petroleum revenues also enhanced Mexico's position in the international arena as the OPEC-driven price shock of 1979 flaunted the apparent power of the oil-producing nations. Although Mexico never became a formal member of OPEC (preferring to have the ambiguous status of official observer), national leaders firmly believed that this economic leverage would provide the basis for a new assertiveness in foreign affairs. As López

Portillo himself liked to say: 'You can divide the countries of the world into two types, the ones that have oil and the ones that do not. We have oil'.[46] Having kept a low diplomatic profile for decades, Mexico was now ready to impose itself on the international scene. As though in reflection of this feeling, Mexico hosted a massive North–South dialogue in the glittering resort town of Cancún in October 1981.

This ebullience became particularly apparent in Mexico's stance toward the evolving crisis in Central America. While the United States was denouncing Soviet and Cuban influence in the isthmus, Mexican officials tended to see political conflicts within the region as the logical response to historic conditions of repression and inequity. In the hope of encouraging negotiated settlements, the López Portillo regime showed public sympathy with revolutionary causes. The Mexican government broke relations with the Somoza regime in Nicaragua well before the insurgent victory in mid-1979, and then proceeded to lend unequivocal support to the Sandinista government. In 1980, Mexico (together with Venezuela) began offering petroleum to Nicaragua on generous concessionary terms. The following year Mexico joined with France to issue a call for recognition of the Salvadoran Democratic Revolutionary Front (FDR–FMLN) as a 'legitimate political force'. This involvement of an extra-continental power in hemispheric affairs violated a long-standing tenet of regional diplomacy, one that the United States had sought to enforce ever since the declaration of the Monroe Doctrine in 1823, and the Reagan administration looked on with sullen disapproval.

In a February 1982 speech in Managua, López Portillo publicly offered Mexico's help to unravel what he called 'three knots that tie up the search for peace' in the region – the internal conflict in El Salvador, distrust between the United States and Nicaragua and hostility between the United States and Cuba. He reiterated the call for a negotiated settlement in El Salvador, proposed a non-aggression treaty between the United States and Nicaragua, and urged further dialogue between the American government and the Castro regime. All by itself, Mexico was thus proposing to assume a major leadership role in regional affairs. Predictably enough, the U.S. response to this initiative was at best lukewarm; a few discussions took place and then withered away.

López Portillo's high-growth economic strategy incurred important

---

[46] Quoted in George W. Grayson, 'Mexico's Opportunity: The Oil Boom,' *Foreign Policy* 29 (Winter 1977–8): 65–89, esp. 65.

costs, one principal drawback being the balance of trade. Although the value of exports increased dramatically, the quantity of imports grew even more. The result was a staggering commercial deficit: $2.1 billion in 1978, $3.6 billion in 1979, $3.2 billion in 1980 and again in 1981. Economic expansion required importation, especially of intermediate and capital goods, and Mexico continued to purchase more than it sold. Such deficits were formerly off-set by two special links with the United States – the tourist trade and border transactions (including exports from *maquiladoras*). But by 1981 tourism yielded almost no surplus at all, as high-income Mexicans spent lavish amounts of money abroad (the over-valued peso made foreign travel cheap), and border industries suffered from the recession in the United States. In 1981 Mexico's overall balance of payments ran up a deficit of $11.7 billion dollars, an enormous sum by any standard – even for a country rich in oil.

Meanwhile, the government itself went into debt. To implement its high-growth approach the López Portillo administration undertook high-cost initiatives that increased the economic participation of the state. In relative terms, the government's deficit went from around 7 per cent of GDP in the 1970s, a level sustained during much of the decade, to 14 percent in 1981 and 18 percent in 1982. The deficit and the balance of payments left only one option: to borrow funds from abroad. Mexico's private businesses and state agencies searched for capital in the international money market. And foreign bankers, apparently bedazzled by the oil discoveries, hastened forward with massive loans. The national debt continued its inexorable climb, from around $30 billion in 1977–8 through $48 billion in 1980 to more than $80 billion by 1982. About three-quarters of this debt belonged to the public sector. Inflation accelerated too. Almost alone among developing nations, Mexico had successfully resisted inflation through the 1960s, keeping annual rates around 5 per cent or less. In the mid-1970s price increases moved up around 20 per cent, still reasonable by international standards, but then they jumped to 30–40 per cent under the high-growth strategies of the López Portillo administration. By 1982 the rate was nearly 100 per cent. This inflationary pattern reduced the purchasing power of the workers and, especially because it came so suddenly, threatened to bring on social tension. 'The bottom had to fall out', said an economist at one of Mexico's biggest banks. 'Nobody expected it so fast.'[47]

[47] *Boston Globe*, 3 October 1982.

It appears that the López Portillo administration committed two major errors in economic policy. One was to place too much confidence in petroleum exports. The extraction and commercialization of Mexico's oil reserves required large-scale investments, so a considerable share of petro-dollar earnings were plowed back into the oil industry. As the energy sector expanded, therefore, the rest of the economy languished. Moreover, the urgent need to create new jobs tempted López Portillo to push for high rates of growth. In addition, the 'no re-election' clause may have lured him into short-run strategies that would achieve tangible results during the course of his non-renewable presidential term. At any rate, Mexico began to spend its petroleum earnings before they were safely in hand. Mexico thus became extraordinarily dependent on its energy exports, which made the country vulnerable to changes in the international price of oil. In mid-1981 a world-wide glut led to sharp drop in prices. Mexico attempted to resist this trend, and internal policy disputes led to the abrupt dismissal of Jorge Díaz Serrano from the directorship of PEMEX. López Portillo eventually had to settle for a price reduction, however, and this brought a significant drop in export earnings. Because of overambitious policies, Mexico fell victim to forces beyond its control.

The second mistake was continued overvaluation of the peso. By 1980 and 1981 the constant drain on dollar reserves (because of trade deficits and capital flight) was exerting pressure for devaluation of the peso. Such a step would reduce imports, increase exports and stem the flight of capital – because dollars would cost more pesos than before. But López Portillo and his advisers did not go along with this, partly because the economy was booming anyway and partly because interest rates were rising on the foreign debt (which required repayment in hard currency). The effect was to build up even more pressure for devaluation and to encourage even more capital flight.

A further important miscalculation concerned the ethics of public life. For various reasons Mexican society had long tolerated the idea of self-enrichment through the possession of political office – what is often called corruption. One practical consequence of this tradition, if not a motive for it, was to permit people of modest background to pursue politics as a full-time career; another was to encourage them to accept the prospect of early exit from high office, thus permitting the turn-over – and the extension of patronage – that helped stabilize the system. But even in Mexico the practice had its limits. And according to wide-spread rumour, López Portillo and his friends transgressed those time-honored boundaries by helping themselves to excessive amounts of the public treasury and in too flagrant a fashion. The President constructed an ostentatious palatial residence for himself and his family on the outskirts of Mexico City, while government officials were reliably reported to lose hundreds of thousands of dollars at gaming tables 'without blinking an eye'. The direct result was to cast the López Portillo presidency under an unprecedented light of general opprobrium. An indirect result was to raise questions about the conduct and legitimacy of the entire political elite.

The political dimensions of an impending crisis began to appear in September 1981, when López Portillo revealed his choice for the presidential succession. Prominent pre-candidates included Pedro Ojeda Paullada, the tough and experienced Secretary of Labour; Jorge de la Vega Domínguez, a versatile politician (and ex-CONASUPO director) in charge of the Ministry of Commerce; Miguel de la Madrid Hurtado, a skilled technocrat and Secretary of Budget and Planning; Javier García Paniagua, the son of ex-defence minister Marcelino García Barragán and the president of the PRI; and, mainly because of his post at Gobernación, the old-time *político* Enrique Olivares Santana. Although it was anticipated that the *destape* would come in October, after the North–South meeting in Cancún, it took place at the traditional time in late September.

The selection was Miguel de la Madrid, a close personal friend (and one-time student) of López Portillo's who had played a prominent part in the formulation of economic policy. Though Budget and Planning had never produced any presidents before, de la Madrid showed every sign of the intellectual and bureaucratic capacity required by the presidency (including a graduate degree from Harvard). He had only one major drawback: a technocrat par excellence, he had never held elective office and had weak connections with the PRI. This made it all the more significant when the president of the party, Garcia Paniagua, lost his job after openly expressing unhappiness over the selection.

The scale of Mexico's economic difficulties became apparent in February 1982, when the López Portillo administration decided to float the peso on the international market – as Echeverría had done in 1976 – and it promptly plummeted from 26 per dollar to around 45 per dollar. Inflation continued its upwards climb. In March the Secretary of Finance resigned. In August the government decreed another devaluation, the peso falling further, to 75–80 per dollar. As a result, Mexico announced that, given its shortage of foreign exchange, it might not be able to meet its debt obligations. The 'Mexican crisis' had suddenly acquired extraordinary importance for the international financial community, requiring its leading representatives – most notably Paul Volcker of the U.S. Federal Reserve – rapidly to assemble an emergency relief plan in order to avoid the incalculable consequences of an outright default by a major debtor nation.[48] In the meantime, López Portillo complained about capital flight, decried the existence of speculation against the peso, and denounced the 'vultures' seeking ill-gotten gains.

In his annual message on 1 September 1982, López Portillo stunned his audience by declaring state expropriation of privately owned banks (foreign-owned banks were exempted). At the same time the government imposed controls on the foreign-exchange rate, set promptly at 70 pesos per dollar for commercial purposes and 50 per dollar for preferential transactions. The left applauded the nationalization, López Portillo predictably claiming his place in history. And though the measure was widely criticized, it did represent a plausible (if unworkable) set of options for the Mexican state. By nationalizing the banks – and, perhaps more importantly, by setting up exchange controls – López Portillo ruptured the time-honored partnership between the state, the private sector and foreign investors.[49] With control over 70 per cent of investment the state could now attempt to go it alone, and in so doing it could consolidate its tenuous alliance with workers and peasants. Thus, López Portillo sought to resurrect and fortify the 'populist' political alternative for Mexico, a model designed to link a mass following with elite leadership through the mediation and guidance of a dynamic and powerful state. In this endeavour the President could count on the collaboration of both traditional *políticos* and nationalistic *técnicos*. In a style reminiscent of Cárdenas, López Portillo added a conspicuous flourish to the final signature for his six-year term in office.[50]

De la Madrid had won the election of 4 July with nearly 75 per cent of the vote, but, as custom demanded, he kept silent until his own inauguration on 1 December. When his opportunity finally came, he roundly criticized 'financial populism' and called for the 'moral renovation' of society and government. The bank expropriation itself was 'irreversible',

---

[48] See Joseph Kraft, *The Mexican Rescue* (New York, 1984).

[49] It would be noted, later on, that nationalization meant that the state would assume both the debts and the losses of companies owned by the banks, but this objective reality had little to do with subjective perception of private investors and foreign lenders. They continued to denounce the measure.

[50] For an insider's description of these events, see Carlos Tello, *La nacionalización de la banca* (Mexico, 1984).

he conceded, but his administration would take the true road to recovery. 'The first months of the government will be arduous and difficult', he warned. 'The situation requires it. The austerity is obligatory'.[51]

De la Madrid appointed a cabinet full of proficient technocrats like himself, retaining Jesús Silva Herzog as Secretary of Finance and reinstating Miguel Mancera (who had opposed the exchange controls) as head of the central bank. Moving with remarkable speed, the new President accepted the conditions of the International Monetary Funds (IMF) for renegotiation of the debt, including a provision that the budget deficit be gradually reduced from nearly 18 per cent of GDP in 1982 to 3.5 per cent in 1985. He lifted price controls on 2,500 consumer items and provided pricing flexibility on 2,000 more, and he floated the peso yet again so that its free-market value fell to around 150 per dollar. With such measures de la Madrid attempted to restore Mexico's credit with the international community and, in so doing, to repair the relationship between the state and the foreign sector.

The President also took steps to revive and reassure the local business community. In sharp contrast to López Portillo's heated denunciation of profit-seeking 'vultures', de la Madrid used his inaugural address to express praise for 'responsible and patriotic entrepreneurs – who form a majority'. Although the bank nationalization could not be reversed, he intimated that the private sector would still have an important role in the economy. 'To rationalize is not to state-ize *(estatizar)'*, de la Madrid insisted. 'We shall not state-ize society'. True to his word, in January 1983 the President sent a bill to Congress that would authorize the sale of 34 per cent ownership in the newly nationalized banks to private investors. In February he announced a plan for extending financial credit to 'productive' enterprises. Later in the year, the government began paying compensation (in ten-year bonds) to former owners of the banks.

De la Madrid was clearly trying to restore Mexico's long-standing ruling alliance: the three-way coalition between the state, the private sector and the foreign sector which had been initially forged by Alemán and had guided the nation on its post-war path to economic growth. The strategy was to consolidate power at the uppermost reaches of the social order, in other words, and to utilize this strength as a means of shaping and implementing policy. From the start, either by necessity or by choice, the de la Madrid administration moved in a conservative direction. This orien-

[51] The full text of de la Madrid's inaugural speech appears in *Unomásuno*, 2 December 1982.

tation posed complications for the country's political class. De la Madrid drew almost his entire cabinet from the ranks of *técnicos,* sophisticated experts whose bureaucratic and technical capacity seemed to provide ideal credentials for executing an austerity program. *Políticos,* the old-time politicians and party bosses, were most conspicuous by their exclusion from the new administration; there was some muttering and grumbling within the PRI, but no outright rebellion. Signals from the military were also unclear, but de la Madrid showered the armed services with lavish praise in his inaugural address, and it was widely thought that the President would go to considerable lengths to preserve intact the silent partnership between civilian rulers and military leaders.

De la Madrid's economic strategy imposed a large cost, and the burden of payment fell on one key social sector: the working class. Throughout 1983 inflation was running at between 70 and 90 per cent, but labour had to settle for wage increases in the region of 25 per cent. The removal of price ceilings and public subsidies raised the cost of basic necessities. In July 1983, for example, the government announced a 40 per cent hike in the price of corn tortillas and a 100 per cent increase in the price of bread. Economists estimated that the real purchasing power of the working class was declining at the rate of 15 to 20 per cent a year.

Urban labour therefore presented a grave political problem. A mid-1983 round of salary negotiations resulted in stalemate and confrontation. Workers in some thousand companies threatened to strike, a prospect averted in most cases only by the postponement of discussions (rather than the settlement of issues). For a while the struggle came out in the open: on behalf of labour Fidel Velázquez called for a wage–price freeze, and in exasperation de la Madrid denounced the idea as 'demagogic'. Conciliation followed, but it was clear that the relationship between labour and the government was under strain.

The food-price increases represented a deliberate attempt to stimulate agricultural development but did not herald the articulation of any large-scale agrarian program. De la Madrid abandoned SAM, along with other 'statist' elements of the López Portillo regime, and in late 1983 replaced it with a modest food-production program. In mid-1985 he followed up with a so-called national programme of integral rural development, which envisaged little more than inflationary adjustments in the guaranteed minimum price for basic commodities (corn, beans, wheat) and some infrastructural investments in rain-fed areas. The emphasis was on enhancing production, not distribution, through market forces and price incentives. The administration cut back the role of CONASUPO and relied instead on the interaction of supply and demand. Agrarian reform, once the centerpiece of revolution, appeared to have lost its place on the national agenda.

In short, de la Madrid's attempt to re-establish and consolidate the ruling coalition ran the risk of alienating the system's social bases of support, especially the urban working class. The peasantry kept silent and would probably stay under control, but doubts remained over the reaction of the middle class, which had became the most vocal and potentially the most volatile of the regime's constituencies. Perhaps in recognition of this, and in a general effort to shore up his support, de la Madrid continued to insist on 'moral renovation' in a campaign widely interpreted as an attack on López Portillo and his collaborators. In late 1983, after months of public rumors, the de la Madrid government went after one of the former president's most prominent associates, bringing charges against Jorge Díaz Serrano, the former head of PEMEX and a senator from Sonora, for alleged participation in a multimillion-dollar fraud. It was later learned that the ex-president's sister Alicia López Portillo was the target of a parallel investigation, but this was soon brought to a halt. A separate indictment led to the eventual extradition from the United States of Arturo Durazo Moreno, nicknamed *el negro,* the former chief of the Mexico City police and close friend of the ex-president. Such accusations bore no precedent in recent history, and they underscored de la Madrid's determination to free his own administration as far as he could from identification with the López Portillo government.

Corruption thus became a major public issue, and complicated Mexico's relationship with the United States, especially with respect to the growing traffic in narcotics. Collaboration between Mexico and the United States had in fact been rather smooth until February 1985, when a U.S. drug enforcement agent, Enrique Camarena, disappeared and was later found murdered – only a year after the State Department had singled out Mexico's anti-narcotics campaign for special praise. After the Camarena affair officials in Washington began to protest that about one-third of U.S. imports of marijuana and heroin came from Mexico and that perhaps 30 per cent of the imported cocaine passed through that country. But it was Mexico's apparent inability to solve the Camarena case, plus a subsequent murder, that led to allegations about corruption and cover-up – most notably, but not exclusively, in a series of unprecedented Senate subcommittee hearings chaired by arch-conservative Republican Jesse Helms in May 1986.

The de la Madrid administration angrily denied accusations of complicity with drug-runners and, indeed, the evidence appeared to support its contentions. Thousands of Mexican policemen and about 25,000 military troops were assigned to the anti-narcotics campaign; hundreds were wounded or killed. Some individual office-holders no doubt collaborated with such powerful narcotics lords as Rafael Caro Quintana, but the political establishment had every reason to oppose the traffic in drugs. The consolidation of narcotics kingdoms threatened to create empires within the empire and fostered a type of corruption which proved counterproductive for political authority. Drug-trade patronage lay outside the control of the regime (in contrast, for instance, to the petroleum bonanza of the late 1970s) and, in a time of declining governmental resources, it posed an unwelcome challenge.

The question of migration to the United States came to a head with passage of what came to be called the Simpson–Rodino Bill, which President Ronald Reagan signed into law in November 1986. Hailed as a major revision of United States immigration policy, the law had two major provisions: economic sanctions against employers who knowingly hired illegal aliens, and an amnesty for undocumented workers who could prove continuous residence in the United States from January 1982. The U.S. Congress also envisioned a 50 per cent increase in the size of the border patrol (which would require a separate budgetary allocation). Implementation of the law did not lead to massive deportations from the United States, as Mexican alarmists had frequently predicted; nor did it result in massive applications for amnesty, as U.S. officials had nervously foreseen. It seemed likely that the law would encourage employer discrimination against workers of Mexican origin or ethnic appearance, but even that was not self-evident. There was a reasonable chance that Simpson–Rodino would not work. Employer sanctions had met with little success when tried before, as in the state of California. There were simply too many loopholes for effective enforcement. In this case, illegal immigration could be expected to resume its mid-1980s pace, with perhaps a million crossings a year but (since most go back to Mexico) an additional *net* immigration of between 300,000 and 500,000 per year. The total number of undocumented Mexicans in the United States would thus increase from around 3 million to 4 or 5 million by the early 1990s.

Partly because of economic pressure from the United States and partly because of his own political reasons, de la Madrid took a cautious approach to foreign policy. In early 1983 Mexico abandoned high-profile diplomacy and joined together with Colombia, Panama and Venezuela – the so-called Contadora group – in order to explore the possibilities for regional mediation of the conflict in Central America. In support of this general strategy Peru, Brazil, Uruguay and Argentina declared their support for the Contadora enterprise. The Reagan administration, on the other hand, continued to show a notable lack of enthusiasm, and it was obvious to all that Contadora could not succeed without the strong U.S. backing. Whatever the final result, Mexico's role in the Contadora group marked a substantial change from both the ebullience of the López Portillo years and, even more dramatically, from the diplomatic cautiousness of the 1950s.

Overall results from de la Madrid's domestic and international policies seemed inconclusive by the halfway mark of his *sexenio,* 1985 proving to be a particularly difficult year. First, it became apparent that the government's economic 'adjustment' plan was meeting with indifferent success. Productivity was picking up but at a modest pace. Labour and the middle classes lost additional real purchasing power as the annual inflation rate continued at around 60 per cent. The total foreign debt was up to $96 billion (from the 1982 level of $82 billion); debt service for the year amounted to $13 billion, but the balance of payments was just over half that, around $7–8 billion. Investment was low and capital flight persisted at around $5 billion. The public deficit for 1985 was around 8 per cent of GDP, not the 4 per cent agreed with the IMF, which was on the brink of holding up payments on fresh loans.

Then came two external shocks. One was a natural catastrophe. At 7:19 A.M., 19 September 1985, Mexico City suffered an enormous earthquake measuring 8.1 on the Richter scale, and the following evening the city was hit by another which measured 7.3. The damage was greatest in the old downtown area, where tumbling buildings took the lives of at least 7,000 persons and maybe as many as 20,000. Well over 100,000 were injured or homeless, as the world looked on in horror and dismay. The citizens of Mexico City responded with generosity and courage, giving instant aid and shelter to the *damnificados* in a spontaneous outpouring which prompted some observers to take note of the emergence of 'civil society'. Direct economic damage was estimated to be at around $4 billion, a sum that debt-strapped Mexico could ill afford; according to one estimate this would amount to a negative impact on the 1985 GDP of minus 3.4 per cent. There was political fall-out too. Amid the rubble were signs of corruption in that some of the collapsed buildings had failed to comply with construction codes. Many Mexicans felt that the government had responded with too little too late, that de la Madrid had not been able to rise to the occasion. There was concern about the excessive centralization in Mexico City, and a wide-spread clamour for having the regent of the Federal District chosen by election rather than presidential appointment. Grass-roots mobilization continued and helped bring down a cabinet minister.

The second external shock was a precipitous decline in the international price of oil. Between December 1985 and July 1986 the average price for Mexico's export mix plunged from \$23.70 per barrel to \$8.90 per barrel, the resulting loss of income from oil sales amounting to approximately \$8.2 billion dollars. This was equivalent to a drop of minus 6.4 per cent in the GDP for 1986. The costs of reliance on international market forces were again becoming clear. In this general context of economic malaise, de la Madrid and his advisers decided to adopt a dramatic shift in policy, undertaking long-term structural reform in terms that were characterized both at home and abroad as the 'liberalization' of the Mexican economy.

There were two major pillars to the programme. One was to reduce and recast the economic role of the state. From 1983 through 1985 the government had sought to reduce public spending – by as much as one-third – but now the de la Madrid administration sought to redesign the state's economic role, principally through a program of 'privatization' (or, as it was known in Mexico, *desincorporación*). Of the 1,115 publicly owned companies his government inherited in late 1982, de la Madrid managed by late 1986 to sell off 96 (including some major ownings in the hotel and automobile business), to merge 46 and to transfer 39 to state governments. The government also closed down some 279 inefficient plants, including a large steel mill near Monterrey. And in the strategic sectors designated for continued government control – petroleum, railroads, electricity, telecommunications – the government undertook a programme of 'industrial reconversion' to improve efficiency. The para-statal sector continued to be large, but the administration was making a decisive move to curtail it.

The second component of the new policy was commercial liberalization and an 'opening up' of the economy. This was most dramatically demonstrated by Mexico's accession to the General Agreement on Tariffs and

Trade (GATT) in September 1986, which meant a long-term commitment to the reduction of barriers to imports from abroad. This amounted to an almost complete abandonment of the post-war policies of ISI. Liberalization had two main corollaries. One was the phasing out of tariffs. In 1982, 100 per cent of Mexico's imports were controlled by the granting of licenses; by 1987, only 9 per cent remained under such a restrictive regime. In general this meant that the Mexican domestic market, long protected for local industrialists, would be opened up to producers in other countries – especially, of course, the United States. The second corollary was the promotion of exports, especially non-petroleum exports. A key element here was a controlled devaluation of the peso – at a rate higher than domestic inflation – to enhance the competitiveness of Mexican industry. (In early 1987 the exchange rate moved beyond 1,000 pesos per dollar; by midyear it was close to 1,400 pesos per dollar.) As a result of these and other measures, non-oil exports began to pick up. Exports of manufactures approached $1 billion per year. Government officials also reported that flight capital of the early 1980s was returning to the country, perhaps as much as $3 billion to $5 billion for 1986–7.

These policies of liberalization amounted to a radical shift in the historic direction of the Mexican economy. Some observers predicted that the de la Madrid administration, so embattled for so long, would go down as a watershed in Mexican history. But in the late 1980s there were at least two formidable obstacles for the Mexican economy: inflation and the foreign debt. Inflation which stood at 105 per cent for 1986 and which, by mid-1987, was running at an annual rate of 140 percent, had a corrosive effect on Mexican society, from its discouragement of investment (and exportation) to its ruinous effect on income distribution. Government officials saw no obvious way to deal with the problem, other than to continue the programme of commercial liberalization and press on with structural reforms. For many economists, inflation was the principal policy challenge of the late 1980s.

For the first half of his administration de la Madrid appeared to regard the foreign debt as a 'liquidity' problem, rather than a structural deficiency, and this emphasis on cash management influenced a series of negotiations with international creditors. In 1983–85 the government achieved a postponement of short-term payments and a reduction of costs ('spreads' above international interest rates went down from around 2.3 per cent to less than 1 per cent). But from 1986 onwards the government began to insist on a resumption of economic growth. Differences of opinion over how to achieve this goal led to the abrupt dismissal in June 1986 of Jesús Silva Herzog, the charismatic finance minister who was seen by many as the logical successor to de la Madrid. (It was not quite clear what the debate was about: rumours indicated that Silva Herzog wanted to propose either a unilateral moratorium on debt service and/or the imposition of a 'heterodox shock' like the *plan austral* in Argentina.) Between late 1986 and early 1987 Mexico managed to negotiate with its creditors a new package that called for fresh loans of $12 billion to help stimulate growth of 3 to 4 per cent. Repayments were to be made over a period of twenty years, and additional funds were to be made available if the international price of petroleum went below $9 per barrel. Even with these terms, the general question persisted: how could Mexico devise a viable strategy for economic growth in light of its debt obligations? By late 1987 the total debt was well over $100 billion. Could Mexico continue to make debt-service payments of $8 billion to $12 billion a year and still meet the needs of its people?

In addition to these economic problems, the de la Madrid government faced serious challenges on the political front. The President's declaration of a 'moral renovation' in his inaugural address had stimulated hopes that he would extend the 1977 reforms and insist on open elections with genuine possibilities for opposition victories. In 1982–3 the PAN was permitted to win significant municipal victories in the north – in Ciudad Juárez, Hermosillo, Durango, Chihuahua and San Luis Potosí – and the hopes for liberalization seemed justified. But then de la Madrid began to equivocate. In the south, the state legislature of Oaxaca voted in August 1983 to remove the moderately leftist mayor of the town of Juchitán, Leopoldo de Gyvés of the Coalición de Obreros, Campesinos, y Estudiantes del Istmo (COCEI). After a violent confrontation, the army ousted the COCEI group from city hall and installed the PRI candidate, who claimed victory in the November elections. Around this time it appeared that Mexico City had reached a compromise solution: it would permit the right to win local elections but not the left.

Yet even this supposition was shattered in 1985, when congressional by-elections and several key gubernatorial contests in the north began to draw considerable attention. The PAN fielded especially strong candidates in Sonora and Nuevo León, and the international media gathered to witness the struggle of the opposition. Whatever the actual results, the PRI and the regime proclaimed almost-total victory, sweeping the seven governorships and all but a handful of seats in the Chamber of Deputies.

The PRI took 65 per cent of the votes, granting 15.5 per cent to the PAN, 3.2 percent to PSUM, and scattering the rest among small parties. As a result of electoral procedures both the PAN and PSUM actually lost seats in the legislature, while insignificant micro-parties stood to benefit. Widespread accusations of fraud ensued as the PRI asserted its capacity to control the electoral process and subjected the opposition to divide-and-conquer tactics.

In 1986 there was more of the same. Elections included four gubernatorial contests, the most hotly contested occurring in the northern state of Chihuahua. As the race between PRI candidate Fernando Baeza Meléndez and the PAN's Francisco Barrios Terrazas neared its end, opposition leaders – from the PAN, the business sector and the Catholic Church – demanded the annulment of the elections, the *panista* mayor of the city of Chihuahua, Luis H. Alvarez, embarking on a protest hunger strike. The authorities responded with petulance, ousting left-wing *pesumista* poll-watchers from the registries in Chihuahua and Ciudad Juárez while the opposition responded by blockading state highways (including the bridge across the border to the United States). Election day proved to be peaceful, however, and the PRI claimed total triumph once again. According to the official count, Baeza defeated Barrios with 64.3 per cent of the vote; the PRI took all the other three races for governor, 106 out of the 109 mayorships and almost all the local deputyships. The political machinery was back to the *carro completo* ('full wagon'), but President de la Madrid lost a good deal of prestige. Either he had given the PRI hierarchy permission to rig the elections, in which case he had given up his campaign for reform, or he had been unable to impose his will on recalcitrant provincial bosses and local *caciques*. Moreover, there was a conspicuous absence of a clear-cut political strategy.

It was in this context that speculation began to mount about the presidential succession of 1987–8. As the time for decision approached, it appeared that this succession would differ from tradition in at least three ways. First, the institutional power of the presidency seemed less overwhelmingly dominant than before: it was still the paramount office in the land, but the travails of the 1970s and 1980s had tarnished its sense of omnipotence. So if de la Madrid had the final word in the selection of his successor, it appeared likely that he would have to listen more closely to other opinions – including that of Fidel Velázquez, the octogenarian labor boss who had managed to keep the unions in line during a period of sharply falling wage rates. Second, a dissident group of *priista* leaders –

including Cuauhtémoc Cárdenas, the son of Lázaro Cárdenas and former governor of Michoacán, and Porfirio Muñoz Ledo, former cabinet minister, erstwhile presidential aspirant and former head of the PRI itself – joined together to form the *corriente democrática* and to call for an opening of the process of presidential succession. Leaders of the *corriente* received brutal criticism within the PRI and the press because a development of this sort had not been seen for decades. Third, the international media would be paying unprecedented attention to the process of succession. The decision might take place behind closed doors, but the whole world would know about it.

Characteristically enough, rumours raced through political and intellectual circles. The removal of Silva Herzog from the cabinet – and the competition – sent shock waves through the political establishment. So did the subsequent designation of Jorge de la Vega Domínguez, the seasoned politician and ex-rival of the President, as leader of the PRI. Some observers said there were four major pretenders. Some said six. The business organization, COPARMEX, issued a remarkable report announcing six plausible candidates for the presidency.[52] But by an unspoken consensus, most attention focussed on three:

Manuel Bartlett Díaz, fifty-one, was the Secretary of Gobernación. The son of a former governor of the state of Tabasco, he had been active in the PRI since 1963 and was thought by many to have convinced de la Madrid of the need to resort to the electoral strategy of the *carro completo.*

Alfredo del Mazo González, forty-four, was the Secretary of Energy and Mines. A UNAM graduate in business administration with extensive overseas study, del Mazo had, like his father, been the governor of the state of Mexico (1981–6). A protegé of Fidel Velázquez, he had a close personal relationship with de la Madrid.

Carlos Salinas de Gortari, thirty-nine, the Secretary of Planning and Budget, had a formidable intellect. With advanced degrees in economics from UNAM and Harvard, Salinas started a career in public administration while in his mid-twenties. His father, a former cabinet minister and ambassador, was a senator in 1982–8. Salinas was widely regarded as a principal architect of the de la Madrid economic policy and an advocate of a strong state.

All these pre-candidates had worked within the system, were relatively young, were cabinet ministers, and had close relations with the outgoing

[52] *Excélsior*, 15 May 1987.

president. But they also shared another characteristic, one that expressed a telling message about the evolution and status of the regime: they were sons of prominent politicians. The system, it appeared, was reproducing itself in the most literal sense. The separation of political from economic elites thus continued to persist, but it was no longer clear that careers in politics would provide Mexican society with a meaningful channel to upward mobility.

Excitement mounted in mid-August 1987 when the head of the PRI, Jorge de la Vega Domínguez, took the unprecedented step of announcing that there were indeed six candidates for the presidential nomination and that they would be invited to make public appearances (*comparecencias*) before the party hierarchy. In addition to Bartlett, del Mazo and Salinas, the list included Ramón Aguirre Velázquez, the regent of the Federal District; Sergio García Ramírez, the Attorney General; and Miguel González Avelar, the Secretary of Education. In alphabetical order, the pre-candidates appeared before an assemblage of PRI notables at that most venerable of occasions, the political breakfast (*desayuno político*), where they gave formal presentations about their visions of the national future. The press and the political community hung closely on each gesture and word, looking for clues to the outcome. There had never been anything quite like this before: did it herald a new process of 'democratization' in the selection of the president, or was it merely a cosmetic change?

To most observers the selection of Carlos Salinas de Gortari meant that de la Madrid had retained control of the process of succession. (It also underscored the political weakness of organised labour.) Indeed, it was widely believed that de la Madrid had decided on Salinas well in advance of the *comparecencias*. The presidential succession of 1988 thus far had complied with previous patterns. Then came the electoral campaign, which was normally an opportunity for acclamation of the official party nominee, but which became much more than that in 1988.

The first major development came with the formation of the Frente Democrático Nacional (FDN), a coalition of leftist parties with the *corriente democrática* in the spring of 1988. Moreover, the Frente decided to put forward a single candidate for the presidency, Cuauhtémoc Cárdenas. The Cárdenas candidacy immediately confronted the ruling establishment with a genuine electoral opposition. Constantly invoking his father's name, Cárdenas sought to rally workers and peasants under a common banner. He appealed to themes of nationalism, sovereignty, justice and reform – in short, to the time-honoured causes of the Mexican Revolution. Claiming that *técnicos* in the administration and *políticos* in the PRI had forsaken the needs of the people, Cárdenas proposed dramatic solutions to the country's economic crisis – including a suspension on petroleum exports and a unilateral moratorium on debt service. The Cardenista candidacy drew impressive crowds throughout the country, and it appeared to pose a plausible threat to the hegemony of the PRI. Meanwhile, the conservative PAN nominated as its candidate Manuel Clouthier, a prominent agribusinessman, former *priista* and firebrand orator. Clouthier developed as his main campaign theme freedom – for religious worship, for private enterprise and for political opposition. He looked for support from the private sector, from the middle classes and – conspicuously – from the newly emergent Catholic Church. Throughout the campaign, spokesmen for the FDN and the PAN joined together in the call for a free and open election in 1988. The opposition thus made the conduct of the election itself one of the primary issues of Mexican politics.

Salinas de Gortari, for his part, developed the theme of 'modernization'. Mexico, he said repeatedly, need not disinherit its national legacies; it must nurture and strengthen its traditions in a constructive fashion. Modernization of the economy would require effective control of inflation, improved productivity and the continuation of structural reform. Political modernization, he declared in an extensive statement on 'the challenge of democracy', must begin with a reform of the electoral code. There should be a stronger, more independent legislature, a better court system and a positive role for the media. He envisioned a strong (but loyal) opposition: 'We want strong and responsible political parties', Salinas proclaimed, in one of his major public statements, 'respectful of laws and institutions, that work in a democratic manner to expand their social bases'. He called for internal reforms of the PRI to include stronger ties to local constituencies, better procedures for selecting candidates and greater opportunities for young politicians. The speech consisted of generalities but nonetheless marked a sharp departure from the triumphal discourse of previous *priista* presidential candidates. 'This is a historic time', Salinas recognized. 'Everyone is clamoring for more democracy'.[53]

Tension mounted as the election approached. Two of Cárdenas' campaign aides were murdered. Many observers feared an outbreak of more generalized violence. However, the day of the election, 6 July, passed in relative tranquillity. Then Manuel Bartlett, still Secretary of Gobernación,

[53] Text of speech to the Comité Ejecutivo Nacional of the PRI (Puebla, July 1988).

announced that the government's computers had broken down for 'environmental reasons'. Opposition spokesmen and numerous observers accused the PRI of rigging the results. In claiming victory, Salinas de Gortari observed, remarkably: 'We are ending an era of what was practically one-party rule and entering a new political stage in the country with a majority party and very intense opposition from the competition'.[54] When the election commission finally declared Salinas to be the winner with a base majority of the vote – 50.4 percent against 31.1 per cent for Cárdenas and 17.1 per cent for Clouthier – the cardenistas immediately claimed fraud and staged some massive protest demonstrations. And the *panistas* called for a brief campaign of 'civic resistance'.

Thus, Salinas began his *sexenio* in a relatively weak position. He could not claim the traditionally overwhelming popular mandate of previous presidents. (Indeed, an abstention rate of 48.4 per cent meant that Salinas won active approval from only about one-quarter of the adult population.) And in view of the disputed returns, he could not claim victory in a totally clean election. Moreover, even according to official figures, the Cardenista movement had established itself as a powerful electoral force in the nation. It remained to be seen whether it could transform itself into a durable, opposition political party. In the Chamber of Deputies, the PRI had 260 seats but the combined opposition had 240. Moreover, the opposition had won four seats in the Senate – including both seats for the Federal District, where Ifigenia Martínez and Porfirio Muñoz Ledo of the FDN claimed decisive triumphs. As the ruling establishment was soon to discover, this heralded a major transformation in the position of the legislature, until then a supine and subordinate instrument of the PRI and the presidency. The new president faced the challenge not only of continuing and extending his predecessor's policy of economic 'liberalisation' in the expectation that this would lead to a resumption of economic growth, but also of political reform; in one way or another, the Mexican people were demanding the democratization of the post-war authoritarian political system.

[54] *Excélsior*, 8 July 1988.

Part Two

CENTRAL AMERICA

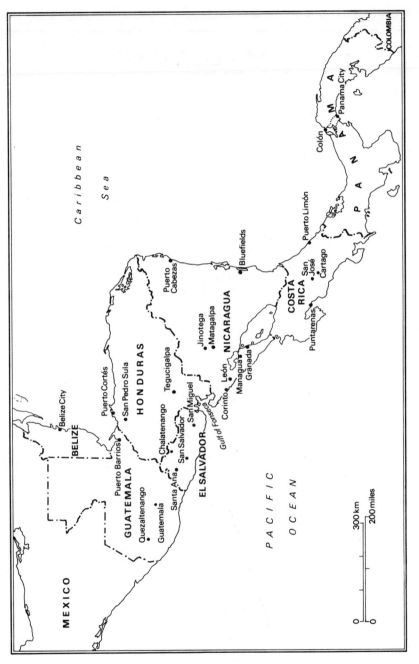

Central America

3

CENTRAL AMERICA SINCE 1930:
AN OVERVIEW

The establishment of stable nation states and permanent economic links with the world market through agricultural – especially coffee – exports took place in Central America during the second half of the nineteenth century. This process occurred first and most successfully in Costa Rica; later, and after much bloodshed, in Guatemala and El Salvador; and belatedly and incompletely in Honduras and Nicaragua. The backwardness inherited from the Spanish colonial period, the cyclical crisis in the international coffee market and the political struggles of the oligarchy for control of the government all slowed down economic growth, social progress and the development of institutional stability. Nevertheless, by the beginning of the twentieth century important changes had taken place in social stratification with the appearance of a coffee bourgeoisie and a small urban middle class, and political life was stable, though not democratic.

In 1914 the total population of Cental America was a little under 4 million, of whom nearly 60 percent lived in Guatemala and El Salvador. The basis of society – the agrarian structure – had three characteristics: large coffee estates controlled by national farmers producing for export; banana plantations, foreign-owned, with a vertically integrated production and marketing structure tied directly to the North American market; and small landholdings belonging to peasants who cultivated basic grains and other products for their own consumption or to satisfy internal demand. (Coffee and bananas accounted for 80 per cent of Central American exports.) The labour market was composed of *mozos colonos*, farmhands tied to the coffee haciendas by lifelong indebtedness; agricultural workers on U.S.-owned banana plantations; and – the largest sector – peasant smallholders, sharecroppers and migrant day-labourers who worked for wages

This chapter was translated from the Spanish by Elizabeth Ladd.

161

during the harvest season. In Costa Rica, this last category did not exist on a significant scale, and in Honduras subsistence farmers were predominant, partly as a result of that country's mountainous terrain.

Before 1930, the advantages of the export agriculture model were never doubted. On the contrary, the high degree of economic specialization and the freedom to sell in the foreign market were seen as a great opportunity for material progress in certain regions and among a few small groups. It is certainly true that a number of important changes came about under the impetus of export production. More than 80 per cent of the railway lines that exist today in Central America had already been built by about 1910. On the Atlantic coast the ports of Puerto Cortés, Puerto Barrios and Limón (in Honduras, Guatemala and Costa Rica, respectively) were renovated to reduce the cost of direct transport to European and North American markets. A financial and banking system was gradually established; before the First World War there were twenty-three banks in the region, most of them based on national capital. Although the electricity system was limited and served only the capital cities of Guatemala, San Salvador and San José before 1917, the telegraph linked the major cities and the most important economic areas of the region.

Central America came under U.S. influence in the late nineteenth century and this intensified when Britain in 1901, under the Hay–Pauncefote Treaty, agreed to diminish its presence there. The United States began to construct an inter-oceanic canal in Panama, which had, with U.S. assistance, secured its independence from Colombia in 1903; the canal was opened in 1914. The United States intervened in Nicaragua in 1912 and remained there, with a brief interruption, until 1933. At the same time, Washington imposed its will on the other Central American republics through military and diplomatic means during various episodes of political instability. After the First World War the U.S. economic presence in Central America was extended beyond investments in agriculture, railways and ports. For example, electricity services in three of the five countries passed into North American hands. More than 75 per cent of foreign trade was to or from the United States (an increase from the pre-war period largely at the expense of Germany). Such developments contributed to a period of relative prosperity, particularly in the 1920s and especially for Guatemala, El Salvador and Costa Rica. The export model became even more firmly entrenched. In the years immediately before the world crisis of 1929–30, income from coffee and bananas accounted for nearly 90 per cent of export revenue in Costa Rica, Guatemala and El

Salvador, and 70 per cent in Honduras and Nicaragua (where the mining of gold and silver remained significant). The 1920s were also characterized by a political stability in which – at least in Costa Rica, under the Liberal 'Olympians' represented by Juan Ricardo Jiménez Oreamuno and Cleto González Víquez; in Guatemala, where José María Orellana and Lázaro Chacón, both Liberals, were successively elected; and in El Salvador under the leadership of the Liberal Meléndez–Quiñónez family – the functioning of the oligarchical structures of control and domination were compatible with a form, albeit limited, of electoral, representative democracy.

When the international economic crisis of 1929 reached Central America, it immediately changed the dynamics of foreign commerce through a drop in international demand for the region's traditional agricultural products as well as in the traditional sales of manufactured goods from more economically developed countries, especially the United States. The impact of the world depression varied from country to country. The highest levels in foreign trade were in fact achieved in Nicaragua in 1926, in Guatemala in 1927, and in Costa Rica and El Salvador in 1928, whereas Honduras did not see its foreign-exchange earnings decline until 1931. Similarly, the lowest point in the depression cycle was experienced in different ways.

It is possible, however, to generalize about the effects of the economic crisis on the region as a whole, although there were certain distinctive features in each country. The depression was not felt locally as a financial catastrophe paralysing economic life; it was experienced as a period of stagnation lasting more than a decade, scarcely interrupted by moments of transitory recovery. Because Central American society generally had agriculture as its economic base and the external market as its dynamic factor, and because more complete indicators do not exist, statistics for the production and export of coffee and bananas or, even better, data on foreign trade more generally are used to show the external origin of the crisis in the form of declining international demand, which recuperated only after 1945 and whose counterpart was a parallel decline in imports. These were the combined effects of the international crisis of the decade and the Second World War at the end of the depression.

As seen in Table 3.1, there was no spectacular crash in regional production or exports, but rather a zigzag pattern, which during the first years showed an average decline equivalent to 50 per cent of the value of exports in relation to the highest point of the preceding decade, and which imposed severe limitations on the capacity to import. The international

Table 3.1. *Central America: Value of Foreign Trade 1930–45 (in millions of current dollars)*

Year	Guatemala		El Salvador		Honduras		Nicaragua		Costa Rica		Central America	
	Export	Import	Export	Import	Export	Import	Export	Import	Export	Import	Export	Import
1930	51.6	33.0	22.0	20.0	54.9	26.0	13.4	16.0	27.5	11.0	169.4	106.0
1931	33.2	26.0	19.0	12.0	55.8	17.0	10.4	12.0	24.1	9.0	142.5	76.0
1932	23.3	15.0	9.0	9.0	55.6	12.0	7.0	7.0	14.4	5.0	109.3	48.0
1933	16.5	12.0	9.0	8.0	60.0	10.0	6.1	6.0	14.0	6.0	105.6	42.0
1934	19.2	12.0	9.0	5.0	52.6	12.0	4.6	5.0	8.2	9.0	93.6	46.0
1935	16.1	15.0	10.0	9.0	17.1	6.0	4.6	5.0	7.3	7.0	55.1	42.0
1936	22.0	18.0	10.0	8.0	11.2	5.0	3.5	6.0	7.8	8.0	54.5	45.0
1937	23.0	26.0	15.0	10.0	12.2	6.0	6.2	6.0	10.8	12.0	67.2	60.0
1938	23.5	26.0	10.0	9.0	15.9	10.0	4.3	6.0	9.3	13.0	63.0	64.0
1939	24.3	24.0	12.0	9.0	22.5	11.0	4.8	7.0	8.6	17.0	72.2	68.0
1940	15.6	20.0	10.0	8.0	22.3	11.0	3.7	8.0	7.0	17.0	58.6	64.0
1941	18.8	19.0	10.0	8.0	21.3	11.0	4.6	12.0	9.8	18.0	64.5	68.0
1942	26.7	14.0	17.0	9.0	20.3	12.0	5.6	8.0	10.2	12.0	79.8	55.0
1943	26.3	18.0	21.0	12.0	9.0	10.0	7.7	16.0	12.2	20.0	76.2	76.0
1944	31.1	21.0	22.0	12.0	19.8	14.0	7.8	12.0	10.4	22.0	91.1	81.0
1945	39.7	23.0	21.0	13.0	27.6	15.0	6.9	14.0	11.5	27.0	106.7	92.0

Source: CEPAL. *América Latina: Relación de Precios de Intercambio* (Santiago, 1976), pp. 35, 43, 45, 49, 53.

collapse of the gold standard in 1931 created problems with the exchange rate; Guatemala and Honduras resisted devaluation, while Costa Rica and El Salvador, after letting their currencies float, devalued between 1931 and 1933. (Nicaragua followed suit in 1937.) The countries most affected by the crisis were Honduras and Nicaragua, and in both recovery was slow and at levels lower than those of the rest of the region. In Nicaragua, moreover, the balance of trade remained persistently unfavorable for fifteen years. Stagnation lifted slightly in 1936–9, and especially in 1937, in Guatemala, El Salvador and Costa Rica, but the paralysis of international commerce precipitated by the war in Europe contributed to the problems of the external sector at the start of the Second World War (see Table 3.1). The levels of foreign trade, public spending and the gross domestic product (GDP) in general recovered only after 1945, and in some cases, such as Honduras, even later.

The existence of an internal market economy was important because most agricultural production and that of the small artisan-manufacturing sector was consumed domestically. It is difficult to make precise calculations of the value of production destined for the foreign market and that which went into domestic consumption; the latter contained an important element of self-consumption which was centred not only in peasant economies but also in the traditional estates whose owners lived on an extensive system of sharecropping. Calculations made for the beginning of the 1940s suggest that on average less than half the value of agricultural production was destined for export trade.[1]

The nature of the agricultural sector was determined by the functioning and relations among its three sub-sectors. The banana industry was modern and controlled by North American capital, its operations internationally integrated. Thus, the banana industry was affected by the crisis not only in the decline in the volume of trade and the fall in the price of bananas but also by changes in investment strategies on the part of the parent company. In the 1930s the United Fruit Company, unable to combat the 'Panama disease' effectively, decided to transfer its plantations to the Pacific region: Tiquisate in Guatemala, and Quepos in Costa Rica.

The second sub-sector was the coffee industry, which had a different level of capitalization. Coffee enterprises were able to continue even with decreased revenues because of the permanent character of coffee cultivation

[1] E. Torres-Rivas, 'Centroamérica: algunos rasgos de la sociedad posguerra', Working Paper of the Kellogg Institute, no. 25 (Washington, D.C., 1984), table 1, p. 49.

and also because of previous experience with depressed cycles followed by periods of prosperity. The decline in income in the coffee sector affected the system of production only in a relative way, by inhibiting the expansion of cultivated areas and improvements in productivity. The decrease in international demand affected coffee earnings, which could be absorbed by the land-ownership structure without affecting basic production resources on the estates.

The third sub-sector was the peasant economy, whose production was distributed more in the form of family self-consumption than through sales of surpluses in local markets. In fact, only this sector of the economy improved its level of production. The crisis stimulated the conditions to strengthen a simple mercantile economy as an alternative to the relative weakness of the mercantile export sector. Increased production of basic grain crops, especially corn and beans, confirmed that the mercantile economy could reappear or invigorate itself wherever independent producers maintained their means of production, the availability of food stimulating domestic demand. Figures for this period indicate that there were times when grain and beans were quite abundant, being especially so, for instance, in 1937. Using logical deductions based on a knowledge of the structure of production, we can conclude that such yields came from small properties. Undoubtedly, it is this information that has enabled Bulmer-Thomas to analyse the diverse mechanisms which palliated the crisis, one of which was the substitution of agricultural imports during the second half of the 1930s.[2] Domestic agriculture grew in importance for some time, and more because of internal conditions that reduced the ability to import than because of governmental decisions.

The absorption capacities of the peasant economies were put to the test when they became a refuge for the rural unemployed masses. As happens in mono-export economies, where dynamic impulses originate in foreign demand, the loss of such impulses translates into a partial decadence in the monetary sector of the internal market, but without catastrophic consequences. Coffee production depended only partly on wage relations, as can be seen from the position of the *mozo colono* in Guatemala, El Salvador or Nicaragua, or the sharecropper in Costa Rica. In both situations coffee producers avoided the problems of paying wages, leaving the matter of maintaining and replacing the labour force as marginal to the cost of production.

[2] V. Bulmer-Thomas, *The Political Economy of Central America since 1920* (Cambridge, 1987), chap. 4.

During this period, too, coffee earnings, derived from and subject to international prices, were relatively independent of the internal cost of production, which only indicated a lower limit; cycles of growth or depression were not reflected in wage levels or other living conditions of the labour force. The standard of living of the peasant population was tied to the level at which production itself yielded enough to support a subsistence economy. Nevertheless, there was unemployment on the national urban level, less visible in the country, where 80 per cent of the population lived.

Government response to these problems in all five countries can be described as a policy of confronting the economic cycle in a traditional and orthodox manner. The traditional element was determined by the culture of the coffee producers, whose mentality, strongly influenced by economic liberalism, led them to insist upon the inefficacious nature of state action. The orthodoxy of policy lay in its application of the principle that state spending stimulates demand only to the extent that it exceeds tax revenues; therefore, fiscal deficit had to be avoided at all costs. Central American governments carried out immediate budget cuts as a consequence of the appreciable fall in fiscal revenues which came largely from taxes on imports and exports. The most surprising development in this regard occurred in the mid-1930s, when the reductions in public spending reached the level where they began to produce small surpluses, which, for example, in Guatemala and El Salvador, accumulated as unspent savings.

Of the five governments, that in Guatemala was the most orthodox, and after 1932 managed to balance the budget, henceforth generating a growing surplus which accumulated unproductively until the end of the war. The government not only reduced public employment, it also cut salaries and instituted a policy of road construction – based on free labour – all of which did nothing to stimulate domestic demand. The other governments were in a different position, and hampered by the same shrinkage of public spending to prevent annual deficit balances, they resorted to internal debt. The budgets of Honduras and Nicaragua were managed at the lowest level of purely administrative expenses, a level so low that the next step would have been total paralysis. The year 1937 saw only a fleeting improvement in foreign trade, but this was important in that it signalled a turning-point after which state spending began a slow growth.

The orthodox attitude in public policy, influenced by the defense of the landowners' interests, ensured that state spending during this epoch of crisis not only failed to address the effects of the depression cycle but also indirectly contributed to them. The growth of debt incurred to cover budget balances always proved unproductive while the governments' contribution to the GDP was always small and, during these years, declining. Programmes of public works, purchase of crops or credit expansion were practically unthinkable. In general, there existed no fiscal policy capable of 'curing' a depression that had foreign origins or of limiting the dislocation caused by a boom in exports when this originated entirely in price movements rather than in the growth of the productivity of labour.

In sum, except for variations of minor significance, the Central American states responded to the economic crisis with a set of orthodox liberal economic policy measures. Their policies (or absence of them) weakened domestic consumption, drastically cutting public spending, reducing salaries or limiting the mobilization of financial resources.

At the same time, as we shall see, a profound fear of social unrest found expression in a defence of the traditional political order by heightening authoritarian mechanisms already deeply rooted in the culture of the region.

The impact of the Second World War on the Central American economies was considerable because Europe was an important market for the region's exports. In the short term the most important consequence was the loss of first the German and then the British markets for coffee and the reorientation of Central American trade towards the United States, consolidating a tendency that had been growing since the First World War. This shift was particularly important because the region's trade balance with the United States was in deficit whereas it had been in surplus with Britain and Germany. Central America was converted not only into a good neighbour but also into a good partner. Among the most important measures was the Inter-American Coffee Agreement (November 1940) that established quotas for the first time for the expanding U.S. market. Banana exports, on the other hand, declined. The reduction or loss of South East Asian markets produced a degree of agricultural diversification through the emergence of 'war crops', such as rubber, basic oils and vegetable fibres, the strategic production of which the U.S. government encharged to the United and Standard Fruit companies in Guatemala, Honduras and Costa Rica. However, the importance of these crops proved to be temporary, and after the war only abacá and African palm continued to be subordinate products of the banana enclaves.

None of the Central American countries was at this time in a position to encourage industrial growth through import substitution. Although the war greatly impeded imports, there was little effort to establish the domestic supply of manufactured goods. By 1944–5 the countries of Central America, especially Guatemala and El Salvador, had perforce accumulated sizeable reserves of foreign exchange and gold which were not employed in productive activity but were largely used to pay the external debt, especially the oldest loans, those advanced by the British. At the same time, the inflow of external earnings contributed to inflation, which was particularly acute in Honduras and Nicaragua.[3] The fiscal problems that had prevailed since 1930 continued, to varying degrees, until 1942, but it was only in Costa Rica under the Calderón Guardia regime that they caused serious problems.

The most important political phenomenon at the beginning of the 1930s was the recrudescence of the peasant war in the north of Nicaragua. As is well known, Nicaragua had been invaded on 3 October 1912 by the United States, when a squadron of warships entered the Pacific port of Corinto and 1,500 marines landed in an effort to end the struggle between Conservatives and Liberals. The North Americans eventually left (August 1925), but Nicaraguan fratricide caused them to return, in larger numbers, in 1926. When this renewed intervention led to what they considered to be a shameful accord between the foreign military forces and the traditional Nicaraguan politicians, Augusto César Sandino and a group of dissident Liberal officers rose up in rebellion in July 1927, opening an intermittent but prolonged civil war.

At the beginning of 1930 the marine units stationed in Nicaragua were concentrated in the cities and left the principal operations of the war in the hands of the National Guard (Guardia Nacional), which they had recently created. The course of the war was irregular, but the offensives carried out by Sandino and his men gained strength during the winter of 1931–2, possibly as a result of the economic crisis and its effects among the impoverished peasantry of Las Segovias, one of Nicaragua's most important coffee-producing areas. U.S. President Herbert Hoover announced his intention to withdraw the last of the marines after the Nicaraguan presidential elections in November 1932. Washington wanted the Nicaraguan government to reach an agreement directly with the Sandinistas or con-

---

[3] V. Bulmer-Thomas, *Political Economy of Central America*, p. 100.

tinue the war without United States military aid. As a result, on 2 January 1933, the day after Dr. Juan Bautista Sacasa took office as president and put Anastasio Somoza in command of the National Guard, the last foreign troops sailed from Corinto. At the beginning of February 1933, Sandino reached a peace agreement with the new liberal government, but a year later, on 21 February 1934, he was assassinated by the National Guard. In the meantime the guerrilla war that developed in Nicaragua had considerable repercussions throughout Latin America but especially in Central America where it inflamed the social discontent arising from unemployment, low wages and shortages caused by the economic crisis.

These factors, without doubt, lay behind the bloody peasant rebellion in the Izalco region in El Salvador in January 1932. However, the uprising and slaughter that followed it should be seen in the context of the election in January 1931 of a popular leader, Arturo Araujo, who in the name of 'laborism' won more than 50 per cent of the vote and defeated the candidate of the powerful coffee oligarchy, Alberto Gómez Zárate. This election, hailed as the only free poll ever held in the country, constituted a popular victory that was rapidly countered by the military coup of December 1931 led by General Maximiliano Hernández Martínez. The rupture of constitutional order created profound internal and international discontent, and, in accordance with the provisions of the Peace and Friendship Treaty signed between the five Central American governments and the United States in 1923, Washington refused to recognize the new regime. However, General Martínez was easily able to hold on to office once the 1932 revolt had been suppressed, eventually obliging the United States to recognize his government in an act that effectively terminated both the 1923 original peace treaty and Washington's policy of boycotting non-elected regimes.

The leadership and programme of the popular rebellion of January 1932 have never been sufficiently clarified, but it was certainly a peasant uprising and in some areas, such as Nahizalco and Juayúa, it was vigorously supported by indigenous communities. For three days well-armed government troops fought the insurrectionary groups armed with machetes and clubs who were overrunning the western part of El Salvador in a random fashion, peace being restored at the price of twenty-five or thirty thousand deaths. The severity of this repression created a climate of terror which extended beyond the frontiers of this small country and lasted for many years.

What happened in El Salvador was not a well-planned revolutionary action but rather a disorganized display of deep popular discontent that was far from an isolated event in the region. The artisanal base of Central American manufacturing and the existence of a vast peasant class effectively confined organized protest to that sector of the agricultural proletariat linked to the banana plantations. The social discontent of a population which lacked traditions of organization and struggle was general but unstructured. In Costa Rica, though, it took on a relatively more systematic and active character when, in August 1934, popular malaise finally led to the banana-workers' strike in the Limón region. This strike lasted for more than forty-five days, enjoyed a broad class-based solidarity and finally turned out to be a decisive event in the social history of Costa Rica since it marked the birth of an independent union movement in that country.

There were also social unrest and protest in the plantation areas of northern Honduras. In February 1932, a broad-based but short-lived strike movement broke out in the Tela Railroad Company as a consequence of the dismissal of eight hundred workers and a general salary cut. The government of Vicente Mejía Colindres initially backed the Honduran workers' demands, fearing that the company's actions – which exacerbated the effects of the economic crisis – would lead to the generalized spread of collective unrest. On the other hand, discontent among the banana-workers in the Izabal zone in Guatemala failed to generate a strike movement or other forms of collective protest. All that remains in the historical record of the social struggles in this country is the pre-emptive repression ordered by President Ubico, alarmed by the news from neighbouring countries. The incipient union movement started by socialist-inspired artisans was destroyed when the government ordered the execution of fourteen militant student and labour organizers and imprisoned more than twenty persons, who remained in jail without judicial process until 1944.

It is necessary to stress that during this period institutional stability was achieved by means of diverse processes which had nothing to do with democratic mechanisms and which were, in fact, as much the results of the depression and its social consequences as of the authoritarian tradition and political *caudillismo*. The most wide-spread opinion among analysts of this era is that the system of oligarchical domination in general was directly threatened by popular discontent, the almost universal reaction being to install military governments which had a great capacity for repression and were legitimated precisely by their ability to keep things under control in the face of the risk of rampant social disorder. With the passage of time the most negative aspects of a political system that seemed to be always on the defensive were reinforced. Central among these was the inability of the regime to tolerate any opposition.

The electoral system which seemed to have been consolidated in the previous decade was *formally* upheld in all the countries except El Salvador, where the coup by General Hernández Martínez was validated in 1932 by the National Assembly, which installed him as president. Even he, however, continued to govern through successive re-elections until his fall in 1944. In Guatemala the Liberal general Jorge Ubico was elected, though without opposition, in February 1931. His position as *caudillo* was soon confirmed when he annulled municipal autonomy, seriously interfered with the independence of the judiciary and generally concentrated power in his own hands. Ubico was reelected in 1937 and again in 1943, after successive modifications of the Constitution. In Honduras General Tiburcio Carías Andino was elected in February 1933, after two previous efforts; like Ubico, he managed to endow the executive power with total authority, centralizing in his hands the control of the country's political life, except for activity in the areas reserved to the jurisdiction of foreign plantation-owners. A constitutional assembly in 1936 promulgated a document modifying the length of the presidential term and authorizing it to continue for six additional years after its legal expiration in 1939; further extensions authorized by the parliament enabled Carías to rule until 1948. In Nicaragua, the government of the Liberal Juan Bautista Sacasa, elected under U.S. supervision in 1932, was overthrown by a coup d'état led by the impatient General Somoza, also a Liberal and Sacasa's nephew. After a brief period of transition, Somoza was elected in November 1936 and became President of Nicaragua on 1 January 1937. Thus began the long period of the dictatorship of this family, which did not end until 1979.

Costa Rica merits separate mention because its democracy, which took the form of liberal *caudillos* elected on the basis of their prestige, acting through small parties of notables (land-owners, lawyers, etc.) and characterized by their capacity to tolerate the existence of oppostition, largely survived the test of the social effects of the depression. In fact, the last liberal *caudillo,* Ricardo Jiménez, was not elected but appointed in May 1932 by Congress, which first proposed him as candidate and then proclaimed him president. The attempt at a coup in Bella Vista, albeit a failure, revealed the limitations already evident in the old oligarchical model. Yet, in February 1936, León Cortés was elected without a major crisis, and in 1940, Dr. Rafael Angel Calderón Guardia likewise assumed the presidency. Calderón's government is notable not so much for his election landslide (84 per cent of the vote), as for the character of his presidential leadership. There are disputes over whether his exceptional social policy was a product of his social christian background in Europe or of his firm alliance with the Catholic Church – at that moment led by Archbishop Sanabria – or his association with the Communist Party. Whatever the case, during his government the Costa Rican Social Security Fund was set up in 1941; and in 1943 a comprehensive labour law was passed and important modifications made to the Constitution, establishing a set of civil rights distinctly advanced for the time. The social reforms of the Calderón Guardia administration were consolidated under that of his successor, Teodoro Picado (1944–8). However, Calderón Guardia's attempt to regain office in 1948 by means of electoral fraud and in the context of violence unusual in the political life of the country, led, as we shall see, to the civil war of 1948.

The military dictatorships set up in the 1930s in four of the region's countries experienced a twofold pressure towards the end of the Second World War which provoked what has been called the 'crisis of the oligarchy'. On the one hand, the international climate provoked by the defeat of European fascism encouraged people to value local democratic experiences; on the other, internal social forces which had been contained for so many years of stagnation and dictatorship now sought to establish a democratic process through elections, party competition and popular organization. The anti-oligarchical programme was not radical in its ideology – it merely sought to re-establish the rule of law – but the struggles against the dictatorships towards the end of the war initially took the form of urban insurrection.

In April 1944, a general strike obliged General Hernández Martínez of El Salvador to resign. This was a multi-class movement, led by professionals of the middle class and young military officers. The campaign failed to become a national movement or introduce profound changes because its leaders were discovered and shot. As a result, the crisis was resolved internally in the armed forces; the decrepit dictator was replaced by his chief of police and later by another hastily elected general, Salvador Castañeda Castro (1945–8). A movement of similar stamp, also led by young military officers, academics, professionals and middle-class businessmen, managed to oust the dictatorship of Jorge Ubico in Guatemala between June and October 1944. This anti-oligarchical movement was more radical and more successful because the generals of the old army of the dictatorship were expelled from the country, the Liberal Party disappeared and the field was open for free popular organization. With the election of Dr Juan José Arevalo in December 1945 a process of reform with broad popular participation was initiated.

The democratic struggles against the oligarchy and military authoritarianism were not triumphant in Honduras and Nicaragua because the social forces mobilized were weak, although the programme was similar to those of the other countries. In Honduras, the 'anti-oligarchic' campaign led by the Liberals assumed a limited dimension and was essentially a battle against the dictator Carías, who had the support of the foreign plantation interests and thus a sufficient base for governmental stability. Nevertheless, social discontent limited General Carías' ambitions; he had no choice but to agree to hold presidential elections in 1948 and to allow the Liberals to participate, although the victor was his Minister of War, Juan Manuel Gálvez. In Nicaragua the truly democratic interests of social renovation, for which a generation of intellectuals and workers had been fighting, were obscured by traditional Liberal–Conservative rivalry. The Conservative Party, through its youth groups, participated actively in the struggle against Somoza's dictatorship, but neither of the parties managed to give its platform a popular anti-oligarchical content. All the same, Anastasio Somoza was obliged to desist from having himself openly re-elected in 1947. Under both national and international pressure, the dictator had Dr Leonardo Arguello elected 19 February 1947, only to remove him on 24 May. Benjamin Lacayo Sacasa was hastily installed, and after twenty-two days of provisional government, elections were held in which another compliant Liberal, Victor Román y Reyes, emerged the victor. Both were relatives of Somoza, who never left his post as chief of the National Guard and became president again in January 1950.

In Costa Rica the liberal democratic experience had deep historical roots, yet the political forms which characterized it seemed to come to an end in the 1940s. It was the end not only of the liberal *caudillos* but also of a style of government. The pre-electoral period of 1947–8 was characterized by a growing intransigence on the part of the government, which disturbed the conciliatory tradition of the country. Never before had there existed the distrust and political violence now manifested by both the government and the opposition. Under considerable political pressure because of Calderón Guardia's plans for re-election, the government ceded control of the National Electoral Tribunal to one of the opposing factions. Elections were held on 8 February 1948, but the results were not known until the 28 February, when the defeat of Calderón's National Republican Party and the victory of Otilio Ulate was announced. On 1 March the National Congress, whose majority favoured Calderón, annulled the presidential elections. Insurrection would not wait, and the "revolution of '48" broke out on 10 March.

The military events of the two-month civil war in Costa Rica are of minor importance compared to the social and political phenomena which accompanied its unfolding and its resolution. In effect, the social policy of Calderón in the early 1940s had constituted a preliminary rupture of the traditional oligarchical order. The so-called social guarantees he introduced had two decisive but contradictory respects: on the one hand, the beginning of the incorporation of the popular masses into political life through a party of the left (the Communists); and on the other hand, Calderón's connection with the clergy, an outcome of his social christian inclinations learned in Europe that broke with a long anti-clerical tradition of liberal inspiration. The anti-Calderón alliance was itself cleft by even deeper contradictions. On one side was the powerful landed-commercial oligarchy based on coffee, which mounted the most militant opposition in defence of their economic and social interests. On the other were the urban middle class intellectuals and politicians, who had entered the political scene more recently motivated by an interest in modernization and change. They were led by José Figueres, Rodrigo Facio and members of various groups who eventually formed the National Liberation Party in 1951. The crisis was above all a crisis within the ranks of the bourgeoisie, yet precipitated by the new role of labour, which at that time reached a level of organization and influence it would never achieve again.

José Figueres, who led the triumphant coalition of the urban middle class and a fraction of the oligarchy, proclaimed himself chief of the Founding Junta of the Second Republic and governed the country for eighteenth months (April 1948 to November 1949). The set of measures taken at this time paradoxically continued the reformist impetus initiated by Calderón and the Communists. For example, Figueres lifted the tax on wheat to lower the price of bread, faciliated wage increases for agricultural workers and established the Consejo Nacional de Producción and the Instituto Costarricense de Electricidad, which nationalized production and reduced the cost of electricity. On 21 June 1948, he imposed a 10 per cent tax on capital and nationalized the private banks; to the present day these are considered the most audacious steps ever taken under reformist inspiration. A new constitution, drawn up by a constitutional assembly with a conservative majority in 1949, did away with the army and established in its place a rural National Guard and urban police forces. Figueres' transitional government was then replaced by that of Otilio Ulate (November 1949 to November 1953), a conservative leader but one of those who participated in the victory over Calderón Guardia. The Partido Liberación Nacional (PLN) was established 12 October 1951 as the result of the fusion of diverse social forces under a social democratic inspiration, an ideology already contained in one of its founding currents. In the elections of 1953, Figueres, as candidate of the PLN was finally constitutionally elected President of Costa Rica (1953–8), and during his term he pursued a reformist policy with even greater vigour, which contributed to the social and economic modernization of the country, the perfecting of strictly electoral processes, and the definition of a new role for the state.

The political changes begun in 1948 favoured not only a broadening of political democracy but also a stage of economic growth based on the diversification and modernization of agriculture and the establishment of light industry based in the urban centres. The nationalization of the banks weakened the links between commercial-finance capital and the coffee exporters, but socio-economic policy did not have a well-defined anti-oligarchic purpose; it promoted a vast programme of modernization of the coffee plantation which benefited all the planters at the same time as it created a co-operative system for marketing coffee in order to limit the commercial monopoly. In essence, this established a new role for the state in active economic intervention in order both to modernize the productive bases of the bourgeoisie and to limit its monopolistic features.

The social policies vigorously pursued by the PLN allowed it to create a new base of support in the country's peasantry. It should, at the same time, be noted that after 1948 the urban labour movement, under the influence of the communist Partido Vanguardia Popular (PVP), was badly defeated and disorganized. In Central American terms the social-democratic ideology and policies of the PLN constituted advanced forms of bourgeois thought, which bore a certain resemblance to the radical reformism of the governments of Guatemala at the time.

Guatemala's experience is distinct in that the new period of democratic life lasted less than a decade. The overthrow of the dictatorship of General Ubico in June 1944 and of his immediate successor General Ponce on 20

October 1944 as the result of a broad-based national movement, was immediately consolidated by the election of a constitutional assembly promulgating a modern constitution with socialist leanings to replace the old liberal-oriented constitution in effect since 1877. A civilian–military junta called elections which Dr Juan José Arévalo won by a landslide. Arévalo's government (1945–51), encouraged the modernization of a socially and culturally backward country, established programs for the promotion and diversification of agriculture, and introduced social security and a labour law; but above all, Arévalo created the conditions for the organization of diverse social interest groups and extended mandatory free public education. He was succeeded by Jacobo Arbenz (1951–4), also elected by a large majority, whose government continued Arévalo's programme but in a more nationalist and radical style.

Between 1951 and 1954 an attempt was made to renovate the old system of land-ownership by imposing an agrarian reform that constituted the most profound challenge to the traditional social order in the entire region. The reform attempted to punish unproductive large land-owners, prohibit any form of personal servitude and utilize the land as a means of production and labor. The implicit purpose was to dismantle the old rural class structure and create an internal market capable of supporting industrial growth under the control of national and state capital. In this sense, Arbenz's programme not only was anti-oligarchic but also contained an obvious anti-imperialist purpose. Probably the most significant feature of the period, begun by Arévalo and intensified by Arbenz, was the importance acquired by union and peasant mobilization and organization.

The expropriation of more than 100,000 hectares of land accompanied by an intense peasant mobilization in Guatemala in the early 1950s was the culminating moment of the anti-oligarchical offensive which swept over Central America during the post-war years. Here mention should be made of two different factors which contributed to the defeat of Arbenz's nationalist programme. One was that the United Fruit Company was the largest land-owner in the country; under the law more than 15,000 hectares of company land were to be expropriated. The other was the Cold War and the confrontation with the Soviet Union which had exacerbated the anti-communist tendencies in U.S. foreign policy and the anti-communism of conservative groups which constituted the internal opposition to the revolutionary reformism of Arbenz and the parties of the Democratic Front.

A conspiracy within the senior ranks of the army nurtured by U.S.

ambassador John Peurifoy was the culmination of a long anti-communist campaign that had an important religious content. This campaign weakened the Democratic Front's political support for President Arbenz, who had to resign on the night of 27 June 1954, after receiving an ultimatum from his Minister of Defence and chief of the armed forces. The form of Arbenz's resignation at the peak of popular mobilization and organization provoked enormous internal confusion and ensured that within a short time the parties and popular organizations would be declared illegal and subjected to brutal repression. The offensive was especially violent against the peasantry, who had benefited from the redistribution of land. Within a week the changes in the armed forces left power in the hands of the leaders of the conspiracy. On 5 August 1954, Colonel Carlos Castillo Armas was named head of state, opening a new stage in the political life of Guatemala.

There was no stable consolidation of power after these events. Castillo was assassinated by one of his own partisans on 26 June 1956, and this unleashed a new crisis in the army. Successive coups d'état and a fraudulent election in 1957 led finally to the election in 1958 of General Miguel Ydígoras Fuentes, who presided over a conservative transition towards political democracy. Freedom of organization, speech and the press were reinstated as Ydígoras tried to impose contradictory measures of national reconciliation that alienated the sympathies of the coalition which had brought him to power. He was removed by a military coup in March 1963.

In Honduras during this period, the election of Juan Manuel Gálvez (1949–54) amounted to an attempt to prolong the Carías regime, although there were a number of important new developments. The first was the great banana strike in May 1954, which started as a simple protest over the dismissal of twenty-five workers at the Tela Railroad belonging to the United Fruit Company and developed into a campaign for higher wages and better working conditions. The favourable attitude towards change and the search for democratic experimentation, both of which took different expression throughout the region, explain why the conflict spread rapidly to the plantations of the Standard Fruit Company, the El Mochito mine, and the entire foreign-owned agro-industrial zone in the region of San Pedro Sula. The conflict, which attracted the active support of more than 40,000 workers, ended in July after sixty-nine days of strike. It was important not only for its victorious conclusion but also because it had decisive effects on the whole of political society, the most important of these being the creation of real possibilities for working-class and peasant organization. This was the starting-point for labour and social security legislation as well as the creation of the Ministry of Labour and the new awareness that the national problem was closely linked to the social problem. The incorporation of labour and, later, the peasantry, as relatively autonomous political forces was a decisive feat in the framework of a backward agrarian society. It must be added, however, that the strike had a negative impact on the labour market, reducing employment on the banana plantations from 35,000 workers in 1953 to 16,000 in 1959, and its effects on production were compounded by a hurricane in December 1954. These events do not fully explain the slowness of overall growth, but they were undoubtedly important given the weight of the fruit plantations in Honduran economic life.

A second central phenomenon of this period was the entry of the armed forces into the political arena. In the elections of 1954 the traditional Liberal and National parties were unable to resolve their differences because neither could claim an absolute majority. Although the Liberals won 48 per cent of the total, a second vote was corrupted by fraud, provoking the intervention of the army, for the first time, as an institution in 1956. It is of some significance that the victor of the new national elections held under military supervision in September 1957 was Dr. Ramón Villeda Morales (1957–63), returning the Liberals to power after twenty-five years of conservative government.

By contrast, political life of El Salvador remained marked by a permanent military presence, both because the army had been a decisive factor in the struggle for power since 1932 and because senior government officials had always come from the military establishment. In the period under analysis, the oligarchical crisis and its counterpart, institutional and democratic modernization, were expressed in the so-called Revolution of '48, a movement of young officers who carried out a coup d'état on 14 December 1948.

Thereafter a variety of measures were taken to improve the economy and state institutions. All of these may be described as conducive to a relative modernization of Salvadorean society, albeit without recourse to the risks of democracy and without touching the economic bases of the coffee oligarchy. In spite of these limitations, the acts of both the revolutionary junta and the regime of Major Oscar Osorio (1950–56) were marked by a willingness for change. A new constitution, promulgated in 1950, gave legal support to the whole of the transformation process. The general climate of this epoch explains why, as in the other countries, the social rights of workers were recognized in the Constitution, in specific legislation, and in the appearance of a more functional concept of the role of the state in the economy and of the changes which the economy should undergo.

Perhaps the most important feature of these years was the effort to promote industrial growth by various means. In this area the construction of the Río Lempa hydroelectric plant, which is the largest in Central America, and the port of Acajutla, which is modern and was built to fortify foreign trade, are significant. Both autonomous state enterprises were built with the participation of the private sector. In fact, the reformist thought of these young Turks continued beyond Osorio's regime, prolonging itself into the first years of the government of Colonel José María Lemus (1957–60). The political life of the country, however, continued to be marked by government repression and a distinctly authoritarian democracy.

During this period Nicaragua also passed through a stage of important economic growth based on cotton exports, which lent a certain legitimacy to the continuation of the regime of Anastasio Somoza. In the middle of his campaign for re-election, however, he was assassinated on 21 September 1956, in the city of Léon. The Somoza family's control over the state mediated through the National Guard (which was in the hands of Anastasio Somoza, Jr.) and the Congress (presided over by Luis Somoza) ensured that the mechanisms of succession were resolved within the family, supported by the Liberal Party against the fierce opposition of groups of independent Liberals and the Conservative Party. The death of Somoza provoked violent repression against the opposition even though the assassination was the personal act of a young poet, Rigoberto López Pérez. Luis Somoza was promoted to president and his election was ratified by Congress in February 1957. He ran a shadow government which profited from the cotton boom and the first investments stimulated by the Central American Common Market. Luis Somoza died a few days before the poll of February 1963, in which the dictatorship of the family was interrupted to allow the election of a friend of the family, René Schick, who helped pacify the growing opposition to the Somozas and create a space for the future ascent to power of Anastasio Somoza, Jr., in 1967.

The end of the Second World War marked the slow and contradictory beginning of a new stage in the economic life of the countries of Central America. The international context was generally favourable because of the recovery of the European economy and the re-establishment of trade and investment links with the United States. In fact, despite minor recessions in 1949 and 1954, Central America benefited from the effects of the longest phase of prosperity ever seen in the world economy. At the same time, post-war economic growth was accompanied by a quantitative and qualitative transformation of Central American society. Most significantly, population growth rates for the entire period 1945–80 exceeded 3.2 per cent. In 1945 the region had a little more than 7 million inhabitants while in 1980 its population was 20 million. Several other socio-demographic changes were also decisive. In particular, the level of urbanization increased from 14 to 43 per cent between 1945 and 1980, expanding in particular the population of the capital cities, which came to account for more than 25 per cent of the total population.

One other phenomenon of the post-war period deserves mention: the role the state began to play in the promotion of development by means of the modernization of its institutions, such as central banks, and the creation of others, such as development banks and public electricity companies.

The importance of the economic changes during the post-war period must be seen in the context of the revival of international trade once the restrictions imposed by the exigencies of the war were lifted. Central America's traditional production, which had continued to respond to internal demand but had been depressed by the decline of the international market, was soon stimulated again from outside.

During the first few years the economic cycle was based exclusively on the rise in international prices and the reopening of traditional external markets. No important productive investment can be attributed to Central American exporters, who reacted slowly through the route of increases in the extent of land under cultivation, adding to the acreage in production. This operation was carried out through the utilization of land that was in the hands of the peasant sector and by substituting export crops for those destined for the internal market. The cultivation of new land and the risks of capital investment in improved techniques appeared only at the end of the period under consideration.

Despite this, the improvement in the value of foreign trade in Central America was the first factor that favourably affected the economies of the region. The increase in the value of the terms of trade (see Table 3.2) until 1954 demonstrates how, for a while, the capacity for exchange in the region improved, and how it had an immediate effect on the more than

Table 3.2. *Central America: Value of foreign trade (in millions of dollars),*
terms of trade and purchasing power of exports (1970 = 100), 1946–58

Year	Exports	Imports	Terms of Trade	Purchasing power of exports
1946	128.4	127.0	93.5	21.2
1947	192.4	197.0	87.7	24.4
1948	238.9	221.0	95.9	29.5
1949	242.1	215.6	108.4	31.8
1950	299.6	233.3	135.0	40.2
1951	343.4	279.7	149.9	43.0
1952	367.9	322.1	144.4	44.5
1953	390.1	338.0	152.7	48.4
1954	410.8	380.8	176.6	48.5
1955	420.0	414.5	159.3	50.7
1956	438.8	469.2	162.1	51.5
1957	469.5	524.9	151.9	54.4
1958	453.6	509.9	132.6	52.8

Source: James W. Wilkie and P. Reich (eds.), *Statistical Abstract of Latin America* (Los Angeles, 1979), vol.20, table 2730, p. 412.

proportional increase of imports which had been held back for a long time, especially during the war years. The most critical case was that of Honduras, whose economic life continued to revolve around banana production. During the Second World War, due to the so-called Panama disease (sigatoka), which affected a large proportion of the plantations, production was almost paralysed and the plantations had to be moved from the Trujillo zone to new lands between San Pedro Sula and La Ceiba. The investments of foreign companies seem to be recorded as capital entries which were not reflected in the growth of either production or exportation. According to Bulmer-Thomas' calculations, the GNP of Honduras, which was $257 per capita in 1929 (1970 prices), fell to $191 in 1939 and only recovered to $225 in 1949, a notable contrast to the figures of neighbouring countries.[4]

The three coffee-growing countries reacted at different times. El Salvador, the largest producer in the region, was the first to take advantage of the new post-war opportunities and by 1949 was already producing 73,000 metric tons of coffee, a quantity not surpassed until 1957, with 83,200 tons. Guatemala started to increase its production from 1951,

[4] Ibid.

when it was 63,000 tons, and maintained a steady growth during the entire period. Costa Rica did not increase levels of production until 1954, and then only very slowly. All the countries benefited from the rise in prices that occurred in the international market, which rose by 600 per cent between 1940 and the peak period reached in 1954–7. At the end of the Second World War (average of 1940–4), the quoted price of a pound of coffee in New York was about 11.7 cents; in 1949 it had risen to 28.7 cents, and between 1955 and 1957 it was worth 57.4 cents.[5]

This period is important not only because the production of a traditional product like coffee increased but also because it witnessed the beginning of a decisive diversification of agricultural commodities such as lumber, cocoa, hemp and, above all, sugar and cotton. The sowing of cotton reached extraordinary levels in El Salvador and Nicaragua and later in Guatemala, and it merits specific discussion both because of its economic consequences and because of its effects on society and politics. The cultivation of cotton changed the rural landscape in important areas of the humid Pacific coast of Central America. The rapidity with which areas were taken over for this product occurred because the lands used were old tenancies which had been devoted to extensive cattle-grazing, estates devoted to 'lease agriculture', land owned by peasants and, of course, unproductive terrain. 'Cotton fever', which began in 1945 in Nicaragua and El Salvador and in 1950 in Guatemala, not only disrupted vast areas traditionally occupied by a peasantry dedicated to subsistence farming combined with the cultivation of basic crops for the market, it also modified the state of unproductive and sharecropping estates, thus shattering the social equilibrium of thousands of peasants. The ecological balance was also altered to an extent that is still not appreciated; old forested areas and pastures were destroyed in the zones of Escuintla and Retalhuleu in Guatemala, La Paz and Usulután in El Salvador, and Chinandega and León in Nicaragua.

The modernization of Central American agriculture began with cotton, which immediately became a conspicuous example of modern agricultural enterprise. The structure of such enterprises has common characteristics in all three countries. The typical cotton entrepreneur was formerly a civil or military functionary, political leader or businessman, and only occasionally a former farmer. This was linked to the role played by the state, which so promoted and protected the planting of cotton that it has been dubbed

---

[5] James Wilkie (ed.), *Statistical Abstract of Latin America*, (Los Angeles, 1980), table 2526, p.340.

'political cultivation'. The industry arose, in effect, through the creation of large state facilities for bank credit plus 'know-how' acquired abroad and, most essentially, by planting on rented lands. This last factor constitutes a novelty inasmuch as the capitalist renting of land converted the cotton planter into an entrepreneur linked to the land in the most modern manner, by means of rent, which formed part of the investment capital.

The production and export of cotton grew at a regional average of 10 per cent during the first years; by the end of the 1950s it accounted for 6.6 per cent of the total of world exports and the third largest production in Latin America. Production reached 843 kilos per hectare in El Salvador, 700 in Guatemala, and 580 in Nicaragua. Egypt, another producer of unirrigated cotton, was producing 520 kilos per hectare during this period.[6] El Salvador initiated a so-called cotton boom which is worthy of note because before 1945 national production was extremely low and available land was relatively scarce. The 13,000 hectares planted in 1945 increased to 40,000 in 1956; in one decade the land area, yield and the value of production increased to occupy the country's entire Pacific coastal region. The growth of productivity was rapid and after 1954 El Salvador had, according to official sources, the highest yields in the world, next to Nicaragua.

It was in Nicaragua that the cultivation of cotton presented the best opportunity for constructing an agricultural economy for export that was modern and had far-reaching social and political implications. In effect, by 1950 Nicaragua was already the primary cotton producer in Central America, with more than 18,000 metric tons, and in 1954 it was exporting more than 47,000 tons. In that decade cotton exports occupied first place, accounting for 35 per cent of total exports. The production and export of this crop consolidated an already important entrepreneurial group, which oversaw the most dynamic period of expansion Nicaragua had ever experienced. Contrary to what has been mistakenly observed about the cotton adventure, capital participation was provided not only by the 'Somoza group' but also by the country's Liberal and Conservative business groups.

In the three producing countries the cultivation of cotton was important not only for high rates of growth in production, which increased from 11 thousand metric tons in 1947 to 110 thousand tons in 1958 (excluding

---

[6] CEPAL, *Análisis y proyecciones del desarrollo económico. El Desarrollo Económico de El Salvador* (Mexico, 1959), p. 21.

cottonseed and its derivatives), but also for the installation of agro-industrial cotton gins and as a source of social transformation on the part of business on the one hand, and the mass of agricultural labor on the other.

It was also during the post-war period that the production of cane sugar and livestock for export was started on a large scale. Both areas constituted significant sources of modernization in agriculture and economic diversification, contributing to the end of the mono-export tradition which had prevailed in most of the societies of the region. The stimulus for the conversion to sugar began before the Cuban quota was re-allocated among the small economies of Central America and the Caribbean. From 1947 the proportion of land planted, production and productivity began to grow slowly, increasing from 96,000 tons in 1949 to 236,000 in 1958. In the following decade volume increased even more and sugar became the third most important regional export. As with cotton, it was Nicaragua which most rapidly developed the modern sugar plantation with an agro-industrial infrastructure and skilled personnel, although Guatemala always had the largest volumes of production and exportation. All five countries became self-sufficient and, after 1953–4, began exporting to the United States. Nonetheless, the regional sugar industry never attained profitable production costs. With the fall of prices on the world market during the 1970s the industry found itself in a state of crisis without foreseeable recovery. Beef production was more successful, with exports beginning after 1955 and growing with North American demand from 3.2 million kilos at the end of the 1950s to 8.6 million in 1972.

The impulse to export agriculture directly provided by the United States aggravated rural domestic imbalances, on the one hand by sacrificing the best land to cattle-grazing and cotton, and on the other, by displacing the cultivation of basic grain crops to poor land and reducing the acreage allotted to the cultivation of products for the domestic market. In other words, the type of agrarian structure which carries with it unequal forms of tenancy was reinforced during this phase; the number of peasants engaged in the process of proletarianization increased, as did the standard of living and opportunities for work. It should not be forgotten that the historical formation of commercial agriculture for export produced a distribution of functions whereby the peasant sector of the economy became the producer of goods destined to feed the national population. The sharecropping economy continued to function in a very backward technological state, without capital resources and with difficult access to the marketplace.

In this regard, one should note the newest tendency towards shortages of foodstuffs like corn, rice, beans and so on. The period under consideration (1945–60) tested the capacity of Central American countries to maintain their self-sufficiency in food production. In fact, despite variations from one country to another, internal market production was already stagnating or in frank recession by 1948. The growth of population and the diminution of the supply of basic foods for popular consumption produced a regression in the nutritional levels of some sectors of the population, and this situation tended to worsen. The production of corn in 1949 was 950,000 tons, of rice 63,000 tons and beans 106,000 tons; in 1958, the total regional production of corn barely reached 1,023,000 tons, with rice at 77,000 tons and beans at 103,000 tons, which meant that the amount available on a per capita basis first stagnated and then decreased in each product category, most notably corn. The average rate of cumulative growth between 1949 and 1959 was 2.58 per cent, but exportable products increased at 7.14 per cent compared with 1.6 per cent for internal consumption.[7]

This picture presents us with paradoxical conclusion: that Central American agriculture had grown at a faster rhythm than that of nearly all other Latin American countries, yet it had not translated into an increase in employment opportunities for the rural population or an improvement in the levels of food consumption for the low-income population in general. At the same time, the growth and transformation of the export sector was based on an agriculture that increased in value not only through rises in prices but also because after the early post-war years, and especially during the 1950s, there were increases in productivity and modernization in some of its sectors.

After 1945 the rate of capital formation was very low, giving the definite impression that these were economies without capital accumulation in the sense that the augmentation of productive capacity did not play any relevant part. After 1950 there was growth in capital investment, closely associated with improvements in the capacity to import, which maintained an ascendant rhythm in spite of the accelerated growth of imports. The process of the slow destruction of urban and semi-rural

---

The statistical information in this section was obtained from CEPAL, *Primero y segundo compendio estadístico centroamericano* (New York, 1957, 1962).

artisanry and its replacement by small- and medium-sized industrial enterprises has not been sufficiently studied. No doubt this phenomenon is connected with the improvement in internal demand resulting from a new political and cultural climate bolstered by a rise in the incomes of the better situated social groups in the structure, the growth of population, and urbanization. Another factor was an improvement in the facilities for obtaining the supply of capital goods, primary materials, fuel and the like, which accompanied the rapid rise in imports throughout the period.

The censuses taken around 1950 record the presence of numerous manufacturing establishments with fewer than five employees, artisanal in character and generally known as 'workshops', which supplied nearly the entire demand for food, beverages, shoes, textiles, wood products, leather goods and so on. In the midst of this sea of tiny enterprises there existed two or three large factories, with ample capital, high concentration of labour and a monopolistic nature. Examples of these are the beer factories which had existed in Guatemala and El Salvador since 1890, a textile factory in Costa Rica, the cement factories in Nicaragua and Guatemala. In addition, there were agricultural concerns which were categorized as industries, the coffee-processing plants, the cotton gins, the sawmills, the rice-threshing plants and so on.

Obviously, the domestic supply of products for immediate consumption was highly restricted, a fact amply demonstrated by the composition of imports after 1945. It is only from the late 1950s that capital goods grow in importance, and during the first decade of the period under consideration, that is to say before the end of the 1950s, one finds no official policy of import substitution. The propensity for external consumption, which grew with both the relative increase in income and the capacity to import, was disadvantageous to the existence of Central American manufacturing and initiated the decline of artisanry, that would become more evident during the era of the Latin American Common Market.

The value of industrial production in the region as a whole amounted to about 12 per cent of the gross domestic product (GDP), with greater development in Nicaragua and Guatemala and less in Honduras and El Salvador. In 1946 the value of the production of food, textiles and beverages was $29 million in Guatemala, $31.7 in Nicaragua, $21.2 in Costa Rica, $7.6 in El Salvador and $6.3 in Honduras. Eleven years later, in 1957, the value of production of the same products for immediate consumption had climbed to $50 million in Guatemala, $73.1 in Nicaragua,

$50.6 in Costa Rica, $35.4 in El Salvador and $17.2 in Honduras.[8] We might add that this represents a modest growth, less in some cases than that in population and insufficient to satisfy the expansion of domestic demand, which relied increasingly on imports. Foreign commerce in Central America expanded, with the import ratio rising from 16.3 per cent in 1950 to 21.1 per cent in 1960.

As we have seen the end of the Second World War marked the beginning of a new stage in the economic history of Central America; the average annual rate of growth of GDP for the region as a whole was more than 5.3 per cent for nearly twenty-five years. However, for the ten years between the late 1950s and the late 1960s – the period known as the 'golden decade' of the Central American economy – economic performance was even better. The factors which invigorated the regional economy in the 1960s were of a diverse nature, and produced important differences among countries and in the nature of the cycle. The establishment of the Central American Common Market (CACM) in 1960 was the principal factor, although this itself was the effect of two other concurrent developments: the relative homogeneity of the regimes, and the growth of the international economy and the recovery of foreign demand. The historical factor – a common colonial experience and union in the immediate aftermath of independence as well as more than a dozen attempts at a Central American union since then – is also important.

Economic integration did not result from the exhaustion of the external sector. Indeed, it was precisely the dynamism of this sector which favoured the process that, announced on 16 June 1951, preceded similar initiatives elsewhere in Latin America. Between 1951 and the signing of the Multilateral Treaty for Free Trade and Economic Integration on 10 June 1958, economic relations were conducted on the basis of short-term bilateral treaties limited to specific goods. The idea of a larger market itself had the programmatic and technical support of the United Nations Economic Commission for Latin America (ECLA/CEPAL), whose pioneering work emphasized the importance of regional planning and the role of the state. At this time both local commercial interests and the politically dominant groups in the various Central American republics favoured the objective of economic cooperation although they had little experience of it and were

---

[8] The value of production in El Salvador and Costa Rica is calculated in 1950 dollars; that of Honduras, 1948 dollars, and Nicaragua, in 1958 dollars. CEPAL, *Primero y segundo compendio estadístico.*

Table 3.3. *Intra-Central American exports: value (in millions of dollars) and percentage of total exports, 1950–87*

Year	Value	% of total exports	Year	Value	% of total exports
1950	8.5	2.9	1970	286.3	26.1
1951	10.7	3.2	1971	272.7	24.6
1952	10.4	2.9	1972	304.7	22.9
1953	11.0	2.9	1973	383.3	23.0
1954	13.4	3.3	1974	532.5	25.2
1955	13.0	3.1	1975	536.4	23.3
1956	14.9	3.5	1976	649.2	21.6
1957	17.6	3.8	1977	785.4	19.1
1958	20.9	4.7	1978	862.7	22.4
1959	28.7	6.7	1979	891.7	19.9
1960	30.3	6.9	1980	1,129.2	25.4
1961	36.2	8.0	1981	936.8	25.5
1962	44.7	8.7	1982	765.5	22.4
1963	68.7	11.7	1983	766.6	21.6
1964	105.3	15.6	1984	719.2	18.9
1965	132.1	17.4	1985	488.4	13.9
1966	170.3	20.4	1986	447.9	11.1
1967	205.6	24.0	1987	525.9	13.8
1968	246.9	26.1			
1969	250.1	25.7			

Source: SIECA, *Series Estadísticas Seleccionadas de Centroamérica* (Guatemala).

unsure as to how to proceed towards it. There is little doubt that the new groups that had come to control state power in the post-war era were far more open to such an enterprise than the landed oligarchy, which, looking primarily to the overseas market did not fully understand its possibilities. Thus political and ideological as well as economic factors converged to favour the signing of the 1958 treaty, which led to the General Treaty of Central American Economic Integration signed on 13 December 1960. The 1960 treaty established a free trade area for a period of five years, laid the basis for a customs union and introduced a series of fiscal, credit and service incentives that promoted the growth in intra-regional trade shown in Table 3.3.

If the original ideas proposed by CEPAL are compared with the final draft of the 1960 treaty, it is evident that several key features had been abandoned, particularly the notion of gradualism and reciprocity as a means by which to establish local industries within the five signatory countries according to a plan for the region as a whole. This shift reflected the interests and influence of the United States as much as those of Central American entrepreneurs. Both were willing to liberate commerce from all restrictions and to reduce the role of the state to that of a mere administrator of free trade.[9] The project of regional co-operation, which fell short of total economic integration, sought to counter the historical deterioration of the agrarian export model by providing employment to a growing supply of labour, raising national per capita income and the standard of living of the urban population, and reducing the external vulnerability that had been determined from the beginning by the nature of the dependent relationship with the world market. In the decade of the 1960s average annual growth of industrial production was in fact 8.5 per cent, almost double the growth rate of the GNP.[10]

It has been rightly said that the project of integration was, above all, a project for entrepreneurs. They were the ones who took direct advantage of it and the ones who in the course of daily events moulded it to suit their needs. Among these investors one must decidedly include North American capital. When we speak of entrepreneurs, we refer as much to businessmen as to a nascent industrial elite, little differentiated in social terms from the agrarian oligarchy. The programme of the 'common market' created an important industrial base without necessitating reforms in the countryside; in both conception and application it included a tacit agreement not to interfere with the great rural interests. According to some, the mechanism of building an economic space out of five small markets postponed the political task of reforming the old rural structure.

In sum, the common market project initially advanced rapidly because the governments agreed without major problems on the establishment of a common external tariff, abatements in taxes on local products, and the promulgation of laws to foment industry. These last created competitive little fiscal 'paradises' for foreign investment. As has been seen, the result

---

[9] In February 1959, Douglas Dillon, U.S. Assistant Secretary of State, 'put an end to the initial U.S. objections, identified Washington's requirements for regional trade in Latin America – the freest possible movement of goods, capital and labour – and moved rapidly to have these applied'. A. Guerra Borges, *Desarrollo e Integración en Centroamérica: del pasado a las perspectivas* (Mexico, 1988), p. 20. On the emergence and development of the Central American Common Market, see in particular SIECA, *El desarrollo integrado de Centroamérica en la presente década*, 13 vols. (Buenos Aires, 1973).

[10] CEPAL, 'Industrialización en Centroamérica 1960–1980', in *Estudios e informes de la CEPAL*, no.30 (Santiágo, 1983).

was an active zone of free trade, the emergence of industries which substituted imports on the most basic level of products for immediate consumption, and a hitherto unknown flourishing of transportation, insurance and other services linked to the growth of new industrial parks.

The programme of economic integration has been the object of eulogies and critiques that sharply contradict one another concerning its significance as a mechanism of growth and development. Today judgments can be made with the benefit of hindsight. During the 1960s the economic policies which sought to foment industry through this programme were successful within apparently inevitable structural limitations. At its peak, more than 85 per cent of the total value of intra-zonal exchange consisted of industrial goods, defined to include commodities for immediate consumption (beverages, food, shoes, shopwork and some textiles). The substitution of imports was, literally speaking, a substitution at the level of assembly, which meant that the co-efficient of imports rose parallel with the growth of industry, at an average rate of 25 per cent in the last five years of the decade. The use of imported capital goods, obsolete in their countries of origin, was novel and saved labour so the manufacturing sector did not utilize an excessive supply of labour. Finally, under the influence of North American policy, a competitive industry was essentially established in the hands of foreign capital, resulting in denationalization and new dimensions of financial dependence.

In the sixties the participation of the agricultural sector in regional production continued to decline, thus ratifying a historical tendency which started after the war. Accordingly, in the middle of the 1970s its share approached a little more than 30 per cent, but it absorbed 60 per cent of the economically active population and contributed about 80 per cent of extra-regional exports (foreign currency). Central American development manifested a cruel paradox; economic growth had always depended on the production and export of agricultural products, but social development in the countryside was sharply limited and contradictory. Agriculture had grown more rapidly than the Latin American average yet this did not improve opportunities for work or the standard of living of rural inhabitants, who are the majority of the population.

No dualist explication is pertinent in examining the modernization of the internal market economy in the hands of small, increasingly impoverished owners. The increases in exportable goods occurred above all in cotton and meat, especially in El Salvador, Guatemala and Nicaragua, and

Table 3.4. *Central America: Increase in volume of
agricultural production, 1950–4 and 1975–6 (in
percentages)*

	Total production	Food	Export products
Latin America	106	124	117
Costa Rica	143	130	142
El Salvador	136	116	188
Guatemala	250	254	309
Honduras	85	68	102
Nicaragua	199	148	337

Source: CEPAL, Cuadro 19, 'El Crecimiento Económico de
Centroamérica en la Postguerra', in 'Raíces y Perspectivas de
la Crisis Económica', *ICADIS,* no. 4:93.

sugar in Guatemala and Costa Rica. But the fact that a high percentage of
the agricultural population continued to receive low incomes meant that
the general process of dynamism created employment or generated income
for other sectors.

The Central American experience in industry as well as in agriculture
(and in general economic growth) provides a good example of how a rise
in wealth in societies with great social inequalities creates greater dispari-
ties. The 'trickle-down' theory has been a myth for many long years. It is
nothing but a wish or an academic hypocrisy. What actually happens is a
permanent 'competitive exclusion' in which the losers are always the
peasants. Agricultural dynamism undoubtedly changed the rural landscape; it modernized important agrarian sectors, creating an entrepreneurship distinct from the traditional image of absentee land-ownership.
On the other hand, the advance of agrarian capitalism caused the disappearance of the *mozo colono* (the peasant whose attachment to the land is
permanent) and substituted temporary agricultural labourers whose position as such is not influenced by whether or not they own a small piece
of land. This semi-proletarianization meant, above all, a relative but
increasing impoverishment. The phenomenon was particularly acute in
Guatemala and El Salvador. In Nicaragua, the displacement of the production of basic grain from the Pacific coast to the interior and its
replacement by cotton created a labour market formed by transient wage-
workers to the degree that the 'salarization' of the rural labour force was
complete by the sixties.

On the political plane the decade of the sixties witnessed repeated defeats of reformist movements of different signatures, expressions of a democratizing will which encouraged popular participation in parties, unions and elections. The failure of gradualist programmes illustrates the crisis of the oligarchical–liberal order, later to become completely bankrupt.

During the last years of the 1950s Latin America as a whole had experienced sluggish growth. The need to open up new channels of development through cooperation was signalled by the establishment of the Inter-American Development Bank in 1961. Concern over this issue was expressed at Punta del Este, Uruguay, in March 1961 immediately following the Kennedy administration's declaration of an Alliance for Progress to stimulate U.S.–Latin American co-operation through economic growth and political democratization in the wake of the challenge presented by the Cuban Revolution. Although the Alliance for Progress resulted in increased loans for Central America and provided greater legitimacy to the idea of agrarian reform and structural change, it also led to a rise in military aid, particularly for Guatemala and Nicaragua, and introduced the doctrine of national security, the concept of the 'internal enemy'. The result of this combination assigned to put brakes on the revolution in Central America was the fortification of counter-insurgent political–military structures and the complete absence of substantive reform.

The most concrete outcome of this set of external and internal conditions in the political arena was the emergence of profoundly repressive governments. These were, however, the result of a certain type of electoral opinion; they respected the alternation of executive power, but only within the narrow circle of military choices. The cycle of these 'facade democracies' began in El Salvador with the creation by the army of the Partido de Conciliación Nacional (PCN), created in the image of the Mexican Partido Revolucionario Institucional (PRI). Although the Mexican party had to some extent resolved the problem of legitimacy by holding periodic elections, and the problem of succession by naming, through secret mechanisms, the candidate who would win, the historical context was very different in Central America. The PCN was created in 1961 following the military coup that put an end to the reformist tendencies of a civil–military junta (1960) and the cautious modernization projects attempted by Colonels Osorio and Lemus (1956–60). This coup marked the installation of a new period of political monopoly by the army, which, in totally controlled elections, secured the election of Julio Rivera (1962–7), Fidel Sánchez (1967–72) and Carlos Humberto Romero

(1977–9). In Guatemala, a similar experience was established with the same sequence of a coup d'état (Colonel Peralta Azurdia, 1963), a constitutional assembly, a new constitution and presidential elections. First to be elected under this system was Julio César Méndez (1966–70) himself a civilian but leader of an essentially military government, which was subsequently controlled directly by officers: Colonel Carlos Arana (1970–4) and Generals Kjell Laugerud (1974–8) and Jorge Lucas García (1978–82). For more than sixteen years El Salvador and Guatemala lived under a military control characterized by the observance of legal formalities. The regimes tolerated limited opposition but only within the parameters of strict rules of the game; Congress was under the control of political forces closely tied to the army, and periodic elections were held in which the parties could elect representatives but not presidents, whose selection was always in the hands of the high military command. This experience was accompanied by a permanent demobilization of popular organization and a general depoliticization of political life parallelled by brutal repression against reformist and radical political forces. As a result of this the union movement, the university (professors and students), sectors of the Church and even the reformist parties themselves, which were temporarily allied with the army, and above all the peasants, were beaten down in a permanent and bloody manner.

The base of these regimes was a solid alliance with the business sector, the economic interests of which were assiduously promoted by official policy. To this was added the multiple support of the United States, which cannot be described solely as military and economic assistance since it also included important cultural and ideological elements within the framework of an explicit objective: security against counter-insurgency.

One result of this was the rejuvenation of the military institution, modernized and trained in special operations, covert activities, intelligence operations on a national scale, and so on, as if waging a war against an internal enemy, although this did not yet exist. Another consequence was the corporate consolidation of the business groups, which perfected their associations so meticulously that they became not only a powerful united pressure group but also a political force with a much higher level of aggressiveness with regard to their economic interests.

The years of this period were also characterized by intense social struggle and efforts to introduce reforms. Between 1964 and 1968 the first guerrilla war was started in Guatemala by a group of ex-rangers from the army after the failed military insurrection of 13 November 1960. Later they were joined by radical groups of students and urban workers and the communist Guatemalan Labour Party itself. The creation of the Thirteenth of November Movement and the Rebel Armed Forces (Fuerzas Armadas Rebeldes, or FAR) did not constitute a military challenge in the strict sense, but it undoubtedly expressed the profound popular discontent produced by the anti-peasant policies of the governments which followed the fall of Arbenz and the deception practiced on the reformist groups by the military coup of March 1963, which, as we have seen interrupted an electoral process and frustrated a democratizing project of institutional normalization.

The entry of the middle sectors into regional political life is an important phenomenon which is associated with the crisis of oligarchic domination in the sense that the latter exercised power on the basis of exclusion. The middle-class groups were not alone; in Central America they invariably favoured popular and union organization, party competition and universal suffrage. Also associated with the parties and organizations of the middle sector were a major intellectual and cultural renewal and the formation of a relatively modern 'public opinion'.

The history of Central America begins to change under these social and political influences, even when fraud – more in the counting of votes than in the elections themselves – preventive coups d'état and repressive violence underscored time and again the weaknesses of the democratic foundations. The electoral history of the region does not exhibit a continuous or ascendant progress, or irreversible phenomena of democratic affirmation.

In Honduras, Ramón Villeda Morales governed with a modernizing hand, re-established a bipartisan system and initiated changes which were always incomplete and backward despite the support of the Alliance for Progress. On 3 October 1963, weeks before the scheduled elections, a group of officers headed by Colonel Osvaldo López Arellano broke the law under unjustifiable pretexts and expelled the civilian president. This coup d'état inaugurated the epoch of full military intervention in politics, bringing Honduras into line with the rest of its neighbours. López Arellano had himself elected president by a constitutional assembly and was promoted to the rank of general. But he found he was facing the most important peasant mobilization in the history of Central America with the mass occupation of large tracts of land which were not only uncultivated but also held under very questionable terms of tenancy. The occupation of state and common lands often revealed them to be illegally possessed by large landlords. The dynamic of the agrarian 'invasions' was paralleled by the organization of several peasant federations whose importance in political life began to be decisive. To alleviate the pressures and the growth of conflicts in the countryside, López Arellano's government promulgated in 1967 a programme of land distribution which affected hundreds of Salvadoran families who lacked title to properties they had occupied in Southern Honduras for a long time.

No one has ever been able to identify the precise and immediate causes of the aptly called 'useless war' between Honduras and El Salvador which broke out in July 1969.[11] Abuses against Salvadorean peasants by the Honduran authorities doubtless occurred, more than 100,000 persons being expelled during a three-month period. Honduras itself suffered from a permanent and substantial commercial deficit with El Salvador as a result of the common market. A football game erupted into a riot, whose seriousness resides neither in itself nor even in the number of supposed deaths that occurred. The Salvadorean Army, which was the better equipped, invaded Honduras but only stayed seventy-two hours because of mediation by the Organization of American States (OAS) and U.S. pressure. The rupture of all relations between the two countries weakened the project of economic integration and established a focus of discord that remained unresolved, owing as much to the frontier's lack of definition as to the continual aggravation of nationalist sentiment. The event seriously affected the structure of Salvadoran exports, 20 per cent of which were directed at the Honduran market, and created a serious demographic-economic problem in the poorest rural region of El Salvador, which was already over-populated.

The event pointed up serious social deficiencies in Honduras, especially injustices in the countryside and the futility of internal conflict. López Arellano first tried for re-election on the pretext that the dangers of a new war required his presence, but he finally accepted a project of national unity proposed by the army, COHEP (Consejo Hondureño de la Empresa Privada) and the union movement. A bipartisan solution was attempted in the Colombian style by electing a president but splitting government posts in a fifty-fifty ratio between the Liberal and National parties. Thus, in June 1971 the aged lawyer Ramón Ernesto Cruz of the National Party was elected. The formula for national reconciliation did not, however, work, more because of the political backwardness of the traditional

---

[11] See Thomas P. Anderson, *The War of the Dispossessed: Honduras and El Salvador 1969* (Lincoln, Neb., 1981); and D. Slutzsky et al., *La Guerra Inutil* (San José, 1971).

caudillos than the senile ineptitude of the President. On 4 December 1972, López Arellano again shattered the feeble legal order that had been achieved, breaking the army's word in open contempt of the bipartisan project for stability.

Nicaragua was no stranger to the reformist projects of the decade, both the kind that adopted a more or less ritual aspect, such as those inspired by the Kennedy Administration and those originating from a real desire for change. The death of President Schick in 1966 created the possibility that the temporary interruption in the Somoza family's control of the government would develop into a longer period of democratic competition. However, the historical opportunity was lost with the electoral imposition of Anastasio Somoza Debayle, who also retained his post as head of the National Guard. At the beginning of 1967, before his election, the most important popular mobilization ever seen in the country was staged to repudiate the electoral fraud in advance. It was especially true of Nicaragua at this time that the geopolitical priorities of the United States favoured neither a civil government nor a democratic perspective.

Nicaragua's history was marked by frequent pacts between the two 'historical' parties, Somoza's Liberals and the Conservatives. In 1972 one of these pacts took place, when Dr Fernando Aguero, the leader of the Conservatives, agreed to act as a member of a triumvirate established to preside over the country until new elections in 1974. The earthquake of December 1972 interrupted this arrangement and must be mentioned because its strictly telluric effects were as disastrous as the ones it had on the political situation in Nicaragua. In the first place, it revealed the internal weakness of the National Guard, which was incapable of maintaining order when what was required was not merely physical repression; it made a shambles of the formality of the bipartisan 'triumvirate', because Somoza immediately had himself elected co-ordinator of the National Emergency Committee, which monopolized international aid and converted itself into an arbitrary executive power; it revealed in a dramatic manner the misery of the popular masses and mobilized them, especially in the city of Managua, where manifestations of external solidarity never reached. These conditions did not prevent Somoza from having himself elected president of the country again in 1974.

The history of this period in Costa Rica follows a more civilized path. The 'war' of 1948 and the succeeding events were the Costa Rican way of settling accounts with the old coffee oligarchy, with its political culture and with the need for institutional and economic modernization. This design was carried out in the context of the new conditions that emerged in the 1950s with the rise of the PLN and the renewed strength of an important generation of politicians and intellectuals, many of whom were militants of this social-democratic current. The force of political tradition permitted the perfection of electoral mechanisms and extended to the construction of a state capable of stimulating growth and development. The governments of Figueres (1953–8), Mario Echandi (1958–62), Francisco Orlich (1962–6), José Joaquín Trejos (1966–70), José Figueres again (1970–4) and Daniel Oduber (1974–8), evince a pendulum swing in the exercise of the electoral process, which included two victories – in 1958 and 1966 – for the opposition.

The renewal of Costa Rican society included the reconstruction of a state which defined its relation to the economy and the society by promoting a social economy where the influence of the market was less disorderly; it strengthened small-and medium-sized businesses, especially in agriculture; it democratized credit, not only with the nationalization of the banks but also with the creation of local juntas to administrate them. There was a broadening of the varieties of coffee and an increase in state control of basic services like electricity, transportation, insurance, telephone service, ports and other services, all through a regime of autonomous and semi-autonomous institutions. The education sector was expanded. Entry into the Common Market, which had been delayed by a persistent isolationist viewpoint on the part of economic groups, permitted a gradual development of light industry that become important by the 1970s. Since Costa Rica is a poor country one can draw the elementary conclusion that it prospered because it had been well administered.

In the middle of the seventies the political crisis completed a long cycle of gestation when it took the form of an armed and massive challenge to the institutional order in Nicaragua, Guatemala and El Salvador. The roots of the crisis were long and diverse and varied from one country to another. What they had in common was a dominant agrarian class which allowed the exercise of power to reside with the army and in the permanent violence of the state rather than in the search for consensus and respect for legality. The emotional and political difficulties of negotiation were compensated for by relative success in the capacity for repression; the struggle for the economic surplus was almost always resolved in the political field rather than in the marketplace despite the liberal roots of the economic culture of the landed class.

If it is true that the crisis was the last expression of a will for social change, the forms it assumed in each country can be described as the collapse of the weak channels of legal participation. In societies that are blocked politically, subordination, whether lived or imagined, is superior as a mobilizing force to economic exploitation as such. Class contradiction is inferior to the rotation between what may generically be termed dominant and subordinate groups. This explains the multi-class character of the social forces expressed through the guerrilla organizations. Nothing could have been farther from the *focos* of the 1960s than these genuinely poly-class coalitions, carriers of a will for radical change more through the experience of mobilization used than through the ends vaguely inscribed in their programmes. The social heterogeneity stimulated a multiple convergence of ideology, which explains this original combination of the theology of liberation, radical Jacobinism and various breeds of Marxism.

The features just described reflect the social and ideological nature of the Frente Sandinista de Liberación Nacional in Nicaragua (FSLN); the Frente Farabundo Martí para la Liberación Nacional (FMLN) in El Salvador (composed of four political–military organizations); and the Union Revolucionaria Nacional Guatemalteca (URNG) (comprising three different-sized organizations).[12] The activity of these guerrilla organizations began with varying degrees of success. The Guatemalan groups had the precedent of 1964–8, but they only appeared between 1975 and 1978 as a strongly established force in the central and northeast highlands. In El Salvador the organizations formed successively between 1971 and 1976, when they began to perform propaganda actions armed with great audacity. In Nicaragua, the FSLN was formed early (1961) but, battered by repression and lost in secrecy, it only became a real presence in December 1974.

The political crisis was neither characterized uniquely by manifestations of armed violence nor confined strictly to guerrilla actions. Before and after peak insurgent activities there were mass mobilizations of unprecedented magnitude, such as the march of the miners in Ixtahuacán (November 1977); the general strike of public employees in 1978; and the agricultural-workers' strike on the south coast (February 1980) in Guatemala. The occupation of the Labour Ministry, the seizure of churches and the general strike of 1977–8 in El Salvador, and the great urban uprisings together with the general strikes that followed the assassination of Pedro

---

[12] These designations correspond to the ones adopted by the unitary organizations after 1979, and not 1977–8.

Joaquin Chamorro in Nicaragua between 1978 and April 1979 reflect the same process. For the most part these mass phenomena were linked to military resistance, although in Guatemala and El Salvador the height of mass mobilization did not coincide with the timing of guerrilla offensives, which would have doubtless provoked a crisis of major, perhaps definitive dimensions. The political crisis reached its breaking point in July 1979 in Nicaragua, almost coinciding with the beginning of the most severe economic crisis since 1930, which punished the Central American societies with the worst breakdown in their republican history.

At the end of the 1970s, it was evident that Central American society and economy were different from what they had been immediately after the Second World War. Between 1950 and 1980 GDP rose from $1,950 million to $7,520 million (1970 prices) and the population from 8 million to 21 million inhabitants. Social stratification diversified in several senses, some calling it more segmented and others more pluralistic. The urban population jumped from 15 to 45 per cent of the total during this period and became 'rejuvenated' in the sense that the age group between fifteen and twenty-four years increased proportionally, especially in the cities. Manufacturing activity also grew from 14.6 to 24.1 per cent of GDP, and in general the productive apparatus was modernized. National integration was achieved through networks of roads, electricity and telephone services, and in 1980 the region had a physical level of communications greatly superior to conditions even ten years earlier as a result of large investments in the infrastructure. Intra-regional commerce reached $1.1 billion in 1980.

Similar advances were not registered in the provision of services in education, labour, health and housing; even those important changes which did take place had specific social limitations due to the excessive sway of the laws of the marketplace, against which the laws of the state were especially weak in Guatemala, El Salvador and Honduras. The dynamic of modernization was limited and exclusive, and social and cultural lag was sometimes concealed by statistical rhetoric or by the urban image of a small group of modern constructions. The traditional structure was not altered but had a modern structure superimposed on it, producing contradictory effects and delays in social change in general.

In the seventies economic problems had begun to escalate as a result of the rise in the price of oil in 1973, the beginning of disorder in the international financial market in 1974, swings in the prices of Central

American export products and several droughts and three natural catastrophes of major proportions in Honduras, Nicaragua and Guatemala. The real growth rate was still an average 5.6 per cent a year, but external vulnerability kept rising (from 16.2 to 27.3 per cent of the co-efficient of imports). From 1981 negative rates of growth were generalized throughout the region.

Import substitution industrialization had experienced a growing dependence upon imported primary materials, intermediate components and capital goods. When the economic crisis took the form of reduced loans, diminished investment and falling prices for agro-exports, the industrial sector was directly affected, prompting a crisis in intra-regional trade (see Table 3.3). Nonetheless, the project of economic integration had been positive in that it stimulated industrial production, modified economic structures, encouraged employment, altered patterns of production and consumption and, above all, introduced new economic, political and cultural linkages between Central Americans. Some of these were later evident in the declarations of the regional presidents at the end of the 1980s (Esquipulas II, August 1987, and Costa del Sol, February 1989) which produced important initiatives towards the solution of political conflict.

Even before the full scope of the post-1979 economic crisis was evident, the situation was exceptionally poor for the majority of the population of Central America. Toward the end of the seventies, 20 per cent of the highest income groups earned more than 50 per cent of the wealth, with substantial variation among countries (see Table 3.5). The social breach widened and the number of Central Americans living in situations of extreme poverty was growing.[13]

After thirty years of steady, though sometimes erratic, growth in per capita income there was a collapse of socially incalculable magnitude. At the end of 1985, per capita income in Costa Rica and Guatemala was the same as it had been in 1972; in Honduras, it had dropped to 1970 levels; and in El Salvador and Guatemala, to 1960 and 1965 levels respectively. External factors unleashed the crisis but their effects were multiplied by the backwardness of the existing social structures and, above all, by the factors that produced profound political instability.

The 1970s produced new economic problems, most particularly the first major oil price rises in 1973 but also the erratic price of coffee and other regional exports. As a result, great importance was given to the use

[13] M. E. Gallardo and R. López, *Centroamérica: la crisis en cifras* (San José, 1986), table 1.8, p. 158.

Table 3.5. *Central America: distribution of income and levels of income in 1980 (in 1970 dollars)*

Strata	Costa Rica		El Salvador		Guatemala		Honduras		Nicaragua	
	Percent	Mean Income	Percent	Mean Income	Percent	Mean Income	Percent	Mean Income	Percent	Mean Income
Poorest 20%	4.0	176.7	2.0	46.5	5.3	111.0	4.3	80.7	3.0	61.9
30% below the median	17.0	500.8	10.0	155.1	14.5	202.7	12.7	140.0	13.0	178.2
30% above the median	30.0	883.0	22.0	341.2	26.1	364.3	23.7	254.6	26.0	350.2
Richest 20%	49.0	1,165.2	66.0	1,535.5	54.1	1,133.6	59.3	796.3	58.0	1,199.8

Source: CEPAL, based on official figures of the countries.

of foreign capital, largely in the form of loans, to avoid fiscal deficits and enable governments not only to compensate for the lack of local investment but also to respond to periodic droughts and a series of natural catastrophes (the Nicaraguan earthquake of 1972; Hurricane Fifi, which hit northern Honduras in 1974; and the Guatemalan earthquake of 1976). By the time of the second major 'oil shock' in 1979 Central America was already registering the impact of the international recession through the fall in its growth rate, which had historically stood at around 5 per cent per annum. Oil purchases, which had accounted for 2.7 per cent of imports in 1970, rose to 21.1 per cent in 1982, accelerating inflation and producing a veritable disaster in the current trade account. Capacity to meet payments on a debt which rose from $895 million in 1970 to $8,456 million in 1980 and $18,481 million in 1987 was radically diminished as exports encountered major problems, interest rates rose and the trade balance worsened. The prospects for development were gravely impeded on every front.[14]

The regional economic recession of the 1980s was most acute in Nicaragua and least pronounced in Costa Rica, which was the only country to register any growth (in 1985–6). Structural adjustment and stabilization measures designed and effectively imposed by the IMF were begun in Guatemala in 1981 and soon applied to all the countries with varying degrees of failure. The objectives of reducing inflation, controlling the fiscal deficit and improving the balance of payments were not even met at the cost of stagnation, this being assured by a fall in imports of more than 50 per cent and sharp cut-backs in government expenditure. U.S. preoccupation with this serious situation led to the establishment of the bipartisan Kissinger Commission and, in 1984, to President Reagan's 'Caribbean Basin Initiative'. However, the tariff concessions under the CBI had little impact on the overall economic crisis in the region.

The fall of the Somoza family dictatorship in July 1979 was a moment of historical proportion in the Central American crisis for a variety of reasons. In the first place, it was not only the end of a long familial, military and hereditary dictatorship but also produced the collapse of a form of bourgeois power and a weak state constructed on very personalized social and economic bases, which made use of non-national, traditional and

---

[14] Inter-American Development Bank, *Progreso económico y social en América Latina* (Washington, 1980–7).

violent political resources. Second, it was the political and military victory of a broad multi-class coalition of national character with a programme for the cultural, moral and political regeneration of a backward society. Third, it was the downfall of a conspicuous expression of U.S. foreign policy expressed through aid and military protection; the power resources of Somoza's dictatorship were basically North American. Finally, it constituted a revolutionary form of resolving the crisis which affected El Salvador and Guatemala, where massive insurrectionary movements were also preparing the way for a take-over of power.

At the beginning of 1980 the combined guerrilla groups in Guatemala amounted to more than 8,000 fighters, with non-fighting civilian support including about 250,000 persons in the over-populated indigenous zones of the central and northeast highlands. The mobilization of the indigenous peoples was the most outstanding feature of the crisis because it raised the question of ethnic-national revindication and, in effect, constituted the largest indigenous revolt since the era of the conquest. In El Salvador the first guerrilla organization grouped in the FMLN included more than 4,000 armed men, a level of organization and discipline superior to that of their counterparts in Guatemala, and a qualitatively different implantation in the population, not least because they were fighting against an incompetent and corrupt army. If they had not immediately received U.S. assistance in massive proportions, the armed forces in El Salvador would have been incapable of resisting the popular insurrection.

The results of the civil wars have been different. In both cases the internal war was the historical result of the 'oligarchical way of conducting politics' and of the deep class divisions within society. The counter-insurgency operations were directed with a 'crusading spirit' against the infidels. The offensive of the Guatemalan army (1981–2) did not annihilate the guerrillas, but it forced them to retreat to their former areas while physically destroying 440 indigenous villages, killing 75,000 peasants and producing a population displacement that affected between 100,000 and 500,000 people. Operation 'Victoria 82' was an act of genocide that destroyed the material and social bases of the indigenous culture. In El Salvador, the FMLN launched its final offensive in January 1981, which failed but did not prevent its consolidation in important zones of the country.

In the midst of these contradictory military outcomes there was an inevitable crisis of the 'facade democracies' based on periodic elections and the consolidation of a counter-insurgent state structure. The crisis occurred first in El Salvador and then in Guatemala. In both cases it began within the army and demonstrated the difficulties of maintaining an alliance in which the military was the axis of power. The coups, against General Romero in El Salvador (October 1979) and General Lucas García in Guatemala (March 1982), opened up a period of successive illegal changes which moved in the direction of transferring power to the political parties. In this 'twist of the fist' they were forced by the pressure of North American policy to 'civilize' the power structure, to present a democratic image based on the reinforcement of a political centre that the counter-insurgency itself had debilitated or destroyed.

Between the first civil–military junta in El Salvador and the last (October 1979 to December 1980), the Christian Democrats had gained strength while in 1982 the banker Alvaro Magaña was installed as provisional president. This was the period in which the North American presence consolidated itself firmly as the most important factor in political power. The U.S. Senate urged the 'legalization' of power and elections were called for a constitutional assembly (March 1982); to everyone's surprise the poll was won by a coalition of parties to the extreme right headed by Roberto D'Aubuissón, although the Christian Democrats emerged from the election as the single most important party in the country. Successive coups d'état in Guatemala (March 1982 and August 1983) also led, under the somber leadership of General Mejía Victores, to constitutional elections (June 1984). The results were similar; a strong representation of rightist parties, yet the Christian Democrats possessing the largest relative majority. There was an orderly retreat of the army to the barracks that looked like nothing less than a military defeat. In May 1984 and December 1986 the Christian Democrat leaders José Napoléon Duarte (El Salvador) and Vinicio Cerezo (Guatemala) were elected president in polls without fraud and with practically no abstentions. For the first time in fifty-five years in El Salvador and twenty years in Guatemala, civilian opposition candidates were victorious.

The democratizing wave in the midst of crisis, war and open U.S. intervention also came to Honduras. The erosion of the military governments who controlled the country from 1971 (López Arellano, 1971–5; Juan Alberto Melgar Castro, 1975–8; Policarpo Paz García, 1978–80) was substantial. The political weariness of the Honduran colonels did not originate in the duties of war. López Arellano and two ministers were denounced on charges of flagrant bribery, after his own government had imposed, for the first time in history, taxes on the production and export of bananas. His successors practised a policy of cautious reform, but they, too, found themselves involved in scandals concerning contraband trafficking in drugs and emeralds as Honduras was converted into an appendix of the international Colombian corruption. Yet as the Sandinista revolution imposed, against its own intent, the militarization of Honduras and the liberalization of the government, there took place a now inevitable Central American ritual of holding constitutional elections to draw up a new Magna Carta and thus hand over the reins of power with a clear legal conscience.

The elections of April 1980 opened the way for the return of civilian government, the return of the Liberals and the reinforcement of U.S. influence. The Carter administration greatly assisted the victory of Roberto Suazo Córdova, and U.S. presence gained a new regional dimension directly articulated against the Sandinista government of Nicaragua.

The strategy of national security reinforced by the obsessive vision of the recently elected President Reagan transformed Honduras not only into a 'sanctuary' for mercenary Nicaraguan bands organized by the U.S. administration, but also into an offensive establishment which included several military bases and a site for the aggressive staging of an endless series of joint manoeuvres that began in 1982. Honduran society has been disturbed in many ways by becoming the seat of various non-Honduran armies and having been converted into the aggressive military axis of U.S. foreign policy. The survival of civilian power under these conditions is only one of the basic formalities which are convenient to maintain and has little to do with the internal crisis of the Honduran army, especially in the Consejo Superior de las Fuerzas Armadas (CONSUFFAA), which forced Generals Gustavo Alvarez Martínez and Walter López out of power and the country.

During the government of Suazo there was a serious confrontation between the executive branch, Congress and the judiciary, which was resolved through a mediation by the army, the unions and the U.S. embassy. Another conflict, internal to the traditional parties and resolved by the intervention of these same entities, produced a virtual end to Honduran bipartisanship. In the presidential elections of 24 November 1985 there were three candidates from the Liberal Party and two from the National, the candidate who had the most votes (Rafael Leonardo Callejas) losing, and Azcona de Hoyo, who had 200,000 votes less, winning because his count was inflated by the votes of all the other Liberal candidates. At any other point in the history of the country, a crisis like this would have rapidly provoked the intervention of the armed forces.

In Costa Rica institutional stability has remained undisturbed, in spite of the fact that the conservative government of Rodrigo Carazo (1978–82) tried to follow a liberal economic policy. Contrary to what was expected, Carazo refused to negotiate with the IMF and permitted the use of the territory by the opposition to Somoza in Nicaragua,. The elections which followed allowed the return of the PLN under Luis Alberto Monge (1982–6), but the economic crisis was already starting to bite and North American policy tried to convert Costa Rica into a key part of its anti-Sandinista offensive. Monge's government acted in a contradictory manner as a result of economic helplessness, U.S. pressure and the general move to the right in Central American politics. In January 1984, Monge proclaimed the permanent, unarmed and active neutrality of Costa Rica, but in August he got rid of important officials who belonged to the progressive wing of his party in order to facilitate the activities of the anti-Sandinistas in the country.

In 1986, in spite of the difficulties experienced in social and economic policy, the PLN won the elections again under the leadership of Oscar Arias in the party's first experience of running against a conservative opposition organized into a party with a clear ideological identity. As this movement consolidated itself, the country would enter into a U.S.-style political model, one of bipartisan structure in which there is little programmatic difference between the parties. The forces of the left in Costa Rica entered a crisis and lost their already slim electoral support.

The most important aspects of Arias' government were his effort to bring the country to a position of effective neutrality and his initiative to achieve peace after calling a meeting of presidents in February 1987 to which President Daniel Ortega of Nicaragua was not invited. Successive efforts culminated in the Esquipulas II meeting held in Guatemala in August 1987, where the five Central American presidents signed a document calling for regional pacification. This proposal received the support of the countries of the Contadora group active since 1983 in favor of peace (Mexico, Panama, Colombia and Venezuela), those belonging to the Support Group (Brazil, Argentina, Peru and Uruguay), the European Parliament, and four of the five permanent members of the United Nations Security Council. Yet it was stubbornly opposed by the Reagan administration, which continued to support and promised increased aid to the mercenary groups known as 'contras'. On this count, the conduct of the United States seemed to be the greatest obstacle to the eventual pacification of Central America.

The situation in Nicaragua in this period was characterized by a set of novel features, some positive, some negative, presented as a total reorganization of society with intensive support among the mobilized masses, directed by the FSLN yet in the framework of respect for private property, aside from that of the Somoza family. The FSLN proclaimed as basic principles a mixed economy, political pluralism and nonalignment; on the basis of these they created a state economic sector and an alliance (the Frente Patriótico Revolucionario, or FPR) which included various parties situated to the right and the left of the FSLN.

Notwithstanding these intentions the dynamic of change in Nicaragua has been limited, on the one hand by the economic and political backwardness of the country and, on the other, by the fierce opposition of the Reagan administration. With the indefinite suspension of bilateral assistance by the United States (February 1981) and the blocking of loans by international organizations (starting in November 1981) the country's economy was slowly paralysed by the difficulty in replacing parts as well as intermediate goods, capital and raw materials. This position illustrates the economic backwardness of a society tied by a thousand strings to the U.S. economy. The collaboration of the private sector was made difficult by these deficiencies provoked from the outside, because the market lost its total decision-making sovereignty in exchange for a growing intervention by the state, because of a new attitude on the part of workers, and even because a bourgeoisie without an army, as one civilian leader noted, is not a bourgeoisie. The fundamental behaviour of the economic system passed from a type consistent with the principle of accumulation to a system for the satisfaction of basic needs of the population and one in which businessmen speculate, decapitalizing their companies and taking resources out of the country.

On the political front, the FSLN constituted itself as a party and the mass organizations formed a broad base of social support through the Comités de Defensa Sandinista. A field of opposing forces formed immediately on which the Consejo Superior de Empresa Privada (COSEP) and the upper levels of the church hierarchy played complementary leading roles. In December 1981, the U.S. National Security Council took the initiative in organizing the so-called contras and initiating a chain of covert actions (including the mining of Nicaraguan ports).

The victories in the political and social arenas were not matched by the development of the economy, which dramatically signalled the limits of the new arrangement. Between the efforts at national reconstruction and the defence of territory a few important events occurred: the conflictive development of the ethnic question (with the Miskitos of the Atlantic coast), in which mistakes made at the beginning later gave way to an original and daring solution: reclaimed autonomy. Political pluralism was put to the test in a backward political culture; the first elections, held in November 1984, were won by the FSLN with 67 per cent, a constitutional assembly was elected and Daniel Ortega voted in as president. Even before the elections it was evident that the opposition lacked a meaningful alternative policy with respect to the revolutionary project. The Reagan administration granted substantial aid – of public and of private origin – to a counter-revolutionary military force which was better organized and financed but which had no ability to govern. The effect of the 'low-intensity war' was nevertheless successful. The Sandinistas secured effective military victories against the contras, especially in 1983–7, but the exhaustion of the economy imposed by the mobilization of resources, the gradual destruction of co-operatives, bridges, schools, numerous civilian deaths, and so on, created an extremely difficult situation for the Sandinista government.

This set of political and economic phenomena constituted a renewed example of the enormous difficulties a small country has to face in order to win national independence and overcome under-development. The war imposed on Nicaragua only made this task more difficult, bringing with it social sacrifice for the population. Agrarian reform and other measures in the countryside contributed to the alteration of social structure and the partial alleviation of production difficulties, but the economic crisis affecting the rest of the countries of Central America afflicted Nicaraguan society in greater measure, and obliged its leaders to seek peace as a condition for any kind of internal arrangement.

By now the Central American crisis possessed an important international dimension involving new actors as U.S. hegemony in the region began to manifest some signs of decline. Significantly, the only diplomatic initiative to endure was the Contadora Accord signed in January 1983 by Mexico, Venezuela, Colombia and Panama in an effort to secure a framework for negotiating the end to the various and distinct conflicts. Although the peace of the region as a whole was never placed in significant danger, the conflicts in Nicaragua and El Salvador did pose a major threat to stability and democracy. In August 1987 the Central American presidents signed the Procedures for the Establishment of a Firm and Lasting Peace in Central America, generally known as the Esquipulas II agreement. This accord led to a series of meetings to consider and resolve the socio-political crises of the region and improve inter-governmental relations. Thus, conversations between the Nicaraguan government and the Contra rebels were held at Sapoá in February 1988, and a year later the FMLN guerrillas made wide-ranging proposals for the cessation of the civil war in El Salvador. Neither initiative seemed remotely likely at the time Contadora was set up. The inauguration of a new president in Washington in January 1989 increased hopes of a more modulated U.S. policy towards the region. Nevertheless, the solution to the crisis depended above all on the political initiatives of the Central Americans themselves.

4

GUATEMALA SINCE 1930

Although the 108,900 square kilometres of its landmass made it smaller than both Nicaragua (148,000) and Honduras (112,000), Guatemala had in 1930 the largest population in Central America (1.7 million). The capital – Guatemala City – had, however, a population of only 130,000 and the country's second city, Quezaltenango (20,000), was no more than a modest provincial town. With a minuscule manufacturing base and an export sector almost completely dominated by coffee (which generated 77 per cent of export revenue) and bananas (13 per cent), Guatemala conformed to the stereotype of a backward plantation economy in which large commercial farms coexisted with a patchwork of small peasant plots dedicated to subsistence agriculture and the provisioning of a limited local market in foodstuffs. On the eve of the depression, GDP stood at $450 million, making Guatemala's economy considerably greater in size than those of the other states of the isthmus. (The second largest was that of El Salvador, with a GDP of $227 million; the weakest, that of Nicaragua with a GDP of only $129 million.) Moreover, Guatemala still retained much of the regional political influence it had enjoyed under Spanish colonial rule, when it was the seat of civil and ecclesiastical administration as well as the centre of commerce for the entire area. Hence, although it was a decidedly small and impoverished state compared to most in Latin America, and was dwarfed by Mexico to the north, Guatemala remained the strongest power in Central America, which constituted a distinct political arena just as much in 1930 as it does today.

The assumption of the presidency by General Jorge Ubico in February 1931 following an election in which he won over 300,000 votes against no competition began a thirteen-year regime of personalist dictatorship that both mirrored those of his regional peers – Maximiliano Hernández Martínez in El Salvador, Tiburcio Carías Andino in Honduras and Anastasio

Somoza in Nicaragua – and continued Guatemala's long-standing tradition of prolonged autocratic government. This had begun early in the republican era under Rafael Carrera (president from 1838 to 1865). Carrera, a man of humble origins, had vigorously upheld a backward-looking conservative order in the face of precipitate liberal efforts to abolish the colonial restraints on the free market. The political and economic chaos that attended independence and the Central American Confederation established in its wake had produced a strong backlash not only among Guatemala City's powerful merchant class, under threat of losing the effective regional monopoly upheld by the Spanish crown, but also among the bulk of the peasantry, which rapidly found the paternalist controls of the colonial regime preferable to the atheism and high taxes associated with liberal 'modernization'. Carrera could, therefore, give his rule what might now be called a populist character, his platform of clericalism, defence of the Indian community, and conformity with the social norms of the imperial order receiving wide-spread support from the mass of the population. Correspondingly, following the collapse of the Confederation, which was irredeemably tarnished as a liberal artefact, the dictator sought to revive Guatemala's control over the weaker states of the isthmus. This had now necessarily to be imposed by occasional intervention rather than through any formal channels, but Carrera was remarkably successful and the country's political influence extended to the Colombian border throughout the middle decades of the nineteenth century.

In the 1870s the advent of coffee and a second generation of liberalism that promoted it through policies of free trade and opening up the market in land – primarily that of the Church and the Indian communities – witnessed no reduction in Guatemala's ambitions as a regional power. The great liberal *caudillos* Justo Rufino Barrios (1873–85) and Manuel Estrada Cabrera (1898–1920) not only preserved an absolutist regime at home but also meddled incessantly in the affairs of their neighbours, although the scope for this was greatly diminished by the consolidation of the United States as a regional power at the turn of the century. Following the overthrow of Estrada Cabrera, who had long been supported by Washington in return for his generous concessions to the United Fruit Company (UFCO) that began to cultivate bananas early in the twentieth century, there was a brief and disorganized attempt to revive the union of Central America, but this came to nought in an era when U.S. marines were being regularly dispatched to impose order in neighbouring states such as Honduras and Nicaragua. If Guatemala remained Central America's strongest power, its political elite could no longer reproduce the regional authority and privileges held under the colony or, indeed, during most of the nineteenth century. The outlook bred of this past was increasingly turned inward, manifesting itself above all in the social arrogance of a provincial seigneurial class.

The rise of U.S. hegemony was not the only factor in Guatemala's introversion. While the oligarchy could afford to harbour ambitions to the south, it viewed its large northern neighbour Mexico with considerable apprehension. Immediately after independence the Mexican General Augustín de Iturbide had made an abortive attempt to take control of the isthmus, and although Mexican liberalism had been welcomed by many of the elite in the 1870s, ideological affinity never erased a residual suspicion about expansionism and, as evidenced by the secession of Chiapas in the 1820s, even annexation. Such a jealously guarded political identity on the part of the white and *ladino* upper classes was greatly fortified by the Mexican Revolution, which traumatized the Guatemalan landlords and sharply curbed any efforts to reduce the authority of the military or relax a particularly rigid social system determined as much by racism as by the demands of the plantation economy. Thus, although the 1920s witnessed a degree of intra-oligarchic dispute and a number of challenges to the contracts conceded to the United Fruit Company, the short-lived regimes of Generals José María Orellana (1921–5) and Lázaro Chacón (1926–30) did not indulge opposition to nearly the same degree as elsewhere in Central America. Ubico's rise to power was as firmly based on his support for United Fruit, the only fruit company operating in Guatemala as well as the single most important representative of U.S. interests and largest employer of waged labour, as it was on his suppression of popular discontent in the wake of the crash of 1929 when he was Minister of War.[1] The economic crisis, it should be noted, had provoked an outbreak of popular mobilization in Central America, and particularly in that region of El Salvador bordering on Guatemala, summoning up fears of a Mexican-style revolt. Hence, although social order was disrupted to a quite modest degree in Guatemala, Ubico experienced little difficulty in gaining oligarchic support for his policy of harsh repression that limited upper-class political life as well as subordinating the lower orders.

---

[1] Details of contracts signed by UFCO and the Guatemalan government are given in Alfonso Bauer Paiz, *Cómo opera el capital Yanqui en Centroamérica: el caso de Guatemala* (Mexico, 1956). This highly polemical text reflects the depth of feeling generated by the company's activities in the late 1940s and early 1950s.

The absence of a system of open and competitive politics within the Guatemalan landlord class, such as the system tenuously established elsewhere in the first decades of the twentieth century, may largely be attributed to the country's large Indian population – some 70 per cent of the total population in 1930 – and the tendency of debt peonage – the principal mechanism for providing coffee plantations with seasonal labourers from the highlands – to strengthen the coercive characteristics of the central state. Although the tasks of engaging more than 100,000 workers for the harvest and then guaranteeing their arrival at the *finca* were technically undertaken by independent *habilitadores* (money-lenders) who dispensed cash advances for local fiestas and when the surplus of corn was low, in both law and practice the state was committed to supporting this system, upon which depended both the country's staple export and general social control in the countryside.[2] The fact that the great bulk of migrant workers came from the eight densely populated 'Indian' departments of the western highlands placed particular importance upon the control of the *jefes políticos* (regional executive officers) of these zones, but even in those areas, such as Alta Verapaz, where plantations had been established in the midst of dense peasant settlement and drew much of their labour force from the locality the *finqueros* depended upon a much higher degree of state support than was the case in El Salvador or Costa Rica. Moreover, at the time Ubico took power German planters concentrated in Alta Verapaz produced more than half the national coffee crop and yet had not converted this economic power into political authority to the extent achieved by their peers in the other two countries. Ubico, who had served as *jefe político* in Alta Verapaz and often enjoyed less than harmonious relations with the local land-owners, was by no means a puppet of the coffee bourgeoisie, although he sought throughout his regime to provide it with optimum conditions during a period of recession. At the same time, he continued Estrada Cabrera's policy of full co-operation with the United Fruit Company in making generous concessions of land and tax exemptions about which both coffee planters, prejudiced by the company's effective monopoly over rail transport and manipulation

---

[2] For a contemporary account of relations in the countryside, see Chester Lloyd Jones, *Guatemala Past and Present* (Minneapolis, 1940). Over the last two decades theoretical and historical work on rural labour relations has advanced significantly. The best historical overview is given in David McCreery, 'Coffee and Class: the Structure of Development in Liberal Guatemala', *Hispanic American Historical Review* 56, no. 3 (1976), and 'Debt Servitude in Rural Guatemala, 1876–1936', *Hispanic American Historical Review* 63, no. 4 (1983).

of freight charges, and the small but burgeoning urban middle class expressed some discontent.

Although Ubico maintained the formalities of a liberal democratic system and even resorted to a further election as well as to a referendum in order to confirm constitutional changes that enabled his continuation in office, he permitted no opposition candidates, scarcely ever convened his cabinets, and employed a formidable secret police force to invigilate not only the population at large but also the army, upon which his power ultimately depended. The jailing of radical activists and the execution of their leaders in 1932 was facilitated by a 'red scare' easily conjured up in the wake of the abortive peasant rebellion across the border in western El Salvador. No less decisive, however, was the regime's repression of more traditional opposition in 1934, when the device of a discovered 'assassination plot' was employed to eradicate the last vestiges of dissident organization with the loss of several hundred lives. On this basis Ubico was able to outlaw all civic organization independent of the government – including the Chamber of Commerce – command large numbers of votes, direct a hand-picked and compliant Congress, and personally undertake the daily supervision of the state, a task greatly assisted by his enthusiasm for the radio and the motorcycle, which made him a much more ubiquitous autocrat than suggested by subsequent literary depictions of the culture of the dictator during this epoch.[3] In other respects Ubico's ability to give full rein to personal eccentricity – such as a proclivity for providing the populace with advice over the airwaves and in the desultory press on issues from cooking to musical taste and mechanics – corresponded more directly to the bitter whimsicality of unencumbered power projected by novels of the genre established by the Guatemalan Miguel Asturias, whose *Señor Presidente* (1946) was in fact modelled on Estrada Cabrera. These activities were also authentic political devices, serving to maximize the potential of personal authority. Over time, of course, both human frailty and the inexorable political logic that places the requirements of collectivities over those of individuals undermine such systems, but for a dozen years Ubico was able to supervise Central America's largest nation-state without significant challenge while lacking either the decisive military victory obtained by General Martínez in El Salvador or the fulsome backing given by the United States to Somoza in Nicaragua. Insofar as it did not derive from such a profound rupture with existing patterns of

[3] Sec Kenneth J. Grieb, *Guatemalan Caudillo: The Regime of Jorge Ubico* (Athens, Ohio, 1979).

government, Ubico's regime was perhaps less remarkable than those of his regional counterparts.

In responding to the economic crisis the Ubico government was far from inactive, seeking to protect the agricultural system and the socio-ethnic structures upon which it rested by a degree of innovation as well as conservation. Between 1927 and 1932 the value of coffee exports fell from $34 million to $9.3 million, and the value of banana exports dropped barely less precipitously. Annual average growth of GDP collapsed from 5.4 per cent in 1920–4 to minus 0.6 per cent in 1930–4 as a result of the decline in world prices, producing great difficulties for coffee farmers, for whom the payment of cash advances to seasonal labourers constituted a major item of expenditure. As plantation wages were cut and prices of basic grains tumbled, peasant farmers became less responsive to the mechanisms of debt-based seasonal labour at a time when economic logic required greater export volume and thus an expanded harvest work force. Predictably, Ubico defaulted on the external debt, left the gold standard but retained the quetzal's parity with the dollar, which was to last until 1984, and reduced state expenditure by 30 per cent in order to avert a progressive fiscal crisis. His response to growing difficulties in agriculture was to transform the principal mechanism for labour supply by abolishing debt peonage – an act undertaken with full exploitation of its 'progressive' and 'democratic' implications – and replacing it in 1934 with what was a far more extensive and directly coercive system based upon the obligation for all those who farmed less than approximately 3 hectares to work between 100 and 150 days a year on the *fincas*. The number of peasants classified by the new decree as 'vagrants' was sufficiently large not only to make good the loss of indebted labourers but also to provide a ready supply of workers for the *corvée*, with which the state undertook an ambitious road-construction programme. At the same time, Ubico bolstered legal protection for landlords, by granting immunity for all crimes committed in defence of property, and he replaced the traditional system of indigenous mayors, who had hitherto co-existed with *ladino* local authorities and received state recognition, with that of centrally appointed intendents. This latter initiative undoubtedly reduced indigenous autonomy and further prejudiced the position of communal culture, which had been under pressure since the liberal revolution of 1871 and the emergence of the coffee estate. On the other hand, it was not an unambiguous assault upon Indian society because the new authorities sometimes proved more resistant to landlords' demands than had Indian leaders, the requirements of the *finca* being balanced by an evident need to protect the subsistence economy upon which it depended for labour and food crops at the same time as the two competed for land and control over resources.

Ubico directed these policies with enough paternalist patronage of the indigenous population to persuade some students of his regime that he enjoyed appreciable popularity among the peasant masses. This is to be doubted. It is nevertheless true that, despite a slow but steady expansion of the frontier of the agro-export plantation, subsistence agriculture remained relatively buoyant after the initial impact of the depression through to the 1950s when the growth first of cotton and then cattle ranching renewed pressure on peasant plots without providing compensatory opportunities for waged labour. In this respect the stagnation of the economy caused by the depression offered a degree of protection for Indian society and the peasant economy (and as under the Carrera dictatorship in the middle of the nineteenth century this coincided with conservative rule). At the same time, the denial of autonomous organization and the enhanced demands on labour through the vagrancy law amounted to more than negotiated and incremental exactions within a traditional division of social and racial power. When Ubico fell in 1944 these were among the first measures to be reversed in the name of democracy, and even after the counter-revolution of 1954 they could not be restored.

As elsewhere in Central America, the Second World War weakened the dictatorship. In economic terms Guatemala was somewhat protected in that Ubico had for some time been reducing commercial ties with Germany because the Nazi regime insisted upon paying for coffee in Askimarks (which could only be exchanged at face value for German goods), while trade with Britain was very modest indeed. The 1940 Inter-American Coffee Agreement provided a guaranteed U.S. market at modest but acceptable prices for the country's primary staple, and the decline in banana exports was to some degree off-set by cultivation of the strategically important crop *abaca* (hemp). At the same time the Guatemalan State received considerable revenue from the management of the extensive coffee estates and other property (nationalized in 1944) of the German nationals Ubico had deported at the start of the war. However, the rapid fall in imports caused by the conflict soon reversed the gradual decline in consumer prices witnessed in the late 1930s. And the middle class, which was particularly prejudiced by war-time inflation, was exposed for the first time in a dozen years to democratic ideals inextricably associated with the Allied campaign. The dictator's sycophantic press could not fully suppress this important external influence, and yet the *caudillo* was unable and unwilling to accept the political consequences of the 'geographical fatalism' that had underpinned his declaration of war on the Axis powers whose ideologies and regimes he so admired. In June 1944, when confronted with street protests by the students of San Carlos University demanding the free election of faculty deans and the rector, Ubico belligerently declared, 'While I am President I will not grant liberty of the press nor of association because the people of Guatemala are not prepared for democracy and need a firm hand'.[4] By this time, however, his regime was gravely threatened not only by the students but also by the bulk of the middle class of the capital and, most critically, by junior army officers dissatisfied with incompetence and corruption in the upper echelons of the military as well as with a broader sense of social stagnation. The students' demonstrations at the beginning of June were met with predictable police repression but over the following weeks they returned to the streets, encouraged by the success of their Salvadorean counterparts in removing General Martínez, clear signs that the Ubico regime no longer had U.S. support, and popular backing for increased demands that extended first to complete university autonomy and then to liberty of the press and association. On 24 June the UN Charter was read to the crowd at a public meeting and a petition was presented to the president signed by 311 distinguished public figures; together these proved sufficient to persuade the ailing autocrat that it was time to stand down.

Ubico's departure from power was precipitate but not the result of a decisive revolutionary moment; he was able to pick out a member of his lacklustre entourage, General Federico Ponce, to replace him and ensured ratification of the succession by Congress. The peasantry did not intervene significantly in these manoeuvres; a few compliant or confused groups manipulated by the authorities endorsed Ponce's accession to power. The working class was still very small, lacked trade unions and desisted from independent action. Even the middle class, which had headed the campaign against Ubico, displayed every sign of being somewhat taken aback by its rapid success, for which there was no obvious next step or political leadership. Prolonged authoritarian government had left a political vacuum. However, the resolutely personalist nature of the dictatorship also deprived the new regime of great authority, political skill or a clear mandate beyond sustaining an *'ubiquismo* without Ubico'. Despite the temporary advantages

---

[4] Quoted in Carlos Samayoa Chinchilla, *El Dictador y Yo* (Guatemala, 1950), p. 176.

gained by conceding the principal demands of the students and sheer relief at the dictator's removal, there was only limited potential for such a policy succeeding for more than a few months; its demise was hastened by Ponce's ineptitude in calling elections in October and then declaring himself the winner with more votes than had been cast. This was, under the circumstances, no more plausible than Ubico's refusal in June to make any concessions to the students. It prompted the junior officers to rebel against a regime that lacked any popular following and was further weakened by the disorganized ambitions of the military old guard.

The password of the military rising of 20 October was *'constitucion y democracia'*, and its leaders – Majors Francisco Arana and Jacobo Arbenz – took the bold step of distributing weapons to civilians supporters, thereby averting the possibility of a popular anti-militarist movement feared by the officer corps. Such an initiative converted a regular military coup, eventually won by dint of a fortuitous artillery hit on the capital's arsenal, into a much broader movement, although at no stage over the following ten years did the military lose its leading role in the management of the state. The rising of October was to all intents and purposes a continuation of the demonstrations of June; it obeyed the logic of the moment in yielding a junta – Arana, Arbenz and a lawyer, Guillermo Toriello – that proclaimed itself strictly provisional and called for free and fair elections for the presidency and a constituent assembly.

The revolt of October 1944 opened a singular decade in Guatemalan political history, the character of which is perhaps better captured in the phrase 'ten years of spring' than in the term 'revolution' that is more often applied to the governments of Juan José Arévalo (1945–50) and Jacobo Arbenz (1951–4). Notwithstanding differences in style and a critical deterioration of relations with Washington following the onset of the Cold War from 1948, those two administrations combined cautious economic reform with an unprecedented extension of civic and political freedoms, and in this respect they may legitimately be distinguished from all subsequent governments, which resorted to authoritarianism and resisted all but the most minimal adjustments to the economy. As a result, the 'revolution', which is remembered by a small but significant portion of the population, has often been viewed in Manichaean terms, by the left as a solitary experience of freedom and progressive redistribution, and by the right as a sobering example of ingenuous reform acting as hand-maiden to communism.

Returning from a decade of exile in the provinces of Argentina, the mild-mannered schoolteacher Arévalo rapidly won broad support for his candidacy because he appeared to personify all the civic virtues associated with democratic government, and his lack of party affiliation was viewed as a distinct advantage for the formation of a broad progressive coalition. Arévalo's victory, by 255,000 out of a total of 295,000 votes, in the elections of December 1944 was the product of individual popularity and the 'bandwagon' effect of his artfully managed campaign rather than any clear ideological preference on the part of the electorate. Although both he and Arbenz sought to build a government on the Mexican model, the reform period was characterized by the relative diffusion and weakness of the political organizations that supported it. Drawn principally from the middle class and promulgating programmes that differed in tactics rather than strategy within a common acceptance of the broad reformist and nationalist motifs of the day, forces such as the Frente Popular Libertador (FPL), Renovación Nacional (RN) and the Partido de Acción Revolucionaria (PAR) were marked by personalism and a failure to establish an organized mass membership, thereby accentuating the role of the presidents who were obliged to negotiate their disputes and orchestrate their deputies. Although there existed throughout this period a more radical current seeking to remedy the absence of a national Communist Party, a great many of the young parliamentarians elected to the new constituent assembly supported Arévalo's idealist 'spiritual socialism' that combined recognizable motifs of secular mysticism with the less familiar cadences of a developmentalist vision:

We are socialists because we live in the Twentieth Century. But we are not materialist socialists. We do not believe that man is primarily stomach. We believe that man is above all else the will for dignity. . . . Our socialism does not aim at an ingenious distribution of material goods or the stupid equalization of men who are economically different. Our socialism aims at liberating man psychologically and spiritually. . . . The materialist concept has become a tool in the hands of totalitarian forces. Communism, fascism and Nazism have also been socialist. But theirs is a socialism which gives food with the left hand while the right mutilates the moral and civic virtues of man.[5]

Such statements heralded a primarily political rather than economic programme for change, but recognition of a spectrum of civil liberties in a country with such entrenched divisions determined by race as well as class prompted significant shifts in the balance of social and productive power.

[5] Juan José Arévalo, *Escritos políticos* (Guatemala, 1945), p. 199.

The charter of 1945 abolished the vagrancy law of 1934 and thereby terminated an epoch in which rural labour had been organized by predominantly extra-market forces. At the same time, suffrage was extended to many of those who had been obliged to work under such systems, but the democratic impulses of the assembly fell short of giving the vote to illiterate women, an appreciable sector of the population. In keeping with the juridical mode of the time, property was declared to be inviolable but also subjected to a 'social function' that provided for state intervention, the prospect of which was viewed with some alarm by landlords already disturbed by Ubico's appropriation of German-owned estates. Building on the Constitution, the new government provided for the holding of municipal elections in 1946 – a measure of considerable importance for a rural population deprived of autonomous organization for over a decade and generally more concerned with local government than that at a national level. The following year Arévalo consolidated the constitutional freedom of association by introducing a comprehensive labour code – the first in Guatemala's history – which guaranteed trade unions and collective bargaining, and established legal norms for working conditions. The prevailing political atmosphere precluded an outright opposition to this singular measure, and it is significant that resistance to it on the part of the United Fruit Company was sustained in the name of democracy because the code permitted the organization of rural workers only on estates of at least five hundred employees when at least fifty wished to form a union, of whose members 60 per cent had to be literate. In imposing such sharp restrictions the government had sought to inhibit wide-spread unionization in the countryside – in 1948 only eleven rural unions were registered – but such an evidently conservative policy was not unjustifiably construed by United Fruit as prejudicial to the interests of large commercial concerns. Under pressure from the company and the State Department, Arévalo amended the statute in 1948, thereby laying the basis for far more extensive rural organization over the following years, although outside the banana enclave this rarely assumed the form of a coherent and politically unified mass movement.

No less apprehensive about the possibilities of the urban labour force trespassing the bounds of legal ordinance, Arévalo was quick to close down the Escuela Claridad, a workers' night-school run by Marxists who were unable to establish an independent Communist Party because the Constitution prohibited parties with international links. In both this measure – repeated in 1950 – and his assiduous insistence that the restrictions as well as the liberties stipulated by the labour code and the constitution be respected, the cautious President was fully supported by Colonel Arana, who, as commander of the army, sought to restrict advances made by the popular movement and often had to be held back from acts of direct repression as workers began to make use of the unfamiliar tactic of the strike. Nonetheless, under Arévalo this was far from a frequent occurrence, and the general rise in wages in both town and countryside derived principally from government initiatives and a generally buoyant economy now liberated from the constraints of the war and benefiting from the postwar rise in the coffee price.[6]

Such conditions amounted to a great deal less than a boom in production, but they did assist the cessation of coerced labour and provide the new regime with some leeway for its reforms under what remained remarkably tight fiscal constraints. Thus, while Arévalo established a state credit institute – one of the very few measures taken in the name of development that antagonized neither local entrepreneurs nor the U.S. government – his personal enthusiasm was much more consistently directed towards precisely those 'spiritual' advances made possible by changes in the superstructure rather than the substance of Guatemalan society. As leader of a 'teachers' revolution', the President found a ready constituency for promoting education, nearly doubling the number of schools and teachers from the level obtaining in 1940. The number of books published and level of cultural activity in the towns underwent a marked increase, while brave attempts were made to establish rural literacy campaigns. By 1954 the standard of education in Guatemala still remained the lowest in the region, those who had been taught to read and write being numbered in the tens rather than hundreds of thousands. Yet even such limited advances had a discernable effect within the country, not least in augmenting the quantity of state employees, whose work increasingly included economic management as the apparatus of intervention – incarnated in the establishment of a central bank – was slowly expanded.

Arévalo's attachment to the cause of Central American union was not uncharacteristic of Guatemalan civilian politics, within which this ideal was more prominent than elsewhere in the isthmus, yet it proved no more successful in practice than had previous endeavours. Support for the 'Caribbean Legion', a loose grouping that held no brief for political union but

---

[6] A sense of both the objectives and the limits of Arévalo's programmes may be gleaned from Leo A. Suslow, *Aspects of Social Reform in Guatemala 1944–1949* (New York, 1950).

congregated non-Communist opponents of dictatorial regimes from the Dominican Republic to Nicaragua, was altogether more adventurous in its open patronage of insurrectionary activity. The Guatemalan president's assistance of the force of José Figueres in the Costa Rican civil war of 1948 contributed to the downfall of less a reactionary autocracy than a Communist-backed populist regime, but it had the effect of temporarily stemming the growing sentiment in Washington that his government was excessively indulgent towards domestic radicals who were exploiting democratic liberties in their campaign against U.S. interests. However, Arévalo's involvement in the Legion's affairs greatly antagonized Colonel Arana, whose ambitions to succeed him as president had been rebuffed by the major parties. Arana had accumulated considerable power by virtue of almost constant activity in suppressing ill-organized revolts against a government with which he felt decreasing sympathy as the impetus of social change began to parallel that of political adjustment. In July 1949, Arana, by this stage widely suspected of preparing his own coup, was assassinated while returning from an inspection of a cache of arms confiscated from Arévalo's colleagues in the Caribbean Legion. Culpability for this act that removed the principal conservative challenger to the reformist regime was generally ascribed to Arana's colleague Arbenz, who despite being Minister of Defense was notably sympathetic to the left and the prospect of introducing more substantial economic reforms. Although responsibility was never proved, a significant portion of the military reacted to Arena's death by staging a major revolt that was defeated only with considerable loss of life and the calling of a general strike by the Confederación de Trabajadores de Guatemala (CTG) under a predominantly Marxist leadership.

The collapse of this rebellion shifted the locus of political activity to the left precisely at a time when the Cold War was setting in and the initial anti-dictatorial impetus evident elsewhere in the region had been brought to a halt. Until 1950, U.S. investment in Guatemala had been increasing, and although the State Department harboured reservations as to Arévalo's ability to control the radical forces within the parties that supported him, Washington's pressure was exercised with a modicum of restraint. With the effective disintegration of the domestic forces of conservatism, the growing strength of the left within the unions, and control of the military in the hands of an officer pledged above all to nationalism but also amenable to its radical interpretation, the U.S. government shifted its policy from lack of sympathy – evident in the arms boycott of 1948 – to increasing aggression, which was by 1953 to take the form of concerted destabilization.[7] This progression was certainly influenced by the replacement of the Truman administration by that of Eisenhower, which saw the promotion to Secretary of State and Director of the CIA of the brothers John Foster and Allen Dulles, who had worked for and held shares in the United Fruit Company, the largest U.S. company in Guatemala. Nevertheless, the State Department was scarcely less preoccupied under Dean Acheson than under Foster Dulles for although the transfer of office from Arévalo to Arbenz in March 1951 introduced policies that thirty years later would seem unremarkable in their objectives of limiting foreign control of infrastructure and effecting a modest redistribution of land, these were undeniably accompanied by greater popular activity and a discernable fortification of the left as the political forces of the middle class that had underwritten the revolution of October 1944 began to lose momentum and break up.

The first signal of a more consolidated approach towards the inequities of land tenure was given by Arévalo's 'Law of Forced Rental' of December 1949. This statute provided for provisional usufruct of some uncultivated lands, but in practice it affected the less densely settled *ladino* zones of the south-east rather than the Indian departments of the *altiplano*. It was under Arbenz, a less 'political' but more administratively resolute leader than Arévalo, that both the policies of the Guatemalan government and the political objectives of some of its supporters became a matter of considerable concern for the United States and the local landlord class. Since its foundation in 1944 the CTG had been led if not comprehensively controlled by the left, personified by Víctor Manuel Gutiérrez, the confederation's secretary-general. This leadership had provoked a split in the union movement, with the more cautious sectors of the urban labour force led by the railway workers clinging to their mutualist past and resisting an overtly political role. However, in October 1951 the undoctrinaire and skilful Gutiérrez achieved a rapprochement, and the establishment of the Confederación General de Trabajadores de Guatemala (CGTG) effectively represented a unification of what was still a very small labour movement – there were fewer than 100,000 members in 1954 – under radical leadership. In 1950 the disparate rural unions were unified in the Confederación Nacional Campesina de Guatemala (CNCG), and on the eve of the counter-

[7] Although written from a deeply anti-communist stance, Ronald M. Schneider, *Communism in Guatemala* (New York, 1958), contains a wealth of detail on the left between 1944 and 1954.

revolution claimed to have 345 affiliates with 256,000 members. Although such figures may have been inflated, they were not grossly exaggerated, and despite the very diffuse and informal character of the rural *sindicatos,* they combined with the communal-based *uniones* to confront the landlords with an unprecedented organization of a peasantry that had hitherto been contained with only very irregular interruptions by a deft mixture of patronage and coercion. The leaders of the CNCG were largely from the middle class, profoundly suspicious of the Marxists heading the urban movement, and in no sense could be described as the 'Bolshevik menace' so often perceived by the large land-owners. However, shortly after the establishment of the CGTG, Gutiérrez was able to reach a tactical accord with the rural leadership largely as a result of the small Communist vanguard having settled its often heated internal disputes and accepted the need for an agrarian reform of a non-collectivist character. Gutiérrez had been at loggerheads over this and other critical issues with José Manuel Fortuny, the leading ideologue of Guatemalan communism and architect of the tactic of 'entryism' inside the Partido de Acción Revolucionaria from 1947. As a result, the small caucus of Marxists had been debilitated for a number of years, and its divisions were not fully healed until the constitutional difficulties of public registration were finally resolved in the formation of the Partido Guatemalteco de Trabajo (PGT) in December 1952. Recognition of this party by the Arbenz government was seen in the United States as tantamount to an official imprimatur of communism, but the organization's militants never exceeded two thousand in number; of these, none served in the cabinet, fewer than half a dozen held senior posts in the civil service and a similar number won seats in Congress. The influence of the PGT derived largely from its members in the leadership of the trade unions, but even there programmatic positions were frequently sacrificed for tactical ends and were in any case rarely out of keeping with a much broader accord between supporters of the government that the primary tasks of the 'second phase' of the revolution lay in an agrarian reform and the curbing of United Fruit's control over the economy, principally through its monopoly of rail transport to the Caribbean port of Puerto Barrios. Although the PGT was anathema to Washington by virtue of its very existence, a more profound threat was seen to lie in the fact that it formed part of a broad consensus that was prejudicial to U.S. corporate interests in the country and thus constituted a challenge to the security of the hemisphere. Insofar as the retiring, upright Arbenz also formed part of this consensus he was doomed to be depicted as a Communist 'stooge'.

It was less from the tenets of communism than from the recommendations of the World Bank's 1950 mission to Guatemala that the Arbenz
government drew many of its economic initiatives, including the building
of a public road to Puerto Barrios to compete with UFCO's railway and the
construction of a state-owned electricity plant that also stood to prejudice
U.S. corporate interests. The World Bank's report had mentioned but not
made detailed proposals for an agrarian reform, which was recognized to
be a major and politically sensitive undertaking. The statistical evidence
of an exceptionally regressive pattern of land tenure presented in the 1950
census indicates why the government felt obliged to confront this issue
and why a constituency for change existed well beyond the ranks of the
radical left: some 2 per cent of the population controlled 74 per cent of all
arable land, whereas 76 per cent of all agricultural units had access to only
9 per cent; 84 per cent of all farms possessed an average of less than 17
acres and 21 per cent less than 2 acres when 9 acres was considered the
minimum size for the sustenance of an average family. The government's
response to this extreme imbalance resulting from the consolidation of the
coffee estates and banana plantations was to adopt a distinctly moderate
proposal for redistribution with the explicit objective of developing capitalist agriculture through building up the 'small farmer' sector while protecting most commercial enterprises. Arbenz himself was scrupulously clear
on this point: 'It is not our purpose to break up all the rural property of
the country that could be judged large or fallow and distribute the land to
those who work it. This will be done to latifundia, but we will not do it to
agricultural economic entities of the capitalist type'. Accordingly, Decree
900 of 27 June 1952 left untouched farms of under 90 acres and provided
extensive exemptions to units over this size on which significant cultivation was undertaken. Moreover, nearly a third of the land distributed was
already owned by the state, so that although a total of 918,000 acres were
expropriated and distributed to 88,000 families in two years, less than 4
per cent of all privately owned land beyond that controlled by UFCO was
affected by the measure. In the highland departments only 15 per cent of
19,000 farms were touched by the law, and there is little evidence of any
reduction of harvest labour supply as a result of it.

Although it drew its inspiration far more from the models of Italy and
Mexico than from those of the Soviet bloc, aimed at increasing production
rather than curbing the power of the landlords, and left almost the entire
productive base of the large commercial farmers untouched, the reform
was resolutely boycotted by the oligarchy. The first concerted effort since

the Liberal revolutions of the 1870s to adjust the terms of landed society in Central America was viewed as a major assault upon the political culture erected upon the traditional hacienda, already under threat from independent peasant organization. Yet, if the opposition of local land-owners proved to be largely ineffectual and failed to coalesce into a signifi-cant political campaign despite the support of the Church, that of UFCO – the enterprise most severely affected by dint of the extent of its uncultivated lands – ultimately proved to be decisive. Over 15 per cent of the 650,000 acres owned by UFCO were marked for expropriation with compensation to be paid in line with the company's 1950 tax declaration. According to the government the corporation was owed $627,527 at $2.99 per hectare, whereas UCFO rapidly gained Washington's support for its counter-claim for $15.8 million, at $75 per hectare. Arbenz's refusal to pay such a sum served to accelerate the U.S. government's campaign against his regime, which could now be attacked for a tangible infraction rather than on the basis of questionable ideological comport-ment. Such a policy was greatly assisted by UFCO's ability to harness much of the U.S. press to its cause, but this itself was not without official assistance and was underpinned by the shrill political atmosphere of the McCarthy years, during which the logic of anti-communism was all-encompassing.

By the end of 1953 the efforts of the State Department to organize a diplomatic offensive against the Arbenz government had effectively been overtaken by plans for direct destabilization and a CIA-supported interven-tion, although these were throughout provided with diplomatic backing through less than subtle tactics in the Organization of American States and the United Nations. Furthermore, at no stage did 'Operation Success' deviate from its objective of presenting Guatemalans as the principal protagonists and Central Americans as the sponsors of the overthrow of a government that, albeit elected, internationally recognized and manifestly in control of national territory and institutions, was now unreservedly denounced as a pawn of Moscow and a threat to the security of the Western Hemisphere. The fact that this government had no allies in Central Amer-ica and could not even rely upon a sympathetic neutrality from states such as Mexico, Argentina and Bolivia, which still followed a foreign policy discernably autonomous from that of Washington, gravely debilitated its diplomatic defence under conditions in which direct physical resistance was broadly accepted to be beyond serious consideration. In this respect Washington's decision to remove Arbenz may be contrasted with the not dissimilar campaign against the Sandinista government in Nicaragua thirty years later.[8]

Notwithstanding this unprecedented situation on the international plane, the final intervention come close to failure. The 'invasion' of Guatemala from Honduras in June 1954 by a group of insurgents led by Colonel Carlos Castillo Armas and supported by air-raids on the capital undertaken by CIA pilots was only assured success once the army, which had hitherto maintained a neutral stance despite reservations as to Arbenz's policies, halted its initial resistance, obliged the President to stand down, and entered into negotiations with U.S. envoy John Peurifoy over the terms of succession. The signal failure to distribute arms to the population, absence of viable preparations for resistance on the part of the unions, and extensive disillusionment within the middle class ensured that once the high command had taken this step further opposition to the intervention was destined to fail. Moreover, so great was Washington's political investment in the operation that it was not prepared to parley for long over its outcome. Castillo Armas, the firm U.S. candidate for the presidency, was installed in office within a matter of weeks and began to oversee a comprehensive dismantling of the reforms of the previous decade.

During the year following the counter-revolution of 1954 there was plenty of evidence, particularly in the countryside, of a 'settling of accounts', but there was more encarceration, exile, politically motivated unemployment and removal of civil liberties from the supporters of the 'revolution' than actual bloodletting. The level of violence cannot plausibly be compared with that prevalent both in Guatemala and elsewhere in Latin America in the 1970s. Nonetheless, the intervention of 1954 opened a new political era in which almost every effort at reform was stalled by a ruling class determined to protect its economic and social interests at any cost. Both the decade-long experience of mounting radicalism and final reliance upon U.S. intervention in order to eradicate it marked the political instincts of the landlords and an emergent urban bourgeoisie; the culture of anti-communism was seeded before the example of Cuba affected the rest of the region. Not only did the civilian elite set its face determinedly against concessions to the lower orders of society but the army, first traumatized

---

[8] The intervention of 1954 and its background are surveyed in detail in Stephen Schlesinger and Stephen Kinzer, *Bitter Fruit: The Untold Story of the American Coup in Guatemala* (New York, 1982), and Richard Immerman, *The CIA in Guatemala: The Foreign Policy of Intervention* (Austin, Tex. 1982).

and then thoroughly purged, undertook a marked and apparently irreversible shift away from its anomalous acquiescence in social change and became increasingly dedicated to the tasks of coercive control. Within fifteen years it had not only regained many of the attributes of the pre-1944 epoch but was also demonstrating itself to be one of the more efficient and most ruthlessly repressive bodies in the subcontinent. At the same time, both the urban working class and the peasantry were subjected to a decisive political and organizational defeat from which there was evidently no easy or rapid means of recovery. The regional and international balance of power in 1954 was such that these developments appeared neither greatly surprising nor, indeed, as decisive as later transpired to be the case. Two Guatemalan generations were to grow up in a political atmosphere that certainly registered distinct, sometimes important, shifts in character but always remained determined by the trauma of the 'liberation'/'counter-revolution', which was consolidated in an extended and predominantly authoritarian regime.

Castillo Armas abolished both the CGTG and the CNCG, cancelled most of the provisions of the 1947 labour code, and withdrew legal recognition from 553 trade unions while devolving nearly all the expropriated private lands to their original owners and handing over control of the state electricity plant to the very U.S. company against which it was originally designed to compete. Generously funded by Washington, which between October 1954 and the end of 1957 disbursed aid of $100 million when grants to the rest of Latin America amounted to less than $60 million a year, the new president argued that an election would be excessively costly. However, because he was the leader of a movement championed as democratic he permitted the holding of a referendum over acceptance of his appointment, gaining the support of 95 per cent of the vote. The extreme vagueness of his 'New Life' programme for social harmony served to veil increasing division within his supporters, unified by opposition to Arbenz rather than agreement over a positive post-revolutionary platform. Yet not even the quasi-fascist convictions of his principal adviser Mario Sandoval Alarcón, leader of the extremist Movimiento de Liberación Nacional (MLN) for the following two decades, could persuade Castillo Armas to run the risk of reverting to coerced labour or formally cancelling the extension of suffrage. Such measures were justifiably viewed as unnecessary for the eradication of the reformist legacy once the agrarian reform and labour organizations had been suppressed. However, the absence of a coherent project on the part of the regime beyond these objectives provoked increased discontent within the *'liberacionista'* camp, and in October 1957, Castillo Armas was killed in an internal feud. Such a precipitate termination of what the United States had presented as a model government was further complicated by the resort of the defunct president's party to fraud in order to thwart the electoral challenge of General Manuel Ydígoras Fuentes, a traditional conservative whose Redención party artfully projected the need for social and political rapprochement, questioned the extent of U.S. influence, and combined appeal to the middle class with the prospect of a return of the old guard of the Ubico era. The electoral fraud of 1957 was to presage resort to this tactic over the ensuing years, but this time it was employed without the backing of the military, which still retained misgivings as to *liberacionista* ambitions and intervened, with U.S. support, to guarantee a new and relatively honest poll the following year, from which Ydígoras emerged as the clear victor.

The Ydígoras administration (1958–63) halted the ascendency of the arriviste hardliners of the MLN, but it did so in the form of a disorganized, backward-looking enterprise increasingly accused of corruption and soon revealed to be both unwilling and incapable of restoring a genuine openness to political life. Ydígoras, once Ubico's Minister of Public Works, undoubtedly possessed more of the flair of a *caudillo* than had Castillo Armas and initially reaped the benefits of his predecessor's repression of the left and the unions, but neither the auctioning of the *fincas nacionales* nor the stentorian revival of claims on Belize (British Honduras) were sufficient to consolidate a new political order at a time when coffee prices were falling and the Cuban revolution was providing an example of radical change comparable to that snuffed out in Guatemala just five years previously. Lacking any consistent ideological appeal and heavily dependent upon distribution of the spoils of office to sustain its supporters, the regime was confronted by a diverse but growing opposition within its second year in power. In November 1960 a military revolt by junior officers dismayed at the degree of official venality and still influenced by the Arbenz period was subdued without great difficulty, but two of the ringleaders – Captain Marco Antonio Yon Sosa and Lieutenant Luis Turcios Lima – failed to surrender and were by 1962 embarked upon a guerrilla campaign in which their military skills were adjusted to the strategy of Castro's insurgents. The establishment of the Fuerzas Armadas Rebeldes (FAR) in three fronts in the eastern departments of Zacapa and Izabal opened a guerrilla war that subsequently underwent important shifts in intensity, strategy and popular support but persisted for over two decades as a central factor in Guatemalan political life. Under Ydígoras this development was still of minor political and strategic importance, but it served to harden the attitude of the military hierarchy as the regime attempted its own electoral fraud – winning all but two seats in the congressional poll of 1961 – and then lost the support of many of these deputies, which obliged the President to rely upon a military cabinet in order to cow the parliamentary opposition and provide protection against the rising number of coup threats.

It is likely that this hybrid administration would have collapsed well before the end of its official term were it not for the growth resulting from the establishment in 1960 of the Central American Common Market (CACM), within which Guatemala was the most powerful economy, and the support given to incumbent elected governments by Kennedy's Alliance for Progress. However, as the elections of 1963 drew near, Ydígoras increased political tension by tabling an income-tax bill and thereby alienating a bourgeoisie notable for its ability to resist even the most minimal fiscal demands. (Guatemala was the last Latin American country to introduce such a tax and would for the next twenty years maintain the lowest level of taxation in the Western Hemisphere notwithstanding repeated attempts by civilian and military regimes to increase both direct and indirect levies in order to expand the capacity of the state.) Moreover, the President appeared, after an initial period of judicial skirmishing, to acquiesce in the candidacy of the still exiled Juan José Arévalo in the approaching poll. Since neither the governing party nor the MLN seemed set to win a majority and several new centrist organizations quickly rallied to Arévalo's cause, this move was perceived by the military high command as little less than tantamount to the restitution of the reform era, a prospect made all the more threatening by the expansion of FAR operations in the countryside. The absence of discernable opposition by Washington to the resulting overthrow of Ydígoras by his Minister of Defence, Colonel Enrique Peralta Azurdia, suggested that even under Kennedy the U.S. government was of the same opinion.

The Peralta Azurdia regime (1963–6) was in many respects a logical consequence of Ydígoras's resort to a military cabinet. It represented an effort by a now well-funded and progressively more confident institution to establish a stable system of political control in the wake of the excessive partisanship and incompetence of Castillo Armas and Ydígoras. Although the view of Peralta and his colleagues was that only the military possessed the capacity to mediate competing interests within the dominant bloc as well as guarantee discipline within the working class and peasantry, they did not seek an exclusively military regime. Instead, the Guatemalan officers took their model in part from the Mexican Partido Revolucionario Institucional (PRI) and in part from from the successful enterprise of their Salvadorean counterparts, whose Partido de Conciliación Nacional (PCN) had to all intents and purposes monopolized office since 1950 through a system wherein limited opposition and congressional representation by non-radical forces was tolerated but tightly controlled elections continued to return the official party to power. The success of the PCN derived in no small degree from the Salvadorean military's ability in the late 1940s to forestall an authentic reform movement of the Guatemalan type by incorporating some of its motifs into their own discourse. The potential for such a strategy was, therefore, much more limited in Guatemala itself, but in founding the Partido Institucional Democrático (PID), Peralta obtained the acquiescence not only of Sandoval's ultramontane MLN but also of the centrist Partido Revolucionario (PR), established in 1958 under Mario Méndez Montenegro, a former leader of the FPL and supporter of Arévalo. The comparably moderate forces of Democracia Cristiana Guatemalteca (DCG) and Francisco Villagrán Kramer's Unidad Revolucionaria Democrática (URD) remained outside this uneasy concordat, lacking the influence to pose a major challenge to it. As a result, they fell foul of the principal device designed to protect the new system enshrined in the Constitution of 1965 – the stipulation that no party could contest elections without previously submitting a list of at least 50,000 members that satisfied the government-controlled electoral commission. Although the traditional means of manipulating the contents of ballot boxes was never jettisoned, this precautionary measure gave the PID and the high command a legal procedure with which to organize an acceptable field of contestants. Hence, in the poll of 1966 only the PR was permitted to present a notionally reformist programme against the trenchantly anticommunist campaigns of the PID and the MLN, the party's inclusion owing less to a genuine breadth in the system – the PGT and almost all independent trade unions remained outlawed – than to the expectation that it would continue its informal alliance with the PID. However, the mysterious death prior to the poll of Mario Méndez Montenegro, whose policy of extreme caution had provoked a number of internal rifts, elevated his brother Julio César to the leadership of the PR and enabled the diffuse forces of the centre-left to close ranks behind a more resolute commitment to reform. Indeed, such was the conviction of Méndez Montenegro's campaign that even the leadership of the FAR endorsed his candidacy in the hope of a democratic opening, even though shortly beforehand the army had captured and executed a score of trade unionists and militants of the PGT – including Víctor Manuel Gutiérrez – with which the guerrilla was allied. Taken unawares by this rapid consensus behind the opposition candidate, the PID felt obliged to recognize Méndez Montenegro's victory, which they could not plausibly deny without jeopardizing the entire project of controlled constitutionalism at its first trial. However, the PR failed to secure an overall majority and the prospective president thus required the endorsement of the outgoing legislature dominated by the right. After a week of private bargaining and a public exchange of threats not witnessed in more than a decade, Méndez Montenegro finally obtained the acceptance of his victory by the MLN and the military. Yet the price he agreed for this – complete non-intervention in the affairs and operations of the army – soon proved to be so high that it effectively reduced his programme to little more than a collection of pious intentions, and his administration to a weakling apparatus incapable of restraining a military counter-insurgency campaign of considerable ferocity.

At the time of the PR's assumption of office in 1966 the guerrilla campaign in eastern Guatemala had been under way for four years and was at its peak.[9] Although the rebel forces were small – at no stage more than three hundred militants – and failed to generate a broad base of peasant support as prescribed by the *foco* theory held by their leaders, they provided an unprecedented challenge to the military and threatened to provoke the rural revolt constantly feared by the landlord class. Yet the guerrillas were not concentrated in the area of greatest Indian population and were badly divided over political strategy, with Yon Sosa, whose operations centred on Izabal, inclining to the advice of Trotskyists in establishing the breakaway MR–13 in March 1965 while Turcios maintained the original FAR on a more orthodox course in alliance with the PGT. Although the FAR had endorsed Méndez Montenegro's candidacy, it rejected his offer of an amnesty once it became clear that the new government could not restrain the operations directed against the guerrillas by Colonel Carlos Arana Osorio from his headquarters in Zacapa. Combining a scorched-earth policy of generalized repression with a U.S.-

[9] For a valuable survey of the guerrilla movement in the 1960s, see Richard Gott, *Rural Guerrillas in Latin America* (London 1971).

sponsored 'civic action' programme whereby certain communities were politically and economically favoured by the army, Arana's campaign resulted in the death of some ten thousand people in the space of five years while close co-operation with MLN militants and the establishment of a system of 'military commissioners' in the villages laid the basis for the death squads of the 1970s and the civil patrols of the 1980s. The similarities of this operation to many of the methods employed in Vietnam owed much to the fact that for a while U.S. strategists considered Guatemala to be a case of comparable severity. However, by 1968 both wings of the guerrilla had been driven into retreat, their reduced forces seeking both protection and a new strategic arena in the capital in direct contravention of the ruralism of the *foco* theory, which had already lost its chief protagonist, Che Guevara, in an even more abortive effort to employ an urban vanguard to awaken the peasantry to revolutionary consciousness in the Bolivian countryside. Turcios had already died – in a car crash – in 1966; Yon Sosa was shot by Mexican troops in the border area in 1970; and the new strategy of executions and kidnappings was soon shown to provoke much greater repression than political support from the populace. For both the guerrillas themselves and their natural constituency the cost of this failure was very high indeed. Yet its lessons were not ignored. The next generation of insurgents, most particularly the Ejército Guerrillero de los Pobres (EGP), was established around a core of survivors from the FAR and on the conviction that immersion in the Indian society of the western highlands in a prolonged campaign of political education and collaboration before initiating combat represented the only viable strategy for a popular revolution in Guatemala.

For some years matters of this nature were to remain part of a suppressed and esoteric culture, but the counter-insurgency campaign of the late 1960s polarized political activity to such a degree that the negotiation of some space for even modest reform was viewed as a doomed venture by all except the most ardent advocates of constitutionalism. Even before Méndez Montenegro's term expired it was evident that the military would no longer brook anything bar the most formal and limited pursuit of democratic politics. Arana's zeal in repression and excessively aggressive political views eventually won a spell of diplomatic exile in Nicaragua – where he was assiduously patronized by Somoza – but the army continued to tighten its control, having a free hand in the declaration of states of siege at the same time as its programme of pacification fortified the confidence of the right wing and nullified the President's efforts to adjust the social and economic legacy of 1954. Government proposals for sales and property taxes were sabotaged with ease, further complicating recovery from the down-turn in the economy and stagnation of the CACM, while the emergence of death squads such as Ojo por Ojo and Mano Blanca hastened the retreat of the centre and left into the semi-clandestine shadows. By the 1970 elections the PR was comprehensively discredited and the right in such ascendency that Arana could return from Managua to campaign on an explicitly repressive platform: 'If it is necessary to turn the country into a cemetery in order to pacify it, I will not hesitate to do so'.[10]

There was no place in such an atmosphere for the degree of indecision and flexibility that had attended the 1966 poll. Threats from the new vigilante groups replaced rejection of membership lists as the most efficacious means of cowing the already disorganized opposition. Arana's victory with the support of some 5 per cent of the population, in an election in which fewer than 50 per cent of registered voters cast a ballot, marked the first of a string of polls in which population disenchantment paralleled the successes of the official, military-sponsored candidate. The diminishing efficacy of such a system was to become apparent within a decade, but in 1970 lack of popularity was manifestly of minor importance to the colonels compared to the aim of eradicating not only the radical left, which was already in disarray, but also any opposition to a regime that was no longer simply defending the social order established in 1954 but upholding the interests of a new generation of commercial farmers and entrepreneurs who had emerged through the CACM and the expansion of the economy beyond the staple exports of coffee and bananas. In pursuit of this objective Arana imposed a state of siege for the first year of his regime, during which more than seven hundred politically motivated killings took place, exiles both official and voluntary abounded, the university was intervened and the military occupied the centre stage of politics. Although the MLN and the paramilitary gangs that it readily admitted to fostering played an important part in the early phase of this activity, many in the army resented the party's autonomous capacity for violence and were scornful of Sandoval's brash political credo, which was so decidedly inquisitorial that it could not serve as a viable vehicle for government. Accordingly, the MLN was progressively reduced to the status of a minor partner as the officer corps used the PID to consolidate an institutional regime. By

[10] *New York Times*, 8 May 1971, cited in Jim Handy, *Gift of the Devil. A History of Guatemala* (Toronto, 1984).

the time of the 1974 elections the success of Arana's offensive was sufficiently evident that Sandoval could be offered the vice-presidency to General Kjell Laugerud, the former chief of staff (of Norwegian extraction).
The main opposition was provided by the DCG, whose leaders tried to
circumvent official impediments to their campaign by fielding a conservative officer, General Efraín Rios Montt, as their candidate. The PR was
now a spent force, and the only other reformist organization of any influence, Manuel Colóm Argüeta's Frente Unido Revolucionario (FUR), was
excluded by the authorities' refusal to accept the validity of its list of
ninety thousand supporters. As in 1966, the logic of the opposition was to
fall behind the most viable challenger, and Rios Montt polled particularly
well, but despite discernable differences within the dominant bloc and the
fact that their principal opponent was renowned for his role in the counter-
insurgency operations of the 1960s, the system functioned without major
flaw. The DCG claimed that 180,000 votes were altered to provide
Laugerud with victory, and the party was sufficiently confident of its
support that for a while a major crisis seemed to be pending. But Rios
Montt bowed to the pressures of his fraternity and accepted a diplomatic
post in Spain in exchange for recognizing Laugerud's triumph.

The events that attended Laugerud's elevation to the presidency may
have persuaded the new incumbent of the desirability of a more modulated
regime. In any event, the need for the degree of inflexibility shown by
Arana was no longer apparent. Moreover, Laugerud was soon at odds with
his predecessor, whose personalism threatened to undermine institutional
unity at a time when military participation in the economy was on the rise
and responsive to a technocratic direction of the type offered by the new
president. As a result, Laugerud permitted a very limited relaxation of the
political climate, allowing some unions to make a public appearance and
accepting a number of DCG policies as valid proposals for economic
growth and social amelioration. For two years it seemed as if the military
might accept some measured qualification to the policies of extreme economic conservatism and political dictatorship, and the Christian Democrats responded by moving closer to the government while rank-and-file
organizations began a tentative process of reorganization. However, in
February 1976, Guatemala was struck by a major earthquake in which
thousands of people were killed and extensive damage caused. Although
administrative chaos was less than that in Nicaragua four years earlier,
control of the National Reconstruction Committee was the object of fierce
and sometimes violent competition within the ruling class, and the after-

Table 4.1. *Guatemala: rural sector, c.1950–c.1975*

	Year	Area (× 1,000 hectares)	Production (× 1,000 metric tons)
Coffee	1950	162	57.6
	1977	270	147.0
Bananas	1950	17	185
	1974	59	450
Cotton	1948–52 average	5	2
	1979	120	146
Sugar	1961–5 av.	32	1,960
	1977	85	6,800
Cattle	1947–52 av.		977 (per 1,000 head)
	1974		1,916 (per 1,000 head)
Maize	1948–52 av.	538	437
	1978	522	760
Beans	1948–52 av.	63	30
	1978	135	80

Source: Edelberto Torres Rivas, 'The Beginning of Industrialization in Central America', Working Paper no. 141, Woodrow Wilson Center (Washington D.C., 1984).

math of the disaster saw an upsurge in political conflict as the military and its right-wing allies sought to contain the effects of independent political and organizational activity in the relief campaign. Renewed recourse to the death squads closed off any potential latitude in the political system and compounded the effects of the deteriorating economy in encouraging the development of a radical opposition that had been dormant since 1968.[11]

In terms of global production the Guatemalan economy advanced considerably between 1950 and 1980. Although the population grew at about 3.2 per cent per annum (from 3.0 million to 7.3 million), so also did GDP (from $767.1 million to $3,067 million) and even GDP per capita (from $293 to $575). In the rural sector this expansion was primarily due to growth in agro-export activity, which in terms of both area cultivated and production, advanced more rapidly than did domestic food crop agriculture. As Table 4.1 demonstrates, the expansion of large-scale commercial agriculture took the form of greater cultivated area as well as improve-

[11] See Roger Plant, *Guatemala: Unnatural Disaster* (London, 1978).

ments in yield, and it was frequently the domestic food crop sector, both subsistence and locally marketed, that bore the brunt of this expansion because the agricultural frontier as a whole moved imperceptibly over these thirty years. Thus, although the size and infrastructure of the economy progressed steadily, distribution of what was still an exceedingly modest national income did so at a notably slower rate with the result that, according to estimates for 1970, the poorest 50 per cent of the population earned only 13 per cent of income (at an average of 73 Central American pesos per head), while the top 5 per cent accounted for 35 per cent (2,023 pesos per capita). In the countryside this disparity was even greater, mirroring the pattern of land tenure too closely for land poverty to be disregarded as a central factor despite complex and plausible technical arguments as to the efficiency of commercial farming. According to the 1979 agricultural census, units of less than 7 hectares accounted for 87 per cent of all farms and yet possessed a mere 16 per cent of cultivated land. At the other end of the spectrum the 482 estates of more than 900 hectares constituted less than 1 per cent of farms whilst possessing 22 per cent of the cultivated land. Perhaps most significantly, 167,000 plots (31 per cent of all farms) were less than 0.7 hectare in size.

The growth in the population and greatly reduced opportunities for temporary labour in the new agro-export sector – neither cotton nor sugar require a harvest work force for as long as coffee does, and cattle-raising produces a minimal labour demand – meant that despite increases in production, overall land–labour ratios fell, income distribution remained markedly regressive, and the degree of landlessness also rose. By the mid-1970s the historic poverty of the rural population of the country had palpably not been alleviated, and for many thousands of peasants it was increasingly being determined by pressure at both poles of the traditional exchange between harvest labour in the lowland plantations and cultivation of a subsistence plot subjected to an unprecedented degree to incursions by cattle ranchers and other commercial farmers, who were expanding their holdings under the law or outside of it. By the mid-1970s per capita grain consumption was, with the exception of rice, one-fifth lower than that in the previous decade, and although the average calorie-intake remained constant over the decade – in the rest of Central America it rose by 4 per cent – that of proteins fell.

The prospects of a rural population in such a position finding some escape in the new urban industrial sector were exceptionally limited, since this, too, had registered a notably uneven form of development. Although between 1950 and 1978 the share of GDP attributable to manufacturing rose from 11.1 per cent to 15.1 per cent and the total value added from $98.0 million to $531.7 million, with nearly half of all foreign investment in 1970 being directed to this sector, the structure of industry remained largely traditional and highly dependent upon foreign inputs and investment. Between 1960 and 1978 perishable goods fell from 86 per cent to only 70 per cent of all production, while capital goods rose from 4.7 to less than 9 per cent. In 1975 only the food, tobacco, textile and wood industries drew more than half their primary materials from the national economy. The nature of production was little transformed from that prevailing at the establishment of the CACM, with an industrial labour force of 219,000 representing only 11.5 per cent of the economically active population (compared with 128,500 and 10 per cent in 1962) and still predominantly concentrated in workshop production (68.4 per cent of workers employed in enterprises with five or fewer workers, against 75.6 per cent in 1962). Expansion of the urban and industrial economy encouraged the growth of the capital as the sole urban centre of metropolitan proportions – in 1980 Guatemala City had a population of 1.2 million, Quezaltenango, the second town, 92,000 – but it had not produced any major social transformation by the time the world recession of the 1980s hit commodity prices, stalled and then reversed growth rates, and provoked an increase in indebtedness highly unfamiliar in an economy traditionally directed along extremely conservative lines. Popular discontent resulting from the inequities of growth was already evident before the onset of economic decline at the end of the 1970s, but it was significantly deepened by the recession, which hit the urban economy especially hard and, as elsewhere in Latin America, compelled a large sector of the labour force to depend upon precarious strategies for survival in the informal economy. Although an economy as backward as Guatemala's had long nurtured such a sector of petty vending and independent marketing of small-scale services, this now expanded considerably, further prejudicing the condition of the majority of a population: 44 per cent were illiterate; 43 per cent were younger than age fifteen and yet only 18 per cent of school-age children were enrolled in education; the average life-expectancy was fifty-six years; the level of infant mortality was officially estimated at 79 per 1,000 live births but generally agreed to be very much higher, particularly in the countryside. Since the government's budget allocated more to military expenditure (22.4 per cent in 1985) than to health (7.5 per cent) and education (13.3 per cent) combined, it is not surprising that indices such as these were broadly perceived to derive not just from the backwardness of the economy and its powerless position in the contracting world market but also from the social policy of a state opposed to redistribution and instinctively inclined to the maintenance of the status quo through force of arms.

The years 1977 to 1983 were marked by open social and political conflict in which both government and military were increasingly hard-pressed to maintain control in large areas of the countryside, and sometimes in the capital itself; the bulk of the 100,000 people estimated to have been killed for political reasons since 1954 lost their lives during this period. In the towns, most particularly in Guatemala City, much of the violence was attributable to the actions of anonymous death squads operating against individual or small groups of activists of opposition parties and unions, but it was primarily the indigenous peoples of the western highlands who suffered its effects. This campaign – for which there are few parallels in the history of twentieth-century Latin America – incorporated the traditional derision shown by the *ladino* towards the *indio,* whose distinct dress, languages and autochthonous customs were, and remain, widely construed as primitive and an impediment to both material progress and the consolidation of a republican and Hispanic culture. Although the period since 1944 had witnessed appreciable *ladinización,* more than 40 per cent of the country's population had one of the five main Indian languages – with more than twenty distinct dialects – as their mother tongue and remained more attached to the society of the sixteen principal ethnic groups than to that of a Guatemalan nation.[12] The preponderance of Indian peasants in the harvest labour force and their overwhelming majority of the population of the eight departments of the *altiplano* region had since the last quarter of the nineteenth century required the managers of the state to negotiate as well as to impose a form of apartheid with limited advantages for the *indio* insofar as it tolerated a degree of cultural autonomy, albeit under persistent pressure. Nonetheless, from the 1950s onwards the expan-

---

[12] Debate over the social character and political dynamics of ethnicity in Guatemala is highly charged and sometimes obscure in its terms of reference. Severo Martínez Peláez, *La patria del criollo* (Guatemala, 1973), remains the most controversial text. For alternative views, see Carlos Guzmán and Jean-Loup Herbert, *Guatemala: una interpretación histórico-social* (Mexico, 1970), and Carol Smith, 'Indian Class and Class Consciousness in Pre-revolutionary Guatemala', Working Paper no. 162, Latin American Program, Woodrow Wilson Center (Washington, D.C., 1984). A quite extraordinary account of such consciousness is Elizabeth Burgos Debray (ed.), *I . . . Rigoberta Menchú* (London, 1983).

sion of commercial agriculture had posed an increasingly serious threat, not solely to communal lands dedicated to the cultivation of local food crops but also to a distinct socio-cultural way of life indivisible from the *milpa* (plot). In the 1970s the pattern of economic growth markedly accelerated this pressure, challenging the indigenous universe and provoking a response both peasant and Indian in its nature. This movement, often unseen at the level of formal and 'national' politics, may in some senses be compared with that of the early independence period in that it sought to defend both a specific economic circuit and a culture; however, it was at the same time a modern phenomenon that incorporated syndicalist organizational forms and adopted unfamiliar political discourses, such as that of radical Christianity as well as the notion of liberation for oppressed peoples.

The most palpable single threat to the indigenous population was the establishment of the Northern Transverse Strip (Franja Transversal del Norte, FTN) by the Laugerud regime in 1976. This project amounted to the declaration of a 'development zone' close to the areas of most dense Indian settlement on the Mexican border and in the department of Izabal on the Caribbean coast. Designed primarily to meet the needs of agribusiness and the petroleum and nickel industries, in which great expectations were invested, the FTN provided extremely generous incentives for capital in a concerted attempt to open a new frontier where the interests of the established peasant economy were accorded minimal protection. The success of the project in attracting both local and foreign enterprises, led to inflated land prices and threw existing patterns of ownership, both legal ones and those based on precedence, into confusion, thus compounding the trauma caused by the earthquake. The FTN represented a signal effort to impose a modern, capitalist economy in the heartland of subsistence agriculture. Yet it was less a break with than an acceleration of the existing tendencies within the rural economy.

After the earthquake the initial advances made by the opposition were modest in character, but the establishment in 1976 of the Comité Nacional de Unidad Sindical (CNUS) and the growth of the Confederación Nacional de Trabajadores (CNT) – which together increased the number of unionized workers from 1.6 per cent to 10 per cent of the labour force between 1975 and 1978 – were developments of some consequence. Moreover, the revival of confidence and militancy frequently took place outside the confines of organized – still less, officially recognized – structures; the protest march of the miners of Ixtahuacán to the capital in November

1977 combined with that of sugar-workers to prompt impressive displays of spontaneous popular sympathy. These examples also provided encouragement for a nine-day strike by 85,000 public-sector workers, many of them middle class, in February 1978 – the single largest instance of industrial action since 1954. In each case the unions were strengthened, although they still remained highly vulnerable to shifts in the popular mood and dependent upon the resolution of rank-and-file militants, the most prominent example of which was the prolonged endeavour of the workers in Guatemala City's Coca-Cola plant to obtain official recognition. This campaign over five years cost the lives of a dozen activists and attracted international attention precisely at the time when the Carter administration was insisting upon greater respect for human rights from its allies. The shift in U.S. policy affected the Guatemalan military in much the same manner as it did their counterparts in the rest of Central America, as well as in Chile and Argentina. But whereas the regimes in El Salvador and Nicaragua were obliged to adjust their repressive tendencies somewhat, the Guatemalans refused to do so and were subjected to an arms embargo. Developing a more autonomous foreign policy and turning to the Southern Cone and Israel for logistical support, the army was able to retain its control without major difficulty in the election of 1978. General Romeo Lucas García was elected in a poll in which 69 per cent of registered voters abstained and 20 per cent of the ballots were spoiled. Colóm Argüeta's FUR and its Social Democratic allies led by Alberto Fuentes Mohr were prohibited from standing, and the DCG won acceptance only by omitting from its platform many of the proposals for which Rios Montt had campaigned in 1974. Lucas had passed over the discredited MLN and picked the respected Villagrán Kramer as his vice-presidential candidate, thereby bestowing upon the official ticket a degree of credibility. But such a move neither persuaded the U.S. government to alter its hardening position nor, indeed, resulted in anything more than the isolation and abuse of Villagrán, who was eventually forced to abdicate his solitary campaign for social consensus and seek exile in Washington.

The absence of any change in policy was sharply reconfirmed in May 1978 when some hundred Kekchi peasant farmers from the town of Panzós, Alta Verapaz, were shot down by the army when meeting in the town square to discuss the defence of their lands threatened by cattle ranchers granted, or claiming, concessions under the FTN. The Panzós massacre is widely and justifiably perceived as opening a new phase of rural confrontation out of which emerged the Comité de Unidad

Campesina (CUC) and a disposition on the part of many inhabitants of the countryside to support the armed organizations of the left. However, it was in Guatemala City that public order first broke down on a major scale when, following a large demonstration earlier in the year against both the Panzós massacre and the assassination of CNUS leader Mario López Larrave, extensive rioting took place in October 1978 against a rise in bus fares. The regime, surprised by the depth of public feeling on this issue, gravely misjudged its impact on an already poor transport system heavily used by workers living on the outskirts of the city. Much less accustomed to controlling angry street crowds than to eliminating individual oppositionists, the security forces were able to reinstate order but with enough difficulty to suggest that the customarily subdued city might once again be the site of unpredictable outbursts of discontent.

Both the public sector strike of February and the riots of October were marked by a lack of control and decision on the part of unions, themselves unaccustomed to managing movements on such a scale. Nevertheless, the events of 1978 encouraged organizational consolidation and underscored the opposition's need for agreement on a broad platform. Early in 1979 steps were taken towards this with the formation of a loose alliance of centrist parties and the major unions in the Frente Democrático Contra la Represión (FDCR) which, despite restricting its demands to those for respect of basic civil liberties, posed enough of a threat to provoke the execution by unidentified gunmen of the Social Democrats' leader Fuentes Mohr as well as, less than eight weeks later, the FUR's Colóm Argüeta, both of whom the military hierarchy viewed as potential victors of the 1982 elections. These were but two further instances of state-sponsored assassination for which Guatemala had long possessed a formidable reputation, but they also marked a readiness to kill both distinguished popular figures and proponents of modest reform as well as the traditional targets on the left. According to the young leader of the DCG, Vinicio Cerezo, 120 of his party's members were killed in the space of ten months in 1980–1 when the Christian Democrats were in sharp competition with the radical currents for popular support. In a political culture such as Guatemala's, the macabre task of disaggregating the death toll by party affiliation is often needed to help identify shifts in government policy.

Although this increase in repression further alienated the Lucas García government from Washington, it was not without a certain logic. In July 1979, Somoza was overthrown in Nicaragua, and in October reformist elements in the Salvadorean army staged a coup to end the PCN regime, some of their number deliberately seeking a rapprochement with a progressively more militant popular movement; the prospect of a break-down of the established order throughout Central America was viewed with great gravity. That the Guatemalan military hierarchy was not absolutely rigid in its response to this threat, which was little less real than it was perceived, may be seen in its decisions in the spring of 1980 to concede most of the demands made in an unprecedented strike by cotton- and sugar-harvest workers supported by the urban unions as well as CUC. The scale of the strike, and its well-organized threat to the most modern sectors of agribusiness, obliged the regime to impose a wage agreement on the farmers, yet, in contrast to the government's climb-down over bus fares, this was later allowed to lapse by default and did not signal any relaxation of the counter-insurgency campaign in the highlands. Such a tactic proved highly efficacious; but what it gained in terms of stealth and the avoidance of further prejudice to the regime's unenviable international reputation was lost in January 1980 in the much publicized police attack on the Spanish embassy, which had been peacefully occupied by a score of Indians seeking the services of Madrid's sympathetic envoy to intercede with the military controlling their villages. The killing of all the demonstrators – including that of the solitary protestor evacuated alive only to be taken from his hospital bed and shot – and the narrow escape of the ambassador himself revived concern abroad about methods to which international opinion had become wearily familiar. Hence, despite the regime's sanguine expectation that the Reagan administration would reopen full and friendly relations, it subsequently proved difficult for the new administration to overcome profound congressional disdain for the Guatemalan military, making full support for the campaign against the left dependent upon a much more substantial political reorganization than the colonels and, indeed, Reagan himself had anticipated.

Such a strategy, clearly signalled by the end of 1981, was delayed by a number of years partly as a result of the military's ability to resist pressure from Washington and partly because the challenge posed by the guerrilla was manifestly serious. Drawing on a ground-swell of sympathy engendered both by economic pressure and by the army's operations, organizations established in the early 1970s – such as the EGP and the Organización del Pueblo en Armas (ORPA) – had succeeded in extending their activity throughout much of the *altiplano*. By 1980 the EGP controlled large tracts of Quiché and Huehuetenango while ORPA's fighters were moving with ease in the departments of San Marcos, Sololá and

Chimaltenango. Concurrently, the very much smaller reincarnation of the FAR had established a presence in the outlying and under-populated Petén region, posing little threat to either the state or economic infrastructure, yet tying down valuable military units. The strategy of armed struggle also gained adherents among a fraction of the much weakened PGT, although this group failed to build an urban campaign of great significance. Such a pattern of support reflected the relatively subordinate influence of the orthodox left in a movement that owed much to shifts in the doctrinal and pastoral attitudes of the rural priesthood, many of whose members had for more than a decade been developing the traditionalist structures of Acción Católica into a much broader and politically independent system of organization of the laity. Although the Guatemalan Church hierarchy was notably more reactionary than those (until 1979) in El Salvador and Nicaragua, where similar developments were taking place, it proved difficult to impede the encouragement of co-operatives, the spread of catechism and novel interpretations of the Gospel in a country noted for popular piety but where Catholicism had for many years been subjected to competition from evangelical Protestantism and where the number of locally born priests was very low. However, the traditional attachment of the military to the mores and hierarchy of the established Church did not stop it attacking what were perceived, often justifiably, as subversive clerics and their proselytising acolytes in the catechist movement. The persecution of the clerics reached such a point that in 1980 the Bishop of Quiché ordered the evacuation of all religious from his diocese in order to assure their safety and to protest the anti-clerical campaign. As both radicalized priests, and many of those who had followed them out of a position of traditional respect into one of political commitment, became treated as enemies of the state, collaboration with guerrillas, who frequently came from local communities and espoused recognizable aspirations, became correspondingly more compelling an option. In those areas where the military had effectively declared what since Vietnam have been termed 'free-fire zones', such collaboration was little less than a strategy for survival. By 1981 this pattern was sufficiently generalized to cast considerable doubt upon the army's control of the western highlands, where the rebels were staging operations on a scale that belied accusations that they were isolated Communist agitators divorced from the local population. The Guatemalan armed forces appeared to be in a situation no better than that encountered by Somoza's National Guard early in 1979, or that of the Salvadorean military at the same time.

The severity of the army's position provoked unease inside both the military and the dominant bloc as a whole. In 1981 garrison officers publicly voiced their misgivings over the lack of a coherent strategy and the poor conditions in which they were obliged to stage a highly exigent campaign while senior commanders appeared to be reaping considerable personal rewards from their management of the state and, in particular, the FTN. Army discontent was somewhat reduced by the appointment of the president's brother, General Benedicto Lucas García, a French-trained officer of some ability, to direct operations. However, the regime's failure to register the extent of disenchantment led it to stage the 1982 elections in customary style, presenting the Minister of Defence, General Aníbal Guevara, as official successor to Lucas García without paying heed to the claims of the junior officers who sought greater institutional participation in political decision-making. This, in turn, provided encouragement for the outcast MLN, which had taken to crying fraud at what seemed to some a rather late stage in its life, while the guerrillas demanded a boycott of the poll and theatened to disrupt it in much of the countryside. In the event, the tactical difficulties of attacking places where numbers of civilians were gathered meant that this disruption did not extend much beyond the traditional degree of popular abstentionism, but Guevara's predictable victory prompted demonstrations of protest by the upper-class followers of the MLN and other small rightist parties which, most unusually, were subjected to less than gentle treatment at the hands of the police. This anomalous situation of a military regime lacking support from the right wing and a significant portion of the officer corps by virtue of professional inefficiency, political dishonesty and economic corruption did not last for long. Within days of the poll a bloodless coup by middle-level officers ousted Lucas García and Guevara. They were replaced with a junta of whom the most celebrated member and eventual leader was General Rios Montt, brought out of retirement to provide the movement with a figurehead who was staunchly anti-communist yet not part of the ruling cabal.

The political character of the junta was initially confused. However, in the subsequent in-fighting the MLN and its allies were excluded from influence, and Rios Montt, who had become a 'born-again Christian' prone to launching into millenarian disquisitions, dedicated himself to a maverick style of government which gave central attention to the counter-insurgency campaign yet also harrassed the upper class with new tax proposals and the prospect of a Bonapartist regime restoring a greater degree of autonomy to the state at their expense. The populist potential in such a project was never realized, partly because Rios Montt was disinclined to abjure his professional proclivities or his vocation as a martinet but largely because he was obliged to dedicate himself principally to defeating the guerrilla. Although a comprehensive eradication of the armed groups in the highlands – now unified on paper but scarcely in practice as the Unión Revolucionaria Nacional Guatemalteca (URNG) – was not achieved, the adoption of an extensive scorched-earth campaign reminiscent of tactics employed in Algeria and Malaysia as much as in Vietnam did succeed in delivering a major blow to the rebels from which it would require several years to recover. This campaign, known as 'fusiles y frijoles' for its policy of relocating friendly communities with a modicum of economic assistance while freely treating those seeking protection from the rebels as if they were enemy combatants, revealed the guerrillas' inability to provide such protection or maintain control over large areas for any length of time. By mid-1983 it was clear that the destruction of many villages, construction of fortified hamlets and enforced conscription of tens of thousands of able-bodied men into poorly or unarmed 'civil patrols' had achieved much success in exploiting the guerrillas' loss of popular confidence, if not sympathy, and reducing their rebellion. Subsequently this system of rural control was further expanded and presented by the army as a complete strategy for rural development, although one of its principal effects was to prevent many communities from having access to their traditional lands and practising the customs attached to them.[13] By 1985 the rebel forces were beginning to regroup and resume operations at a more modest level, but the abrupt set-back they had suffered stood in stark contrast to the ability of their Nicaraguan and Salvadorean comrades to sustain, respectively, a successful insurrection and a prolonged resistance against the state's forces. This further reduced the prospects of a regional radical upsurge that a few years before had seemed imminent but was now sorely threatened by Washington's obvious preparedness to intervene militarily in Central America.

The requirements of containing the domestic insurgency prompted not only Rios Montt's regime but also those that followed it to pursue a foreign policy little more amenable to the amicable Reagan than it had been to Carter. Already accustomed to a degree of distance from Washington, the military studiously desisted from enthusiastic support for U.S.

[13] Christine Krueger, 'Security and Development Conditions in the Guatemalan Highlands', Washington Office on Latin America (Washington, D.C., 1985).

plans to revive the regional military alliance Consejo de Defensa Centroamericana (CONDECA) and give the battle against communism a truly regional character. No less reactionary than their peers, the Guatemalan officers were not prepared to sacrifice their own precarious advantages for what they often considered to be questionable logistical and political enterprises, and although manifesting unrefined contempt for the Sandinistas, they were also prepared to adopt a pragmatic approach towards the new Nicaraguan government once it became clear that neither it nor Cuba was providing the URNG with significant material support. However, both the political traditions of the ruling class and the experience of the military tended towards close collaboration with the United States, and there was little dissent from the view that the regime could not permit differences in appreciation of the region's strategic position to prejudice both ideological affinity and the resolution of mounting economic difficulties. Within a year of Rios Montt's taking power, it was clear that he was incapable of negotiating such a delicate balance, especially since his unpredictable conduct had diminished support not only among the bourgeoisie but also within the high command. His eventual removal, in August 1983 at the hands of General Humberto Mejía Victores, was widely anticipated and corresponded to a resurgence of confidence within a ruling bloc temporarily thrown into confusion by the events surrounding the 1982 election. Mejía's return to the established mode of military government in greater collaboration with the business sector and a desistence from flamboyant pronouncements was, however, carefully shorn of the excessive partisanship witnessed under Lucas García, and provided a secure guarantee that compliance with Washington's desire for the restitution of civilian rule would be undertaken in a disciplined fashion, retaining full operational independence for the military and excluding the forces of the left from the *apertura* (opening). Although somewhat perplexed by the profusion of party-politicking that ensued, and more deeply concerned at another sudden outburst of street protests in the capital caused by the deteriorating economic situation (most sharply illustrated by the collapse of the sixty-year parity of the Quetzal with the dollar), the high command gravely stuck to its pledge, overseeing elections to a constituent assembly in 1984 and a further poll for the presidency and a new congress in 1986. This second, and more important, contest was handsomely won in the second round by Vinicio Cerezo and the DCG, which finally reached office after thirty years. Having taken advantage of the many candidacies on the extreme right in the first round, in the second round the DCG represented the obvious choice for those discontented with the existing order. In keeping both with its political traditions and with a resolutely pragmatic assessment of the prevailing balance of forces, the party held back from any move towards judicial investigation of the violation of human rights by the military – although it did take some limited action against sections of the police – and sought to exploit support from more prescient commanders aware of the international conditions in order to obtain a working neutrality from the majority of the officer corps inclined to a glowering scepticism. At the same time, Cerezo studiously avoided raising the issue of an agrarian reform because this more than any other single issue threatened to destroy the tenuous concordat that had permitted him to take office.[14] Benefiting from a clear margin of electoral support from a populace that had apparently voted for a policy of social rapprochement and an end to the violence, backed by a conservative administration in Washington anxious to maintain civilian governments in the region, and exhibiting exceptional caution, the new government offered the prospect of ending a long history of reactionary control. Nonetheless, such a scenario was not so different from the attending Méndez Montenegro's victory in 1966, and many commentators expressed reservations as to its chances of success. The failure either to curb the army's operations or to present a substantive programme of economic improvement for the peasantry and the urban poor suggested that a resurgence of popular organization and radical demands – already witnessed in the protests in Guatemala City in the autumn of 1985 and evident in the countryside within weeks of Cerezo's assumption of office – could not be discounted. If the pattern of politics since 1954 had indeed been subjected to major adjustment, it remained open to doubt whether the underlying tensions in Guatemalan society could be contained for any length of time simply by the adoption of formal democratic procedure.

---

[14] The background to the 1985 elections and first phase of the Cerezo presidency is succinctly but critically analyzed in James Painter, *Guatemala: False Hope, False Freedom* (London, 1987).

5

EL SALVADOR SINCE 1930

During the first three decades of the twentieth century the economy of El Salvador became the most dynamic in Central America. Unlike the rest of the region, El Salvador had no banana enclave, but the success of its coffee economy was such that the country gained a reputation as 'the Ruhr of Central America'. The efficiency of the coffee sector owed a great deal to the capacity of a new generation of landlords to exploit the comprehensive alienation of communal lands in El Salvador's central zone in the years which had followed the Liberal revolution of 1871. The altitude and fertility of these lands was particularly well suited to the crop, and because El Salvador is by far the smallest Central American state (21,040 square kilometers) while possessing a large population – even in 1930 it was approaching 1.5 million – the density of settlement was extremely high and the opportunities for peasant migration correspondingly low. As a result, large numbers of rural inhabitants were not so much physically displaced as deprived of their status as small freeholders or members of the municipal commune and converted into waged harvest labourers or *colonos* paying labour rent for subsistence plots on the edges of the new coffee *fincas*. Thus the Salvadorean agro-export sector was unique in the isthmus in that it was blessed with a high availability of local labour. Moreover, the remarkably rapid and all-encompassing alienation of common land – the Church, that other traditional target of nineteenth-century liberalism, possessed very little rural property – encouraged an early concentration of commercial estates and propelled the formation of one of the most compact and confident landed oligarchies in the world.[1] The landed oligarchy of El Salvador is often referred to as 'the fourteen families', although in

[1] For discussion of this process, see David Browning, *El Salvador: Landscape and Society* (Oxford, 1971), and Rafael Menjivar, *Acumulación originaria y desarrollo del capitalismo en El Salvador* (San José, 1980).

251

1930 there existed sixty-five large commercial enterprises and some three hundred fifty estates of more than 100 hectares, which is large by Salvadorean standards. Four decades later, well into an era in which agrarian reform had elsewhere ceased to be 'subversive' and was included in the mildest of political programmes, the distribution of land was still the most inequitable in Latin America while the economic power of the oligarchy remained concentrated to an impressive degree: twenty-five firms accounted for 84 per cent of all coffee exports and forty-nine families possessed farms of more than 1,000 hectares.[2]

The conversion of El Salvador into an oligarchic state and an agro-export economy based on private property was by no means a smooth process. It depended as much upon the exercise of class and ethnic violence as it did upon the entrepreneurial zeal and political confidence so celebrated in the opening years of the new century. Indeed, it was in El Salvador that Liberalism had first been challenged by Indian resistance in the aftermath of Central American independence; in 1833 the popular uprising led by Anastasio Aquino had required the deployment of troops from outside the province and wide-spread repression before social order was restored and the *ladino* state secured. In the 1870s and 1880s the expropriation of common land provoked a series of local revolts, residual violence being higher than that attending similar measures in the rest of the region. This conflict prompted the formation of a powerful army that simultaneously provided some protection against Guatemala, with which relations were always strained, and supported the regional designs of Liberalism, for which El Salvador had long been a spiritual home. Internal and external dependence upon armed force sustained for a while a political culture based upon the coup d'état, yet if the Salvadorean landlords lagged behind those of Costa Rica in subduing upstart army officers and introducing government by civilian grandees, they were not far behind. Within a decade of its establishment by coercive means, the Liberal state was provided with a comprehensive legal apparatus; and by the turn of the century, political life had been freed from both military intervention and the

[2] The character and development of the oligarchy have yet to be analysed exhaustively. However, much useful information and suggestive discussion may be found in Robert Aubey, 'Entrepreneurial Formation in El Salvador', *Explorations in Entrepreneurial History*, second ser., vol. 6 (1968–9); Everett Wilson, 'The Crisis of National Integration in El Salvador, 1919–1935', unpublished Ph.D. dissertation, Stanford University, 1970; Eduardo Colindres, 'La tenencia de la tierra en El Salvador', *Estudios Centroamericanos* 31 (1976); Manuel Sevilla, 'El Salvador: la concentración económica y los grupos del poder', Cuaderno de Trabajo no. 3, Centro de Investigación y Acción Social (Mexico, 1984).

instability this cultivated. The economic resource and political confidence of landed capital was fully manifested in the monopoly over office held by the Melendez and Quiñonez families, who passed the presidency calmly between each other through formal elections and in a manner comparable to that of the Costa Rican 'Olympians'.

So assured was this regime that even after the Mexican Revolution, towards which it displayed a notably unflustered attitude, the oligarchy was prepared to sanction a degree of popular organization, in the towns, at least, albeit of a severely supervised nature. In the 1920s artisanal guilds were permitted to operate, legislation was introduced to regulate the conditions of urban workers, and reformist opponents of the Liberal order were allowed to compete for office. When the boom years of the 1920s were brought to an abrupt end, however, the Salvadorean oligarchic regime was revealed not as a stable and organic means of social control capable of mutating into 'tradition' but as an extraordinarily fragile construction which had been built upon the exceptional performance of the agricultural economy, the termination of which it was unable to survive.

The distinctiveness of the Salvadorean agricultural system, in contrast to that of Costa Rica, for example, lay in the absence of a buoyant class of medium-sized farmers and the abundance of land-poor harvest workers. The dominance of the *finqueros* was based less on their indirect control of an internal market in coffee than on the direct control they exercised over land and production. This system may also be contrasted with that in Guatemala insofar as labour control in El Salvador depended much less upon moving large numbers of temporary Indian labourers to the plantations from separate zones of peasant settlement and subsistence agriculture, than upon supervision of workers living on or near to *fincas* where they were employed, either for the harvest or throughout the year. On the one hand, the weakness of what might be termed a 'middle peasantry' made landlord domination less the product of a negotiated hegemony than that of direct and emphatic control. On the other hand, both the relatively low importance attached to the 'Indian question' – by 1930 indigenous culture in El Salvador was limited to the regions around Izalco and Santiago Nonualco – and the marginal need for extensive coercive mechanisms to ensure a supply of labour reduced the tendency of the state towards centralism and authoritarianism. After the subjugation of the conflict that attended the first phase of appropriation, the role of the army in maintaining order was increasingly replaced by paramilitary forces – particularly the National Guard (Guardia Nacional) established in 1912 – which were often based near major farms and were more directly answerable to individual land-owners than was the regular military.

This rural regime was marked by neither flexibility nor a philanthropy beyond that normally associated with an omnipotent but prescient *patrón;* wages and conditions on Salvadorean estates were among the poorest in the region and contributed towards the relative efficiency of the export economy. However, the maintenance of a coherent system of political control at the level of the state depended not only upon stable terms of competition within a very small capitalist class but also upon the restriction of social contradictions to the locus of the *finca*. By 1930 it was evident that this second condition no longer obtained as a peasantry in particularly onerous circumstances, even by Central American standards, began to manifest a wide-spread discontent. The Liberal order, already losing momentum, entered a period of crisis, and late in 1931 the landlord class withdrew from government, accepting the claims of the military to direct control of the polity. At the same time, the structure of the coffee economy ensured that the oligarchy continued to exercise the social power of a formidable ruling class, including that of veto over the economic policy of regimes which remained in the hands of the army, with one short break, from 1932 to 1982. Nowhere else in the isthmus was such a division of power so clear and systematized, or so much in contrast with the pattern of politics up to the 1930s. One of its characteristics – evident from the late 1970s as much as in the early 1930s – was a marked incidence of conflict within the dominant bloc in times of social crisis when the concession of political power by the landed bourgeoisie to the military could no longer be guaranteed to support their economic interests.

The origins of this singular division of power may be located in the turbulent weeks between November 1931 and February 1932, when the failure of a reformist Liberal administration to contain popular discontent caused by the collapse of the economy in the world depression led to a military coup and then, at the end of January 1932, to insurrections in both San Salvador and the western regions of the country. The suppression of these rebellions was of such ferocity that what became known as La Matanza could be described as the single most decisive event in the history of Central America until the overthrow of Somoza in Nicaragua in July 1979. It traumatized both the peasantry and the oligarchy, laying the basis for a fifty-year regime that, notwithstanding prolonged periods of general tranquillity, drew its underlying strength from the memory, both real and cultivated, of the violence of 1932 and the fear that it might recur. When this fear was realized in the civil war of the 1980s, some of the vestiges of 1932 were still plainly visible in the low level of armed conflict in those areas where the revolt had taken place, as well as in the extreme reluctance of the landlords to accept a civilian regime pledged to reform and strongly sponsored by Washington in preference to proponents of open militarism and unabashed conservatism.

In 1930 the Salvadorean economy was more narrowly based on coffee than any other in the region. During the 1920s high prices had prompted both an extension of the agricultural frontier close to its limits – 90 per cent of land under coffee in 1960 was under coffee in 1930 – and concentration on a single crop that was considered risky by more than cultivators of sugar, *henequen* and cotton. The fall in the price of coffee – from 25 cents a pound in 1925 to 9 cents in 1935 – as a result of the world depression had, therefore, a catastrophic effect and generated wider and more directly politicized social conflict than that witnessed elsewhere in Central America. Income from exports in 1932 was less than half of that in 1926, the average annual growth rate for 1930–4 was -0.7 per cent, and by 1939, after several years of gradual recovery, GDP per capita was still below that of 1929. Although there is evidence that the *cafetaleros* (commercial coffee farmers) held back from collecting the harvest of 1930, the most logical response to the crisis was to maximize the volume of exports, cutting wages to the increased harvest labour force required by expanded production. Thus, despite lay-offs of permanent workers, some extension of plantation lands, the calling-in of debts and tightening of terms of tenantry, the principal economic cause of popular unrest in the countryside appears to have been the sharp reduction in pay, which was cut from 75 to 15 centavos per day in two years. This measure provoked a series of rural strikes in 1931, markedly increasing political tension and providing growing support for the Federación Regional de Trabajadores de El Salvador (FRTS), which had been established in 1924 but which from 1930 was sharpening its activity under the direction of the newly formed Partido Comunista de El Salvador (PCS) led by the veteran agitator Agustín Farabundo Martí. The party itself, however, was very much less popular than the Partido Laborista (PL) recently founded by Arturo Araujo, a maverick member of the ruling class whose adoption of a vague but robust reformism had enabled him to win the presidency in 1931 despite profound oligarchic misgivings as to the outcome of an open poll. The greater advance of trade-union organization in El Salvador than elsewhere in the region during the 1920s had already obliged the Liberal governments to engage in some pre-emptive populist activity, but Araujo took this tendency to its limit in economic circumstances which precluded the possibility of both meeting popular expectations and safeguarding the interests of the landlords. Hence, although the President retained a strong personal following, his government soon lost its sense of direction and authority in the face of strikes and demonstrations, while the military began to manifest unfamiliar signs of disquiet and the oligarchy chafed under its failure to secure a devaluation of the currency. When, in December 1931, the army finally rebelled, principally because it had not been paid for months, few were surprised. Only Araujo loyalists were completely dismayed because even the PCS, which had strenuously opposed the government, did not believe that the coup presaged any major change in the political system as a whole. This view soon proved to be gravely mistaken when the new head of state, Araujo's Minister of War, General Maximiliano Hernández Martínez, withdrew his promise to hold elections in January 1932 after the voting lists had been drawn up and campaigning was well advanced. One persuasive interpretation of Martínez's timing in this manoeuvre was that it enabled the army to identify supporters of the PL and PCS, drawing them into the open before embarking upon their repression. In all events, the cancellation of the poll gave the proponents of insurrection within the PCS support for a hastily planned and several times postponed urban revolt. It also drove the leadership of the peasantry around Ahuachapán and Izalco towards a rebellion that had some links with the PCS but was at root an independent movement in pursuit of both immediate economic amelioration and a more deeply seated defence of the region's embattled communal culture.[3]

The urban uprising of 22 January 1932 was suppressed within a matter of hours because news of its preparation had already reached the high command; isolated mutinies by radical conscripts had already been contained and several important Communists, including Farabundo Martí, detained some days previously. The subsequent campaign of persecution in San Salvador was extended to supporters of Araujo and members of artisanal guilds who often had nothing to do with the rebellion. The adoption of a policy of summary execution of known opposition elements

---

[3] The events of 1931–2 are discussed in some detail in Thomas P. Anderson, *Matanza: El Salvador's Communist Revolt of 1932* (Lincoln, Neb., 1971); Rafael Guidos Vejar, *Ascenso del militarismo en El Salvador* (San José, 1982); Roque Dalton, *Miguel Marmol* (New York, 1987).

and extensive incarceration of suspects effectively decapitated the radical movement – Farabundo Martí was shot after a brief court martial – and was emphatic enough to eradicate all vestige of independent popular organization for a dozen years and to hamper its progress for a further two decades thereafter. In the west of the country – there was no fighting in the east – the jacquerie led by Indian *caciques* managed a somewhat less fleeting existence in that it exercised control over a number of small settlements for up to forty-eight hours. It was, nonetheless, directed without strategic ambition and in the traditional mode of peasant revolts, devoid of the 'Bolshevik' characteristics often ascribed to it, manifesting a notable reluctance to damage religious property, and generally preoccupied with imposing justice on individual representatives of the state and the landlord class in a brief flurry of disorganized and almost carnival repudiation of the regime of the *cafetaleros*. The level of violence inflicted by rebel forces almost entirely bereft of firearms was, however, quite low; fewer than fifty people died at their hands.

Apprehension over the consequences of both the economic collapse and the cancellation of elections had prompted the U.S. and British governments to dispatch warships to Salvadorean waters. Some Canadian marines were briefly disembarked. But this outside force was rapidly ordered to retire following Martínez's insistence that the army and civilian vigilantes had the revolt under control within two days. In the light of subsequent developments, this proved to be something of an understatement because the retreat of the rebels began on the first full day after their insurrection and was rapidly converted into a rout as the troops and 'fraternities' of irregulars organized by landowners exacted an awesome revenge for the challenge to a social order based not only on the coffee *finca* but also on a belligerently *ladino* republic. Given the summary and extensive nature of this repression, it is not surprising that assessment of its human cost has become the subject of rather macabre debate; but if the figure of 40,000 deaths presented by the opposition movement of the 1980s is often deemed too high, it is evident that the razing of villages and liquidation of many of their inhabitants throughout February 1932 produced a toll that may reliably be said to be in the tens of thousands. The impact of such attrition was no less cultural than political; it threw the peasant *cofradías* (socio-religious brotherhoods) into confusion and effectively suppressed the wearing of Indian clothes, which was now considered by the rural population to be a provocative act of cultural resistance – and rightly so since although the revolt was denounced as communist by the regime, for many local *ladinos* it was a revolt of primitive *naturales* against whom a genocidal solution was not beyond the realm of reason.

Although much of the violence of the spring of 1932 was undertaken by civilian vigilantes – the forebears of the death squads of the 1970s – its political outcome was the confirmation of the army's claim to office; and because the army remained a backward, garrison-based force lacking an institutional system for political decision-making, power stayed firmly in the hands of its commander, Martínez, who consolidated a regime of pronounced personalism. The decisiveness of the general's direction of operations enabled him to impose a number of limited constraints upon the oligarchy. He readily accepted its demands for a devaluation and weathered the difficulties of suspending the external debt within weeks of coming to power, but he later cut interest rates, established a central bank and withdrew rights of issue from private institutions, imposed exchange controls and provided for state participation in a credit bank. None of these measures severely prejudiced entrepreneurial interests, but some restricted short-term profitability and laid the basis for a modest state intervention in the economy, albeit usually in close collaboration with the powerful corporate associations of the bourgeoisie such as the Asociación del Café, which was transformed in 1942 into the Compañía Salvadoreña del Café and subsequently remained little less than a parallel economic cabinet through its control of the coffee market. By the end of the 1940s this process of modest qualification to a completely free-market model had proved to be sufficiently advantageous to the landlords and their commercial partners that they tolerated Martínez's introduction of some protectionist measures on behalf of an artisanate bereft of corporate representation and still in need of tariffs to assist recovery from the effects of the depression. There was nothing particularly adventurous in such initiatives – the exceptional economic conditions of the 1930s drew similar measures from equally conservative regimes in the region – and they never reached the point at which the land-owners' control of economic policy, through the relevant cabinet portfolios, or its capacity for non-compliance, through its representative bodies, came under serious challenge. (Indeed, this did not occur until the tabling of a bill for agrarian reform in 1976.) There was no further agitation over the exchange rate, which was maintained at its 1935 level of 2.5 colones to the dollar for more than fifty years.

Martínez ruled El Salvador for more than twelve years (1932–44) in a style broadly comparable to that of his peers in the neighbouring states, through a cycle of unopposed re-elections and with the retention of no more than a veneer of democratic procedures. It should, however, be noted that over time this became a formality of some consequence insofar as the Salvadorean military, unlike their counterparts in many South American countries, never fully jettisoned the protocols of the Liberal constitutional system. Under Martínez the survival of this political form was both ensured and yet evacuated of substance by a narrow concentration of personal power combined with a no less marked eccentricity of character that was later lampooned for its ostentatious mysticism – the President was an ardent advocate of theosophy and did not lack confidence in his ability to tap supernatural powers – but which also served to create an aura of unpredictability and distinctiveness around the person of a *caudillo* who could by no means be considered a mere cipher of the oligarchy. The predictability of his electoral successes sometimes provoked ill-fated stabs at revolt by disgruntled senior officers, but even before Washington reversed its refusal to recognize de facto regimes in 1936, Martínez's position was extremely secure. Thereafter it appeared little less than unassailable until the final stages of the Second World War. By this time the enforced expansion of trade with the United States had compensated for the very low level of direct U.S. investment and bestowed upon Washington an unprecedented degree of influence in El Salvador, albeit more circumscribed than in any other Central American state except Costa Rica. This influence was employed to reinstate a modicum of popular participation in the political process without at the same time undermining the landlords or threatening the army. Such an objective in the mid-1940s (as in the 1950s), pursued by Roosevelt by means short of direct intervention, was exceptionally difficult – arguably impossible – to achieve, but it nonetheless greatly debilitated a dictatorship which had declared war on the Axis on the basis of geographical necessity rather than ideological repudiation and increasingly at odds with the democratic sentiments of the 'Four Freedoms' propounded by the Allies.

By the time Martínez's authority appeared to be slipping in 1943 – a year in which, on the one hand, a tax on coffee exports agitated the *finqueros,* and, on the other, the railway-workers managed to revive their union – his dalliance with the fascist powers in the late 1930s had become but a minor feature of growing discontent with a long-standing and narrow autocracy, most forcefully expressed in the middle class, which had been hit particularly hard by the sharp rise in consumer prices induced by the war. By Central American standards the urban middle sector in San

Salvador was large and, despite a dozen years of obligatory absence from public life, not lacking in political traditions. Moreover, agitation over the corruption and bureaucratic inefficiency stemming from the favouritism inherent in Martínez's personalist regime found a strong echo in the ranks of the army, where many officers felt threatened by the President's growing patronage of the paramilitary forces, which were commanded by regular officers but not answerable to the Minister of War. When, early in 1944, the inflexible *caudillo* instructed a compliant Congress to amend the constitution to allow him yet a further term in office, he succeeded in maximizing antipathy towards his government. In April a section of the officer corps staged a revolt that was subdued only with difficulty by the National Guard and the execution by firing squad of the ringleaders, none of whom could be described as radical. Such a move, unprecedented in the history of the modern Salvadorean army, increased hostility between the various security forces, and outraged not only the victims' colleagues but also the urban populace at large. The students and doctors of the capital declared a civic strike, which did not last long but engendered enough support to persuade the President that he could no longer rely upon the army, Washington or popular acquiescence. However, both the cautious approach of the U.S. Embassy, which refused to support either side, and the desire of a majority of officers for a conservative and institutional succession restricted the immediate outcome of the anti-dictatorial movement to Martínez's replacement by a trusted colleague, General Andrés Ignacio Menéndez.

The strike of April 1944 was staged in support of the military dissidents and against Martínez rather than the ruling class as a whole; there was no significant movement in the countryside, and the working class played only a subordinate role. Although this was the first of a series of popular anti-dictatorial mobilizations in Central America during 1944 and opened a short but active period of political competition, there was no instant upsurge in radical activity once Martínez had gone and Menéndez had announced new elections for the autumn. The initially cautious mood appeared to confirm expectations of a restitution of the system that had obtained up to 1931. However, the accumulating impetus of the candidacy of Dr Arturo Romero, who gained the endorsement of the Communist-backed and rapidly expanding Unión Nacional de Trabajadores (UNT) despite his espousal of a programme less radical than that of Arturo Araujo's Partido Laborista, raised fears inside both the military and the oligarchy of uncontainable mobilization following an almost victory for Romero at the polls. Such apprehension was deepened by the removal of General Ubico in Guatemala in June and the popularly backed military coup of October. Thus, when a large crowd gathered in the central plaza of San Salvador on 21 October 1944 precisely to celebrate the Guatemalan revolution, Menéndez finally bowed to the pressure from his colleagues and permitted a pre-emptive coup by Colonel Osmín Aguirre, one of the leaders of the repression in 1932. The resulting massacre in the city centre within six months of Martínez's departure not only marked a return to the methods of the ex-president but also underscored the extreme vulnerability of any effort to sustain a civilian political system without the unambiguous imprimatur of the army. Attempts to stage a second general strike and then to invade the country from Guatemala were suppressed without quarter even, as in the case of the ill-organized student invasion, when the opposition was middle class and far from extremist. Aguirre's coup imposed unity on the military apparatus and ensured that no civilian candidate stood in the elections of January 1945, the 'overwhelming majority' of votes being cast in a manner quite distinct from that envisaged by the United Nations, for an old ally of Martínez, General Salvador Castañeda Castro, heading the aptly named Partido Agrario (PA).

Castañeda presided over a four-year holding operation during which time the Cold War set in and the international conditions for a return to democracy deteriorated under the weight of a pervasive anti-communism. The same period also witnessed a steady economic recovery as coffee prices were freed from war-time agreements, opening possibilities of agricultural diversification and encouraging ideas of some industrial development. This encouraged a degree of differentiation within a capitalist class which, although exceptionally tight, was not fully integrated and had always incubated some tension between landlords and merchants. Competition rarely went much beyond sectoral tussles over positions in the markets, but within such a compact community it had enough resonance to disturb unity over the prospect of a simple retreat to the restrictions of the Martínez years. This was politically reassuring yet also out of keeping with the new phase of economic growth. Moreover, many junior officers who had supported the coup of April 1944 considered that of October, with its personalism and rejection of an institutional system of apportioning office and regulating policy, to have defrauded them. Hence, when Castañeda endeavoured in 1948 to prolong his lacklustre regime, he was overthrown in what became known as 'the majors' coup', which marked both a consolidation of the military around the objectives of the 1944 revolt and a clear shift towards modernizing the style of control. A regime of complete political prohibition and economic conservatism moved towards one that promoted an increased level of state intervention in the economy, tolerated a number of closely watched-over urban unions and civic associations, accepted some political competition within the middle class as well as the oligarchy, and gave a degree of support to those elements of capital seeking to invest in new sectors of agriculture, particularly cotton, and the manufacturing industry. The principal figure in this movement was Colonel Oscar Osorio, who manoeuvred diligently and forcefully to establish the Partido Revolucionario de Unificación Democrática (PRUD) in 1949 as the military-sponsored official party of government that would in 1961 mutate with little change beyond that of title into the Partido de Conciliación Nacional (PCN), which ruled until 1979.

The junta that held power until 1950 was young, middle-class and technocratic, initially attracting wide-spread sympathy for the military in what was seen as a reprise of April 1944. But the *apertura* that many expected was never granted. Anti-communism remained resolutely at the centre of a system that replaced Martínez's narrow autocracy with a more dynamic style of domination predicated upon the belief – as expressed by Colonel José María Lemus – that 'the only truly efficient way to achieve [social and economic] equilibrium and avoid the evils of dangerous doctrines is to promote broad transformative doctrines within the framework of co-operation between government, the capitalists and the workers'.[4] *Transformismo* was a much-used term in Central America at this time, yet although the Constitution of 1950 included stipulations in favor of agrarian reform and the 'social function' of all property, the Salvadorean officers desisted from implementing the former in the countryside and implemented the latter only with great caution in the towns. The new regime could be described as anti-oligarchic only insofar as it confirmed Martínez's exclusion of civilians from political power and adjusted the terms of that exclusion to incorporate some statist and developmentalist currents. This fully assuaged Washington, while absolute prohibition of popular organization in the countryside and tight control of the urban unions through both co-optation and direct coercion ensured that for the mass of citizens, the system was only marginally different from its predecessors.

The governments of Oscar Osorio (1950–6) and José María Lemus

---

[4] Quoted in Robert E. Elam, 'Appeal to Arms: The Army and Politics in El Salvador, 1931–1964', unpublished Ph.D. dissertation, University of New Mexico, Albuquerque, 1968, p. 146.

(1956 – 60) consolidated military power in a period of generally buoyant coffee prices, agricultural diversification and some modest growth in manufacturing. The election of 1956 was, as usual, contested by parties of the civilian right, but the PRUD received 93 per cent of the votes once a reshuffle in military appointments had ensured full institutional support for the official candidate. Such a reassuring result enabled Lemus to start his period in office with great confidence and to relax some of the controls imposed by Osorio. However, towards the end of the decade coffee prices began to fall and the example of the Cuban Revolution excited the enthusiasm of the students, who subjected the government to increasingly vociferous opposition through their union, and the newly established reformist party named after the movement of 1944, the Partido Revolucionario de Abril y Mayo (PRAM). At first Lemus attempted to field this challenge with some flexibility since the alliance built around the PRAM won the mayoralty of the capital and five other towns in the spring of 1960 elections. Nevertheless, government refusal to permit any opposition victories in the congressional polls only encouraged their campaign to the point at which, in August 1960, Lemus declared martial law and sent the army into the university. These measures, and the vigorous clamp-down that ensued, signalled a refusal to accept a genuinely independent and active opposition. Although Communist influence and the economic slump certainly caused consternation within the officer corps, there was a lack of unanimity over the wisdom of restricting political participation so tightly. Hence, when a section of the army overthrew the now highly unpopular President in October 1960 and established a junta with civilian technocrats and sympathizers of democratic reform, there was apprehension but no immediate resistance from more conservative elements. Yet, once it became clear that the junta would permit the left to stand in new elections, this caution was rapidly reversed and the counter-coup led by Colonel Julio Rivera in January 1961 received majority military support for its restitution of institutional government. Just as in 1944, when open elections and civilian government emerged as a tangible possibility, political concessions by the military were soon curtailed. However, Lemus' precipitate prohibition of all authentic opposition not from the right was henceforth adjusted by the newly formed PCN to permit some congressional and municipal representation as a form of safety-valve and to refurbish the image of the regime within the Alliance for Progress. The Partido Demócrata Cristiano (PDC), established in 1960, was permitted to win fourteen congressional seats against the PCN's thirty-two in 1964, and in

1966 one of the party's young leaders, José Napoleón Duarte, was allowed to take the mayoralty of San Salvador which he soon converted into a platform for the PDC's policy of social rapprochement and measured reform.[5] On the other hand, the Partido de Acción Renovadora (PAR), which had had a tenuous existence since the late 1940s to be revived under a new leadership in the early 1960s, was banned in 1967, having won 29 per cent of the vote on the basis of a much more extensive programme of reforms. Its effective successor, the Movimiento Nacional Revolucionario (MNR), led by Guillermo Manuel Ungo, was allowed to contest the poll of 1968 on a Social Democratic platform that included the call for an agrarian reform – not a leading item on the PDC agenda – but it lacked great popular appeal and failed to win any seats in 1970, which may well have guaranteed its continued existence.

The presence of an opposition was integral to the PCN regime, which continued to exploit its control over elections to maintain a 'continuist' system of government under the presidencies of Colonels Julio Rivera (1961–7), Fidel Sánchez Hernández (1967–72), Arturo Molina (1972–7) and General Carlos Humberto Romero (1977–9). Although the more devout and philanthropic aspects of Catholic social policy promulgated by the PDC, or demands for redistribution emanating from the Social Democrats, were at times unsettling and threatened to attract considerable support, their mere existence served to sustain the appearance of democracy and kept the system from being a full-fledged dictatorship, even though it was guaranteed by the regular army at elections and more generally upheld by the paramilitary forces. From the end of the 1960s these were assisted by a powerful, semi-official organization known as ORDEN, which functioned principally as a vigilante force in the countryside. In contrast to previous bodies of this type, ORDEN was designed to have a mass membership, and many who joined it were less attracted by its reactionary ideology than by the possibility of minor official favours or often simply the need to protect themselves against persecution, usually at the hands of the National Guard, which firmly suppressed dissident activity and ensured the prohibition of independent rural unions.

In the 1960s, rural unions often originated from the co-operatives and communal associations sponsored by the Church, posing little ostensible threat to the established order until rising violence and support for the

[5] The origins and development of the PDC are analysed in one of the very few published studies of a Central American political party: Stephan Webre, *José Napoleón Duarte and the Christian Democratic Party in Salvadoran Politics, 1960–1978* (Baton Rouge, 1979).

'preferential option for the poor' in the pastoral work and theological convictions of many rural priests engendered potent currents that acquired organizational autonomy in the 1970s.[6] Radical Catholicism was perhaps stronger in El Salvador than elsewhere in Central America, and it matched the influence of the secular left in politicizing rural labour and the students, if not the urban working class. By the mid-1970s this was plainly depleting the rank-and-file support built up by the PDC, but it did not deprive the party of large numbers of tactical votes in elections where the left either could not or would not stand. The strength of the movement was nowhere more clearly signalled than in the positions adopted at the end of the decade by Archbishop Oscar Arnulfo Romero, a cleric of hitherto conservative persuasion who, on the basis of his forceful condemnation of violence, was considered by the military and the right to be a major hindrance and, with somewhat less justification, an active supporter of the left. The shock caused by Romero's volte-face paralleled that generated by the scale of rural organization, which, because it remained largely outside the pattern of formal national politics, diffuse, and almost by definition absorbed with local tactics, was not for a long time perceived by the military as posing a markedly greater threat than the tame co-optational entities out of which it grew. As a consequence, efforts to establish an agrarian reform against landlord opposition were pursued with minimal energy and the demands of the centrist opposition for a strategic resolution to the rural question generally dismissed as demagogy. When, however, it was recognized that an authentic challenge existed in the countryside, the political instincts of the armed forces were permitted to run free in a repressive campaign that frequently compounded rather than cowed opposition.

In the towns, particularly San Salvador, the marked growth of manufacturing and regional trade in the 1960s prompted by the Central American Common Market (CACM) provided some space for trade-union expansion. Moreover, although the number of organized workers remained very low and many of these were enrolled in federations controlled by government supporters, independent action such as the general strike of 1967 reflected an erratic trend towards militancy and away from the mutualist traditions of the artisanate.[7] That this was still vulnerable to co-optation as well as coercion may be seen in the wide support for the government's invasion of

---

[6] Carlos Cabarrús, *Génesis de una revolución* (Mexico, 1983); Jenny Pearce, *Promised Land: Peasant Rebellion in Chalatenango, El Salvador* (London, 1985).
[7] See Rafael Menjivar, *Formación y lucha del proletariado* (San José, 1982).

Honduras in the 'Soccer War' of 1969, when nationalist fervour captured the PDC, which enjoyed appreciable support among workers, and elicited minimal opposition from the Communist Party (PCS), which was the major leftist force inside the unions.

This conflict had little to do with clashes during various football matches in the first round of the World Cup, and was aggravated less by border disputes than by El Salvador's considerable commercial superiority over Honduras and the large number of Salvadorean migrant workers in that country. The imbalance in trade resulted from Salvadorean exploitation of its already existing advantages under the more favourable commercial climate given by the CACM, but emigration from densely populated and intensively farmed El Salvador had provided its oligarchy with a valuable safety-valve for many years. More than half a million people had left the country since 1930, the majority to Honduras. This population provided a ready target for the embattled Honduran regime of Colonel Osvaldo López Arellano, which sought both to resist Salvadorean economic hegemony and to reduce popular opposition by appropriating the lands of Salvadorean settlers for redistribution. At least 100,000 migrants were driven back to their homeland, and this produced long-term problems that far outweighed the short-term political gain of a momentary boost to Salvadorean nationalism. Many of these refugees had trade-union experience from working the Honduran banana plantations, and most necessarily sought to re-establish their lives in the capital since the prospects for rural labour were now far worse than when they had left the country. The size of the influx was in itself a problem, but many of the refugees were less inclined to be grateful for their deliverance than discontented by the absence of opportunities that attended it, which was also a factor of some consequence. The capacity of the urban economy to absorb more labour was already exhausted, and the war effectively ended the CACM. More immediately the regime's resettlement programme provided little or no relief.

Thus, not only was a strategic outflow of poor Salvadorean workers brought to an abrupt halt by the war with Honduras, but a large number of displaced and dispossessed people were added to the expanding population of the shanty-towns around the capital, accelerating an already visible process of 'marginalization'. Between 1950 and 1980 the country's urban population grew from 18 per cent to 44 per cent of the total – an average increase by regional standards – and that of the city of San Salvador from 116,000 to 700,000 – this, too, by no means exceptional in Central

America. However, by the mid-1970s the department of San Salvador, containing more than a fifth of the national population, had a population density of 843 per square kilometre against a national average of 170, itself five times the Central American average. Thus, although the social conflict of the 1970s and 1980s could not be explained plausibly just by population density, which had been high for centuries, it was the case that this phenomenon was reaching chronic proportions and creating in the political centre of the country conditions of settlement that both exacerbated the economic difficulties of the mass of the people and promoted extra-occupational patterns of unrest and organization. As with the rapid expansion of the student population – by 1974 more than 30,000 were enrolled in the Faculty of Humanities alone – a major new political constituency came into being and unsettled the familiar socio-political balance between town and country.

The war with Honduras generated a crisis within the PCS, which was seen by many radicalized youth as incapable of providing a decisive challenge to the regime. Continued devotion to the 'peaceful road to socialism' through elections and cautious work in the unions were in keeping with Moscow's advice – increasingly harmonious with that issuing from Havana – and the organizational instincts of a party that had been all but destroyed by the adoption of an insurrectionary strategy within two years of its birth. Critical of this approach and of the 'idealist' belief that democracy could be obtained with the support of a 'national bourgeoisie' of anti-oligarchic entrepreneurs, the secretary-general, Salvador Cayetano Carpio, together with several important union and student leaders, left the party to establish a 'politico-military organization', the Fuerzas Populares de Liberación – Farabundo Martí (FPL), in 1971. This guerrilla organization did not begin operations immediately, because it rejected the *foco* theory derived from the Cuban example as well as notions of rapid insurrection in favour of a strategy of 'prolonged people's war' on the Vietnamese model. In the 1972 a more middle-class and adventurous group of disenchanted PDC supporters broke from legal politics to set up the Ejército Revolucionario del Pueblo (ERP) on the basis of a more militarist *foquismo*. Internal disputes over the validity of this model of an elite vanguard bringing the masses to revolutionary consciousness through example more than organizational collaboration reached a bloody apogee in the execution by the ERP leadership of the distinguished writer Roque Dalton in 1975. Supporters of Dalton's criticisms of the ERP subsequently formed the third major guerrilla force, the Fuerzas Armadas de Resistencia Nacional

(FARN) on more cautious political and military lines. The relatively late emergence of these groups in El Salvador compared with the rest of Central America may be attributed in large part to the fact that although there appeared to be some prospects for democratic progress in the 1960s, these were progressively reduced over the following decade as the PCN prevented the reformist opposition from obtaining office despite, or more probably because of, their growing popular support.

Since the principal mechanism for this containment continued to be government manipulation of the polls – particularly flagrant in those for the presidency in 1972 and 1977 – the pattern of polarization tended to follow the electoral calendar, popular discontent at scarcely credible opposition defeats provoking significant break-downs in public order as well as accumulating a more general disenchantment with the political system as a whole. Although the parties of reform might be criticized for a misguided belief in their ability to take office or cajole the regime into introducing progressive change, they acted with appreciable skill in seeking to exploit the opportunities available to them. By forming the Unión Nacional Opositora (UNO), the PDC, MNR and the Unión Democrática Nacionalista (UDN) – effectively a front for the outlawed PCS – not only suppressed what were little more than tactical and confessional differences between themselves but also presented the government with an impressive challenge behind the candidacy of the able Duarte, supported by the less colourful but more intellectual Ungo. Indeed, so high were expectations of a UNO victory in 1972 that when Colonel Molina was finally declared the winner by less than 10,000 votes after a suspiciously abrupt suspension of public information on the count, a section of the officer corps was prompted to stage a coup. Although the rebels refused to distribute arms to civilians, they were defeated only after troops from neighbouring states organized in the Central American Defence Council (Consejo de Defensa Centroamericana, CONDECA) were flown in to assist the disorganized loyalist forces and the ever-faithful paramilitary police. Duarte had hesitated to support the rising and held back UNO followers from staging their own street protests, but he was deemed too threatening an opponent to be afforded further guarantees and was arrested, severely beaten and exiled to Venezuela. The treatment administered to one of the most talented leaders of Latin American Christian Democracy enhanced his profile abroad and greatly increased his popularity at home.

The Molina regime, though shaken by the events of 1972, did not thereafter impose markedly tighter control than had its predecessor. It even reduced pressure on the formal opposition in an effort to maintain its participation in the system. This temporary relaxation was most evident in the regime's preparedness to acquiesce in opposition control of some congressional committees. Although this was won more by tactical skill than official concession, such acquiescence enabled the presentation in 1976 of a bill for limited agrarian reform which the government did not immediately block. However, the oligarchy staged a resolute resistance through its principal pressure groups – the Asociación Nacional de Empresas Privadas (ANEP) and the Frente de Agricultores de la Región Oriental (FARO) – thwarting the proposed legislation and signalling to the high command that the limits of concession had been exceeded. This stance was brutally supplemented by the growing activity of right-wing vigilante groups (death squads) such as FALANGE and the Unión Guerrera Blanca (UGB), which undertook selective assassinations and established a pattern of repression that was henceforth to be a sadly persistent feature of Salvadorean life.

Both the ground yielded to the opposition and the Molina regime's own disposition to countenance some form of reform in the rural sector drove the military farther to the right. The PCN candidate for the 1977 poll, General Romero, was an extreme conservative. In an effort to protect its candidate against a reprise of the events of 1972, UNO put forward a retired officer, Colonel Ernesto Claramount, who represented a minority liberal current within the military. This forced the hierarchy to carry out a frantic reorganization of army commands in order to assure support for an official candidate more resolute in his convictions than skilled in defending them. However, the scale and clumsiness of the machinations employed to return Romero both before and during the poll provoked the occupation of the capital's centre by his opponent's followers, wide-spread street violence and a short-lived general strike. Although the guerrillas were responsible for some of this activity, much of it stemmed from popular organizations and trade unions whose members had voted for UNO but were inclining to direct action in pursuit of both economic and political objectives. The post-electoral repression of 1977 assisted the growth of this tendency because President Romero, unlike his predecessor, maintained and increased coercive control, courting a rupture with the Carter administration as official government forces, ORDEN and the death squads embarked upon a violent campaign against both the orthodox left and the Catholic radicals which had already begun to construct broad-based popular organizations, fronts or 'blocs' around the much smaller guerrilla groups: the Bloque Popular Revolucionario (BPR) (1975) for the FPL; the Ligas Populares – 28 de Febrero (LP–28) (1977) for the ERP; and the Frente de Acción Popular Unificada (FAPU) (1974) for the FARN.[8] These bodies were still in fierce dispute over political and military strategy and unable to stage more than small-scale operations, usually against individuals connected with the oligarchy or military. But in the wake of UNO's manifest failure to secure reform through constitutionalism, the extension of the left's influence and growing acceptance of armed struggle were not without a certain logic. This, combined with continued sectarian divisions, gave rise to a string of organizations which were to compete for popular support until, with the country standing on the verge of civil war early in 1980, they were forced into unification.

It is certainly true that the final collapse of the PCN regime as a result of the coup of 15 October 1979 was influenced by developments at a regional level, particularly the Nicaraguan revolution of July but also the poor and deteriorating relations between the Romero regime and Washington as a result of Romero's suspension of constitutional guarantees and reluctance to halt escalating violence by the military and its informal allies, who were not afraid to promise the liquidation of the country's entire Jesuit order unless its members left. However, the momentum of domestic conflict had reached such a point by mid-1979 that a major political crisis appeared inevitable in any event. The acquiescence of the United States in a change of regime merely facilitated a relatively bloodless and essentially pre-emptive coup initiated by reformist junior officers but soon captured by less ambitious conservative rivals to Romero anxious to meet the accumulating radical challenge with both a more resourceful strategy and badly needed U.S. economic and logistical support. Romero had been obliged to lift his state of siege earlier in the year, yet this proved insufficient to stem the tide of strikes, demonstrations and guerrilla operations; both the suspension of the Constitution and its restitution in unaltered circumstances confirmed the exhaustion of the PCN strategy of combining repression with formal liberties. Neither was adequate by itself, and when organized separately they simply cancelled each other out. An essentially tactical arrangement had decomposed into confusion whereby the populace was aggrieved at the absence of proclaimed freedoms and insufficiently cowed by the violence. The younger officers behind the

---

[8] Latin America Bureau, *El Salvador Under General Romero* (London, 1979).

October coup generally associated with Colonel Majano sought to provide space for negotiation (although, unlike their forebears in 1944 and 1961, they held back from promising immediate elections). In this they enjoyed the tacit support of Washington, still shocked by the overthrow of Somoza and concerned to avert open military rule. Nonetheless, the reformists remained a minority inside the army and enjoyed even less support in the powerful paramilitary forces; and since the radical left refused to halt popular mobilization or abdicate armed activity – only a truce was agreed – on the basis of changes in the military hierarchy, conservative officers were able to harness the logic of maintaining public order to their rapidly organized campaign to sabotage economic concessions. For both internal and external reasons it proved impossible to resolve these tensions inside the dominant bloc with any speed. As a result, although the reformists progressively lost authority, political conflict within the military and ruling class endured long after El Salvador had entered a low-level but prolonged and very brutal civil war in which the military and oligarchy were ranged against a popular bloc composed of the majority of the erstwhile legal opposition and the organizations of the radical left.

In economic terms the outbreak of major social conflict in El Salvador in 1979 was perhaps more predictable than even the Nicaraguan revolution; the steady increase in production and agro-exports during the post-war period had been matched by a no less impressive tendency to reduce access to land for subsistence, prompting increased unemployment and under-employment and a regressive distribution of income in the countryside more pronounced than in the rest of Central America and certainly beyond hope of significant alleviation from growth in the urban economy. Between 1950 and 1980, GDP grew from $379.6 million to $1,526 million at an annual average rate of 5.2 per cent while the population expanded at 3.3 per cent. The increase in GDP per capita from $185 to $289 over this period appeared to indicate an improvement in the wealth of the population at large consonant with a threefold increase in the number of vehicles, fourfold rise in paved roads and in the number of telephones, and other infrastructural advances of a similar order. Yet if the global stock of wealth had increased faster than that of people and the forces of production had advanced considerably, the impression of a comprehensive modernization was belied by the indices for income distribution and land tenure. In 1977 the wealthiest 6 per cent of the population earned as much as the poorest 63 per cent. In 1975, 41 per cent of rural families were completely landless, 34 per cent farmed less than 1 hectare (insufficient for subsistence) and 15 per cent possessed less than 2 hectares.[9] Moreover, although since before the turn of the century, the Salvadorean peasantry had been much more restricted in its access to plots of land than had small farmers in neighbouring states, land poverty had accelerated appreciably since the late 1950s as commercial estates dedicated to both coffee and new crops such as cotton and sugar as well as cattle-ranching occupied greater space within a virtually static agricultural frontier. The rise in production that supported the post-war growth in GDP may be explained in part by better yields – that for coffee rose from 655 kilos per hectare in 1950 to 1,224 in 1977 – which also had the effect of at least maintaining demand for harvest labour. However, while the expansion of land under coffee was relatively modest – from 112,000 in 1950 to 147,000 hectares in 1977 – that under cotton more than trebled (to more than 60,000 hectares) while sugar increased by comparable degree (to 38,000 hectares) and the area in pasture for cattle – the sector that demanded least labour and most land per unit – rose by 50 per cent. In many cases this expansion was achieved at the direct cost of peasant holdings on the periphery of established coffee country and outside the traditional zones of large estates. Although cotton was an established crop and could be extended on the basis of existing patterns of tenure, the rise in cattle-raising trespassed deep into the less fertile and marginal lands that had hitherto provided a modicum of space for subsistence. This expansion did not produce an absolute stasis in the domestic food crop acreage – which may be broadly but not exclusively associated with peasant agriculture – but it did impede growth in land cultivated for the domestic market. Between 1948 and 1978 land given over to maize expanded by 30 per cent; to beans, by 23 per cent; and to rice, by just 12 per cent. Modest improvements in yield assisted increases in production of 75 per cent, 43 per cent and 67 per cent respectively over a period when El Salvador's population nearly trebled in size.[10] Thus, while harvest labour demand was maintained and agro-exports grew in both volume and value, the subsistence economy declined relative to both the commercial estates and the population. The import of increasing quantities of basic grains was necessary to maintain levels of consumption.

[9] Ministerio de Planificaíon, 'Distribución del ingreso y gasto por deciles de hogares', (San Salvador, 1981); Censo Agropecuario, 1975, cited in J. Mark Ruhl, 'Agrarian Structure and Political Stability in Honduras', *Journal of Inter-American Studies* 26, no. 1 (1984): 47.

[10] Edelberto Torres Rivas, 'The Beginnings of Industrialization in Central America', Working Paper no. 141, Latin American Program, Woodrow Wilson Center (Washington, D.C., 1984), p. 17.

Lacking virgin lands in which to settle or even a culture of socio-economic 'refuge' comparable to that sustained by the Indian farmers of Guatemala, the expanding Salvadorean peasantry was caught in a pincer movement between loss of opportunities for direct cultivation and those for temporary waged labour. This by no means compelled a break-down in rural order, still less open revolt, but it did aggravate discontent with the landlord regime while dislocating large numbers of rural labourers from the economic and social controls of the *finca*, opening the traditionally cautious political consciousness of the peasantry to the unsettling influence of local priests, schoolteachers and lay activists opposed to the established order. The sharp contrasts in the human condition in El Salvador, where the wealth of the landlord class was as impressive and as ostentatiously paraded as anywhere else in Latin America, were naturally prone to excite sentiments of Jacobin egalitarianism as much as resignation to an historic and unremovable order.

As we have seen, a significant proportion of the rural population moved either permanently or temporarily to the towns as the manufacturing sector began to grow. Between 1950 and 1977 industry expanded by an average of 6.3 per cent a year. The share of GDP attributable to manufacturing production rose from 12.9 per cent to 18.7 per cent, which was high by regional standards. Much of this growth took place under the CACM in the 1960s when the share of foreign, principally U.S., investment in manufacturing rose from 0.7 per cent in 1959 to 38.1 per cent in 1969.[11] Such progress was not of the type envisaged by many planners in the period after the Second World War insofar as there was very little heavy industry – capital goods accounted for 8.6 per cent of production in 1978 – and the bulk of output (64.7 per cent) was of perishable commodities frequently related to agricultural production. Nevertheless, the amount of locally produced inputs was lower than this structure might suggest, the textile industry importing 45 per cent of its raw materials and the paper industry nearly 90 per cent. This, combined with the 'assembly and finishing' character of many of the new enterprises, limited the trickle-down effects of sectoral growth to the rest of the economy. Furthermore, since much of the new industrial plant was foreign-owned and capital-intensive, the overall rise in the labour force (from 87,300 in 1962 to 118,000 in 1975) was much more modest than that in production

---

[11] Gert Rosenthal, 'El papel de la inversión extranjera directa en el proceso de integración', in *Centroamérica hoy* (Mexico, 1976), p. 125.

and masked a fall in the size of the working class relative to the economically active population as a whole (from 10.2 per cent to 9.3 per cent) as well as the fact that nearly half of this manufacturing labour force was still employed in artisanal workshops of five employees or less.[12] Thus, not only did industrial growth fail to supply alternative employment for most of those leaving the countryside, it also resulted in the properly 'proletarian' character of the urban labour force being diminished from the early 1960s onwards – a matter of no little importance for sociological theories of revolution. The influence of assembly-line and factory syndicalism cannot by any means be excluded from the urban unrest of the late 1970s, but these were often subordinate in terms of both numbers and political impetus to the role of radicalized white-collar and skilled workers (particularly the teachers and power workers), the impoverished 'self-employed' in the informal sector, and locally based community organizations that usually dominated the plebeian fronts to the fore in popular mobilization until open activity was halted by repression following the general strike of August 1980. Nonetheless, it is of some consequence that once a modicum of public organization and activity again became possible after the elections of 1984, the trade unions, particular those in the white-collar and public sectors, revived remarkably quickly, suggesting that urban discontent could not be reduced simply to a revolt of a marginalized lumpenproletariat.

It is evident that neither economic stagnation nor mere poverty caused the social conflict of the late 1970s, the former because it simply did not occur until the civil war had begun – and the international economy entered recession – and the latter because poverty in itself was no novelty in Salvadorean society nor as great as in Honduras, which remained relatively free of violence, although undoubtedly people were getting poorer faster than ever before. What lay behind the collapse of a social order established a century before was a process of concerted growth dominated by the export sector that dislocated tens of thousands of rural labourers from the security of both their lands and harvest wages but failed to replace this disaggregation of the peasantry with a process of socially stable and economically compensatory urbanization. This imbalance not only accelerated impoverishment but also created a significant population devoid of 'pure' class character, often geographically as well as socially mobile, outside established circuits of control, and subjected to decreas-

[12] Ramón Mayorga, *El crecimiento desigual en Centroamérica* (Mexico, 1983), pp. 60–6.

ingly efficacious strategies for survival. This population cannot be accounted as exclusively urban or rural since the symbiosis between town and countryside is too strong in El Salvador, as later became evident in the relatively fluid exchange between the two spheres in terms of military operations. In this respect, at least, the crisis was as 'modern' as it was traditional, combining features of the late twentieth century (the guerrillas' use of video for propaganda and education) with those familiar for centuries (the struggle over land; cultural antipathies; inter-communal violence).

Between October 1979 and January 1980 there was considerable confusion in Salvadorean politics as a junta combining both reformist and conservative officers, representatives of the legal opposition (including the PCS), the oligarchy, and some sectors of the radical bloc endeavoured to agree upon policy while the military continued to attack popular demonstrations. By the end of 1979 those reforms the progressive elements had managed to introduce were plainly being stalled by the right, and the refusal of the military to accept government control over its operations resulted in the resignation of all the reformists except members of the PDC. In January 1980 the plebeian fronts held a large demonstration in the capital to mark the anniversary of the 1932 rising and the formation of the Coordinadora Revolucionaria de Masas (CRM), which unified the popular organizations and was joined two months later by most of the reformist parties and many unions to form the Frente Democrático Revolucionario (FDR). Henceforth the FDR acted as the principal political body of the opposition. This consolidation of the popular bloc was hastened by the assassination of Archbishop Romero in March, a crime widely attributed to the paramilitary forces nurtured on the periphery of the army and publicly lauded by extremist politicians of the right, such as Roberto D'Aubuisson, who considered as subversives even those depleted and cowed representatives of reform still in government. Romero's death indicated how far such forces were prepared to go in their campaign against reform, and it split the PDC, a minority leaving both government and party on the grounds that it was no longer politically possible or morally acceptable to collaborate with the right in order to fortify the centre against the left. The majority of the party, however, continued to support their leader José Napoleón Duarte, who was receiving support from Washington for his vehement campaign against his old UNO allies for being the dupes of Communism. The opposition retorted with equal predictability that he had made common cause with those who not only oppressed the people but had also tortured and exiled him when he championed democratic rights.

Although Duarte was henceforth vilified by the left and centre as a puppet, he maintained a position independent of the extreme right and most of the military in that he insisted upon an agrarian reform as a necessary means by which to reduce polarization in the countryside. Since the Carter administration supported this strategy and the high command was now prepared to accept it as the price for much-needed U.S. logistical backing, a still disorganized oligarchy failed to impede its formal introduction in May 1980. The reform subsequently underwent a very chequered history in that redistribution of large coffee estates either fell outside its compass or was postponed *sine die,* and the conversion of a number of less efficient and 'over-sized' haciendas into co-operatives often amounted to little more than an alteration of deeds, since sabotage and violence impeded a genuine adoption of control by the labourers. There was some progress in granting title to small plots, but this proceeded far more slowly than planned and certainly did not produce the stratum of small capitalist farmers envisaged by the U.S. planners in charge of the programme. Harried particularly by the forces of the right but also sometimes by those of the left, the recipients of long-awaited lands were largely incapable of realizing a significant change in their circumstances while the great majority of the rural population remained excluded from the reform. Yet even those limited steps that were taken proved anathema to the landlords, who began to exercise their de facto powers of veto with the help of officers who accepted the reform as a requirement of U.S. support but whose political instincts were to hinder any change in the traditional order. The exceptions to this rule were notable for their small number, but as the war became more extended some of the more able commanders not known for their progressive views began to accept the programme on purely logistical grounds.

Even before this attitude began to take root, the oligarchy was being obliged by the thrust of the junta's policies to move beyond spoiling operations and stage a political challenge for formal office. This was compelled both by the fall of the PCN and Washington's strategy of making military support conditional upon at least the promulgation of some social reforms, a quid pro quo greatly facilitated by the PDC's presence in the junta but justifiably viewed by the extreme right as susceptible to adjustment should it gain power and the left-wing challenge continue to perturb the U.S. administration. The establishment of the Alianza Republicana Nacional (ARENA) under the leadership of the reactionary populist Roberto D'Aubuissón may, therefore, be seen as the first genuinely independent intervention of the landlord class in open political competition since 1932, a development that was somewhat obscured by the adoption of modern methods of campaigning in the style of U.S. parties to complement the power of patronage and retribution over voters employed by, or vulnerable to, the party's leading supporters. ARENA's unqualified repudiation of economic reform and advocacy of a purely military solution to the conflict was nothing if not simple and coherent – the electoral appeal of which was often underrated by its opponents – and it effectively obliged Washington to desist from any major challenge to the landed bourgeoisie. Yet if D'Aubuissón's well-publicized connections with the death squads and chilling proclamations engendered diplomatic embarrassment, his opposition to the government lent some credibility to the notion that formal political competition existed in El Salvador, thereby facilitating the presentation of both the government and its legal opponents as constituting a democratic system worthy of protection against Communist subversion.

The programme drawn up by the Coordinadora Revolucionaria de Masas (CRM) in January 1980 and adopted by the Frente Democrático Revolucionario (FDR) a few weeks later was not a charter for Communism, but it did include a comprehensive agrarian reform and the nationalization of strategic economic infrastructure as well as the banks and foreign trade. (These last two measures were, in fact, implemented in part by the junta on rational capitalist grounds, and although they were resisted by the oligarchy, were allowed to stand when the right was in control of the constituent assembly and presidency in 1982–4.) Although the FDR contained a number of powerful and openly Marxist bodies seeking some form of socialism through revolutionary change, none of its members was in a position to impose a programme of socialist transformation or indeed considered it viable in even the medium term, and the alliance had been made possible only through agreement on a 'popular democratic' platform that postulated a social policy comparable to that held by UNO in the early 1970s. Yet under the conditions of extreme violence obtaining from early 1980 the political methods of the FDR predictably took on a more radical tone, and opposition strategy increasingly came under the influ-

ence of the guerrilla groups. This shift began following the failure of the
general strikes of June and August 1980 when the reformists were obliged
to accept that there was no alternative to armed struggle.

The establishment of a combined military command in the Frente
Farabundo Martí para la Liberación Nacional (FMLN) in the autumn of
1980 marked the end of a period of ambiguity in opposition tactics and
the beginning of a civil war in which some 70,000 people lost their lives
over the following six years. The precipitate attempt by the FMLN to
stage a 'final offensive' in January 1981 not only provoked greater U.S.
intervention but also obliged the guerrilla to alter its tactics from a
predominantly urban and insurrectionary approach to a more rural and
low-level campaign punctuated with occasional large-scale attacks, particularly in the north and east of the country. The rebels were strongest in
Chalatenango (where the FPL was dominant), Morazán (ERP-dominated)
and around the Guazapa volcano to the north of San Salvador (where all the
groups possessed forces), although a total force of perhaps 7,000 combatants had the capacity to harass an army over 30,000-strong beyond these
zones and particularly in the rich farming country around San Miguel and
San Vicente. Under the Reagan administration military assistance to El
Salvador was substantially increased but also limited in its efficacy by the
army's lack of experience in combat, the low quality of the officer corps,
and the proclivity of the paramilitary forces for killing unarmed peasants.
Such resort to the traditional methods of control greatly prejudiced the
international image of the regime and prompted the French and Mexican
governments to recognize the FMLN-FDR as a representative political
organization. Yet even though the Salvadorean military acquired a formidable reputation for both inefficiency and brutality, the waging of a war of
attrition did eventually reduce the inhabitants of combat zones to strategies for survival beyond that of supporting the guerrilla. Thus, by the end
of 1982 it was evident that although it had established a remarkable
capacity for resistance, the rebel army lacked the ability to defeat the
military in the foreseeable future.

In the spring of 1982 elections were held for a constituent assembly
which produced a working majority for a revived PCN and ARENA over
the PDC, which had dominated the junta under Duarte's provisional
presidency. Unable to halt the poll, the guerrilla was now faced with a
regime that was certainly more conservative than its predecessor but could
also claim to have a popular mandate. Even though such claims were
rebutted with evidence of electoral irregularities that appeared convincing

to many beyond the rebel ranks, and despite the fact that the change in administration barely affected military operations, the poll did mark a shift in political conditions insofar as it opened up a second sphere of contest. This was boycotted by the FDR on the plausible grounds that since so many of its leaders and supporters had been killed there was no possibility of its being permitted to participate without precipitating a massacre. The notion that a political competition between parties of the right under the conditions of a civil war constituted a genuine democratic process was subjected to much scepticism both within the country and abroad, especially given El Salvador's questionable electoral traditions. On the other hand, it was apparent that however insufficient a reflection of public opinion, the restitution of the formalities of democratic government was a major development. This opened tensions inside the opposition on both tactical and ideological grounds, differences inside the left only finally being resolved following the death of two veterans of the FPL – Cayetano Carpio and Mélida Anaya Montes. As a result of these disputes, early in 1984 the FDR issued a new programme that was appreciably less radical than that of 1980; it suppressed concrete economic and social objectives and concentrated upon the mechanisms for a ceasefire and the establishment of a provisional government combining representatives of both the existing regime and the FDR. The opposition continued to denounce the formal political system as a charade, but the Reagan administration's decision to stage a concerted campaign against the left in Central America and the retreat of the embattled Sandinista government in Nicaragua from its early logistical support for the rebels indicated that expectations of a victory achieved in the short term and by military means were misconceived. The shift towards negotiation was further encouraged when, in May 1984, Duarte narrowly beat D'Aubuissón (by 54 per cent to 46 per cent of the vote) in an election that, although neither free of suspect practices nor reflective of the sympathies of a considerable section of the population, did nevertheless indicate a widespread desire for peace. By campaigning in the name of rapprochement, Duarte was able to match the well-funded and agile anti-communist crusade staged by D'Aubuissón, and although Washington made no secret of its preference for the PDC, the extent of the slaughter, economic crisis and forced migration undoubtedly convinced many to vote for what seemed the quickest and least terrifying path to terminating hostilities. However, if the exhaustion of the populace stemmed the progress of the radical right, expectations that the war would now be halted dissipated rapidly as Duarte, threatened by the powerful and suspicious high command and lacking U.S. support for negotiations, rejected proposals for a ceasefire and a new government, made by the rebels at the town of La Palma in November 1984. For the next two years peace talks foundered upon the president's insistence that the opposition lay down its arms without condition and the rebels' refusal to accept these terms as anything distinct from surrender. As the economy continued its steep decline, Duarte lost both popularity and authority, and the military failed to extend its containment of the FMLN to a decisive victory. The prospects of a government victory appeared as distant as those of a resolution that favoured the rebels who, confronted with absolute opposition from Washington, were unable to escape the logic of a *guerra popular prolongada* that offered their supporters no relief from violence and economic hardship.

Under such conditions, which produced a death toll of some 70,000 between 1980 and 1988, both sides had reason to consider the merits of the regional peace plan proposed by President Oscar Arias of Costa Rica in February 1987 and ratified, in amended form, by the regional heads of state in August of that year as the Esquipulas II agreement. Although both the armed forces and the FMLN remained profoundly reluctant to countenance concessions on the part of their political allies, President Duarte was unable to escape the logic of his earlier initiative to negotiate, while the left, now under pressure from Managua and Havana to display strategic flexibility, perceived the need to broaden its campaign on both domestic and diplomatic fronts.

The obstacles confronting a negotiated settlement were more substantial than in Nicaragua – where the Contra rebels had failed in their military campaign and remained almost entirely beholden to Washington – or, indeed, in Guatemala – where the Union Revolucionaria Nacional Guatemalteca (URNG) was too weak to expect reasonable terms from a civilian administration which was patently cowed by the military. Yet the political leadership of the Salvadorean opposition had never fully rejected the electoralist road or entirely dedicated itself to the capture of state power through insurrection. Equally, the civil war had greatly prejudiced the economic interests which challenged Duarte from the right and which now perceived some advantage in launching a nationalist campaign against the government's dependence on the United States, not least perhaps because this opened up the possibility of conducting an independent overture to the guerrillas. Although both the level of violence and the degree of ideological polarization underwent no diminution, it became apparent that U.S. involvement in Salvadorean affairs had produced some unforeseen consequences.

The strength of ARENA's conservative challenge to the PDC was not immediately obvious because the Christian Democrats secured control of Congress in 1985 and their opponents remained tarnished abroad by D'Aubuissón's association with the death squads. However, the Duarte administration was hamstrung by more than its extreme dependence upon U.S. aid, which by 1988 amounted to half the national budget. Although the army was bolstered by U.S. assistance, it was the government that suffered from its failure to translate this into victory over the guerrilla. At the same time, North American largesse provided ample opportunity for official corruption, which particularly damaged a confessional party that made much of its high moral purpose. Moreover, from the time that Duarte had obtained the provisional presidency his party had excused its failures in terms of the extreme right's control of the judiciary and, after 1982, the legislature; after 1985 such an explanation appeared threadbare indeed to those who had voted for the PDC, which failed to develop an organized popular movement based on its voters and then began to suffer from divisions within its elite. ARENA, by contrast, was able to stage a significant recovery as the government failed to realize the promises made between 1981 and 1984. As a result, the extreme right scored a sweeping victory in the legislative elections of 1988. Recognizing that this paved the way to ousting the PDC from the presidency in the poll of March 1989, the ARENA leadership turned its attention to improving its international image and making some gesture towards a negotiated settlement of the conflict so as to placate regional concerns as well as the preoccupations of many voters. These moves ran directly counter to the party's frequent calls for a 'final' military solution to the civil war, suggesting it had registered the importance of U.S. influence but was unwilling to alter its fundamental outlook. This, certainly, was the interpretation of many when D'Aubuissón was replaced as party leader by Alfredo Cristiani, a mild-mannered coffee grower who, educated in the United States, soon proved to be an extremely adroit advocate of the 'modern' ARENA in Washington.

Faced with a number of important developments both within the country and in Central America as a whole in 1987–8, the left responded with some unexpected initiatives of its own. In the autumn of 1988 the FDR leaders Guillermo Manuel Ungo and Rubén Zamora returned openly to San Salvador, secured personal guarantees and announced that they would participate in the March 1989 election in the name of Convergencia Democrática (CD), which, they claimed, would win a free and fair poll. The military leadership of the FMLN effectively dissociated itself from this move but desisted from directly attacking it. Then, as the election campaign got under way, the FMLN itself took the lead by proposing a postponement of the poll for six months as the principal basis upon which a cease-fire might be established, the left reincorporated into legal political life, the military dramatically reduced in size, U.S. military aid cut, and a true electoral test held. For a while the new Bush administration seemed prepared to consider discussion of this offer, and ARENA displayed even more willingness than the PDC to negotiate with its enemies. However, the FMLN's terms proved to be too steep and the initiative rapidly foundered. The guerrillas returned to their campaign to sabotage the poll but failed to impede Cristiani from easily beating the PDC candidate, Fidel Chávez Mena, while the CD predictably returned a very low vote.

In one sense these developments deepened the complexities of Salvadorean political life and appeared to open up possibilities not seen since the onset of the civil war in 1980–1. Yet even at the height of the manoeuvres it was difficult to envisage a stable resolution of the conflict in local terms. Indeed, ARENA's victory appeared to herald a return to the oligarchic mandate, uniting a fiercely reactionary dominant bloc under a reluctant but decisive North American imprimatur. A decade of bloody strife had failed to reduce political activity, but the practice of politics had equally proved incapable to putting an end to war.

6

HONDURAS SINCE 1930

In the first century after independence from Spain Honduras fought a mainly unsuccessful battle to overcome the constraints on national integration imposed by its geography.[1] The country's high mountains and narrow, steep-sided valleys had crippled internal communications, inhibited agricultural development and produced a marked localism in national politics. In the late 1920s, the land frontiers with Guatemala, El Salvador and Nicaragua were all still in dispute, leading to occasional military conflict, while the lack of national integration encouraged neighbouring governments to intervene in Honduran affairs. Even the off-shore territories were subject to the same centrifugal tendencies; the Bay Islands, recovered from Great Britain in 1860, remained largely autonomous, sovereignty over the Swan Islands was disputed with the United States, and possession of several islands in the Gulf of Fonseca was contested with El Salvador and Nicaragua. The country's difficulties were compounded by the size of its population. The 1930 census estimated the number of inhabitants at 854,184, giving a population density of less than 20 per square mile. The overwhelming majority were scattered throughout the rural areas, leaving the capital Tegucigalpa with a mere 40,000 souls. Large areas of eastern Honduras were virtually uninhabited.

Geography had given a different twist in Honduras to the liberal reforms which swept Central America from the 1870s. While Liberal *caudillos* implemented and participated personally in programmes to foster coffee and other agro-exports in the neighbouring republics, in Honduras Presidents Marco Aurelio Soto (1876–83) and Luis Bográn (1883–90)

---

[1] Richard Harding Davies tells the story of a Honduran congressman who demonstrated the nature of his country's geography by crumpling up a page of letter-paper, dropping it on his desk and declaring 'That is an outline map of Honduras'. See Richard Harding Davies, *Three Gringoes in Venezuela and Central America* (New York, 1896), p. 73.

emphasized mining, both becoming shareholders themselves in newly formed companies. Mining, on which the colonial economy had been based, offered the chance of eliminating the commercial disadvantage implied by poor internal communications since the high value-to-weight ratio of the leading minerals (silver and gold) reduced the relative importance of internal transport costs (almost prohibitive in the case of coffee). Furthermore, it was hoped that a mining boom might provide both the incentive and the fiscal resources with which to carry out long-overdue improvements in the communications system.

Some Honduran nationals participated in the recovery of mining after the liberal reforms, but the most successful ventures – stimulated by generous legislation – were foreign-owned, the New York and Honduras Rosario Mining Company acquiring a dominant position by the end of the century. The active promotion of foreign *direct* investment was no accident, because Honduras had been effectively excluded from the international bond market since the early 1870s as a consequence of a financial scandal, which became a cause célèbre and deeply scarred a whole generation of the political elite. The Honduran government had in the late 1860s raised three loans with a face value of nearly £6 million to construct an inter-oceanic railway link in a brave, if naive, attempt to improve communications and foster national integration. The scheme collapsed in 1872 with only fifty miles of track complete when it became clear that the Honduran government had been swindled; by the mid-1920s capitalization of unpaid interest had left Honduras with an external public debt of nearly £30 million – one of the highest in the world on a per capita basis.

The collapse of the railway venture led subsequent Honduran governments to hold exaggerated expectations of the impact of mining on national integration. The industry certainly expanded, but generous concessions limited the fiscal impact and the government's road-building programme remained pitifully undeveloped. Only one bank (Banco de Honduras) emerged in response to the mining boom, and the main beneficiary outside the mining sector was the small commercial enclave dominated by Arab, French and German merchants. Poor communications continued to inhibit the growth of a marketed surplus from agriculture and Tegucigalpa was the only capital city in Central America not served by a railway.

With this dismal background in view, it is not difficult to understand the enthusiasm with which successive governments greeted the overtures of foreign-owned banana companies at the turn of the century. The banana industry had been developing slowly since the 1860s with foreign ships calling at the Bay Islands and the Atlantic coast ports to purchase bananas from local producers. Growth was impeded, however, by transportation problems and the new breed of foreign entrepreneurs offered to develop railroads, improve port facilities and diversify exports in exchange for land and tax concessions. Since the land at the time appeared to have no other use, and since the fiscal privileges demanded were similar to those awarded to foreign-owned mining companies, the entrepreneurs were warmly received.

The first to enter Honduras in 1898 were the Vaccaro brothers, whose firm later became the Standard Fruit and Steamship Company. Four years later, in 1902, a similar concession was awarded to William Streich, but lack of funds forced him to sell his business to Sam Zemurray a few years later. Zemurray formed the Cuyamel Fruit Company in 1911, and the following year the United Fruit Company (UFCO) entered Honduras with the granting of concessions to two subsidiaries – the Tela and Truxillo Railroad Companies. These three companies (the Cuyamel, Standard Fruit and UFCO) soon came to dominate both the production and export of bananas and were responsible for the extraordinary boom which took Honduras to the position of the world's leading banana exporter by 1928. By that time more than a thousand miles of railways had been laid and even the sixty miles (ten had been added since the 1880s) belonging to the National Railway were managed by Zemurray's Cuyamel Fruit Company.

The price paid for this rapid expansion was high. Competition among the banana companies for government favours at first exacerbated the personalism and localism of Honduran politics. There were few, if any, elections in the first two decades of the century in which the competing candidates were not backed by rival companies. In the absence of alternative sources of funds, the companies became lenders of last resort and the successful candidate was expected to ignore irregularities in the implementation of existing contracts or award even more generous concessions. Tax privileges soon reached a point where the amount exempted far exceeded total government revenue from all sources, while duty-free imports sold through company stores undermined the fledgling manufacturing sector. Indeed, the few examples of industrial development by the end of the 1920s mainly represented diversification by the fruit companies themselves.

The spectacular growth of the banana industry did not solve the problem of poor communications inherited from the nineteenth century. By the end of the 1920s, an unpaved road linked Tegucigalpa with the Pacific port of San Lorenzo, but the centre of economic gravity was now firmly on the northern (Atlantic) coast, which was still not connected to the capital by road or rail. The banana zones on that coast were the purest form of enclaves with ports, railroads, telegraphs, and so on under foreign control and labour frequently imported (from the West Indies and El Salvador); a bank (Banco de Atlántida) founded by Vaccaro Bros. provided primitive financial services and the U.S. dollar (backed by gold) circulated freely, while the rest of Honduras remained on the silver standard in a rare example of bimetallism. One of the few links with the rest of the economy was provided by the fruit companies' lawyers, all Hondurans, who frequently doubled as politicians in remote Tegucigalpa.

The U.S. government had cast a jaundiced eye over Honduran internal affairs on several occasions since the turn of the century. Intervention by both Nicaragua and Guatemala had been one factor behind the decision to hold the conference of all Central American states in Washington in 1907 that produced the ill-fated Central American Court of Justice and a Treaty of Peace and Amity. Washington was also concerned by the geometric growth of the external public debt owed to European holders of the railway bonds, and in 1910 dollar diplomacy was invoked by Secretary of State Philander Knox to shift the debt from European to U.S. hands. The U.S. administration was thwarted, however, by Zemurray; he financed a revolution to topple the Honduran president, who favoured U.S. fiscal intervention.

Not for the first time, therefore, the State Department found itself at loggerheads in Honduras with one of the fruit companies, but a more active intervention was delayed until 1924. The presidential elections of 1923 had produced a three-way split with no candidate securing an outright majority. Congress refused to endorse any of the candidates, the outgoing President López Gutiérrez declared himself dictator and civil war ensued. This civil war, like its predecessors, might have been left to run its course if the U.S. administration had not recently persuaded all Central American countries to sign a new Treaty of Peace and Amity. U.S. prestige was, therefore, on the line, with the result that the marines entered Tegucigalpa in March 1924 and Sumner Welles was despatched to call a conference of the conflicting parties. The outcome was the Pact of Amapala, signed in May, which provided for the election to the presidency of Miguel Paz Barahona, one of the few participants in the 1923 election who had not participated in the civil war.

The marines departed almost as swiftly as they had arrived and Honduras entered on a period of stability such as it had not enjoyed since independence. This, however, was due not so much to U.S. intervention as to the growing maturity of the Honduran political system. The Liberal Party had gradually risen above the extreme factionalism of the nineteenth century into a political machine with national pretensions. The Liberals' opponents had finally coalesced into a genuine political party with the launch of the National Party in 1923. The two parties were distinguished less by the nineteenth-century ideological disputes between liberals and conservatives than by the conditions under which armed revolt was regarded as legitimate, the National Party demonstrating the greatest reluctance to use force as a means of settling political disputes.

Ironically, it was the National Party's presidential candidate – Tiburcio Carías Andino – who resorted to arms after the 1923 elections, but he did so only after López Gutiérrez had declared himself dictator. Both Carías and the National Party later demonstrated realism in accepting the stipulation of the Pact of Amapala that Paz Barahona (Carías' vice-presidential running mate) should be elected president. A more severe test for the National Party came when the Liberal candidate, Dr Vicente Mejía Colindres, defeated Carías in the 1928 presidential elections and became the first incumbent in Honduran history to win the presidency in peaceful elections against an official candidate. This rare experience was repeated in 1932, when Carías defeated the Liberal candidate in the October presidential elections. In the elections of both 1928 and 1932 the two parties presented a single candidate, giving the winner not only a plurality but also an outright majority. This made congressional intervention unnecessary and avoided the complications which had so frequently led to civil war in the past.

The period of relative stability that began in 1924 made possible the resolution of several problems from the past. In 1926, Congress ratified an agreement settling the outstanding external debt arrears; all unpaid interest was cancelled and the balance of the principal (£5,398,370) was to be paid off over thirty years with payment guaranteed by the consular revenues administered through the National City Bank of New York. These terms were not onerous, and Honduras was one of the very few Latin American countries not to default on its external debt in the 1930s.

Furthermore, the agreement permitted the Honduran government to return to the international capital market, and in February 1928 a loan was arranged with a U.S. bank to consolidate the public debts owed mainly to the fruit companies.

The renewed access to external finance might have increased the government's room for manoeuvre with the fruit companies, but the sale in December 1929 of Zemurray's Cuyamel Fruit Company to UFCO left the Mejía Colindres administration facing just two giant multinational firms: UFCO and Standard Fruit. The balance of power was revealed clearly during this administration when Congress first uncovered numerous irregularities in company behaviour that were ignored by the President and then failed to reverse Mejía's approval of contracts giving the fruit companies the right to utilize certain national waters without compensation. The sale of the Cuyamel Fruit Company did, however, have one desirable side effect: it ended the dispute between Zemurray and UFCO over concessions in the north-west of the country which had brought Honduras and Guatemala close to war in 1928. A treaty was signed between the two countries in 1930, and the boundary was settled by arbitration in 1933.

The banana boom had pushed specialization to the point where bananas accounted for nearly 90 per cent of Honduran exports at the end of the 1920s. Furthermore, the production of bananas formed such a large part of agricultural output that banana exports constituted around one-third of the gross domestic product (GDP). This dependence on one crop left the economy desperately vulnerable not only to fluctuations in the world market for bananas, but also to decisions by the two fruit companies on their global allocation of resources. The impact on Honduras of the world depression was therefore very severe, although it was delayed until 1931–2 by the decision of the fruit companies to concentrate production initially on their low-cost Honduran divisions.

The fall in the world price of bananas – nothing like as steep as for coffee – at first made no impact on Honduras. Since the 'price' was a book-keeping entry between different subsidiaries of the same vertically integrated firms, the returned value from banana exports was unaffected. By 1932, however, the companies were trying to transfer some of the burden to their Honduran divisions through a reduction in nominal wages and in the prices paid to independent producers. In the face of a series of strikes by the unorganized labourers (trade unions remained illegal in Honduras until the mid-1950s), the companies made some concessions on non-wage issues but were able to force through the salary reductions.

The artificial nature of the export price made the value of exports a meaningless statistic, but the value of imports started to fall after the fiscal year 1929/30 for a variety of reasons.[2] First, the fruit companies imported less as investment plans were shelved; second, the rest of the economy was not immune to the impact of world depression and, third, the dollar price of imports was itself falling. As a result of all these factors, customs duties fell and the government faced a major fiscal crisis in the run-up to the 1932 elections. Two foreign loans were arranged through UFCO with the Canal Bank and Trust Co. of New Orleans, but not for the first time in Honduran history public-sector salaries were 'postponed' and the floating debt (a euphemism for unpaid salaries) jumped from zero in 1929 to 8.1 million lempiras in 1933.[3]

THE CARIATO (1933–48)

When he finally assumed the presidency on 1 February 1933, Tiburcio Carías faced a very difficult situation. A rebellion launched by several of his Liberal opponents the previous November had still not been completely crushed, and the expenses of civil war had added to the fiscal crisis inherited from the Mejía Colindres administration. The decline in banana exports, which in turn reduced imports, government revenue and the general level of economic activity, was expected to continue and the fruit companies (especially UFCO) were pressing for favours from the government to off-set the impact of the world depression on the sharp decline in their global profits.

In the previous decade, Carías had done his best to establish an element of representative democracy in Honduras and end the cycles of civil war. The Liberal rebellion launched in November 1932 showed that the old habits had not yet died out, although neither Mejía Colindres nor the Liberal presidential candidate – Angel Zúñiga Huete – were directly implicated in the revolt. Faced with this challenge, Carías reverted to type and exploited the state of siege imposed as a consequence of the civil war to move against his political opponents. Zúñiga Huete went into exile in Mexico (not to return until 1948), gangs of convicts (with iron balls

---

[2] The fiscal year ended 31 July. This was changed to a calendar-year basis at the end of the 1930s.

[3] The lempira had been made the Honduran unit of account in 1926 by act of Congress, although the act did not go into force until 1931. The lempira was fixed at the rate of two per U.S. dollar, while the previous unit of account (the peso) had fluctuated around the same value since 1918. At the time of writing, the lempira is still fixed at two per dollar, giving Honduras the longest period of exchange-rate stability in Latin America, with the exception of Panama.

chained to their legs) were employed on public works in the capital city, the authority of Congress to criticize the executive was progressively reduced, and local autonomy for mayors and municipalities was replaced by a much greater degree of central government control.

New presidential elections were due in October 1936, but shortly before that date Congress converted itself into a constituent assembly, extended the presidential term from four to six years and confirmed Carías in office until the end of 1942. This exercise in *continuismo* similar to that witnessed in El Salvador and Guatemala was taken a stage further in 1939 when Congress extended Carías' term in office to the end of 1948. The Cariato, as President Carías' sixteen years in office are known, finally broke the Honduran tradition of weak governments, civil wars and rapid presidential succession, although this was achieved at the expense of the nascent democracy which had begun to develop between 1924 and 1932.

Earlier Honduran presidents had attempted *continuismo*, but none had enjoyed Carías' success. This was due to various factors, perhaps the most important being the weak leadership provided by the Liberals, who remained loyal to the exiled Zúñiga Huete, incapable of exploiting the opportunities created by the arbitrary nature of Carías' rule and by the hardships of the depression years. A faction of the National Party led by Venancio Callejas split from Carías in 1936 over the new constitutional proposals, but a Callejas–Zúñiga pact signed in 1938 never commanded much respect. Even the unprecedented public demonstrations against the dictatorship in 1944, inspired by similar events in neighbouring republics, failed to galvanize the Liberal Party into decisive action. Zúñiga Huete failed to win the support of President Arévalo, Guatemala's champion of the anti-dictatorial Caribbean Legion, and the most vociferous campaign against Carías came from the more radical Partido Democrático Revolucionario Hondureño (PDRH), formed in 1947 to fight the dictatorship. The Liberals presented the same slate in the 1948 presidential elections as they had done in 1932, withdrawing only days before the vote through a combination of repression and fear of defeat.

While the Liberals were clearly expected to be the first line of defence against Carías' *continuismo*, the second could safely be assumed to be the armed forces. Occasional revolts occurred, the most serious in 1943, but Carías showed all his political skills in his relationship with the military and began the process of professionalizing the army which was completed by his Minister of War and presidential successor Dr. Juan Manuel Gálvez. As early as 1933 Carías established a training school for corporals and sergeants, and introduced obligatory military service in 1935; military officers began to receive U.S. training in 1942, following the entry of both the United States and Honduras into the Second World War. Carías purchased three war planes in 1934, having learned the importance of air power in the 1932–3 civil war where the services of the newly formed Transportes Aereos de Centroamérica (TACA) were used to support the government; additional military hardware was provided during the war by the Roosevelt administration. Carías also received support from neighbouring *caudillos;* General Maximiliano Hernández Martínez, the Salvadorean dictator, helped Carías during the civil war in the hope of breaking his own regime's diplomatic isolation, while General Jorge Ubico in Guatemala arranged for the murder of both a Liberal revolutionary (General Justo Umaña) and a leading Honduran Communist (Juan Pablo Wainwright).

The Cariato gave Honduras its longest period ever of political stability, but it was order without progress. Not only were the first tentative steps towards democracy sacrificed, but it also proved impossible to reverse the country's economic decline. At the end of the Mejía Colindres administration, the gross domestic product (GDP) per head was second only to that of Costa Rica in Central America; in 1934 the figure was exceeded by Guatemala and in 1937 by El Salvador, and in 1942 Honduras became the poorest republic in the region (and in all mainland Latin America) when it was overtaken by Nicaragua.[4] The healthy trade surplus which Honduras had enjoyed every year since 1925–6, and which enabled the government to maintain the lempira's parity with the U.S. dollar, finally disappeared in 1936–7, the shortage of domestic currency forcing the authorities to start importing U.S. notes and coins after 1942 to maintain monetary circulation.[5]

The root cause of these economic difficulties was the decline of the banana industry from the spectacular peaks it had reached at the start of the 1930s. At first the reduction was due to adjustment by the fruit companies to world recession – aggravated by serious flooding in 1934 – but by 1936 sigatoka disease had entered Honduras from the Caribbean

---

[4] See V. Bulmer-Thomas, *The Political Economy of Central America Since 1920* (Cambridge, 1987), table A.3.

[5] The Honduran trade balance is very sensitive to the price used to value banana exports. Since 1947, it has been customary to value exports at market prices which – if applied to the pre-war years – yields a large trade surplus in every year. Before 1947, however, Honduran authorities worked with a price which corresponded roughly to the local currency costs of the fruit companies; on this basis, a trade deficit was first recorded in the fiscal year 1936–7.

and wreaked havoc with banana plantations. No sooner had the companies developed a spray to counteract the spread of the disease than Honduras was plunged into the Second World War. The fruit companies' shipping fleets were requisitioned by the U.S. Navy with the result that Honduran banana exports in 1942–3 stood at 10 per cent of the 1929–30 peak. Exports, imports and general economic activity fell in line with the trend for bananas. By 1943 (its lowest point) GDP per head was 36 per cent below its peak in 1930.

The collapse of banana exports occurred despite the generous policy adopted towards the fruit companies by the government. President Carías, his Minister of War (Juan Manuel Gálvez) and the president of Congress after 1939 (Plutarco Muñoz P.) were all allied to UFCO (Gálvez and Muñoz as company lawyers), but Standard Fruit was equally successful in wriggling out of contractual obligations. Both companies collaborated closely in the 1930s, Standard Fruit accepting with equanimity its role as junior partner, and land titles were swapped in an effort to rationalize company holdings. In 1941 UFCO founded the prestigious School of Pan-American Agriculture and in the following year the company obtained a concession allowing the Truxillo Railroad Company to ship railway lines and other equipment to neighbouring countries in flagrant breach of the original contract.

The decline of the banana industry did lead to some agricultural diversification through a re-allocation of resources; the output of cereals, vegetables and other fruits all increased in the 1930s, but this could not compensate for the collapse of banana production, and the fruit companies retained firm control over both land and means of communication in the northern departments. The backwardness of the economy in general, and agriculture in particular, was captured vividly by a U.S. mission, led by E. M. Bernstein, which reported on monetary and credit conditions in 1943 at the invitation of the Carías government. The report, written in appropriately soothing terms, took the authorities to task for the weakness of banking institutions, the lack of attention to agriculture, the high cost of loans and the virtual anarchy surrounding the process of monetary emission in the absence of a central bank.[6]

The Cariato may have neglected economic development, but Carías could not ignore the fiscal crisis he had inherited from his predecessor.

---

[6] See E. M. Bernstein et al., *Informe de la Misión Técnica y Financiera sobre condiciones monetarias y de crédito en Honduras* (Tegucigalpa, 1943).

With payment on the domestic debt suspended since 1932 and public employees' salaries often unpaid, Carías was forced to use draconian measures. A loan was negotiated through UFCO with the Canal Bank of New Orleans, public-sector pay was reduced by 20 per cent (with a further 5 per cent deducted as payment to the Partido Nacional) and exchange control was introduced in 1934. This last measure was intended to generate exchange profits for the treasury rather than eliminate a shortage of foreign exchange (which was still plentiful), but it also served to restrict access to imports. The same purpose was served by tariffs introduced in 1934, although the following year a bilateral trade agreement with the United States forced on Honduras by Cordell Hull undermined the impact of the new trade restrictions; the tariff was revised again in 1983, following the Salvadorean example, with three scales designed to discriminate against countries enjoying a surplus on trade with Honduras. By 1937 Carías felt confident enough to force through a drastic reduction in the domestic debt, creditors receiving a mere 7 per cent in cash on the face value of their bonds. Coupled with the revenue-raising measures just described, this change produced an approximate fiscal balance from 1937 onwards while the tariff increases provided a stimulus for import substituting industrialization, a small number of modern factories opening their doors during the Cariato. War-time inflation – a product of import scarcity and monetary expansion – also stimulated fiscal receipts and permitted the government not only to carry on reducing the external debt (under the 1926 agreement), but also to lower the internal debt.

Despite Carías' neglect of economic development, some progress was made. The communications problem began to be solved during the Cariato. TACA was rewarded with a generous concession for its part in the civil war and within a few years internal air services were the most sophisticated in Central America. Then the outbreak of hostilities in Europe increased U.S. interest in highway construction in Central America; Honduras qualified for a two-thirds grant from the Roosevelt administration for its share of the Pan-American Highway and U.S. engineers completed the road link around Lake Yojoa, which finally connected Tegucigalpa with the national railway and the northern coast.

Honduras also played a part in hemispheric efforts to replace U.S. strategic imports cut off by hostilities in Asia. UFCO converted some of its banana plantations to the production of rubber, *abacá* and African palms, these programmes coming on stream by 1945. The country also collaborated in a U.S.-sponsored scheme to export fruits and vegetables to the Panama Canal Zone. Shortages of imports led to the expansion of forestry, the development of cotton production and the re-establishment of sugar-refining (sugar-milling had closed during the depression), all these products being exported on a modest scale after 1945.

The Second World War also brought an unexpected bonus for Honduran coffee producers in that the 1941 Pan-American Coffee Agreement gave the country a generous quota which had doubled by the end of the war. The improvement in communications, the post-war recovery in world prices and the greater availability of seasonal labour at harvest time as a result of demographic pressures all contributed to the emergence of Honduras as an important coffee-exporter, and by the end of the Cariato coffee production was twice its level at the beginning. With the return to normal commercial conditions after 1945, banana exports also recovered and stood at nearly half their peak level by the end of the Cariato. As a result, the Honduran economy enjoyed a modest boom in the last five years of the dictatorship, although GDP per head in 1948 was still below the pre-war peak.

Tiburcio Carías has frequently been grouped with the other long-serving dictators of Central America in the 1930s and 1940s, but there were differences between *caudillo* rule in Honduras and elsewhere.

The Cariato was not as tyrannical as *caudillo* rule in the neighbouring republics. Some leading Liberals continued to hold important positions, the Liberal press was generally allowed to function and the exile of the party leader, Zúñiga Huete, was self-imposed. Some of Carías' departmental governors, notably Carlos Sanabria in Colón, were petty tyrants, but Carías himself never shared his fellow *caudillos'* enthusiasm for European fascism, and Honduras' declaration of war on the Axis powers in December 1941 was not as cynical as some. Equally, Carías did not seek to dominate political life after his withdrawal from the presidency in 1948. Although he ruthlessly crushed the wave of protests against his rule in 1944, he had resolved as early as 1945 not to stand for re-election, and U.S. pressure was only of marginal importance in this decision. His handpicked successor, Juan Manuel Gálvez, stood uncontested in the presidential elections of October 1948 but subsequently demonstrated a certain degree of autonomy from the ex-dictator. Carías, furthermore, accepted his defeat in the 1954 presidential elections, when the Partido Nacional was split, without recourse to civil war. These differences should not, however, be exaggerated. Carías could be exceedingly ruthless when he felt it necessary, and the labour movement was given short shrift in a long dictatorship made worse by economic decline. The best that could be said for the Cariato was that it gave Honduras its longest period without civil war since independence.

Caudillo rule left unresolved a number of key issues. The relationship with the fruit companies, particularly UFCO, remained very unsatisfactory; the multinationals contributed virtually nothing to fiscal revenue as a result of the numerous concessions, yet they succeeded in evading most of their contractual responsibilities pleading in mitigation the state of the world economy. The weak fiscal position and the subordinate role of the government undermined the scope for economic diversification and left the economy dependent on an industry which appeared to be in structural decline. For most of the Cariato the fruit companies remained the lender of last resort, and foreign loans often depended on UFCO's support.

The 'commanding heights' of the Honduran economy (bananas, mining, external trade, railways, air transport and modern manufacturing) were still in the hands of foreigners at the end of the Cariato, the urban commercial sector was under the control of 'los Turcos'[7] and the one bright spot (coffee) had been developed by small- and medium-sized growers without political influence. The local political elite, including Carías, limited their economic activities to cattle-ranching, real estate or internal trade-activities which were safe from foreign competition. Yet the absence of a land-owning oligarchy, in contrast to El Salvador and Guatemala, was not without its advantages; the vast majority of rural Hondurans (with the exception of the relatively well-paid banana proletariat) still had access to land, and *ejidal* (communal) land ownership was widespread. The Cariato did not provide an alternative to the enclave development symbolized by the fruit companies, but at least it had not closed down all the options.

CAPITALIST MODERNIZATION AND SOCIAL REFORM
(1949–63)

Juan Manuel Gálvez, president from 1949 to 1954, seemed an improbable candidate for the task of modernizing Honduras. As a former attorney for UFCO and Minister of War under Carías, he was expected to maintain the political stability achieved under the Cariato and change little else. Gálvez, however, laid the foundations for capitalist modernization and

---

[7] 'Los Turcos' was the name given to Arab immigrants from the Levant, many of whom arrived on Turkish passports after the First World War.

social reform and his work was continued by the three succeeding governments. By 1963, when the military seized power, Honduras had enjoyed
fifteen years of almost unbroken social and economic progress under both
Partido Nacional and Liberal Party rule. These changes – modest even by
Latin American standards – were almost revolutionary in the Honduran
context and prevented the state from becoming too closely identified with
any single interest group. Although far from democratic and still dominated by *personalismo,* the political system moved away from the repressive
model of neighbouring republics and came closer to the Costa Rican
example, where well-organized pressure groups competed for official
favours.

Gálvez began a six-year period of rule by introducing an income-tax
law – the first in Honduran history – which obliged the fruit companies
to pay 15 per cent of their profits to the government. Although UFCO
only agreed to this long-overdue reform in exchange for fiscal concessions
on its non-banana operations (e.g., *abacá* production), the change was
dramatic; in its first full year (fiscal 1950–1), the new tax provided nearly
20 per cent of government revenue with most of the receipts coming from
the fruit companies. The tax was raised again in 1955 to 30 per cent
(following the Costa Rican example) and the fruit companies ceased to be
the lender of last resort. While the relationship between the companies
and the state was still very unequal, the income tax was the single most
effective way of increasing the returned value from banana exports.

Gálvez also turned his attention to the weaknesses in the banking and
financial system identified so clearly in the 1943 Bernstein mission. With
support from the International Monetary Fund (IMF), a central bank was
established in 1950 with a monopoly over the note-issue and exchange
transactions and the resources necessary to guarantee the circulation of the
lempira. For the first time, the Honduran currency was available in sufficient quantities to meet the demands of trade, while international reserves
were more than sufficient to guarantee the rate of exchange with the U.S.
dollar. A state development bank (Banco Nacional de Fomento – BNF)
was also founded in 1950 to support the economic (particularly agricultural) diversification neglected hitherto by the private banks.[8] The BNF
was given the resources to provide storage and marketing facilities, mate-

---

[8] A private bank (Banco Capitalizadora) was founded in 1948 with Salvadorean capital; this ended the
duopoly exercised over Honduran banking for nearly forty years by the Banco Atlántida and Banco
de Honduras, but did not at first contribute much to economic diversification.

rial inputs and technical advice, so that lending did not need to be restricted only to large-scale farmers.

Armed with higher fiscal revenues and aided by grants from U.S. agencies, the Gálvez administration turned to the neglected area of public works. The entire first chapter of a glossy book issued to commemorate Gálvez' years in the presidency was devoted to municipal drains – a sharp reversal of Honduran governments' usual priorities.[9] The most important progress came in the field of highway construction with feeder roads reaching into the agricultural frontier in the south, west and east of the country and major improvements in the railway–road link connecting the Atlantic with the Pacific coast via Tegucigalpa. Important advances were also made in electricity production and telecommunications, providing Honduras with the minimum social infrastructure necessary for capitalist modernization.

Capitalist development in Honduras had traditionally depended primarily on foreign initiative, but under the Gálvez administration a small national bourgeoisie began to emerge linked to agricultural diversification and urban growth. The banking reforms and improved communications helped production of coffee, basic grains, timber and meat. The increase in cotton production on the south coast (stimulated by the construction of the Pan-American Highway) was at first promoted largely by Salvadorean entrepreneurs, with the raw material being sent to El Salvador for ginning, but after the BNF set up a ginning plant Honduran participation increased. Agricultural diversification reduced the relative importance of bananas, whose contribution to exports finally dropped below 50 per cent in 1954. Industrial development was also stimulated, albeit from a very low base, by the Gálvez reforms and by the rapid growth of the urban population, which, particularly in San Pedro Sula and Tegucigalpa, far outstripped the population growth for the whole country. In 1950 nearly 20 per cent of the 1.37 million Hondurans could be classified as urban.

The reform movement under Gálvez was primarily of a developmentalist character and stopped far short of genuine political pluralism. The climate of repression under Carías was relaxed, political prisoners were released and the Liberal Party was free to operate normally, but the Gálvez administration harassed the small Marxist movement, banned the PDRH in 1952 and sided unequivocally with U.S. efforts to overthrow the Arbenz regime in Guatemala. Legislation favouring workers was passed in

[9] See *La Obra del Doctor Juan Manuel Gálvez en su Administración, 1949–1954* (Tegucigalpa, n.d.).

1952, but trade unions and strikes were still illegal, and Honduras remained outside the International Labour Organization (ILO), having abandoned its membership in 1938 under Carías.

The news, therefore, that a strike had been launched in April 1954 by workers belonging to one of the UFCO subsidiaries was greeted with unconcealed hostility by the Gálvez administration. This strike over pay and conditions occurred at a particularly tense moment in Central American history with the counter-revolutionary army of Carlos Castillo Armas assembled in Honduras and poised to invade Guatemala. Furthermore, an illegal Communist Party was formed in April by a faction of the banned PDRH and Communists were inevitably blamed for causing the strike. Gálvez arrested and imprisoned the leaders of the strike committee, and under intense pressure from the government the workers elected new, more moderate, leaders. But the strike spread to other activities on the northern coast and even found an echo in Tegucigalpa. The new anticommunist leadership gained the support of the American Federation of Labor (AFL) and the Gálvez administration began to press UFCO to reach a settlement. This was finally agreed on 9 July, a few days after the fall of Arbenz and the victory of the U.S.-supported counter-revolutionary forces in Guatemala.

In narrow economic terms, the strike was a pyrrhic victory for the workers. The modest wage increases (10–15 per cent) were swamped by wide-spread dismissals as both UFCO and Standard Fruit halved their work force over the next five years in response to production difficulties and the emergence of Ecuador as a major banana exporter. Yet the strike won legal recognition for the workers' right to organize and reversed UFCO's opposition to the existence of trade unions, which had been used by successive Honduran governments to resist progressive labour legislation. Within a short period, Honduras had rejoined the ILO and recognized 1 May as International Labour Day, while unions – under the watchful eye of the AFL – developed quickly along the northern coast and soon spread to the inland urban centres.

The 1954 strike also coincided with preparations for the October presidential elections. The Liberal Party had been revitalised under the leadership of the educationalist Dr Ramón Villeda Morales, but the Partido Nacional had been split by the decision of Tiburcio Carías to seek the presidency again. A breakaway faction – Movimiento Nacional Reformista (MNR) – led by Abraham Williams, vice-president under Carías, led to a three-way contest in which the Liberals won a handsome plurality but not a majority. In the time-honoured tradition, the losers refused to take their seats in Congress, a quorum could not be formed and Julio Lozano Díaz, who had succeeded to the presidency upon the retirement (on grounds of ill health) of Gálvez on 16 November, declared himself acting chief executive.

Lozano's intervention was at first welcomed by the three political parties. It avoided bloodshed and could be used to prepare the ground for fresh elections. Furthermore, Lozano maintained the reform programme of the previous few years, providing continuity with the Gálvez administration. The vote was extended to women and a Fundamental Charter of Labour Guarantees was introduced in 1955, covering virtually all aspects of labour relations from minimum wages to collective bargaining. In the same year, a national economic council later to become the Consejo Superior de Planificación Económica (CONSUPLANE) was founded to provide the rudiments of economic planning long before the Alliance for Progress would make this a condition for aid disbursal. Lozano, however, soon made it clear that he had no intention of handing over power in free elections, organized his own party (Partido Unión Nacional, or PUN), exiled Villeda Morales, and called elections for a constituent assembly in October 1956, which the PUN claimed to win with nearly 90 per cent of the 'vote'.

The other three political parties joined forces to protest against the Lozano dictatorship, but they were powerless to prevent it. The armed forces, on the other hand, had both the means and the motive to intervene. The professionalization of the military begun under Carías had accelerated during the Gálvez administration; funds for training and equipment had been poured in by U.S. administrations, concerned at the security implications of the Guatemalan Revolution. Honduras signed a military assistance pact with the United States in 1954, establishing the close relationship between the armed forces of the two countries, which has survived to this day. The unconstitutional character of the Lozano regime was an affront to the constitutionally minded officers of the Honduran armed forces, and within two weeks of the constituent assembly elections Lozano had been ousted by a military triumvirate including a son of former president Gálvez.

The military intervention was quite unlike the *cuartelazo* politics of the civil war eras. The military intervened as an institution and in defense of the constitution, promising fresh elections within a year. Moreover, it earned universal respect by keeping this promise. Nonetheless, military intervention came at a price; the armed forces demanded from the winners of the elections a high degree of autonomy for the military and the right to intervene in future in the event of a constitutional crisis. This privileged military position, established in the Constitution of 1957, accounts for many of the peculiarities of the Honduran political system in the last three decades.

The constituent assembly elections held in September 1957 produced an overwhelming victory for the Liberals. Villeda Morales, who had been posted to Washington by the military triumvirate and had calmed U.S. fears about his alleged Communist sympathies, assumed the presidency at the end of the year in indirect elections – three years after narrowly missing victory in direct elections. The new president went out of his way to accommodate the military, most of whose officers owed their positions to the Partido Nacional under Carías and Gálvez. Indeed, the suspicions held by some sections of the armed forces about Villeda Morales were the main reason for the President's agreeing to share power with the military under the Constitution of 1957 with disputes to be settled by Congress.

Villeda Morales' six-year presidential term (1957–63) saw a major extension of the reform programme undertaken by his predecessors. His more enthusiastic supporters claimed that Villeda Morales had introduced social democracy to Honduras and laid the foundations for genuine political democracy. Villedismo, however never fully surpassed the *personalismo* which had plagued Honduran politics since independence, and the President was more concerned with the threat to hemispheric security from Castro's Cuba than with that to political freedom from reactionary despotism in the neighbouring republics. The Liberal Party remained a loose amalgam of competing factions whose character was determined primarily by the man in charge. Thus, Villedismo could not survive Villeda Morales, and the party had to wait nearly twenty years before a new Liberal president emerged with the authority to stamp his own personality on the party machine.

The social reforms begun after the 1954 banana strike were extended in a variety of ways by the Villeda administration. The Labour Code of 1957 incorporated and extended the Labour Charter of 1955 and, after two failed attempts, a Law of Social Insurance was enacted in 1962. Coverage was at first limited to workers in the central district, but the principle of social security had been established and the proportion of the labour force receiving benefits rose steadily in the next two decades. Almost all labour disputes were settled through the conciliation procedures laid down in the

Labour Code. Industrial development was promoted through a Ley de Fomento Industrial, passed in 1958, giving fiscal advantages to new firms. Honduras also signed the 1958 Tripartite Treaty with Guatemala and El Salvador which provided for tariff reductions on intra-regional trade and preceded the formation of the Central American Common Market (CACM) in 1960.

Manufacturing growth was rapid under Villeda Morales and maintained the rhythm of the previous decade. Between 1948 (the last year of the Cariato) and 1963 (the last year of Villeda Morales' presidency), the share of manufacturing in GDP doubled to more than 14 per cent with foreign participation by no means dominant. Yet the years of Villeda's presidency were difficult ones for the Honduran economy; technical problems plagued cotton production in the late 1950s and the fall in coffee prices after the Korean War discouraged new coffee plantings. Some success was achieved in expanding meat exports to the United States, and sugar exports were boosted by the allocation to Honduras after 1960 of part of Cuba's U.S. sugar quota, but the continuing difficulties of the banana industry hung like a millstone round the economy's neck and kept the growth of real GDP well below that recorded in neighbouring republics. Honduras remained the poorest country in Central America and mainland Latin America.

Both the fruit companies experimented with new disease-resistant varieties of bananas after 1960 and the industry's fortunes began to recover. The massive dismissals after the 1954 strike were not reversed, however, and unemployment among banana-workers became a very serious problem. The government experimented with peasant colonization schemes on disused land handed back by the fruit companies, but social unrest in the banana zones continued and access to land for many families outside the zones was curtailed by the growth of agricultural export diversification (particularly cattle-raising and meat exports). With the help of dismissed banana-workers and the active participation of Communists, a militant peasant union – Federación Nacional de Campesinos Hondureños (FENACH) – was formed to press for radical changes in the land-tenure system. In 1962 the government responded with an agrarian reform law administered by the Instituto Nacional Agrario (INA), while the AFL and the anti-communist regional labour federation (Organización Regional Interamericana de Trabajadores, or ORIT) hurried to counter the influence of FENACH by helping to establish a rival peasant union, Asociación Nacional de Campesinos (ANACH). The agrarian reform law was not well

received by the fruit companies, which were able to force through a
number of amendments more favourable to their interests, but the measure remained on the statute book, providing a safety valve which could be
opened or closed over the following years according to social conditions.
Agrarian reform has never been radical in Honduras, but it was always
more than a token concession to the Alliance for Progress and ultimately
effected a significant minority of the peasantry.

Villeda Morales feared the consequences of the Cuban Revolution, but
the real threat to his regime came from the traditional right. A series of
minor revolts culminated in an uprising by the National Police in July
1959, which was suppressed with some difficulty. In retaliation, the
President created a separate Civil Guard subject to presidential control
(unlike the National Police, which had been subject to the control of the
armed forces). Clashes between the 2,500-strong Civil Guard and the
armed forces became frequent and contributed to a sharp deterioration in
the relationship between the military and the Liberal government. A
further rift was provoked when the party adopted as its presidential candidate for the 1963 elections Modesto Rodas Alvarado, a protégé of Zúñiga
Huete in the 1940s and a man of known anti-militarist sympathies. The
prospect of six years of Rodismo was too much for many officers, and the
military, led by air force colonel Osvaldo López Arellano, overthrew
Villeda Morales shortly after the President had agreed to disarm the Civil
Guard and only ten days before the scheduled elections.

MILITARY RULE (1963–82)

The military regime, headed by López Arellano, was not recognized by
President John F. Kennedy (to whom Villeda Morales had appealed personally at the moment of the coup), but the anti-communist stance of the new
government produced a change of heart on the part of the Lyndon Johnson
administration following Kennedy's assassination. This second military
intervention completed the transformation of the armed forces as an institution and confirmed the army's role as a key actor in Honduran political
life.

The real reason for the coup was the military's fear of an election victory
by Rodas, who had committed the Liberal Party to revise the Constitution
of 1957 and re-establish civilian control over the armed forces. Both Rodas
and Villeda Morales went into exile, the former maintaining the loyalty of
the Liberal Party through his well-organized Rodista faction, while the

latter's Civil Guard was abolished and replaced by a police organization (Cuerpo Especial de Seguridad) subject to military control. The anti-communism of the military government was not all rhetoric designed to win U.S. support. Communists had helped to set up FENACH and had penetrated the union of Standard Fruit workers (SUTRASFCO). The new government promptly outlawed FENACH and purged SUTRASFCO, imposing restrictions on the rest of the labour movement. At a regional level, López Arellano joined forces with the neighbouring military governments to form CONDECA, a mutual defense pact with strong anti-communist overtones, supported by the U.S. administration and in 1965 Honduras sent troops in support of the U.S. invasion of the Dominican Republic.

These initiatives, coupled with the underfunding of INA and the low priority given to land reform, confirmed the conservative nature of the new regime and won for it the enthusiastic support of the traditional land-owners. Such an alliance might have been sufficient to maintain an iron grip on affairs in neighbouring Guatemala or El Salvador, but in the Honduran context it represented a relatively weak coalition. Indeed, it was not until 1966, with the formation of the Federación Nacional de Agricultores (FENAGH), that the land-owners established institutional representation for their class interests. López Arellano, however, was able to consolidate his hold on power through a tactical alliance with the Partido Nacional, now unified under Ricardo Zúñiga A., who saw an opportunity to settle scores with the rival Liberal Party. The tactical and opportunist nature of the alliance was underlined by the fact that López Arellano had formed part of the junta which had paved the way for the Liberal government of 1957, in which he had occupied the post of Minister of Defence.[10] The new alliance with the Partido Nacional, however, was superficially effective and served to 'legitimise' López's rule, although the constituent assembly elections of 1965 were marred by fraud and strong-arm tactics orchestrated by the Mancha Brava – a shadowy para-military group linked to the Partido Nacional and the armed forces. The Partido Nacional majority in the new Assembly introduced a new constitution confirming the autonomy of the armed forces and promptly elected López Arellano (now promoted to brigadier general) as president for six years.

López's initial identification with the traditional land-owners and most conservative elements in Honduran society earned him the opposition not

[10] He was not originally a member of the junta, but joined it in 1957.

only of the organized labour movement but also of the new industrial groups. Within a few years, these two groups had made common cause and forged a powerful alliance with which the opportunist López was prepared to negotiate. This transformed the nature of political loyalties in Honduras: military rule in the 1970s acquired a reformist, almost populist, character which stood in marked contrast to the conservatism of the 1960s. Even in the 1960s, however, military government avoided the reactionary despotism so apparent in neighbouring countries; the reforms of previous governments in fiscal, labour and social policy were allowed to stand and in some cases were even extended.[11]

The purge of Communists from the organized labour movement strengthened the 'free and democratic' unions linked to ORIT and supported by the United States. Within a year of the 1963 coup, a national Confederación de Trabajadores de Honduras (CTH) had been formed, bringing together the banana-workers of the north coast, the unions of the central district and the peasantry organized in ANACH. The purged SUTRASFCO also joined the CTH, which was affiliated to ORIT and the International Federation of Free Trade Unions. The new confederation faced some competition from Social Christian peasant unions, organized on the south coast with the support of the Catholic Church, but this was not sufficient to challenge its hegemonic position at the national level.

The coup of October 1963 coincided with a resurgence of export agriculture in Honduras. Banana production soared as a result of the introduction of new varieties, while cotton, coffee, beef and sugar all benefited from improved world prices and greater credit availability. Demand for new land to support this expansion rose, driving up rents and leading to disputes over access to *ejidal* and national lands. The peasant organizations called on the government to revitalise the land-reform programme – virtually stalled since the coup – and began to undertake land invasions in support of their claims.

The main focus of peasant agitation was the agrarian reform agency INA, which in five years (1962–6) had distributed land to a mere 281 families. In a gesture designed to reduce the unpopularity of his regime, López appointed in 1967 as head of INA Rigoberto Sandoval Corea, who was also placed in charge of national planning. This proved a shrewd move because Sandoval managed to promote land reform without provoking

---

[11] The López government introduced, for example, a 3 per cent retail sales tax in December 1963 – the first government to do so in Central America.

excessive opposition from FENAGH or the fruit companies through the creation of co-operatives that often produced export crops.[12] Thus, the reformed sector did not undermine the export-led model favoured by the government and most of the land was obtained through 'recovery' of *ejidal* or national properties rather than through expropriation of private estates.

While the revival of INA and the land-reform programme reduced tensions in the rural areas, urban opposition to the regime was growing. The entry of Honduras into the Central American Common Market had undermined the government's income from import duties, the main source of revenue, and had obliged the López regime to introduce new taxes. These fell particularly heavily on urban areas, provoking a storm of protests in 1968, when the government introduced a new range of taxes on consumer goods and raised tariffs (in line with other Central American countries) on extra-regional imports. A general strike was called only to be met with a state of siege that soon forced it to be called off, but the strike cemented the informal relationship between the CTH and the industrialists of the Consejo Hondureño de la Empresa Privada (COHEP) who were also opposed to many features of the government's economic policies. This improbable alliance between workers and urban capitalists, both losers under the economic policies favoured by López in the 1960s, drove a wedge between the property-owning classes in Honduras and prevented the consolidation of a united anti-labour policy among the political elite.

The industrialists, with their main stronghold in San Pedro Sula, took exception to the way in which the CACM appeared to discriminate against Honduras. Although exports from Honduras to the rest of Central America had expanded since the CACM's formation, they had risen much less rapidly than exports by other CACM members to Honduras. As a result, the Honduran trade balance with the rest of Central America had turned negative at the start of the decade and increased in size in every year thereafter. Furthermore, many Honduran exports to CACM were agricultural goods sold at prices not unlike those ruling in world markets, whereas imports from CACM consisted of industrial goods whose price reflected the high common external tariff imposed by all CACM members. Honduras, the industrialists argued, had paid a high price for CACM membership and the rules of the game needed to be changed to serve the interests of the weaker members.

---

[12] These co-operatives, organized in 1970 by the Federación de Cooperativas de la Reforma Agraria de Honduras (FECORAH), often received financial support from state banking institutions and in some cases sold their output to the fruit companies for marketing.

With its close ties to traditional agricultural interests, the López regime at first paid little attention to the complaints of the industrialists, which surfaced as early as 1965. The trade deficit with CACM had to be paid in dollars, but the boom in agro-exports in the first half of the 1960s provided ample foreign exchange. This position soon changed, however, as cotton exports fell in response to falling prices after 1965 and banana exports hit their peak in 1967. Foreign exchange was now more scarce and the government joined the chorus demanding special treatment for Honduras within CACM.

The other CACM members were not insensitive to these Honduran requests, and by March 1969 agreement had been reached on a system of fiscal incentives for the region, which would have allowed Honduras to offer special privileges designed to attract foreign and local investment into its manufacturing sector. However, this concession soon became irrelevant since Honduras withdrew from the common market in December 1970, following the war with El Salvador, and proceeded to negotiate non-reciprocal bilateral trade treaties with Costa Rica, Guatemala and Nicaragua.[13]

The war with El Salvador in July 1969 was caused by a variety of factors, of which dissatisfaction with the functioning of CACM was only one. Salvadoreans had been migrating to Honduras in search of land and jobs for many decades, but two-thirds of the estimated 300,000 migrants who had entered Honduras since the 1890s had arrived since 1950. The overwhelming reason for Salvadorean out-migration was a desire for land, but land pressure had accelerated rapidly in Honduras, leading to an increase in the number of *microfincas* (farms smaller than one hectare) and landless workers. Tension over access to land was exacerbated by the unresolved dispute between Honduras and El Salvador over the border, which was still undefined for much of its length, but the flames were well and truly fanned when INA announced in March 1969 that the beneficiaries from the land-reform programme would be restricted to those of Honduran birth and that Salvadoreans without legal title would be expelled. The extremes of nationalist passion surrounding the World Cup qualifying matches between the two countries provided the final straw, and the Salvadorean army responded to the expulsion of their countrymen by invading Honduras on 14 July.

[13] The treaties allowed Honduras duty-free access to other countries, while permitting Honduras to charge tariffs on imports from these countries. Trade with El Salvador, however, remained blocked throughout the 1970s.

The war brought little glory to either side, and the Honduran army was rescued from an embarrassing humiliation only by the early intervention of the Organization of American States. A cease-fire was agreed, but diplomatic relations were broken and the border remained closed to normal commerce, jeopardizing Salvadorean exports to Nicaragua and Costa Rica. Although López Arellano's air force performed with some distinction, scoring a direct hit on Salvadorean oil-refining facilities in Acajutla, the President's authority was badly dented by the war, which provided the catalyst for the realignment of political forces in Honduras that had been simmering for some time.

The war had created a strong feeling of national unity in Honduras with all the political, business and labour organizations (except the Communist Party) responding to the call for patriotism. Within a few months of the war, COHEP had called a meeting of the 'Fuerzas Vivas', bringing business and labour leaders together with leading public officials. The meeting led to informal contacts with the President, who still clung to hopes for his own re-election. The discussions continued throughout 1970 and by the end of the year agreement had been reached on a political pact under which the traditional parties would unite behind a single non-political candidate in the 1971 elections leading to a government of national unity.

The agreement satisfied López, who was to be left in charge of the armed forces, but it failed to meet the demands of the traditional parties. It was therefore modified to allow for competition between the parties for the presidency, with the winner committed to appointing public officials on the basis of merit rather than party affiliation. Even this proved too much for the Liberal and National parties, however, and the day before the March 1971 elections, the pact was once again revised to allow for an equal sharing of the top government posts between the two major parties. Nevertheless, the Political Plan for National Unity (or *pacto,* as it was widely called) still committed the new administration to implement the reform programme thrashed out in the Fuerzas Vivas meetings.

The winner of the elections was the National Party candidate, Ramón Ernesto Cruz, who secured 49.3 per cent of the popular vote. A lawyer by training, the elderly Dr Cruz was neither politically nor temperamentally suited to leading a government of national unity committed to implementing a wide range of reforms. Sandoval Corea was replaced as head of INA by a Conservative, peasant unrest was met with severe repression, and the Partido Nacional, with Ricardo Zúñiga occupying the key post of Minister of Government and Justice, concentrated its efforts on securing partisan control of the state bureaucracy. It became clear very quickly that the new administration was incapable of rising above the limitations of traditional party rivalries. Respect for civilian rule was badly dented, the workers' movement threatened a major demonstration in support of the original aims of the *pacto* and on 4 December 1972 the military intervened, with López Arellano once again becoming chief of state.

The collapse of the national unity government weakened the prestige of both traditional parties and left the military free to develop an informal alliance with COHEP and the labour movement, both of whose interests were promoted during the first (populist) phase of military rule. Decree No. 8, introduced before the end of 1972, provided for the transfer or forced rent of idle land; the landowners' organization (FENAGH) protested strongly and was able to force through some modifications to the law, but the pace of land reform accelerated with 11,739 families benefiting in the first two years (1973–4). The introduction of a new Agrarian Reform Law on 1 January 1975 took the process a stage further with upper limits set on the size of private landholdings and more explicit criteria established for determining idle or underutilized land. All the same, delays in implementing the law gave some large landowners a chance to subdivide their holdings, improve efficiency and escape the application of the law to themselves.

The second López administration, clearly influenced by the reformist military experiment in Peru, also addressed the question of national economic development in the post-CACM environment. A fifteen-year development plan published in January 1974 provided for state participation in the primary sector and co-operation with COHEP on new industrial ventures. A wide variety of parastatal organizations were set up, which were largely autonomous and free to raise funds on the international capital market. With competition from the rest of Central America much reduced and now aided by state support, the manufacturing sector grew rapidly and increased its share of GDP during the 1970s, while the exploitation of the country's enormous forest resources was pushed ahead under the watchful eye of the state Corporación Hondureña de Desarrollo Forestal (COHDEFOR).

The populism of General López concealed a weakness in his position inherited from the poor performance of the armed forces in the war with El Salvador. The junior officers, who supported the reform programme, agitated for a new command structure, designed to share power with the chief of state. The Consejo Superior de las Fuerzas Armadas (CONSUFFAA) was

reorganized in March 1975 and took advantage of General López's tempo-
rary absence from the country to appoint Colonel Juan Alberto Melgar
Castro as head of the military. General López remained chief of state, but
he was forced to resign this post as well the following month when the
Wall Street Journal reported that he had received a bribe from UFCO (now
United Brands) to ensure that the government would lower the new export
tax on bananas imposed by the Unión de Países Exportadores de Banano
(UPEB), to which Honduras belonged.

CONSUFFAA, its authority now firmly established, appointed Melgar
Castro as chief of state – replacing him as head of the armed forces with
Colonel Policarpo Paz García. The collective nature of military rule was
now clear, the chief of state being reduced to the first among equals.
This shift was important because Melgar Castro – allied to the Partido
Nacional – had conservative instincts, although the impetus in favour of
the reform programme from other directions was still strong. Thus,
Melgar Castro appointed Sandoval Corea as head of INA and the land-
reform programme continued until Sandoval's resignation in 1977, after
which it slowed considerably.

The scandal over the bribe from United Brands offered the Honduran
government an excellent opportunity to establish the relationship with the
fruit companies on a more equal basis. Nationalist feelings were running
high and the government took control of the north coast docks, set up its
own marketing agency for bananas, Corporación Hondureña de Bananos
(COHBANA), acquired railway lines from the companies, expropriated
fruit company lands under the agrarian reform law and made the multinationals subject to the new export tax. The fruit companies, particularly
United Brands, were in no position to argue, not least because three
decades of export diversification had reduced their importance, the banana
share of exports falling to 25 per cent by the end of the 1970s. However,
the companies were by no means crushed and managed to fight off the
challenge from COHBANA, while negotiating reductions in the export
tax when international banana prices weakened.

Under Melgar Castro the military began to address the vexed question
of a return to civilian rule. A Presidential Advisory Council set up early in
1976 was given responsibility for preparing an electoral law leading to
constituent assembly elections. The prospect of handing over power to the
discredited civilians divided the military, which was also split over the
slower pace of agrarian and other reforms. Allegations that high officials
were involved in drug-smuggling and other misdemeanours provided the

justification for another change of government; CONSUFFAA intervened in mid-1978 to replace Melgar Castro by a triumvirate headed by Paz García.

The new government showed little sympathy for the progress recorded in agrarian, fiscal and social policy and had no desire to implement a new reformist programme. Its top priority was to engineer a peaceful return to civilian rule under terms acceptable to the military, a task made all the more urgent by the social upheavals in neighbouring El Salvador and Nicaragua. With the Carter administration also exerting pressure for a return to civilian rule, constituent assembly elections were set for April 1980.

The Constituent Assembly elections in 1980 marked the start of a transition to civilian rule and the end of nearly two decades of direct military government. The 1960s were notable for the high level of administrative incompetence (many foreign grants, for example, went undisbursed), the 1970s, for corruption and public scandals. Yet the long period of military rule had witnessed a steady improvement in Honduran social and economic indicators from their abysmally low levels at the beginning of the 1960s.[14] And the second half of the 1970s had coincided with the fastest economic growth ever recorded in the country. The military withdrew from direct rule with its prestige still intact – and on terms acceptable to the high command.

The elections for the Constituent Assembly were expected to produce a conservative majority because the military had worked closely with the Partido Nacional for almost twenty years. An important obstacle, however, to military collaboration with the Liberals was removed when Modesto Rodas Alvarado died at the end of 1979. Although the Rodista faction survived under the leadership of Roberto Suazo Córdova, it lost its anti-militarist character and the new Liberal leadership went out of its way to assuage fears among senior officers of a return to civilian control of the armed forces. The triumvirate no longer had a preference between the two traditional parties and the Liberals, led by Suazo Córdova, scored an impressive electoral victory. The Constituent Assembly determined that the president would be chosen by direct elections for a term of four years. In the November 1981 presidential elections Suazo Córdova for the Liberals won by a clear majority over Ricardo Zúñiga for the Partido

---

[14] Between 1961 and the early 1980s, the illiteracy rate fell from 53 per cent to 40 per cent of the adult population; urbanization jumped from 23 per cent to 37 per cent; and life expectancy rose from forty-four to sixty-two years.

Nacional.[15] In January 1982, therefore, Suazo Córdova became the first civilian president since the ill-fated Dr Cruz.

CIVILIAN RULE SINCE 1982

The transition to civilian rule had been conducted in a manner and on terms acceptable to the military, which was left with a great deal of autonomy and continued to adopt a high profile during the 1980s. The appointment of General Gustavo Alvarez Martínez as head of the armed forces following Suazo Córdova's election brought to power a man with marked authoritarian tendencies and strong anti-communist credentials; Alvarez helped to establish the Asociación para el Progreso de Honduras (APROH), an organization with a corporatist (almost fascist) character. During the first two years of Suazo Córdova's rule, Alvarez steadily gathered the reins of power into his own hands. The civilian government was powerless to resist, but Alvarez's ambitions and his apparent desire to drag Honduras into a war against the Sandinistas in Nicaragua disturbed his fellow officers in CONSUFFAA. In a swift and well-planned move, Alvarez was sent into exile in March 1984, the air force commander, General Walter López, taking his place as head of the armed forces. Soon afterwards, APROH folded and the threat of another period of direct military rule receded. It was, however, significant that, just as in 1956, it was the armed forces which had preserved constitutional rule while the civilian government had been little more than a spectator.

The natural reluctance of the military to retreat to the barracks after the 1980 elections was given additional impetus by the deterioration in the security situation. The civil war in El Salvador drove thousands of Salvadoreans back across the border into Honduras as refugees while the Salvadorean guerrillas used the *bolsones* (demilitarized pockets of disputed territory in the border zones) to regroup their forces. The search for a peace treaty with El Salvador, pursued fruitlessly for most of the 1970s, was given new emphasis by U.S. concerns over guerrilla successes. A peace treaty was signed in December 1980 with unusual haste, leaving the border to be defined at a later date and paving the way for co-operation

---

[15] The small Christian Democratic Party (founded in 1970) and the Honduran Patriotic Front (a broad coalition of left-wing groups) were not allowed to participate in the November 1980 elections. Only the small Partido de Innovación (PINU), founded in 1970 during the national unity dialogue, was allowed to compete against the National and Liberal parties. (It secured a mere 3.5 per cent of the vote.) Both the Christian Democrats and the Patriotic Front were permitted to take part in the November 1981 presidential elections.

between the armed forces of both countries to defeat the guerrilla threat.[16]
A mild echo of the Salvadorean guerrilla movement was heard in Honduras itself when three small guerrilla groups attracted publicity with a wave of kidnappings, hijackings and bank robberies. They were, however, no match for the security forces and lacked popular appeal; although Honduran democracy was a far cry from being perfect, it offered sufficient scope for reform and peaceful change to deter all but the most determined from entering the ranks of the guerrilla movement. By 1984, the guerrilla threat had virtually disappeared, resurfacing from time to time in the remote eastern provinces of Mosquitia.

The security threat presented by the Honduran-based opponents of the Sandinista regime in Nicaragua was a much more serious matter because it raised the possibility of a war between the two countries. The border with Nicaragua had been finally settled in 1960, following a ruling by the International Court of Justice, but the rugged terrain and lack of access roads made the frontier virtually impossible to police. After the fall of Somoza in July 1979 the rump of the Nicaraguan National Guard fled across the border to Honduras, contenting themselves at first with cross-border raids motivated by little more than revenge. However, the consolidation of the FSLN (Frente Sandinista de Liberación Nacional) regime and Sandinista blunders in the Atlantic coast provinces of Nicaragua swelled the numbers of these 'contras' during 1980 and 1981 and produced considerable tension between Honduras and Nicaragua over their presence on Honduran territory.

The growth in the number of contras coincided with a sharp deterioration in the relationship between Nicaragua and Washington. A decision was taken by the Reagan administration in November 1981 to authorize CIA covert operations against the Sandinistas with the funds channelled to the contras. The ostensible purpose was to interdict arms supplies from Nicaragua to the Salvadorean rebels through Honduras, but the real aim was destabilization of the Sandinista regime. At the same time, the United States military began a long series of joint manoeuvres with its Honduran counterpart; thousands of U.S. troops were trained to fight in the difficult Honduran terrain and a large number of U.S. military bases were constructed.

The logic of U.S. geopolitical priorities provided little opportunity for

[16] The treaty provided for a border commission to determine the frontier throughout its length. If (as happened) the members of the commission could not reach agreement after five years, the dispute was to be submitted to the International Court of Justice for arbitration.

strengthening Honduran civilian rule, especially since Washington's leading local ally was General Alvarez, who shared the Reagan administration's concern over the consolidation of the Sandinista regime. Alvarez's fall in 1984 did not end Honduran military cooperation with the United States, but there was a change of emphasis. The U.S. military base at Puerto Castilla, used for training Salvadorean troops, was closed and the contras were forced to adopt a lower profile. The new Honduran military leadership may have shared Alvarez's distaste for the Sandinistas, but they were not prepared to embark on a war against a Nicaraguan army of far greater strength. Throughout his presidency Suazo Córdova protested feebly that there were no contra bases on Honduran soil. This denial, flatly contradicted by the evidence, earned the Honduran government little respect in international circles, although there was not much else it could do.

As the Reagan administration drew to a close, its Central American policy in disarray, the Honduran government felt able to assert itself more visibly against the contras. President José Azcona Hoyo, who as the Liberal Party candidate had won the presidential elections at the end of 1985,[17] at first limited his demands to a request for an international peace-keeping force to police the border with Nicaragua; by early 1989, however, the Honduran government felt able to join forces with the rest of Central America under the Arias peace plan in calling for the disbanding of the contras and an end to U.S. military support for 'irregular forces'.

U.S. pressure against the Sandinistas and the use of Honduran territory for U.S. military bases left the weak civilian administration with virtually no freedom in foreign policy. Only in domestic policy, therefore, could it establish its identity, and the reform programme, stalled since the late 1970s, received some attention. Land distribution under the agrarian reform law began again, although the main thrust of the programme (financed by the U.S. Agency for International Development, AID) was giving title to peasants with insecure property rights. However, the government's opportunities for carrying out major reforms were sharply cur-

---

[17] In April 1985 Suazo Córdova triggered a consitutional crisis by attempting in the first place to succeed himself, then to name his successor. The crisis was resolved only after the application of strong pressure by the military. In the November 1985 presidential elections the Liberal party fielded four candidates, the National party three. The Liberals secured a dubious victory because the leading Liberal (José Azcona Hoyo) polled fewer votes than the leading National party candidate (Rafael Leonardo Callejas). Azcona was declared the winner because the combined vote of the four Liberal candidates exceeded that of the three National party candidates. When Azcona succeeded Suazo Córdova as president in January 1986 it was, however, the first time since 1933 that one constitutionally elected president had succeeded another.

tailed by the economic recession, which coincided with the beginning of civilian rule. The deterioration in the external terms of trade and the second oil crisis at the end of the 1970s opened up a huge trade deficit that was financed by borrowing from abroad at high nominal (and real) interest rates. The public external debt, which had been kept within tolerable levels during most of the 1970s, became a serious burden on the economy, and capital flight – a response mainly to the growing regional crisis – aggravated the balance of payments problem. The outgoing military government signed stand-by agreements with the International Monetary Fund in February 1980 and August 1981, but both were suspended when the authorities failed to meet fund targets for the public sector deficit.[18]

The Suazo Córdova government proved much more successful than its predecessor at implementing adjustment and stabilization policies, although this required observance of both IMF guidelines and AID priorities. The authorities, however, insisted on maintaining the parity of the lempira against the dollar despite enormous pressure from U.S. donor institutions; this left non-traditional exports relatively uncompetitive and in a weak position to exploit the opportunities available under the Caribbean Basin Initiative, but it avoided the high rates of inflation which had exacerbated social tensions in neighbouring countries.[19]

The fall in real GDP and real GDP per head during the worst years of the recession (1982–3) was much less severe in Honduras than in the rest of Central America. Indeed, the return to modest rates of growth after 1983 (helped by massive U.S. economic and military assistance) enabled the country to close some of the gap between itself and the rest of the region. By 1988 real GDP per head was comparable to levels in El Salvador and Nicaragua (where civil war had taken an awful toll), but was still far below the average for Latin America. Under IMF prodding, the Suazo Córdova, and later Azcona Hoyo, governments tackled the deteriorating fiscal situation with some courage and raised government revenue's share of GDP to 16.3 per cent by 1987 – a tax effort comparable to that in several major Latin American republics.[20] Yet Honduras was unable to

---

[18] For further details, see V. Bulmer-Thomas, 'The Balance of Payments Crisis and Adjustment Programmes in Central America', in R. Thorp and L. Whitehead (eds.), *The Debt Crisis in Latin America* (London, 1987).

[19] The Caribbean Basin Initiative, launched by President Reagan in 1982 and formally inaugurated 1 January 1984, offered duty-free access for twelve years on a wide range of non-traditional exports to the U.S. market for most Central American and Caribbean countries.

[20] See Inter-American Development Bank, *Economic and Social Progress Report: Latin America* (Washington, D.C., 1988), table C-1.

generate sufficient resources to service its foreign debt without sacrificing all efforts in favour of reform, and a moratorium was declared at the beginning of 1989.

Thus, Honduras retained during the difficult years of the 1980s the reformist thread which had run through its history since the Gálvez administration. With the possible exception of the populist phase under López Arellano (1972–5), the pace of reform had always been modest and had occasionally ground to a halt, but the direction of change was clear. In matters of labour policy, social legislation, agrarian reform and fiscal effort there was a sharp contrast by the end of the 1970s between Honduras and its immediate neighbours. This contrast provided Honduras with a certain immunity from the subsequent regional crisis, although the country could not escape all the shock-waves emanating from the epicentres in Nicaragua and El Salvador.

The ability of backward Honduras to implement a reform package where more economically advanced countries had failed owed a great deal to its peculiar agro-industrial structure. The absence of a powerful domestic land-owning oligarchy placed foreign capital, particularly the fruit companies, as the key obstacle to reforms. Hondurans of all social classes could unite behind a package of reforms in which the main losers were the fruit companies. (This helps account for the successful introduction of the income tax in 1949 and labour legislation after 1954.) The weak Honduran state had been a poor match for the fruit companies while alternative sources of funds were unavailable and bananas occupied such a key role in the economy, but the post-war period coincided with the emergence of new sources of foreign borrowing (e.g., the World Bank) and the diversification of the economy through the expansion of coffee and cotton.

If Washington had identified with the fruit companies, as happened in Guatemala under Arbenz, the passage of reform measures would have been far more difficult. The State Department, however, had cast a jaundiced eye on the fruit companies in Honduras ever since the disastrous episode in 1910 when dollar diplomacy was thwarted by Sam Zemurray. There were no Cold War reasons to favour the fruit companies under Gálvez and the U.S. Department of Justice filed a civil anti-trust suit against UFCO in 1954. The rapid rise of trade unions with Communist participation, after 1954, presented a major challenge for Cold War strategists in Washington, but successive Honduran governments showed themselves as keen as any U.S. administration to purge the Marxists from positions of influence: both

Honduran and U.S. governments recognized that a 'free and democratic' labour movement could be a source of strength. The post-war rise of an influential agro-export class, symbolized by the formation of FENAGH, posed a potential threat to the reform programme in the mid-1960s, but by then the labour movement was firmly established under anti-communist leadership and the new industrial class competed with FENAGH for government favours. This prevented too close an identification between government and agro-exporters (a major problem in neighbouring countries).

The Honduran reformist experiment failed most obviously in the field of democracy. The political system suffered many weaknesses, not least the overwhelming influence of the military, and lacked credibility as a fully functional democracy. In contrast to El Salvador and Guatemala, the problem could not be identified with the incorporation of an influential Marxist left into the democratic process, because in Honduras the latter remained of marginal importance. Politics in Honduras was dominated by two traditional parties, loose coalitions of warring factions committed to *personalismo* and united only behind the lure of power and access to the spoils of office, which proved incapable of moving with the times and continued to be an obstacle to effective presidential leadership. The cause of democracy in Honduras in the 1980s after the return to civilian rule was not helped by the tension between the United States and Nicaragua. U.S. geopolitical priorities led to a massive build-up in the quantity and quality of the Honduran armed forces as a strategic bulwark against the Sandinistas. The U.S. military presence, semi-permanent from 1983, led to a close collaboration with the Honduran armed forces over counter-insurgency strategy, which largely by-passed civilian members of the government. The emphasis on security increased the importance of the military in internal affairs, at a time when the consolidation of democracy demanded its return to the barracks. Although the armed forces respected the constitution after 1984 and left the civilian government in charge of most aspects of economic and social policy, political progress in Honduras remained fragile.

7

NICARAGUA SINCE 1930

In 1930, more than a century after independence from Spain, the status of Nicaragua as a sovereign nation was in doubt. Occupied by U.S. Marines almost continously since 1912, the country had effectively lost its political independence; indeed, a vocal minority favoured annexation by the United States. With U.S. officials responsible for most aspects of fiscal and monetary policy, Nicaragua had also lost its financial autonomy. The economy was relatively weak. The export sector (based on coffee, bananas, timber and gold) remained the driving force of the economy but lacked the dynamism of neighbouring countries: exports earned a mere $10 million a year. As a result, Nicaragua, with a population of only 680,000, had the lowest income per head in all Central America. Lack of government resources had hindered the spread of public education and the vast majority of the population remained illiterate. Moreover, the task of national integration was not yet complete. The eastern provinces bordering the Caribbean sea remained unconnected by road or rail to the capital, Managua, and the English-speaking inhabitants of the Atlantic coast, whose formal link with Great Britain had only been broken in 1894, continued to regard 'the Spanish' on the western side of Nicaragua as representatives of a foreign country.

THE U.S. MILITARY OCCUPATION

By virtue of its location and unusual geographical features, Nicaragua has excited the interest of outside powers since the earliest days of Spanish colonial rule. During most of the nineteenth century after independence, it was taken for granted by interested parties that a future inter-oceanic canal would be built through Nicaragua, since the easily navigable San Juan River and Lake Nicaragua would limit major construction works to the narrow strip of land separating Lake Nicaragua from the Pacific Ocean. There was intense rivalry between Great Britain and the United States for control of such a canal until the Clayton–Bulwer Treaty of 1850 bound both powers to reject exclusive control over any such project. However, under the Hay–Pauncefote Treaty of 1901, Great Britain acknowledged its reduced influence in Central America and ceded to the United States exclusive control and protection over any canal it should build. President Theodore Roosevelt's recognition of Panamanian independence in 1903 and the construction of a canal across the isthmus (completed in 1914) did not lessen U.S. geopolitical interest in Nicaragua. On the contrary, the stability of countries close to Panama acquired a new significance and it became more important than ever to prevent rival powers from acquiring control of any canal route through Nicaragua. The administrations of the first decades of the twentieth century never renounced the idea of a Nicaraguan canal under U.S. control. Indeed, surveys were carried out at frequent intervals until the early 1930s.

Relations with José Santos Zelaya, the Liberal president of Nicaragua (1893–1909) were, therefore, of special interest to the U.S. State Department. Zelaya granted generous concessions to U.S. entrepreneurs active in Nicaragua's mining, timber and banana industries, but his relationship with the State Department was badly strained by his interventions in the affairs of neighbouring republics (particularly Honduras) and his flirtations with Germany and Japan regarding a possible canal through Nicaragua. Hence, when a Conservative revolt broke out on Nicaragua's eastern seaboard in 1909, the administration of President William Howard Taft was quick to exploit it and force the removal of Zelaya. However, the succession was not smooth and the outbreak of civil war brought U.S. marines to Nicaragua in 1912.

The arrival of the marines put the military seal on a process of U.S. intervention that had begun in October 1910 with the despatch of Thomas C. Dawson, U.S. minister at Panama, to Managua. The 'Dawson agreements', signed in 1911, assumed that a precondition for political stability in Nicaragua was financial stability, and it was taken for granted that this could not be achieved without close U.S. supervision. Thus began the long period of U.S. intervention in Nicaragua's financial affairs, which survived the Good Neighbor Policy of the 1930s and did not finally end until the 1940s. The State Department secured the support of its Nicaraguan political allies for financial intervention by promising a $15 million loan from U.S. banks, the terms and conditions of which were enshrined in the Knox–Castrillo Treaty of 1911. The U.S. Senate, however, rejected the treaty on three occasions, so the Nicaraguan government had to make do with a more modest 'interim' loan of $1.5 million, while financial intervention went ahead despite the absence of the treaty. By the end of the decade, the framework for fiscal and monetary supervision was firmly in place. A U.S. Collector General of Customs was in charge of customs duties, the first claim on which was external public debt service; European bondholders were therefore assured of prompt payment and any possible need for European intervention in defiance of the Monroe Doctrine averted. A National Bank was established with a majority of shares held by U.S. bankers in order to maintain the new currency (the córdoba) at par with the U.S. dollar and keep Nicaragua on a gold exchange standard with reserves held in New York. The bankers also purchased a majority shareholding in the National Railway and, although the Nicaraguan government bought them out in 1924, both the National Bank and the National Railway continued to have a majority of U.S. directors on their boards with the headquarters of both organizations located in the United States.[1]

Following the infamous Bryan–Chamorro Treaty of 1916[2] the State Department pushed through new financial plans in 1917 and 1920 that provided for even closer control of Nicaraguan fiscal affairs. A High Commission was established (with majority U.S. membership) and given control over part of the Nicaraguan government's budget (including public works) and powers to supervise changes in customs duties – a not insignificant function in a country where taxes on external trade accounted for at least 50 per cent of government revenue. The State Department was also instrumental in setting up three commissions, with strong U.S. representation, to adjudicate claims arising out of civil disturbances during the first three decades of the century.

Financial supervision – to the relief of the State Department – was cheap. Neither the bankers nor the U.S. government became major credi-

---

[1] In 1929, the bankers Brown Bros. & Co and J. & V. Seligman & Co resigned. Their place as fiscal agent for the National Bank and the Pacific Railroad was taken by the International Acceptance Bank of New York.

[2] The Bryan–Chamorro Treaty (signed in 1914, but not ratified by the U.S. Senate until 1916) gave the United States, in perpetuity, exclusive proprietary rights for construction, operation and maintenance of an inter-oceanic canal. It also granted the United States a ninety-nine-year lease on the Corn Islands off the Atlantic coast and for a naval base in the Gulf of Fonseca. In return, the United States paid the Nicaraguan government $3 million, most of which was required to be used in settlement of debt arrears. See I. J. Cox, *Nicaragua and the United States (1909–1927)* (Boston, 1927), p. 845.

tors to the Nicaraguan government, whose public external debt continued
to be mainly in the form of bonds owed to Europeans; U.S. foreign
investment – both direct and portfolio – was less important in Nicaragua
than in any other Latin American country except Paraguay.[3] The connections of Philander Knox (Secretary of State in the Taft administration)
with a U.S.-owned mining company in Nicaragua raised some eyebrows,[4]
but the U.S. government could plausibly claim that its motives for intervention in Nicaragua were not economic. Financial supervision was also
effective. The córdoba remained roughly at par with the U.S. dollar
during the difficult years of the First World War and even survived the
worst years of the depression after 1929. The public external debt was not
only serviced promptly, but also declined in nominal terms during the
1920s as repayments exceeded new borrowings. Under the restrictions
imposed by the Collector General of Customs, the High Commission and
the bankers, the government avoided the worst excesses of deficit finance
observed in the Zelaya period, while both the National Bank and the
National Railway became highly profitable.

The assumption in the Dawson agreements, however, that financial
stability would bring political stability, proved quite false. Within a few
months of the withdrawal of U.S. marines in 1925, civil war had broken
out again. Moreover, there was an additional complication in that the
Mexican government was supporting the Liberal opposition led by former
vice-president Juan Bautista Sacasa in its bid to regain power; in addition
to the other reasons advanced in favour of intervention, the U.S. government now had to consider the possible loss of prestige that would result
from a 'Mexican' victory. The U.S. Marines therefore returned again to
Nicaragua in 1926 and in May 1927 a peace treaty between the Liberals
and the Conservatives was signed under the supervision of Henry Stimson,
a former U.S. Secretary of War. This time, as a further precondition for
political stability the State Department demanded the abolition of all
Nicaraguan armed forces (including the police) and their replacement by a
non-partisan National Guard staffed initially by U.S. officers, modelled on
the National Guard in U.S.-occupied Haiti, soon to be adopted in the
Dominican Republic, and designed to overcome the deep divisions in

[3] See E. Kamman, *A Search for Stability: United States Diplomacy Toward Nicaragua, 1925–1933* (Notre
Dame, Ind., 1968), pp. 220–4.

[4] Philander Knox represented at various times the Nicaraguan mining concern La Luz and Los
Angeles Company, owned by the Fletcher family. A clerk from this company, Adolfo Díaz, became
president of Nicaragua on three occasions during the U.S. occupation.

Nicaraguan society between Liberals and Conservatives by convincing the opposition party that it could come to power by electoral means without resorting to force. The peace treaty was not signed by all the Liberal leaders. Augusto César Sandino, who had returned from Mexico in 1926 to join the Liberal revolt and had risen to the rank of general in the army led by José María Moncada, refused to submit to any treaty which left the U.S. Marines in Nicaragua. Sandino took to the hills of Nueva Segovia in northern Nicaragua with a band of thirty men.

The first test of the new order came in the presidential elections of 1928. The electoral contest, like all those since the fall of Zelaya, was supervised by U.S. Marines, but this time the outcome was not a foregone conclusion. The Liberal Party fielded their war hero General Moncada, who secured a narrow victory over his Conservative rival in a hard-fought contest with high voter participation. The Liberal Moncada proved just as anxious to co-operate with U.S. officialdom as his Conservative predecessors, and the 1930 congressional elections, also supervised by U.S. Marines, produced a Liberal majority. In January 1931, Henry Stimson – now Secretary of State in the Hoover administration – announced that U.S. forces would finally withdraw from Nicaragua after the presidential elections of November 1932.

Stimson had become convinced that political stability had finally been achieved in Nicaragua. The U.S. administration had found, somewhat to its surprise, that most of the Liberal leaders were sensitive to U.S. perceptions of the region and willing to accommodate U.S. interests in their policies. The outstanding exception, Sandino, had been denounced by his own Liberal party and Stimson was confident that Sandino could be contained – if not defeated – by the National Guard, which would remain under the command of U.S. officers until the withdrawal of the marines. Domestic opposition in the United States against the presence of marines had increased for both economic and political reasons, while Latin American condemnation of the occupation had grown since discontent had first surfaced at the Sixth Pan-American Conference in Havana in 1928. Last, but not least, the collapse of world trade after 1929 left the Panama Canal with ample spare capacity, so that the need for a second canal through Nicaragua (the right to which had been secured through the Bryan–Chamorro Treaty) was not so pressing. (The last survey of the Nicaraguan canal route was carried out in 1932.)

The legacy of more than two decades of almost unbroken military intervention in Nicaragua was not a happy one. The State Department's supporters could claim some positive gains: financial stability had been achieved; the elections of 1928, 1930 and 1932, conducted under U.S. supervision, were among the freest in Nicaraguan history; the State Department was no longer seen to favour one party (the Conservatives) over the other and could now do business with a new generation of Liberals, making a policy of non-intervention feasible. On the other hand, financial stability had been achieved only by sacrificing Nicaragua's economic development. In modern parlance, growth was sacrificed for the sake of prompt service on the debt. In the decade up to 1926–7 on average more than one-third of government annual expenditure was spent on servicing the debt; following the formation of the National Guard in 1927, military expenditure became a heavy charge on the budget, absorbing nearly 30 per cent in 1929–30; expenditure on public works – a residual under the financial plans after all other expenses had been paid – was so low, a U.S. financial expert commented in 1928:

There is very little to show for such sums, and it is probable that substantial portions, though credited to public works, have been diverted to other purposes, as in the case of public instruction funds. Highways have absorbed the bulk of public works disbursements, yet not a mile of first-class highway exists in the republic outside of certain recently paved streets in the Capital. Other portions of public works funds have been devoted to the construction or repair of public buildings, but here again accomplishments are not in accordance with appropriations.[5]

The U.S. intervention also distorted the perceptions and behavior of the Nicaraguan elite. An entire generation had become accustomed to the idea of U.S. intervention; the vast majority of the Nicaraguan elite – in government and business – not only accepted U.S. intervention as inevitable but welcomed it as desirable. In 1927 the Nicaraguan finance minister proposed that the United States should extend its fiscal control to include internal taxation as well as customs duties, that a board of estimates with a majority of U.S. citizens should prepare the nation's budget and that a U.S. comptroller should supervise all government expenditures. In the same year, President Adolfo Díaz repeated his offer (first made in 1911) to amend the Nicaraguan constitution to allow the United States to intervene almost at will in return for a modest loan. Indeed by the end of the 1920s the U.S. administration was somewhat embarrassed by this obsequious attitude which it had itself engendered.

The Hoover administration's decision to withdraw the marines from

---

[5] See W. Cumberland, *Nicaragua: an economic and financial survey* (Washington, D.C., 1928), p. 106.

Nicaragua anticipated Roosevelt's Good Neighbor Policy, but a U.S. policy of non-intervention in Nicaraguan affairs was not credible. Fiscal supervision continued as before and the Bryan–Chamorro Treaty giving the United States rights to a canal route together with military and naval bases was still in force. Moreover, it was not believed by the Nicaraguan elite, who for nearly twenty-five years had been mastering the art of interpreting U.S. preferences as a means of political self-advancement. It continued to be assumed that the State Department had its favourites and that the latter would win any contest; political success therefore depended on convincing the public that an individual or faction enjoyed implicit U.S. support.

THE IMPACT OF THE DEPRESSION

By the time the U.S. Marines finally withdrew from Nicaragua – the last left on 2 January 1933 – difficulties had increased considerably as a result of the world economic crisis. The Nicaraguan economy on the eve of the 1929 depression was heavily dependent on exports, which in turn were dominated by coffee; over half these exports went to the United States, while the latter supplied nearly two-thirds of imports. Customs duties and surcharges on these imports accounted for the bulk of government revenue, while external trade also determined to a large extent the level of activity in commerce, transport and services.

Despite the presence of many foreign entrepreneurs, the coffee sector was characterized by inefficiency and low yields; the republic's coffee had not achieved a reputation for high quality – in contrast to Costa Rica, El Salvador and Guatemala – and the price received by growers was lower than in the rest of Central America. These prices peaked as early as 1925, but the precipitate decline did not begin until after 1929. In the first two years (1930 and 1931), the volume of exports was sustained at pre-depression levels, but a poor harvest in the 1931–2 season contributed to a 49 per cent drop in the volume exported and the value of coffee exports in 1932 was only 25 per cent of the level in 1929.

Nicaragua's other exports (mainly bananas, timber and gold) were not as badly affected by the depression as coffee was, but the latter's importance was sufficient to pull down total export earnings from $11.7 million in 1928 to $4.5 million in 1932. At the same time, under the watchful eye of U.S. fiscal intervention, these reduced foreign exchange receipts were still expected to pay for the service charge on the public external debt, which remained the same in nominal terms. This required a cut in imports even more savage than that for exports; imports fell from $13.4 million in 1928 to $3.5 million in 1932. This reduction was achieved without breaking the parity of the córdoba against the U.S. dollar, although Nicaragua did abandon the gold exchange standard and introduced exchange restrictions in November 1931 under a Control Board composed of the U.S. Collector General of Customs, the U.S. manager of the National Bank and the Nicaraguan Minister of Finance.

The public debt (internal and external) was therefore serviced promptly, although amortization of the external debt was partially suspended from 1932 onwards. Nicaragua joined Argentina, Honduras and the Dominican Republic as the only Latin American countries to meet interest payments in full on the foreign debt during the 1930s. Nicaragua's room for manoeuvre, however, was even less than for these other republics, because in addition to the priority given to the public debt, additional expenditure had to be found for training and recruiting the National Guard. The government of President Moncada desperately tried to protect government revenues by introducing customs surcharges,[6] but fiscal receipts still declined from 5.6 million córdobas in 1928–9 to 3.8 million in 1932–3, and the share of receipts committed to the National Guard and debt service rose to 50 per cent by the time the U.S. Marines withdrew.

This critical situation was made even worse by the disastrous earthquake which struck Managua in March 1931, killing a thousand people and destroying virtually all government buildings. The government negotiated a series of emergency loans in 1932, 1933 and 1934 with the National Bank in order to finance the work of reconstruction and the reduction of arrears in public-sector salaries, but expenditures on health, education and road construction virtually ceased and lay-offs among government employees became common. The Banco Hipotecario, set up by the Moncada government in October 1930 to help the farm sector, closed in 1931 before it could start operations and did not reopen until October 1934. Gross domestic product (GDP) per head fell by 32.9 per cent in real terms between 1929 and 1932, the sharpest drop in Central America.[7] Furthermore, the withdrawal of the marines – whose numbers had exceeded 5,000 in January 1929[8] – deprived Nicaragua of a valuable source of purchasing power just as the

---

[6] These surcharges increased the average tariff rate from 34 per cent in 1928 to 50 per cent in 1953.
[7] See V. Bulmer-Thomas, *The Political Economy of Central America since 1920* (Cambridge, 1987), table A3.
[8] They were reduced to 1412 by January 1931 and 910 by the time of the final withdrawal on 2 January 1933.

depression began to have its greatest impact. GDP per head continued to fall and reached its nadir in 1936, by which time it was the lowest in Central America and one of the lowest in all Latin America.

THE SANDINO EPISODE[9]

The withdrawal of the U.S. Marines in January 1933 left Sandino and his army, the Ejército Defensor de la Soberanía Nacional de Nicaragua (EDSN), still at large. In six years of fighting, neither the U.S. Marines nor the U.S.-officered National Guard had been able to destroy the EDSN, despite the use for the first time of aerial bombardment in support of ground troops by the U.S. military. The EDSN, which reached a maximum of 3,000 members (many of whom were part-time), scored some spectacular military successes, including the destruction of the Fletcher family's La Luz y Los Angeles mine, but its base of operations was mainly confined to the remote and thinly populated provinces of Nueva Segovia, Jinotega and Zelaya.[10]

Sandino, who had left Nicaragua in 1920 following a violent incident, had worked for U.S. companies in Honduras, Guatemala and Mexico – an experience which gave him an inside view of the operations of foreign (U.S.) capital in Latin America. He returned to Nicaragua in 1926 inspired, as we have seen, by the Liberal revolt which followed the first withdrawal of U.S. troops. After the return of the marines, Sandino refused to surrender under the terms of the agreement proposed by Stimson in May 1927. Sandino's purpose in launching a Guerra Constitucionalista was ostensibly the restoration of constitutional government in Liberal hands under Juan Sacasa. But Sacasa accepted the Stimson–Moncada pact, and in November 1928, Moncada himself won the presidential elections for the Liberals. Sandino's objective therefore became the defence of national sovereignty, which required at the very least the withdrawal of all U.S. troops. However, the defence of national sovereignty, in a country where two decades of U.S. military occupation had created an extensive network through which U.S. interests were represented, was no simple matter.

The Coolidge and Hoover administration saw Sandino purely in mili-

---

[9] The original meaning of an 'episode' is 'an interval between two choric songs in Greek tragedy'; this seems highly appropiate.

[10] The military aspects of the Sandino episode are competently discussed in Neil Macaulay, *The Sandino Affair* (Chicago, 1967).

tary terms and described him in official communiqués as a bandit, although he was addressed as General Sandino in letters sent to him by representatives of the U.S. military occupation. The U.S. public, meanwhile, received much of its news about Sandino from the Nicaraguan representatives of United Press and Associated Press, the first of whom was the U.S. Collector General of Customs and the second his U.S. assistant.[11] However, when an excess of confidence on the part of U.S. officers resulted in a series of military reversals, North American public opinion began to be affected by the reports of dead or wounded marines. The U.S. administration therefore switched to a policy under which the National Guard rather than the marines would bear the brunt of the fighting, and approval was even given to the formation of a highly partisan group of *auxiliares* to supplement the work of the supposedly non-partisan National Guard.

The consequence of this shift in policy was that the bulk of casualties was borne by Nicaraguans on both sides. Between 1926 and 1933, 136 marines died, but only 47 fatalities were the result of combat action against the EDSN – an average of one every seven weeks.[12] This low figure meant that Sandino's goal of defending national sovereignty had to be achieved by Nicaraguans killing Nicaraguans – a position which underlined the difficulty of prosecuting a nationalist cause in a country where the imperialist power could rely on national agents to defend its interests.

Although Washington saw Sandino as a bandit, public opinion in Latin America regarded him as a hero and symbol of the struggle against the 'Colossus of the North'.[13] Anti-interventionist sentiment in Latin America reached a peak between the Sixth Pan-American Conference in Havana in 1928 and the Seventh in Montevideo in 1933, coinciding with Sandino's campaign, which attracted a wide regional following and found an echo in Europe, Asia and even North America.

Until the end of 1928 Sandino's key representative was the Honduran poet and politician Froylán Turcios, who edited the widely distributed review *Ariel*.[14] However, Turcios broke with Sandino after a dispute that

---

[11] See C. Beals, *Banana Gold* (Philadelphia, 1932), pp. 304–5.

[12] The remaining deaths were due to the following causes: murder (11); accidents (41); suicides (12); disease (24); and shot while resisting arrest (1). See Macaulay, *The Sandino Affair*, p. 239.

[13] Sandino's struggle elicited an extraordinary number of books, articles and pamphlets throughout Latin American from as early as 1927. For an excellent example of these writings, deferential in tone, see Instituto de Estudio del Sandinismo, *El Sandinismo – documentos básicos* (Managua, 1983), pp. 211–31.

[14] *Ariel* was named after a novel by the Uruguayan José Enrique Rodó, written in 1909, which symbolized the struggle between Latin America and the United States. See Hugo Cancino Troncoso, *Las raíces históricas e ideológicas del movimiento Sandinista: antecedentes de la revolución nacional y popular Nicaragüense, 1927–1979* (Odense, 1984), p. 56.

underlined the difficulties found by Sandino in developing a consistent strategy for the defence of national sovereignty. Turcios wrote to Sandino in December 1928, following the election of Moncada as president, to propose a peace treaty under which Moncada would request the immediate withdrawal of U.S. troops and Sandino would then lay down his arms and recognize the Moncada government in return for the latter's commitment to restore the constitution and suppress all unconstitutional edicts and contracts.[15] Sandino rejected this proposal out of hand – hence the resignation of Turcios as his representative – but within two weeks he had written to Rear Admiral Sellers, U.S. Navy Commander, Special Service Squadron, and Brigadier General Logan Feland of the U.S. Marine Corps to say that he would only reach a peace agreement with General Moncada, 'since the latter – being a member of the Liberal Party, which he betrayed – can correct his mistakes through the commitment which he is in a position to make with us, on behalf of the Nicaraguan people and the Liberal Party itself, to respect the proposals which our army will make at a suitable opportunity'.[16]

Sandino was therefore unclear whether his objective of national sovereignty could be achieved by restoring constitutional government under Moncada (or some other representative of the Liberal Party) or whether it required the elimination of all those traditional institutions (including the Liberal Party) which had collaborated with U.S. imperialism. The latter was a much more radical position towards which both the Alianza Popular Revolucionaria Americana (APRA) and the Communist International wished to push Sandino. For APRA, founded by the exiled Peruvian Víctor Raúl Haya de la Torre in Mexico in 1924, Sandino's war symbolized the struggle of the whole Latin American continent for national sovereignty, independence and social equity. Froylán Turcios was named as honorary Aprista and the Peruvian Esteban Pavletich was despatched to Nueva Segovia in 1928 to join the EDSN. Pavletich gained Sandino's confidence and accompanied him on his extended sojourn in Mexico from June 1929 to May 1930, intended to broaden the base of support in Latin America for his struggle. It was from APRA that Sandino borrowed the term 'Indoamericanismo' and his plan to hold a regional conference in Argentina in order to promote an internationally controlled Nicaraguan canal leaned heavily on APRA's scheme to wrest control of the Panama Canal from the United States.

Sandino also borrowed from APRA's social analysis, claiming on one

---

[15] Turcios' letter is printed in full in S. Ramírez (ed.), *El pensamiento vivo de Sandino*, 2d ed. (San José, 1976), pp. 156–8.
[16] See Ramírez, *El pensamiento*, p. 155.

occasion for example, that: 'neither extreme right nor extreme left is our slogan. For that reason, there is nothing illogical in our struggle being based on the co-operation of all social classes without ideological labels'.[17] This analysis appeared consistent with Nicaraguan social reality since the low level of economic development had generated only tiny pockets of proletarians (e.g., in banana plantations and mines) while the bulk of the labour force (more than 80 per cent in the 1920 census) was engaged in agriculture and only a small proportion were landless labourers. Equally, the officers of the EDSN – both Nicaraguans and other Latin Americans – were drawn heavily from the petty bourgeoisie. However, Sandino sometimes spoke in class terms. In a 1930 letter, made famous since the Nicaraguan Revolution of 1979, he wrote that 'with the intensification of the struggle and the growing pressure from the Yankee bankers, the waverers and the timid – because of the form the struggle now takes – are abandoning us; only the workers and peasants will carry on to the end, only their organized strength will achieve victory'.[18] A year later, in a letter written to one of his closest officers, Pedrón Altamirano, he claimed that the Sandinista movement should disassociate itself from all bourgeois elements on the grounds that it was in their interests to favour a humiliating accommodation with the United States.

Such positions reflect the influence on Sandino of the Communist International and the Liga Anti-Imperialista de las Americas, which was founded in 1925, not as a Communist organization but with Communists playing a leading part in its activities. It was through the League that Sandino came into close personal contact with some of the key Latin American Communists of the day, such as the Venezuelan Gustavo Machado, who visited Sandino in Las Segovias, and – more importantly – the Venezuelan Carlos Aponte and the Salvadorean Agustín Farabundo Martí. Both Aponte and Martí joined the EDSN in 1928 and both rose to the rank of colonel, Martí in particular gaining the confidence and close friendship of Sandino.

Sandino was not a Communist and his occasional use of Marxist phraseology and class analysis was more a reflection of his desire to retain the support of the League than a genuine commitment to class struggle. The differences finally surfaced at the end of 1929, during Sandino's ten-month sojourn in Mexico and just before his interview with the Mexican president Portes Gil.

---

[17] Quoted in R. Cerdas Cruz, *Sandino, el APRA y la Internacional Comunista* (Lima, 1984), pp. 65–6.
[18] See Cerdas Cruz, *Sandino*, p. 106.

By early 1930, the break was complete and the Communist International began to denounce Sandino as a traitor who had become a petit-bourgeois liberal *caudillo*. Abandoned by both Turcios and the Communist International together with its front organizations, Sandino was now more isolated than ever and from mid-1930 had to deal with the confused political situation in Nicaragua surrounded by officers of outstanding courage and military skill but minimal political experience.

Following Sandino's return from Mexico in May 1930, the EDSN's military successes were substantial and clearly enjoyed considerable backing from the population surrounding its bases of operations, although support in the major cities was much less secure. Sandino's call for a boycott of the elections of 1928, 1930 and 1932 together with the EDSN's campaign of disruption were not successful; in every case the turn-out was extraordinarily high.[19] Sandino failed to build a political wing of the EDSN in the main cities: the Partido Laborista (PL), set up in León in 1928 and led by Dr Escolástico Lara, collapsed soon afterwards, while a similar fate greeted the pro-Sandino Partido Liberal Republicano (PLR) set up in Managua. A year before the 1932 elections, Sandino proposed Horacio Portocarrero — a Nicaraguan living in El Salvador — as president of a provisional government, but this initiative also failed to gain support.

These political disappointments contributed to Sandino's uncertainty regarding his relationship with the traditional political parties, particularly the Liberals. At times, he appeared to regard the entire political elite as hopelessly corrupted by U.S. imperialism and incapable of defending national sovereignty. Yet in this, as in so many other areas, he was not consistent, and his dilemma was compounded by the victory of the Liberal candidate, Juan Sacasa, in the presidential elections of November 1932. Sacasa became president on 1 January 1933, the day before the last of the U.S. Marines withdrew, and although he felt betrayed by Sacasa, Sandino could not ignore the change in circumstance which was made even more dramatic by Sacasa's appointment of Sofonías Salvatierra, a Sandinista sympathizer, as Minister of Agriculture.

Salvatierra headed the Grupo Patriótico, formed in 1932 to promote peace between Sandino and the government. Negotiations began in December 1932 and the peace protocol proposed by Sandino on 23 January

---

[19] In 1928, the voters numbered 133,633 out of an electorate of 148,831 — a turn-out of 88.8 per cent. See Kamman, *Search for Stability*, p. 166, n49. In the 1932 presidential elections the vote dropped to 129,508.

1933 made it clear that the 'defence of national sovereignty' included an end to U.S. fiscal intervention, revision of the Bryan–Chamorro Treaty and reorganization of the National Guard to bring it within the Nicaraguan Constitution.[20] Astonishingly, the final peace treaty – signed in Managua on 2 February – made no mention of these questions. Instead, Sandino settled for a treaty in which the EDSN agreed to surrender its arms in return for access to state lands along the Río Coco, a personal bodyguard for Sandino of a hundred men (subject to review after one year) and a commitment by the government to a public-works programme in the northern departments for a minimum of one year.

Sandino later claimed that he had agreed to this treaty to avoid giving the U.S. authorities an excuse for a third military intervention. The treaty, however, left unresolved all the issues of non-military U.S. intervention in Nicaragua and in particular ignored the unconstitutional character of the National Guard. Within days, there were clashes between the National Guard and former members of the EDSN, Sandino refusing to surrender the rest of his weapons on the grounds that the Guard was not a duly constituted authority and could not therefore receive his arms. This infuriated the Guard's officer corps, and their fury turned to fear, when – in response to a temporary state of siege imposed by Sacasa in August following a series of violent explosions in the main Guard arsenal – Sandino offered to come to the rescue of the government with a force of six hundred armed men. The tension rose sharply at the beginning of 1934, and the senior Guard officers, led by their Jefe Director Anastasio Somoza García secretly agreed to take advantage of a planned trip to Managua by Sandino in February to assassinate both him and many of his supporters. The ruthless destruction of the remnants of the EDSN and their agricultural co-operatives in the northern provinces virtually erased the memory of Sandino for many years. Only two members of his army played an important part in the guerrilla struggles in Nicaragua from the late 1950s onwards and, ironically, Nicaraguans were forced to rely on a book ghost-written by Somoza for any reference to Sandino's writings.[21] The lessons of the Sandino episode were, however, clear for that small group of Nicaraguans – mainly students – determined to keep the memory alive: first, the defence of national sovereignty could not be restricted to ending

[20] See G. Selser, *Sandino* (New York, 1981), pp. 161–2.
[21] See A. Somoza, *El verdadero Sandino o el calvario de las Segovias* (Managua, 1936).

U.S. military intervention, and, second, the traditional political elite in the Conservative and Liberal parties could not be trusted to defend the national interest.

THE CONSOLIDATION OF SOMOZA'S RULE (1934–51)

The timetable for withdrawing the marines announced by Stimson in January 1931 accelerated the formation of the Nicaraguan National Guard. It was intended, as we have seen, to be non-partisan. However, given the intense rivalry between Liberal and Conservative families in Nicaragua, this goal was never realistic, especially because political loyalties in Nicaragua had a strong regional dimension.[22] The objective of a non-partisan National Guard was rendered even less realistic by the short time allowed for training the Nicaraguan officers. The military academy set up by the marines had graduated only 39 officers by March 1932 – nine months before withdrawal – when the estimated minimum requirement was 178. The U.S. director of the National Guard, Calvin B. Matthews, felt that these officers were too young and inexperienced to fill the higher ranks, but the determination of the State Department not to delay the evacuation of the marines meant appointing Nicaraguans to the highest posts without proper military training. An agreement was therefore reached at the U.S. legation in Managua on 5 November 1932 (the day before presidential elections) that the Liberal and Conservative presidential candidates would each nominate an equal number of persons from his party who would be acceptable replacements for the U.S. Marine officers. Outgoing President Moncada would then appoint the nominees of the successful candidate after the election and the incoming president would choose the new chief of the National Guard from among their ranks. The 'non-partisan' character of the Nicaraguan constabulary was therefore established on the basis of the political loyalties of its senior officers – a contradiction in terms.

Sacasa's victory in the November 1932 elections guaranteed that Liberal nominees would fill the top posts in the Guard. Moncada's preferred candidate for the post of the Jefe Director was Anastasio Somoza García, who had supported the 1926 Liberal revolt, served as the President's

[22] The city of León was the Liberal stronghold, while the Conservative base was Granada. Managua had become the capital in the nineteenth century in response to the bitter rivalry between these two cities.

personal aide and later, after a brief period of disgrace, as his Undersecretary of Foreign Affairs.[23] Moncada's choice of Somoza was undoubtedly
influenced by the support Somoza enjoyed in the U.S. camp from the time
he attracted Stimson's attention as an interpreter at the 1927 peace conference; by the end of 1932 both the U.S. minister, Matthew Hanna, and the
U.S. National Guard chief were convinced that Somoza was the man for
the job. Sacasa, however, was unconvinced, his first choice being the
Liberal veteran General Carlos Castro Wassmer. Yet because Castro was
unacceptable to both Moncada and the U.S. officials, Sacasa was obliged to
choose from an approved list of three candidates including Somoza.[24]
Under duress he chose Somoza, his niece's husband. From the start, therefore, the relationship between Somoza and Sacasa was strained, with Somoza confident in the knowledge that he enjoyed U.S. support.

The assassination of Sandino by the National Guard in February 1934
temporarily weakened Somoza's position, but Sacasa was unable to capitalize on this, and the young Jefe Director survived his greatest crisis and
emerged greatly strengthened. Somoza had personally promised the new
U.S. minister, Arthur Bliss Lane, that he would not move against
Sandino, and his actions effectively obliged Sacasa to retaliate by replacing
several of the officers implicated in the crime with new appointments,
many of whom were his relatives, and by temporarily adopting the title
commander-in-chief. Somoza, however, was only required to repeat his
oath of loyalty in the presence of the diplomatic corps. Despite repeated
requests by Minister Lane, Washington refused to make any public declaration discouraging Somoza from undermining the Sacasa government,
while the Jefe Director 'leaked' a series of stories suggesting not only that
he had ordered the killing of Sandino, but that he had done so in league
with U.S. officials. Somoza cultivated the image of himself as Washington's man and the stony silence from the State Department encouraged
Nicaraguans to believe the image was true. Sacasa's position was made
even weaker when the United States, following its recognition of the
Martínez dictatorship in El Salvador in 1934, announced that it was
abandoning its non-recognition policy under the Washington treaties of
1923. Moreover, when in 1935 Sacasa's wife informed Lane that her
husband was going to ask Somoza to resign as head of the National Guard
and that aircraft from El Salvador and Honduras would bomb his headquar-

---

[23] See B. Diederich, *Somoza and the Legacy of U.S. Involvement in Nicaragua* (London, 1982), pp.
13–14.
[24] See R. Millett, *Guardians of the Dynasty* (Maryknoll, N.Y.), pp. 134–5.

ters if he refused, the State Department intervened quickly to stop the President's plan.

Sacasa's position was further prejudiced by the continued weakness of the economy. World coffee prices remained at one-quarter of their pre-depression peak, while sugar exports suffered from U.S. refusal to allow Nicaragua a sizeable sugar quota under a reciprocal trade treaty.[25] Banana exports, which had challenged coffee in terms of importance at the beginning of the 1930s, started to fall sharply after 1933 under the impact of disease, and by 1943 they had disappeared completely. Within its limited means, the government did what it could: in 1934 the Banco Hipotecario finally began operations favouring coffee growers with a credit policy designed to avoid the need for foreclosures. In the same year the Caja Nacional de Crédito Popular (Monte de Piedad) was established to channel loans to small farmers at very low rates of interest. Two laws were passed (Ley de Habilitaciones and Ley de Usura) to ease the problems of the farm sector, and by the end of 1934 producers were receiving a modest premium over the official rate of exchange for their exports. The value of exports remained deeply depressed, however, throughout Sacasa's term of office (1933–6), pushing down imports and contributing to a permanent crisis in government revenue.

Sacasa's difficulties did not automatically work to Somoza's advantage. A rally held in 1934 while Sacasa was abroad was a failure. And Somoza's control of the National Guard was not yet fully assured. Furthermore, Somoza's presidential ambitions were thwarted by two provisions in the Constitution; the first stated that the head of the National Guard could not be a presidential candidate, while the second demanded a lapse of six months before any relation of the incumbent could himself succeed to the presidency. Somoza explored all manner of ways of circumventing these provisions, including the formation of a special constituent assembly to change the rules, but the lack of trust between himself and Sacasa produced no results.

Somoza was therefore forced to bide his time and concentrate on building a political machine. He formed a gang of thugs, Camisas Azules, consciously modelled on Mussolini's black and Hitler's brown shirts, and used his paper *La Nueva Prensa* to float the idea of his presidential candidacy. Somoza's real breakthrough came in February 1936 when he inter-

[25] The treaty was eventually signed in 1936, after Secretary of State Cordell Hull had applied economic pressure on Nicaragua to lower tariffs on a number of imports.

vened in a taxi driver's strike provoked by petrol shortages. His conciliatory attitude succeeded in ending the dispute, contrasted sharply with Sacasa's abrasive position, and won him the praise of both labour and business leaders. The following month, U.S. minister Lane was replaced by Boaz Long, who proved to be much more warmly disposed towards Somoza and his presidential ambitions. By May, Somoza felt strong enough to provoke a confrontation with Sacasa's cousin in charge of the Acosasco fort at León. The President reacted with unusual speed ordering his cousin to resist and calling an emergency meeting of Liberal and Conservative leaders to select Leonardo Argüello as a joint candidate in the November presidential elections.

Somoza was unperturbed. His National Guard units overpowered Ramón Sacasa in the Acosasco fort, leaving Somoza in complete military control of the country. Sacasa resigned on 6 June 1936 and three days later a compliant Congress nominated Dr Carlos Brenes Jarquín as interim president. The elections were postponed until December and in November Somoza resigned as Jefe Director of the National Guard so that his ascent to power could remain within the constitution. The Partido Liberal Nacionalista (PLN) was formed to launch Somoza's candidacy, which was also supported by a faction of the Conservative Party. The opposition called for U.S. supervision of the elections, and withdrew when this was not forthcoming. However, Argüello's name remained on the ballot paper and he secured 169 votes to Somoza's 107,201. The president-elect then resumed control of the 3,000-strong National Guard and combined the posts of Jefe Director and president from 1 January, 1937.

Support for Somoza was nothing like as strong as the voting figures suggested. The traditional political elite, which had previously seen in Somoza a means for pursuing its own ambitions, now began to realize that his dominant position posed a threat, while some members of the National Guard were unhappy at the President's handling of military affairs. Somoza, however, possessed an efficient intelligence system, enabling him rapidly to consolidate his position within the Guard and to divide his political opponents. He provided huge wage increases for the Guard's members and began the construction of both an air force and a navy under National Guard control. The Guard's functions were expanded to include control of internal revenue and the national railroad, while its grip on postal, telegraph and internal radio services together with control of immigration and emigration was tightened, providing innumerable opportunities for members of the force to supplement their salaries as well as to maintain social control.

Somoza's response to the threat from the traditional political elite was more subtle. Although he sometimes resorted to strong-arm tactics, including the arrest at a rally in 1937 of fifty-six members of the Conservative Party, Somoza recognized that these did not offer a long-term solution. He therefore adopted a series of measures to reverse the stagnation of agriculture since the economic interests of the traditional elite – Liberal and Conservative – were bound up with the fortunes of this sector. The most important measure was the series of devaluations, beginning in March 1937, which took the córdoba (¢) from par to five per U.S. dollar by the end of 1939 and gave a huge stimulus to agricultural exports, especially coffee, which was only partially off-set by new taxes on exports and exchange rate transactions designed to boost government revenue. The banking system was encouraged to finance new crops and both cotton and sesame production rose rapidly. Somoza also passed legislation favouring foreign investment; gold exports, in particular, increased sharply as a consequence. He did not, however, neglect his own economic interests; a 5 per cent tax on all public-sector salaries, a 1.5 cents per pound tax on beef exports and a share of foreign mining profits were all assumed to pass through his hands.

These economic measures produced a steep rise in the cost of living. Food retail prices increased by 124 per cent between 1937 and 1939 and those on fixed incomes suffered accordingly. The National Guard, however, was protected by large salary increases and the traditional elite benefited from the higher nominal prices for agricultural products. Elite opposition to Somoza began to crumble and Leonardo Argüello, his erstwhile opponent in the presidential elections, took the lead in unifying the Liberal Party behind the new Nicaraguan *caudillo*. Flushed by his success, Somoza persuaded Congress at the end of 1938 to turn itself into a Constituent Assembly, which extended the presidential term from four to six years without re-election (except for the present incumbent). A few months later, the Assembly reverted to the National Congress, and in one of its first acts declared Somoza president for eight years until May 1947.

His national power base secure, Somoza now turned to the Roosevelt administration, which had invited him for a state visit to Washington in 1939. Somoza secured from Roosevelt most of his demands: assistance in training officers for the National Guard at Nicaragua's Academia Militar, loans from the Export-Import Bank to purchase U.S. goods, and financial and material support to construct a road designed to link the English-speaking Atlantic region with the more densely populated Pacific provinces. The trip was of inestimable value to Somoza since it confirmed the wide-spread public belief that the Jefe Director enjoyed the support of the White House and could therefore not be overthrown without risking Washington's ire. In Nicaragua, non-intervention and the Good Neighbor Policy led to the endorsement of a president whose venality and ruthlessness were well known to U.S. officials.

The outbreak of the Second World War created serious problems for the Nicaraguan economy and temporarily raised the prospect of a revolt against Somoza. Under the inconvertible Aski-mark system, Germany had steadily increased its trade with Nicaragua during the 1930s. The loss of the German and European markets after 1939 was not at first compensated by increased purchases from the United States. At the same time, Somoza's suspension of constitutional guarantees and imposition of a state of siege created wide-spread resentment. The exile community, led by the Conservative Emiliano Chamorro, attempted a challenge but a swift shake-up of the National Guard – including the dismissal of Chief of Staff General Rigoberto Reyes – kept Somoza firmly in control. A lend-lease agreement with the United States in October 1941 provided the National Guard with modern equipment worth $1.3 million, greatly weakening the prospects for any revolt staged by the traditional Nicaraguan method of a poorly equipped volunteer force of exiles invading the country.

The entry of the United States into the war in December 1941 gave Somoza many opportunities to demonstrate his support for the Roosevelt administration at very little cost. Nicaragua immediately declared war on Japan, Germany and Italy, and the United States was invited to build naval and air bases in the republic. The government participated in U.S. schemes to supply the Panama Canal Zone with fruits and vegetables, while work on the Pan-American Highway (two-thirds funded by the Roosevelt administration) proceeded rapidly. Nicaragua promoted rubber production in the Atlantic region as part of the hemispheric effort to provide U.S. access to strategic raw materials formerly obtained from the Far East. Coffee production stabilized under the quota allocated to Nicaragua by the Inter-American Coffee Agreement, while gold exports soared.

Exports almost trebled in value between 1938 and 1944, but imports suffered from shipping and other shortages and only doubled in value. As a result, Nicaragua's gold and foreign-exchange reserves rose steadily during the war, pushing up the money in circulation and contributing to a noteworthy increase in prices. The creation of a Price Control Board headed by the U.S. Collector General of Customs, did little to restrain prices, which rose by 325 per cent between 1939 and 1945. On the other hand, price control coupled with import restrictions created enormous opportunities for graft by the Somoza family, the value of whose fortune rose rapidly during the war. By its end, Somoza was alleged to control fifty-one cattle ranches, forty-six coffee plantations, two sugar plantations, an airline, a gold mine, a milk plant and factories producing textiles, cement and matches. Much of this property had come into his hands as a result of expropriation of enterprises owned by Axis nationals.

The rapid rise in the cost-of-living index created resentment among urban workers, whose numbers had grown during the war. The traditional elite, on the other hand, resented Somoza's use of price and import controls to enrich himself at their expense. Even the Roosevelt administration began to question the wisdom of its support for Somoza when he unveiled his plans for re-election in 1947. All these factors combined to produce a real threat to the Somoza regime from 1944 onwards, but the lack of unity among his opponents, together with the dictator's undoubted tactical skill, enabled the dynasty to survive the greatest challenge to its existence until its overthrow in 1979.

Since the taxi drivers' strike of February 1936, Somoza had enjoyed posing as the friend of organized labour. His inclusion of minor social reforms in the Constitution of 1938 had contributed to the difficulties of the Partido Trabajador Nicaragüense (PTN), founded in 1931 as the party of organized labour. The PTN leadership subsequently divided over the attitude the labour movement should adopt towards Somoza, and the party dissolved itself in 1939. During the war Somoza invited Lombardo Toledano, the Mexican Marxist labour leader, to Nicaragua, and he frequently promised to introduce a Labour Code which became a central demand of both pro-Somoza labour groups and the Partido Socialista Nicaragüense (PSN), formed in 1944 by former leaders of the PTN. The attitude of these groups was not, however, one of confrontation with Somoza, who, for his part, manoeuvred to secure labour endorsement of his plans for re-election.

The attitude of the traditional elite, who felt they had more to lose from the dictator's continuation in power, was more hostile. Somoza's decision early in 1944 to seek re-election split the Liberal Party and led to the formation of the Partido Liberal Independiente (PLI) which made common

cause with the Conservatives to launch a strike designed to bring down
Somoza in mid-1944. The labour movement, still hopeful for the Labour
Code, did not, however, support the strike, which was also undermined
by the announcement of Irving Lindberg, U.S. Collector General of Customs and head of the Price Control Board, that any business participating
in the strike would be expropriated.

Washington, which had not authorized Lindberg's intervention, was
also anxious to prevent Somoza's re-election. His requests for additional
weapons in 1944 and 1945 were refused and strong pressure was brought
to bear. Yet the dictator did not yield until the end of 1945, by which
time the PLI and the Conservatives had agreed on Enoc Aguado as their
joint presidential candidate. Somoza invited the aged Leonardo Argüello,
his opponent in 1936, to represent the Somocista cause and Argüello duly
won a handsome election victory in May 1947. However, the new president demonstrated a surprising degree of independence and immediately
began to attack Somoza's power base in the National Guard by reassigning
officers. The dictator was shaken, but recovered his composure rapidly and
carried out a coup d'état within the month removing Argüello and ensuring that Congress chose Somoza's uncle, Victor Román y Reyes, as interim
president.

This move provoked a major crisis since the Truman administration
refused to recognize the new regime even after it had adopted a new constitution with strong anti-communist provisions. Recognition of the Román y
Reyes government at the end of 1947 by the governments of Costa Rica and
the Dominican Republic marginally reduced the isolation of the regime,
but the Truman administration stood firm until March 1948, when Somoza
played his trump card by invading Costa Rica in support of President
Teodoro Picado, whose government was backed by the Communist Party, in
the Costa Rican civil war. The Truman administration was keen to see the
elimination of Communist influence in the Costa Rican government and
persuaded Somoza to withdraw his troops in return for recognition of the
Román y Reyes regime, a step that was formally taken following the meeting of the Organization of American States (OAS) in April 1948. For the
next thirty years, successive U.S. administrations never again wavered in
their support of the Somoza family.

Meanwhile, Somoza had turned on his erstwhile allies in the labour
movement. The Labour Code of 1945 was ignored, the PSN outlawed,
and organized labour was so effectively crushed that it played no significant role until the 1970s. The student opposition, through which the

memory of Sandino had been kept alive, was undermined by closing universities and selective imprisonment. The traditional elite, however, were treated quite differently. Following a series of tactical agreements a pact was signed in 1950 by Somoza and Emiliano Chamorro under which the Conservative Party would be guaranteed one third of the seats in Congress together with representation in government and the judiciary. Most importantly the elite was guaranteed 'freedom of commerce', which meant that the Somoza family would share the benefits of economic growth with the traditional ruling classes. The 1950 pact paved the way for a presidential contest between Somoza and Chamorro, that duly provided the former with a further six-year term.

By 1951, at the start of his last presidential term, Somoza's rule had been firmly consolidated. He had thwarted all efforts to unseat him by deftly playing off one opponent against the other. Except in 1947–8, when he turned on the labour movement, he did not rely on extensive repression preferring exile and temporary imprisonment to weaken his opponents. He had manoeuvred his way around U.S. opposition to his continuation in power, appealing to the military against the State Department when necessary. Nicaragua remained a backward country with a weak export sector and limited opportunities for capital accumulation, but the 1950 pact finally resolved the division of labour between the Somoza family and the traditional elite and ensured the latter's support for the regime for the next twenty years.

ECONOMIC TRANSFORMATION AND THE FOUNDATION OF THE SOMOZA DYNASTY

The Nicaraguan economy on the eve of the Somoza–Chamorro pact was virtually stagnant; real GDP per head was still below the level of the late 1920s and virtually unchanged since 1941.[26] Real income per head was not only the lowest in Central America but also the lowest in Latin America except Haiti.[27] For almost a century, Nicaragua had followed an export-led model with only the most modest of results; exports in 1949 were a mere $23 per person (compared with $63 per person in Costa Rica) and this figure falls to a derisory $15 if gold exports (a virtual foreign enclave) are excluded. However, from 1949 to 1970, the Nicaraguan economy grew faster than

---

[26] See V. Bulmer-Thomas, *Political Economy of Central America*, table A3.
[27] See CEPAL, *Series históricas del crecimiento de América Latina* (Santiago, 1978), Cuadro 2.

any other Latin American country's (including Brazil's); by the mid-1960s
real GDP per head had overtaken the rest of Central America (except Costa
Rica) and climbed to the middle of the Latin American rankings. In the
same period (1949–70), Nicaraguan exports grew by 667 per cent – an
annual rate of 10.2 per cent – compared with 178 per cent for Latin America as a whole, so that exports had jumped to $98 per person by 1970, the
second highest figure in Central America (after Costa Rica) and one of the
highest in Latin America.

This transformation of the economy was not a smooth process. It was
subject to marked cycles: the first half of both the 1950s and the 1960s
were periods of exceptional growth followed in each case by five years of
modest economic expansion. Both the rapid expansion and the cycles were
dictated by the fortunes of the export sector, which added several new
products to the list of traditional exports.

The first such product was cotton, which had made a brief appearance
in the export list in the late 1930s. In 1949 cotton accounted for less than
1 per cent of exports; by 1955, this proportion had reached 38.9 per cent,
making cotton more important than coffee (34.9% per cent) or gold (10.2
per cent). This was followed by a period of retrenchment, caused by lower
world prices and technical difficulties, until a second boom in the first half
of the 1960s lifted the volume of cotton exports fourfold in the five years
up to 1965. The increase in beef exports after 1958 was almost as spectacular. The cattle industry, a traditional stronghold of the Conservative elite
based in Granada, was transformed by the introduction of modern
abattoirs and an efficient transport system; the Somozas played a pioneering role in beef exports to the United States, which rocketed from zero in
1958 to nearly $30 million by 1970, equivalent to 15 per cent of total
exports. The success of beef as an export product was followed in turn by
sugar, which benefited from the re-allocation of Cuba's U.S. sugar quota
after 1960. In this case the main beneficiary was the Conservative Pellas
group, the principal shareholders in the San Antonio sugar mill, although
the Somoza family by the end of the 1960s owned two of the six mills
operating in Nicaragua.

The boom in agro-exports was made possible by economic policies
which gave absolute priority to this branch of agriculture. Until the
córdoba was officially devalued in 1955 (from 5 córdobas to 7 córdobas per
U.S. dollar), agro-exporters were able to convert their dollar earnings to
local currency at the favourable free-market rate. Following the devaluation (the last until 1979), Nicaraguan farmers enjoyed exceptional price

stability, which kept input costs firmly under control. They also benefited from the weakness of rural trade unions, the failure to apply the 1945 Labour Code to agricultural workers and the absence of minimum rural wages (at least until 1962), which, coupled with demographic pressures, guaranteed adequate supplies of labour, even at harvest time, at a fixed real wage. Last, but not least, the allocation of credit was deliberately distorted in favour of agro-exports, which were subject to a maximum charge of 2 per cent (compared with 8 per cent for other commercial bank credits) for much of the period.

Agricultural products were not the only source of Nicaragua's export boom. The creation of the Central American Common Market (CACM) in 1960 provided the basis for a rapid increase in manufactured exports to the rest of the region. Many of these products, such as cooking oil and textiles, were based on the new agricultural exports, but others were the more familiar import-intensive 'finishing-touch' consumer goods that had become immensely profitable as a result of the new tariff structure adopted by CACM. Multinational capital (mainly from the United States) was attracted to Nicaragua by these industrial opportunities, underpinned by exceedingly attractive tax treatment as well as by the opportunities for profit in the commercialization of agricultural exports, the production of which, however, generally remained in national hands.

The cotton boom at the start of the 1950s was so profitable that the beneficiaries soon found themselves in possession of a large financial surplus. This stimulated the creation of two privately owned financial institutions outside the control of the Somoza family. The first, Banco de América (BANAMER), was founded in 1952 by a group of Granada-based businessmen led by Silvio F. Pellas, a member of the Conservative elite. The second, Banco Nicaragüense (BANIC), began operations in 1953 with the main shareholders linked to León and the Liberal Party. The new banks played a key role in the establishment of modern capitalism in Nicaragua. They robbed the Somoza family of its virtual monopoly over the allocation of scarce credit, each bank building up a series of enterprises in different sectors under the full or partial control of shareholders, so that it became possible to identify two dominant groups in the Nicaraguan economy outside the Somoza family. The BANAMER group, the BANIC group and the Somoza family all had major interests in agricultural exports, manufacturing and commerce, while the first two groups enjoyed a privileged position (at least until the early 1970s) in construction.

The Somoza family continued to enjoy a special status in relation to public financial institutions, a position strengthened by the creation in 1953 of the Instituto de Fomento Nacional (INFONAC) and by the establishment in 1966 of the Banco de la Vivienda. Nevertheless, the establishment of BANIC and BANAMER provided an opportunity for the traditional elite and a small group of new entrepreneurs to share in the benefits of economic transformation. As a result, the resistance of the bourgeoisie to the consolidation of Somoza's rule in the 1940s on the grounds of unfair competition was overcome and did not re-emerge until the mid-1970s.

The benefits of the economic transformation after 1950 were nevertheless very narrowly distributed: in the late 1960s 1 per cent of depositors accounted for nearly 50 per cent of savings deposits.[28] At the same time, the rapid transformation of agriculture produced a major social upheaval since the expansion of the new export products occurred not on the frontier (towards the Atlantic coast) but in the settled Pacific coast departments. As a consequence, some of the peasantry were driven towards less fertile lands in the frontier regions, others were reduced to the status of landless agricultural workers, while a third group migrated towards the cities (notably Managua).

This social upheaval was mirrored in other parts of Central America, but its impact in Nicaragua was particularly dramatic because the pace of transformation was more rapid than elsewhere and because the effort to introduce reforms to off-set the impact of social upheaval was particularly feeble. Although a land reform law was passed and a National Agrarian Institute established in 1963 under the influence of the Alliance for Progress, its impact was minimal. Equally, the Instituto Nicaragüense de Comercio Exterior e Interior (INCEI), set up to promote production of agricultural goods for the home market, was rendered incapable of stimulating domestic production and increasing food security because of a lack of resources. A minimum-wage provision was added to the Labour Code in 1962, but the rates were set so low as to have no appreciable effect on wages received, while the social security programme launched in 1957 never extended outside the city of Managua.

The social upheavals accompanying the economic transformation during the 1950s and 1960s never seriously troubled the Somoza dictatorship. On the contrary, the distractions provided by profitable economic opportunities for his traditional opponents in the Conservative and Inde-

---

[28] See John Morris Ryan et al., *Area Handbook for Nicaragua* (Washington, D.C., 1970), p. 312.

pendent Liberal parties enabled Somoza García not only to rule with a minimum of repression but also to found a dynasty – a combination no other Caribbean Basin dictator of those years succeeded in achieving.

Somoza's two legitimate sons, Luis and Anastasio ('Tachito'), had been groomed for the succession for many years. The eldest son, Luis – an agricultural engineer by training – had played a key role in helping to break the international isolation of the dictatorship in the 1947–8 period, while Anastasio had returned in 1946 from military training at West Point to enter the National Guard. A third (illegitimate) son, José, had entered the Guard as early as 1933 as an enlisted man but had been promoted to officer rank by the 1940s. Luis entered Congress in 1950 and by early 1956 had acquired the key position of First Designate, thus ensuring that a Somoza would fill the presidency if anything should happen to his father. Anastasio, meanwhile, had become acting Jefe Director of the National Guard with José promoted to the rank of major.

Somoza's control of the Nicaraguan state apparatus was secure by the mid-1950s. However, he still faced an external threat from the Caribbean Legion, a loosely knit organization of revolutionaries dedicated to the overthrow of regional dictatorships and whose greatest triumph was provided by José Figueres' victory in the Costa Rican civil war. Figueres did not forget his debt to the Legion and in April 1954 was implicated in a plot by Nicaraguan exiles, led by Emiliano Chamorro, to assassinate Somoza. Although this plot was easily foiled, Somoza was temporarily prevented from retaliating against Figueres by his involvement in the overthrow of the left-wing government of Jacobo Arbenz in Guatemala in May 1954. Somoza had long played the anti-communist card with enthusiasm and had been rewarded with substantial U.S. military equipment, an agreement setting up a U.S. Army mission and a U.S. military assistance program. In return, Nicaragua now provided training centres and other logistical support for Guatemalan counter-revolutionaries. The fall of Arbenz left Somoza free to retaliate against Figueres and in January 1955 the National Guard supported an invasion of Costa Rica by an exile force. Figueres countered with the formation of a volunteer army and a diplomatic offensive that prompted the U.S. military in Panama to come to his rescue and the Organization of American States to offer a mild condemnation of Nicaragua's role in the invasion. Somoza, however, had made his point; by September the two leaders had signed a Pact of Amity and Treaty of Conciliation between their countries and the Nicaraguan dictatorship ceased to be troubled from outside.

The assassination of Somoza in September 1956, after he had obtained the Liberal Party's nomination for a further presidential term, occurred, therefore, at a time when the dictatorship was under no serious internal or external threat. The succession was relatively smooth and was made easier by misleading reports from the U.S. military hospital in Panama, where Somoza had been flown at the personal intervention of the U.S. ambassador, that the dictator would recover. Luis became acting president; Anastasio, Jefe Director of the National Guard; and Colonel Gaitán, who had ensured the loyalty of the National Guard during the tense days after the assassination, was exiled for his pains to Argentina as ambassador.

Luis Somoza formalized his grip on the presidency through fraudulent elections in February 1957 which were boycotted by all the opposition except the puppet Partido Nacionalista Conservador (PNC). The Partido Social Cristiano (PSC) was created in reaction to these elections and received support from younger Conservatives dissatisfied with their party's inability to make any political impact on the dictatorship. The run-up to Luis' six-year term was marked by considerable repression – including the imprisonment of Pedro Joaquín Chamorro, editor of *La Prensa,* and Dr Enoc Aguado, defeated presidential candidate in 1947. Yet, once he was in office, Luis Somoza made it clear that he wanted to modernize Nicaragua as well as to maintain the hegemony of the Somoza family. It is significant that, however cosmetic they may have been, all the major socio-economic reforms of the post-war period occured during his six-year term (1957–63). Moreover, the press became relatively free and in 1959 the constitutional ban on re-election was restored.

The treaty with Costa Rica in 1955 may have ended Figueres' challenge to the dictatorship, but the Cuban Revolution brought into existence a potentially more serious threat. At the same time, it gave the dynasty a great opportunity to play the anti-communist card and curry favour with the Eisenhower and Kennedy administrations. As early as the middle of 1959, only six months after Castro's triumph, Luis Somoza was accusing Cuba of aiding efforts to overthrow his regime and Nicaragua played a leading role in the Bay of Pigs fiasco in April 1961, providing bases for the troop-lift and air attacks. This support for the United States was far from disinterested since the Cuban Revolution provided the inspiration for the more radical opponents of the Somoza dynasty: the Frente Sandinista de Liberación Nacional (FSLN) was formed a few months after the Bay of Pigs by a group of Nicaraguan exiles led by Carlos Fonesca Amador.

Despite the numerous plots against the dynasty, Luis Somoza felt sufficiently confident to engineer the victory of an outsider in the February 1963 presidential elections. His candidate, René Schick, was chosen by the Liberal Party at the insistence of the Somoza family in preference to more popular figures, the Conservative candidate, Dr Fernando Agüero, withdrawing as soon as it was clear that electoral fraud would guarantee Schick's victory. Schick was a puppet, but he managed to irritate Anastasio Somoza by subjecting a National Guard officer accused of murder to judicial process and by intervening to ensure the exile rather than imprisonment of Carlos Fonseca Amador. The Jefe Director, who had never found his brother's theory of indirect rule convincing and felt vindicated by Schick's behaviour, resolved to stand for election in February 1967.[29]

The prospect of another Somoza in the presidency provoked the opposition to mount its most serious challenge to the dictatorship since 1944. The Conservatives, the PLI and the PSC united to form the Unión Nacional Opositora (UNO) to fight the election behind the candidacy of Dr Fernando Agüero. The size of UNO's rallies and the certainty of electoral fraud convinced the opposition leadership that a popular movement could be mounted to bring down the dynasty. A rally of between 40,000 and 60,000 people was held in Managua in January 1967, but the National Guard remained loyal to the Somoza family and dispersed the crowd with heavy casualties. Anastasio Somoza duly won the elections the following month and resumed the directorship of the National Guard. Like his father, he now controlled the two key institutions in Nicaragua and a further restraining influence was removed when his brother Luis died in April 1967.

The legal opposition was crushed by the events of 1967, and the FSLN was unable to establish a base in either the urban or the rural populations. With his opponents demoralized, the young Somoza returned to his father's idea of a pact with the opposition to give them minority representation in return for their acceptance of Somoza family hegemony. The agreement, in which the U.S. ambassador played a decisive role, was reached in March 1971 and provided for the formation of a three-man ruling junta composed of Fernando Agüero together with two Somoza appointees. This Junta was to rule the country from May 1972 to December 1974, when new presidential elections would be held. The pact split the opposition

---

[29] Within two days of Anastasio Somoza's endorsement by the Liberal Party, Schick died and was replaced by Lorenzo Guerrero, who served the remaining few months of the presidential term.

but was duly implemented and left Somoza, still Jefe Director of the National Guard, firmly in charge. He enjoyed the full support of the Nixon administration, faced a weak and divided legal opposition and a minuscule threat from the revolutionary left; when he vacated the presidency, he had every reason to believe that he had been just as successful as his father in guaranteeing the survival of the dynasty.

COLLAPSE OF THE DYNASTY

Unlike the Somoza–Chamorro pact of 1950, the Somoza–Agüero agreement did not consolidate the authority of the regime. On the contrary, the reaction to the pact marked the first stage in the disintegration of the dictatorship. The success of Somocismo had rested on several pillars: a strong National Guard, loyal to the Somoza family; unconditional U.S. support; a tacit alliance with the most powerful sections of the bourgeoisie; and a political party system in which the opposition – in return for freedom of the press and radio and a minimum of repression – generally observed strict limits in the challenge it mounted against the regime. The dictatorship also relied upon a Catholic Church that endorsed its political programme and preached only to spiritual needs.

Both the political-party system and the traditional role of the Catholic Church were ruptured by the Somoza–Agüero pact. The Catholic Church, led since 1968 by Archbishop Miguel Obando y Bravo, refused to endorse the accord and signalled its entrance onto the political stage through a series of pastoral letters critical of the dictatorship. Christian base-communities had been springing up in Nicaragua since the late 1960s and the Catholic Church, as elsewhere in Latin America, had become much more conscious of social questions, although this concern was not so apparent among the Protestant churches dominant on the Atlantic coast. The Conservative Party, the traditional focus of legal opposition to Somocismo, was badly shaken by Agüero's decision to collaborate with the regime and split into four groups. Even the Somocista Liberal Party was affected because the pact virtually guaranteed Somoza the presidency for a further seven-year term in the scheduled 1974 elections and deprived outsiders of a chance of high office. Dr Ramiro Sacasa, a relative of Somoza who had served in various government posts, duly resigned from the party to form the Partido Liberal Constitucionalista (PLC).

Somoza might have weathered these difficulties, but the earthquake that destroyed Managua on the night of 23 December 1972 further undermined support for the regime. For three days Somoza was unable to control the National Guard, which went on an orgy of looting; law and order was briefly in the hands of the troops provided by the United States and a group of Central American countries under the 1964 military agreement known as CONDECA (Consejo de Defensa Centroamericana). The notion of the Guard's invincibility and unquestioning loyalty to the Somoza family was badly shaken; some of the regime's opponents were persuaded that a coup from within the Guard was a possibility, while the militants of the FSLN were convinced that their strategy of armed struggle could indeed succeed.

Somoza responded to the crisis by establishing a National Emergency Committee and dropping the hapless Agüero from the now powerless triumvirate. As head of the committee, Somoza was in a position to determine the allocation of the generous relief funds with which the international community had responded to the earthquake disaster. The resources were spent in a manner involving massive corruption (particularly by the National Guard) and favoured existing or new Somoza industries, the family acquiring important new interests in land development, construction and finance. The tacit alliance with the bourgeoisie began to break down under the charge of *competencia desleal* and members of the BANIC and BANAMER groups, together with the private sector umbrella organization Consejo Superior de Empresa Privada (COSEP), complained that Somoza was using his privileged position to expand his family interests at the expense of the rest of the private sector.

The earthquake also revived the labour movement after twenty-five years of quiescence. The cost of living leapt 20 per cent in the year 1972–3 under the impact of imported inflation as well as domestic shortages provoked by the earthquake. Real wages for all Nicaraguan workers inevitably declined, but the construction workers in Managua were in a strong position to demand salary adjustments; their strike in 1973 was largely successful and marked a triumph for the labour confederation (Confederación General de Trabajo Independiente, or CGTI) formed by the illegal Socialist Party in the 1960s.

Since the crushing of the labour movement in 1948, the labour force had expanded rapidly and wage earners formed a growing proportion of the total. The emphasis on agro-exports had produced a marked rise in the size and importance of the rural proletariat while many small farmers felt threatened by the growth of large-scale agro-enterprises. This presented opportunities for the dictatorship's political opponents, but labour organizations (particularly in rural areas) met with stiff resistance from employers backed by the National Guard. The success of the construction workers gave a new lease of life to the organized labour movement, and the FSLN was particularly quick to exploit the new opportunities registering its greatest successes in rural areas.

Somoza's decision in 1974 to seek (and inevitably win) a further seven-year presidential term provided the catalyst for a regrouping of the opposition forces. The result was the Unión Democrática de Liberación (UDEL) which was led by Pedro Joaquín Chamorro, and which brought disgruntled Conservatives and Liberals (notably Sacasa's splinter group) together with the PLI, the PSC, the PSN and the CGTI. This was the broadest opposition group yet formed against Somocismo, involving both pro-Moscow Communists and representatives of the traditional elite, and it marked an important change from the sectarianism and personalism of the past. Nevertheless, UDEL excluded the FSLN, who denounced it on orthodox Marxist lines for class collaboration, and did not receive endorsement from U.S. officials, who remained loyal to Somocismo and disturbed by the presence of Communists in the opposition. Equally, it did not receive support from all sections of the private sector.

The private sector may have resented the *competencia desleal* of the Somoza group after the 1972 earthquake, but complete anti-Somoza solidarity was undermined by the existence of plenty of profitable opportunities. After a period of relative stagnation from 1969 to 1972, the Nicaraguan economy experienced rapid growth again in 1973 and 1974 as a result of post-earthquake reconstruction and a sharp recovery in the fortunes of export agriculture. Standard Fruit re-entered the country in 1972 and banana exports accelerated rapidly, while cotton began its third post-war boom in 1970 with cotton exports reaching a peak in the middle of the decade. The cost of fertilizers, however, had soared as a result of the 1973 oil crisis and the expansion of cotton could take place only through the incorporation of new lands. This put pressure on domestic food production, which declined in per capita terms, and the high levels of inflation after 1972 made the situation facing the rural labour force (40 per cent of whom were landless) more and more intolerable.

The formation of UDEL presented a challenge to both Somoza and the FSLN. UDEL gave prominence to the FSLN's older rival, the PSN, and it advocated a strategy of tactical class alliances which the FSLN had consistently rejected. The Marxist line of the Frente did not rule out the possibility of membership by non-Marxists, particularly radical Catholics, but the FSLN's hostility was still very profound towards the Nicaraguan bourgeoisie and its collaboration with Somoza. The minuscule FSLN therefore undertook a spectacular kidnapping of leading members of the Nicaraguan elite at the end of 1974, which brought it to national (and international) prominence and re-asserted the Frente's strategy of armed struggle as an alternative to UDEL's emphasis on a broad anti-Somoza alliance and dialogue.

The kidnappings obliged Somoza to meet almost all the Frente's demands, including the release from prison of several of its leaders. As a result the humiliated dictator unleashed the most ferocious wave of repression since the foundation of Somocismo. Although the dynasty was prepared to use force where necessary – notably in 1948, 1956–7 and 1967 – indiscriminate repression had not been the hallmark of either Somoza's father or brother, both of whom had tolerated some press and radio criticism of the regime and had usually released their opponents from prison after a discreet period. Anastasio, however, was unsympathetic to such sophistication and responded to the kidnappings by imposing a state of siege, martial law, press censorship and a campaign of terror under the control of the National Guard. The result was international condemnation by human rights groups, which brought Somoza to unwelcome prominence in the Carter administration's foreign policy at the beginning of 1977; at the same time, Nicaragua's private sector – the boom years now ended – began to distance itself from the regime. New tax increases were greeted with a call for a boycott by COSEP, capital flight began in earnest in 1977 and the regime was forced to rely on foreign borrowings, much of it from U.S. banks, in order to finance the government deficit and maintain currency stability.

The wave of repression did succeed in weakening the FSLN, which split into three groups. Significantly, two of these *tendencias* – the Tendencia Proletaria (TP) and Guerra Popular Prolongada (GPP) – assumed that the Nicaraguan revolution would be a long, drawn-out struggle involving patient ideological work among the urban (favoured by TP) and rural (favoured by GPP) masses. The third *tendencia* felt that the internal Nicaraguan situation had disintegrated so rapidly that the FSLN should press for an immediate full-fledged insurrection. This Tendencia Insurreccional (TI), led by Daniel and Humberto Ortega, was therefore obliged to accept the necessity for tactical alliances with non-Marxist opponents of the regime in order to ensure the success of the insurrection. This position prevailed within the leadership of the FSLN, the TI (or 'Terceristas', as they were also labelled) receiving a further boost when it engineered the formation in October 1977 of a group of twelve distinguished Nicaraguans (*los doce*) who insisted on the FSLN's participation in any post-Somoza regime. In the same month, the Terceristas attempted a national insurrection, but it was easily defeated by Somoza and publicly condemned as premature and adventurist by the other two tendencies.

Under pressure from the Carter administration, Somoza – who had barely recovered from two heart attacks – lifted the state of siege in September 1977. This provided the signal for a wave of protests against the regime. Yet Somoza still felt fairly secure. The National Guard was loyal and had showed, against the Terceristas, that it could be effective against a guerrilla attack; U.S. economic and military aid was still flowing, despite the criticisms of the Carter administration; and Somoza's opponents – Marxist and non-Marxist – were still far from united. The situation changed dramatically, however, with the murder in January 1978 of Pedro Joaquín Chamorro – editor of *La Prensa,* charismatic leader of UDEL and a lifelong opponent of the Somozas. The assassination, in which Somoza's son and heir apparent was implicated, produced a wave of strikes and spontaneous uprisings. More significantly, it galvanized the opponents of the regime into dialogue and produced in a few months an anti-Somoza unity which had not been achieved in the previous four decades.

By May 1978 the unification talks had produced a new organization in the Frente Amplio Opositor (FAO), which embraced UDEL together with the remaining factions of the Conservative Party. Private-sector support for the FAO was secured by the participation of the Movimiento Democrático Nicaragüense (MDN), formed in March by Alfonso Robelo, a leading Nicaraguan businessman and critic of Somoza. The FSLN was not a member of the FAO, but *los doce* agreed to join, thereby guaranteeing the Frente at least a minority position in a post-Somoza government if negotiations succeeded in removing the dictator.

The FSLN, still a minuscule and divided organization of fewer than a thousand members, ran the risk of being marginalized by the FAO despite the presence of *los doce.* However, the spontaneous uprisings of January and February had strengthened the position of the TI and opened the way for unification with the other two *tendencias* (that was finally achieved in March 1979). The Frente's answer to the FAO was the formation in July 1978 of the Movimiento Pueblo Unido (MPU), which included student and youth organizations, Communists and socialists (now weaned from UDEL) and the small labour organizations controlled by the Marxist left (including the Asociación de Trabajadores del Campo [ATC] established in 1977 by the Frente). The MPU, however, lacked the broad appeal of the FAO and represented a defensive move by the Frente in response to the success at unification of the non-Marxist anti-Somocistas.

By mid-1978, therefore, there were two clearly defined alternatives to Somoza, the non-Marxist FAO and the Marxist MPU. The FAO united the traditional opponents of the regime with the private sector and the Christian Democrats (PSC). It used strikes by the private sector to weaken the regime, enjoyed some support within the Carter administration (which suspended arms supplies to Somoza in 1978) and was confident that it could provide a transition to a post-Somoza regime through negotiations or mediation. The MPU, by contrast, pinned its hopes on armed struggle and a nation-wide insurrection, relying on a direct appeal by its mainly Marxist organizations to the most disadvantaged groups in society.

The FAO's position was not helped by a certain ambivalence in the Carter administration towards Somoza. Responding to pressure from Somoza's many friends in the U.S. Congress, President Carter wrote to the dictator in mid-1978 congratulating him on an improvement in the human rights situation at the same time as his aides were trying to assemble support for a package which would lead to the resignation of the dictator, retention of the National Guard and exclusion of the FSLN – a package rapidly dubbed 'Somocismo without Somoza'. The FAO's position was further weakened by the Frente's seizure of the National Palace, which housed the Nicaraguan Congress in August. This action badly humiliated Somoza and triggered off a wave of spontaneous uprisings in September, convincing the Insurrecionistas – now dominant in the Frente and the MPU – of the correctness of their strategy. The seizure of the palace and the subsequent uprisings, although defeated by the National Guard, swelled the ranks of the FSLN so that by the end of the year their numbers had reached 3,000 compared with 10,000 for the Guard.

The challenge from the FSLN gave a new urgency to those looking for a negotiated solution, above all the FAO and the Carter administration. The former's policy of strikes and business closures had not succeeded in crippling the dictatorship, which continued to receive substantial foreign loans (including a major loan from the International Monetary Fund in May 1979), while the latter began to take seriously the revolutionary challenge posed by the Frente and MPU. Even Somoza was finally forced to acknowledge the logic of negotiations and agreed to accept a U.S. initiative under which an OAS team (formed by the United States, the

Dominican Republic and Guatemala) would mediate between him and the FAO. The team began work in mid-October and immediately ran into difficulties over both Somoza's insistence on serving out his term until 1981 and Washington's desire to retain a political role for Somoza's Liberal Party and the National Guard. By the end of October, *los doce* – the only link between the FAO and the Frente – had resigned from the FAO. The following month the Frente, which had watched the mediation process with deep suspicion, returned to armed struggle, prompting the FAO to accept Somoza's call for direct negotiations. This provoked further resignations from the FAO, so that by the beginning of 1979 the initiative had shifted dramatically to the insurrectionary strategy advocated by the Terceristas. The mediation effort finally collapsed when Somoza refused to accept the OAS terms for a national plebiscite on his continuing in power.

In February 1979 the FSLN seized the opportunity afforded by the collapse of the negotiations to broaden its base of support by forming the Frente Patriótico Nacional (FPN), which included *los doce,* the PLI and the Partido Popular Social Cristiano (PPSC), which had split from the PSC in the mid-1970s. The programme of the FPN had a much broader appeal than earlier documents associated with the FSLN and MPU, and it provided the basis for political collaboration with the remainder of the FAO, including the private sector. There was no doubt, however, that the failure of negotiations and the drift towards insurrection had raised the FSLN – formally united in March 1979 – to a dominant position within the anti-Somocista coalition.

The final offensive was launched at the end of May. By this time, the Somoza regime was internationally isolated; several Latin American countries had withdrawn recognition and the Sandinistas were receiving arms through Costa Rica from Panama, Venezuela and Cuba. The Carter administration made a final effort to resurrect its 'Somocismo without Somoza' project but was decisively defeated in the OAS, which accepted the guarantees on political pluralism, a mixed economy and non-alignment offered by a five-member junta appointed by the anti-Somoza alliance in June. The dictator resigned and handed over power to the unknown Francisco Urcuyo on 17 July, his departure to Miami prompting the final disintegration of the National Guard. The victors marched into Managua on 19 July ending a war which had cost an estimated 50,000 lives out of a population of some 3 million.

The events leading up to the fall of Somoza demonstrated the importance of unity in the struggle against the dictatorship. The broad coalitions, first UDEL and later the FAO, had shown the depth of opposition to the Somoza dynasty but had failed to mobilize sections of the labour movement and relied too heavily on U.S. support to persuade the dictator to step down. On the other hand, the FSLN and the MPU had made important progress in incorporating the labour movement into the struggle (particularly rural workers) and posed a direct military challenge to the dictatorship by the end of 1978, but their militants were still no match for the heavily armed National Guard. The failure of negotiations and the collapse of the mediation effort left the FAO with no alternative other than co-operation with the Frente or rapprochement with Somoza; that it chose the former is a tribute to the political skills of the FSLN and the contempt in which the Somoza dictatorship was held.

The new alliance which emerged after February 1979 finally brought together all the social and political groups opposed to the dictatorship. The urban youth, students and workers, were attracted to the FSLN by its courage and daring, most accepting its authority and leadership in the armed struggle. By June, the number of militants trained and equipped by the Frente was sufficient to challenge the National Guard on military grounds, while the dictatorship had become completely isolated politically. Although many groups within the broad alliance had reservations over the wisdom of co-operation with the Frente, the strategy was devastatingly effective in undermining both Somoza and Somocismo.

THE CONSOLIDATION OF SANDINISTA RULE

The flight of Somoza and the collapse of the National Guard signalled a total military victory for the anti-Somocista coalition, but the price paid was a ravaged economy in which GDP fell by 26.4 per cent in 1979 in addition to the decline of 7.8 per cent in 1978. International reserves had been completely drained out of the country, and Somoza had left a $1.6 billion debt, much of which had never been invested in Nicaragua and could not be serviced. Agricultural exports were badly affected by the civil war – cotton planting was reduced to the levels of the early 1950s – and inflation leapt to 60 per cent as a consequence of severe shortages.

Now that the dictator had fallen the anti-Somocista coalition also began to experience difficulties.[30] The agreement reached in Costa Rica (the

---

[30] Somoza was assassinated in Paraguay in September 1980; circumstantial evidence suggested that his murder was the work of the FSLN.

Puntarenas Pact) called for the five-member Junta to establish political
pluralism, a mixed economy and a non-aligned foreign policy. The first
goal would be underwritten by a Council of State with minority FSLN
membership and free elections to be called at some unspecified date, while
a non-partisan national army would be constructed to replace the National
Guard. The FSLN, however, had emerged from the insurrection in a much
stronger position than the groups with which it had made a tactical
alliance and which had failed to obtain any guarantees from them regarding implementation of the programme agreed at Puntarenas. The Sandinistas enjoyed undisputed control of the battle-hardened military forces
which had defeated the National Guard, whose rump had fled across the
border to Honduras. Thus, the FSLN, which only a year before had still
been a very small and divided organization, was in a highly advantageous
position to determine the initial stages of the Nicaraguan Revolution
through its grip on military power – and its hidden majority on the
Junta. Daniel Ortega was the only avowed member of the FSLN on the
Junta, but Moises Hassan – a leader of both the MPU and the FPN – was
a close sympathizer and Sergio Ramírez had been a secret, non-combatant
member of the FSLN since 1975.

The first step taken by the FSLN was the construction of a standing
army, the Ejército Popular Sandinista (EPS), and a police force, Policía
Sandinista. As their names imply, these organizations were highly partisan; they laid great stress on political education and training was largely in
the hands of Cubans and Eastern Europeans. (Offers of help in training
from the United States, Panama and Venezuela were politely, but firmly,
refused.) Opposition to the construction of a partisan army, a clear breach
of the Puntarenas Pact, was muted until the end of 1979, when Bernardino Larios (a former National Guard officer) was replaced as Minister of
Defence by Humberto Ortega – a member of the FSLN National Directorate and commander-in-chief of the EPS. By the end of 1980, the EPS
exceeded the size of the National Guard at its peak and, following the
introduction of conscription in 1983, leapt to more than 60,000 with
recruits passing into the reserves after their two years of service.

The cabinet appointed by the Junta in July 1979 gave the key economic
portfolios (with the exception of agrarian reform) to representatives of the
private sector. These ministers faced the daunting task of renegotiating
the foreign debt, co-ordinating foreign aid through the Fondo Internacional de Reconstrucción (FIR) and channeling credit to the private and
public sectors. In the initial stages progress in this area was relatively

smooth; foreign lending from bilateral, multilateral and commercial sources was substantial and the debt was successfully rescheduled in two stages on generous terms. The government's priorities were laid out in a document known as 'Plan-80'; special emphasis was placed on the recovery of agro-exports, wage increases were held below the rate of inflation and real GDP rose by 11 per cent in 1980 and a further 5.3 per cent in 1981.

In the early stages of the economic recovery programme, the main challenge came not from the private sector but from the ultra-left. These groups felt that the essentially conservative nature of the government's economic policy (even the Somocista Labour Code was not repealed) represented a betrayal of the revolution and they reacted by provoking strikes and demonstrations. The FSLN responded harshly, using the state of emergency to imprison the ultra-left leaders and ban their organizations early in 1980, while making some concessions to land invasions led by the pro-Sandinista ATC. The agrarian-reform programme was accelerated in mid-1981, when a law was passed to permit expropriation of under-utilized or abandoned non-Somocista properties, but efficient agro-exporters were left unaffected and no upper limit was placed on farm size (unlike in El Salvador).

In some respects the reconstruction of the shattered economy was the easiest stage of the revolution for the government because both the FSLN and the private-sector groups in the anti-Somocista coalition were in broad agreement on what was required. The nine-member National Directorate of the FSLN in which the three *tendencias* were equally represented, remained committed to the goal of socialism in Nicaragua, but this was seen as a long-term objective. For both theoretical and practical reasons it was recognized that the private sector had an important part to play in the work of reconstruction. The Directorate argued, however, that the long-term objective could not be postponed altogether and the first step was the creation of a dynamic state sector (Area Propiedad del Pueblo, or APP); this was achieved through the expropriation of all Somocista properties together with the nationalization of financial institutions, foreign trade and national resources (including mining).

These measures, which would have provoked major private sector opposition in other Latin American countries, produced hardly a ripple in Nicaragua. The Somocista properties, which included 20 per cent of the arable land and some of the most efficient farms and factories, were clearly the spoils of war, while the financial institutions – drained by capital flight – were bankrupt. The expropriated agricultural properties, producing many agro-exports, were turned into state farms under the direction of a new Ministry of Agrarian Reform, and by 1980 the APP had control of 34 per cent of GDP.

Despite the moderate nature of economic policy in the first stage of the revolution, the private sector umbrella organization (COSEP) was in open conflict with the government by the end of 1981, with several of its leaders in prison or exile and one killed. The strained relationship was not so much because of the economic policy of the government (although as early as November 1979, COSEP had publicly aired its concern over the future of private enterprise) as of the political programme of the Sandinistas. The flight of Somoza had led to the total collapse of the old political institutions and the National Directorate of the FSLN, all of whom were Marxists with profound respect for the Cuban Revolution, proceeded to reconstruct the Nicaraguan state along the principles of democratic centralism. This left little room for political influence, or even power-sharing, by the private sector.

The repression during the last years of the Somoza regime had made it difficult for the FSLN – or any other party – to develop mass organizations. In 1977, the Frente had set up associations for both rural workers (the Asociación de Trabajadores del Campo, or ATC) and women (the Asociación de Mujeres ante la Problemática Nacional, or AMPRONAC), but they had not yet risen to the status of mass organizations by July 1979. Sandinista control over urban labour, the small peasantry and the urban petit-bourgeoisie was less secure at the time of the revolution, and the Frente faced competition among all these social forces from the other political parties and their trade-union affiliates. By the end of 1981 the position had changed dramatically. The Central Sandinista de Trabajadores (CST) had acquired a dominant position among urban labour, the pro-Sandinista Unión Nacional de Agricultores y Ganaderos (UNAG) was gaining a strong foothold among the small- and medium-size peasantry, the ATC had consolidated its position among the rural landless workers and the women's association (the Asociación de Mujeres Nicaragüenses 'Luisa Amanda Espinoza', or AMNLAE) had made great strides. The neighbourhood Comités de Defensa Sandinista (CDS), modelled on their Cuban equivalents, had acquired major importance as a result of their role in food rationing and the organisation of militias. The non-Sandinista 'mass' organizations had been reduced to a handful of small labour federations linked to various opposition parties.

The success of the Sandinista mass organizations provided the key to the subsequent consolidation of Sandinismo and was made possible by a variety of factors. First and foremost, by thwarting the creation of popular organizations Somocismo had left a *tabula rasa,* allowing the most dynamic forces in the revolution to start from scratch. Second, the Sandinistas thwarted efforts by their left-wing rivals to gain a foothold among the unorganized masses. Third, all efforts by foreign governments (particularly the United States) to help establish non-Sandinista mass organizations were resisted. Last but not least, public recognition that support for Sandinismo could bring positive results (e.g., ration cards issued by the CDS) was a powerful stimulus for membership in one of the mass organizations.

The Frente's grip on political institutions was increased by a number of cabinet changes at the end of 1979 and changed qualitatively in April 1980, when the composition of the Council of State was announced. Instead of the minority Sandinista position agreed in the Puntarenas Pact, the Frente with its mass organizations now enjoyed an absolute majority. Elections, it was also announced, would not be held for five years. Furthermore, by forming an alliance (Frente Patriótico Revolucionario, or FPR) with sympathetic political parties (including the PLI), the Sandinistas weakened still further the opportunities for the private sector and its political representatives to influence policy. Shorn of power, their two members on the Junta (Alfonso Robelo and Violeta Chamorro) resigned to be replaced by two non-Sandinistas, Arturo Cruz and Rafael Córdoba acceptable to the Frente. Robelo's efforts to turn his MDN into a major opposition party were thwarted by the Sandinistas, and he soon left Nicaragua to become a leader of the counter-revolution.

The private sector was visibly shaken by the departure of Robelo, but the FSLN acted quickly to provide reassurances on the future of private enterprise. The Directorate, both publicly and privately, distinguished between the 'patriotic' and the 'treacherous' bourgeoisie, stressing that the former had a role to play in the economic sphere. With some reluctance, COSEP participated in the Council of State until late in 1980. By that time, the relationship between the Frente and COSEP had deteriorated badly as a result of complaints that the private sector had abused its freedom by engaging in decapitalization and capital flight. Tough penalties were introduced for decapitalization, foreign-exchange controls were reinforced and in September 1981 the Junta introduced a state of economic and social emergency, under which several COSEP leaders were imprisoned.

Intervention by the Mexican government led to an improvement in the relations with the private sector in 1982, but by then the Sandinistas faced opposition from a variety of other quarters. Sandinista troops over-reacted to a riot in the Atlantic coast town of Bluefields in September 1980, driving large numbers of Miskitos and other ethnic minorities into the armed counter-revolution. The Atlantic coast population, which had been largely ignored by Somoza and had played virtually no part in the insurrection, objected to the crude efforts by the Sandinistas to incorporate them into the Nicaraguan revolution. The relocation by force of many Miskitos raised questions internationally regarding Sandinista respect for human rights, and it took the Frente several years to adopt a more flexible policy designed to drive a wedge between the Atlantic coast's desire for autonomy and the counter-revolution's efforts to end Sandinista rule.

The Frente's most formidable opponent was always the Reagan administration. The National Directorate assumed that a confrontation with the United States was inevitable but hoped that it could be postponed until after the consolidation of Sandinismo. From the start the Carter administration had grave misgivings about the Frente and looked with disfavour on Nicaragua's abstention in the United Nations vote condemning the Soviet invasion of Afghanistan. The use of Cubans to train the EPS and their presence in large numbers during the 1980 literacy campaign was not well received, and the administration noted with displeasure the close ties established in March 1980 with the Soviet Union. Nevertheless, President Carter was determined to avoid a repeat of the Cuban fiasco twenty years earlier and pushed through a not insubstantial aid programme (to which Congress insisted on adding a series of humiliating amendments which undermined whatever goodwill the aid programme might have generated).

President Reagan had made clear his total opposition to the Sandinistas even before taking office in January 1981. Once in office, however, he proceeded with caution. His first step was to suspend the aid programme, which was severed completely following allegations that the Sandinistas were heavily involved in supplying and training the guerrillas in El Salvador. The economic pressure was increased in 1982, when multilateral organizations with strong U.S. participation ceased lending to Nicaragua, whose U.S. sugar quota was cancelled in 1983. A trade embargo was finally imposed in 1985, but by that time trade between the two countries was already much reduced.

Despite the rhetoric, the Reagan administration was, like its predecessor, uncertain how to handle the Sandinistas, although the President himself never wavered in his desire to remove them. It was clear to all, with the benefit of hindsight, that the few months prior to the fall of Somoza had represented the best chance for a U.S. administration to influence the course of the Nicaraguan revolution. That chance had now passed and the administration was left with the power to weaken the Sandinistas but not overthrow them. Policy wavered between offers of a 'Finnish solution' and military pressure through the use of proxy troops. The latter option gained strength after the President gave approval in November 1981 for covert CIA operations against Nicaragua designed to destabilize the Sandinistas and interdict the supply of arms to the Salvadorean guerrillas.

The CIA set about organizing the undisciplined bands of former National Guardsmen ("contras") who had fled to Honduras in July 1979 and subsequently extracted revenge on the Sandinistas through cross-border raids. By the end of 1981, their numbers had been swollen by volunteers disillusioned with the Sandinista revolution (many from the Atlantic coast), although the military leadership remained firmly in Somocista hands. This control prevented a successful unification of all the anti-Sandinista forces, some of whom – notably Edén Pastora, who abandoned the revolution in July 1981 – refused to collaborate with the Honduran-based contras and established their own guerrilla campaign in Costa Rica. Under CIA influence, the contras became a more serious threat to the Sandinistas, although in open combat they were no match for the EPS (armed with Soviet and Cuban equipment since 1981). The discovery in 1984 that the CIA had mined Nicaraguan harbours, damaging foreign ships, temporarily weakened U.S. congressional support for the contras, but an unprecedented personal campaign by President Reagan had led to an increase in funding by 1986. By then, however, it was clear that the contras lacked the capacity to hold any Nicaraguan territory permanently, let alone overthrow the Sandinistas, while support for the contras had driven the Reagan administration into numerous violations of both international and U.S. domestic law.

The tension between the Reagan administration and the Sandinistas was viewed with increasing concern by other countries. The Nicaraguan revolution enjoyed overwhelming international support in its early days and the FSLN had won the support of the Socialist International (SI) within which the Sandinistas had observer status. The disillusionment of Costa Rican and Venezuelan social democrats over the course of the revolution led to a serious crisis in the SI in 1982, but the official policy remained one of critical support for the revolution and several SI leaders, notably Spain's Felipe González, acted as unofficial intermediaries between the Sandinistas and the Reagan administration. Other Latin American countries viewed with horror the prospect of U.S. military intervention in Central America and the Contadora group (Mexico, Venezuela, Colombia and Panama) was formed in January 1983 to seek a peaceful solution to the regional crisis. This group devised a twenty-one-point programme of demilitarization and democratization that all Central American countries would have been required to sign. However, the Acta de Contadora did not win the support of the Reagan administration, which did not welcome any agreement that might leave the Sandinistas in power, and despite its formal support for Contadora Washington was able to undermine the process of negotiations through its regional allies (Costa Rica, El Salvador and Honduras). Contadora was broadened in late 1985 by the formation of a support group (Argentina, Brazil, Uruguay and Peru), but by then tension between Nicaragua and its neighbours was so great that there was little chance of agreement on a peace treaty even without U.S. misgivings. The Reagan administration, for its part, launched bilateral talks in Mexico with the Sandinistas in mid-1984, but these broke down in early 1985 in an atmosphere of mutual recrimination and distrust.

The impasse between Nicaragua and its neighbours was made some-what easier following the election of Oscar Arias Sánchez as president of Costa Rica in 1986. After an uncertain start to his presidency, Arias committed himself to a negotiated solution among the five Central American governments with the Contadora group playing only a secondary role. The Arias plan, launched in February 1987, was endorsed by all five Central American presidents in August of the same year and held out the prospect of an end to the regional crisis. It committed each Central American administration to a dialogue with opposition groups through a National Reconciliation Commission, to an amnesty for those who had taken up arms against the government and to an end to outside military support for 'irregular forces'.

As far as Nicaragua was concerned, the Arias plan implicitly acknowl-edged the legitimacy of the Sandinista government and promised an end to civil war in return for a significant degree of political pluralism and democratization. The plan therefore went against the preferences of Presi-dent Reagan, but his administration — weakened by the scandals surround-ing the sale of arms to Iran and the illegal diversion of funds to the contras — was unable to carry its Central American policy through Congress where the Democratic Speaker Jim Wright was increasingly active in shuttle diplomacy between Washington and Managua. The Reagan administration tried to maintain the contras in existence despite a renewed congressional ban on military aid, but the Arias plan gathered momentum and a cease-fire was signed in March 1988 between the Sandinistas and the contras in Nicaragua. This cease-fire survived with only minor infringements into the Bush administration at the start of 1989, by which time it was clear that the contras – deprived of U.S. military assistance – were close to collapse. In February 1989, at the third meeting of the Central American presidents under the Arias plan, a decision was taken unanimously to adopt measures leading to the disbandment of the contras and the Sandinistas felt sufficiently confident to advance the electoral calendar and hold elections in February rather than November 1990.

The Nicaraguan economy was seriously undermined by U.S. pressure, but economic performance was not helped by many of the policies adopted by the government. Faced with an exchange rate which became progressively overvalued, non-traditional exports steadily declined; agro-exports were protected by policies designed to supply inputs at a price which guaranteed a positive return, but they could not be protected from falling world prices and total export earnings had fallen to $200 million in 1988 compared with $646 million in 1978. The system of food subsidies used to protect the real incomes of the urban poor became unmanageable as inflation widened the gap between producer and consumer prices, so that the fiscal deficit reached intolerable levels. Efforts by the government to phase out the subsidies in 1985 and 1986 pushed inflation into three-digit figures without curbing the fiscal deficit, which by then was determined primarily by defence spending in response to the contra threat. The growth of black markets accelerated in response to high inflation and official controls, encouraging migration to Managua and a boom in unlicensed petty commerce. Official channels of distribution were increasingly by-passed, production declined almost continuously after 1981 and real GDP per head in 1988 (in which year the country was hit by a hurricane) was back to the level of the 1950s and the lowest in Central America.

By the beginning of 1989, inflation was running at over 100 per cent per month and the Sandinistas faced the prospect of a complete collapse of the monetary and financial system. Orthodox measures to halt inflation could no longer be avoided and – gambling on the collapse of the contras – the Sandinistas began to lay off thousands of public-sector workers including members of the armed forces, putting at risk their chances in the 1990 presidential elections. The exchange rates in the official and parallel markets were brought closer together and for the first time in many years relative prices began to acquire a semblance of rationality, although the private sector remained extremely reluctant to invest in view of the continuing economic and political uncertainties.

Nicaragua's economic difficulties did not prevent the further consolidation of Sandinismo. The early years of the revolution had yielded substantial advances in health, education and literacy (a highly successful literacy campaign had been adopted in 1980), which were only partially reversed during the years of economic decline. These achievements and the growth of the mass organizations gave the Frente a solid base among the workers and peasants it regarded as its natural constituency; the EPS, the militias and the reserves gave the government a potential military strength of around 300,000 – a huge proportion of the adult population. The state of emergency reintroduced in March 1982 was regularly extended and gave the authorities considerable powers to control or suppress dissent. The opposition daily *La Prensa* survived in heavily censored form until 1986, when it was closed for eighteen months. With television under state control and independent radio subject to severe restrictions, the FSLN gradually acquired a dominant position over the means of communication.

The Frente did not, however, seek or achieve the total elimination of internal opposition. Just as the Sandinistas believed in a patriotic or democratic bourgeoisie which would collaborate with the economic priorities laid down in state planning, so they also hoped for the emergence of a loyal opposition which would accept Sandinista hegemony in the new political institutions. The decision to bring forward the elections by one year (anticipating by two days the re-election of President Reagan in November 1984) forced the issue and seven parties (including the FSLN) ranging from the ultra-left to the right-of-centre registered. The government's efforts to involve The Coordinadora Democrática, which represented a right-wing coalition formed in the Council of State in 1982, failed, and the Coordinadora withdrew from the elections. The elections gave the FSLN the presidency (Daniel Ortega became the chief executive) and a solid two-thirds majority in the new National Assembly, where the other political parties played the role of official opposition with varying degrees of reluctance. A new constitution drafted by the Assembly went into force in January 1987 with power heavily centralized in the hands of the President.

The elections clearly revealed the limitations of the opposition parties and left the Catholic Church as the major force resisting the consolidation of Sandinismo. The hierarchy had been weakened in the early years of the revolution by the growth of the popular Church and the presence of several radical priests in the government. However, with his promotion to the rank of cardinal Archbishop Miguel Obando y Bravo began to criticize the government with the same doggedness he had used against Somoza and attracted large crowds to his public sermons. In their dealings with the hierarchy the Sandinistas alternated between repression and dialogue, while hoping – perhaps naively – that the Church would respect and uphold national laws (including conscription). Freedom of religion itself, however, was not an issue between the State and the Church.

Another source of opposition to the Sandinistas came from within the mass organizations themselves. In its first five years the agrarian reform programme had been used to build up state farms, develop co-operatives and give title to the small peasantry with insecure property rights. The top priority had been the maintenance of agro-exports, and although the state farm sector began to decline after 1982, the number of landless workers receiving individual title was very small. Pressure from the ATC and UNAG in 1985 forced a change of policy from the government; the agrarian reform law was amended in January 1986 to conform to the new policy, and thousands of landless peasants received titles to land which in many cases had been previously used for agro-exports. The change was dramatic; within a short period, the conservative Nicaraguan reform programme had been radicalized affecting a majority of the rural labour force. At the same time the new programme threatened to undermine the last remaining sources of export earnings and widen still further the trade deficit.

The U.S. embargo did not cripple Nicaraguan trade with Western countries, and exports, in particular, remained diversified. Nonetheless, dependence on the socialist countries for strategic imports (e.g., oil) and balance-of-payments support had steadily increased. The Soviet Union repeatedly made it clear that it would not underwrite the economic and financial costs of the revolution, as it had done in Cuba, but the geopolitical logic of the tension between Nicaragua and the United States obliged the Russians to increase their commitment year after year. By the beginning of 1989 Nicaragua was receiving special terms from the socialist countries for its agro-exports, had became an observer at COMECON meetings and hoped eventually to be a full member. Western European bilateral aid was still flowing to Nicaragua, which was a beneficiary of multilateral EC aid under a co-operation agreement signed in 1985 with Central America, but its relative importance was declining.

The adoption of the Constitution in January 1987 completed the institutionalization of the Sandinista revolution. If judged by the public commitment to political pluralism, non-alignment and a mixed economy, the revolution had failed since these features were present only in a heavily distorted form. Yet Nicaragua had not become a second Cuba and the Frente could claim with some justification that Sandinismo had created a new Nicaragua rather than another Cuba. The Sandinistas had neither the will nor the capacity to administer all branches of production and individual titles to land (which could be inherited but not sold) were firmly established in agriculture; large-scale private producers in agriculture and industry were tolerated, subject to numerous restrictions on prices, credit and foreign exchange, while a handful of multinational companies continued to do business in Nicaragua and the Constitution promised a new foreign investment law. Criticism of the regime was possible within strict limits and the rudiments of a loyal opposition had emerged in the Assembly; foreign relations were maintained with a wide variety of countries and diplomatic ties still existed with the United States, but the relationship was closest with the socialist countries and Nicaragua's voting pattern conformed closely to Cuba's in the United Nations.

The construction of a new Nicaragua did not, however, mean that the Sandinistas had succeeded in resolving the accumulated problems from the past. The FSLN appeared unwilling to cede power through elections; the dream of a non-partisan armed force, first voiced by the United States in the 1920s, remained remote. The Sandinistas had hoped to build an economy less dependent on primary exports and world market conditions, but had been reduced to managing a stagnant economy, swollen foreign debts and massive balance-of-payments deficits. The Frente retained considerable popular support, yet production levels and real wages were far below their peaks before the revolution, while fiscal and monetary orthodoxy had given way to printing money and accelerating inflation. The Atlantic coast population remained distrustful of rule from Managua and their integration into Nicaraguan life was still far from complete.

None of those who opposed the consolidation of Sandinismo could draw much satisfaction from the record of their own efforts. The Frente's allies in the struggle against Somoza had shown extraordinary naiveté; the contras had indulged in appalling human rights violations without achieving any military success; the legal political parties weakened themselves through internal dissensions. The formation of a bloc of 14 parties to contest the 1990 elections was based on the most fragile unity, although it did at least offer a chance of defeating the FSLN by electoral means. The Carter administration lost a golden opportunity to promote democracy in Nicaragua by failing to force the resignation of Somoza one year earlier, while the Reagan administration stretched the Western alliance to its limit through its unilateral aggression against Nicaragua.

It was not only the Sandinistas' opponents whose judgement was frequently at fault. The National Directorate of the FSLN misjudged the Nicaraguan bourgeoisie by imagining that its 'patriotic' component would continue to produce and invest once deprived of access to political power as well as foreign exchange. The mixed-economy strategy was therefore prejudiced from the start, but the Sandinista state lacked the resources to take over the private sector's role. The leaders of the Frente sometimes exhibited a poor grasp of the subtleties of international diplomacy, depriving Nicaragua of part of its foreign support quite unnecessarily. The Directorate allowed Nicaragua's history to influence unduly its relations with the United States, whose leaders were clearly uninterested in or ignorant of past U.S. interventions in Central America.

The history of Nicaragua since 1930 has been, and remains, a tragic one. An accident of geography has given Nicaragua all the costs of superpower attention without any of the benefits. Local difficulties, which in a less sensitively placed country would have been ignored by outside powers, have provided an excuse for U.S. intervention. The Somozas understood the limitations on Nicaraguan sovereignty implied by the country's geographical location, and the founder of the dynasty showed himself to be a tactical genius in his manipulation of domestic opponents. His younger son, however, lacked the father's flair and brought into disrepute the country's client status. By the time of the revolution, few Nicaraguans were willing to re-establish the old order even without the Somoza family. The Sandinistas' attempt to create a new order allotted a role to the United States which was inconsistent with its superpower status, while the Reagan administration's attempts to humble the Sandinistas took no account of national pride. By the beginning of 1989, despite the determination of President Bush to give a lower foreign policy priority to Nicaragua, it was clear that – as long as the Sandinistas remained in charge – it would take many years to develop the relationship between the two countries on a harmonious basis.

8

COSTA RICA SINCE 1930

In 1930 Costa Rica, with a landmass of 50,000 square kilometers (more than twice the size of El Salvador), had a population of scarcely half a million inhabitants. The capital, San José, had 50,000 inhabitants; no other town had a population of more than 8,000. More than 60 per cent of the economically active population of some 150,000 worked in agriculture. Production revolved around the cultivation of coffee, which was exported principally to the United States and the United Kingdom. The cultivation of bananas, the second most important export product, was controlled by the United Fruit Company. The country also exported cocoa beans, although in smaller quantities, to practically all of Europe. These three crops accounted for 94.3 per cent of Costa Rica's total income.

The traditional coffee economy had produced a social pyramid with the plantation workers at the base and the growers and exporters, the latter primarily of German descent, at the apex. The coffee growers and merchants also controlled credit, directly or indirectly, through the private banking institutions. Between the two extremes of the pyramid was an important group of small and medium-sized producers who maintained a relative social and economic independence, which had great significance in the national political system.

The development of banana production from the end of the nineteenth century on the Atlantic coast, together with the economic impact of the First World War, had produced some social and economic differentiation, but this was still of a secondary order. A new stratum of waged labour clearly began to take shape during this period, although it remained diversified and could not be strictly described in terms like 'working class' or 'proletariat' more appropriate to developed societies. Less noticeable,

This chapter was translated from the Spanish by Elizabeth Ladd.

but potentially more significant, was the emergence of a middle-class business sector during 1930s. The need to find substitutes for imported products which could not be obtained because of the world crisis and the search for new fields of production combined to stimulate intellectual nuclei which questioned the existing order, criticized the coffee oligarchy and foreign capital (especially North American capital) and sought fresh strategies for national development. The first stage in this process was the emergence of a generation of young people that was strongly influenced by Communism and *aprismo,* and evolved from a populist orientation to a Marxist-Leninist radicalism, founding the Costa Rican Communist Party in 1931. This movement was followed almost immediately by another which leaned more towards the reformist and nationalist currents contained in *aprismo.* This group founded the Centro para el Estudio de los Problemas Nacionales (Centre for the Study of National Problems) in 1940 under the intellectual leadership of Rodrigo Facio (1917–61); it later united with the political movement of José Figueres' Partido Acción Demócrata to establish the Partido Liberación Nacional (PLN) in October 1951, following the civil war of 1948.

Both these movements emerged from a tightly controlled social and political system. Except for the short dictatorship of the Tinoco brothers (1917–19), Costa Rican politics was dominated for the first thirty years of the century by two paternalistic and personalist liberal parties led by Cleto González Víquez and Ricardo Jiménez. The former, known in the country as Don Cleto, had already been president in 1906–10, and his second term (1928–32) was one of transition between the undisputed domination of the coffee growers and the rival groups whose emergence was accelerated by the crisis and who questioned the distribution of power in Costa Rica for the next two decades. It was, however, the third and last administration of Jiménez, better known as Don Ricardo (1932–36), which had to bear the brunt of the crisis.

Although the country had already undergone some democratic change, such as the introduction from 1902 of reforms which changed the traditional voting system into a universal, secret and direct ballot, politics remained under the control of the large coffee growers, importers and bankers, who were strongly linked together by financial and family ties. Contrary to the experience of the rest of Central America, the dominant elite in Costa Rica participated directly in the play of power rather than delegating it outright to the military or to outsiders.

The electoral campaign of 1931 was fought along traditional personalist lines. Even though the Costa Rica economy was feeling the first effects of the crisis, the election centred on well-known political figures who belonged to the dominant social group. Of the organizations contesting the poll of February 1932 the Republican Party's Carlos María Jiménez won 22 per cent; the National Republican Party's nominee Ricardo Jiménez won 46.6 per cent; and the remaining 29.1 per cent of the vote went to the Partido Unión Republicano (PUR) candidate Manuel Castro Quesada, who was backed by bankers and land-owners, and financed principally by Fernando Castro Cervantes, a well-known capitalist closely associated with the United Fruit Company. As expected, none of the candidates obtained the absolute majority required, and the final result produced a tense situation which culminated in a desperate attempt by Castro Quesada to seize power by taking over the Bella Vista garrison on the morning of 15 February 1932, the day after the elections. The ensuing armed encounter confirmed Ricardo Jiménez's victory at the ballot box and was consolidated with an amnesty for the rebels. What the country sacrificed in peace and order, the new administration gained in legitimacy and authority.

The Communist Party was not permitted to participate in these elections under its own name and nominated candidates only in the municipal elections, in the name of the Workers' and Peasants' Bloc. The party had been founded on 16 June 1931 by a group of law students who had formed ties with the artisans' and workers' guilds that already existed in Costa Rica. Although the party declared itself part of the Third International, this was not really the case. After the failures sustained in Nicaragua with Sandino, who in 1931 was declared a traitor who had sold out to imperialism, and in El Salvador with Farabundo Martí, who was disowned as a renegade after the massacre of 1932, the Comintern had abandoned the region, leaving the newborn Communist Party of Costa Rica in an orphaned state that would prove to be its salvation. The Communist movement had decisive importance in contemporary Costa Rican history out of all proportion to its size and without rival in the rest of the Caribbean, except Cuba.

The crisis which struck the country at the beginning of the 1930s created favourable conditions for the development of the Communist Party. After the coffee boom of 1924–29, the price of coffee registered a continuous decline. Taking 1929 as a base year with an index of 100, exports declined to 87 in 1930, 83 in 1931 and 43 in 1932. Taking 1925 as a base year with an index of 100, the price of coffee in London fell from

81 in 1930 to 43 in 1933. Banana exports declined from 7,323,481 bunches at a total price of $5,492,611 in 1928 to 2,908,836 bunches at a price of $1,493,512 in 1935. The impact on public finances was immediate. In round figures, revenues dropped from 35 million colones in 1929 to 23 million in 1932, rising to 26 million in 1934. The years 1930, 1931 and 1932 showed the largest fiscal deficit, creating conflict over the use of unbacked money for fiscal purposes. Imports declined from $20 million in 1920, of which $4 million was for raw materials, to, respectively, $11 million and $2.3 million in 1930, and $6 million and $1.7 million in 1932. Obviously such a marked deterioration in imports in general – and imports of raw materials in particular – indicates the general deterioration of the national economy and the grave decline in standard of living. Unemployment became particularly acute; according to official statistics which some considered too low, 27,000 persons were directly or indirectly affected. Of the unemployed, 75.65 per cent were agricultural workers and 19.67 per cent industrial workers.

Free of what Rómulo Betancourt (later president of Venezuela and at that time a member of the Communist Party of Costa Rica), called 'the ukases and incompetence of the International', the Costa Rican Communists brought the demands of the emerging social sectors into a national political system that demonstrated the necessary flexibility to assimilate them, albeit not without tension and violence. In August 1934 the Communist Party led a major banana strike on the Atlantic coast in the midst of social disturbances throughout the country. The final result, in spite of repression and resistance, was a clear improvement in the standard of living and working conditions of the banana-workers and the opening of a political breach in the liberal system in favour of free unionization and the right to strike.

The national political system, which throughout its evolution had demonstrated some significant autonomy from the dominant economic groups, demonstrated a capacity for reform and adaptation to new circumstances. By permitting the new political groups to formulate their demands, and even allowing many of these to be channelled through the Communist Party, the regime effectively legitimized itself and provided space for modernization. While it maintained an internationalist rhetoric with respect to the USSR, Costa Rican Communism observed in its internal policy an advanced reformist and social democratic line, oriented more towards the correction of abuses and excesses than towards a complete change in customs and practices. This opened up a political perspective which was unique in Latin America, excepting Cuba and Chile. On the one hand, the internal conditions of the country encouraged the formation of multi-class alliances for the achievement of urgent reforms and the promotion of a kind of protectionist nationalism, particularly with regard to the United States. On the other hand, from 1936 the Comintern's strategy coincided with the practice of the Costa Rican Communist Party, insofar as it sought to universalize the experience of the popular fronts in Europe. This consolidated both the local tendencies of the party and its subordination on the international front to the anti-fascist and anti-imperialist tasks so important to Comintern.

Contrary to what might be expected of a country as small and isolated as Costa Rica, the international situation enormously complicated internal politics. The German links of many of the principal coffee-growing and exporting families, the presence of pro-Franco and pro-Mussolini sectors in their respective communities and the volume of Costa Rican trade with the Axis countries, especially Germany, created serious difficulties for any internal alliance which sought not only the acceptance of internal reforms but also an anti-fascist foreign policy. Nevertheless, the urgent need for reforms forced the party into various attempts at political alliances. The first of these was with President Ricardo Jiménez, the indisputably brilliant leader of Creole liberalism, during the electoral campaign of 1939. A second, and far more important, alliance was formed in 1941–2 with the government of President Rafael Angel Calderón Guardia and Archbishop Monsignor Víctor M. Sanabria, leader of the Catholic Church. This pact lasted until the end of the government of Teodoro Picado (1944–8).

The rise of fascism had an especially acute impact on local politics in 1936, when the outbreak of the Spanish Civil War provoked strong confrontations and affected the election of 1936, won by León Cortés (1936–40). As the absolutely anti-communist candidate of the Republican National Party, Cortés won 60 per cent of the total vote and easily defeated the National Party's candidate, Octavio Beeche, an old conservative lawyer; the Communist Party, which campaigned as the Workers' and Peasants' Bloc, gained only 5 per cent of the vote.

The political sympathies of important national leaders for the political experience of Italy and Germany strengthened traditional family and financial ties that already existed between those countries and the coffee growers and exporters. Germany had become one of the principal buyers of Costa Rican coffee (18.9 per cent) and cocoa (80 per cent), and had indicated that it would purchase 40 per cent of the 1939 coffee crop.

Germans were not only the principal coffee growers but also owned 80 per cent of the sugar mills; the expatriate community continued to be bolstered by immigration, and some of its members had risen to occupy key positions in León Cortés' administration. Nevertheless, Cortés himself was less a fascist than attracted by German administrative efficiency, the authoritarian tendencies of which was not entirely alien to his centre-right political philosophy.

It is true, that Cortés praised those German elements who were clearly identified with Nazism, and even allowed them to implement anti-semitic policies from their public posts, particularly with regard to immigration and commercial activities of the Jewish minority in the country. However, he never tried seriously to modify the traditional political system, and his practice in the 1939 electoral campaign was no different from that of his predecessors. Cortés used all the power available to him to minimize the electoral results favourable to the Communists, and he undermined the candidacy of Ricardo Jiménez, then allied with the Communists, thus assuring the landslide victory of the official candidate, Dr Rafael A. Calderón Guardia, who obtained 90 per cent of the vote and who would soon become Cortés' strongest adversary and an ally of the Communists.

A variety of social and political sectors were represented in the government of Calderón Guardia: Cortés' own followers, representatives of national capital, elements of Francoist orientation, and a new group of young people who were seeking to promote institutional and political reform. This amalgam was rapidly split apart by the outbreak of the war. Educated in Belgium and inspired by progressive Catholic theology, Calderón Guardia opted firmly for a democratic alliance against the Axis. This placed him in opposition to the principal coffee families, who imposed such a comprehensive isolation or the President – personal, political and social – that he was forced to enter into an alliance with the Communist Party, his only electoral adversary in 1939. This alliance, although not alien to his mode of thinking in its social reform objectives, contradicted the very essence of his traditional Catholic conception of state and society.

The Calderón–Communist alliance placed the government on the side of the Allied powers whose incessant pressure soon produced concrete actions against the German minority in the country. And not only pro-Nazi elements were affected; persecution was generalized against all persons of Italian and German extraction. With external aid, the government drew up so-called blacklists, which were used to send whole families to camps located inside the country and in the United States. Those included in the blacklists had their goods confiscated in an arbitrary manner and were subjected to multiple abuses, giving rise to wide-spread administrative corruption that was predictably encouraged by the growing crisis of subsistence and the shortage of imported goods provoked by the war.

As the government's isolation from the sectors which had supported it in the election became more accentuated, the alliance with the Communist Party was legitimized by the entry of the USSR into the war against the Axis and by the atmosphere of reform in inter-American relations which Roosevelt's New Deal had created. This domestic and foreign situation also coincided with the Holy See's naming of Monsignor Víctor M. Sanabria (1899–1952) as archbishop of San José and head of the Costa Rican Catholic Church. A man of scarcely forty-two years, superior intelligence and sharp wit, well versed in the social doctrine of the Church and in the country's history, and a consummate politician came to the forefront of a church whose following constituted an absolute majority in the country. He naturally identified himself with the anti-Nazi forces, and he followed a coherent doctrine that led him to repudiate Marxism, although without fearing it or seeing it simply as an object for excommunication. When the Communist Party dissolved itself on 13 June 1943 and became the Partido Vanguardia Popular (PVP), its secretary-general, Manuel Mora, sent a public letter to the archbishop, obviously by prior agreement, asking if he believed there was any obstacle to prevent Catholic citizens from supporting, collaborating or allying themselves with the new party. Monsignor Sanabria answered the same day, assuring him that Catholics could subscribe to the programme and join the new group with no twinge of conscience. This did not, however, prevent Sanabria from taking the initiative to dispute the hitherto unchallenged jurisdiction over the unions enjoyed by the Communists. He sponsored the formation of the Confederación de Trabajadores Rerum Novarum under the direction of Father Benjamin Núñez, who would later become its leader, and the leading opposition activist José Figueres. Nevertheless, Sanabria's participation in the government alliance was decisive, both for the triumph of social reform and for Calderón Guardia's decision to participate actively in it to the end.

This alliance of government, Catholic Church and Communist Party in Costa Rica in the 1940s was more complex than it appeared, there being latent conflicts of fundamental nature within and among each of the factions that only came to light much later. The pact marked the beginning of a period that can be called the 'era of the enemy alliances', which lasted until shortly after the victory of the rebels in the civil war of 1948. On one side was the old coffee oligarchy, opposed to Calderón Guardia's anti-German policy, his social reforms and alliance with communism, irritated by the corruption in public administration and indignant over the government's electoral fraud. Allied with the oligarchy were the small business sectors, which possessed a distinct social and political programme but kept it in abeyance during the struggle against Calderón Guardia and the Communist Party.

The social reforms promulgated by Calderón Guardia's administration took a predominantly constitutional form. First, a new chapter was added to the 1871 constitution, whereby the rights of freedom of association, unionization and strikes were guaranteed, the state's obligation to support production and assure a just distribution of wealth was recognized, and workers were insured against illness, old age and death by a social security system that also provided maternity care. This system was financed through tripartite obligatory contributions by the government, employers and the insured, and was managed by a new independent body, the Social Security Fund. The right to be given notice and to collect unemployment benefits in the case of unjust dismissal was established, as were the rights to paid annual vacations, extra pay for overtime, and the like. The inclusion of these rights alongside the classical individual guarantees in the Constitution was opposed by capitalists – and by the U.S. embassy. However, the reforms still lacked a concrete mechanism for implementation, and a variety of specific laws needed to be passed to put the general principles outlined in the Constitution into effect. And the Calderón coalition faced the threat of defeat in the election of 1944.

Within the opposition to the Calderón–Communist government there were sectors, particularly the members of the Centre for the Study of National Problems, which supported social reform but rejected the procedures used to promote it as well as the political uses to which it was being put by the government. In the words of a leading opposition spokesman, the journalist Otilio Ulate, the reform was simply the 'opium of social guarantees', and the opposition candidate in the 1944 poll, ex-president León Cortés, announced his intention to have it repealed if he won. Indeed, this danger was so real that the anti-Communist union leader Benjamin Núñez voted for the government candidate, Teodoro Picado, simply to protect the new legislation.

Picado was unable to muster the sympathy and support enjoyed by

Calderón Guardia. A cultivated man, historian, lawyer and teacher, but of weak character, he was incapable of matching the political prowess of Cortés. Although the alliance with the PVP guaranteed him the support of important groups, his forces were distinctly inferior to those of the opposition. As a result, the government resorted to violence by armed bands and the intervention of the police in favour of the official candidate. The appearance of Communist 'shock troops', justified by the party as self-defense, exacerbated a political climate that was violent and intransigent, and contributed to the growing lack of legitimacy of the electoral institutions.

Some politicians – the PVP leader Mora among them – sought a candidacy of national consensus. But both Picado and Cortés refused to renounce their candidacies despite the fact that in September 1943 Congress approved the new Labour Law, which then ceased to be a major campaign issue. A joint procession led by President Calderón Guardia, Manuel Mora and Archbishop Sanabria in an open car through the streets of San José served only to unite the opposition behind Cortés. Picado, however, won the election of 13 February 1944 with 82,173 votes to Cortés' 44,435. But the evidence of fraud and popular support for the opposition suggested a very much closer result than was formally declared.

The North American perspective on events in Costa Rica during the Second World War and until 1948 was not always coherent or free of contradictions. At first, the U.S. view of the nature of the PVP coincided with that of other sectors, particularly that of Archbishop Sanabria. The small but important Communist Party was seen not to fit precisely into the rigid mould of the other Latin American Communist Parties, and it was perceived as possessing an ideology closer to that of the Congress of Industrial Organizations (CIO) in the United States than to that of the Third International. This view was, however, soon modified by the party's aggressive attitude towards capital, both national and foreign, particularly the United Fruit Company and the Electric Bond and Share Company, where conflict with the unions had become especially acute.

The dissatisfaction of local and U.S. capitalists was the determining factor which finally led the State Department to change its attitude towards the PVP, although less quickly than its embassy in Costa Rica since from the viewpoint of the general struggle against the Axis powers, the internal alliance between Communists and the Calderón Guardia and Picado administrations did not seem particularly strange or alarming. It should be remembered that in the same period a similar alliance was formed in Cuba under the government of Fulgencio Batista. In the case of Costa Rica a distinction must be made between the changes in U.S. attitude that arose from internal pressures, originating above all from local U.S. investors, and those modifications which came about as a result of the Cold War. Although the final consequences were the same, the different sources of similar behaviour permit an explanation of the vacillations that characterized U.S. policy towards Costa Rica, especially during the administration of Dr Calderón Guardia.

The legitimacy that the alliance against the Axis had conferred on the pact with the PVP disappeared definitively with the end of hostilities and beginning of the Cold War. Trips by opposition leaders, especially Otilio Ulate, to the United States and Europe brought the growing conflict between the United States and the Soviet Union to the forefront of Costa Rican public opinion and gave the opponents of the Picado regime a chance to denounce the danger of world communism and the lack of trustworthiness of its pacts and alliances. The development of the Cold War and the increase of U.S. pressure undoubtedly shook the alliance and augmented the misgivings of the Communists, although they still did not clearly understand the full nature of the changing international situation.

Less obvious, but no less important was the fact that the break-up of the wartime global alliance against the Axis powers effectively destroyed the only political project that existed within the Costa Rican regime. The reforms sponsored by the Communists were oriented towards a total restructuring of the state and national society that required the exceptionally favourable conditions provided by the world-wide struggle against fascism. When these conditions ceased to exist, the project collapsed. The Calderonistas lacked their own political project. They vegetated behind the Communist Party's programme, allowing the conflict with the opposition, to develop into the prospect of either the simple restoration desired by the traditional coffee sectors, or the dominion of the small business sector, whose political-military leader was José Figueres.

The expulsion of Figueres from Costa Rica in 1942, which the government accomplished by invoking reasons of national security and his possible connections and sympathies with Nazism, led to a period of exile in the United States, Mexico and Guatemala. His expulsion took place under circumstances about which there were contradictory explanations. According to Figueres' own version it was a simple matter of persecution by President Calderón Guardia, but according to Manuel Mora, it was the result of a direct action by the U.S. embassy. This version has not been corroborated by documents from the Department of State archives in Washington, although it is explicitly recounted in the memoirs of Ivonne Clays Spoelder, then Dr Calderón Guardia's wife. Politically opposed to the Calderón Guardia brothers, Figueres supported the candidacy of León Cortés in 1944 through his own political organization, Democratic Action, and, as a candidate for Congress, was a direct victim of the electoral fraud that gave victory to Picado.

In July 1943, Figueres had participated in the creation of a revolutionary Central American force to overthrow the dictatorships in the region, since Costa Rica was considered the best place to start the crusade. In this spirit, Figueres combined his struggle against the Calderón–Communist government with regional objectives of larger scope. His plans were greatly helped by the overthrow of the dictatorship of Jorge Ubico and the Guatemalan elections of December 1944, which brought Juan José Arévalo to the presidency of that country. It was under Arévalo's aegis that the so-called Caribbean Pact was formally signed on 16 December 1947 in Guatemala City.

In spite of his nationalist and anti-imperialist tendencies, Arévalo kept the same Central American policy as his dictatorial and reactionary predecessor in an effort to secure Guatemalan hegemony in the region. Figueres' plans fitted perfectly into this perspective because the signers of the pact promised to create a Central American Republic after overthrowing the existing military dictatorships. The fact that the government of Costa Rica had a progressive social policy and was allied with the Communists, who in Guatemala supported Arévalo's government, did not deter Guatemalan support of Figueres. The traditional theme of Central American union around the colonial Captaincy General prevailed over new themes of social policy and universal suffrage, which became a means and not an end.

These international alliances produced true political paradoxes. Arévalo's government, democratic, socially advanced and supported by the Guatemalan Communists, was opposed to that of Teodoro Picado, which was similar in character and had suffered in the past at the hands of Ubico, who had supported Cortés in the 1944 elections. Arévalo now supported Figueres, who had become the leader of the armed branch of the Costa Rican opposition movement headed first by Cortés and then, after his death, by Otilio Ulate. Moreover, in his zeal to promote Central American union, Arévalo sought the support of the conservative government of

Canstañeda in El Salvador, provoking understandable apprehension on the part of the governments of Carías in Honduras, Somoza in Nicaragua and Picado himself in Costa Rica. Both Picado and Somoza thus had a double fear: on the one hand, of the prospect of Guatemala's hegemony over the isthmus, and on the other, of the support that Arévalo lent to political groups who were seeking the armed overthrow of the governments of both countries. This forged the conditions for an alliance between Nicaragua and Costa Rica which contradicted those maintained internally by Picado (pro-communist) and Somoza (anti-communist). This paradoxical situation was heightened by the fact that there was no direct or immediate involvement by the United States in the behaviour of the governments concerned.

In Costa Rica, U.S. policy leaned clearly against Picado and in favour of the opposition, and therefore against the Communist Party. Washington's formula for a solution in this case was to see Picado step down through a victory by the opposition, guaranteed by armed pressure on the part of Figueres, but without giving the latter the chance to take power or fulfil his promises under the Caribbean Pact. In this way Arévalo would remain in a state of confrontation with the rest of Central America, the Caribbean Pact would be aborted, Nicaragua's hands would be free and the Costa Rican political situation would be satisfactorily resolved. However, the history of Costa Rica and the other Central American nations had its own dynamic.

Two great political-electoral coalitions came face-to-face in the elections of February 1948. The first consisted of the government and its Communist allies; with ex-president Calderón Guardia the official candidate. The second comprised the conservative Democratic Party, the centrist and liberal National Union, and the social-democratic group that was the fruit of the fusion of the Centre for the Study of National Problems (led by Rodrigo Facio) and José Figueres' Partido Acción Demócrata; Otilio Ulate was the opposition presidential candidate. The nation was deeply divided in a political climate which exacerbated hatred and promoted violence. Ulate used the slogan 'If he's for Calderón, don't talk to him, don't buy from him and don't sell to him'. Government officials used brutal police methods against the opposition, which had the effect of radicalizing rather than intimidating them.

The union movement was also divided between the Confederación General de Trabajadores Costarricenses (CGTC) and the Confederación de

Trabajadores Rerum Novarum. The first was effectively the union branch of the PVP; it supported the government of Picado and Calderón Guardia, mobilized itself around themes of social reform and labour legislation and would be an important factor in the organization and mobilization of the militia in the civil war that followed the elections. The CGTC was led by Rodolfo Guzmán, educated in the Moscow union school in 1933, and Jaime Cerdas Mora, founder of the Communist Party and one of the principal leaders of the banana strike of 1934. The Confederation's principal strength lay among the banana-workers, although it also had important organizations in the city among shoemakers, construction-workers and bakers.

Rerum Novarum, on the other hand, resulted from Archbishop Sanabria's attempts to create an alternative union inspired by the social principles of the Church. Its supposed purpose was neither to divide the labour movement nor to advocate an anti-communist policy, but to offer all workers, Catholic or not, a non-confessional, non-communist avenue for social revindication. Yet Sanabria had sent its leader, Benjamin Núñez, to the United States to study sociology and become acquainted with union organizations, and Núñez soon acquired a strong anti-communist attitude that led him to identify with the opposition and particularly with José Figueres and his group. Another leader of Rerum Novarum (and future president of Costa Rica), Luis Alberto Monge, was even more closely tied to Figueres. Rerum Novarum relied on the financial support of large national capitalists who sought to weaken the Communists, and on U.S. labour organizations, which were then seeking to expand into Latin America. The two confederations were driven into irreconcilable positions by the conflict of 1948. Núñez was a prominent figure in the civil war and became Minister of Labour in the junta government which was established after Figueres' victory. He promptly and predictably ordered the dissolution of the CGTC, but at the same time he was unable to stem the decline and ruin of Rerum Novarum itself, which never recovered from its politicization in the period prior to the civil war.

The economic situation had begun to improve at the end of the world war. The average price per kilo of exported coffee had risen from $0.35 for the crop of 1944–5, to $0.60 in 1947–8; the value of coffee exports increased from $7,488,761 to $14,189,041. Nonetheless, during this period the trade deficit rose from $15 million in 1945 to $25 million in 1947. The principal imports were related to the production of food, beverages and tobacco, with an increase in capital goods for agriculture, industry and commerce in 1946–7. In 1948 agriculture accounted for 43 per cent of the GDP, commerce 14.7 per cent, services 10.9 per cent, and industry 7.6 per cent. The public sector represented 10.9 per cent of GDP while the national debt stood at $56 million, with $30.2 million in foreign debt.

The government coalition had tried to secure popular support by pushing forward social welfare measures such as the construction of low-cost housing. Nevertheless, neither this nor other measures were able to prevent the deterioration of the regime's popularity, obliging the government to rely heavily upon its control of the repressive apparatus and the Congress, where the Calderón–Communist alliance continued to hold the majority.

The experience of the electoral fraud of 1944 remained acute and placed the opposition's demand for guarantees for a clean election at the centre of politics. The Communists had formulated an Election Code which finally came to regulate the electoral process. But this code then proved unsatisfactory to the opposition. It was not until after the strike of 22 July 1947 led by the business sector that the government gave in to opposition pressure and granted electoral guarantees, which some of its own partisans considered to be nothing less than the surrender of the electoral machinery to the opposition.

This produced a situation where the traditional fraud and manipulation of votes and ballot boxes were a subject for complaint not only by the opposition but also by the government itself. The leaders of the PVP, in particular, had detected illegal movement of voters, exclusion of citizens from the list of registered voters, and so on. Yet, when Otilio Ulate defeated Calderón Guardia, the tendency of the Communists was to accept the electoral results since the PVP itself had elected twelve congressmen out of a total of forty-five, not counting those who had been elected from Calderón's camp. This, however, was not the attitude of its Calderonista allies who had been defeated at the polls. And, finally, partisan interests prevailed over sober political analysis and institutional concerns. Thus, both the losing Calderonistas and the PVP, which on its own had won nearly a third of the seats in Congress, dedicated their efforts to getting the elections results annulled.

In conditions of acute tension that required little to trigger off violent conflict, this was the immediate cause of armed confrontation.

This domestic conflict interacted with another of international character which was no less complex. On one side were the promises Figueres had made in the Caribbean Pact to take advantage of the Costa Rican situation – 'the most convenient and easiest to utilize' – to overthrow the government and begin toppling the dictatorships of Nicaragua, Honduras and the Dominican Republic; to unite Central America under the clear hegemony of Guatemala and Juan José Arévalo; and to promote the formation of new national entities and federations in the Caribbean with greater economic, social and political power. Counterposed to this was Somoza's policy, which sought to block both the actions of the Caribbean conspirators and those of the United States itself, which sought to remove him from power and impose a form of democracy in Nicaragua superintended by the trustworthy National Guard. In Costa Rica, by contrast, the United States was seeking not so much Picado's departure and Ulate's victory – the policy they ended up following – as they were the separation of the Communist Party from the government. Thus, on 22 March 1948 Somoza and the U.S. business attaché, Mr Berhaum, proposed a plan to President Picado to eliminate both Figueres and the Communists with the use of Nicaraguan troops. This proposal was not entirely novel: two years earlier Léon Cortés had offered Picado a pact of support to his government as long as it terminated its alliance with the Communist Party and expelled it from the government. The death of Cortés in March 1946 put an end to the first project; Picado's loyalty to his Vanguardista allies aborted the second.

Armed conflict became the only possible solution to the confrontation. Although there existed within the insurrectionary forces some support for a peaceful solution and negotiations which could prevent more bloodshed, especially on the part of Ulate himself and Mario Echandi, the dominant influence was that of José Figueres, who was determined to go forward with the fighting not only on the national level but on the regional one as well, in accordance with the Caribbean Pact. The insurrectionists mobilized their sympathizers on the basis of slogans linked to electoral freedom, universal suffrage, respect for election results and fear of the Communist threat. On the other hand, social reform, the threat of the repeal of the Labour Law and, paradoxically, denunciation of electoral fraud, were the arguments mobilized by the government and its Vanguardista allies.

The elections themselves had taken place on 8 February 1948. Ulate and the PUN received 54,931 votes while Calderón Guardia's National Republican Party won 44,438. The declaration of the winner could not, however, be made unanimously, as required by law; it was declared by majority because the president of the electoral tribunal refused to cast his vote on account of the circumstances in which the count had been held. The other two members of the Tribunal made their declaration on 28 February. Calderón Guardia presented an immediate demand for nullification to the Congress, which according to the constitution had to make the final decision by 1 March. In the legislative session on that day, in the midst of an unruly street demonstration, Congress agreed by majority vote to annul the presidential elections.

On 12 March there was an armed uprising on Figueres' estates south of San José, located in the mountains separating the capital from the Valle del General, which was promptly taken by the rebel forces. There was also an uprising in San Ramón, to the north of the capital, led by Francisco J. Orlich, but the military actions on this front were less important than those in the south, where the main fighting was centered. The insurrectionists needed to control San Isidro del General in order to possess an airport from which to transport arms and men, which were being sent from Guatemala in accordance with the Caribbean Pact. The rebel presence in the mountains enabled them to cut communications between San Isidro and the capital and maintain an open supply line with Arévalo's government. Shortly afterwards, the anti-government forces attacked the city of Cartago and took it. At the same time, with forces formed by Costa Ricans and Dominican, Honduran and Nicaraguan soldiers from the Caribbean Legion, they took Puerto Limón on the Atlantic coast.

While the Communists, who were bearing most of the burden of the fighting (Calderón Guardia did not call out his partisans until 12 April), maintained that they had enough men and a portion of the arms needed to surround Cartago and overthrow Figueres, Picado's government admitted defeat and decided to seek a formula for surrender. On 12 April, the President called a meeting of the diplomatic corps to solicit their co-operation to save San José. Immediately a delegation of diplomats met with Figueres in Cartago when he presented them with certain demands that produced considerable apprehension in the political circles surrounding Ulate, since the rebel leader required that he himself be named president, which of course implied the recognition of the annulment of the elections in which Ulate had been elected. This was the first symptom of the division which was to occur later when the rebel opposition triumphed.

This issue threatened the talks which began the next day, 13 April, at the Mexican embassy under the auspices of the diplomatic corps, with the participation of Picado and, among others, Manuel Mora of the PVP and

Father Benjamin Núñez for the so-called Army of National Liberation (Ejército de Liberación Nacional). The negotiations were proceeding normally when the U.S. ambassador, Nathaniel Davis, announced that Picado's government had asked Somoza to intervene in Costa Rica and that Nicaraguan troops were already in the town of Villa Quesada, at some distance from the Nicaraguan frontier. The National Guard had attacked the positions of some of the rebels, making it clear that the protestations of 'neutrality' in the conflict and claims that the intervention was only to safeguard the Nicaraguan frontiers from revolutionary actions were palpably untrue. The most serious aspect was that the Somoza regime attempted to legalize its intervention with a request and authorization supposedly submitted to him by President Picado – the version given by the Nicaraguan dictator to the other American governments who were then meeting at the Ninth Inter-American Conference in Bogotá. In Costa Rica, Picado denied Somoza's interpretation, although he did not deny that he had sent Dr Calderón Guardia's brother to ask Somoza to secure his own frontiers in order to prevent people passing from one side to another. At the same time, Rómulo Betancourt, representative of Venezuela at the meeting in Bogotá, and an ally of Figueres, had submitted a petition to the Nicaraguan government asking it to refrain from interfering in the internal affairs of Costa Rica and to withdraw its troops from Costa Rican territory.

The forces supporting the government came from three sources: the PVP militia, which were well disciplined, numerous and combative, but less well armed; the forces of the government itself, which were better armed but without the fighting spirit of the PVP militia and suffered the disadvantages of a policy of sabotage from within on the part of President Picado's brother; and the Calderonista groups, disorganized, mainly billeted in the cities, with a leadership that oscillated between the hopes for Nicaraguan intervention and fear of exile. The fact that after hostilities ended, boxes of modern weapons that had never been used were found in the defeated government's headquarters, while the Vanguardista militia was using single-shot rifles, and that many of these weapons had been taken from the country's arsenals and sold or given by the Minister of War to the National Guard of Nicaragua, the country in which he had sought asylum, clearly demonstrates the importance of the internal divisions in the pro-government alliance. For reasons such as these the peace negotiations could not be restricted to the legal government only but had to include the PVP, which was not only independent from the military point of view but also effectively held political control of the government by the end of the conflict.

On 18 April parallel negotiations were held between Father Núñez, Figueres and Manuel Mora for the purpose of offering additional guarantees that would put an end to hostilities. This led to a meeting on the front line of battle between these three plus Carlos Luis Fallas, the PVP military commander, called at the last minute by Mora to confirm his version of what was said there. The meeting gave rise to what was known as the Pact of Ochomogo. Although no document was signed – no facilities existed at the meeting place – general lines of conduct were agreed upon for the victors. These related particularly to the conservation of the social guarantees and the Labour Law and the legality of the unions and of the Popular Vanguard Party itself. All this was formulated in a private letter that Núñez, following Figueres' instructions, gave to Mora, to which express reference is made in point 6 of the Pact of the Mexican Embassy, which, dated 19 April, put an end to the armed struggle. Father Núñez' letter to the Communist leader Mora carries the same date.

The signing of the Mexican Embassy Pact, later denounced by the victors, put an end to the armed struggle. A transitional government was formed under Santos León Herrera, and almost immediately replaced by a junta headed by Figueres that named itself the Junta Fundadora de la Segunda República.

The establishment of the junta led by Figueres (1948–9) marked the beginning of a political schism in the victorious group. The ideological and political homogeneity within the junta was not complete, nor was there total unity among those who were not in the junta. Yet two clearly defined political centres stood out from the very beginning among the winners. On one side was the political sector around the elected president, Otilio Ulate, of conservative and centrist character, with considerable popular support. On the other was the military sector, led by Figueres, of a populist, reformist character, self-defined as social-democrat and yet lacking in popular support.

Figueres' group, organized in the government junta and with a small contingent in the Constitutional Assembly under the banner of the Social Democratic Party, tried to push through a genuine program of social, educational, financial, economic and institutional reform. The idea of a second republic, of a new and modern role for the state in society and the economy, responded to the urgent needs of an ascending middle class with a business vocation, and clashed with the limited horizons of the traditional elite, who believed that the downfall of Calderón-communism meant the re-establishment of its ascendancy.

The project for a new constitution presented by the Social Democrats combined diverse ideological elements: the populist and nationalist thought of Víctor Raúl Haya de la Torre and *aprismo* plus the moderate distributionist currents of English socialism, North American pragmatism, and the social progressive features of Colombian liberalism. The experiences of Chile and Uruguay provided important institutional models for state decentralization and modernization. These currents coincided with the search for new entrepreneurial and productive horizons beyond the traditional agro-export model. Based above all on the work of Rodrigo Facio, Alberto Martén, and the intellectuals of the Centre for the Study of National Problems, a variety of programs in the areas of education, economy, finance and administrative decentralization sought to open a new social and political project for Costa Rica.

Ulate's group was organized around the PUN (Partido Unión Nacional) and its newspaper *Diario de Costa Rica.* The most prominent capitalists were already beginning to express themselves through *La Nación,* founded in 1946, which was not specifically identified with any political party but represented the traditional conservative tendencies of the country and the interests of the large agricultural, commercial and exporting groups, both national and foreign. Ulate, for his part, was not at all opposed to social change. On the contrary, he perceived the importance and significance of the changes which had taken place in the preceding decade and was responsive not only to the demands of the most important capitalist sectors but also to small and middle-sized producers. As a result, there was later acute friction between him and the representatives of large capital, who eventually withdrew their support. On the other hand, the doubts and reservations about Figueres' real intentions were resolved through the so-called Ulate–Figueres Pact, in which Figueres promised to hand out power to Ulate in eighteen months, postponable, eventually, to twenty-four months.

The junta proscribed the Communist Party (the PVP), had the CGTC declared illegal for being an instrument of the Communist Party, and effected the dismissal without compensation of the partisans of the previous regime, in both private business and the government. It also established special tribunals to try supporters of the defeated alliance. In this initial period there was serious strife over the promises Figueres had made in the Caribbean Pact and over the presence in the country of armed foreigners, who were trying to incite revolutionary international ventures. This was the cause of a protest by some military men in the government itself, headed by the Minister of Public Order (responsible for the police), Edgar Cardona, who attempted a coup d'état against the junta known as 'El Cardonazo' on 2 and 3 April 1949.

During Figueres' government some of the ideas which later would play a central role in national politics were clearly outlined, such as nationalization and development of the electricity industry, and the revision of the country's economic and fiscal relations with the United Fruit Company. From the political and social point of view, however, the most important measure was the nationalization of the banks decreed on 21 June 1948, along with a 10 per cent tax on capital over $50,000. This was the central instrument which permitted the development of the new business sector, politically united in what would later become the Partido Liberación Nacional (PLN) since the growth of this business sector had hitherto been stalled by the financial control that the agro-export and commercial-import groups exercised over private banking and credit.

The coffee oligarchy did not have time to savour its illusory triumph of 1948. Its young Social Democrat allies asserted their independence almost immediately. As early as the battle for Cartago, in the middle of the war, Figueres had rejected attempts by some capitalists to get him to repeal the Labour Law and the social guarantees. A few weeks after Figueres had triumphed, he proceeded to break up the financial monopoly and the social and political influence of the great coffee growers and traders, who were tightly linked by family relationships and most heavily affected by these nationalizing measures of the de facto government. A key factor of their social and political power thus passed to the state, not as a neutral entity but as an effective instrument of development for the emerging political-entrepreneurs.

The reaction of those affected by this policy was to see it as 'communist', not last because of its supposed links with the Caribbean Pact. This distrust grew as illusions about repealing such measures evaporated and the new arrivals in power broadened their base of social support, and stood out as a group who sought hegemony, through a nationalist strategy, over Costa Rican society and politics. The profound nature of the changes was not understood at the time, either by the conservative allies of the previous era, who saw only communism in Figueres and his international allies, or by the Communists, who felt only the repression and anti-communism that surrounded the junta.

One of the most questionable aspects of the governmental actions of the junta revolved around the management of public funds. The lack of proper legal ordinances, the decision to indemnify Figueres for damages to his property during the war, and the issuing of the so-called Decree 80, which empowered Daniel Oduber to dispose of public funds without control or regulation, soon surrounded Figueres'administration with the suspicion of corruption. This was naturally magnified by those who opposed the junta, both those defeated in the civil war and also the junta's own temporary allies, who were beginning to distrust Figueres and the junta and were readying their weapons for the next political fight.

Another aspect which should be stressed is the conflict that broke out between the junta and the Church, especially when the government attempted to sign an agreement which would create seven bishoprics and two archbishoprics. This was a clear attack on the ecclesiastical leadership of Monsignor Sanabria because of his ties with the previous regime. Furthermore, the leader of the Catholic Church continued to intervene to oppose the abuses being committed against the losers in the civil war; he was decisive in halting an attempt to shoot the leaders of the Communist Party, who were imprisoned in the central penitentiary, which was due to take place at the same time as a group of Communist union leaders on the Atlantic coast were being shot at El Codo del Diablo on the railway to Puerto Limón.

In December 1948, the junta was confronted by a bold attack organized by Calderón Guardia from Nicaragua and sponsored by Anastasio Somoza. Foreseeing the threat posed to him by Figueres and his allies in the Caribbean Pact, Somoza took advantage of the desire for revenge prevalent among the Costa Rican exiles to launch them on an invasion and create a border conflict between the two countries. Somoza sought both to alarm the U.S. Department of State and to warn Figueres against any aggression against him. As soon as the Nicaraguan dictator had secured his own interests and distracted Figueres, he abandoned Calderón Guardia and withdrew from the calculated alliance he had promoted exclusively for his own interests. The defeated Calderón Guardia chose to go into exile in Mexico and wait for another opportunity for a military coup, which occurred fruitlessly, in 1955. Meanwhile, he asked his followers to abstain from participating in the 1949 elections for the National Constituent Assembly. This made it particularly difficult for sectors of his own party, some independents and the Communists, to participate in and influence the Assembly.

The National Constituent Assembly was installed on 15 January 1949 and dominated by Ulate's PUN, which had obtained thirty-four delegates while Figueres' Social Democrats managed to elect only four. In spite of the abstention of the Calderonistas, the Constitutional Party, reputed to be of Calderonista tendency, obtained six seats.

Although Calderón Guardia decided to boycott the election and place his hopes in insurrectionary activity, his former Communist allies were opposed to this line and reached certain understandings with individuals who participated under the banner of the Constitutional Party. These elections, then, marked the beginning of the underlying schism within each of the enemy coalitions of the civil war. On the victorious side there was evidence of profound ideological divergence. The political initiative lay with Ulate and his followers, and not with Figueres and his supporters, in spite of their prestigious military triumph. On the losing side, the Communists emphasized social programmes and internal democratization, which in its current form excluded them from operating legally in the political system and forced them to struggle for legal recognition; their Calderonista allies sought new alliances with Caribbean tyrannies, alarmed by the Caribbean Pact, which was aimed against them and which had converted Figueres' regime into a destabilizing factor for Nicaragua, the Dominican Republic and, more recently, Venezuela, under the control of Marcos Pérez Jiménez.

The basis of discussion in the Constituent Assembly was not the plan for a new constitution presented by the Social Democratic Party, which proposed a much more modernizing, regulationist and innovating document, but rather amendments to the charter of 1871. To this were added various corrections and reforms that attempted to synthesize the dramatic social innovations and institutional experiments of the previous ten years. The new constitution introduced a system of autonomous and semi-autonomous institutions, opening the doors to an inexorable process of administrative decentralization and state intervention that began almost immediately. It also limited the presidentialist regime which had hitherto prevailed, and it introduced guarantees for the secure tenure of public employees. In a decisive departure from the rest of Central America, a Superior Electoral Tribunal was established as the fourth power of the state to manage all electoral matters in an exclusive manner. Efforts were made to eliminate corruption in the re-election of presidents and deputies, and civil rights were strengthened, both in reference to the protection of individual and social rights and specifically with regard to the administrative relations between the individual and the state. The equality of the sexes was recognized and women were granted the right to vote. Nevertheless, the Constitution reaffirmed the Junta's previous ban on the organization of parties which could be identified with the activities, programmes or international links of the Communist Party; this prohibition remained in force until 1974.

The constitution abolished the army as a permanent institution. Although Figueres had already disbanded the military, constitutional confirmation of this act was decisive for the democratic future of Costa Rica and distinguished it sharply from its neighbours. While the army as such had begun its decline during the first term of Cleto González before the First World War, and by 1948 had been reduced to a small mobile unit that was dissolved in the middle of the civil war by the Minister of War, its abolition by constitutional law prevented the victorious group from installing itself in power with its own army at the end of the war. At the same time, the old liberal tradition of division of powers was fortified with the recognition of the independence of the judicial power. Both measures were the culmination of a complex historical process which made the existence of the army unnecessary and existence of an autonomous judicial power unavoidable. Like the abolition of the army, both were decisive for the democratic development of Costa Rican society, in sharp contrast with the rest of Latin America and Central America in particular.

The new constitution also ratified the activity of the state in production and in the distribution of national wealth, by strengthening the mechanisms for its intervention in areas of public interest. Without being cemented into any law, the conviction existed, both in the Constitutional Assembly and in the society at large, that it was necessary somehow to link economic and social development to political democracy.

The old coffee oligarchy and its allies failed to adjust to the new situation and simply followed the initiatives of others. Except for the figure of Ulate, with whom they soon broke, they found no leader who could supply them with unity and a sense of purpose. Equally, Calderón Guardia's group sought little more than political restoration and economic compensation for the persecution of which they had been victims. The Communists were crushed both by the harsh internal repression that ensued after the civil war and by the rapid advance of the Cold War, which was already making its mark on the political climate in Latin America. This left the future to the young political entrepreneurs who created the PLN in 1951 with José Figueres at its head. In founding the new party,

Figueres relied on his recent military victory, the absence of a strong opponent in the electoral field and a team of enterprising men who had their own political plans for the country. Figueres and Ulate had agreed to accept the results of the presidential elections of February 1948 in which Ulate had been elected. However, they annulled the election of congressmen, which had given the Calderón-communists the majority of seats. This was a political arrangement among winners, in which Figueres, albeit reluctantly, handed power to Ulate in spite of his feeling that the latter represented forces and interests contrary to his real political and social programme.

The Ulate administration (1949–53) encountered a climate favourable to economic recovery. Internationally, European reconstruction had favourable repercussions on world trade, and the Korean War contributed to the improvement in the price of coffee. Agricultural exports continued to be the mainstay of national economic activity, with coffee and bananas together representing 89.2 per cent of the total value of exports in 1951. Industry employed a little more than 10 per cent of the economically active population, while agriculture accounted for more than 50 per cent of the work force. Mechanization in agriculture was minimal, and the weight of the international market was highly significant in the national economy and public finance. In 1949, 16,603,580 kilos of coffee had yielded $11,087,136, at an average price per kilo of $.0667; by 1952 the average price per kilo stood at $1.147 and the quantity exported at 21,194,786 kilos, producing a total value of $24,323,613.

Although it had had a precarious and dependent agro-export base, the national economy showed dynamism and growth, facilitating the political and institutional process generated after the civil war and the constitutional assembly. In patronizing this incipient modernization the Ulate administration possessed two advantages: it had no real political opposition, since this oscillated between the illegal Communist Party and a tarnished and exiled Calderonism; and the financial and economic situation permitted a healthy reordering of the state and of public finances. The administration had the means to promote key institutions like the Costa Rican Institute of Electricity, the Central Bank and the National Council of Production – key mechanisms in the new interventionist state – as well as the Costa Rican Social Security Fund, while maintaining the value of the colón and a fiscal surplus, which would never recur after 1953. Ulate also managed to reduce the public debt – internal and external – of the central government from $403 million in 1950 to $328 million in 1953.

The Ulate administration carefully preserved its neutrality in the face of the electoral challenge that gained strength with the foundation of the PLN on 12 October 1951 under the undisputed leadership of José Figueres. Thus began a project conceived a year earlier in Rome, by three persons who would later be presidents under the new party's banner: Figueres, Francisco J. Orlich and Daniel Oduber. Besides the PLN, two other new political formations emerged: the Partido Unión Nacional (PUN) and the Partido Demócrata (PD). The first, whose blue flag had flown over the united opposition headed by Otilio Ulate in 1948, was reorganized in 1952 by Mario Echandi, Minister of Foreign Affairs in the Ulate administration and the principal aspirant to the party's nomination. The second, which brought the most powerful capitalists together, finally selected Fernando Castro Cervantes as its presidential candidate. Owner of substantial assets, Castro Cervantes was trusted by the United Fruit Company and could rely on the support of the moneyed group which increasingly gravitated towards *La Nación,* a paper which was careful, however, to avoid letting electoral bias colour its steadfast defence of more permanent interests. A fourth party attempted to enter the contest under the name Partido Progresista Independiente, nominating Joaquín García Monge, a distinguished educator and intellectual who had studied in Chile and was founder and director of the *Revista Repertorio Americano,* an important cultural magazine. The PVP supported his candidacy in an effort to evade its outlaw status but in spite of the respect in which García Monge was held, the party was declared illegal and excluded under Article 98 of the Constitution.

Much of the electoral debate revolved around the PLN and the controversial figure of Figueres, who was increasingly accused of being a Communist, of having secret pacts with international soldiers of fortune, and of having indulged in administrative corruption in the exercise of power. It soon became evident that capital supported Castro Cervantes, forcing Echandi to join forces with the PD and run only as an independent candidate for congressman in San José. Eventually both the PVP and Calderonism backed Castro Cervantes, motivated more by resentment against Figueres than by the ideological and social content of the contending factions. The elections in which women voted for the first time, were held on 26 July 1953. The result clearly favoured Figueres, who captured 123,444 votes, 65 per cent of the total cast.

Ulate held a non-binding referendum at the same time as the general elections, in order to change from eight to four years the period a president had to wait before running for office again. This referendum was approved by a large majority, but the outcome was not respected by Figueres and his group. The legislative assembly, where the matter had to be ratified closed the door to the constitutional amendment and thus to the eventual return of Ulate to power. This precipitated a confrontation between Ulate and Figueres, after which they were irreconcilably opposed to each other.

With the rejection of this constitutional amendment the PLN clearly revealed its intentions to control national politics in opposition to both its adversaries and its former allies in the civil war. This provoked the formation of diverse and contradictory electoral alliances against the party in power. For the conservative sector, Figueres was a Communist because of his ties with Rómulo Betancourt and his statist policies, which was only possible 'in Russia and Costa Rica'. When Ulate broke definitively with Figueres he dusted off old documents from Betancourt's first exile in Costa Rica, during which he was a militant in the Communist Party, and used them to attack Betancourt's friendship with Figueres. Even to the Calderonistas, Figueres' nationalizing tendencies looked suspicious and seemed to bring him closer to their old Communist allies. Thus the PVP's isolation was doubly intensified. All this in turn confirmed the PLN's independent identity and forced an alliance between the wealthy conservative groups and the Calderonistas, who lacked any political program of their own other than the defeat of Figueres.

The economic conditions in which the new government came to office were favourable. The average price per kilo of exported coffee rose from $1.193 in 1953 to $1.483 in 1956 although a fall in quantum exports in that year meant that revenue from coffee sales was only marginally above that for 1953. Nonetheless, during the first PLN administration movement in the volume and prices of coffee exports usually compensated each other. The PLN administration addressed itself to demanding fair prices for export products from the consumer countries and denounced those aspects of commerce that were unfavourable to Latin American development in general. This policy led to friction with Washington, which also distrusted Figueres' efforts to modify the terms of the economic relations between the Costa Rican state and the United Fruit Company at a time when the company was in confrontation with the Guatemalan government of Jacobo Arbenz. In negotiations with the banana company, Figueres managed to raise the government's share of United Fruit's profits from 15 per cent to 30 per cent. He also obtained an increase in wages as part of his policy of strengthening consumption and developing the internal market for the new business sector.

The Figueres administration used its congressional majority to modernize and stabilize the state apparatus through administrative specialization and expansion of the autonomous institutions. The state began to offer all kinds of services, developing the communications network, undertaking important energy projects, and extending education throughout the country. The state thus became a large employer of the electoral constituency of the new party, and a mechanism for social and economic advancement for the rising middle sectors of society. Between 1950 and 1958 the economically active population grew by 2.77 per cent per annum while employment in the public sector grew by 7.44 per cent. The state also became a large market for goods and services, highly conditioned by political and electoral considerations. Between 1950 and 1953 public investment had an 18 per cent share of the GDP, but in the period between 1954 and 1958 it passed the 22 per cent mark, the share of autonomous institutions and the Ministry of Public Works being particularly pronounced.

This strategy had been elaborated by the Centre for the Study of National Problems as well as by Figueres himself, and it was now strengthened by the explicit adoption of the Keynesian economic thought. The nation's wealthy were considered 'timid and cowardly, incapable of boldly undertaking new economic enterprises', in the words of Rodrigo Facio, the government seeking to compensate for their organizational and psychological weakness with state intervention. The financial lever for this was the nationalization of the banks, which was to supplement the economic resources available for the emergence of a new business sector oriented to internal consumption in industry, agriculture and services through the policy of higher salaries and the increasing consumption of goods and services by the state apparatus.

The financing of the modernization effort was based principally on the imposition of indirect taxes, which contributed 48 per cent of the government's revenues, as opposed to direct taxes, which accounted for 12.6 per cent in the period between 1946 and 1958. The other major factor in finance was the internal and external debt: in 1953 the public sector owed $380,980,000, and in 1956, $452,384,000, of which over a quarter was external debt.

The growth of the state was not entirely Figueres' work. The phenome-

non of state expansion and institutional diversification had been present in
Costa Rica since the 1920s, became more accentuated in the 1930s, and
was evident in the process which took place from 1941 to 1948. What
distinguishes Figueres' project is that both he and his group linked the
process directly to the emergence of a new sector of entrepreneurs who
sought to use the State to modernize the nation and form an internal
market. They tried to consolidate their political and social hegemony
through a populism which, with the state as employer, would supply
them with a permanent social and electoral constituency. They already had
influence with the peasantry. The new measures created a rising middle
sector, both private and bureaucratic, which needed the power of the state
for its own development.

The Figueres administration encountered political conflict on two
fronts. Internationally, its head-on collision with the dictatorships of the
Caribbean led it in 1954 to abstain from participating in the Tenth Inter-
American Conference in Caracas, where the Guatemalan regime of Arbenz
was condemned, and to refuse to fraternize with Somoza and other dictators at the Presidents' Conference in Panama. In addition, its constant
demands for better prices in the world market, and its friendliness towards
exiled politicians, including Rómulo Betancourt of Venezuela and Juan
Bosch of the Dominican Republic as well as numerous Nicaraguan exiles,
brought it into opposition with their respective tyrannies and with certain
sectors in the United States. Nevertheless, on the advice of a few liberal
North American friends like Adolf E. Berle and others, Figueres made
important efforts to improve his image in the United States, especially
among the Democrats. He even paid large sums to a public relations
agency to promote his image as a champion of democracy, which proved to
be particularly useful at the time of the armed invasion against his government in 1955. Until that time only Somoza among the heads of state in
Central America had bothered to cultivate an image and try to influence
U.S. public opinion.

On the national level, the overwhelming PLN majority in Congress
clashed with an especially capable opposition, in which the agility and
aggressiveness of Mario Echandi played a critical note. Echandi earned the
hatred of his adversaries and the sympathies of the Calderonista masses,
who saw the true expression of their own sentiments in his attacks against
the government. They forgot that the fiery legislator had been a highly
placed leader in Ulate's camp in the 1948 election, an active opponent in
the civil war and Minister of Foreign Affairs in Ulate's government. The

weakness of the Figueres administration before this implacable opponent grew day by day while Echandi, without a programme but with great technical skill, exploited the government's errors. Perhaps his lack of a programme helped Echandi to knit together those political forces whose common denominator was opposition to Figueres and his party. In all events, a somewhat oligarchic but simple and witty political style helped him to capture widespread popular sympathy and would later give his own administration a traditionalist republican flavour.

In the judgement of the Calderonistas both external and internal conditions were propitious for the removal of Figueres from power through armed action. They were encouraged in this view by growing support from the the public, who frequently booed ministers in the stadiums and protested openly against government measures. Externally, a recalcitrant anti-communism was spreading through Latin America and legitimizing the tyrannies of Trujillo, Pérez Jiménez and Somoza. The conspirators believed that Washington would support the new alliance of populist Calderonism and conservative capital. The Calderonistas explicitly rejected the former alliance with the PVP and their clandestine rebel radio constantly attacked Figueres for his supposed alliance with Communism. The return of Calderón Guardia was considered virtually a fait accompli.

Somoza exploited this situation no less astutely, as he had done that in December 1948. Now he had the support of the other dictators in the Caribbean, and was again ready to test his relations with the U.S. government as far as he could in order to stay in power, if necessary by securing the overthrow of the decidedly threatening government in San José. Nevertheless, Somoza had a clear conception of his purposes, and once the challenge to his own regime was suppressed, he was quite prepared to coexist with the Figueres government. This was not the case with Calderón Guardia, who wanted above all else to overthrow Figueres and was prepared to go to extremes in search of this objective.

The *coyotepes* – as the calderonista insurrectionists were called from the town in Nicaragua where they were trained – entered Costa Rica in January 1955, but their military actions did not meet with the success the rebel leaders and their allies had hoped for. The people remained passive in the face of aggression that did not respond to their needs or their spirit. Moreover, the operation had a strong foreign association which the government stressed, appealing to the inter-American organizations to intervene to pacify the frontier, if not to condemn Nicaragua. The invasion proved to be a fruitless venture from the beginning and only served to help the government recover its lost prestige. The United States took the side of Figueres' constitutional government and demonstrated its repudiation of Somoza's actions through the symbolic sale of three fighter planes at a dollar apiece. The Organization of American States sent forces to seal the frontier and disarm the rebels, who returned to Nicaragua defeated once more and betrayed by Somoza. (When he saw the firm attitude of the United States and the imminent failure of the invasion, Somoza suspended the shipment of arms and logistic support he had promised.) Calderón Guardia, who lost an eye in the fighting, decided to go into exile in Mexico again, burdened by the military failure and the humiliation of an alliance with the tyrants.

The PLN tried to take advantage of the moment to subordinate congressional opposition, especially that of Echandi. The government accused him and another Calderonista congressman of being in collusion with the invaders, stripped them of their parliamentary immunity and had them indicted for treason. Scandalous acts of disrespect and violence occurred during and after this session, and when Echandi decided not to offer any defence against baseless charges, he won a complete pardon from the highest court in the country. His opposition colleagues in Congress decided not to attend the legislative sessions until both congressmen's rights were restored, a situation which lasted for eight months. The victory was thus a shared one: militarily and politically, the government was the victor, but Echandi had also second a political and personal triumph, which enabled him to defeat the two other contestants for the opposition candidacy. He then entered the 1958 election as the sole, and highly popular, opponent to the PLN.

Liberationism, by contrast, presented a divided front. Jorge Rossi, a conservative ex-Minister of Finance and aspirant to the PLN nomination, withdrew from the party denouncing acts of fraud against him and founded the Partido Independiente, which nominated him as its presidential candidate. Another sector, more clearly linked with what was beginning to be called the party machine, nominated Francisco J. Orlich. Figueres, in open defiance of the election laws, lent his support to Orlich, an old comrade-in-arms on whose estate the party had been founded.

The national political system was still very weak. One sector of the populace felt excluded from the political contest and had to support candidates who were not strictly speaking their own although the Calderonistas, many of whose leaders remained in exile, registered their congressmen with the Republican Party. The Communists, who tried to participate under the name Partido Unión Popular, were once again declared illegal and had to limit themselves to choosing among the candidates that the system allowed to participate. Appreciable progress had been made towards cleaner and more democratic electoral processes, but to make further advances it was necessary to remove one giant obstacle: the national divisions and political intolerance that derived from the military confrontations of 1948 and 1955.

The elections were held on 2 February 1958 and 229,543 voted. Echandi obtained 46 per cent of the vote, Orlich, 43 per cent, and Rossi 11 per cent. The president-elect took office on 8 May. However, he lacked a majority in the Legislative Assembly since the anti-PLN vote remained divided between congressmen of Echandi's PUN and Calderón Guardia's Republicans. The independents and Liberationists responded by forming a powerful parliamentary bloc made up of the most able men of both parties, who had been divided more by purely electoral considerations than by profound ideological differences.

Contrary to expectations, Echandi's term was characterized by moderation, a spirit of dialogue and respect for the law. The new president's clear purpose was to complete the consolidation of the rule of law, respect public opinion and give substance and stability to the institutions that had emerged from the new constitution.

Echandi's most difficult task, however, was to heal the divisions caused by the military struggles of 1948–9 and 1955. Surprising some by his lack of vengeance and angering others who did not want to see his administration commit a dangerous act of Calderonista restoration, the President took a major step in this direction by permitting the return to Costa Rica of Calderón Guardia. The return of the 'Doctor' was the cause of one of the largest popular demonstrations seen in the country. The event showed that Costa Rican democracy needed to include that third of the Costa Rican population who identified with 'the eight-year regime', as the administrations of Calderón Guardia and Teodoro Picado were pejoratively called. Special courts ordered the return to the Calderonistas of property which had been seized after the civil war, and those prisoners who had been sentenced at the same time by the so-called Tribunal of Immediate Sanctions were released.

Echandi's failure to obtain a parliamentary majority was compounded by the quality and belligerence of the opposition congressmen, and it was only the President's skill and experience that enabled him to exclude the PLN from the presidency of the Legislative Assembly which was a key post because it controlled the composition of the parliamentary committees. The government was also severely taxed by the banana strike of 1959 on the Pacific coast, where the workers demanded pay for a thirteenth month from the banana company. An agreement was eventually reached whereby the government paid the wages for that year, but the strike demonstrated the recovery of the unions in the banana zone and opened a new phase of tough collective bargaining by labour with foreign companies. At the same time, the situation on the Nicaraguan frontier remained unstable, not least because Figueres continued to instigate and participate in conspiracies against Somoza. The Nicaraguan government captured an arms cache in Punta Llorona, and produced evidence that PLN leaders had participated in their transfer. A few exiled Nicaraguans tried to carry out military actions against Somoza, and he retaliated by detaining a Costa Rican Airlines plane. Echandi, who was maintaining cautiously cordial relations with the dictator, took a firm stand against Somoza's action and forced him to return the airplane. When a Costa Rican officer who was a close friend of the President was killed in a frontier incident, Echandi further hardened his stance towards this kind of activity.

In his relations with communism, which were aggravated by the victory of Castro in Cuba, Echandi took care not to apply the administrative procedures which were provided for in the constitutional prohibition against the Communist Party and which seriously limited individual guarantees. The President began the practice of having the Department of the Interior return publications which were confiscated by the customs service; he allowed the radio broadcast of a speech by Manuel Mora, banned under the Figueres administration, and increasingly left it to the courts to decide the precise meaning of the prohibition against Communists participating under their own party name in elections. In the meantime, he permitted the opening of the PVP party headquarters, the holding of assemblies and meetings, and the publication and circulation of the party paper. Even after Costa Rica broke off relations with the revolutionary regime in Cuba (over the execution of supporters of Batista) Echandi tried to prevent illegal anti-Cuban military activities.

The Cuban Revolution activated the agrarian question in Costa Rica although there was relatively little real grass-roots pressure, as opposed to party propaganda, over the issue. The concentration of property was undeniable – estates of more than 2,400 hectares accounted for only 0.11

per cent of all farms yet occupied 26.56 per cent of the arable land – but the problem still did not produce serious social conflict.

The general elections of 1962 saw the old rivals from the civil war era return to the fray with their own parties. Otilio Ulate, candidate of the National Union, obtained 14 per cent, Calderón Guardia of the National Republican Party won 35 per cent, and Francisco J. Orlich, candidate of the PLN, triumphed with 50 per cent of the vote. The left-wing Popular Democratic Action also ran, although its aim was primarily to secure a radical presence in Congress after so many years of political ostracism.

In the early 1960s the urgent task was no longer democratic consolidation – this had been secured by Echandi – but economic development. The country was suffering from adverse international economic conditions. The prices of coffee, bananas and cocoa were in decline. Exports, which had grown by 6.6 per cent per annum between 1951 and 1957, grew by only 2 per cent in 1962. To this was added the eruptions of the Irazú Volcano during 1963, 1964 and 1965, which affected the coffee crop and disturbed all agricultural production in the central meseta. The gross internal product had seen an average rate of growth of less than 4 per cent between the last year of Figueres' government and the end of the Echandi administration.

The Orlich administration (1962–6) adopted the goals of the Alliance for Progress, which led to a significant inflow of capital from multilateral organizations and initiated a policy of external indebtedness, which was tied during this initial stage to the creation of favourable conditions for production and investment. Industrialization was seriously promoted, first by implementing a law for industrial protection and development passed in 1959, and later through the entrance of Costa Rica into the Central American Common Market (CACM).

The negotiations and studies for the creation of the Central American Common Market had been started by the United Nations Economic Commission for Latin America (CEPAL) in 1951 and lasted until 1958. However, U.S. pressure ensured that the project, which was cemented in 1960 with the signing of the General Treaty of Economic Integration and the creation of the Central American Bank of Economic Integration, finally took shape without CEPAL's most nationalist proposals. This created the dilemma for Costa Rica of whether to accept a project practically imposed by El Salvador and Guatemala, and motivated by North American interests, or to remain outside the common market. The Echandi administration had attempted bilateral negotiation and a gradual entry which would avoid a sudden inrush of competing foreign capital free of the social charges that burdened Costa Rican investment, and preserve an internal market for national capital. In the prevailing international economic situation, and under pressure from an expanding labour market – the result of a demographic explosion which was a reflection of improvements in health and other living conditions in the country – a pure and simple objection to integration was insufficient.

The PLN by contrast, was impatient to join the process of economic integration in Central America, and on 23 July 1962, as soon as the elections were over, President Orlich expressed the willingness of Costa Rica to become part of the Central American Common Market. From the economic point of view, entry into the CACM meant the adoption of import substitution, based on the use of a technology which, although outmoded in its countries of origin, was sufficiently advanced in the underdeveloped Costa Rican economy to undermine the utilization of the abundant labour force, whose employment was supposedly one of the principal objectives of the integrationist policy. Investments were not regionalized and ended up competing between the member countries. The sum total of the five feeble markets of the participating countries excused them, for the moment, from having to develop a true internal market through reforms in agriculture. The blow to public finances was no less destructive. In the zeal to compete for foreign investment with the other countries of the CACM, the principal weapon used was tax exemption through the application of the incentives built into the Law of Industry. This gave rise to a chronic fiscal crisis which culminated a few years later in general economic crisis.

The CACM produced significant social differentiation within national society. There was an increase in local entrepreneurs who participated in the Market under fiscal protection and those who established ties with foreign capital. In the wake of this limited industrial expansion a new working class developed, with working conditions and social relations that were different from those that had traditionally prevailed. The special characteristics of this stratum made the organization of strong unions in the private sector very difficult, and union activity continued to be concentrated in the areas of banana production and the public sector.

Although a certain symbiosis was subsequently to be established with the traditional coffee-growing and agro-export group, the new entrepreneurs tied to the CACM initially encountered a climate of confrontation originating in the costly policy of industrial protectionism. The new entrepreneurs and managers were unable to consolidate an independent political identity and therefore began to enter the existing political parties. Through this route and from the areas of the state which they managed to control, they subsequently exerted considerable influence over economic policy.

The Orlich government, besides pursuing international policies in the interests of the coffee sector, attempted to pursue a policy of development from within by fostering the national production of bananas in the Atlantic zone while simultaneously negotiating with multinational banana corporations interested in investing in Costa Rica. The monopoly the United Fruit Company had held in the national production of bananas was thereby broken. By 1975, 41 per cent of a much-increased banana production was controlled by national enterprises. Nevertheless, commercialization remained in foreign hands: COBAL, first controlled by German capital and later by United Brands, brought 95 per cent of its export crop from national producers; BANDECO, first owned by the West Indies Company and later by Del Monte Corporation, 55.5 per cent and the Standard Fruit Company, a subsidiary of Castle and Cook, 44.1 per cent. United Fruit Company, by contrast, only acquired 3 per cent, producing 97 per cent of its exports on its own plantations. While this generated an important new entrepreneurial sector, its principal social effect was the development of a belligerent agricultural proletariat which, when added to that of the Pacific coast, would strengthen Communist unionism until the crisis of 1984.

The diversification of production embraced other activities, such as sugar exports, favoured by the redistribution of the Cuban quota among Latin American countries producing sugar cane, and the export of meat and cattle. This generated new and larger revenues in foreign currencies, a certain level of industrialization – sugar mills, meat-processing plants, and the like – and, in the case of livestock, which was extensive, the development of large properties and systematic deforestation. There were also ventures into cotton and pineapples, which together with livestock consumed the greater part of external credit aimed at promoting agricultural production.

Following a clear policy of expansion of public spending and state intervention, the Orlich administration created a series of new autonomous institutions, which were financed in part by increasing the foreign debt. This had serious repercussions on the independence of the government, particularly in relations with the United States, and was probably one of the reasons why Costa Rica sent civil guards to the Dominican Republic to support the North American intervention in 1965. The implementation of these policies also led the Orlich government to increase tax rates, to stop paying the state's quota to the Social Security Fund, and to begin the practice of financing public works with government bonds – which would be out of control by the end of Oduber's administration (1978) and create a crisis during Carazo's term in office (1978–82).

The elections for Orlich's successor were held on 6 February 1966. The PLN was unified electorally but manifested growing differences between its most prominent leaders. Its candidate was Daniel Oduber, a brilliant politician who had been a founder of the Centre for the Study of National Problems, Secretary of the government junta of 1948 and the administrator of Decree 80, which had been central to the management of public funds. Oduber had also been president of the Legislative Assembly and Minister of Foreign Affairs in the Orlich administration. A lawyer who had studied in France and Canada, he occupied the third-ranking position, after Figueres and Orlich, in the party hierarchy. The opposition, on the other hand, was obliged to undergo a political transition in order to control the elections as a united force. This meant dispensing with the historical candidates of the main parties and selecting a compromise candidate in Professor José J. Trejos Fernández, a liberal economist and academic by profession and a man of great equanimity and tolerance.

The opposition attempted to organize the campaign around the issues of Communism and corruption, accusing Oduber of symbolizing both. The PLN laid great stress upon the experience of 1948 and championed its own record in government. This gave the opposition the opportunity to denounce PLN continuism, Trejos openly challenging the post-1948 model by supporting private banking and affirming the principle that the state should only intervene where private persons could not or would not do so. The Communists tried to participate in league with the Partido Alianza Popular Socialista, whose proposed candidate was the former Liberationist military leader Marcial Aguiluz, who had left his former party and allied himself with the PVP. However, in October 1967 the party was again declared illegal following a motion of the PLN and a nearly unanimous vote in the Legislative Assembly.

This was perhaps the closest election in national history: Trejos Fernández obtained 222,810 votes (50.5 per cent) and Oduber 218,590 (49.5

percent). In spite of this, the Legislative Assembly, which was elected together with the local governments on the same date as the presidential election, remained under the control of the PLN, which secured twenty-nine seats. Unificación Nacional, as the opposing alliance was called, elected twenty-six congressmen; a paramilitary rightist group, which soon disappeared, electing the remaining two.

The new administration inherited a public debt, excluding the debt owed to the Costa Rican Social Security Fund, of more than $870 million; the external debt stood at $100 million. Trejos Fernández responded by imposing a policy of austerity and containment of public spending. Employment was directed towards the private sector, producing friction with both Ulate and Calderón, who were under pressure from their respective electoral constituencies to provide jobs in the public domain. In accordance with his idea of the state as complementary to private enterprise, Trejos tried to repeal the state monopoly of banking. This initiative opened a particularly heated debate, which culminated on 23 July 1967 when the project was rejected.

The administration provoked further controversy when, in April 1970, it approved a contract with the multinational aluminum company ALCOA. The agreement was denounced in student circles and by the left in general as being unfairly one-sided and contrary to the national interest. Among those in the National Assembly who opposed it was Rodrigo Carazo, who exploited this issue to the full in developing his own political platform and ambitions. When congressmen from both parties approved the contract by a majority, the Legislative Assembly building was stoned and almost burned down by students on 24 April. Although there were riots in the capital and clashes with the police, the contract was immediately ratified by the executive. Nevertheless, having undertaken no work in the area in question, ALCOA soon withdrew and terminated the contract.

The political consequences of this event were significant. In the first place, it effectively suppressed the practice, inherited from the era of banana contracts, of granting concessions to foreign companies, guaranteeing them special privileges and compromising the sovereignty of the state. Second, it encouraged the student movement as well as other popular sectors to look for political alternatives to Communism and Castroism, encouraging the formation of a variety of leftist organizations from 1970 onwards.

The Trejos admininstration's economic policy was at first greatly complicated by a significant fall in coffee prices. Between 1966 and 1968 the average price per kilo of coffee exported fell from $0.959 to $0.806, although a modest increase in the volume of exports avoided a major fall in revenue. The price improved slightly from 1969, and by 1970 stood at $1,057 per kilo, further increases in volume exported producing an income from coffee sales that was, at $73 million, some 50 per cent higher at the end of the Trejos government than at its start. In 1969 total investment stood at $173.3 million, with $36.7 million, or 21.1 per cent, directed to the manufacturing sector. Thus, despite the generally unfavourable situation in coffee prices, the economy exhibited some dynamism as a result of the Trejos administration's policy of containing public spending, stabilizing government finances and slowing the growth of the state sector. Nevertheless, by 1970 the crisis of the Central American Common Market was already manifest.

In the elections of 1 February 1970 two ex-presidents, José Figueres and Mario Echandi, faced each other although neither of them had won their nominations easily. Figueres had succeeded in persuading Daniel Oduber to postpone his aspirations to stand for a second time, but Rodrigo Carazo, hitherto a political protégé of Figueres, had the impertinence to put up his own name at the convention and ran against the old *caudillo*. Carazo obtained a third of the votes, which intensified the conflict to such a point that he was practically expelled from the PLN. A little later he founded the Partido Renovación Democrática around his charismatic figure.

In Echandi's case, there were two great difficulties to overcome: the support pledged to Ulate's candidacy, and the attempts by a few Calderonistas to nominate their own candidate. Although Echandi managed to isolate Ulate from the capital, from his Executive Committee, and even from the National Assembly of his own National Union Party, the invectives launched by the veteran of 1948 succeeded in sharply impairing the credibility of Echandi's candidacy. At the same time a schism within the Calderonista ranks gave birth to the Partido Frente Nacional, and although the strength of the new party diminished as the campaign progressed, its mere existence, added to Ulate's efforts, irreparably weakened Echandi's chances against Figueres. Even Calderón Guardia himself was unable to overcome the effects of the division through a vigorous campaign in support of Echandi. By then Calderón's health was failing, and at the end of 1970 his rich and adventurous life came to an end.

The 1970 election was notable for the fact that the Christian Democrats participated as a party for the first time, and that the Communist Party,

Partido Acción Socialista, was able to compete. This was because although the Supreme Electoral Tribunal considered that it fell under the prohibition of Article 98 in the constitution, the Legislative Assembly did not become aware of the situation in time and did not decree its proscription by the two-thirds vote required by the law. Figueres, who had been closely linked with proscription in 1948, now requested that the Communists be completely legalized. (In fact, Figueres had not been in agreement with the legal prohibition of the Communist Party after the civil war although he accepted the majority decision of the rest of the members of the government junta, which was radically anti-communist.) It is noteworthy that thanks to the intervention of Luis Burstin, Figueres' physician, who had been a militant member of the Communist Party and very close to Manuel Mora, a close relationship had been established between Mora and Figueres. The two agreed that Mora would see to it that the Soviet Union purchase Costa Rica's coffee surplus, which was saleable only in new markets, in exchange for which the price and commissions would be distributed among the new coffee exporters, and the excess profits used to finance the cost of Figueres' campaign. Figueres, for his part, promised to legalize the Communist Party and establish diplomatic relations with the Soviet Union. The election results gave Figueres victory with 54.78 per cent of the vote while Echandi obtained 41.17 per cent and the other three candidates received less than 2 per cent.

Between 1961 and 1971 there had been a significant degree of concentration of income in the intermediate strata of society, and it was evident that the middle and upper sectors had become concentrated in secondary and tertiary activities. There was an increase in the number of professional employees, many of whom now worked for the state or in large private companies. Likewise, there was an increase in the relative percentage of waged workers in the secondary sector, reducing the corresponding number of workers employed in agriculture which had itself undergone appreciable differentiation with the appearance of important nuclei of national entrepreneurs in livestock, sugar cane, bananas and, later, rice, bolstering the growth of management groups in industry, both national and multinational.

Thus, during nearly ten years of the Central American Common Market the middle sectors had strengthened their presence in society and the state. Furthermore, the process of industrialization and modernization in agriculture had augmented the numbers of the proletariat, from 48.1 per cent of the economically active population in 1960 to 55.1 per cent in 1970. In his electoral campaign Figueres championed not only the democratic system, and especially the independence of the judiciary, but a fairer distribution of wealth and the struggle against extreme poverty, which, in his judgment, threatened the outbreak of violence within Costa Rican society. In addition to winning the presidency, Figueres had an overwhelming majority in the Legislative Assembly that comprised the thirty-two PLN congressmen, two Communist deputies (one of whom was Manuel Mora) and the Christian Democrats, who were in many aspects an extension of the government party. The government also controlled nearly all the municipalities. Moreover, as a result of a confidential arrangement with the Calderonista leader Francisco Calderón Guardia, the administration was able to control the autonomous institutions by introducing Law 4646, which guaranteed four seats for the government and three for the major opposition party on the boards of directors.

With such resources at his disposal, Figueres was able to create the Instituto Mixto de Ayuda Social (IMAS), whose mission was to eliminate extreme poverty in Costa Rica over a ten-year period. He introduced family allowances, expanded the coverage of social security (which rose from 46 per cent of the population to 85 per cent in 1978) and promoted higher education, increasing the number of universities to four, with a student body of 48,000, which represented 2.16 per cent of the country's population. Figueres also acquiesced in the proposal by a sector of the PLN to establish the Corporación Costarricense de Desarrollo (CODESA), and he ensured that the economic independence of the judiciary was constitutionally consolidated by allotting it a fixed percentage of the national budget. Figueres fulfilled his agreement with Manuel Mora; he established relations with the Soviet Union to the opposition of the right and the applause of the left, and legalized the Communist Party, repealing paragraph 2 of Article 98 of the Constitution.

On the other hand, the government soon found itself involved in several scandals, the most important of which was caused by the government's protection of the international fugitive Robert Vesco, for whom President Figueres himself wrote a defence speech. The financier, who had been charged in the United States for laundering money, financed part of the PLN election campaigns in 1970 and 1974, and set up a newspaper of social democratic leanings, *Excelsior,* to compete with *La Nación.* Yet the Vesco affair was only the most infamous of the series of financial and political scandals connected with the expansion of the state and welfare services that created a constant deficit in the state budget and an increase in public debt.

The rise in the price of petroleum struck home in 1973, but no preventive measures were taken. The resources of the Costa Rican Oil Refinery (RECOPE) were committed to financing the construction of stadiums and playing fields and recreational facilities in the ports. The government resorted to deficit and debt, in the thousands of millions, first in colones, and later in dollars.

In spite of his control over the executive power, the Legislative Assembly, the municipalities and the autonomous institutions, Figueres felt that he had not been able to govern as freely as he wanted. He declared that the Costa Rican state had grown too large, and was impossible to control. In his judgement, a de facto government like that of 1948 ought to be established for a period of two or three years in order to introduce reforms without legal or bureaucratic impediments, the normal system of elections every four years being reestablished thereafter.

In the elections of February 1974, the opposition to the PLN again failed to unite behind a single candidate. In addition to Daniel Oduber for the PLN and Fernando Trejos Escalante for Unificación National, there were six other candidates including a Christian Democrat; Rodrigo Carazo for the new Renovación Democrática party; Jorge González Martén for the Partido Nacional Independiente (PNI) which sought to champion the interests of integrationist managerial sector; and Manuel Mora for the Partido Acción Socialista.

Opposition to the PLN was not the only source of division. The Communist Party for the first time had to face the emergence of other political groups whose convictions were more or less close to their own. To their left stood the Movimiento Revolucionario Auténtico with a Castroist orientation, and the Costa Rican Socialist Party; and to their right, the Partido Frente Popular, which only presented candidates for Congress.

The divisions within the opposition assured Daniel Oduber victory with 43.44 per cent of the vote (just under 300,000 votes); the Unificación Nacional candidate received 30.39 per cent, Carazo won 9.1 per cent, and González Martén 10.9 per cent. On the left, Mora obtained 2.4 per cent, the Socialist Party 0.5 per cent – the same as the Christian Democrats.

Upon taking office, the new president, much to Figueres' annoyance, made a speech around the theme 'Down with corruption', thereafter introducing a series of policies with remarkable speed. Oduber completed the universalization of social security, established his own programme of family assistance, and extended state services and the network of public roads. He increased the purchase of land to be distributed among the peasants, and stimulated the modernization of communications and the production of electric power. By 1978 health services, which in 1970 covered barely 46 per cent of the population, had expanded to cover 86 per cent, infant mortality dropped to 21 per thousand in 1978 while life expectancy passed the seventy-year mark.

Politically, the Oduber administration (1974–8) broke the alternation of power and was effectively the second part of a Liberationist administration of eight years (1970–8). At the same time, the PLN lacked a clear congressional majority, and although it was often able to reach agreement with Unificación Nacional, the other emerging parties subjected the government to sharp criticism. The government relied heavily on a significant rise in the price of coffee, from $1.384 per kilo in 1974 to $4.721 in 1977, which was unprecedented in the country's history and propelled total sales from $124.8 million to $319.2 million over the same period. The government also utilized internal and external credit for expansion during the international crisis of 1974–5. This, in turn, contributed towards the exhaustion of the programme of the PLN despite the singular efforts to promote an entrepreneurial state. This policy was linked to the appearance of a second generation of party leaders composed not of entrepreneurs who needed political power for their own modernization projects ('political entrepreneurs'), but of politicians and bureaucrats who wanted to enter the productive sphere in order to broaden their jurisdiction and private capital. This group may be termed 'entrepreneur-politicians' or a 'bureaucratic bourgeoisie'.

It soon became clear that the principal representative of the first generation of PNL political-entrepreneurs continued to be ex-president Figueres, while the second generation was represented in political and ideological terms by Daniel Oduber and in social terms by Luis A. Monge, whose successful electoral slogan in 1982 was that his only business had been the PLN.

The continuous exercise of political power by the PLN between 1970 and 1978 allowed this new social segment to launch the political programme of the entrepreneurial state, one of whose principal manifestations was CODESA. This corporation was created from the perspective that the state would develop projects in a number of economic areas where the private sector might have an interest but lacked the necessary resources. In order to avoid foreign control over these areas, the state would make the initial investment and, once the business was making a profit, would pass it back to the private sector. Those sectors of the economy that were considered vital would remain directly in the hands of the state. Nevertheless, in practice the postulates of the law establishing CODESA were very rarely followed. In addition to undertaking infrastructural activity, such as the production of hydrocarbon alcohol and cement, CODESA engaged in others where private enterprise had failed and still others in which its errors, losses and poor standards caused political and financial scandals. Thus, the nationalist ethic behind certain aspects of the entrepreneurial state and CODESA was profoundly compromised by economic confusion and suspicions of corruption.

With this transformation to the entrepreneurial state, the public sector was expanded once again, assuring for the new bureaucratic bourgeoisie, the income – from high salaries, tax exemptions, expense accounts, cars, house, credit and so on – and prestige that had previously been reserved for successful private businessmen. The financial sources for this political project included an increased public deficit and increases in tax rates on producers and citizens, an exaggerated and excessive external debt, bond issues and a rise in the internal debt. Thus the size of the investment, the concentration of capital, the privileges deriving from the essential nature of public enterprises, converted an entrepreneurial politician sector, unfamiliar with the real and substantive notions of profitability, efficiency, waste-trimming and satisfactory performance standards, into a dangerous competitor for the traditional private business sectors and, eventually, into an incontrovertible adversary.

Public sector entrepreneurialism deepened the segmented nature of the state. Each bureaucracy sought to protect itself though the feudalization of its institution. Institutional particularism was the dominant theme in matters of policy, pensions, salaries, commissions, permits, vacations, and so on. Differentiation arose not only between the institutions but also within them, reproducing the general social differentiation between the poor, the middle-income and the rich. At the same time, there was a manifest lack of coordination, and chains of command dissolved into hierarchical formalities incapable of changing policy. The state thus grew at an accelerated and a disorganized pace; it covered every facet of the social life of the country, reinforcing the image of a government with a giant body and a weak head.

At the end of the Oduber administration, Figueres announced that the country did not know where public affairs ended and private affairs began, thus legitimizing the suspicions of corruption against the government. Furthermore, he expressed his belief that Monge, the Liberationist candidate in the elections of 1978, would be defeated by the opposition. Since the constitutional reform of July 1969 expressly prohibited the re-election of a president, Figueres was able to make such provocative statements without prejudicing his own political ambitions. He therefore broke free from the traditions of his party to declare that the Costa Rican state was not only corrupt but also bureaucratic and indeed ungovernable.

Oduber's term ended not only in a fiscal crisis but also one of parties, ideologies and the nature of the State. The outgoing president's entrepreneurial state was a stillborn experiment. Symbolically, this took on a tone true to magic realism when his successor opened and closed, on the very same day, the installations of CATSA, the largest sugar center for the production of anhydrate alcohol in the country, property of CODESA.

Despite the participation of eight candidates, the 1978 poll centred on two principal groups: the Partido Unidad, whose candidate was Rodrigo Carazo, and the PLN, led by Luis A. Monge. Both the PNI and Unificación Nacional were abandoned by their supporters because of their supposed collaboration or complicity with Oduber; neither was able to elect a congressman to office. The PVP joined several small leftist groups under the name Pueblo Unido. The election was a clear victory for Carazo, who obtained 50.5 per cent of the vote against 43.8 per cent for Monge. The PVP obtained 2.7 per cent, and Unificación Nacional, which claimed to represent authentic Calderonism and counted Francisco Calderón Guardia among its leadership, only 1.7 per cent. The name of Calderón Guardia and his electoral heritage, however, were preserved by the opportune shift of several family members and important leaders, especially the son and widow of Dr Calderón Guardia, to the Partido Unidad, which they themselves had helped to create.

President Carazo had been a leader of the PLN, and his economic policies were influenced by those of his original party, although they also contained neo-liberal tendencies and a very marked personalist manner in decision-making. Carazo also presided over an incoherent alliance which tended to side with the Partido Liberación Nacional on certain issues, and as soon as he took office he found himself without a parliamentary faction of his own. The congressmen elected by the new Partido Unidad had different loyalties to those the leadership of the alliance, and the administration soon found itself isolated in the face of severe internal and external problems that it could not control.

Through the alternation between the principal parties every four years, the Costa Rican state had found a corrective factor for the excesses in spending and public investment by the governments of the PLN. Prudent rectifications in fiscal and monetary matters, and more sober utilization of governmental spending and external resources, brought equilibrium to public finance and the national economy. This process was interrupted by the election of the succeeding PLN administrations of Presidents Figueres and Oduber and then that of President Carazo, who had the same political and ideological origins as his predecessors. The Carazo administration thus failed to introduce the kind of corrective measures that might have rescued the financial situation of the country. The President did not put the currency on sound basis, failed to advance vigorous new policies, cut public spending or consolidate a consensus around the government that might have put an end to the abuse of internal and external credit.

Such failure was all the more marked in view of the gravity of the economic crisis the country suffered in this period. The GDP growth rate fell from 6.4 per cent in 1979 to 0.8 per cent in 1980, −2.3 per cent in 1981 and −7.3 per cent in 1982. The external public debt rose from $1 billion in 1979 to $3.7 billion in 1982. Exports, however, followed a different rhythm: in 1978 they stood at $1 billion as against $1.3 billion in imports; and in 1980 exports were $1.2 billion and imports $1.65 billion. Inflation advanced at an accelerated pace from 7.8 per cent in 1979 to 81.8 per cent in 1982. The colón lost its value in a similar pattern; in 1981 the real devaluation of 51 per cent was the largest in the country's economic history. In the first two years of the subsequent administration, the currency was devalued by 23 per cent, the figure for 1984 and 1985 being 9.6 per cent and 12.7 per cent respectively.

This economic crisis led to a series of open clashes between Carazo and the IMF and other international organizations, creating a climate of tension in foreign affairs that was greatly aggravated by the war in Nicaragua, which impinged directly on Costa Rica. Despite heading an avowedly conservative coalition, Carazo decided to give outspoken support to the insurrection against Somoza's regime. Combining the personal inclinations of the President with the legitimate policies of the state on the international level, and protected by the traditional anti-Somoza sentiments of the Costa Rican people, the Carazo regime became directly involved in the conflict. The prospect of a generalized instability that the fall of the Somoza regime implied was ignored, as was the impact that the illegal shipment of arms and personnel implied in a society like Costa Rica, which lacked adequate resources and mechanisms to manage and control the situation.

The crisis, however, was even more profound, and one of its clearest manifestations was the absence of political leadership. The older generation had lost its most outstanding leaders: Calderón and Ulate had already died; Figueres was now old and neutralized by Daniel Oduber; Mora not only carried the burden of his age, but his leadership was seriously questioned within his party, leading, in December 1984, to a major split in the PVP and a weakening of its union organizations. The conflict which occurred that year with the removal of Manuel Mora from the Party's general secretariat was encouraged by the Soviet embassy, which considered Mora to be weak and reformist at a time when Moscow was advocating a radical policy in Central America and total support for the Nicaraguan revolution. The party divided into two factions, one of which, led by Humberto Vargas and Arnoldo Ferreto, relied on the approval of the Soviet Union. With the take-over of the Central Committee by Vargas and Ferreto, Mora immediately founded a new organization, the Costa Rican National People's Party, with the political support of the Cuban government, and with the advantage that he maintained control over the finances of the old party. The group led by Vargas and Ferreto continued to use the name and flag of the PVP and organized a strike on the banana plantations of the southern Pacific coast, with a view to proving its national strength and dominance over the unions. This occurred at the same time as the United Fruit Company decided to cease banana cultivation in Costa Rica. The strike only encouraged the company in its plans, and was a complete disaster. The closure of the banana industry dissolved a long-standing concentration of workers, and the union movement lost its strength in the country. The blame for these events fell on the PVP, but the popular sectors punished the left as a whole, which failed to achieve even 5 per cent of the vote in the election of 1986.

Thus the general crisis of the Costa Rican state and the Costa Rican economy was exacerbated by a crisis of the Costa Rican political system, marked by both an absence of leadership and a neutralization of the different factions into which society had become divided. The problems were so profound and varied that they required a national consensus, or at least a consensus among key social forces, in order to overcome the exhaustion of post-war political strategies. As the regional conflict in Central America deepened and the role of the United States within it grew, what came to be questioned was the very viability of Costa Rica as a sovereign, independent nation with its own cultural and historical profile.

In 1982 the political pendulum swung back towards the PLN, which once again presented Luis A. Monge as its presidential candidate. Monge was a former union leader with Benjamín Núñez, and had been a Social-Democrat delegate to the constitutional convention in 1949. He possessed long-standing ties with the United States and now found support among the electorate for a close alliance with the U.S. embassy, which was strongly opposed to Carazo.

The Partido Unidad, oppressed by the weight of the Carazo administration and by the crisis for which the government was blamed, nominated as its candidate Rafael Angel Calderón, the son of Dr Calderón Guardia and ex-Minister of Foreign Affairs under Carazo. Also participating were the Movimiento Nacional, with ex-President Echandi as candidate (he had been exempted when the constitutional prohibition against presidential re-election had been written), the PVP and its allies under the United People's Coalition, and two parties, the Democratic Party and the Independent Party, which lacked a clear political and ideological profile. The PLN won 58 per cent of the votes; the Partido Unidad received 33.6 per cent; Echandi's Movimiento Nacional only 3.8 per cent; and Pueblo Unido 3.3 per cent.

The problems inherited by the new Monge administration were serious, but the PLN victory was great enough to allow it to attempt profound and radical changes in society, the economy and the state. This, though, was not the new president's calling, and he governed in a listless fashion, which by the end of his administration produced a multitude of very serious political scandals. Perhaps the greatest of these was on the international front, when Monge declared a policy of neutrality, yet allowed the anti-Sandinista activities of the Reagan administration to take place on Costa Rican soil with the full knowledge of the government.

The Monge government enjoyed the apparent good fortune of being able to exploit the exceptional regional situation, which attracted an uncommon involvement of foreign agencies and governments channeling important financial resources to Central America that, under other conditions, would perhaps have been directed to different places. Thus the total amount of new resources from external financing received by the public sector alone rose from $469.4 million in 1981, to $494.2 million in 1985. When these figures are added to the overdue amounts in debt service and its scheduling, they came to a grand total of $4,132 million between 1981 and 1985. This foreign aid permitted and even encouraged the continuation of the paralysis and stagnation of the previous period. The privileges derived from state employment continued, although, under pressure from the international lending agencies, Costa Rica would have to abandon momentarily some of the most sordid and critical aspects of the entrepreneurial state model and make room for the impetuous and disorderly emergence of a private finance sector, closely linked to these same agencies.

The absence of significant rectifications and the artificial climate which produced this generous U.S. aid did nothing to impede the transfer of the cost of the crisis to the weakest economic sectors and the middle classes, which were directly affected by the stagnation of production, the fall of real income, high taxes and debt service. Between 1979 and 1982 real income declined by between 30 and 40 per cent. In 1982, income reached its lowest level and inflation reached 9 per cent, its highest level, while production fell 7 per cent. It is estimated that even if production had not declined, the national gross income would have been 12 per cent less as a result of unfavorable exchange rates and payments to meet the external debt.

External economic aid was attached to clearly neo-liberal policies which sought the denationalization of the economy and its reorientation on the basis of simple fiscal equilibrium, geared towards the production and export of non-traditional goods. In other words, the objectives of these policies did not lie in resolving the crisis of the country and re-establishing a healthy direction for its development, but rather in ensuring at any cost that it would meet its obligations to the international banking system, in accordance with the bias characteristic of the agreements with the International Monetary Fund.

For the international agencies this responded to a clear logic which saw everything (loans, structural adjustments, letters of intent, etc.) from the perspective of liberalizing the economy, reducing the sphere of public investment and facilitating the fulfilment of servicing the public debt. While the external public debt showed, in millions of U.S. dollars, capital gains of $207.0 in 1982, $609.1 in 1983, $454.5 in 1984 and $491.7 in 1985, the debt service actually realized was, for the respective years, $169.0, $637.7, $315.4, and $563.1, leaving the balance of net external resources at $38 million for 1982, −$28 million for 1983, $139 for 1984 and −$71.4 for 1985.

From the national point of view, the problem was much more complex than the heavy burden of debt service. The criteria of comparative international costs used to evaluate the profitability of a productive sector led to the eventual liquidation of entire branches of the economy. Dependency on the flow of external resources made the slightest regression critical in its effects, and the national economy became chronically dependent on the goodwill and distribution of aid from the international agencies and friendly countries.

Such a state of affairs postponed the solution of structural problems, but it did re-establish confidence and preserve social peace. This was less the result of the government's own initiative than of U.S. policy to make financial concessions and grant aid so as to secure a degree of tranquillity and non-military influence within Central America. At the same time, the emphasis of foreign aid on the private sector raised the possibility that its principal beneficiaries might accumulate sufficient economic and political authority to break the existing impasse and establish a new hegemony. The weakening of the state monopoly on banking in 1984 strongly suggested that the balance of forces was moving in this direction.

However the private financial sector lacked autonomous economic power. Basically speculative in character, its activities were heavily dependent on the flow of external economic aid after 1982. Since very little of this aid was directed to the public sector the new financiers certainly had access to unusual resources. Yet the dependence on external aid and the favouritism that went with it were naturally conditioned by fluctuations in the aid itself and by the international economic situation. Thus, when the favourable character of these changed for the worse, the impact on the local financial sector was immediate. This began to happen quite quickly. Second, the objective limits on the opportunities for productive investment, beyond transactions in foreign money and state securities, played a negative role. Much speculative activity involved foreign currency transactions, in many cases skirting the restrictions established by the Central Bank. These and other activities provoked financial scandals and numerous bankruptcies, which eroded public confidence in the new financial groups and indirectly strengthened the national banking system.

Although the economic crisis, regional conflict, and expansion of foreign influence produced an unprecedented challenge during the 1980s, they also helped to promote the values of the Costa Rican democratic way of life. The country's indices of health and education remained among the highest in Latin America; the regime of political parties, free elections and respect for human rights constituted true accomplishments on the part of a people which had learned, in the midst of scarce resources and the inherent problems of its underdevelopment and dependency, how to preserve its profile as sovereign, democratic and independent.

The 1986 election victory of the PLN candidate Dr Oscar Arias brought into relief the national, democratic and pacifist nature of Costa Rica. The new president diligently sought to resolve the ambiguities of the Monge government, most particularly in the field of foreign relations. In February 1987, Arias presented a plan to secure the cessation of the civil wars and foreign armed intervention in the region. For this he was awarded the Nobel Peace Prize, and the peace plan was formally adopted by Central America's presidents in August 1987. This initiative by no means succeeded in immediately quelling the fighting and only modestly reduced Costa Rica's vulnerability to destabilization from abroad. Nevertheless, it produced a palpable shift in the regional balance of forces and political atmosphere, introducing a modicum of Costa Rican equanimity into the violent affairs of its neighbours. In the wake of this celebrated enterprise in foreign policy, the overriding challenge that remained was to secure a strategy that would resist the decay of the considerable accomplishments of Costa Rican society, overcome the adverse conditions that had prevailed for the previous decade, and provide a dynamic basis for economic welfare and political democracy in the last years of the century.

Part Three

THE CARIBBEAN

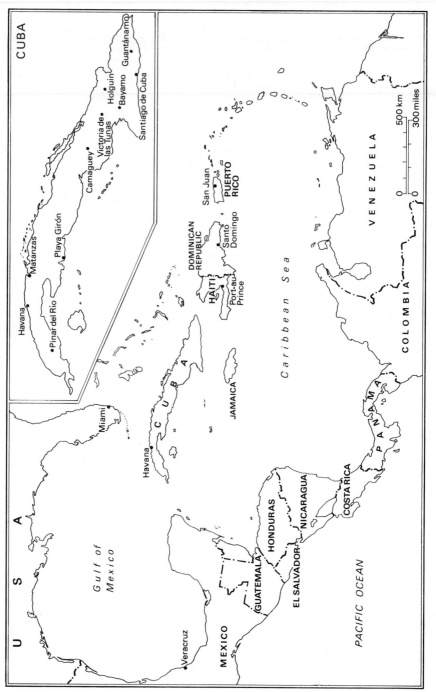

The Caribbean

9

CUBA, c. 1930–59

No part of Cuba escaped the ravages of the war with Spain that ended in 1898. From the eastern mountains across the central plains to the western valleys, the scene of desolation and devastation was the same. It was a brutal conflict in which the opposing armies seemed determined more to punish the land than prosecute the war, practising pillage of every kind for almost four years. More than 100,000 small farms, 3,000 livestock ranches and 700 coffee *fincas* were destroyed. Of the estimated 1,100 sugar mills registered in 1894, only 207 survived. Property-owners, urban and rural, were in debt and lacked either access to capital or sources of credit.

This devastation was neither unforeseen nor unplanned. In fact, it was the principal purpose for which Cubans, who understood well the political economy of colonialism, had taken up arms. It was indeed a war against property, and by 1898 separatist tactics had vindicated the goal of separatist strategy: Spain was on the brink of collapse. But the success of the Cuban military campaign did not produce the desired political results. Rather, it precipitated United States intervention, and at this point all the Cubans' plans went awry. They had thrown everything into the campaign against Spain. Victory over Spain left them exhausted, weak and vulnerable.

Armed intervention led to military occupation, at the end of which, in May 1902, the United States had effectively reduced Cuban independence to a mere formality. The Platt Amendment denied the new republic treaty-making authority, established limits on the national debt and sanctioned North American intervention for 'the maintenance of a government adequate for the protection of life, property and individual liberty'. The reciprocity treaty not only bound Cuba's principal export commodity, sugar, to a single market, the United States, but also opened key sectors of the Cuban economy – agriculture (especially sugar and tobacco), cattle-ranching, mining (especially iron), transportation (especially railways), utilities (gas, electricity, water, telephones) and banking – to foreign, mainly U.S., control.

By the beginning of the second decade of the twentieth century, whereas total British investments stood at $60 million, largely in telephones, railways, port works and sugar; French investments at $12 million, principally in railroads, banks and sugar; and German investments at $4.5 million, divided between factories and utilities; United States capital invested in Cuba exceeded $200 million. Under the reciprocity treaty preferential access to U.S. markets for Cuban agricultural products served to encourage Cuban dependency on sugar and, to a lesser extent, tobacco, and to increase foreign control over vital sectors of the economy. Reciprocity also discouraged economic diversification by promoting the consolidation of land from small units into the latifundia and concentration of ownership from local family to foreign corporation. And the effects of reciprocity were not confined to agriculture. The reduction of Cuban duties, in some instances as high as 40 per cent, opened the island to North American imports on highly favourable terms. The privileged access granted the U.S. manufacturers created a wholly inauspicious investment climate for Cuban capital. Even before 1903 the dearth of local capital and depressed economic conditions had combined to prevent development of national industry; after the reciprocity treaty prospects for local enterprise diminished further. North American manufactured goods saturated the Cuban market and hindered the development of local competition. Many firms could not compete with United States manufactures, and business failures increased.

Within a decade of the War of Independence the United States had become a pervasive presence in Cuba, totally dominating the economy, thoroughly penetrating the social fabric and fully controlling the political process. The ubiquity of this presence served to shape the essential character of the early republic.

Cuban politics acquired a distinctively distributive quality soon after independence. Because much of the national wealth rapidly passed into the hands of foreigners, political office guaranteed successful office-seekers and the retinue of their supporters access to the levers of resource and benefit allocation in the only enterprise wholly Cuban – government. Re-election violated the intra-elite protocol implicit in the electoral method of circulating public office. Monopolization of public office by one party, or one faction of a party, threatened to block access of others to the sinecures of state. Insofar as public administration under the republic served as a principal source of livelihood for the elites, elections institutionalized a process among power contenders by which participants shared, more or less equally, a guaranteed cyclical access to government. Indeed, so vital was the preservation of this system that the presidential succession precipitated armed protest in 1906, after the re-election of Tomás Estrada Palma, and again in 1917 against Mario G. Menocal.

Resistance to the re-election of President Gerardo Machado for a second term in 1928 came from the traditional Conservative and Popular parties, but also from within his own Liberal Party. In 1927, Carlos Mendieta broke with the party and established the Unión Nacionalista, openly opposed to presidential re-election. Other well-known party leaders, such as the disaffected Liberals Federico Laredo Bru and Roberto Méndez Peñate and the former Conservative president Mario G. Menocal, protested against re-electionism and fled into exile to organize opposition to Machado.

However, the challenge to the *machadato* did not originate principally from the established parties. New forces were stirring in Cuban society. By the 1920s the first republican-born generation of Cubans had reached political maturity and found the republic wanting. National disillusionment found expression first in the marketplace of ideas, in university reform, new literary and artistic currents, and fresh perspectives on history. Disillusionment gave way to disaffection as hopes for cultural regeneration fused with visions of political redemption. The political agenda expanded to include anti-imperialism, nationalism and social justice, but it was primarily against banality of national politics and the improbity of public officials that this generation directed its ire. In March 1923 radical intellectuals published a manifesto denouncing corruption in government. A month later the Junta de Renovación Nacional Cívica published a lengthy denunciation of graft, corruption and fraud. In August the veterans organization joined former officers of the old Liberation Army with dissident intellectuals to demand political and administrative reforms. Discontent spread to other sectors of society. In 1923, university students organized into the Federacíon Estudiantil Universitaria (FEU). Labour militancy increased as trade unions expanded at both provincial and national levels. In 1925, workers organized the Confederación Nacional Obrera de Cuba (CNOC), the first national labour organization. In that same year, the Cuban Communist Party (PCC) was founded.

Intellectuals, students and labour had pushed dissent beyond the limits of traditional partisan politics and into the realm of reform and revolution.

The very content of the national debate had changed. The republican generation was possessed of a peculiar redemptive mission, one that had as its goal the total regeneration of the republic – one, too, that challenged as much the assumptions upon which Machado governed as it did Machado's government.

Nevertheless, in 1927, through a combination of intimidation, coercion and bribery, Machado eventually secured the joint nomination of the traditional parties for a second term. *Cooperativismo,* as the arrangement became known, joined the Liberal, Conservative and Popular parties behind Machado's candidacy for re-election. More important, it ended all semblance of party independence and political competition, the traditional sources of anti-reelectionist violence. Later in 1927 Machado also secured congressional passage of a resolution amending the Constitution to extend the presidential term of office by two years. And in November 1928, unopposed as the *candidato único,* Machado won re-election to a new six-year term.

In many ways the re-election of Machado represented a collective response by the traditional political elites to the profound changes overtaking Cuban society. *Cooperativismo* was itself a necessary coalition among the embattled traditional parties designed to overcome the mounting challenge to the old order. For thirty years, the veterans of the nineteenth-century wars for independence had dominated the island's politics, bargaining among themselves political accommodations to ensure their continued pre-eminence. In 1928 this political community of interests found its logical conclusion in the *cooperativista* consensus. Indeed, *cooperativismo* promised to stabilize intra-elite politics at a time when the politicos were themselves under siege and facing the most serious challenge to their thirty-year rule of the republic.

The re-election of Machado in 1928 certainly served both to deepen opposition and give focus to dissent. But it was the world depression that accelerated political confrontation and intensified social conflict. Sugar production, the fulcrum upon which the entire Cuban economy balanced, dropped 60 per cent. In mid-1930 economic conditions deteriorated further when the United States enacted the Hawley–Smoot Tariff Act, a protectionist measure that increased duties on Cuban sugar. (The Cuban share of the U.S. market shrank from 49.4 per cent in 1930 to 25.3 per cent in 1933.) Sugar producers struggled to remain solvent by lowering wages and cutting production through labour lay-offs. The *zafra* was reduced to a sixty-two-day harvest, only two months' work for tens of thousands of sugar-workers. Some 250,000 heads of families, representing approximately 1 million people out of a total population of 3.9 million, found themselves totally unemployed. Those fortunate enough to escape total unemployment found temporary work difficult to come by and wages depressed. Pay for agricultural workers declined by 75 per cent, wages in the sugar zones falling as low as twenty cents a day. In some districts labourers received only food and lodging for their work. Wages for the urban proletariat decreased by 50 per cent as commercial, banking and manufacturing failures reached record proportions. In 1930 the government announced drastic salary cuts for all public employees except the armed forces, and the first of a series of redundancies in the state sector was imposed the following year. Members of the well-established middle class, particularly those professional groups that had traditionally found security and solvency in the civil service and public administration, were among the newest arrivals to augment the swelling ranks of the unemployed.

By 1930, as the full effects of the economic crisis reverberated across the island, virtually all sectors of Cuban society were at odds with the Machado government. In March 1930 a general strike organized by the outlawed CNOC and supported by 200,000 workers paralysed the island; in September a student anti-government protest resulted in violence and the closing of the university. As mass demonstrations spread, union membership expanded strikes halting production in key sectors of the economy including cigar-manufacturing, metallurgy, construction and textiles, in 1929 and 1930. The 1930 general strike ended only after fierce repression, arrests, torture and assassinations becoming commonplace. Increased repression did not, however, reduce resistance. On the contrary, opposition to Machado increased. A desultory warfare broke out in the countryside, the torching of canefields destroying millions of *arrobas* of cane. Armed bands operated throughout the interior, ambushing trains, cutting telephone and telegraph wires and attacking isolated Rural Guard posts. In November 1930, the government proclaimed a state of siege throughout the island. Army units in full combat dress assumed police functions in provincial cities and towns. Military supervisors displaced civilian governors in Pinar del Río, Matanzas, Las Villas, Camagüey and Oriente, and army tribunals superseded civilian courts. Constitutional guarantees were restored on 1 December but suspended again ten days later. Repression depended upon an extensive police apparatus: a secret police was organized – the Sección de Expertos, specialists in the method of torture – while the Partida de la

Porra served as a government death squad. Cuba assumed the appearance of an armed camp under a regime for which neutrality was suspect and the slightest criticism was subversive.

The organized opposition responded in kind, several groups taking up arms to challenge Machado. The ABC consisted of intellectuals, professionals and students, organized in clandestine cells and committed to creating conditions of revolution through systematic use of violence against the government. The Organización Celular Radical Revolucionaria (OCRR) also adopted a cellular structure and adopted armed struggle and sabotage as the means to overthrow Machado. In 1931 an ideological dispute within the Directorio Estudiantil Universitario (DEU) resulted in the formation of the Ala Izquierda Estudiantil (AIE) which, dedicated to the radical transformation of Cuban society, formed 'action squads' of urban guerrillas and carried the struggle into the streets. The PCC expanded its revolutionary activities as well as asserting leadership over key trade unions, most notably CNOC. In 1932, sugar-workers established the first national union, the Sindicato Nacional Obrero de la Industria Azucarera (SNOIA) while women's resistance groups, university professors, and normal-school teachers and students joined an underground network dedicated to armed struggle against Machado. By the early 1930s, the crisis was moving beyond a political settlement. As economic conditions deteriorated and social unrest spread, the struggle against Machado was changing daily into a movement seeking more to overturn a system rather than overthrow a president.

In 1933 Cuba quivered at the brink of revolution. Sixty per cent of the population lived at submarginal levels of under $300 in annual real income; another 30 per cent earned marginal wages between $300 and $600. Early in the year exiled opposition leaders organized into a revolutionary junta in New York and called for a national revolution to remove Machado. The Cuban ambassador to Washington acknowledged privately to the State Department that the beleaguered Machado government faced serious political trouble and appealed to the new Democratic administration for immediate U.S. support. Otherwise, he predicted somberly, 'chaos would result, the sort of chaos that might easily require the United States to intervene in a military way'.[1] However, Washington

---

[1] William Phillips, 'Memorandum of Conversation with Cuban Ambassador', 5 May 1933, File 550 S.S. Washington/415, General Records of the Department of State, Record Group 59, National Archives, Washington, D.C. (hereinafter cited as RG 59).

was unwilling to entertain the idea of armed intervention in 1933. Having committed his administration to a Latin American policy based on the notion of a 'good neighbour', Franklin Roosevelt was unwilling to inaugurate a new phase in hemispheric relations by sending troops to Cuba. Washington favoured instead a negotiated political settlement in which Machado would resign before the expiration of his term in 1935, thereby permitting a coalition of moderate political groups to form a provisional government.

Developments in Cuba concerned the United States in another way. The U.S. was also concerned by the fact that its grip over the Cuban economy was slipping. In the three decades since the signing of the reciprocity treaty, a series of developments had altered U.S.–Cuban trade patterns. The tariff law of 1927 launched Cuba on an import substitution program, increasing self-sufficiency in a variety of products formerly imported, including eggs, butter, lard, shoes, furniture and hosiery. U.S. exports to Cuba also suffered from increased foreign competition as the depression and the drop of Cuba's purchasing power combined to make the island a price market and opened the door to the importation of cheap commodities from Europe and Japan previously supplied by the United States on a quality basis.

The effects were substantial. Between 1923 and 1933, Cuban imports from the United States declined from $191 million to $22 million while Cuban exports to the United States decreased from $362 million to $57 million. The U.S. share in Cuban imports diminished from 74.3 per cent during the First World War to 66.7 per cent in 1922 and 61.8 per cent in 1927. By 1933 it had decreased to 53.5 per cent, and Cuba had dropped from sixth to sixteenth place as a customer for U.S. exports. The U.S. Department of Agriculture estimated that the loss of Cuban markets for foodstuffs alone meant the withdrawal of 817,267 acres from agricultural production in the United States. Exports to Cuba of raw materials and manufactured products other than foodstuffs dropped from $133 million in 1924 to $18 million in 1933.

The purpose of U.S. policy in Cuba, thus, was twofold: first, to end conditions of political instability and, second, to recover control over Cuban markets. To these ends the State Department appointed Sumner Welles as ambassador to Cuba. Welles' instructions directed him to offer the 'friendly mediations' of the United States for the purpose of securing a 'definite, detailed, and binding understanding' between the government and the opposition.[2] And early in June, Welles secured the agreement of the government parties and moderate opposition, including the ABC, OCRR and the Unión Nacionalista, to participate in discussion.

Through the early summer the actual purpose of Welles' mission to Havana remained unknown and undisclosed. Methodically and patiently, Welles maneouvred the mediations towards the twin objectives of persuading Machado to resign and thus bring the Cuban political crisis to a peaceful conclusion. Yet these were only the means. The objective was to end the revolutionary threat to the institutional structures upon which Cuban elites ruled, and upon which U.S. hegemony rested, and to establish a government in Cuba that would renegotiate a new reciprocity treaty, thereby restoring North American primacy in Cuban's foreign commerce. 'The negotiation at this time of a reciprocal trade agreement with Cuba . . . ', Wells wrote from Havana, 'will not only revivify Cuba but will give us practical control of a market we have been steadily losing for the past ten years not only for our manufactured products but for our agricultural exports'.[3]

Machado had outlived his usefulness. The order and stability which he had provided during his first term, and which had won Washington's support for his re-election, had collapsed. The anti-Machado struggle had stepped beyond the bounds of conventional political competition and generalized into a revolutionary situation. After nearly five years of sustained civil strife it had become apparent that Machado could not restore order. His continued presence was now the greatest single obstacle to the restoration of order and stability. In late July, Welles informed the unsuspecting President that a satisfactory solution to the crisis required him to shorten his term by one year. Machado responded first with incredulity and then with rage. He convened a special session of Congress to repudiate the proposed settlement, vowing to remain in power through his full term of office.

In the days that followed, Welles worked to undermine Machado's domestic support as a means of forcing him into early retirement. If Machado fell solely through North American pressure, the traditional political parties, discredited by their collaboration with Machado, faced the prospect of drastic reorganization, at best, or complete suppression — as many opposition factions demanded. The success of an internal revolt

[2] Cordell Hull to Sumner Welles, 1 May 1933, U.S. Department of State, *Foreign Relations of the United States, 1933*, 5 vols. (Washington, D.C. 1941), 5:285.
[3] Sumner Welles to Cordell Hull, 13 May, 1933, 833.00/3512, DS/RG 59.

against the government similarly threatened the old party structure with extinction by subjecting Machado supporters to political reprisals from the regime's opponents. Support for the ambassador's recommendations, however, carried some assurances that the parties would survive the *machadato*. In early August, therefore, the leaders of the Liberal, Conservative and Popular parties endorsed the mediator's proposals and introduced in Congress legislation designed to expedite Machado's departure.

Welles moved next against the diplomatic underpinnings of the Cuban government and threatened Machado with the withdrawal of North American support. He insisted that under the terms of the Platt Amendment, Machado had simply failed to maintain a government adequate for the protection of life, property and individual liberty. The continuation of these conditions, Welles warned Machado, would require U.S. intervention. To Washington, Welles recommended the withdrawal of diplomatic recognition if, at the end of a reasonable period, Machado continued to resist early retirement. He assured the State Department that this would obviate the necessity of an armed intervention by making it impossible for Machado to survive in power much longer.

In mid-summer the struggle between the U.S. ambassador and the Cuban President assumed a new urgency. On 25 July bus drivers in Havana organized a strike in protest against a new government tax. Within a week a clash between the protesting drivers and the police resulted in sympathy strikes among taxi drivers, streetcar operators and truck drivers. The transportation strike in the capital spread to other sectors and within days all movement of people and goods came to a halt. By the end of the first week of August, the general strike had acquired the full proportions of a revolutionary offensive and Welles and Machado had acquired a much more formidable adversary that threatened to sweep aside both the regime of Machado and U.S. hegemony.

Machado and Welles recognized the gravity of the strike and turned immediately to defuse the deepening revolutionary situation. Each took extraordinary steps to end the strike. Machado conferred with the leadership of the PCC and CNOC, offering the party legality and the CNOC recognition in exchange for their support in ending the strike. It was an opportunity seized by the Communist Party. Under the terms of the agreement, the government released labour leaders and Communists from prison and proclaimed the legality of the PCC upon the end of the strike. The party leadership, in return, issued return-to-work orders. In fact, however, both Machado and the PCC misjudged conditions. The government believed the party controlled the strike; the PCC believed the government to be stronger than it was. But the strike had evolved beyond the Communist control and the government was beyond salvation.

For Welles, Machado's departure could no longer wait until May 1934, the date set for the President's early retirement. His resignation was required immediately. The ambassador would later recall that the 'ominous signs provided by a paralyzing strike' necessitated a 'radical solution' to the Cuban problem to 'forestall the cataclysm which otherwise was inevitable'.[4] On 11 August, Welles reported a confidential talk with Secretary of War and former army chief General Alberto Herrera in which he offered Herrera the presidency in exchange for his support in a quick resolution of the crisis. This arrangement was a direct invitation to the armed forces to impose a political settlement.

The army was already predisposed to act. Indeed, the armed forces had a considerable stake in the outcome of the political conflict. The mediations had not inspired confidence within the high command while rising anti-militarism among the opposition had contributed to a general restlessness among the officer corps. Opposition groups used the negotiations as a forum to denounce the military, the ABC advocating a reduction in the size of the military establishment and restrictions on army authority. One report circulating throughout Havana suggested that the opposition planned to reduce the army from 12,000 to 3,000 officers and men. Business and professional groups, troubled by the excessive taxation required to support the military, similarly advocated reductions in the army. As a result, army intervention in August 1933 was not unconditional. The armed forces acted only after having secured in advance assurances from opposition leaders, to which Welles subscribed, that the subsequent government would respect the integrity of the military. A 'strictly confidential' memorandum pledged that the armed forces would be maintained without any alteration until 20 May 1935, the scheduled expiration of Machado's second term. The proviso further stipulated that 'members of the said armed forces . . . cannot be removed from their positions nor punished' in any way inconsistent with the existing laws.[5]

On 12 August, the army demanded and secured Machado's resignation.

---

[4] Sumner Welles, *Two Years of the 'Good Neighbor' Policy,* Department of State, Latin American Series No. 11 (Washington, D.C., 1935), pp. 8–9.

[5] 'Memorandum', 11 August 1933, enclosure in Orestes Ferrara to Sumner Welles, 12 August 1933, File (1933) 800, U.S. Embassy, Cuba, Correspondence, Record Group 84, Records of the Foreign Service Posts of the United States, U.S. National Archives, Washington, D.C.

Herrera's succession was, however, resisted on grounds that the Secretary of War was too closely identified with the fallen president. Undeterred, Welles continued to pursue an orderly and constitutional resolution of the crisis. All *machadista* cabinet members except Herrera resigned. Herrera then served as provisional president only long enough to appoint as Secretary of State Carlos Manuel de Céspedes, who was something of a political non-entity – or 'statesman', as he loftily described himself – an inoffensive compromise candidate who lacked affiliation with any political party or political tendency. Herrera then resigned to permit Céspedes to succeed as president.

The Céspedes government set in sharp relief the contradictions generated during the *machadato*. The Welles mediations had served to legitimize the formerly outlawed anti-Machado groups and guarantee their inclusion in the new government. On the other hand, the timely desertion of the dictator by the former government parties guaranteed them a political role in post-Machado Cuba. The distribution of government portfolios to representatives of such diverse factors as the ABC, the Liberal Party, the Unión Nacionalista, the Conservative Party, the OCRR and the Partido Popular, previously implacable adversaries, served to institutionalize the unresolved disputes of the *machadato*.

The difficulties confronting the new government were not, however, confined to internal contradictions. The departure of Machado had produced an immediate halt to government repression, and the change of governments clearly reduced national tensions and eased mounting revolutionary pressures. But Cuba remained in the throes of the depression, and the social and economic dislocations that had plunged the *machadato* into crisis continued unabated after 12 August. Strikes persisted as the new mood of labour militancy extended across the island. The organizations that had earlier boycotted the mediations – principally those sectors of the anti-Machado opposition that aspired to something more than simply a change of presidents – found the Céspedes solution wholly unsatisfactory. Many of these groups, including the two student organizations, the DEU and the AIE, and the Communist Party, had toiled too long in the pursuit of revolution to settle for a palace coup as the denouement of their political labour.

There were other problems for Céspedes. Public order had broken down. The rioting produced by Machado's flight continued intermittently through August, the mobs dispensing revolutionary justice to suspected *machadista* officials. Army and police authorities, formerly the object of popular enmity, now moved to control civilian excesses only tentatively, if at all. Many officers feared that strict enforcement of order under Céspedes would serve only to revive anti-army sentiment among those former opposition groups now in power. This military morale was in any case at a low level. Senior officers lived in fear of arrest and reprisals for their part in the *machadato* while junior officers eagerly awaited the promotions certain to follow the purge of *machadista* commanders. Non-commissioned officers and enlisted men grew increasingly restive as rumours foretold of impending pay cuts and troop reductions.

The end of the Céspedes government came from a most improbable and unexpected source. On the evening of 3 September sergeants, corporals and enlisted men of Camp Columbia in Havana met to discuss their grievances, the deliberations ending with the preparation of a list of demands to be submitted to the commanding officers. The officers on duty, however, declined to discuss the demands of the aroused soldiery and instead retired from the army post. Suddenly, and unexpectedly, the troops found themselves in control of Camp Columbia and in mutiny. The NCO protesters, under the leadership of Sergeant Fulgencio Batista, exhorted the troops to hold the post until the army command agreed to review their demands.

The soldiers' protest immediately received support from anti-government groups. In the early hours of 4 September, student leaders of the DEU arrived at Camp Columbia and persuaded the sergeants to expand the movement. Civilian intervention changed the nature of the NCO protest and transformed a mutiny into a putsch. The 'sergeants' revolt', as the mutiny later became known, was originally possessed of less ambitious objectives. The sergeants planned a demonstration only to protest against service conditions, specifically poor pay, inadequate housing facilities and rumoured cuts in the enlisted ranks – not the ouster of the officer corps or the overthrow of Céspedes. Having unexpectedly found themselves in a state of mutiny, and effectively in rebellion against the government, there was little enthusiasm to return to the barracks under the existing regime. The students offered an alternative. It was a coalition of convenience, not without flaw, but one that offered rebellious troops absolution and dissident civilians political power. Out of this tentative civil–military consensus emerged a revolutionary junta composed of Ramón Grau San Martín, Porfirio Franca, Guillermo Portela, José Irizarri and Sergio Carbó.

The transfer of the revolutionary junta from the Camp Columbia barracks to the presidential palace served to shift the locus of authority in Cuba. Power passed to those forces long situated at the fringes of the republican polity – radicals and nationalists – who saw themselves as the agents of a historical imperative as well as the instruments of a popular mandate. On the morning of 5 September, a political manifesto announced the establishment of a new Provisional Revolutionary Government and proclaimed the affirmation of national sovereignty, the establishment of a modern democracy and the 'march toward the creation of a new Cuba'.

The forces of old Cuba responded with more than indignation to the September usurpation. The established government parties that earlier had deserted Machado as a means to survive the discredited regime once again faced persecution and extinction. So too did the ousted *machadista* army officers who, for all their efforts to secure immunity from post-Machado reprisals, now found themselves vulnerable to prosecution and imprisonment. Representatives of business and commercial sectors recoiled in horror at the change of governments and openly predicted the collapse of the Cuban economy. Nor was it only old Cuba which opposed the revolutionary junta. New political groups, including the ABC and the OCRR, organizations that previously had paid dearly to attain political power in post-Machado Cuba, faced an abrupt and inglorious end to their debut in national politics. A government composed of radical students and created by mutinous soldiers had the immediate effect of uniting in opposition those political forces which had earlier been rivals in power.

The provisional government faced its most formidable adversary in the person of Sumner Welles, the U.S. ambassador. The coup had undermined constitutional legality and overthrown conservative authority, both of which had been arduously defended by Welles. The ambassador was neither slow to react nor unequivocal in his response. His immediate recourse was to recommend, unsuccessfully, U.S. military intervention in order to restore Céspedes to power. Welles deliberately characterized the new government in terms calculated to arouse suspicion and provoke opposition in Washington. The army had fallen under 'ultra-radical control', Welles cabled Washington, and the government was 'frankly communistic'. Irizarri was characterized as a 'radical of the extreme type' while Grau and Portela were described as 'extreme radicals'.[6]

---

[6] Sumner Welles to Secretary of State, 5 September 1933, 837.00/3757, RG 59, and 'Memorandum of Telephone Conversation Between Secretary of State Hull and Welles', 5 September 1933, 837.00/3800, RG 59.

Early opposition to the provisional government produced a number of immediate changes. In mid-September, the junta dissolved in favor of a more traditional executive form of government under Ramón Grau San Martín. Fear that the combination of political intrigue and disarray in the army command would result in the collapse of public order prompted the government to promote Fulgencio Batista to the rank of colonel and appoint him as army chief. He was instructed to commission new officers in sufficient numbers to maintain stability in the armed forces. In early October, the government proclaimed the former officers deserters and ordered their arrest, thereby paving the way for a total reorganization of the army under Batista. This certainly strengthened the position of the provisional government. But the purge of the old officer corps was also a political triumph for the army and a personal victory for Fulgencio Batista. And this deepened the contradictions within the provisional government. Students and soldiers remained inextricably bound together in the original transgression against constituted authority, and they shared mutual interests in the fortune of the provisional government, if only because they shared a common fate if it failed. Nevertheless, the gap between them widened after 4 September. The students carried Cuba into the realm of experimental government, not least because this was the first administration of the republic not formed with Washington's support. Reform proved to be intoxicating, and for one hundred days the students devoted themselves with exalted purposefulness to the task of transforming the country. Under the injunction of 'Cuba for Cubans', the new government proceeded to enact reforms laws at a dizzying pace, committing itself to economic reconstruction, social change and political reorganization. The new government abrogated the Platt Amendment and dissolved all the *machadista* parties. Utility rates were lowered by 40 per cent and interest rates reduced. Women received the vote and the university secured autonomy. In labour matters, government reforms included minimum wages for cane-cutters, compulsory labour arbitration, an eight-hour day, workers' compensation, the establishment of a Ministry of Labour, and a Nationalization of Labour decree requiring that 50 per cent of all employees in industry, commerce and agriculture be Cuban nationals. In agricultural affairs, the government sponsored the creation of *colono* associations, guaranteed peasants permanent right over land they occupied and inaugurated a program of agrarian reform.

As the students continued to advance on their 'march to create a new Cuba', the army became an increasingly reluctant escort. Military support of the provisional government was always more an expression of self-interest than a function of solidarity. This was the government that had sanctioned the sergeants' sedition and validated hundreds of new commissions, a government from which the new army command derived its legitimacy. But it was also true that the new leaders of the army were anxious for an immediate political settlement, if for no other reason than to institutionalize their recent gains. The army command saw little to be gained by social experimentation except a prolongation of uncertainty. Indeed, many *septembrista* commanders perceived the student projects as hazardous ventures, ill-conceived programs of a government upon whose solvency they depended to legitimize ill-gotten commissions.

These fears were skillfully exploited by Welles. By mid-autumn, he shifted his attention away from promoting unity among anti-government factions to encouraging division among its supporters. An astute observer of Cuban politics, Welles was well aware of the deepening contradictions within the provisional government. The sergeants' revolt, Welles reminded Washington, did 'not take place in order to place Grau San Martín in power'. He added that the 'divergence between the Army and civilian elements in the government is fast becoming daily more marked' and as Batista's influence grew 'the power of the students and Grau San Martín diminished'.[7] Another political coalition, Welles reasoned, one capable of constituting itself into legitimate government and willing to ratify the *septembrista* army command, could persuade Batista to abandon the government that had originally conferred military legitimacy on an army mutiny.

For the second time in as many months, Welles appealed directly to the army to overturn a government that had fallen into North American disfavour. On 4 October, days after the arrest of the former officers, the ambassador reported having had a 'protracted and very frank discussion' with Batista. Now characterizing Batista as the 'only individual in Cuba today who represented authority', Welles informed the army chief that he had earned the support of 'the very great majority of the commercial and financial interests in Cuba who are looking for protection and who could only find such protection in himself'. Political factions that only weeks earlier had openly opposed him, Welles explained, were now 'in accord that his control of the Army as chief of staff should be continued as the only possible solution and were willing to support him in that capacity'.

---

[7] Sumner Welles to Secretary of State, 5 October 1933, 837.00/4131, RG 59.

However, the only obstacle to an equitable arrangement, and presumably recognition and a return to normality, the ambassador suggested, 'was the unpatriotic and futile obstinacy of a small group of young men who should be studying in the university instead of playing politics and of a few individuals who had joined with them for selfish motives'. In a thinly veiled warning, Welles had reminded Batista of the tenuous position in which affiliation with the government placed him: 'should the present government go down in disaster, that disaster would necessarily inextricably involve not only himself but the safety of the Republic, which he had publicly pledged himself to maintain'.[8]

Welles' comments could not have been interpreted by Batista in any other fashion than an invitation to create a new government. There meetings served also to underscore the uncertainty of Batista's position. Non-recognition continued to encourage opposition and resistance. There remained a danger that a revolt would topple the provisional government and lead to the nullification of the *septembrista* army command and arrest of the former sergeants. Nor had prospects of a U.S. military intervention entirely passed, further raising the possibility that the United States would return Céspedes to power. Batista's authority within the armed forces was also threatened by his continued support of a government diplomatically opposed abroad and politically isolated at home. His command over the army rested on the sanction of a provisional government facing an uncertain future. Batista was simply one of four hundred recently promoted non-commissioned officers whose rank and appointment depended on a political settlement in Havana compatible with – or at least not hostile to – the new army hierarchy. As long as the *septembrista* officers remained identified with a government lacking legitimacy and deprived of the authority to underwrite permanently the promotions of 4 September, they risked sharing the ultimate fate of a regime opposed at home and abroad. Batista's own position within the army depended on his ability to legitimize the new commissions through a political settlement satisfactory to organized political and economic groups and Washington.

The end was not long in coming. In December, Welles reported with some satisfaction that Batista was actively seeking a change in government owing to his apprehension of a conspiracy within the army, the persistence of anti-government intrigue and fear of a North American intervention. In

[8] Ibid.

January 1934, Batista withdrew army support from Grau and backed the old disaffected Liberal politician, Carlos Mendieta. Within five days, the United States recognized Mendieta. Supported diplomatically abroad and with established political backing at home, the new government moved immediately to ratify the new army commissions. Decree Number 408 formally dissolved the old National Army and proclaimed in its place the newly organized Constitutional Army. The new army was to consist of all officers, non-commissioned officers and enlisted men on active duty at the time the decree was promulgated.

The forces of change released during the *machadato* did not abate with the passing of the Grau government. On the contrary, they found new forms of expression. The ancien regime had certainly found renewed life in new army chief Batista and old Liberal leader Mendieta, but not without renewed challenge. Most immediately, the reform program of the short-lived provisional government acquired institutional vitality with the organization in 1934 of the Partido Revolucionario Cubano (PRC/Auténtico) while, under the leadership of Antonio Guiteras, formerly Grau's minister of government, radicals formed a clandestine revolutionary organization, Joven Cuba. Eschewing electoral politics, Joven Cuba adopted armed struggle as the principal means to combat the Batista–Mendieta government. Assassination, bombings and sabotage again became the dominant mode of political opposition. Student opposition resumed with the reopening of the University of Havana in 1934. Anti-government demonstrations and labour protests once again became commonplace. Between 1934 and 1935 more than one hundred strikes flared up across the island.

In March 1935 momentum for revolutionary change assumed formidable proportions when an anti-government general strike plunged the island into crisis. Unlike August 1933, however, the government was neither willing to negotiate with labour nor reluctant to persecute participants. Proclamation of martial law announced a reign of terror that lasted through late spring. Strike leaders were arrested, many were tortured and assassinated, others fled into exile. Unions were outlawed and the university was occupied. In the weeks that followed military firing squads executed civilian dissidents. In May 1935 the army killed Antonio Guiteras.

The 1935 general strike was the last revolutionary surge of the republican generation. It collapsed after only a few days but its effects lasted through the decade. Most immediately, the severity of the military repression caused dissension in and then the dissolution of the ruling coalition. By the end of March, Mendieta found his support reduced to his own faction in the Unión Nacionalista and the military. Within months, he too, resigned. In a very real sense then, the strike achieved its desired effect but did not accomplish its principal objective. The Mendieta government did indeed collapse but in so doing created a political vacuum filled by Batista and the armed forces. Virtually every branch of government passed under army control. Military supervisors replaced provincial and municipal officials, the army command purging striking civil servants and establishing control over every division of public administration. The army emerged as the most important source of patronage and public employment. Batista was now the single most dominant political force on the island.

Batista's prestige increased throughout the 1930s as he restored order and stability. Washington found in the Pax Batistiana sufficient cause to continue diplomatic support for the dictator's puppet presidents and shadow governments: José A. Barnet (1935–6), Miguel Mariano Gómez (1936), and Federico Laredo Bru (1936–40). Nor did Batista's opponents of the 1930s recover. The tempest of the decade had blown itself out. Many of the most prominent opponents of the Batista–Mendieta regime had lost their lives in 1935. Others sought personal security in exile or departed Cuba to carry the banner of revolution to other lands, most notably Spain. Revolutionary groups had been shattered and crushed. When the university reopened in 1937 classes resumed uneventfully. The PRC/Auténtico turned to electoral politics and devoted itself to the arduous work of constructing a new party infrastructure and developing grassroots support. Moreover, by the end of the decade, the Communisty Party had made peace with Batista. After 1938, the party adopted a reformist and openly collaborationist posture, consolidating control over the trade unions and gaining legal status in exchange for political support of the Batista-backed government. Its newspaper was published and distributed publicly, and by the late 1930s the party appeared on the electoral rolls. Communist control over the trade-union movement expanded, culminating in 1939 with the establishment of the Confederación de Trabajadores Cubanos (CTC).

In some measure the restoration of social tranquillity was due to the programs pursued by the new army command. Certainly Batista transformed the Cuban army into an effective apparatus of repression. At the same time, however, the military leadership practised graft and corruption on a scale previously unknown in Cuba although Batista himself was interested in more than either political power or personal wealth. He committed the armed forces to a wide range of social programmes, starting in 1937 with the inauguration of the civic-military school system, under which sergeants served as schoolmasters throughout the countryside. These *misiones educativas,* designed to disseminate information concerning agriculture, hygiene and nutrition to rural communities, inaugurated a rudimentary education network in the interior. The army operated a thousand schools in which day sessions were devoted to the education of children and evenings to adults. By the late 1930s the army command had created an extensive military bureaucracy assigned exclusively to the administration of social programmes. A Three Year Plan was inaugurated to reform agriculture, education, public health and housing. One important effort of this was to provide the programmatic basis for Batista's direct entry into national politics at the end of the decade.

Economic conditions improved through the 1930s. Gradually Cuban sugar recovered a larger share of the U.S. market, although it would never again attain the prominence it enjoyed during the late 1910s and early 1920s. Under the terms of the Jones–Costigan Act of 1934 the United States lowered the protectionist tariffs on sugar imports, substituting quotas for tariff protection as the means to aid domestic sugar producers. The law empowered the U.S. Secretary of Agriculture to determine the annual sugar needs of the nation, whereupon all sugar-producing regions, domestic and foreign, would receive a quota of the total, which was based on the participation of sugar producers in the U.S. market for the years 1931–3. The selection of these years was unfortunate for Cuban producers, for it was precisely this period – the years of Hawley Smoot – in which the Cuban share of the U.S. market was the smallest. Nevertheless, the Cuban participation in the U.S. market increased slightly from 25.4 per cent in 1933 to 31.4 per cent in 1937. These were years, moreover, in which Cuban overall sugar production expanded, and the value of the expanded production increased. Between 1933 and 1938, Cuban sugar output increased from 1.9 million tons to 2.9 million tons, with the corresponding value increasing from 53.7 million pesos to 120.2 million pesos.

This slow economic revival, no less than the slight restoration of the Cuban share of the U.S. market, was not without a price. Under the terms of the new 1934 reciprocity treaty negotiated by the Mendieta government, Cuba secured a guaranteed market for its agricultural exports in return for tariff reductions to a large variety of commodity lines and the reduction of internal taxes on U.S. products. Concessions granted by the United States covered thirty-five articles; Cuban concessions affected four hundred items. Tariff reductions granted to Cuban items ranged from 20 per cent to 50 per cent; tariff concessions to U.S. products ranged from 20 per cent to 60 per cent. The new agreement also specified that the enumerated tariff schedule could not be altered as a result of changing money and currency values.

The new treaty certainly contributed to Cuban revival since the country's principal export, sugar, was the item most favored by the 1934 agreement. The U.S. tariff on Cuban raw sugar was reduced from $1.50 to 90 cents per pound. Reductions were also made on tobacco leaf as well as cigars and cigarettes, honey, fish, products, citrus, pineapples and other agricultural goods. At the same time, however, the 1934 treaty dealt a severe blow to Cuban efforts at economic diversification. Scores of agricultural and manufacturing enterprises, many of which had arisen in the aftermath of the 1927 customs-tariff law, were adversely affected. More broadly, the new treaty allowed U.S. trade adjustment to changing market conditions in Cuba, and ultimately re-established U.S. primacy in the Cuban economy. Cuba was again linked closely to the United States, thereby returning the island to the patterns of pre-depression dependency. The total value of North American imports increased from $22.6 million in 1933 to $81 million in 1940; the U.S. portion of Cuban imports for the same period increased from 53.5 per cent to 76.6 per cent.

The renegotiation of the reciprocity treaty was accompanied by the renegotiation of the Permanent Treaty, the legal form of the Platt Amendment. With the exception of provisions for United States use of the Guantánamo naval station, the long-standing affrontery to Cuban national sensibilities was removed. Henceforth, U.S.-Cuban relations would be conducted formally between 'independent though friendly states'.

By the end of the decade, the passing of the economic crisis and the return of political stability, particularly with acceptance of electoral politics by the Auténticos and the Communist Party, created a climate auspicious for constitutional reform. Batista's political position was firmly established and could only be enhanced by his identifying himself with the demands for reform. Indeed many of the measures enacted by the ill-starred Grau government continued to enjoy considerable national popularity. Furthermore, the old Constitution of 1901 remained permanently stigmatized in Cuba since it contained as an organic part the odious Platt Amendment. Hence, a new constitution promised to make a break with the past and institutionalize the gains of post-Machado Cuba.

A constituent assembly representing the full spectrum of political affiliation, from old *machadistas* to the PRC and Communists, convened in 1939 to draft a new constitution. It provided the forum for renewed debate over virtually all the key issues of republican politics. Nor did political alignments determine the direction of the debates. The pro-government coalition included the discredited Liberals and moribund Unión Nacionalista as well as the Communist Party. The opposition was led by the Auténticos and included the ABC and supporters of former president Miguel Mariano Gómez. Thus, ideology tended to transcend partisan affiliation, left-liberal delegates frequently joining forces to form voting majorities against conservatives, without regard to affiliation with government or opposition blocs. The net result was the promulgation in 1940 of a remarkably progressive constitution which provided for the use of referendum, universal suffrage and free elections and which sanctioned a wide range of political and civil liberties. The charter's social provisions included maximum hours and minimum wages, pensions, workers' compensation, the right to strike and state guarantees against unemployment.

For all its enlightened clauses, the Constitution of 1940 remained substantially a statement of goals, an agenda for future achievement. The absence of provisions for enforcement meant that the new Constitution would remain largely unrealized. At the same time, it soon occupied a place of central importance in national politics since it served alternately as the banner through which to mobilize political support and the standard by which to measure political performance. Many of the objectives of the 1930s found vindication in the new Constitution, which also provided the foundations for legitimacy and consensus politics for the next twelve years. Cuban politics would henceforth turn on partisan promises to interpret most faithfully and implement most vigorously the principal clauses of the Constitution.

The promulgation of the new constitution also set the stage for the celebration of presidential elections in 1940. Batista stepped out of uniform and Grau San Martín returned from exile to challenge his old rival. The campaign was vigorously waged, and the election was certainly among the most honest in the nearly four decades at the republic's history. Batista secured more than 800,000 votes to Grau's 575,000.

The Batista presidency (1940–44) had several salutary effects. Most immediately, it ended the anomalous situation whereby effective political power was transferred from constitutional civil authority to the army chief of staff. The 1940 election served to reinvest the constitutional office of the presidency with the power and prestige that had accrued to Batista personally. The demands on Batista the president were no longer the same as the demands on Batista the army chief. He had acquired a larger constituency and accumulated debts to the political coalition that had carried him into office. Batista now presided over the return of patronage and political appointment to the presidential palace. In early 1941 custom-houses, long a source of military graft, were transferred to the Ministry of the Treasury. Army-sponsored education projects passed under the authority of the Ministry of Education. Supervision over lighthouses, maritime police, merchant marine and the postal system returned to appropriate government ministries.

These developments came as a rude jolt to the old *septembrista* command, long accustomed to the exercise of more or less unchecked authority. Many officers viewed the Batista presidency with great expectation, as a logical conclusion to a decade of army pre-eminence. The transfer of army perquisites to civil authority, therefore, quickly aroused the ire of the senior *septembrista* officers and military confidence in Batista declined. Friction between Camp Columbia and the presidential palace increased, and in early 1941 erupted into a short-lived revolt of senior officers. The collapse of the army plot raised presidential authority to a new high. Scores of *septembrista* officers was retired; others received new assignments abroad. A year later the size of the army was reduced and budget allocations cut. By the end of his term, Batista had restored constitutional balance of power and re-established civilian control over the armed forces.

Batista had also the good fortune of serving as a wartime president. Cuba's entry into the war in December 1941 served to facilitate trade agreements and loan and credit programs with the United States. The decline of sugar production in war-torn Asia and Europe spurred Cuban producers. Between 1940 and 1944 the Cuban crop increased from 2.7 million tons to 4.2 million tons, the largest harvest since 1930. The value of Cuban raw sugar production for the same period also increased, from 110 million pesos to 251 million pesos. Cuba was also the beneficiary of several important trade deals with the United States. In 1941 both countries signed a lend-lease agreement whereby Cuba received arms shipments in exchange for U.S. use of Cuban military facilities. In the same year, the United States agreed to purchase the full 1942 sugar crop at 2.65 cents per pound. A second agreement similarly disposed of the 1943 crop. With the continued revival of sugar production, the economy moved out of a state of lethargy, public works programmes expanded and prosperity returned.

The war was not an unmixed blessing. Prices increased and shortages of all kinds became commonplace. The lack of shipping and risks of transporting goods across the Atlantic severely restricted Cuban trade with Europe. Cuban cigar-manufacturers lost the luxury markets of Europe, and no amount of increase in the export of tobacco leaf to the United States could compensate for this. Tourism registered a marked decrease, the number of travellers falling from 127,000 in 1940 to 12,000 in 1943. As a result, there was sufficient dissatisfaction to generate a lively political debate in 1944, when presidential elections was scheduled. The government candidate, Carlos Saladrigas, campaigned with the active support of Batista. He was opposed by Ramón Grau San Martín in a spirited campaign with Saladrigas extolling the Batista administration and Grau recalling nostalgically his one hundred days of power in 1933. Indeed, the mystique of Grau as well as the appeal of the Auténticos was primarily derived from those heady and exalted days of 1933. In 1944, Grau promised more of the same, and an expectant electorate responded. In the June poll Grau obtained more than one million votes, sweeping five out of six provinces, losing only Pinar del Río. After more than a decade of unsuccessful bids for political power, Grau San Martín and the Auténticos had finally won a presidential election.

The Auténtico victory raised enormous popular expectations in the reform program that had served as both the legacy and promise of the PRC. However, neither the Grau government (1944–48) nor his successor Carlos Prío Socarrás (1948–52) was able to meet Cuban expectations. The Auténticos had spent the better part of their political lives as victims of persecution, imprisonment and forced exile. From the earliest political stirrings against Machado in the 1920s, through the revolutionary tumult of the 1930s and the disappointing electoral set-backs of the early 1940s, the first republican-born generation had been banished to a political wilderness. Their debut in Cuban politics had been as inglorious as it was impoverishing. By the mid-1940s, idealism had given way to cynicism, and public office no longer offered the opportunity for collective improvement as much as it provided the occasion for individual enrichment. Government fell under a siege of new hungry office-seekers, and their appetite was voracious. For the first time, Auténticos acquired control over the disposal of lucrative posts and privileges. Embezzlement, graft, corruption and malfeasance of public office permeated every branch of national, provincial and municipal government. Political competition became a fierce struggle to win positions of wealth. Politics passed under the control of party thugs, and a new word entered the Cuban political lexicon: *gangsterismo*. Violence and terror became extensions of party politics and the hallmark of Auténtico rule.

The number of persons on the government payroll more than doubled in size, from 60,000 in 1943 to 131,000 in 1949. By 1950, some 186,000 persons, 11 per cent of the work force, occupied active public positions at national, provincial and municipal levels of government; another 30,000 retired employees were on the state payrolls. An estimated 80 per cent of the 1950 budget was used to pay the salaries of public officials. Pensions accounted for another 8 per cent of national expenditures. The Auténticos responded to their electoral success with considerable uncertainty, fearful that their tenure would be brief and their rule temporary. These circumstances served to distinguish PRC corruption from the practices of its predecessor, emphasis being given to immediate returns and spectacular graft. Grau was accused of having embezzled $174 million. The outgoing Minister of Education in 1948 was believed to have stolen $20 million. The Minister of Finance in the Prío government was accused of misappropriating millions of old bank notes scheduled for destruction.

That these conditions prevailed, and indeed so permeated the institutional fabric of the republic during the Auténtico years, was in no small way a result of the post-war prosperity enjoyed by the Cuban economy. The economies of sugar-cane producers in Asia and beet-growers in Europe were in ruin. During World War II world sugar production declined by almost 60 per cent, from a combined cane and beet production of 28.6 million tons in 1940 to 18.1 million tons, and it was not until 1950 that world production overtook pre-war levels. As world production fell and prices rose the opportunities for Cuban producers were palpable. This boom never quite reached the proportions of the 'dance of the millions' following the First World War, but it certainly produced a level of prosperity not known since those years. Between 1943 and 1948, Cuban sugar production increased almost 50 per cent, from 2.8 million tons to 5.8 million tons. By 1948, sugar had come to constitute a high of 90 per cent of the island's total export value.

Good times came to Cuba in dramatic form. Sugar exports accounted for a nearly 40 per cent increase in national income between 1939 and 1947. Record sugar exports and simultaneous import scarcities caused by the war produced a large balance-of-payments surplus, averaging more than $120 million annually between 1943 and 1947. Domestic industrial and commercial activity increased over the decade while government revenues from taxation rose from $75.7 million in fiscal year 1937–8 to $244.3 million in 1949–50. Food prices increased almost threefold between 1939 and 1948 and the cost of living rose more than twofold. Inflation would have been more acute if it had not been for the wartime import scarcities and the willingness of many individuals and institutions to keep the better part of the savings in idle balances. The money supply increased 500 per cent between 1939 and 1950 while the cost of living rose only 145 per cent. Over roughly the same period the dollar, gold and silver holdings of the national treasury rose from $25 million to $402 million; the net balance abroad from $6 million to more than $200 million; and the public's dollar holding from $14 million to $205 million.

Post-war economic opportunities were squandered not only by corruption and graft but also by mismanagement and miscalculation. Few structural changes were made in the economy, the chronic problems of unemployment–under-employment and a weak agrarian order remaining unaltered. The economy began to decline by the late 1940s, and only a temporary reprieve provided by a rise in the price of sugar occasioned by the Korean War delayed the inevitable crisis. The problem of inflation increased and capital generated by the post-war prosperity war either invested abroad or mismanaged at home. 'Much of the savings of Cubans', the International Bank for Reconstruction and Development reported of these years, 'has gone abroad, been hoarded or used for real estate construction and for speculation'.[9] Between 1946 and 1952 the Cuban gross fixed investment as a percentage of gross income was only 9.3 per cent (in Argentina it reached 18.7 per cent, in Brazil 15.7 per cent and in Mexico 13.4 per cent).

Of course, these developments were not entirely new. They had long been associated with the boom-or-bust mentality of the Cuban sugar economy. But in the late 1940s and early 1950s such conditions had far-reaching implications. The fact that sugar continued to dominate the Cuban economy persuaded potential investors to retain large portions of

[9] International Bank of Reconstruction and Development, *Report on Cuba* (Baltimore, 1951), p. 7.

their assets in liquid form. It contributed to fostering the desire for quick profits and it discouraged new investments and economic diversification. Cuba continued to depend upon an export product in which competition was especially intense, the decline of rival producers as a result of the war engendering a false sense of security. In fact, the economy was not growing fast enough to accommodate the estimated annual 25,000 new jobs required to meet the growing numbers of people entering the labour market. These problems would have challenged even the most enlightened administration. They were historical and structural, and defied easy solution. The Auténticos, however, were far from enlightened. These were years that began with great hope and ended with disappointment and disillusionment.

At the same time, conditions were generally difficult for the Communist Party, now renamed the Partido Socialista Popular (PSP). Collaboration with Batista had gained the party access to the cabinet, and in the 1944 elections the PSP obtained three seats in the Senate and ten in the lower house. By the 1948 elections the party could claim some 160,000 supporters. But PSP fortunes declined markedly during the Auténtico years. The Cold War undermined PSP influence, and the Auténticos lost no opportunity to expand their power. They moved against the Communist-controlled trade unions and by the late 1940s had established PRC control over key labour organizations. The government confiscated the PSP radio station and continually harassed the party newpaper. But even as PSP influence declined, the party remained an effective political force.

The apparent indifference with which the PRC leadership viewed the historical mandate of 1933 and the electoral triumph of 1944 created dissent and tension within the party. By 1947, PRC misgovernment resulted in an open rupture when Eduardo Chibás, a prominent student leader in 1933, broke with the Auténticos and organized the Partido del Pueblo Cubano (Ortodoxo). In claiming to uphold the ideals of the 1930s, the Ortodoxos became generally associated in the popular imagination with economic independence, political freedom, social justice and public honesty. Perhaps the most gifted orator of the era, Chibás articulated public grievances and crystallized popular discontent against the incumbent Auténticos in a campaign that thrived on spectacular accusations and disclosures of high level government corruption. Chibás contributed powerfully to a final discrediting of the Auténtico administration, undermining what little remained of public confidence in government leadership. However, Chibás' suicide in 1951 produced instead mass disillusionment, resignation and indifference despite the fact that the Prío government remained substantially weaker after its three-year bout with the fallen Ortodoxo leader. Thoroughly disgraced, politically weak, morally bankrupt, the Auténticos presided over a discredited government and a demoralized body politic.

Batista would later derive enormous satisfaction in recounting the details of his return to power in 1952. Within one hour and seventeen minutes, he boasted, the military conspirators overturned the Auténtico government. And, indeed, the *cuartelazo* of 10 March unquestionably owed much of its success to the organizational prowess of its planners. At 2:40 A.M. the rebels seized all the capital's principal army posts, from which military units moved into the city to garrison strategic positions. Bus and rail stations, airports, docks, electricity plants, radio transmitters, banks and offices of government ministries passed into army control. Later that morning city residents awoke amid rumours of a coup and turning to radio broadcasts heard only uninterrupted music. Telecommunication service to the interior was interrupted. Sites of potential protest demonstrations against the coup passed under military control. The university and opposition press offices were closed. Local headquarters of various unions and the Communist Party were occupied, and leading activists arrested. Constitutional guarantees were suspended.

The ease with which Batista and the army executed the plot and consolidated power, however, reflected considerably more than adroit application of conspiratorial talents. The effects of nearly a decade of graft, corruption and scandal at all levels of civilian government had more than adequately paved the way for the return of military rule in 1952. The *cuartelazo* simply delivered the coup de grâce to a moribund regime. Indeed, general indifference to the coup underscored the depth of national cynicism with politics. The discredited Autfentico government possessed neither the popular confidence nor the moral credibility to justify an appeal for popular support; its overthrow simply did not warrant public outrage. On the contrary, for many the coup was a long-overdue change. To business and commerce Batista pledged order, stability and labour tranquillity. To the United States he promised respect for foreign capital. To political parties he promised new elections in 1954.

The Auténtico and Ortodoxo parties proved incapable of responding effectively to Batista's seizure of power. The Ortodoxos were leaderless and the Auténticos could not lead. After 1952 Cuba's two principal parties became irrelevant to a solution of the political crisis. In much the same way that the crisis of the 1930s had brought about the downfall of the traditional parties, events in the 1950s contributed to the demise of the Auténticos and Ortodoxos. Both parties, to be sure, duly condemned the violation of the 1940 Constitution, but neither party responded to the army usurpation with either a comprehensive program or compelling plan of action. The little opposition that did arise originated largely outside the organized political parties, principally from ousted military officers, splinter political groups and personalistic factions of the major parties. Once again, however, a new generation of Cubans responded to the summons and filled the political vacuum.

The early challenges to the *batistato* failed, and failed without much fanfare. An abortive plot, the routine arrest of café conspirators, the quiet retirement of dissident army officers, were not the stuff to arouse the national conscience or inspire national resistance. The attack on Moncada barracks in Santiago de Cuba led by Fidel Castro in July 1953 also failed, but it was the dimension of its failure that distinguished it from its ill-starred predecessors: the plan was as daring as its failure was spectacular. It served to catapult Castro into contention for leadership over the anti-Batista forces and elevated armed struggle as the principal means of opposition in the mid-1950s.

The much anticipated elections of 1954 offended all but the most cynical *batistianos*. The major political parties in the end refused to participate and the leading opposition candidate withdrew. Running unopposed, obtaining a majority of the mere 40 per cent of the electorate that voted, Batista won a new term of office. After 1954 those moderate political forces that had counted on elections to settle national tensions found themselves isolated and without alternatives. One last effort to negotiate a political settlement of the deepening crisis occurred in 1955 when representatives of the moderate opposition arranged a series of conferences with Batista. The Civic Dialogue, as the discussions became known, sought to secure from the President the promise of new elections with guarantees for all participants. He refused. The stage was now set for armed confrontation.

The first response was not long in coming. Late in 1955 student demonstrations resulted in armed clashes with the army and police, and the repression which followed persuaded student leaders of the necessity to organize a clandestine revolutionary movement, the Directorio Revolucionario. A year later, an insurgent group of Auténticos took up arms and attacked the Goicuría army barracks in Matanzas. In 1957, after an unsuccessful assassination attempt against Batista, the Directorio Revolucionario also turned to rural insurgency and organized a guerrilla front in Las Villas province known as the II Frente Nacional del Escambray. It was, however, in the Sierra Maestra mountains of Oriente province that the fate of the Batista regime was being determined.

Within three years of the attack on Moncada, Fidel Castro had organized another uprising in Santiago timed with his return from Mexico aboard the small yacht *Granma,* but the revolt of 30 November 1956 was crushed well before the *Granma* crew set foot on Cuban soil. Moreover, alerted to the arrival of the expeditionaries, government forces overwhelmed the landing party at Alegría de Pío in southern Oriente, reducing the force of some eighty men to a band of eighteen. Having failed in a dramatic bid for power, deprived of arms, ammunition and supplies, the *Granma* survivors sought refuge in the southeastern mountain range.

The character of the guerrilla campaign which followed conformed to the geopolitical setting of the Sierra Maestra. Castro and his men commenced operations in a peripheral region of the island where the politico-military presence of the government they were committed to overthrowing amounted to no more than isolated Rural Guard outposts. In waging war against the Rural Guard, however, the rebels attacked both the local power-base of the Batista regime and the symbolic expression of Havana's presence in the Sierra Maestra region. For decades, Rural Guard commanders arbitrarily terrorized rural communities. Hence, however modest rebel successes against the rural constabulary may have seemed, they did pose a serious challenge to Havana's politico-military authority in Oriente province.

The group of *Granma* survivors attracted early recruits from the mountain population, and with this slightly augmented force the insurgents mounted their early offensives. By January 1957, the rebel force was sufficiently strong to overpower the Rural Guard post at La Plata; in a second action in May 1957 the guerrillas defeated the Rural Guard station at El Uvero. News of insurgent victories kept Cubans alive to the struggle unfolding in the Sierra Maestra and attracted new recruits to the guerrilla camp. Rebel operations also forced government forces to leave the security of the cities to give chase to the rural insurgents. In the process the arbitrary manner in which the government conducted field operations served further to alienate the rural population and generate additional support for the guerrilla force.

Insurgent victories forced the government to concede enclaves of liberated territory throughout Oriente. Throughout 1957 and early 1958 the size of the rebel army increased and field operations expanded. By mid-1958, a fifty-man column under Raúl Castro had established the Second Front in northeastern Cuba, consolidating several rebel bands operating in the region. A column of some thirty-five men under Juan Almeida subsequently opened another front in the area around Santiago de Cuba and likewise succeeded in consolidating and augmenting insurgent forces. In April 1958, Camilo Cienfuegos left the Sierra stronghold with a small patrol of eight or ten men. Still another column under Ernesto Che Guevara operated east of Turquino peak.

The expanding struggle in the countryside was accompanied by growing resistance in the cities. Urban underground groups, most notably the Civic Resistance movement, coordinated acts of sabotage and terror in Cuba's principal cities. As kidnappings and assassinations increased the regime responded with increasing ferocity, which served to increase its isolation.

Anti-government opposition was not confined to civilian political groups. By the mid-1950s dissension had become rife within the armed forces. Batista's return to power had signalled the wholesale transformation of the army command, old *septembrista* officers, many of whom had retired in the previous years of Auténtico rule, returning to positions of command. Political credentials and nepotism governed promotions and commands in the early 1950s, Batista virtually dismantling the professional officer corps. The return of *septembrista* officers produced widespread demoralization among younger commanders who were proud of their academy training and took umbrage at appointments that made a mockery of professional standards and placed the old sergeants in positions of command.

In April 1956 the first of a series of army conspiracies jolted the government. The plot led by Colonel Ramón Barquín implicated more than two hundred officers, including the most distinguished field commanders of the army. In the subsequent reorganization some four thousand officers and men were removed, reassigned and retired. In September 1957 another conspiracy resulted in a mutiny at the Cienfuegos naval station that was part of a larger plot involving the principal naval installations across the island. In the same year conspiracies were uncovered in the air force, the army medical corps and the national police. By the late 1950s, then, Batista was facing both mounting popular opposition and armed resistance with an army that was increasingly politically uncertain and professionally unreliable.

The Cuban crisis during the 1950s went far beyond a conflict between Batista and his political opponents. Many participants in the anti-Batista struggle certainly defined the conflict principally in political terms, a struggle in which the central issues turned wholly on the elimination of the iniquitous Batista and the restoration of the Constitution of 1940. But discontent during the decade was as much a function of socio-economic frustration as it was the result of political grievances. By the 1950s sugar had ceased to be a source of economic growth and lacked the capacity to sustain continued economic development. Yet all sectors of the Cuban economy remained vulnerable to the effects of price fluctuations in the international sugar market. The decline in sugar prices between 1952 and 1954 precipitated the first in a series of recessions in the Cuban economy in the course of the decade. At the same time the effects of the reciprocity treaty of 1934 had taken their toll, impeding in Cuba the industrial development characteristic of other Latin American countries during the post-war period. Such local industry which did exist had to face strong foreign competition with little or no tariff protection and there was little incentive to expand manufactures beyond light consumer goods, largely food and textiles. With the Cuban population expanding at an annual rate of 2.5 per cent, and 50,000 young men alone reaching working age every year, only 8,000 new jobs were created in industry between 1955 and 1958.

Investment patterns were at once a cause and effect of these conditions. Investment in industry did not keep up with the availability of domestic savings. At the same time considerable sums of capital were transferred abroad, principally in the form of profits on foreign investments in Cuba and through Cuban investments outside the island. Few Cubans invested in government securities or long-term stocks, preferring liquidity, principally in short-term funds in banks abroad or safety-deposit boxes at home. The few long-term investments made were principally in U.S. stocks. By 1955 investment in real estate exceeded $150 million, most of it in southern Florida. In contrast, U.S. capital controlled 90 per cent of the telephone and electricity services in Cuba, 50 per cent of railroads and 40 per cent of sugar production. Cuban branches of U.S. banks held 25 per cent of all bank deposits. Indeed direct U.S. investment in Cuba, which had declined during the depression, expanded steadily after the Second

World War, reaching a peak of $1 billion ($386 million in services, $270 million in petroleum and mining, $265 million in agriculture and $80 million in manufacturing) in 1958.

Not only did labour's share of net income decline during the 1950s – for example, from 70.5 per cent of 66.4 per cent between 1953 and 1954 – but unemployment and under-employment increased. By 1957, the best year during the middle 1950s, 17 per cent of the labour force was generally classified as unemployed, while another 13 per cent had been reduced to under-employment. In the sugar industry, one of the principal sources of employment for Cuban labour – it employed an estimated 475,000 workers, approximately 25 per cent of the labour force – some 60 per cent of the workers were employed for six months or less, with only 30 per cent employed for more than ten months. The average sugar-worker was employed for less than one hundred days of the year. As unemployment increased so, too, did resistance to measures raising productivity. Sugar-workers successfully opposed mechanized cutting and bulk loading, cigar-workers were able to limit mechanization and dock-workers put up fierce resistance to it. Successive labour laws through the 1940s and 1950s all but made the dismissal of workers impossible and job security became an issue of paramount importance. One result of all this was to reduce further the ability of Cuban exports to compete successfully in international markets.

Significant distinctions existed within the Cuban labour force. Agricultural workers typically earned less than 80 pesos a month, which compared unfavourably with an average industrial wage of approximately 120 pesos a month plus pension allowances and other fringe benefits, particularly if a worker was employed by a major company or belonged to a strong union organization. Moreover, rural Cuba enjoyed few of the amenities and services that had come to characterize life in the island's cities. On the contrary, the one-third of the population which lived in the countryside suffered abject poverty and persistent neglect. Only 15 per cent of rural inhabitants possessed running water as compared with 80 per cent of the urban population. Only 9 per cent of rural homes enjoyed electricity as compared with 83 per cent of the urban population. Medical and dental personnel as well as hospitals and clinics tended to concentrate in the cities while a combination of poverty and isolation served to exclude the countryside from virtually all access to educational services. The national illiteracy rate of 20 per cent concealed that of 40 per cent in the countryside while in Oriente province it was more than 50 per cent. The peasantry lived at the margins of society and outside the body politic. Nor were these conditions likely to change soon. Vast areas of rural Cuba were held in latifundia farms. Twenty-two large sugar companies operated one-fifth of the agricultural land, much of this in reserve for the prospective periodic boom that planters so eagerly awaited. Cattle ranches also accounted for vast acreage, from which large numbers of peasants were excluded as either workers or owners.

By the mid-1950s even the Cuban urban middle class felt itself in crisis. To be sure, Cuba enjoyed one of the highest per capita incomes in Latin America ($374), ranked in 1957 second after Venezuela ($857). Only Mexico and Brazil exceeded Cuba in the number of radios and televisions per one thousand inhabitants. The country ranked first in telephones, newspapers, and passenger motor vehicles. Daily average food consumption was surpassed only by Argentina and Uruguay. Consumption of foreign imports, principally U.S. products, increased from $515 million in 1950 to $649 million in 1956 and $777 million in 1958. Middle-class Cubans, however, found little personal comfort in statistical tallies that touted their high level of material consumption and placed the island near the top of the scale of per capita incomes in Latin America. The United States, not Latin America, was the Cuban frame of reference. Cubans participated directly in and depended entirely on the United States economic system in much the same fashion as U.S. citizens, but without access to U.S. social service programmes and at employment and wages levels substantially lower than their North American counterparts. The Cuban per capita income of $374 paled against the United States per capita of $2,000, or even that of Mississippi, the poorest state, at $1,000. (And in 1956 Havana ranked among the world's most expensive cities – fourth after Caracas, Ankara and Manila.) This disparity was the source of much frustration, particularly as middle-class Cubans perceived their standard of living fall behind the income advances in the United States. Per capita income in Cuba actually declined by 18 per cent, for example, during the recession of 1952–4, neutralizing the slow gains enjoyed during the immediate post-war period. In 1958, Cuban per capita income was at about the same level as it had been in 1947. By the late fifties middle-class Cubans, initially deposed to support Batista, were in many ways worse off than they had been in the twenties.

Batista's continued presence in power compounded the growing crisis by creating political conditions that made renewed economic growth impossible. As the International Commission of Jurists later concluded, 'administrative dishonesty and political illegality' were in 1958 the most important obstacles to economic development.[10] Political instability and conflict were playing havoc with the economy. After the short boom between 1955 and 1957 tourism was once again in decline, and the insurgency was halting the flow of dairy, vegetable and meat supplies from the countryside to the cities. Shortages caused the prices of basic staples to soar while sabotage and the destruction of property further contributed to economic dislocation. Sugar production dropped. Indeed, by 1958 the insurgency had reached its most advanced stage in the three eastern provinces that accounted for more than 80 per cent of the total sugar land and more than 75 per cent of the annual crop. Shortages of gasoline and oil brought railroads, trucking and sugar mills to a standstill. It was in 1958 that the 26 of July Movement opened a war against property and production across the island as a means to isolate Batista from the support of economic elites, both foreign and domestic. The message was clear: conditions of normality would not return until Batista departed. In February the guerrilla leadership announced its intention to attack sugar mills, tobacco factories, public utilities, railroads and oil refineries. The destruction of the sugar harvest in particular emerged as the principal goal of insurgent strategy. 'Either Batista without the *zafra* or the *zafra* without Batista', the 26 of July intoned again and again. In March the rebel army command reported having applied a torch to every cane-producing province on the island, destroying an estimated 2 million tons of sugar. As early as September 1957, the resident *New York Times* correspondent in Havana cabled that commerce, industry and capital, 'which have wholeheartedly supported President Batista since he took over the Government in 1952, are growing impatient with the continued violence in the island'.[11] By 1958, this impatience had turned to exasperation.

Cuba was on the verge of revolution through most of 1958. In July representatives of the leading opposition groups met in Caracas to organize a united front and develop a common strategy against Batista. The Pact of Caracas established Fidel Castro as the principal leader of the anti-Batista movement and the rebel army as main arm of the revolution. As the conference in Caracas convened, Batista launched his most formidable offensive against the guerrillas in the Sierra Maestra. Every branch of the armed forces participated in the offensive, an estimated 12,000 troops

[10] International Commission of Jurists, *Cuba and the Rule of Law* (Geneva, 1962), p. 25.
[11] *New York Times,* September 15, 1957, 4, p. 11.

moving on the Sierra Maestra. Air force squadrons bombed and strafed suspected rebel-held regions while naval off-shore units pounded the south-eastern mountain range. But by the end of the summer the government offensive collapsed, signaling the beginning of the disintegration of the Cuban armed forces. The army simply ceased to fight as desertions and defections reached epidemic proportions. Retreating army units became easy prey for advancing guerrilla columns. Demoralization turned to fear and, ultimately, panic.

The guerrillas launched their counter-offensive in late summer. Within weeks government forces in the eastern half of the island found themselves engulfed by the swelling tide of the armed opposition, isolated from relief and reinforcements as provincial towns and cities fell to guerrilla columns. Local military commands surrendered, often without firing a shot. Loyal troops sought desperately to return west in advance of the revolutionary current that moved inexorably toward Havana from the east.

Two things were now clear; the Batista regime was doomed, and the 26 of July movement under Fidel Castro had established clear hegemony over all the revolutionary factions. In the summer, only months before the fall of the regime, the Communist PSP, which had been proscribed during the second Batista government, had allied itself with the 26 of July Move-ment. This conversion to Fidelismo won the party several key positions within the 26 of July, most notably within the rebel army columns of Raúl Castro and Ernesto Che Guevara, positions later to serve as the basis of expanding PSP authority in post-revolutionary Cuba.

By 1958, Batista had acquired one more adversary: the United States government. The year began inauspiciously for the Cuban government when, in March, Washington imposed an arms embargo, a move tanta-mount to the withdrawal of support. The suspension of arms shipments contributed to weakening Batista's hold over his supporters, both civil and military, especially since it was declared on the eve of the government's spring offensive. For the better part of the 1950s, Batista had retained army loyalty with assurances that he enjoyed unqualified support from Washington. After March 1958, the army command was no longer sure. According to U.S. ambassador Earl E. T. Smith, intimations that Wash-ington no longer backed Batista, had 'a devastating psychological effect' on the army and was 'the most effective step taken by the Department of State in bringing about the downfall of Batista'.[12]

---

[12] Earl E. T. Smith, *The Fourth Floor* (New York, 1962), pp. 48, 107.

The year 1958 was also an election year, providing Batista with an opportunity to demonstrate to Washington that democratic processes were still capable of functioning, civil war notwithstanding. But to the suprise of few, government candidate Andrés Rivero Agüero triumphed, the electoral hoax further weakening Batista's position both at home and abroad. The victory of the official candidate disillusioned the few who still hoped for a political end to the armed insurrection. Army officers personally loyal to Batista, disheartened by the prospect of a transfer of executive power, lost their enthusiasm to defend a leader already replaced at the polls. Washington rejected outright the rigged presidential succession and announced in advance plans to withhold diplomatic recognition of Rivero Agüero, which undermined political and military support for the regime.

In fact, Washington had already determined to ease Batista out of office. The crisis in 1958 recalled that of 1933 in that the incumbency of an unpopular president threatened to plunge the island into political turmoil and social upheaval. Once again Washington sought to remove the source of Cuban tensions as a means to defuse the revolutionary situation. In early December the State Department dispatched financier William D. Pawley to Havana to undertake a covert mission. The United States, Pawley later recalled, urged Batista 'to capitulate to a caretaker government unfriendly to him, but satisfactory to us, whom we could immediately recognize and give military assistance to in order that Fidel Castro not come to power'. On December 9 Pawley held a three-hour conference with Batista, offering him an opportunity to retire unmolested in Florida with his family. The U.S. envoy informed the President that the United States 'would make an effort to stop Fidel Castro from coming into power as a Communist, but that the caretaker government would be men who were enemies of his, otherwise it would not work anyway, and Fidel Castro would otherwise have to lay down his arms or admit he was a revolutionary fighting against everybody only because he wanted power, not because he was against Batista'.[13] Batista refused.

Even as the United States sought to persuade Batista to leave office, the revolutionary momentum had sealed the fate of the regime. The failure of the government offensive and the success of the guerrilla counter-offensive had a galvanizing effect on Cubans, provoking spontaneous uprisings

---

[13] United States Congress, Senate, *Hearings Before the Subcommittee to Investigate the Administration of the Internal Security Act and Other Internal Laws of the Committee on the Judiciary: Communist Threat to the United States Through the Caribbean*, 86th Cong., 2d Sess. (Washington, D.C., 1959–60), pt. 10, p. 739.

across the island. Large amounts of arms and equipment fell into the control of civilians in the wake of the army retreat, including artillery, tanks and small arms of every type. In the closing weeks of 1958, both the ranks of the urban resistance and the guerrilla columns increased rapidly. By December 1958 the Batistiano army command in Santiago reported that 90 per cent of the population supported guerrilla actions. At about the same time, spontaneous uprisings in Camagüey overwhelmed local army detachments. In the decisive battle of Santa Clara, Guevara's column received decisive assistance from the local population. At the time of the government's summer offensive the guerrillas numbered some 5,000 officers and troops. By January 1959, the rebel army numbered some 50,000.

Batista's expendability was the signal for military intrigue. The army that had ceased to fight in the countryside had become the focal point of political intrigue in the cities. By December no fewer than half a dozen conspiracies were developing in the armed forces. During the early hours of 1 January 1959, as guerrilla columns marched across the plains of central Cuba, General Eulogio Cantillo seized power and appointed Supreme Court Justice Carlos Piedra as provisional president. The 26 of July Movement rejected the coup and demanded unconditional surrender to the rebel army. Pledging to continue the armed struggle, Fidel Castro called for a nationwide general strike.

With the news of Batista's flight, army units throughout the island simply ceased to resist further rebel advances. Cantillo complained to the U.S. embassy that he had inherited the command of a 'dead army'. Seeking to revive the moribund war effort, Cantillo summoned the imprisoned Colonel Ramón Barquín and relinquished to him command of the army. Barquín ordered an immediate cease-fire, saluted the insurgent 'Army of Liberation', and surrendered command of Camp Columbia and La Cabaña military fortress to Ernesto 'Che' Guevara and Camilo Cienfuegos. A week later Fidel Castro arrived in Havana.

10

CUBA SINCE 1959

Fulgencio Batista had been the dominant figure in Cuban national affairs for a quarter of a century. He had ruled Cuba, directly or indirectly, since the military coup of 4 September 1933, except for an interlude of Auténtico rule from 1944 to 1952. He had seemed confident and powerful until the last weeks of his last presidency. But suddenly Batista was gone. On New Year's Eve 1958 he quit, taking with him much of the top echelon of his government. A new leader, young and bearded, who for two years had led a guerrilla war in eastern Cuba, gradually spreading the influence of his forces to the western provinces, slowly assuming the leadership of the urban and the rural resistance to the Batista regime, marched into Havana. Audacious and effective in his military campaign and political skills, persuasive and commanding in his public speech, Fidel Castro had become the leader of the future. Power had passed, somewhat unexpectedly, to a new generation of Cubans.

In January 1959 the old regime collapsed in Cuba and a revolution came to power. The old rules of the game no longer applied and the armed forces that had shaped the life of independent Cuba for so long had crumbled. The rebel army became the defender of the new revolutionary state, sweeping aside the parties that had structured political life in previous decades. Only the Communist party (Partido Socialista Popular, PSP), which had been banned by Batista in the 1950s but reappeared in 1959, was left intact. The fall of the old regime required that new norms, rules and institutions be devised to replace those that had collapsed or been overthrown. The history of Cuba during the next thirty years addressed the needs of revolutionary creativity, the persistent commitment to create order out of revolution, the need to uphold a revolutionary faith in the implementation of that new order.

457

THE CONSOLIDATION OF REVOLUTIONARY POWER
(1959–62)

Cuba has always been buffeted by the winds of international affairs. Geographically in the heart of the American Mediterranean, it has been coveted by the major powers over the centuries. With the end of four hundred years of Spanish colonial rule and the establishment of United States primacy in 1898, Cuba's link with the United States became the virtually exclusive focus of Cuban internationl relations during the first half of the twentieth century.

In 1959 the U.S. government viewed with concern the affairs of a country that seemed uncharacteristically out of its control. Cuba mattered to the United States because of both its strategic location and its economic importance. The United States operated a naval base at Guantánamo under the terms of a 1903 treaty that recognized nominal Cuban sovereignty but guaranteed the United States the right to operate the base for as long as Washington wished. Despite subsequent Cuban protests, the United States retained the base. While U.S. military forces had not been stationed in Cuba outside Guantánamo for several decades and U.S. government officials had played a reduced role in internal Cuban politics, in the 1950s the U.S. ambassador remained the country's second most important political figure after the President of the Republic. In 1959 the value of U.S. investments in Cuba – in sugar, mining, utilities, banking and manufacturing – exceeded that in every other Latin American country except Venezuela. The United States also took about two-thirds of Cuban exports and supplied about three-quarters of its imports. (And foreign trade accounted for about two-thirds of Cuba's estimated national income.)

Fidel Castro, the 26 of July Movement, which he led, and other revolutionary forces that had participated in the revolutionary war, sought to affirm Cuban nationalism. In the symbols used and histories evoked, in the problems diagnosed and solutions proposed, there was a strong emphasis on enabling Cubans to take charge of their history. There was, however, during the revolutionary war only a limited criticism of U.S. government policies and the activities of U.S. enterprises in Cuba. Castro had bitterly criticized the modest U.S. military assistance initially extended to the Batista government under the formal military agreements between the two countries, but this aid was eventually cut. Castro had also spoken of the expropriation of the U.S.-owned public utilities. However, in the later phases of the guerrilla war, for tactical reasons, Castro seemed to back off from any expropriation proposals.

In the early months of the Revolution there were three principal themes in Cuban-U.S. relations. First, there was mistrust and anger over U.S. criticism of events in Cuba. The Cuban government brought to trial many who had served the Batista government and its armed forces; most of these prisoners were convicted and many were executed. The trials were strongly criticized, in both Cuba and the United States, for observing few procedural safeguards to guarantee the rights of the accused as well as for the severity of many sentences. Fidel Castro and other Cuban government leaders were offended by this, and they denounced their critics in the U.S. mass media (especially the wire services) and the U.S. Congress. The onset of poor relations between Cuba and the United States from January 1959 stemmed from this clash between the values of justice and retribution of revolutionaries and the values of fairness and moderation of a liberal society even toward its enemies.

The second major factor was the Revolution's initial impact on U.S. firms operating in Cuba. The frequency of strikes increased sharply in 1959 as workers sought gains from management under the more favourable political situation. Foreign-owned firms were affected by such strikes and in some cases the question of their expropriation arose. A strike at the Royal Dutch Shell petroleum refinery, for instance, raised the question of the expropriation of British property, authorized by a law issued by the rebels in retaliation for British military sales to the Batista government. Fidel Castro obtained generous concessions from Shell in exchange for forgoing expropriation 'at this time'.[1] Comparable pressures from below affected the revolution in the countryside. The Agrarian Reform Act (issued May 1959), moderate in many respects, was also strongly nationalist. The Instituto Nacional de Reforma Agraria (INRA) was more willing to intervene in labour–management conflicts when farms were foreign-owned, and to suspend the strict application of the law in these cases to expropriate foreign-owned land. Such local agrarian conflicts soured U.S.-Cuban relations.

The third feature of this period was changing Cuban attitudes to new private foreign investment and official foreign aid. On 18 February 1959 Prime Minister Fidel Castro publicly welcomed foreign capital and on 20 March 1959 acknowledged the ample availability of aid. On 2 April 1959

[1] Fidel Castro, *Discursos para la historia* (Havana, 1959), 1: 50–2, 75–81.

the Prime Minister announced that on a forthcoming trip to the United States he would be accompanied by the president of the National Bank and the Ministers of the Treasury and of the Economy to seek funds for Cuba. This trip to the United States in April 1959 became a deadline for making decisions that the overworked revolutionaries had hitherto postponed. Did Cuba's new government want a close relationship with the United States? Was this revolution committed to a Cuba open and profitable for multinational firms? Could its leaders make a genuine and radical revolution with the support of the United Fruit Company, Coca-Cola, the Chase Manhattan Bank or Standard Oil? Would Fidel Castro accept the economic austerity preached by the International Monetary Fund (IMF), embrace U.S. vice-president Richard Nixon, and proclaim U.S.-Cuban friendship at the gates of the Guantánamo naval base? En route to the United States Castro told his economic cabinet that they were not to seek foreign aid from officials of the U.S. government, the World Bank or the IMF, with whom they might speak during their visit. The purpose of the trip, therefore, changed from acquiring aid for capitalist development to gaining time for far-reaching transformations the specific form of which was still uncertain. There is no evidence that the United States, or these international financial institutions, denied aid to Cuba that its government had requested. In fact, Cuba did not ask them for aid. Had such aid been requested and granted, it would have tied Cuba's future closely to the world capitalist economy and to the United States because of the conditions ordinarily attached to such aid in the 1950s. A small number of revolutionary leaders, therefore, concluded well ahead of the rest of the citizenry that it was impossible to conduct a revolution in Cuba without a major confrontation with the United States. A revolution would require the promised extensive agrarian reforms and probably a new, far-reaching state intervention in the public utilities, mining, the sugar industry and possibly other manufacturing sectors. Given the major U.S. investments in these sectors, and United States hostility to statism, revolution at home would inevitably entail confrontation abroad.

The approval of the Agrarian Reform Act was followed in June 1959 by the first major cabinet crisis, which resulted in the departure of the moderates. U.S. ambassador Philip Bonsal presented a formal U.S. government protest on 11 June complaining of irregularities and abuses in the early implementation of the Agrarian Reform Law against U.S. firms. The head of the Air Force, Pedro Luis Díaz Lanz, quit at the end of June and fled to the United States, charging Communist infiltration of the government. President Manuel Urrutia was forced out in July, leaving no doubt that Prime Minister Castro was Cuba's uncontested leader. The question of communism was also an issue for Urrutia, who had stoutly defended the government against charges of communism while accusing the Communists of attempting to subvert the Revolution. Urrutia was replaced by Osvaldo Dorticós (who would serve as president until 1976). The question of communism also mattered for the slowly evolving links with the Soviet Union. The first official contacts with the Soviet Union were made in Cairo by Ernesto 'Che' Guevara in June 1959, although at this stage Soviet–Cuban trade was as insignificant as it had been before the Revolution. Relations with Moscow changed qualitatively from October 1959. And Soviet deputy prime minister Anastas Mikoyan visited Cuba in February 1960 to sign the first important bilateral economic agreement between the two countries and to promote other relations.

U.S.-Cuban relations continued to deteriorate during the second half of 1959. Disputes over Communist influence in the government became frequent and intense. Washington's view of the Cuban government soured as Castro sharpened the vituperative tone of his remarks about the United States. In early March 1960 a Belgian ship *La Coubre,* loaded with arms and ammunition for the Cuban government, exploded in Havana harbor. Prime Minister Castro accused the U.S. government of sabotage. Publicly, the U.S. government protested. Privately, on 17 March 1960, President Dwight Eisenhower authorized the Central Intelligence Agency (CIA) to organize the training of Cuban exiles for a future invasion of Cuba.

The pace of deterioration in U.S.-Cuban relations quickened in the spring and summer of 1960. In late June the Cuban government requested the foreign-owned petroleum refineries to process crude oil it had purchased from the Soviet Union. When the companies refused they were expropriated. At the same time, a newly amended sugar act was making its way through the U.S. Congress. A clause in the bill authorized the President to cut off the Cuban sugar quota; the bill was approved by 3 July. On 5 July, the Cuban Council of Ministers authorized the expropriation of all U.S. property in Cuba. On 6 July, President Eisenhower cancelled Cuba's sugar quota. On 15 July the newly established Bank for Foreign Trade became Cuba's sole foreign-trade agency. On 7 August the expropriation of all large U.S.-owned industrial and agrarian enterprises was carried out, and on 17 September all U.S. banks were confiscated. On 19 October the U.S. government prohibited exports to Cuba except for non-subsidized foodstuffs and medicines. On 24 October, Cuba expropriated all U.S.-owned wholesale and retail trade enterprises and the remaining smaller U.S.-owned industrial and agrarian enterprises. The United States withdrew Ambassador Philip Bonsal on 29 October. U.S.-Cuban diplomatic relations were finally and formally broken in the waning days of the Eisenhower administration in January 1961.

In contrast, Cuban–Soviet relations improved markedly during this period. On 9 July 1960, Prime Minister Nikita Khrushchev declared that Soviet missiles were prepared to defend Cuba 'in a figurative sense'. The first formal military agreement between the two countries was signed within weeks as the Soviet Union pledged to 'use all means at its disposal to prevent an armed United States intervention against Cuba'.[2] This increasing military collaboration between Cuba and the Soviet Union predictably heightened U.S. government hostility towards Havana.

The swift and dramatic changes in U.S.-Cuban relations were paralleled by the reorganization of Cuba's internal political and economic affairs, one consequence of which was a massive emigration to the United States. Washington favoured this emigration through special programs with the aim of discrediting the Cuban government. From 1960 to 1962 net out-migration from Cuba amounted to about 200,000 people, or an unprecedented average of well over 60,000 per year. Most emigrants came from the economic and social elite, the adult males typically being professionals, managers and executives, although they also included many white-collar workers. On the other hand, skilled, semi-skilled and unskilled workers were under-represented relative to their share of the work force, and rural Cuba was virtually absent from this emigration. This upper-middle- and middle-class urban emigration was also disproportionately white. Henceforth, a part of the history of the Cuban people would unfold in the United States. The first wave of emigrants, in part because they could transfer their skills to new workplaces, would experience relative economic and social success over the next thirty years. Politically, they would constitute a strong anti-communist force often sharply at odds with prevailing political opinion among other Spanish-speaking communities in the United States.

In late 1960 and early 1961 the would-be Cuban-Americans were still just Cubans, exiled from their homeland and planning to return. As the United States and Cuban governments came to blows during the second half of 1960, Washington became more interested in assisting the exiles to

[2] *Revolución*, 21 July 1960, 1.

overthrow the Castro government. The exiles, however, were deeply divided. Those who were once close to the Batista government were repelled by those who had worked with Fidel Castro during the rebellion or in the early months of his government, although they had broken with Castro over the question of communism and other issues; this antipathy was fully reciprocated. Did Cuba need a restoration or a non-communist transformation? There were many shades of opinion within each side of this fundamental cleavage, personality conflicts further complicating relationships. The U.S. government required a unified Cuban exile leadership if the efforts to overthrow the Castro government with a minimum of U.S. intervention were to succeed.

On 22 March 1961 several key exile leaders agreed to form the Cuban Revolutionary Council presided over by José Miró Cardona, who had been the first prime minister of the Cuban revolutionary government in January and February 1959. Prominent members of the Council included Antonio ('Tony') Varona, former prime minister (and opponent of Batista), as well as Fidel Castro's former Minister of Public Works, Manuel Ray. Manuel Artime, a former lieutenant of the rebel army, was to be the political chief of the invasion force and José Pérez San Román the military commander. Upon the overthrow of the revolutionary regime the Council would become the provisional government of Cuba under the presidency of Miró Cardona. The exiles' Brigade 2506 completed its training in Nicaragua and Guatemala.

The administration of John F. Kennedy inherited the plan for this invasion when it came to office on 20 January 1961. Those who pressed for an invasion used the analogy of covert U.S. support for the overthrow of Guatemalan president Jacobo Arbenz in 1954: effective, at low cost to the United States and with no direct involvement of U.S. troops. Supporters of the invasion argued that it had to proceed soon before Castro's government received enough weapons from the Soviet Union to defeat the challenge. On 3 April the U.S. government published a 'white paper' accusing Castro and his close supporters of betraying what had been an authentic revolution. In the U.S. government's view, Cuba needed a non-communist transformation. President Kennedy agreed to let the CIA-trained invasion force go forward, provided that U.S. forces were not used.

On the morning of 15 April planes piloted by Cuban exiles bombed several airfields in Cuba, creating much panic but little damage. The police responded by imprisoning tens of thousands of suspected dissidents. On Monday morning, 17 April 1961, Brigade 2506 landed at Girón beach on the Bay of Pigs in south-central Cuba. The Cuban government mobilized both its regular armed forces and the militia. Led personally by Fidel Castro, they defeated the invasion force within forty-eight hours and captured 1,180 prisoners. The prisoners were held for trial and interrogation by Castro and others on Cuban national television; they were eventually ransomed for shipments of medical and other supplies from the United States late in 1962. As recriminations began within the Kennedy administration and exile groups in the aftermath of the invasion's failure, Castro triumphantly announced that Cuba's was a consolidated socialist revolution able to defeat its enemies within Cuba as well as the superpower to its north.

If the making of a radical revolution in Cuba required a break with the United States, the defence of a radical revolution in the face of U.S. attack demanded support from the Soviet Union. On 2 December 1961, Fidel Castro proclaimed that he was a Marxist-Leninist and that he would be so until death. In July 1962 Raúl Castro, the armed forces minister, travelled to Moscow to secure additional Soviet military backing. On the Soviet side, the possibility of stationing strategic missiles in Cuba seemed to be a political and military coup. A Soviet strategic base in Cuba would parallel U.S. bases ringing the USSR, and the reaction time and accuracy of a Soviet nuclear attack on the United States would be improved. The 'figurative' missiles of July 1960 became the real missiles of October 1962. The USSR eventually installed forty-two medium-range ballistic missiles in Cuba, and as U.S. intelligence sources gathered information on this President Kennedy was persuaded that the Soviet Union and Cuba sought a major change in the politico-military balance with the United States. On 22 October, Kennedy demanded the withdrawal of Soviet 'offensive missiles' from Cuba and imposed a naval 'quarantine' on the island to prevent the additional shipment of Soviet weaponry. Kennedy also demanded the withdrawal of Soviet strategic bombers and a commitment not to station Soviet strategic weapons in Cuba in the future.

The world held its breath. Not since the dropping of nuclear bombs on Hiroshima and Nagasaki had nuclear warfare seemed so imminent. Poised on the edge of war, the two superpowers jockeyed over their military relationship. The crisis ended when, without prior consultation with Cuba, the Soviet Union backed down, pulling out all its strategic forces in exchange for the pledge that the United States would not invade Cuba. The United States made that pledge conditional on UN verification of the Soviet withdrawal of strategic weapons, but a furious Fidel Castro refused to allow on-site inspection. In fact, although a formal U.S. pledge to desist from invading Cuba would not be made, an 'understanding' came to govern U.S.-Soviet relations over Cuba. The Soviet Union was not to deploy strategic weapons in Cuba nor to use it as a base of operations for nuclear weapons. The United States, in turn, would not seek to overthrow Castro's government. Thus the Cuban missile crisis was a major victory for the U.S. government, since it publicly humiliated the Soviet government over the central question of the day, and yet it also sealed the end of U.S. influence in Cuba. Both Fidel Castro and his exile opponents lost the total support of their superpower allies, but the former would eventually recognize the he had gained much more because his rule was saved by the wisdom of Soviet actions.

As peace returned to the Cuban countryside at the beginning of 1959, the economy began to recover. The revolutionary government sought to stimulate economic growth and, at the same time, to pursue its redistributive goals by altering the structure of demand. The real wages of non-agricultural workers rose sharply, and urban rents for lower-rent dwellings were slashed by as much as 50 per cent. Early in 1959, the government seized all property that had belonged to former president Batista and to his close associates. For the first time in Cuban history the state acquired a major role owning and directly operating productive activities. Unlike most other major Latin American countries, Cuba had not developed an entrepreneurial state sector of the economy before 1959; consequently, there was very little experience about how it might be operated. These problems were to be compounded after 1960 when many managers were dismissed, emigrated or were arrested.

The experiment with a mixed economy was brief because, as we have seen, the Cuban government socialized most of the means of production during its confrontation with the United States. That confrontation need not have affected Cuban-owned business, but on 13 October 1960, 382 locally owned firms, including all the sugar mills, banks, large industries, and the largest wholesale and retail enterprises, were socialized. Three days later the Urban Reform Act socialized all commercially owned real estate. The 1959 Agrarian Reform Act had destroyed Cuban-owned as well as foreign-owned latifundia although it still permitted small- and medium-sized private farms. Because many Cuban entrepreneurs had close connections with the United States and were presumed to oppose the revolutionary government, the survival of revolutionary rule seemed to require that management and ownership pass to loyal revolutionaries, however technically incompetent they might be. These actions also reflected a self-conscious decision to socialize the economy even though the Revolution's socialist character would not be proclaimed officially until April 1961. Such decisions were justified on the grounds of national security and also because direct ownership and control over the means of production were deemed necessary for economic planning. Economic centralization was viewed as a rational step to generate economic growth. The revolutionary leaders were not compelled to socialize the economy: they acted autonomously and, in their view, prudently to implement an ideological vision of the society they wished to build. Power had to be concentrated in the hands of the few to achieve the aspirations of the many: that was at the heart of the evolving ideology.

The turning-point in internal Cuban politics occurred in October and November 1959, months before the break with the United States, or the first treaties with the Soviet Union. On 15 October, Raúl Castro, Fidel's younger brother, became defence minister (a title changed later to Minister of the Armed Forces), a post he held thereafter. Raúl Castro had had a distinguished military career. He was primarily responsible for the organization and development of the Cuban armed forces and their eventual victories at the Bay of Pigs and in overseas wars, the military being the one undoubtedly effective organization created in the first thirty years of revolutionary rule. He also assumed the post of second-in-command to his older brother in all affairs of state, civilian as well as military, playing an important role in the revitalization of both party and government in the 1970s. Raúl was Fidel's formally designated successor in case of death, with the power to enforce the succession.

On 18 October 1959, Rolando Cubelas – the 'unity' candidate with Communist support – defeated Pedro Boitel, the candidate of the 26 of July Movement at the university, in the elections for the presidency of the Federación Estudiantil Universitaria (FEU) after intervention by Fidel Castro, and aligned the FEU with the shift toward Marxism–Leninism. (In 1966, Cubelas would be arrested for plotting to assassinate Fidel Castro, for which it seems he had the support of the U.S. Central Intelligence Agency.)

On 19 October, Huber Matos, military commander of Camagüey province and one of the leading figures of the revolutionary war, resigned along with fourteen officers over the rising influences of communism in the regime. When Matos was arrested the entire 26 of July Movement executive committee in Camagüey province resigned and its leader was detained. Matos spent two decades in prison; his courageous resistance in jail and his unwillingness to collaborate or to bend to the will of his captors became a symbol of strength to the opposition.

In November the Confederación de Trabajadores Cubanos (CTC) held its tenth congress to select a new leadership. The 26 of July Movement's slate had a clear majority. The government pressed for 'unity' with the Communists, but the congress delegates refused and when Fidel Castro addressed the congress his words were interrupted by the chanting of 'twenty-six, twenty-six'. He attacked those who would use that label 'to stab the revolution in the heart'.[3] He argued that the revolution's defence required avoiding partisan quarrels; he asked for and received authority from the congress to form a labour leadership. He picked the 'unity' slate, including the communists.

At the end of November most of the remaining moderates or liberals in the Council of Ministers, including Minister of Public Works Manuel Ray and National Bank president Felipe Pazos were forced out of office. Of the twenty-one ministers appointed in January 1959, twelve had resigned or had been ousted by the end of the year. Four more would go out in 1960 as the revolution moved toward a Marxist-Leninist political system. The elimination of many non-communists and anti-communists from the original coalition, along with the regime's clash with business, were the internal ingredients of the transformation of the revolution's politics. A new leadership consolidated centralized and authoritarian rule. With those who had experience of government in opposition, only the old communists had the political and administrative experience to make the new system work.

As internal and international conflicts deepened during 1960 and 1961 the government developed its organizational apparatus. Having obtained control over the FEU and the CTC, the leadership established a militia with tens of thousands of members to build support and to intimidate internal enemies. The Federación de Mujeres Cubanas (FMC) was also founded in August 1960 and the Comités de Defensa de la Revolución (CDR), which eventually encompassed millions of members, were established in September 1960. Committees were set up on every city block, in each large building, factory or work centre (eventually, CDRs would be dismantled in

[3] *Revolución*, 23 November 1959, 4.

work centres so as not to duplicate the work of the labour unions) in order to identify enemies of the Revolution for the state's internal security apparatus. Gossip became an arm of state power. The Asociación de Juventud Revolucionaria (AJR) was launched in October 1960, merging the youth wings of the old Communist Party, the Revolutionary Directorate, and the 26 of July Movement. A few years later the AJR became the Unión de Jóvenes Comunistas (UJC), the youth affiliate of the Communist Party. The Associación Nacional de Agricultores Pequeños (ANAP) was founded in May 1961; it excluded the medium-sized farm owners (whose property would be expropriated in 1963) and sought to cut across the divisions that existed between producers of various commodities.

A new Communist party was founded in the summer 1961. Called the Organizaciones Revolucionarias Integradas (ORI), it was created through the merger of three pre-existing organizations: the 26 of July Movement, the Revolutionary Directorate, and the old Communist Party, the PSP. The first two of these had by this stage become phantom organizations: the Revolutionary Directorate had been deprived of much independent power after January 1959, while the battles for control over the university students' federation and the labour unions had crippled the 26 of July Movement's capacity for independent political activity. PSP members brought several advantages to the ORI. They were bridge-builders between the rest of the leadership and the Soviet Union. They had some theoretical knowledge of Marxism–Leninism, in contrast to the rest of ORI, and they had long experience of party politics as well as the organization of mass movements. The PSP had run the CTC during its first decade and party militants were the only ORI members with prior government experience, having served in Congress in pre-revolutionary years and contributed ministers (including Carlos Rafael Rodríguez) to Batista's war cabinet in the early 1940s. As a result, they initially dominated the ORI.

The organization of party cells, selection of party members, and all promotions and dismissals had to be cleared through the office of the powerful Organization Secretary, veteran PSP leader Aníbal Escalante. Party cells asserted their authority over administrators, and a preliminary system of political commissars was introduced in the armed forces. Membership in the party, moreover, emphasized recruiting those who had belonged to the older political organizations; recruitment of genuine newcomers was not encouraged. Escalante gave preference to his old PSP comrades, who knew best how to organize a party and were personally loyal to him. This proved unacceptable for old 26 of July members and especially to the military commanders of the guerrilla war. In March 1962, Fidel Castro denounced Escalante for 'sectarianism', removed him from the job as organization secretary, and exiled him to Czechoslovakia. A massive restructuring of the ORI followed; about half the ORI members were expelled, many of them from the PSP faction. New efforts were made to recruit members not only from the pre-existing organizations but also from among those who had been too young for political activity before 1959. The scope of party authority in the armed forces was drastically limited; henceforth, military commanders would have supreme military and political authority within the armed forces. In 1963 the ORI's name was changed to the Partido Unido de la Revolución Socialista (PURS).

In 1962, revolutionary power had become consolidated, although the leaders would not realize this for some years. The threat from the United States began to recede as a consequence of the settlement of the missile crisis. Fidel Castro had established his mastery of Cuban politics and his pre-eminence over all rivals. The organization of revolutionary rule beyond his charisma was under way, even though it would become effective only in the 1970s. Opponents of the regime took up in arms in every province in the first half of the 1960s, being especially strong in the Escambray mountain region of Las Villas province. Thousands of Cubans died in this renewed civil war (1960–5), the rebels including the peasantry of southern Matanzas province as well as those whose social and economic interests were more obviously at stake. They were, however, thoroughly defeated by 1965. (With many like-minded Cubans emigrating, the regime, in effect, exported the opposition.) The main task had become the management of the economy, the rapid decline of which imperilled the accomplishment of other government goals.

ECONOMIC POLICIES AND PERFORMANCE

Following the establishment of a command economy under conditions of political crisis, early economic policy in revolutionary Cuba sought development through rapid industrialization. Cuba's overwhelming dependence on the sugar industry was seen as a sign of under-development. As Che Guevara, Minister of Industries and architect of the strategy, put it, 'there can be no vanguard country that has not developed its industry. Industry is the future'.[4]

---

[4] *Obra revolucionaria* 10 (1964): 14.

Central state ministries were established and a development plan was formulated with help from many sources but especially from the Soviet Union and East European countries. Cuba was utterly unprepared, however, for a centrally planned economy. It lacked technical personnel (now in the United States or prison) as much as statistics. The plan for 1962 and the plan for 1962–5 were both fantasies. Data did not exist to formulate them and knowledge of economic management was primitive. The plans called for the achievement of spectacular growth targets. Instead, the Cuban economy collapsed in 1962. The government froze prices and imposed rationing for most consumer products. The ration card, a fixture in Cuban life ever since, combines two important aspects of the government's economic performance: relative failure to generate economic growth coupled with relative success in protecting the needs of the poorest Cubans and reducing inequalities in access to basic goods and services. Redistribution policies sought not only to enhance the purchasing power of the poor but also to curtail that of the rich. Wage scales set maximum as well as minimum salaries. In a suprising move the government changed the currency overnight; those who did not have their funds in state banks could not exchange old for new pesos. Their savings were worthless.

The Cuban economy fell further in 1963. Sugar production was down by over a third of its 1961 level as a result of the government's drastic policies to diversify away from the crop. Production elsewhere in agriculture and industry also suffered. Imports of machinery and equipment for accelerated industrialization, coupled with the decline of revenues from sugar exports, created a balance-of-payments crisis. In June 1963, Prime Minister Castro announced a new strategy which once again emphasized sugar production and slowed down the efforts toward industrialization. The strategy of sugar-led development was reaffirmed in 1964 when the Soviet Union and Cuba signed their first long-term agreement that guaranteed better, stable bilateral sugar prices and, eventually, Soviet subsidies above world market prices for Cuban sugar.

The government's strategy called for increasing sugar production until 10 million tons of raw sugar would be produced in 1970. This policy was opposed by a number of technicians and administrators in the sugar industry, but they were overruled. The 1970 sugar production target became a point of pride, a demonstration that Cubans could take charge of their history against all odds. Just as the impossible dream had been achieved in the late 1950s when Batista was overthrown, so would another be achieved at the end of the 1960s as committed revolutionaries demonstrated that they could raise the level of sugar production from 3.8 million tons in 1963 to 10 million tons in 1970. The doubters would be proven wrong again.

The new strategy was complicated, however, by a top-level debate on the nature of socialist economic organization. One side, led by Minister of Industries Che Guevara, argued that the part of the economy owned by the state was a single unit. Money, prices and credit should operate only in dealing with Cuban consumers or foreign countries. The market law of supply and demand could and ought to be eliminated to move rapidly toward communism. Central planning was the key. All enterprises would be branches of central ministries. All financing would occur through the central budget by means of non-repayable interest-free grants. All enterprise deficits would be covered by the state. Buying and selling among state enterprises would be simple accounting transactions. Money would be a unit of accounting but would not be used to assess profitability. Material incentives (wage differentials, bonuses, overtime payments) to labour would be phased out. The central government would allocate resources by planning physical output and would set all prices needed for accounting.

The other side argued that the part of the Cuban economy owned by the state was not a single economic unit but a variety of enterprises independently owned and operated by the state. Transfers from one enterprise to another did involve buying and selling, with profound implications for the allocation of resources. Money and credits were needed to maintain effective controls over production and to evaluate economic performance. Enterprises had to meet their own production costs and not simply be bailed out for their deficits by the central bank; they had to generate their own funds for further investment, maintenance and innovation. Material incentives to labour were essential to maintain productivity and quality and to reduce costs. If the first model required extraordinary centralization, the second required more economic autonomy for each firm.

The debate was eventually resolved when Che Guevara left the Ministry of Industries in 1965 (to be engaged in revolutionary campaigns in Africa and in South America until his death in late 1967) and the ministry was divided into its former sub-components. Some of Guevara's political allies in other ministries lost their jobs. However, Guevara's policies were generally adopted, and their implementation was carried out to extremes. Much of the calamity in economic performance in the late 1960s is due to Guevara's flawed vision as well as to the administrative chaos unleashed by

Fidel Castro and his associates, as Castro himself would recognize in a dramatic speech on 26 July 1970 when the Cuban economy lay in ruins.

The radical model required the fuller centralization of the economy. As early as 1963 a second Agrarian Reform law was issued to expropriate the middle-sized farms of the rural bourgeoisie that had remained after the implementation of the 1959 law. By the end of 1963, the state owned 70 per cent of all land, and only small farms remained in the private sector. The climax of collectivization came with the 'revolutionary offensive' of the spring 1968 when consumer service shops, restaurants and bars, repair outfits, handicraft shops, street food outlets and even street vendors passed to state ownership and management. Except in a limited way in a small part of the agricultural sector, no economically productive activity could take place in the late 1960s without going through a government agency. It was the time of the state as hot-dog vendor, ice-cream parlour, barber and radio repairman. Although an illegal black market developed, for vegetables as well as for plumbing services, the government had put the economy in a strait jacket.

Paradoxically, as the economy became thoroughly centralized, the means for central planning and control were abandoned. In the late 1960s there were neither real year-to-year national plans nor any medium-term planning. From late 1966 onwards only sectoral planning occurred, but on a limited basis and with little effort to reconcile the often conflicting claims on the same resources from unconnected enterprises and projects. A central budget was also abandoned, not to reappear until a decade later. Fidel Castro launched an attack on 'bureaucratism' which crippled the capacity of several central agencies. Financial accounting and auditing were discontinued; statistics were kept only in physical quantities (e.g., pairs of shoes). It became impossible to determine the costs of production for most items.

The changes in labour policy were equally dramatic. The phasing out of material incentives was to be coupled with a renewed emphasis on moral incentives: the revolutionary consciousness of the people would guarantee increased productivity and quality and reductions in cost. Workers would be paid the same regardless of variations in effort or quality. Those who worked overtime would be expected to do so voluntarily and would not receive extra pay. Money was seen as a source of capitalist corruption. This change in policy occurred in the wake of a major structural change in the labour market. Whereas Cuba had suffered a persistently high rate of overt unemployment before the Revolution, this had been reduced quickly in the early 1960s and been transformed into a labour shortage. Many of the formerly unemployed had been put to work in state enterprises. Productivity per worker plummeted as employment rose and production declined. Inefficiency and under-employment were institutionalized in the new economic structures. And yet this was also an extraordinary human achievement; it allowed most able-bodied Cubans the dignity of some work and the commitment to use their talents in a constructive way.

Economic performances was complicated by another change in the structure of the labour market. Because of the highly seasonal nature of the all-important sugar industry, pre-revolutionary employment patterns had suffered sharp seasonal oscillations. Workers worked very hard when they were employed to save for the expected unemployment during the 'dead season'. When the revolutionary government guaranteed employment (or sufficient unemployment compensation) throughout the year to all able to work the pre-revolutionary structural incentive to work hard weakened. Thus the revolutionary government succeeded in eliminating a perpetual source of misery – the fear of destitution as a worker stimulus – but this was not replaced by new effective incentives for high-quality work. As material incentives were removed on top of these structural changes, the problem of low and declining worker productivity worsened, as did labour shortages. No moral exhortations were incentive enough.

Since moral incentives proved insufficient to stimulate production and productivity the government engaged in mass mobilization for work in the sugar fields and other sectors of the economy. These so-called volunteers – who often lacked the right to refuse – were deployed throughout the country rather ineffectively. They were supplemented by a substantial portion of the personnel of the Cuban armed forces. Having defeated the internal counter-revolution by 1965, the armed forces committed themselves to directly productive economic activities including the harvesting of sugar cane. Military officers became harvest supervisors as the desperate effort to produce 10 million tons of sugar in 1970 combined with the shift towards radical economic policies and reliance on revolutionary consciousness. A new revolutionary citizen was to have emerged to lead Cuba to economic emancipation.

The economy was recorded as having produced 8.5 million tons in 1970 (by juggling the artificially low 1969 figures): the highest in Cuban history but still 15 per cent below target. Between 1968 and 1970 the Cuban economy was badly dislocated as resources were shifted among sectors without regard to the cost of achieving the impossible dream, the central government's actions promoting chaos while labour was coerced to work under military discipline without adequate rewards. Production in cattle-raising and forestry declined from 1968 to 1970, as did over 68 per cent of all agricultural product lines and over 71 per cent of all industrial product lines; even the fishing sector, the best performer under revolutionary rule, showed more declines than increases.

By 1970 Cuba's economic growth performance was dismal. Two sharp recessions had marked the beginning and end of the decade, the intervening years showing only a modest recovery. The standard of living was extremely spartan, and discontent surfaced at all levels. To his credit, Prime Minister Castro took personal responsibility for the disaster and changed economic policies in the first half of the 1970s.

Relief for the Cuban economy came from an unexpected quarter: the world sugar market. Prices for sugar in the free world market soared from an annual average of 3.68 cents of a dollar in 1970 to 29.60 cents in 1974. Given that sugar exports had continued to account for about four-fifths of all exports, this prize bonanza alone accounts for much of Cuba's economic recovery in the first half of the 1970s. The government also moved to reform internal economic organization by adopting and adapting the Soviet economic model. Central macro-economic planning reappeared in the early 1970s, enabling Cuba to adopt its first five-year plan in 1975. The first plan (1976–80) proved too optimistic and many of its targets were not reached (the growth rate was one-third below plan) since it had been based on the assumption that world sugar prices would remain higher than proved to be the case in the late 1970s. Nonetheless, it was more realistic than anything the government had adopted before. A central budget was again designed and implemented from 1977. Financial accounting and auditing were reinstituted, and material incentives received renewed emphasis as various reforms in monetary, price and wage policies sought to align supply and demand more accurately. The Soviet Union also channelled considerable resources to bring the Cuban economy afloat again.

One indication of how badly organized the Cuban economy had been in the 1960s is that many of the new measures formulated early in the 1970s could not be implemented until the late 1970s or early 1980s. Delays were also caused, however, by some opposition to the liberalization of the Cuban economy. And yet, as the 1980s opened, farmers were allowed to sell the surplus to their state quotas in markets where prices were unregulated and transactions were between private persons; this also occurred in handicraft markets and in the after-hours and weekend contracting of services. At long last one could hire a plumber or buy tomatoes without dealing with a bureaucracy. State enterprises received greater autonomy to contract labour directly rather than depending wholly on the central labour agency. A new management system was gradually adopted and implemented in the late 1970s and early 1980s to provide managers with more autonomy and authority. It allowed each enterprise to retain some profits to distribute to staff and workers at the end of the year and to improve the enterprise and its working conditions. Wage differentials, overtime pay and bonuses came to play a major role in labour incentives. Higher wages were paid for better-quality work, productivity improvements, cost reduction and longer hours.

The economy prospered almost spectacularly during the first half of the 1970s, Cuba's growth rate in those years comparing well with that of the world's leading growth performers. However, the economy stagnated during the second half of the decade except for 1978. The third major severe recession under revolutionary rule was under way by mid-1979, encouraging the outburst of emigration in 1980 just as the prolonged recession of the late 1960s increased the emigration of those years.

Weak economic performance at the beginning of the 1980s put pressure on the country's foreign-debt service payments. Although Cuba has not been a major borrower in the international capital markets, its hard-currency foreign debt in 1982 was about $3 billion. When foreign trade became more concentrated with the Soviet Union exports generated less revenue for servicing the hard-currency debt. The ensuing negotiations with European, Arab and Japanese bankers led to policies that decreased consumption levels in the early 1980s in order to meet Cuban debt obligations.

One major difference between these two periods of economic performance was the price of sugar. Although it rose steadily from 1970 to 1974, it fell to an average of about 8 cents per pound during the second half of the 1970s. After a short-lived rise in late 1980 and early 1981 the world price of sugar fell to the 6- to 8-cent level. Moreover, troubled by its own weak economic performance, the Soviet Union in 1981 cut by one-sixth the price it paid for Cuban sugar while continuing to raise the prices it charged for its exports to Cuba. Cuba's terms of trade with the Soviet Union in 1982 – when Cuba had to reschedule its debts with market-economy lenders – were one-third lower than in 1975. The recovery of the price the Soviets paid for Cuban sugar in subsequent years prevented a more severe economic crisis, even if the Cuban–Soviet terms of trade remained well below what they were in the mid- to late 1970s. Sugar prices remain closely related to the swings in Cuban economic performance, underscoring the commodity's persistently central role in the economy.

The adoption of some economic reforms in the early 1970s had quick and positive results, but by the late 1970s productivity improvements were more difficult to attain. Fidel Castro told the third party Congress in 1986 that Cuba still suffered from 'the absence of comprehensive national planning for economic development'. He added that the new management system, after a good beginning, had 'no consistent follow-through to improve it. The initiative was lost and the creativity needed to adapt this system to our own conditions – a system largely taken from other countries – never materialized'. Even 'the budget continued to be ineffective. Rather than regulating spending, it, in effect, promoted it'.[5]

To address these problems, in April 1986 Castro launched a process that he called 'rectification'. Cuba was the first communist regime in the late 1980s to back off from market mechanisms in order to improve production and efficiency. Castro denounced heads of state enterprises for having become apprentice capitalists. He lashed out at the lure of 'vile money'. To stamp out the curse of the market, in May 1986 the government banned the farmers' markets that had been legalized in 1980. Other anti-market measures were adopted and Castro lashed out against the reliance on bonuses to motivate the workers, calling once again for moral incentives to build a better society. The fact that the economy fell into a recession in 1986–7 partly reflected the inefficacy of these measures to rid Cuba from the vestiges of capitalism. There was, however, another enduring problem. The second half of the 1970s was also the period of the two major African wars and of the deployment of large numbers of Cubans overseas, which relied on the mobilization of reservists. A majority of Cuban troops in Ethiopia, about four-fifths of the Cuban troops in Angola and almost all Cuban personnel in Grenada were reservists at the peak of the wars and the U.S. invasion. Given the desire to win the wars and to perform well overseas in military roles, some of the best managers, technicians and workers were taken from the home economy for the overseas army, contributing to a decline in productivity and efficiency in various sectors since the

[5] *Granma Weekly Review,* 16 February 1986, special supplement, 6, 7.

late 1970s. Although the number of Cuban troops in Ethiopia was reduced sharply by the mid-1980s, more than 30,000 Cuban troops remained in Angola in the late 1980s.

The Cuban revolutionary government sought to generate economic growth from the moment it arrived in power but except for the recovery of the early 1970s these policies did not succeed. There was no growth at all during the 1960s. The economy's performance after 1975 failed to reach many planned targets. It generated only modest real economic growth and suffered a major recession as well as serious international debt problems. The structure of production diversified only a little. Sugar remained king, generating about four-fifths of export revenue. However, the government had also implemented a strategy of import substituting industrialization, evolving gradually in the 1970s and continuing in the 1980s – decades after such strategies appeared in most major Latin American countries. Cuba's factories now provided a wider array of light- and medium-industry products. However, their inefficiency and the poor quality of their products remained a problem while non-sugar agricultural production continued to perform poorly with few exceptions (eggs, citrus fruits). Cuba has been unable to diversify its international economic relations to any great extent: there was overwhelming dependence on one product (still, sugar cane) and one country (now, the Soviet Union). The tendency in the late 1970s and early 1980s was to retain dependence on both.

On the other hand, government economic performance was impressive with respect to redistribution. There was a strong and generally successful commitment to provide full employment for all able-bodied citizens (despite the reappearance of overt unemployment in the 1970s, reaching 5.4 per cent in 1979), even at the cost of under-employment and inefficiency. Equally, access to basic goods at low prices was provided through the rationing system, even at the cost of subsidizing consumption. The government's policies in the 1960s dramatically reduced inequalities between social classes and between town and country. The improvement in the rural poor's standard of living was outstanding. The trend in the 1970s and 1980s toward greater use of material incentives led to a new inequality that stimulated good managerial and worker performance. Nevertheless, the leadership retained its commitment to meet the basic needs of its people, and Cuba remained a very egalitarian society by Latin American standards.

SOCIAL TRENDS

Cuba underwent a demographic transformation after the Revolution came to power. There was a 'baby boom' in the early 1960s, the crude birth-rate increasing by about a third compared to the late 1950s; then the crude birth-rate stayed above 30 births per 1,000 population from 1960 to 1968. The principal explanation for the baby boom is probably the improved economic conditions for lower-income Cubans resulting from redistributional policies and improved health facilities in the rural areas. Increased wages, an end to overt unemployment, reduced rents and guaranteed access to basic necessities, including education and health care, provided a 'floor' for all Cubans. At the same time, the government launched a campaign to promote marriages, including the legalization of the many pre-existing consensual unions. Contraceptive supplies, previously available from the United States, were cut off by the U.S. trade embargo. The emigration broke up families and opened up new opportunities for relationships for those remaining in Cuba. The emigration of doctors and other health-care personnel reduced opportunities for abortion, as did the more effective enforcement of a pre-revolutionary law restricting abortion.

The initial impact of the baby boom was masked by emigration. Population growth rates declined in the early 1960s, but when the first wave of emigration was shut off at the time of the missile crisis the growth rate reached the highest level since the 1920s: over 2.6 per cent per year. The baby boom also began to have a dramatic impact on the primary school system, which had to expand overnight, and on the delivery of other social services to the young. The government's ability to deliver such services is a striking demonstration of its commitment to support the young even in years of economic decline.

The baby boom was followed by a baby bust. The crude birth rate was reduced by half between the end of the 1960s and the end of the 1970s, when the population growth rate was one-third of what it had been in the mid-1960s. As a result of the emigration outburst, there was a net decline in population in 1980, when Cuba's age pyramid showed that the population aged fifteen to nineteen (the peak of the baby boom) was 50 per cent larger than the population aged twenty to twenty-four (born just before the Revolution). One consequence of the baby boom was to allow the government regularly to station 35,000 young men in its overseas armed forces. The population under age five (the 'baby bust') was somewhat smaller than the population aged twenty to twenty-four, and it was one-third smaller than the population aged fifteen to nineteen. The baby bust had as many implications for social services as did the baby boom; one initial effect was Cuba's ability to export primary school teachers to work overseas in foreign-aid missions. In the long run, the baby bust might have made it more difficult for Cuba to station its armies overseas in the 1990s.

Cuban fertility had been declining gradually before the Revolution. The high level of social modernization probably contributed to the renewed fertility decline, but its magnitude and suddenness in the 1970s could not be explained with reference to long-term processes alone. The new fertility decline began in the late 1960s with the economy's sharp deterioration. However, it continued unabated during both the economic recovery of the first half of the 1970s and the economic slow-down at the end of the decade. The economy's poor performance is a necessary but insufficient condition for explaining the fertility decline. In 1964, restrictions on abortion were eased. Abortion became legal and easy, Cuba's abortion ratio (the number of abortions per 1,000 pregnancies) rising steadily from the 1960s so that by the end of the 1970s two out of five pregnancies were ended by abortion. Only Bulgaria, Japan and the Soviet Union had a higher abortion ratio. Indeed, abortion probably became the main birth-control method. While the number of abortions doubled from 1968 to 1978, the number of live births fell by two-fifths. Other means of contraception, however, also became more available within the national health system and these contributed to a fertility decline too. After the sharp increases of the previous decade the marriage rate stabilized in the mid- and late-1970s, but the divorce rate quadrupled from its pre-revolutionary level, about one in three marriages ending in divorce throughout the 1970s. It is likely that the greater incidence of divorce helped to reduce the birth rate. The continuing severe housing shortage also discouraged marriages because couples did not wish to live with their in-laws, or if they did, there was rarely space to house children. The permanent stationing of some 50,000 Cubans overseas in the late 1970s must also have contributed to reduce fertility.

According to the 1981 national census, there were 9,706,369 Cubans living in Cuba, one-fifth of whom lived in the city of Havana – a slightly smaller proportion than in the 1970 census. Cuba had become an urban country. While the level of urbanization increased slowly between 1953 and 1970 (from 57 per cent to 60 per cent), it jumped to 69 per cent in 1981. Urban growth also occurred outside the capital. While Havana grew 7.7 per cent from 1970 to 1981, Victoria de las Tunas grew by 58 per cent and Holguín and Bayamo by more than 40 per cent. Seven other cities grew by more than 24 per cent in that period, and the number of towns with a population of 95,000 or more doubled in the 1970s. In short, urbanization occurred mostly outside the primate city (Havana), a rare outcome by Latin American standards.

The experience of women changed considerably under revolutionary rule. As we have seen, women were more likely to get married, get divorced and have an abortion. They were much more likely to have children during the 1960s than during the 1970s. The proportion of women in the labour force also doubled from the late 1950s to the late 1970s, when they accounted for 30 per cent of the labour force. This resulted, however, from a gradual increase rather than from an abrupt change brought about by the Revolution. The increased entry of women into the labour force reflected an evolving social modernization although some government policies may have helped it. By contrast, the participation of Cuban women who emigrated to the United States increased much more and much more quickly: proportionately, twice as many Cuban-origin women in the United States than in Cuba were employed in the labour force in 1970, when a majority of Cuban-American women but only a quarter of Cuban women were in the labour force.

Some Cuban government policies discouraged female incorporation into the labour force. The government reserved certain categories of jobs for men on the grounds that women's health would be impaired were women to be engaged in those occupations, although no evidence was released to justify that policy. As the young 'baby boom' workers entered the labour force rapidly, government policies sought to maintain a constant sex ratio in the labour force instead of helping the proportionate incorporation of women.

There was an impressive increase in the numbers of women throughout the educational system. Women were represented at levels comparable to their share of the population in formerly predominantly male professional schools at the university, such as medicine, the natural sciences and economics. Although they remained under-represented in engineering and agronomy and over-represented in primary and secondary school teaching and in the humanities, a fundamental shift had occurred. The government, however, imposed quotas to limit the increase in women's enrolment in certain professional schools such as medicine on the grounds that women were more likely to interrupt their careers and that women doctors would be less suitable for service in the armed forces.

Women's participation in politics lagged considerably. Women accounted for only 13 per cent of the Central Committees of the Communist Party of Cuba chosen in 1980 and 1986; there were no women in the party Secretariat and no women in the top government organ, the Executive Committee of the Council of Ministers. The first woman entered the party's Political Bureau in 1986: Vilma Espín, Raúl Castro's wife and president of the Women's Federation. Women were also under-represented at the middle ranks of leadership. Surveys suggested the persistence of sexual stereotypes in the home (despite government efforts through a Family Code approved in the mid-1970s to equalize status between spouses in the family), the workplace and in politics. Women and men clung to traditional female roles.

There was little research on race relations after the Revolution. Because Cuba's black and mulatto population was disproportionately poor, and because the poor benefited disproportionately from government policies, blacks were likely to have benefited from such policies. Available surveys suggested stronger black than white support for the government; until 1980 blacks were greatly under-represented among Cuban exiles. The 1980 emigration outburst included urban blacks in numbers comparable to their share of the urban population. The government eliminated the few racially discriminatory legal bars that existed before the revolution but this had modest impact. The government sought to include the symbolism of Cuba's African heritage at the forefront of the justifications for Cuba's actions in African countries. However, the gaps between whites and blacks may not have changed as much during the past decades. For example, although health standards for the entire population improved, the relatively higher vulnerability of blacks to diseases (especially parasitic diseases that afflict poor populations) continued. The gap in access to health care between whites and blacks did not change much either, despite the undoubted gains in this regard for most Cubans.

Perhaps because the leaders of the revolutionary movement in the 1950s were disproportionately white and because they continued to command the heights of power, blacks were greatly under-represented in the top organs of government and party. The level of black representation changed little from before the revolution – when Batista was Cuba's first mulatto president – to the 1986 party congress when President Castro declared it a matter of party policy to increase the black share of top party organs; whereas one-third of the total population was black (1981 census), the black share of the 1986 Central Committee was just one-fifth. Only in elections to local municipal assemblies were blacks apparently represented in numbers comparable to their share of the population.

Since the government claimed to have solved racial problems, it became subversive to argue that they persisted even if in modified form. The government banned associations of black intellectuals and politicians that had existed before the Revolution. A number of those who insisted there were still serious racial problems in Cuban society, or distinctive intellectual issues among Afro-Cubans, became exiles.

Cuba's educational transformation was the revolutionary government's most impressive achievement. The government advanced Cuba's social modernization by the sharp reduction of illiteracy (down to 12.9 per cent in the 1970 census and to 5.6 per cent in 1979), starting with a major campaign in 1961 which was continued through the extensive adult education system. The government expropriated all private (including Church-affiliated) schools. After difficulties during the 1960s, the government accomplished virtual universal attendance at primary schools. Average educational levels in the labour force jumped from bare literacy in the 1964 labour census to sixth grade in the 1974 labour census and to eighth grade in the large 1979 demographic survey. In 1979, two-fifths of the adult population had completed the ninth grade and two-thirds the sixth grade.

The boom in primary education reflected both government conscious policy and the need to accommodate the baby boom. By the late 1970s, primary school enrolments had begun to decline as a result of the baby bust. From 1974–5 (the peak year in primary school enrolment) to 1980–1, primary school enrolment (including preschool) fell 20 per cent. The remarkably adaptive school system increased junior high school enrolment by 121 per cent and senior high school enrolment by 427 per cent over the same period. Between 400,000 and 700,000 people per year were enroled in adult education schools during the 1970s.

The primary school system reduced – but did not eliminate – the differences in access to quality education between urban and rural Cuba. A generous programme of scholarships also helped to reduce class differences in access to education at the post-primary levels. There were a number of serious problems of quality in Cuban schools during the 1960s – high drop-out rates, low levels of teacher training, poor student and poor teacher performance in the classroom. Although some of these problems remained, the qualitative improvement in the 1970s matched the still excellent quantitative performance inherited from the 1960s. Many people deserved credit for these accomplishments, including Fidel Castro, whose concern with education was a key feature of the government's commitment. However, the long-serving vice-president of the Council of Ministers and Minister of Education, José Ramón Fernández, deserved special mention. He skilfully managed the transition from the baby boom to the bust, the adjustments and expansions of enrolment, and the marked improvements in the quality of education, notwithstanding the problems, that, as he recognized, still remained.

Higher education had a more tortuous history. Enrolment declined in the 1960s, to increase only in the next decade. Faculty ranks were decimated by politically inspired dismissals and emigration. Most students were enroled only in night school, where the quality of the instruction and the experience ranged from poor to variable because many teachers were overworked, resources were limited and there were too many students. There was a strong technical bias to higher education that encouraged enrolment in engineering and discouraged it in the humanities. The academic study of the social sciences was neglected, and that which was undertaken avoided contemporary issues of political significance within Cuba. Since 1959, however, there had been superb historiographical scholarship whose crowning glory was Manuel Moreno Fraginals's trilogy on the sugar mill in the eighteenth and nineteenth centuries (*El ingenio*). Good historiography stops generally around 1935, just before the beginning of the subsequently embarrassing alliance between Batista and the Communist Party.

The universities were organized on a broad 'industrial model', to train professional personnel in a hierarchical system. They de-emphasized the development of the liberal arts or the possibility of active intellectual criticism of major political, social, economic or cultural problems. Many of Cuba's leading writers of the 1960s and 1970s lived overseas (Guillermo Cabrera Infante, Severo Sarduy, Reinaldo Arenas, Heberto Padilla, Edmundo Desnoes, Antonio Benítez Rojo, among others) or had died (Alejo Carpentier and José Lezama Lima). Political criteria were among the factors in making decisions on student admissions even to non-political professions such as medicine and despite the fact that the universities and the Academy of Sciences emphasized applied technical research. Medical research, and research on the agriculture and processing of sugar cane, both with long pre-revolutionary traditions, were the major areas of scientific achievement.

Although Cuba had a high level of literacy (about three-quarters of all adults) and relatively high levels of school enrolment before the Revolution, these had stagnated in the middle third of the twentieth century. The revolutionary government thus took up the task of educational modernization where it had been left in the 1920s to institutionalize an educational revolution that was rightly the pride of its people and government and an outstanding example of sustained commitment to other countries. Cuban schoolteachers ably served their country's foreign policy and the needs of ordinary students over three continents. The educational system, however, was inhospitable to political and intellectual dissent; it restricted freedom of expression and repressed many critics. The fruits of education and culture were thus curtailed. For this tragic loss, Cuba served as a negative example of the uses of government power to limit the full development of human potential.

Government policies and performance in the area of health care also registered appreciable success. The government quickly established health care as the right of every citizen, expanding the system of free provision that had existed before the Revolution. There were early advances in the rural areas, improving the delivery of health care and narrowing the gap between town and country. However, general performance deteriorated during the 1960s compared to the quite highly developed pre-revolutionary health system, this trend largely resulting from the worsening health care in the cities, where most people lived. Many doctors and other health-care professionals left the country and because they had been concentrated in Havana the capital suffered disproportionately. Existing medical services and facilities were disrupted by political and military mobilizations. Inefficient production of medicines and the disruption of ties with the United States led to a shortage of medical supplies which had a particular impact on upper-income urban consumers with access to and resources to buy imported medicines. The emergency health-care training program to replace the departing exiles was uneven in quality, and the health system was affected as much as other areas of state enterprise by the disorganization of the 1960s.

During the early 1960s the general as well as the infant mortality rates worsened. The infant mortality rate (deaths under age one per 1,000 live births) rose from thirty-five in 1959 to forty-seven ten years later, the rates for major diseases also worsening during these years. The commitment of government budgetary resources to urban health care faltered as resources were channelled to the rural areas. Indeed, until the early 1970s the performance of the health-care system was not unlike that of the Cuban economy: much better in redistribution among social classes and geographic regions than in growth. By the mid 1970s, thanks in part to preceding economic improvements, the system made great advances. The infant mortality rate fell to 18.5 per 1,000 by the time of the 1981 census, and morbidity rates fell across the spectrum of serious diseases. It must be remembered, however, that Cuba already had a rather mature health-care system on the eve of the Revolution. Thus, six of the top eight causes of death were identical in 1958 and in 1981; heart disease, cancers, diseases of the central nervous system, influenza and pneumonia, accidents and early childhood diseases. On the other hand, although acute diarrheic diseases, homicides, tuberculosis and nephritis were among the top ten causes in 1958, they had been replaced by suicides, diabetes, congenital malformations and respiratory diseases by 1981. These changes brought Cuba closer to the typical health profile for an industrial country in ways that could have been predicted from Cuba's long-term pattern of health-care modernization.

At the start of the 1980s the government's most significant accomplishment in health care remained the reduction of inequality in access to health care among social classes and regions. Havana's advantage over eastern Cuba narrowed. The set-backs of the 1960s were overcome and health standards genuinely improved, building on the good but insufficient levels of the 1950s. Cuba posted talented health-care personnel in three-dozen countries the world over. Some of these programmes sold their medical services to host governments, earning foreign exchange for Cuba's transnational state enterprises. Most such programmes, however, were free of charge to the recipient country.

The revolutionary government's poor performance in housing construction resulted from insufficient production, inefficiency and disorganization in the construction and construction-materials industries. The government did not give high priority in the allocation of construction resources to meeting the housing needs of the population. Its principal goals in this area included the building of hospitals, schools and military installations and the deployment of some of the best construction teams overseas.

In the late 1940s and early 1950s, with a population half of that three decades later, pre-revolutionary Cuba built almost 27,000 housing units per year. In the early 1960s, the rate fell to just over 17,000 units per year; very little housing was built in the radical period of the late 1960s. During the first Five Year Plan (1976–80), just over 16,000 housing units per year were built. The trend in the late 1970s was towards a decline in the rate of housing construction at the same time as more construction workers were deployed overseas and the Cuban armed forces expanded: Cuba built almost 21,000 housing units in 1973 (the peak year since 1959) but not even 15,000 in 1980.

The housing situation was alleviated somewhat by the emigration. From 1959 to 1975, emigration made available about 9,300 units on the average per year; during those same years, average housing construction was about 11,800 units. This meant that about one-third of the new demand for housing went unsatisfied each year. Considering that much of the pre-revolutionary housing stock was already in deplorable condition and that there was much evidence that thousands of housing units collapsed out of poor maintenance, Cuba faced a terrible housing problem in the 1980s. The housing shortage and the resultant overcrowding have been among the major causes for Cuba's high divorce rate and rapidly declining fertility rate.

POLITICS AND GOVERNMENT

The central figure in Cuba's revolutionary politics was Fidel Castro, his leadership remaining charismatic in the sense that it depended on the conviction that he did not depend on election by his followers but had been 'elected' by a supernatural authority or some 'historical force'. He also depended on the citizenry's sharing that conviction. Castro's sense of mission was a persistent theme in his many public statements. The concluding phrase to the edited version of his defence at his trial for attacking the Moncada barracks on 26 July 1953 provided the first major statement of this belief: 'Condemn me; it does not matter to me. History will absolve me'.[6] History-as-god elects the revolutionary leader to act with and for his followers. Or, as he put it in perhaps the most difficult speech of his government career when he reported publicly on the economic collapse of

---

[6] English text in Rolando Bonachea and Nelson P. Valdés (eds.), *Revolutionary Struggle, 1947–1958: The Selected Works of Fidel Castro* (Cambridge, Mass., 1972), vol. 1.

the late 1960s: 'If we have an atom of value, that atom of value will be through our service to an idea, a cause, linked to the people'.[7] The cause, the idea, history incarnate, elects the leader to rule. Castro's sway over his associates and many ordinary citizens has been the single most striking political fact of contemporary Cuban history.

Castro's political style emphasized active engagement as opposed to theoretical pursuits. It also highlighted the power of self-discipline and conscious action, as opposed to the pre-revolutionary Communists who were waiting for objective conditions to ripen to launch their revolution when Castro's forces swept into power and in contrast to those economists who argued that the strategy to produce 10 million tons of sugar in 1970 was madness. Subjective will was the fundamental resource for revolutionary leaders to overcome objective obstacles in war, politics or economics. A vanguard, an elite, must lead the people and awaken them to their historical responsibilities. Moreover, only the maximum possible effort toward the optimal goal was worth pursuing. The apparently unattainable goal was alone worthy because it was clear that the revolutionary consciousness of women and men provided the essential margin for victory. An activist, determined vanguard would reach for the future – and conquer it.

This approach to politics brought the Cuban Revolution to power and led the revolutionary government to undertake a number of successful activities, ranging from victory in the battlefields of the Horn of Africa to the overcoming of illiteracy. It also led to some disasters and tragedies, of which the economic and social experiments of the late 1960s provide the best general example. But many other smaller projects were also disasters, responding to a whim or a passing thought of Castro's to which subordinates dedicated themselves with fervour and commitment for no sensible purpose. This style of leadership bred intolerance toward critics, dissenters, or even those who were just somewhat unconventional. This style of rule rejected out of hand the hypothesis that the great leader's policies might be in error – until disaster struck.

Revolutionary rule was legitimized not only by charisma but also by performance. Cuba, its new leaders said from the moment they seized power in 1959, had been delivered from a terroristic, corrupt, abusive and illegitimate political system. Fidel Castro's consummate oratorical skills – alternately mellow and fierce, jocular or insulting towards his enemies,

[7] *Granma Weekly Review*, 2 August 1970, 6.

thoughtful or emotional, learned and complex before professional audiences or simple, funny and tender in dialogue with schoolchildren – became one of the Revolution's most powerful weapons. He commanded the airwaves of radio and television in a country where both were well established by 1959. He moved incessantly throughout the country as a revolutionary prophet touching, moving, educating and steeling his people for combat: to struggle for a new life, a better future, against known and unknown enemies.

The government continually emphasized its redistribution to the benefit of lower-income people, and especially the better-implemented policies in education and health care. Even when government leaders acknowledged the failure of economic growth strategies, they stressed the gains accomplished in redistribution and social services. A social cleavage, much clearer than at any other point in Cuban history, became the basis for majority support for revolutionary rule in the difficult days of the early 1960s. Nationalism was a further source of legitimacy, affirming the cultural, political and historical integrity of the Cuban nation and emphasizing the unity of the people rather than the legitimacy which might have been derived from any one segment such as the proletariat. Nationalism gained further strength from the struggle against the U.S. government. The class enemies became 'worms'; the foreign enemies 'imperialists'.

In the absence of national elections from 1959 to 1976, or of other effective organizational channels to voice grievances and opinions, charisma, political deliverance, redistribution and nationalism were the pillars on which the right to rule was claimed. The Revolution itself, and its maximum leader, were self-legitimating, although this claim was certainly not universally accepted.

The mass organizations taken over in 1959 or created in 1960–1 have since mobilized the population to build political support for the government and to deter internal enemies. While they respond principally to centralized direction, they were by the 1970s exhibiting interest-group tendencies. The ANAP, in particular, was a strong lobbyist in defence of private peasant interests in the early 1960s and again from the mid-1970s to the mid-1980s. It has sought higher prices, easier credits and freer markets for peasants, and it has tried to curtail the forcible expropriation of peasant land by the state. Only in the radical period of the late 1960s was the autonomy of this and the other organizations virtually destroyed. The FEU was dissolved between December 1967 and 1971;

the height of radicalism tolerated none of the autonomy or dissent typical of university students. By the 1970s, however, even the CDRs (Committees for the Defense of the Revolution) had changed. While their paramount task remained 'revolutionary vigilance', they also adopted other community self-help missions. The mass organizations participated in most campaigns, both effective and ineffective, launched by the leadership. Among their most successful tasks were the reduction of illiteracy and of diseases subject to control through mass immunization campaigns. The CDRs were just as effective in this as they were in political control. The FMC played a prominent role in the sharp reduction of prostitution and the re-education and incorporation of former prostitutes into a new life.

The role of the labour unions in the late 1960s was to support management. Unions were directed to struggle to increase production and productivity, to exceed the goals set in the economic plans, to organize competition ('emulation') among workers to accomplish official aims, and to reduce costs. Workers were to rise above narrow and temporary interests, such as better wages and better working conditions, to sacrifice themselves for the good of the people. Labour was exhorted to heroic efforts and to respond to moral incentives, voluntary work becoming a euphemism for unpaid overtime work. In August 1969, President Osvaldo Dorticós denounced the 'abuse of overtime and the deceit of overtime', but his was a lonely voice and he had little power notwithstanding his title.[8] In 1970 Fidel Castro produced the best epitaph for the unions in this period: 'Unfortunately, for the last two years, our workers' organizations have taken a back seat – not through the fault of either the workers' organizations or the workers themselves but through our fault, the party's fault, the fault of the country's political leadership'.[9]

By the second half of 1970 the workers had taken enough. They staged a general 'strike'. Strikes had been illegal since the early days of the revolution so the leadership described the 1970 event as 'large-scale absenteeism'. Although apparently uncoordinated, some 400,000 workers, a fifth of the work force, stayed away from work in August and September 1970 on any given day. In Oriente province, the cradle of the revolution, a majority of agricultural workers were absent from work in August 1970, and more than a fifth were still staying away in January 1971 even though

[8] 'Discurso del Presidente de la República, Dr. Osvaldo Dorticós Torrado, en la escuela de cuadros de mando del Ministerio de la Industria Ligera', *Pensamiento crítico* 45 (October 1970): 148.
[9] *Granma Weekly Review,* 4 October 1970, 2.

the new sugar harvest was under way. The elections in local labour unions in autumn 1970 were the freest and most competitive since 1959. Many controls over the election process were lifted. Approximately three-quarters of the local labour leaders elected at that time were new to the job. The changes in policy inaugurated in the first half of the 1970s thus responded, in part, to the 'leading role of the proletariat', forcibly communicating to the government that radical policies were no longer acceptable to labour.

As the conditions of labour improved in the early 1970s so were political controls re-established over the unions. By the time of the Thirteenth Labour Congress in 1973 elections by acclamation (rather than by secret ballot) for unopposed slates had reappeared. Representation at labour congresses came to favour the union bureaucracy, with only a minority of seats reserved for delegates elected at the grass roots. While the role of the unions in defence of the interests of the workers was emphasized anew in the heyday of the 1970 union elections, the more conservative approach prevailed again by 1973. Unions could make specific criticism of 'concrete' matters that were going wrong, but they were supposed to stay away from more autonomous political behaviour.

By the end of the 1970s, the membership of the mass organizations stabilized. The CDRs and the FMC encompassed about four-fifths of the adult population and of the adult women, respectively. Whereas the proportion of the relevant populations that belonged to these organizations rose until the mid-1970s, they remained fairly constant thereafter, subsequent growth in membership resulting mostly from demographic change. It became clear that about one-fifth of adult Cubans wanted nothing to do with the mass organizations, and vice versa.

Membership in the mass organization in the 1980s had become a prerequisite for a successful life in Cuba. Responsible positions were open only to those who were integrated into the revolutionary process by their membership in one or more such organizations. It was likely, therefore, that some proportion of the members did not support the regime but belonged to the mass organizations simply to make their own life easier; a substantial proportion of the 1980 exiles, for example, had belonged to such organizations. Some of the organizations, especially the labour unions, allocated certain resources: only those judged to have been vanguard workers had the right to acquire such consumer durables as sewing machines, refrigerators or television sets, and only they had priority access to scarce housing. Other workers could not acquire such goods even if they had the money.

The mass organizations thus became controllers of access to the good life — or at least to a bearable life.

The mass organizations and other political and bureaucratic institutions were subordinated to the party, a relationship which is made explicit in the Constitution of 1976. In the autumn of 1965, the party's name was changed again to the Communist Party of Cuba (PCC). At the same time, Fidel Castro unveiled the first one-hundred-member Central Committee, along with two smaller organs: the Political Bureau, responsible for the making of basic political decisions, and the Secretariat, charged with their implementation. Nevertheless, the party's influence remained limited for the balance of the decade. Not until the early 1970s were serious efforts made to turn it into an effective ruling Communist Party.

The party's first Congress was held in December 1975, the preparatory work for which was a major step forward to institutionalize PCC rule. The Congress approved party statutes, a programmatic platform and a number of statements or 'theses' on various subjects of national policy. It approved the draft of the new national Constitution, which was approved by a popular referendum in 1976. The Congress also approved the first five-year plan and other economic policies. The Central Committee was renovated and expanded to 112 members with a dozen alternates; new authority and activity were vested in the Political Bureau and Secretariat. Indeed, Cuba could be said to have had a functioning, ruling Communist Party only from the early 1970s when the preparations for this Congress were begun. A second party Congress was held in December 1980 and a third in February 1986. Each monitored, passed judgement, and largely ratified the previous half-decade's policies, renewing membership of the key party bodies, and approving new economic policies (including the second and third five-year plans) for the half-decade ahead.

The party's size grew from about 15,000 in 1962, when Aníbal Escalante fell, to 50,000 at the time of the foundation of the Communist Party in 1965. There were just over 100,000 members in 1970; slightly more than 200,000 on the eve of the first Congress; 434,143 on the eve of the second Congress; and 523,639 on the eve of the third Congress. In 1980 about 9 per cent of the population aged twenty-five and older belonged to the party.

The principal change in the composition of the Central Committee was the decline in the military's share of the membership, down among full members from 58 per cent in 1965 to 17 per cent in 1986. The bureaucracy's share of the Central Committee remained remarkably constant at about one-sixth of the membership until 1980, rising to more than one-quarter in 1986. The military's loss has been the politicians' gain. The share of professional politicians (including leaders of mass organizations) in the Central Committee rose from 17 per cent in 1965 to 41 per cent in 1986. The Central Committee membership was thus increasingly reflecting the need for routine government skills.

The military understandably had much influence in the 1960s. Cuba had rearmed quickly and massively to fight the United States. Many military commanders were the heroes of the revolutionary war of the late 1950s and had fought successfully against the internal counter-revolution and at the Bay of Pigs. Led by Raúl Castro, the armed forces had become the only truly well-organized segment of Cuban society in the 1960s. The military organized the party within its ranks, retaining political authority under the command and leadership of the officers, four-fifths of whom were party members by the early 1970s. The armed forces possessed the routine and procedure necessary for party-building whereas these were often lacking in civilian sectors in the radical period of the late 1960s. As a result, the government often relied on the military to perform social, economic and political tasks. These 'civic soldiers', competent in a wide array of fields, were consequently predominant in the party's ranks at all levels in the 1960s.

As the civilian party grew in the 1970s many 'civic soldiers' were transferred fully to civilian tasks, the armed forces concentrating on their military expertise and shedding many (though not all) strictly non-military activities. As the radical period faded, non-military modes of organization expanded, but the decline in the military share of the Central Committee did not mean that individuals who had been officers were removed from it. On the contrary, the rate of turnover in Central Committee membership has been slow, and those who left the armed forces to serve in civilian party or government posts in the 1970s and 1980s remained Central Committee members.

The share of top party organs accounted for by the old Communist Party (PSP) members remained at about one-fifth, albeit declining slightly over time (former PSP members were generally older than the rest of the leadership and more likely to have failing health). Particularly in the 1960s, the PSP share was affected by the factional splits among top leaders, of which the two most dramatic were the dismissal of Aníbal Escalante as party Organization Secretary in 1962 and the uncovering of a 'microfaction' (also linked to Escalante) in 1968. PSP influence declined markedly in the late 1960s.

In late 1967, the top leadership discovered what was called a 'microfaction' within the Cuban Communist Party. It was composed primarily of former PSP members who believed that government and party policies at home and abroad were wrong. Led by Aníbal Escalante, the microfaction developed ties to Soviet and East European government and party officials. Once uncovered, those who belonged to the Central Committee were dropped; many others were expelled from the party, and the leaders of the microfaction were sent to prison for their crimes of opinion and association, although they had taken no other steps that could be construed as counter-revolutionary. Since their diagnosis of mistaken Cuban policies would eventually prove correct, they were punished for having the right insights at the wrong time.

Microfactionists or not, most former PSP members supported close relations with the Soviet Union and correct relations with most governments. They opposed attacks on Latin American Communist parties and were wary of guerrilla movements; they believed in the need for material incentives during a period of transition to socialism and considered that labour unions had to play a more prominent role in politics. The microfactionists argued that mere reliance on the will and on subjective assessments was imprudent and that it was necessary to understand objective conditions in Cuba and abroad. Arguing that central planning, budgets, financial cost-accounting and other such tools were essential to build socialism, they were skeptical of mass-mobilization campaigns that sought to replace these conventional policies. The microfaction demanded the greater use and institutionalization of party organs and other political organizations, supporting the reintroduction of elections and a Constitution. Former PSP members were not the only ones who held these beliefs, but they constituted the most obvious 'faction'. The changes in policies in the 1970s followed these PSP preferences quite consistently not because the old politicians had defeated their rivals of an earlier day but because Fidel Castro and his close associates became persuaded of the wisdom of their arguments.

Former PSP members who, unlike Aníbal Escalante, remained loyal to Fidel Castro, emerged with special influence in the 1970s, Blas Roca and Carlos Rafael Rodríquez being two of the party's long-standing leaders. Roca took charge of the drafting of a new constitution and other basic legislation as well as overseeing their implementation. He made decisive contributions to institutionalization in the 1970s. Rodríguez was the intellectual architect of the change in internal and international economic policies; in the 1970s and 1980s his advice was influential from relations with the United States to policies towards the arts and letters.

Among others who contributed to government reorganization, institutionalization and improved performance in the 1970s were education minister José Ramón Fernández, armed forces minister Raúl Castro, foreign trade minister Marcelo Fernández, Central Planning Board president Humberto Pérez, and interior minister Sergio del Valle. Marcelo Fernández, dismissed in the midst of the 1979–80 crisis, had diversified economic relations and had succeeded in thoroughly undermining the U.S. economic embargo policies against Cuba. Humberto Pérez had the thankless task of informing the government of basic economic truths, reorganizing the economy from the debacle of the 1960s. He endeavoured to bring supply and demand into balance, adopt the mechanisms common to centrally planned economies, stimulate increases in efficiency and productivity, and promote cost reductions, while seeking to enhance managerial and worker participation in economic affairs. The poor performance of the economy should be attributed to the difficulty of these tasks rather than to Pérez's inadequacies. Nonetheless, he was dismissed in 1985, when overall economic co-ordination tasks were given to Osmany Cienfuegos.

Interior minister Sergio del Valle's work cannot be assessed easily. His responsibility remained throughout to repress the opposition and to retain full political control at all costs. However, del Valle deserves credit for softening the harshness of authoritarian controls that had existed in the 1960s. According to the government's official figures, the number of political prisoners fell from about 20,000 in the mid-1960s to 4,000 in the mid-1970s, and to as few as 1,000 when del Valle was removed from his post in the midst of the 1979–80 crisis. The incidence of torture declined and changed in character during del Valle's tenure. Physical torture virtually disappeared and prison conditions improved although psychological torture remained an occasional tool. The police began to observe procedural safeguards to protect the rights of the accused. In the revitalized court system in the late 1970s, cases would be dismissed for lack of evidence or for violations of established procedures. The persistence of many internal security measures was still, of course, subject to criticism at the end of del Valle's tenure, but he had professionalized his service, enhanced the rule of law, and reduced arbitrariness.

Important changes in the organization of the government were introduced in the first half of the 1970s. In November 1972 the Council of Ministers was reorganized to create an executive committee comprising the Prime Minister and all the deputy prime ministers, each of whom would supervise several ministries. The executive committee became the government's key decision-making organ. An experiment in local government was also introduced in 1974 in Matanzas, one of Cuba's six provinces. These procedures would be applied with some variations nationwide under the constitution approved in 1976.

The Constitution of 1976 mandated the establishment of a new National Assembly with legislative powers, these having been vested in the Council of Ministers between 1959 and 1976. The National Assembly would elect the Council of State to function when the assembly was not in session. The president of the Council of State would also become the head of state and serve as head of the government (president of the Council of Ministers). Fidel Castro became head of state replacing Osvaldo Dorticós. Unlike other socialist constitutions, Cuba's requires that the head of state and the head of the government be the same person, a typical Latin American pattern.

A new political and administrative division of the national territory was also implemented in 1976. Instead of the six provinces inherited from the nineteenth century (Pinar del Río, La Habana, Matanzas, Las Villas, Camagüey, Oriente) there would be fourteen: Pinar del Río, La Habana, city of La Habana, Matanzas, Cienfuegos, Villa Clara, Sancti Spíritus, Ciego de Avila, Camagüey, Las Tunas, Granma, Holguín, Santiago de Cuba, and Guantánamo. The Isle of Pines, soon to be renamed the Isle of Youth, became a special municipality. The regions into which the provinces had been subdivided were abolished. There would be 169 municipalities. The most dramatic changes were the splintering of Oriente and of Las Villas provinces into four and three new provinces, respectively.

The Constitution also established elected provincial and municipal governments. The 1976 nationwide elections were the first since 1959. The only direct elections, however, were for members of the municipal assemblies, who themselves elected the executive committee for each municipal assembly, the delegates to the provincial assemblies, and the deputies of the National Assembly. Assembly membership at all levels was a part-time position, members retaining their jobs while serving on the assemblies. The National Assembly normally met twice a year, each session lasting two or three days. Such conditions made it a weak counterpart to government and party organizations.

The electoral law, and some of the procedures in the Constitution itself, further limited the impact of these changes. Self-nomination for elections was impossible and candidates were only nominated in assemblies by a show of hands. Campaigning by the candidates was prohibited; they could not address issues. Only the Communist Party, or the government, could campaign and address the issues, making it impossible for critics to exchange views and information. They could not associate as a party because the Constitution accorded that right only to the PCC. The party and government published biographies of the candidates, who could not veto what may be included in those biographies. At times the only recourse to avoid public humiliation, if nominated against the party's wishes, was to withdraw from an election contest.

The electoral law strengthened the party's control over the higher offices. The lists of nominees for provincial delegates, for executives at the municipal and provincial levels, and for national deputies, was prepared by nominating commissions led by the party. Party members accounted for more than nine-tenths of the membership of the National Assembly. Moreover, provincial delegates and National Assembly deputies did not have to be elected directly by the people to the municipal assemblies in the first instance. The nominating commissions might put forth anyone judged worthy. Approximately 44.5 per cent of National Assembly deputies elected in 1976 to a five-year term had never faced the electorate directly.

The municipal, provincial and national assemblies played a modest role in politics. Their effective powers were far less than appears from a reading of the Constitution. Debate in the National Assembly on the bills that could be used to control the executive branch, such as the annual plan or budget, was perfunctory and votes were typically unanimous. At the provincial or municipal levels, the constraints of extremely limited budgets and the extraordinary authority reserved for central state organs had limited assembly effectiveness. Nonetheless, the National Assembly featured freer and somewhat influential debates on issues other than macroeconomic policy or foreign and military policy. On such matters as common crime, environmental protection and family legislation deputies had some influence over the content of bills. At the local level, the job of municipal assembly delegates was not unlike that of an ombudsman. These delegates gathered citizen complaints and sought to break through bureaucratic obstacles to improve the delivery of government services to their constituents. Indeed, the contacting of public officials to solve local needs – the hallmark of political machines – became one of the most effective means of political participation in Cuba.

The stimulation of citizen complaints to correct local government errors, and the satisfaction of some demands, marked a fundamental difference between politics in the first fifteen years of revolutionary rule and those thereafter. Such protests had been limited, and at times repressed, in the earlier years when the only permissible mode of political participation was mass mobilization. In a more institutionalized authoritarian setting, the regime now relied on subtler policies. At the local level citizens were allowed – at times encouraged – to voice criticisms of specific problems; for such purposes, Cuba now had considerable freedom of expression. The authoritarian constraints, however, limited freedom of association at all levels. Critics of the regime were not allowed to associate in protest or criticism of government policies. Moreover, even at the local level, more general or abstract criticism of the government was frowned upon.

Further constraints on freedom of political expression existed at both the provincial and the national level. Since the spring of 1960 all mass media had been in state hands. Except for occasional letters-to-the-editor that resembled the specific criticism of local problems just mentioned, the mass media provided relentless (and often dull) support for regime policies and activities. There was somewhat greater though still limited freedom of expression to publish artistic and scholarly materials. In 1961, Fidel Castro summarized the regime's cultural policies in an ambiguous phrase: 'Within the revolution, everything; against the revolution, nothing'.[10] Material opposed to the revolution was not published; that which was not explicitly critical of the regime but produced by its known opponents was also not published. Material produced by those whose behaviour was judged unconventional and unacceptable by the government (e.g., actual or rumoured homosexual behaviour) had an uncertain fate; homosexuals suffered greatest hostility in the late 1960s and again in 1980. There was, however, some freedom of expression for persons who supported the Revolution politically and who wrote on topics other than those bearing on contemporary politics.

Especially in the 1960s, Cuba's policies did not emphasize 'socialist realism' as the dominant form of artistic production. In contrast to the

---

[10] Fidel Castro, *Palabras a los intelectuales* (Havana, 1961).

Soviet Union, there was freedom to choose artistic and literary forms. By the 1970s the government was giving preference in exhibitions and publications to those who focused on 'the socialist reality', although this could still be done through some forms of abstract painting. One troubling feature of government policies towards artists and scholars was the possibility that policy might shift and that what appeared 'safe' to an author might not to the censor. Thus, self-censorship, rather than cruder measures, became the main limitation on artistic and scholarly freedom of expression.

One form of intellectual political activity with a modest history was the exposition of theoretical Marxism–Leninism. The main texts in courses on Marxism–Leninism were the speeches of Fidel Castro and other home-grown products. However, after the 1970s more serious efforts were made to disseminate the more abstract theoretical knowledge of Marxist-Leninist classics through the party schools and publications and through research and writing in the universities and the mass media. There was a more conscious effort to relate these theoretical writings to the specific concerns of contemporary Cuba. The main national daily newspaper, *Granma*, the official organ of the Communist Party, founded in autumn of 1965 from the merger of the newspapers of the 26 of July Movement (*Revolución*) and of the PSP (*Noticias de Hoy*), usually devoted a page to articles on theoretical and historical topics. Marxism–Leninism became a required subject in the universities for all professions.

As the 1980s began the regime had clearly consolidated its rule. It might be described as a consultative oligarchy under an undisputed leader. Fidel Castro retained the pivotal role that had marked Cuban politics since 1959, but his delegation of some responsibility to close associates gave the regime a more oligarchic, rather than simply personal, quality. There was an established elite interlinked at the top of party, state and government organs. Eleven of the sixteen members of the Political Bureau elected at the Second Party Congress in December 1980 were also members of the Council of Ministers; fourteen of the Political Bureau members belonged to the Council of State (where they constituted a majority). Of the fourteen members of the executive committee of the Council of Ministers, eight were also Political Bureau members. By the 1986 third party Congress the need for greater delegation was recognized. Although every Political Bureau member retained one other major elite post, only six of the fourteen were simultaneously members of the Councils of State and of ministers as well. Still, between two and three dozen people now occupied all the significant top jobs in party, state and government organs.

There now existed more clearly differentiated second and subsequent echelons of leadership where organizational specialists – in contrast to the generalists at the very top – predominated. These appointments specialized in technical economic issues, military matters or party questions, but they interlocked less. Historical factional splits, inherited from the prerevolutionary period, also became less important. There was a fair opportunity for intra-elite debate and for the exercise of some influence through the party's Central Committee, the National Assembly and the routine relationships of enterprise managers to central ministries.

The political system concentrated decision-making powers very heavily at the top. Despite some trends towards decentralization in the mid-1970s, Cuba had still a highly centralized political system, where most fundamental decisions were made by a relatively small number of people in Havana, most of whom had held high posts for nearly thirty years. Power relations became more institutionalized than they had been in the 1970s thanks to the changes in the party, the mass organizations and the institutions of economic policy-making and implementation, especially central planning.

At the bottom of the political pyramid about one-fifth of the adult population was excluded from effective participation in the mass organizations because they were considered – by both themselves and the authorities – opponents of the regime. Although the levels of political repression against such people declined markedly in the 1970s, they increased again in late 1979 and 1980. Sergio del Valle was replaced as Minister of the Interior by his predecessor Ramiro Valdés, who restored, though not in full, some of the harsh internal security policies of the earliest years of the revolutionary rule. The Minister of Justice, the Attorney General, and the president of the Supreme Court were also replaced in the same period. They were responsible for the more 'lenient' exercise of police and court power earlier in the 1970s; they were more 'liberal' within the context of an authoritarian regime. In 1979–80 the government re-emphasized the pre-eminence of its power against social and political dissidents. (Valdés was dismissed as interior minister in December 1985 and from the Political Bureau in February 1986).

At the intermediate levels, managers now had greater discretion in the work place to hire, fire and discipline workers. They gained new, but limited, authority to dispose of enterprise profits, and they began to demand more powers. The mass organizations began to display some interest-group features, above all the ANAP lobby on behalf of the private peasantry but also, though less effectively, FMC, the women's federation. In such an increasingly hierarchical political system, established practitioners of organizational politics such as the armed forces could claim a rising and disproportionate share of national resources, justified not only by the 'internationalist' missions acquired in the second half of the 1970s but also by new U.S. threats in the 1980s.

One effect of the revolution in the 1960s was to break the correlation between social class background and political power. Many of the formerly powerful were dead or imprisoned, or had emigrated. Many of the newly powerful came from humble origins; the revolution dramatically accelerating the circulation of elites in the early 1960s. By the 1980s, however, there was mounting evidence of correlations between positions of power and social rank, institutionalized revolutionary rule greatly diminishing the circulation of elites. Revolutionary leaders who were strikingly young – late twenties and early thirties – when they seized power in 1959, had aged, but their identities had changed little. The average age of the Central Committee had been increasing about one year per year. New Central Committee members tended to come from the same generation and the same types of background. There was little real renewal.

Oligarchy and hierarchy had been reinforced under institutionalization but more effective means for consultation were also developed. Gone were the days when the only means of consultation was raising hands at a public rally in response to Fidel Castro's persuasive exhortations. From the local to the national level, there was now a more systematic effort to consult those who might be affected by new policies, especially at the middle and top ranks of power. Consultation had become the main channel for interest group lobbying, although it was little more than symbolic in dealings with the mass of the population, and it clearly possessed the potential to attenuate the remaining arbitrary features of the authoritarian regime.

'Demand for orderliness', President Castro told the second party Congress, 'should never be neglected in a revolution'.[11] He thus summarized the response of his government to the tumultuous events of 1980: economic crisis, political opposition and repression, and massive emigration. He also signalled the increased importance of political stratification and order as concerns of the leadership. The question for the years ahead would

---

[11] *Granma Weekly Review*, 28 December 1980, 13.

be whether the new demands for orderliness in the revolution competed with, overcame, or excluded the demands for a revolution within the revolution: the great slogan of the late 1960s. Were the dreams of the late 1950s, which turned the revolution into a national epic for many Cubans, to be realized through rising political and social stratification? Would Cuba respond in the future more to order or to revolution?

INTERNATIONAL RELATIONS

Still threatened by the United States after the settlement of the missile crisis in 1962 – Washington boycotted all economic relations with Cuba and sought to enlist the assistance of other governments to strangle Cuba's economy and thereby bring down its government – and still uncertain over the extent of Soviet commitment, the Cuban government fashioned a global foreign policy to defend its interests. The survival of revolutionary rule in Cuba, the leadership's top priority, required a foreign policy that was both global and activist. Cuba built a large and capable foreign service skilled in diplomacy, international economics, intelligence and military affairs. From the outset, the leadership also sought to use foreign policy to obtain resources for Cuba's social and economic transformation. The relationship with the Soviet Union was the centerpiece of both these priorities. At the same time, Havana sought to maintain good relations with as many governments as possible throughout the world. This policy, consistent with the effort to break out of the isolation that the U.S. government was seeking to impose on Cuba, held open the possibility of economic relations with non-communist countries. Another priority was to expand Cuba's influence over international leftist movements, whether formally organized in Communist parties or not. Cuban leaders believed they had led a genuine revolution to power. The establishment of Marxism–Leninism in Cuba, unlike in most of eastern Europe at the end of the Second World War, was not the by-product of the country's occupation by the Soviet armed forces. This home-grown Caribbean revolution, moreover, had not been led by the old Communist Party. Cuban revolutionaries thought they had some fundamental insights into how Third World revolutions might emerge and evolve toward Marxism–Leninism: in short, they could teach the Soviets a thing or two about how to support revolutions in the closing third of the twentieth century.

The Cuban leaders were interested not just in influence but also in the actual promotion of revolutions. Their future would be more secure in a world of many friendly anti-imperialist revolutionary governments. Revolutions, moreover, were on the cutting edge of history, and the future belonged to those who analyzed it correctly and acted accordingly. It was not enough to allow history to unfold – that had been the error of the old Communists – for peoples must make their own history, even if they cannot do so exactly as they please. It was the duty of revolutionaries to make the revolution. However, this position was often difficult to reconcile with the need to retain diplomatic relations with the broadest possible number of governments.

In the mid-1960s the Cuban government developed an independent foreign policy that brought it often into conflict with the Soviet Union. Cuba supported revolutionary movements vigorously in many Latin American countries and in Africa. Cuba gave material assistance to revolutionaries in most Central American and Andean countries, to those fighting the Portuguese empire in Africa, and also to friendly revolutionary governments such as those of the Congo (Brazzaville), Algeria and North Vietnam. In January 1966 Cuba hosted a Tricontinental Conference, from which were founded the Organization for Solidarity with the Peoples of Africa, Asia and Latin America (OSPAAL) and the Organization for Latin American Solidarity (OLAS). Based in Havana and staffed by Cubans, both supported revolutionary movements. Cuban leaders sharply criticized those who did not take up the armed struggle to bring about revolutionary victory; most Moscow-affiliated Communist parties in Latin American countries were assailed for their excessive caution, if not their cowardice.

If armed struggle was the way forward, then the Moscow-affiliated Venezuelan Communist Party, Castro declared, committed treason when it sought to end Venezuela's guerrilla war in 1967 and to reintegrate itself into more normal politics. But the commitment to the armed struggle, though essential, was not enough. Some who refused to conform to Cuban policies (as the revolutionary Yon Sosa in Guatemala) were denounced as Trotskyites. Cuba wanted to promote revolution, but it wanted even more to maintain and expand its influence over the left. It was willing to split the left, internationally and in particular countries, to maintain its primacy, even at the cost of jeopardizing revolutionary victory. These policies brought Havana into conflict with other governments, especially in Latin America. When Cuba was caught actively assisting Venezuelan revolutionaries the Venezuelan government brought charges of aggression that led to Cuba's condemnation under the terms of the Inter-American Treaty of Reciprocal Assistance (the Rio Pact) in 1964. Collective hemispheric sanctions were imposed on Cuba, requiring all signatories to suspend political and economic relations with Cuba. The United States and all Latin American countries (except Mexico) complied.

These policies also brought conflict to Soviet–Cuban relations. In addition to the conflict over the role of Moscow-affiliated Communist parties, Cuban leaders – especially the Minister of Industries, the Argentine-born hero of the revolutionary war, Ernesto 'Che' Guevara – criticized the USSR for its superpower behavior, and niggardly help to the Cuban Revolution. Soviet and East European products were called 'old junk'. The Cuban government seemed to hold its Soviet ally in contempt as an unrevolutionary country at home and abroad. Cubans had taken up the fallen standard of revolution. When the Cuban leadership linked the USSR and its allies to the microfaction, a Cuban–Soviet confrontation erupted early in 1968. The Soviet Union retaliated by slowing down the rate of delivery of petroleum products to Cuba, forcing the revolutionary government to impose a drastic rationing of petroleum products. The Soviets also withdrew most of their technical advisers. After difficult negotiations, the crisis was overcome in the summer 1968 when Prime Minister Castro unexpectedly acknowledged on television that he was about to endorse the Soviet and Warsaw Pact intervention in Czechoslovakia. This was the historic turning point in Soviet–Cuban relations, the subsequent improvement reaching its peak in co-operation in the African wars of the late 1970s.

Foreign policy faced other sharp problems in the late 1960s. The death of Che Guevara and other members of the Cuban Communist Party's Central Committee in the heartland of Bolivia where they had gone to spark a revolution represented a significant set-back. More generally, the strategy of promoting revolution through armed struggle failed throughout Latin America, consolidating either democratic regimes, as in Venezuela, or dynastic tyrannies, as in Nicaragua. Non-violent strategies that promised change appeared more viable: a left-leaning military government came to power in Peru late in 1968 and a broad coalition of the Chilean left won the presidential elections in 1970.

Cuban relations with the People's Republic of China also soured during the mid-1960s. Notwithstanding the many similarities in outlook and policy between the leaderships and despite the considerable Chinese economic aid to Cuba in the early 1960s, relations deteriorated when the Chinese leadership demanded full Cuban support in the Sino-Soviet dispute and lobbied Cuban military and party personnel directly. When the economies of both countries deteriorated in the mid-1960s there was intensified commercial conflict, and although trade and other relations were never cut off altogether, they were sharply reduced. Bilateral political relations continued to be poor after early 1966.

Despite these difficulties, the most fundamental priorities of Cuban foreign policy were met. Revolutionary rule survived, in itself a remarkable achievement. The pattern of policy gave priority to good relations with the Soviet Union over support for revolution. The Cuban government could not have survived in power without Soviet support, which had increased since the late 1960s. A major agreement signed in December 1972 postponed until January 1986 payments of interest and principal on all Soviet credits granted to Cuba before January 1973, repayments then being extended into the twenty-first century. (In fact, in 1986 repayments were deferred for several more years). Soviet credits to cover bilateral trade deficits for 1973–5 were granted free of interest, with the principal to be repaid from 1986. Between 1960 and 1974 Soviet subsidies of bilateral trade deficits with Cuba totalled approximately $3.8 billion. These deficits would have been larger if the Soviet Union had not also subsidized Cuban sugar exports to the USSR during most years, to the tune of about a billion dollars during the 1960s. In 1976, in partial reward for Cuba's military daring and success in Angola, the Soviet Union again agreed to subsidize Cuban sugar sales through a complex formula that stipulated a price five or six times greater than that prevailing on the world market. In addition, the Soviet Union subsidized the price of the petroleum it sold to Cuba and of the nickel it bought from Cuba. After 1976, Soviet subsidies remained at a very high level, accounting for no less than a tenth of Cuba's gross product per year.

These subsidies predictably tightened Cuban–Soviet trade relations. Whereas commerce with the USSR accounted for an average of 45 per cent of Cuban trade up to 1975, it exceeded 60 per cent in the early 1980s. Cuban trade also increased with Eastern European countries when they agreed to subsidize sugar prices. These shifts were also caused by Cuba's difficulties in trading with hard-currency markets (most Cuban trade with the Soviet Union and East Europe is, in effect, barter trade with imputed prices). In addition, Cuba has received Soviet assistance for economic development projects, the training of Cuban technical personnel in the USSR, and the stationing of Soviet technical advisers in Cuba.

A notable element of Soviet assistance to Cuba was military. In addition to the military shield provided by the Soviet Union against the United

States, Moscow developed the Cuban armed forces into Latin America's premier military establishment. No other armed force in the region could match the skill, experience and sophistication of the Cuban army and air force. The Cuban navy was the only service whose development still lagged. Soviet arms transfers were free of charge, the equipment and modernization of the Cuban armed forces reaching its peak in a large build-up during the early 1980s.

A new phase of Soviet–Cuban military co-operation opened with Cuba's decision to send eventually 36,000 troops to support the Popular Movement for the Liberation of Angola (MPLA) in the civil war that broke out in that country in 1975–6. Although Cuba's entry into that victorious war would not have been possible without Soviet support, the chronology of engagement, the pattern of deployment and the testimony of key witnesses suggest that Cuba and the MPLA – rather than the USSR – took the major decisions. In January 1978, responding to a request from the Ethiopian government faced with a Somali invasion that had occupied a substantial portion of Ethiopian territory, thousands of Cuban troops, supported and led by Soviet and East German officers in addition to Cuban officers, helped repel the Somali invasion. The pattern in this case suggests that the Soviet Union and Ethiopia took the lead in formulating and implementing these policies.

In short, the Soviet–Cuban alliance by the 1980s was close and complex, responding to the perceived interests of both allies, respecting the independence of each and allowing each to formulate its own policies in close collaboration with the other. Although Cuban victories in African wars would not have been achieved without Soviet support, it is also true that Soviet victories would not have been achieved without Cuban forces.

Appreciable success was registered in improving state-to-state relations in general. Even in the years of a radical foreign policy in the 1960s, Cuba had maintained good trade relations with several Western European states. The case of Franco's Spain was noteworthy. From 1963 until Franco's death in 1975, Cuba had excellent economic relations with that country, desisting from the promotion of revolution there in order to maintain a mutually valuable official relationship. Cuba also retained correct diplomatic relations with the Mexican government, eschewing the temptation to support anti-government leftist protests in 1968–71. In the early 1970s Cuba moved steadfastly to improve its relations with most governments. Economic relations with Western European countries and Japan improved further as the Cuban economy recovered from the ravages of the 1960s. In 1975 the collective inter-American political and economic sanctions were lifted, and several Latin American countries developed trade relations with Cuba. Mexican and Argentine trade with Cuba became important over the next five years, and even relations with the United States began to improve. Washington voted to lift collective sanctions and modified its own legislation to eliminate third-party sanctions embedded in U.S. economic embargo policies against Cuba. The Ford administration and the Cuban government held bilateral discussions in 1975, and although these talks were interrupted by the Angolan war, they were resumed in 1977 at the beginning of the Carter presidency. The new talks led to a series of modest bilateral agreements and to the establishment of diplomatic 'interest sections' by each country in the other's capital city. Although most of these procedures endured, relations began to deteriorate again in the wake of Cuba's entry into the Ethiopian–Somali war in 1978.

Cuban relations with Africa and Asia also improved in the 1970s. Cuba had joined the so-called Non-aligned Movement in 1961, and despite its increasingly close military alliance with the Soviet Union, Cuba became the movement's leader for a three-year term at the 1979 summit meeting of heads of state in Havana. Relations with these countries were significantly influenced by the deployment of thousands of Cubans serving in foreign-assistance missions. In the early 1980s some 15,000 Cubans served in overseas civilian missions in some three dozen countries; tasks in construction, health and education predominated.[12] In addition, about 35,000 troops and military advisers (including security experts) were ordinarily posted overseas in about two dozen countries (most were in Angola and Ethiopia). Relative to Cuba's population, the overseas armies represented a larger deployment than that of the United States at the peak of the Vietnam war. Cuba's sizeable military deployment in Angola endured for the same length as the U.S. wartime commitment in Vietnam.

---

[12] Cuban foreign assistance missions have operated in the following countries, among others, at the request of their governments: Chile, Peru, Panama, Nicaragua, Jamaica, Guyana, Grenada, Suriname, Algeria, Libya, Ethiopa, Somalia, Uganda, Tanzania, Seychelles, Zambia, Ghana, São Tomé and Príncipe, Mozambique, Angola, Zimbabwe, Congo, Nigeria, Benin, Burkina, Faso, Malagasy, Burundi, Equatorial Guinea, Guinea, Guinea-Bissau, Cape Verde, Sierre Leone, Mali, South Yemen, Syria, Iraq, Vietnam, Laos, and Kampuchea. In some of these, such as Libya and Iraq, Cubans are paid for their services, often working on construction or public-health projects, so that the relationship resembles that of a transnational firm selling services rather than foreign assistance.

The most decisive new initiative in foreign policy was the support from 1977 for the Sandinista insurgency against Anastasio Somoza's rule in Nicaragua, the first substantial commitment to promote insurgency in the Americas in a decade. After revolutionary victory in Nicaragua in July 1979, Cuba developed extremely close relations with the Sandinista government and also with the revolutionary government that came to power in Grenada in March 1979. Havana sent several thousand civilian and military personnel to Nicaragua and several hundred to Grenada. By its own admission, Cuba also provided political, military and economic support to the insurgents in El Salvador, especially in 1980 and early 1981.

Revolutionary success in Nicaragua was the first in Latin America since the Cuban revolution itself. It frightened neighbouring governments and, above all, that of the United States, which, following the inauguration of Ronald Reagan in January 1981, once again threatened Cuba with military invasion. Cuban reservists fought courageously (though to no avail) against the U.S. troops that invaded Grenada in October 1983 – the first such military clash in a quarter of a century.

If many internationally active Cubans fought bravely for their country in African fields and served foreign-assistance missions in three continents, nearly a million Cubans showed courage in breaking with their government, surmounting its controls and emigrating. The first wave of emigration occurred, as we have seen, in the immediate aftermath of the Revolution and came to an abrupt end in 1962; the second, from late 1965 until it tapered off early in the 1970s. The third wave of emigration occurred in one dramatic outburst in the spring of 1980. After several thousand Cubans had broken into the Peruvian embassy in Havana, the government allowed Cuban-Americans from the United States to come in small boats across the Florida Straits to Mariel harbor to pick up friends and relatives, provided they were also willing to ferry to the United States a substantial minority of people whom the Cuban government called 'scum'. These were rounded up by internal security forces or released from Cuban jails for what amounted to deportation from their own country. After Havana, Miami now became the city with the largest Cuban population.

The Cuban Revolution had burst on the world from a small Caribbean island, gradually becoming one of the central issues in international affairs. Cuba's foreign policy succeeded in ensuring the survival of revolutionary rule and obtaining resources from the Soviet Union. It had influence over many African governments but was less successful in turning insurgencies into revolutionary governments in the Americas. Its leaders commanded world attention; its policies had to be monitored by statesmen everywhere; its people could be found throughout the globe. The stage of the Cuban Revolution had become universal as its concerns and policies impinged on millions of its friends and foes in many countries.

11

THE DOMINICAN REPUBLIC SINCE
1930

THE TRUJILLO ERA, 1930–61

On 23 February 1930, the government of President Horacio Vásquez in the Dominican Republic was overthrown by a coup d'état led by the commander-in-chief of the army, General Rafael Leónidas Trujillo. Unlike other military uprisings headed by *caudillos* during the nineteenth century and the early part of the twentieth century, this coup marked a definitive rupture with the traditional political order. The Dominican people were forced to submit to a totalitarian dictatorship that lasted for thirty-one years, during which the personal interests of the dictator were fused with those of the Dominican state itself. Never before in the history of Latin America had a single ruler been able to impose such a comprehensive control over the minds and properties of his people.

A nation which had endured more than a hundred 'revolutions', uprisings and coups d'état during the seventy years between its definitive separation from Haiti in 1844 to its occupation by the United States in 1916 was subjugated to a long-lasting tyranny capable of surviving the economic crisis of the 1930s as well as the upsurge of democratic sentiment following the Second World War and brought to an end only by the assassination of the tyrant in 1961.

The key to understanding the longevity and stability of Trujillo's thirty-year regime lies in the general disarmament imposed by the U.S. Marines, who governed the country from May 1916 until July 1924. This disarmament destroyed forever the power and influence of the traditional guerrilla leaders and made possible the establishment of a professional national police force obedient only to the central government. This force assisted the foreign troops in their pacification campaigns by implement-

This chapter was translated from the Spanish by Elizabeth Ladd.

ing repression against the peasant movements which had been organized in the eastern region of the country to combat foreign intervention.

When the marines withdrew in 1924 they left behind a national government comprising the most active politicians from the era preceding the occupation and presided over by a former *caudillo,* Horacio Vásquez, who quickly placed the supreme command of the military in the hands of men who were unconditionally loyal to his party, the Partido Nacional (PN), among them Captain Rafael Leónidas Trujillo. In 1927, when Vásquez violated the constitution by extending his presidential mandate from 1928 to 1930 Trujillo was appointed commander-in-chief of the National Army.

The political crisis generated by the President's determination to be re-elected in May 1930 soon degenerated into an open conspiracy against Vásquez by the opposition party, the Coalición Patriótica de Ciudadanos, whose leaders convinced the commander-in-chief to betray Vásquez and join them in overthrowing the government. They had no idea that General Trujillo had his own political ambitions and that after deposing Vásquez, on 23 February, he would use his military power to intimidate his opponents and run uncontested in rigged elections after a violent electoral campaign had forced the opposition to retire from the race. In May 1930, Trujillo was elected president almost unanimously with the votes of less than half the national electorate.

The United States had very little room to manoeuvre in this process. Although U.S. diplomatic representatives had tried to prevent the coup d'état, once confronted with the fact they accepted Trujillo as a guarantor of political stability and the most plausible alternative to revolution. Haiti was then still ruled by a U.S. military government, and the fact that Trujillo was a former officer trained by the U.S. Marines Corps was a guarantee that both parts of the island would remain in peace. During the entire time that Trujillo governed the Dominican Republic, the United States considered him a better option than his enemies from within or without. He therefore enjoyed U.S. support except for a two-year period after the end of the Second World War when several liberal officials in the Department of State who were hostile to Trujillo objected to his regime and tried unsuccessfully to have him removed from power.

Rafael Trujillo, born in 1891, came from a lower-class family of mixed Spanish, Creole and Haitian blood in the village of San Cristobal about 30 kilometres from the capital city, Santo Domingo. In 1918 he joined the then Dominican National Police, which had been organized by the U.S. occupying forces to liquidate both *caudillos* and the revolutionary groups and pacify the country. Trujillo learned new methods of military organization and discipline which had been introduced into public administration by the North Americans. Thanks to his sense of discipline and his outstanding intelligence, he learned his job quickly and rose rapidly within the force, which had changed its name to the National Guard by the time the U.S. Marines left the country, and which was renamed the National Army in 1927.

As he advanced in rank, Trujillo used his growing power as a local commander to make a fortune arranging deals involving the purchase of food, clothing and supplies for the soldiers. He was a ruthless officer who intrigued to have his main enemies removed from the army, so that when he became commander-in-chief in 1927, he was already both rich and extremely powerful. By 1928 his investments in urban land and properties were so extensive that he was identified as having an unscrupulous zeal for wealth very uncommon in a society where economic activity still focussed on the traditional possession of land and agriculture. Trujillo had gradually turned the army into a personal enterprise and a tool to serve his own interests. In 1927 the army's budget closed with a deficit, Trujillo being unable to account for how the money had been spent that year. In 1929, when an administrative-financial study of the country was made by a North American team hired by President Vásquez to modernize various government departments, the channels through which Trujillo had diverted funds from the military budget to his own pockets were discovered. In spite of the commission's recommendations to correct the situation, and the demands by several political leaders from the official party to remove Trujillo from his position, President Vásquez continued to support him without suspecting that Trujillo was conspiring with his enemies and would overthrow him a few months later.

Once he had gained political power, Trujillo eliminated economic competition and established a series of state monopolies. In a 1931 he imposed a monopoly on the production and sale of salt by using his position as president to pass a law prohibiting the traditional production of sea salt so the public would have to consume salt from the Barahona mines, which he himself controlled. Once the monopoly was established, the price of salt rose from 60 cents to $3 per hundred pounds, which according to contemporary reports, yielded profits for Trujillo of about $400,000 a year. The salt monopoly was followed by another on meat, control of the slaughterhouses in the city of Santo Domingo adding some $500,000 a year to his income. The rice monopoly, which Trujillo instituted by prohibiting the importation of rice and requiring Dominicans to buy local rice distributed by his own company, raised the price from about 6 cents to 12 or 15 cents per pound according to the quality. Trujillo extended his economic control by monopolizing the sale and distribution of milk in the capital and establishing a bank for cashing government checks that was managed by his wife María Martínez who oversaw a system whereby public employees paid a percentage of their wages so they could cash their checks in advance. During subsequent years the money accumulated from these initial enterprises enabled Trujillo to buy stock in several existing companies, eventually seizing them from their owners. In one instance he forced the owners of an insurance firm to sell out to him, the renamed 'San Rafael' company henceforth receiving all government insurance contracts. In the case of the tobacco factory Compañía Anónima Tabacalera, the biggest in the country, the owners were in the first place forced to sell shares to Trujillo and then later obliged to yield nearly all the assets of the company to him. The Tabacalera remained until the very end of the Trujillo regime the only producer of cigarettes in the country. With these and many other business ventures, which ranged from prostitution to fruit exports, commissions on concessions for public-works contracts and a 10 per cent deduction from public employees' salaries for his political party, the Partido Dominicano (PD), whose accounts he managed personally, Trujillo had become the richest man in the country by the end of his first presidential term in August 1934. For the rest of his life he would use political and military power to line his own pockets and enrich members of his family and his closest supporters.

Although Trujillo always viewed government as a means for personal aggrandizement, his followers attempted to provide his regime with an ideology based on the idea of national reconstruction. It was argued that until 1930 the Dominican Republic had been a backward and stagnant country, politically divided by the permanent strife between *caudillos* and humiliated by foreign diplomatic and military intervention. Trujillo, by contrast, had started a process of revival based upon political unification and the development of the country's resources. The collapse of the prices of its principal exports meant that for several years after the 1929 crash the country was left without enough foreign exchange to pay for the most essential imports or to amortize its public debt, much less to carry out a program of development. But once the economy began to recover around 1938, the Trujillo government embarked upon the most grandiose program of public works and construction ever realized in the

Dominican Republic, reviving long-standing projects for highways, bridges, irrigation canals – and agricultural settlement. Tens of thousands of abandoned hectares of land were reopened and given by the state to thousands of peasants. Thanks to the colonization programs, which were in reality an incipient agrarian reform, agricultural production grew in every sector, making the country self-sufficient in rice, corn, beans and other foodstuffs.

Trujillo's government made its deepest mark on the Dominican economy by fostering industrialization. From 1910, the high prices of exported Dominican products in the world market had generated a rapid rise in demand for consumer goods that local production was unable to satisfy. During the First World War small factories and workshops had proliferated, taking advantage of the scarcities produced by the war. The artisan class almost disappeared after the war, however, when in 1919 the U.S. military government imposed a customs tariff that eliminated all duties on more than seven hundred consumer products imported from the United States. The Dominican market was flooded with imported manufactures which ruined most local producers. Even though the Vásquez regime which followed the withdrawal of the Marines in 1924 tried to correct this situation by imposing consumption taxes on such imported articles, not until after Trujillo became president of the republic was an explicit industrialization policy implemented.

The Trujillo government was directly spurred by the scarcity of imports created by the depression of the thirties. In April 1934, the first Industrial Tax Exemption Law was introduced to attract capital to industry and serve as a legal incentive for the new industrial investments Trujillo wanted to establish in his determination to become the most important industrial entrepreneur in the Dominican Republic. Although this law was short-lived, Trujillo's leadership was the main factor behind the establishment of new industrial plants to produce shoes, beer, tobacco, alcohol, pasta and vegetable oil organized during the years preceding the Second World War. In addition, many other small factories and workshops were created during the depression years under the sympathetic eye of the government. Most such new establishments were very small since the country's population in 1935 was fewer than 1.3 million inhabitants. Nevertheless, they represented a diversified manufacturing base which served to substitute imports and used locally produced raw materials. The towns of Santiago, Puerto Plata and San Pedro de Macoris, with a more vigorous artisan class and a hinterland containing a richer peasant class than Santo Domingo, became more developed industrial centers than the capital itself, a trend that Trujillo sought to halt, especially once the old city of Santo Domingo changed its name to Ciudad Trujillo in 1936.

In 1942, Trujillo modified the constitution to allow the executive power to grant special incentives and tax holidays to new industrial enterprises created with the purpose of substituting imports and saving foreign exchange. He, of course, was one of the principal beneficiaries of these measures, associating himself with groups of national and foreign businessmen who either joined his companies or were forced to allow him to join those of their companies which had been established for years and had already demonstrated their profitability. Trujillo's partners were Spanish, Syrian-Lebanese or Dominican merchants and industrialists who had participated in the first phase of import substitution at the beginning of the century. The growth of Trujillo's economic empire expanded thanks to a new scarcity of imported manufactured goods during the Second World War, a shortage which he, using his capital and that of his associates, was able to satisfy by creating new industries. After the war the Dominican Republic profited from the world-wide demand for tropical products, particularly during the years of the Korean War. The growth of Dominican exports – sugar, cacao, coffee, tobacco, bananas – generated enough revenue to increase internal demand, and this brought with it a natural incentive to further industrialization. Thus, after the Second World War the Trujilloist industrial complex was further expanded by the opening of new factories for cement, chocolate, alcohol, beverages, liquors, paper, cardboard, processed milk, flour, nails, bottles and glass, coffee, rice, marble, medicines, paint, sacks, cord and knitted goods, textiles, clothing and sugar. Almost all industries created during these years, including those in which Trujillo was not a direct partner, were granted special concessions and tax exemptions as well as being protected by the government from labour unrest, trade-union demands and foreign competition. Most of the new modern plants were established in or around Ciudad Trujillo, thus converting, in less than fifteen years, the old administrative capital into an industrial and commercial center which attracted increasing waves of immigrants from the interior of the country.

During the period from 1938 to 1960 the number of manufacturing establishments in the Dominican Republic almost doubled; capital investment multiplied nine times; the number of workers and employees grew almost two and a half times; the amount paid in salaries by the industrial sector was ten times more in 1960 than it was in 1938; the value of national raw materials used by the manufacturing sector multiplied four-teen times; expenditure on fuel and lubricants went up twenty-two times; industrial sales multiplied more than twelve times from $13.3 million to $164.4 million, an impressive growth in a twenty-two year period. And these figures do not include the massive investments made by Trujillo in the sugar industry.

Sugar was one of Trujillo's biggest industrial ventures. With sugar prices depressed throughout the thirties, Trujillo never considered taking charge of the sugar industry. By the end of the Second World War, however, the enormous profits being reaped by the foreign owners of sugar mills which had been in existence for more than half a century inevitably attracted his attention. In 1949 Trujillo began to build a modest sugar mill, the Central Catarey, on some land he owned on the outskirts of Villa Altagracia, twenty-five miles from Santo Domingo. Within a year he had already started construction of the Central Río Haina, which he hoped would be the largest sugar mill in the country. In the years that followed, Trujillo used state and personal funds to buy most of the foreign mills operating in the country, thus establishing himself as the largest sugar producer in the Dominican Republic. He launched a bitter nationalist campaign against the foreign domination of the sugar industry and in-creased pressure on the foreign sugar companies through onerous export taxes which convinced the owners that the best way out for them was to sell. By 1961 the only mills he still had not bought were those of the Casa Vicini and the Central Romana. (The sale of the latter, the property of the South Porto Rico Sugar Company, was interrupted by the assassination of the dictator in May.)

Trujillo's government had also acquired the National City Bank, which he made into the Banco de Reservas in 1941, and the Compañía Eléctrica (later the Corporación Dominicana de Electricidad). The dictator was also the biggest land-owner in the country, his estates including cattle ranches as well as extensive forest reserves, which he exploited through well-known figureheads and which enabled him to monopolize the country's timber market. Trujillo's economic empire grew to such volume that at the end of his life in 1961 he controlled nearly 80 per cent of the country's industrial production and his firms employed 45 per cent of the country's active labour force. Combined with his absolute control of the state, which employed 15 per cent of the labour force, this meant that nearly 60 per cent of Dominican families depended on his will in one way or another. It was commonly said that during his regime the situation reached such extremes that the Dominicans could not obtain food, shoes, clothing, or shelter without creating a profit in one way or another for Trujillo or his family.

When Trujillo came to power in 1930, in the middle of a general economic crisis, the country's financial limitations were directly associated with its obligations under the U.S.-Dominican Convention of 1924, which not only prohibited the raising of new loans and customs tariffs without U.S. consent but also stipulated that the distribution of customs revenues should be carried out by the United States through the General Customs Office, whereby 50 per cent of customs revenues was deducted to pay the external debt. In 1931, Trujillo's government began negotiating with the United States for a moratorium that would allow the Dominican Republic to pay only interest on the debt as long as the world economic crisis lasted. These negotiations yielded positive results and allowed Trujillo to count on larger resources than he would have enjoyed under the terms of the Convention of 1924.

At the same time the Dominican government began negotiations with the United States over the restoration of the right to administer its own customs office, which had been under U.S. administration since 1905. This agreement was delayed for several years, not least because it was difficult to convince the bondholders that they would continue to enjoy the same guarantees for repayment of the debt. But finally, on 24 September 1940, Trujillo, who had already served two terms as president and had now been named ambassador to Washington, and Cordell Hull, U.S. Secretary of State, signed a treaty modifying the Convention of 1924 to the effect the henceforth the Customs Office would no longer operate under the direction of the U.S. government and its offices and branches would become part of the Dominican public administration system. This treaty, known as the Trujillo–Hull Treaty and ratified 15 February 1941, was the object of an enormous government propaganda campaign presenting Trujillo as the restorer of the country's financial independence. Government apologists exploited the scandalous and depressing financial history of the country to depict Trujillo as a saviour who had been able to restore the sovereignty of a republic that had been mutilated by the foreign administration of customs. In fact, while the administration of customs now passed into Dominican hands, under the terms of the arrangement all funds collected by the Dominican government in the customs houses had to be deposited in the National City Bank of New York, which had a branch in Santo Domingo, so that one of its officers, who represented the bondholders, could distribute the money between the Dominican government and the foreign creditors. Meanwhile, the foreign debt which stood at $16 million dollars in 1930 fell to $9.4 million in July 1947, when it was paid off in full from reserves accumulated during the Second World War.

A further long-standing issue that Trujillo sought to resolve and exploit was that of the permanent Haitian settlement in Dominican territory. For more than a century Haitians had been peacefully settling on agricultural lands abandoned by Dominicans during the Haitian–Dominican wars in the mid-nineteenth century. Despite Dominican efforts to reach an agreement with Haiti, it had proved impossible to solve the problem of the border. The treaty of January 1929 eventually established the demarcation of the frontier, yet tens of thousands of Haitian peasants continued to live on the Dominican side in the southwest and the northwest while others worked as labourers in the sugar industry in the southeast of the island, or earned a living as domestic servants, farmers or small businessmen in many towns of the interior.

The Haitians living near the border were completely marginal to Dominican society, and the territory they occupied effectively functioned as an extension of Haiti. Haitian currency circulated freely in the Cibao, the main agricultural region of the country, and in the south it circulated as far as Azua, only 120 kilometres from Santo Domingo. This was anathema to Trujillo, who at the beginning of October 1937 travelled to the frontier and on 4 October issued the extraordinary order that all Haitians remaining in the country be exterminated. In the days following, some 18,000 Haitians died. The only ones who survived were those who managed to cross the border and those protected by the sugar mills, which did not want to lose their labour force.

The mass-murder of the Haitians produced an international scandal and elicited condemnation from all Latin America and the United States. It also produced a considerable consternation and fear among the Dominican people. After a dramatic series of protests, investigations and diplomatic mediations, the case was closed in February 1939 when the Dominican government paid the Haitian government $525,000 as compensation for damages and injury occasioned by what were officially termed 'frontier conflicts'.[1] Trujillo's government tried to present the slaughter as a simple

[1] The agreement was first reached on 31 January 1938, when the compensation was fixed at $750,000, of which Trujillo paid $250,000 in advance. He then sent to Port-au-Prince a special envoy who, after bribing some of the Haitian's government politicians, managed to bring down the second and final payment to $275,000 in February 1939, for a total compensation payment of $525,000.

frontier incident between Dominican peasants and Haitian livestock thieves which had occurred when the Dominicans, tired of being robbed, decided to attack the Haitians and managed to kill some of them. Nonetheless, the act was widely recognized as one of genocide.

In 1941, the government launched a major program of 'Dominicanization' of the frontier through the construction of towns along the new line of demarcation and the establishment of military posts to prevent further Haitian penetration. In the years that followed, the Dominicanization of the frontier turned into a kind of national crusade to regain those zones which had been lost more than a century before and which the Dominicans had been unable to win back, first because of the Haitian invasions during the wars of independence and later because of frontier commerce. Within a few years the frontier was indeed repopulated by Dominican families who were granted lands in the many new agrarian colonies. The Catholic Church was invited to join this campaign and the Jesuit order sent its priests to the frontier outposts to bring into Christianity those people who were formerly under the influence of Voodoo. Linked by numerous roads and crossed by irrigation canals, the frontier became a permanently populated zone integrated into the general production system of the country. This fact served to reinforce Trujillo's claims that he was the true saviour of the country's traditional Hispanic and Catholic essence.

In political terms the Trujillo regime achieved a remarkable stability despite many conspiracies and the invasions organized by exiles in the years after the Second World Was. Constitutionally, Trujillo was President of the Republic for four terms, the first of which ran from 1930 to 1934 and the second from 1934 to 1938. Although there were no legal provisions against the indefinite re-election of the president, he stepped down in 1938 and sponsored the election of Jacinto B. Peynado, who until then had been his vice-president. When Peynado died in 1940 he was replaced by his vice-president, Manuel de Jesús Troncoso de la Concha. According to some sources, Peynado and Troncoso de la Concha were elected in 1938 because the United States opposed Trujillo's re-election on account of the slaughter of the Haitians. Yet the diplomatic correspondence of the period does not substantiate this view, and only indicates the existence of persistent rumours regarding the displeasure of the U.S. government towards the possible continuation of Trujillo's presidency. In all events, once the programme to Dominicanize the frontier was under way and with five years in which to forget about the conflict, the U.S. government did not object to Trujillo's becoming president for a third term, now for five years, in 1942, nor to his re-election to another five-year term in 1947. In 1952 he imposed his brother Héctor B. Trujillo as president, and in 1957 had him re-elected – as in all presidential elections since 1934, virtually unanimously. Héctor Trujillo acted as president until August 1960, when he resigned because of the international crisis facing the government over the economic sanctions imposed on it by the Organization of American States (OAS) after his brother tried to assassinate Rómulo Betancourt, the president of Venezuela. Joaquín Balaguer, who had been vice-president, then became the new puppet president.

Of the two abortive invasions carried out by Dominican exiles – that of Luperón in June 1949 and that of Constanza, Maimón and Estero Hondo in June 1959 – only the latter succeeded in creating severe problems for the regime. This was largely because the new Cuban government led by Fidel Castro supported the rebels and thus held out the promise of an important revolutionary alliance. The invading army was composed mainly of Dominican exiles and some military commanders who had accompanied Castro in the Sierra Maestra. But once they arrived to the Dominican territory they were quickly defeated by Trujillo's army and almost all the expeditionaries lost their lives. From then on, Cuban radio stations continuously broadcast messages encouraging the Dominican people to revolt against the dictator. Encouraged by these messages, many people started to conspire but most were promptly discovered, and by mid-1960 the jails were full of hundreds of political prisoners from every social class. The government stepped up its long-standing practices of terror and espionage, torturing and killing many who opposed the government. Among those killed in 1960 were three sisters from the respected Mirabal family, whose husbands had been jailed for participating in the original conspiracy which led to the June 1959 invasion. The assassination of the Mirabal sisters on 25 November 1960 provoked wide-spread condemnation of Trujillo and greatly sharpened the crisis into which his government had entered as a result both of the failed invasion and the OAS sanctions imposed following the attempt on Betancourt's life.

By this stage it was the conviction of many in Washington that if Trujillo continued in power and the economic conditions of the country continued to deteriorate under the OAS sanctions, the Dominican Republic might face a Communist take-over similar to that in Cuba. The Eisenhower administration had already been reducing its support for Latin American distatorships, and this policy was confirmed in 1961 by the new

Kennedy administration, which established contacts with high-ranking conspirators from within the regime itself. Encouraged by such backing, a group led by ex-general Juan Tomás Díaz, a childhood friend of Trujillo who had lost his rank and had fallen from the dictator's grace because of his sister's political opposition, plotted to shoot Trujillo while he was on his way to his 'Hacienda Fundación' in San Cristóbal. On the evening of 30 May 1961, after several frustrated attempts, the plotters finally killed Trujillo following a dramatic car chase on the highway connecting San Cristóbal and Santo Domingo.

The assassination of the dictator took place while the regime was in disarray as a result of the economic sanctions imposed by the OAS the year before, and although popular opposition was growing because of the attacks Trujillo had launched in recent months against the Catholic Church after it refused to grant him the title of Benefactor of the Church, which he wanted to add to those of 'Generalísimo', 'Benefactor of the Fatherland' and 'Father of the New Fatherland'. The economic sanctions had greatly aggravated the crisis affecting the Dominican economy since 1958 as a result of the fall of the prices of its principal export commodities. Indeed, the country had been experiencing a significant outflow of capital since 1955, when Trujillo spent more than $30 million in the construction of an international fair to commemorate his twenty-five years in power. Following that, Trujillo lowered the country's international reserves by paying cash to foreign investors for the purchase of several sugar mills and all the electricity plants of the country which were nationalized in the late 1950s. After enjoying an outstandingly strong balance-of-payment situation for more than fifty years, the government had to make recourse to the International Monetary Fund (IMF), and in mid-1959 it signed a stand-by agreement for $11.5 million which provided for import restrictions and other monetary controls. However, the guerrilla invasion of June 1959 scared many of Trujillo's relatives and associates, who immediately began to transfer their savings to foreign banks, and it also prompted Trujillo to spend more than $80 million in weapons and military supplies. When Trujillo died in 1961 his family had about $300 million in accounts outside the country. His companies functioned and made profits because they enjoyed every possible government protection. Many paid no taxes; their workers were paid very low wages; and some used public employees, members of the army and convicts, as workers. In those cases where a company was showing a loss, Trujillo would sell it to the state at a profit. When the company recuperated its losses, he would buy it back again at a profit. The notion that Trujillo made the Dominican state into a private business is not far from the truth.

Although the regime consistently retained a constitutional facade and had a National Congress, senators and deputies were 'elected' by the only political party which existed in the country, the Partido Dominicano, following the personal recommendations of the dictator. Before being appointed, senators and deputies signed a resignation letter with no date, which was delivered to the dictator so that they could be removed according to political convenience. Many radio stations, the only television station and the two major daily newspapers were directly owned by the dictator and his relatives, who used them to stifle all expressions of opposition and to glorify the accomplishments of the regime. Over the space of three decades the impact of such ideological controls was considerable, several generations of Dominican schoolchildren being educated with textbooks that entirely rewrote national history to exalt Trujillo, whose praises were likewise sung in a massive output of popular songs and poems. All this amounted to much more than the suppression of dissent; it conditioned the minds of hundreds of thousands of citizens who were reduced to mere subjects.

The dictator's absolutist patrimonialism did not, of course, exist in a social vacuum. The industrialization which began during the Second World War and continued without interruption until 1960 altered the purely administrative character of the city of Santo Domingo, converting it to a manufacturing center which attracted tens of thousands of Dominicans from the country and cities of the interior in search of jobs. This pattern of internal migration was echoed on different levels in the rest of the country's urban centers, so than by 1960 only 60 per cent of the population lived in the countryside, in contrast to a rural population of 84 per cent in 1920. Improvements in health services and sanitation also made urban life more attractive to many peasants and labourers who, lured by the hope of finding work in one of the new industries, began to form for the first time an ample urban labour market which would supply Dominican industry with a cheap labour force in the years to come. The construction of hospitals, training of hundreds of new doctors, implementation of intensive anti-parasitic disease campaigns, and the introduction of antibiotics at the end of the 1940s radically reduced the mortality rate and fostered greater fertility among Dominican women, to such an extent that the years following the Second World War marked the beginning of a demographic explosion. As late as 1944, Dominican politicians still thought the country was under-populated and for more than fifteen years encouraged child-bearing by offering incentives to large families although the 1950 census registered 3 million inhabitants in contrast to scarcely a million in 1920. Many praised the government of Trujillo for this demographic growth, which they believed was a sign of social maturity and development. It also provided local workers for the Dominican economy, which for centuries had been limited by a permanent shortage of indigenous labour.

The population expansion required the government to enlarge its bureacracy and extend public services. Although an army of some 20,000 soldiers was a heavy burden for the Dominican economy, it was also an important source of employment – and provided opportunities for social advancement – for impoverished peasant youngsters. There was also an increase in school enrolment and the number of university-educated professionals. It is noteworthy that the University of Santo Domingo, which had been reorganized in 1932 and had maintained a student enrolment of about a thousand for many years, saw its enrolment grow to three thousand students at the end of the 1950s, and it regularly graduated around a hundred professionals each year, supplying the country for the first time in its history with a new middle social stratum which would assume political and economic leadership once the Trujillo regime ended. Many of the professionals who graduated during the last ten years of Trujillo's era left the country to study abroad or to perform diplomatic duties, and returned with new ideas; others brought back technical skills vital to the accelarated growth over the following decades.

Despite the economic buoyancy obtaining from the end of the Second World War until 1958, the majority of the Dominican population of 4 million enjoyed only marginal access to the nation's sources of wealth. In 1960 it was apparent that the health service was inadequate; the schools could not handle the population growth and illiteracy had increased. The cost of living had risen while real wages remained stagnant; unemployment was growing in the cities while Trujillo's tiny family oligarchy drained the country of capital that could have been reinvested in the creation of new jobs. Equally, the rural economy had entered into decline, several hundred thousand hectares of land falling into the hands of landlords who increased their holdings at the expense of traditional peasant lands. It is notable that during the 1950s urban groups, recently enriched by industrial development, often used their savings to buy rural properties as a means of acquiring economic security and social prestige. The rural prolerariat had expanded as a result of the government's pro-fertility policies and had become progressively impoverished through the loss of land. Sixty per cent of the population still lived in the countryside, but the establishment of marginal urban settlements accelerated as an enormous mass of men and women without jobs or land settled in the peripheral zones of the principal cities. These *chiriperos* came to constitute a ready market for the contracting of cheap labour in the modern urban economy.

It might be argued that in 1930 Trujillo came to rule over a traditional two-class, peasant-based, backward society, and when he died in 1961 he left a society in transition yet still under-developed, a capitalist economy deformed by monopolistic industrial growth which, by placing the control of the country's resources in the hands of an absolutely unscrupulous family, deprived the nation of even those limited opportunities for balanced economic development possessed by other Latin American countries.

THE POST-TRUJILLO ERA

Trujillo's death on 30 May 1961 initiated an intensive process of political democratization which culminated in free elections on 20 December 1962, the first of their kind since 1924. These elections were organized by a provisional government (Consejo de Estado) composed of seven members and were won by Juan Bosch, the candidate of the Partido Revolucionario Dominicano (PRD, founded in Cuba in 1939), who had spent his adult life in exile during Trujillo's rule and who returned to the country in 1961 together with the rest of the exiles. The constitutional government came to power on 27 February 1963 without a clear plan of economic development. Bosch's general ideas on economic development were of the reformist and populist type he had learned in Costa Rica and Cuba in the fifties. But for many in the Dominican Republic these ideas were too advanced, and Bosch was soon labeled Communist or pro-Communist by businessmen and industrialists.

The Dominican economy had started to recover in 1962 thanks to the emergency plan put into operation by the Consejo de Estado with the help of the Alliance for Progress. Nevertheless, most entrepeneurs preferred to wait until the new constitutional government took office and offered firm guarantees for new investment. Notwithstanding the anticommunist rhetoric of the extreme rightist groups, even those industrialists who did not trust Bosch gave him the benefit of the doubt and were

willing to support his government and to make new investments. The
political liberty and the climate of optimism offered by the new constitutional government as it tried to put public finances in order opened up
debate as to the best way to accelerate development. The Consejo de
Estado had been entirely responsive to industrial interests, but Bosch's
new government was not so tractable, and within two months the
Asociación de Industrias de la República Dominicana challenged him to
define his economic policy. The Asociación de Industrias had been created
in 1962 by the most important industrial entrepeneurs, some of whom
had flourished during the fifties thanks to the extraordinary economic
growth of the post-war years, but who had lacked the privileges enjoyed
by Trujillo's enterprises. Others had simply been favourites of Trujillo or
were partners in some of his enterprises and had managed to survive the
wave of confiscations that took place between 1961 and 1962 as Trujillo's
monopolies became the property of the state. The first president of the
association was Horacio Alvarez, a soft drinks manufacturer and a member of one of the oldest Dominican families linked to nearly all the
governments of the last hundred years, and influential under the Trujillo
regime. Alvarez, like most of the Trujilloist industrialists, had been
protected by the Consejo de Estado and had participated in the electoral
campaign against Bosch. Many entrepreneurs now formed the Acción
Dominicana Independiente (ADI) and established a common front with
the Consejo Nacional de Hombres de Empresa (CNHE) against Bosch's
government. The principal objective of the CNHE at that time was to
overthrow Bosch, and to this end they raised money for the ADI's directors who, in association with clerical groups on the extreme right, began
to organize large concentrations of peasants at 'meetings of Christian
reaffirmation' to protest against Communist infiltration in the republic
and against Bosch's government, which they accused of leading the country into communism. These, of course, were the days of an intensive
continental propaganda campaign against the Cuban Revolution. The
Dominican Republic had welcomed hundreds of Cuban exiles, especially
businessmen and clerics, who were waging an active propaganda campaign against Fidel Castro and who erroneously associated the Bosch
government, whose reformist social-democratic philosophy they considered a threat to their interests, with the Castro regime.

Day by day, opposition to Bosch grew. His total lack of comprehension
of the Dominican reality after twenty-five years in exile led him into
conflict with every social group, including his own party. Within a few

months the President found himself completely alone, and no one defended his government when the business groups eventually called a commercial and industrial strike that paralysed the country for several days and signalled to the military that the time was ripe for the coup d'état they had been planning for several weeks. On 25 September 1963, Bosch was deposed and replaced by a Triumvirate whose members were large corporate executives and lawyers, and whose cabinet was made up of entrepreneurs and lawyers with ties to the Dominican world of business. The Triumvirate's rhetoric was, from the beginning, both anti-Trujillo and anti-communist.

As a de facto regime created by a military coup the Triumvirate was extremely unpopular and only able to stay in power with the support of the United States and the Trujilloist generals in the armed forces, to whom the Triumvirate granted the most outrageous privileges. Under the monetary policy of free exchange designed by the International Monetary Fund and accepted by Bosch, imports had reached unprecedented levels, creating serious balance-of-payments problems and inflation. The position was further aggravated when the Triumvirate permitted the military to establish a national commissariat to sell contraband foreign manufactured goods brought into the country by air force planes. Again the government had to turn to the International Monetary Fund to borrow $25 million to offset the deficit in the balance of payments. The adjustments imposed by this new stand-by agreement were compounded by a crisis in agricultural production produced by a severe drought that lasted almost a year. Constant strikes by workers in state enterprises and by taxi drivers, and equally frequent student demonstrations, obliged the Triumvirate to keep the police in the streets to quell disturbances and arrest political leaders, workers and students.

Forced to operate in secrecy, the democratic political parties turned to conspiracy with Bosch, now exiled in Puerto Rico, and a group of young officers who had been on the fringes of power and wanted a return to a constitutional regime. At the same time, Joaquín Balaguer, the last of Trujillo's puppet presidents formed the Partido Reformista with cadres from the only political party of Trujillo's time, the Partido Dominicano. When Bosch and Balaguer entered into an alliance, the Triumvirate was left without any significant political backing. Civilian groups on the right organized a new party called the Partido Liberal Evolucionista and called for immediate elections to re-install the Triumvirate legally, it being an open secret that the president of the Triumvirate, Donald Reid Cabral, had an understanding with them to run for president in the September 1965 elections. The elections were to be held without the participation of Bosch and Balaguer, the leaders of the two largest political forces in the country, although Reid Cabral was counting on the support of a faction of Bosch's Partido Revolucionario Dominicano (PRD) that believed the only way to resolve the political crisis was to hold elections.

Both Bosch and the Christian Democrats (organized into a political party early in 1962), however, had agreed to denounce the elections and mobilize public opinion in favour of a 'return to constitutionality without elections', a formula that meant nothing less than the overthrow of the Triumvirate. This position was publicly supported by the small but influential Dominican Communist Party, and by a good portion of the unions and student groups. When the conspiracy was finally discovered on 24 April 1965, no one came forward to defend the Triumvirate. On the contrary, rich and poor alike, poured into the streets to celebrate its downfall, which was mistakenly announced over radio and television ahead of time, giving rise to a serious crisis within the armed forces, which were divided into those who wanted Bosch's return to office without elections to finish his constitutional term and those who wanted to form a military junta to replace the Triumvirate and eventually call new elections.

Reid Cabral manoeuvred vainly in an effort to secure military support. Within twenty-four hours the military men who had backed him before made him a prisoner in the National Palace and began to negotiate with constitutionalist military officers. When they could not reach a rapid agreement, the military leaders who had initiated the conspiracy distributed weapons to their civilian supporters. On 25 April 1965 civil war broke out in the city of Santo Domingo. Leftist groups and Bosch's followers organized guerrillas to destroy the old Trujilloist army, which had been kept intact by the Consejo de Estado, Bosch and the Triumvirate, and which had overthrown the first democratic regime elected in nearly forty years under the pretext of a Communist threat. After three days of intensive combat in the streets of Santo Domingo, the constitutionalist forces managed to defeat the troops of the regular army and prepared to launch the final attack on the air base at San Isidro, which was the principal focus of resistance to the movement to restore Bosch. The military posts in the interior watched and waited, under the control of their old military commanders, but the attack against San Isidro never materialized. In order to stop Bosch from returning to power and 'to prevent the emergence of a second Cuba in America', U.S. President Johnson on 28

April 1965 ordered 42,000 U.S. Marines to the Dominican Republic, under the pretext of saving lives and protecting North American interests in the country. Hence, what began as a civil war ended as an international crisis linked to the U.S. military escalation in Vietnam, U.S. policy against Cuba and later, to the declared U.S. intention of saving democracy in the Dominican Republic.

The city of Santo Domingo was now divided into two zones occupied by the opposing armies. The constitutionalist army was composed of several hundred officers and men from the regular armed forces aided by several thousand men and women who had been given arms at the beginning of the revolt and had organized themselves into dozens of 'constitutional commando units' to defend the old colonial city and its surrounding neighbourhoods built at the beginning of the century. On the other side were the Dominican army, navy and air force, assisted by troops from the United States, Brazil, Honduras and Paraguay, countries which, after manipulating the Organization of American States, had managed to form a so-called Inter-American Peace Force to make the unilateral intervention of the United States appear legal, although the action was in violation of the OAS charter as well as that of the United Nations.

In spite of the superiority of the foreign forces, the conflict could not be resolved through military action; the United States had to negotiate an end to the revolt and the departure of foreign troops. Between May and September 1965 there were in fact two governments in the Dominican Republic: one composed of the constitutionalists and presided over by the military leader of the revolt, Colonel Francisco Caamaño; the other was headed by one of Trujillo's assassins, General Antonio Imbert Barreras, a declared enemy of Bosch and of the Communists, whom the United States installed quickly so they could manipulate local politics. When the civil war ended, after four months of intensive negotiations alternating with bloody battles in the streets of Santo Domingo, both governments resigned and a new provisional government was installed with a mandate to hold free elections in May 1966. A basic feature of the Act of Reconciliation of 3 September 1965, which put an end to the civil war, was that the military constitutionalists were to be reintegrated into the barracks and their leaders appointed to diplomatic posts. The United States had managed to reconstitute the Dominican military as a force directly under its command and entirely dependent on the United States government for the payment of its salaries and the provision of its clothing, food, munitions and equipment.

The normalization of Dominican life begun with the signing of the Act of Reconciliation was to be carried out by the provisional government presided by Héctor García Godoy, a career diplomat and businessman chosen after stormy negotiations between the contending parties. It was agreed that the occupation troops would remain in the country until a new constitutional government was in power. The two leading candidates were Joaquín Balaguer and Juan Bosch, both of whom returned from exile and proceeded to reorganize their parties, now in competition. Balaguer's Partido Reformista soon gained the support of Trujilloist army officers and the right, who sponsored a terrorist campaign against Bosch's Partido Revolucionario Dominicano (PRD) in which more than 350 of its political activists were killed between January and May 1966. Bosch himself was not allowed to go out of his house to campaign and had to address his constituency in daily speeches broadcast through the radio. In effect, the campaign simply extended the civil war, and very few military constitutionalists were accepted back by their old comrades in arms. Dozens were assassinated either during the transitional months of the provisional government or after Balaguer was elected President of the Republic on 16 May 1966. Life in the city of Santo Domingo took several months to return to normal as the open combat of the civil war was replaced by a long wave of anti-communist terrorism and the operations of leftist urban guerrilla groups made up of members of the old constitutionalist commandos who were still in possesion of weapons and who believed it possible to make the revolution from the streets by killing police and soldiers.

The Dominican Republic suffered for nearly eight years under the terror imposed by Balaguer's anti-communist forces.[2] In order to make the role of the regular armed forces less visible, Balaguer organized a paramilitary group called 'La Banda' made up of deserters from the leftist parties and professional assassins paid out of the military's intelligence budget. More than four thousand Dominicans lost their lives in terrorist acts between 1966 and 1974, the campaign ending only when the leadership of the leftist parties had been wiped out and the parties completely disorganized. However, the reduction in repression was also determined by Balaguer's bid for re-election in May 1974, in an effort to create the impression of political normality in response to the international outcry in favor of civil

---

[2] Balaguer was 're-elected' in 1970 after wide-spread use of terror against the opposition. The PRD did not offer a candidate. Balaguer ran unopposed.

rights that began in 1973 after a campaign by the Partido Revolucionario Dominicano in Europe, Latin America and the United States.

After the 1974 elections terrorism was used only selectively since the leftists were so debilitated that they no longer constituted a threat to the regime. Colonel Francisco Caamaño had been assassinated in February 1973 after being taken prisoner in the mountains while trying to establish a guerrilla *foco* similar to that attempted by Che Guevara in Bolivia. Following the civil war Caamaño had left the country for London as military attaché to the Dominican embassy, and from there he had gone clandestinely to Cuba where he remained for several years indoctrinating and training himself for the day when he would return to the Dominican Republic to launch a socialist revolution. When he reached the Dominican mountains in February 1973 eight years after the revolt of 1965, the country had changed enormously. The army had been re-trained for guerrilla warfare, and the country itself had been transformed by economic recovery and the policy of industrial growth and accelerated urbanization which gave rise to a middle class with a degree of affluence never before known in Dominican history. Many of Caamaño's old comrades had changed during these eight years as they watched their colleagues fall victims to the government's terrorism. Others joined the world of business in an expanding economy which between 1970 and 1974 achieved the highest growth rates of any Latin American country.

Most of the survivors of the parties of the left were co-opted by Balaguer through various mechanisms: the engineers and kindred professionals received public works contracts from the state while the intellectuals and professionals were mollified by the appointment of more than a thousand professors to the state university. Balaguer handed these jobs to members of leftist parties in order to keep them employed and, at the same time, under observation. The militants of the left were offered jobs in any of the thousands of public projects under way or the many new companies which emerged during the years of the economic boom. Even the Dominican Communist Party was utilized by Balaguer in his agrarian reform programmes which put an end to large landholdings in the country's rice districts after 1972. Members of the Communist Party were converted into the principal ideologues of the government's agrarianism and into a channel of communication between the governments of Balaguer and Fidel Castro. They were so effectively neutralized by the government that they were allowed to leave and re-enter the country freely, publish their newspaper and magazines and hold their meetings publicly. As a reward for its

co-operation and peaceful activities, the Communist Party was legalized in
November 1977. The government presented the pacification of the country after the civil war as one of Joaquín Balaguer's great political achievements. The cost was extremely high in terms of human lives, but Balaguer
always took pride in his heroic feat and referred to it boastfully in his
speeches.

When Joaquín Balaguer assumed the presidency in June 1966, the Dominican government was dominated by some four hundred North American functionaries and advisers who worked at all levels of public administration; the military was practically managed by a North American military
team of sixty-five men; the Ministry of Agriculture was controlled by forty-
five North American technicians who made practically all the decisions; the
National Police and security forces were advised by fifteen experts on matters of public security, a third of them members of the CIA. Other government departments, such as the Oficina de Desarrollo de la Comunidad and
the Instituto Agrario Dominicano worked together with North American
advisers, as did the Ministry of Education. These advisers put considerable
pressure on their Dominican counterparts to follow political or administrative policies emanating from the Agency for International Development
(AID) or the U. S. embassy. The civil war had created such a power vacuum
that fiscal revenues practically disappeared because neither of the warring
governments was capable of collecting taxes. If it had not been for the
massive economic aid poured in by the United States, the country would
have been totally paralysed. Dominicans became accustomed to but resent-
ful at their country's enormous dependence upon North American aid,
which became the principal instrument of U.S. control after the departure
of the foreign troops.

The quantity of money the North Americans poured into the Dominican Republic between 1966 and 1973 was enormous in proportion to the
size of the country's economy. Between April 1965 and June 1966 the
republic received about $122 million, most of it in the form of gifts
granted with the purpose of staving off bankruptcy. In each of the
following three years, that is, during the rest of Balaguer's first term as
president, this aid increased to $133 million a year, most of which was
in the form of long-term loans for development programmes. These loans
were negotiated through AID and on more than one occasion they came
under the jurisdiction of Public Law 480, a special credit programme for
the acquisition of food. From June 1969 to June 1973 the aid fell to $78
million a year, most of which also came under the application of Public

Law 480. The country's economic dependence on foreign aid, especially during the period from 1966 to 1970, was truly remarkable, and there is no doubt that without direct injections of cash and the sugar quota offered by Washington the country could only have survived under a policy of extreme austerity accompanied by a dangerous rise in unemployment. During this period direct foreign aid from the United States and income from the sugar quota accounted for 32 per cent of the country's revenues in foreign currency. A large portion of the national budget in these years was used to cover salaries, the bulk of investments being made with foreign-aid funds, which meant that the program of public investments was effectively determined by the decisions of AID, the Inter-American Development Bank and the World Bank. One condition of the aid was that it assign resources of the National Budget as matching elements for programs financed with North American aid. The Dominican government, however, was resistant to designating funds for these projects, finding it more politically useful to allocate its resources towards those investments which had a proven political impact, such as public works, where the outcome of the investment was visible and generated employment quickly.

AID's resources were generally oriented towards agricultural development, while the Dominican government made investments in the urban sector. The only interest the government had in AID's funds was the receipt of foreign currency, to assist the balance of payments. Before 1972, the year which marked a visible change in the government's agrarian policy, Balaguer's tendency to sacrifice rural development to the simple expedient of staying in power was notable and explains the slow growth in agricultural production during the seventies.

Although it gave low priority to social and economic development programmes and squandered expenditures which led to frequent friction with Washington, the Dominican government accepted what the North American government offered because Balaguer and his advisers knew they had little or no alternative. This became evident every time the Dominican government had to negotiate a favourable sugar quota in order to obtain foreign currency to pay for its imports. The quota was the object of intense lobbying in both Washington and Santo Domingo by Dominican officials, and in 1973 President Balaguer offered his resignation to President Nixon – not to the Dominican Congress – in case he constituted an obstacle to securing the sugar quota. Balaguer, of course, did not resign; the requested quota (700,000 tons) was obtained, and as a result he was able to reinforce his government's economic position and show that the United States was backing him politically. The sugar quota was a matter of particular importance during Balaguer's first two terms, during which the average price of the country's main source of export revenue was much higher in the U.S. market than in the world market. In 1966, for example, the sugar quota meant additional revenues of $53.5 million, which would not have entered the country had it sold its sugar on the world market. In the succeeding years until 1971, this figure remained more or less stable ($55.9 million in 1967; $76.7 million in 1968; $50.2 million in 1969; $48.6 million in 1970; $43.5 million in 1971). But in 1972 world prices took a considerable leap upwards and the difference in income was only $12.9 million. In 1973 the Dominican Republic realized no advantage by exporting its sugar to the United States; rather, it was at a disadvantage in not having sold it at the high prices in the world market. In 1975 and 1976 as prices on the world market soared, the Dominican Republic received the highest export income in its history and the government accumulated enormous reserves of foreign currency, which masked the profound contradictions of an economy that had been growing very rapidly but in an unbalanced fashion. U.S. aid and the quota became practically unnecessary for financing Dominican imports.

In 1966 U.S. aid and the quota together represented 47 per cent of all income in foreign currencies; in 1972 they accounted for only 8.77 per cent. This reduction indicated both that the country had recovered from the crisis of 1964–7 and that the recovery had only been possible thanks to foreign aid that had been used to stimulate the country's economy to an unprecedented level. Other factors central to the economic take-off included the growth of sugar production, which was stimulated by ever larger quotas, and foreign and domestic investments whose promoters, aware of Washington's continuing political support of the Dominican government, risked capital in the mining, industrial, banking and service sectors. Yet although foreign investment grew in absolute terms, proportionally it remained at about the same level as in 1964 in relation to domestic investment, that is, about 35 per cent of the total.

Private investment and foreign aid supplied a major injection of capital into the Dominican economy. Between 1966 and 1971 about $1 billion were invested in the country, a substantial part being directed to important sectors such as mining and energy. The conditions granted by the Dominican government to these investments were always extremely generous. Falconbridge Dominicana, for example, a North American capital enterprise operating under Canadian cover and dedicated to the exploitation of nickel in the central region of the country, invested about $205 million guaranteed by the United States against every type of political risk, particularly expropriation. More modest but important foreign operations such as the Rosario Dominicana gold company, the Dominican Oil Refinery jointly owned by Shell and the state, and the dairy products industry operated by Nestlé, obtained substantial advantages when negotiating their installation contracts with the Dominican government, in the same way that the multinational corporation Gulf and Western received substantial incentives for its sugar and tourist operations during Joaquín Balaguer's presidency. The Dominican government frequently explained publicly the need for foreign investment to finance Dominican development. Every time politicians from inside or outside the government raised their voices to ask that North American investment be limited, regulated or expropriated, Balaguer responded by defending it, pointing to what he called the 'geopolitical destiny' of the Caribbean, meaning that because of the sheer size of the United States the Dominican Republic would always be its satellite in the region since the North Americans would never permit another Cuba in the Caribbean.

Balaguer's opinions were widely shared in the Dominican Republic. People remembered that the United States occupied the country in 1916 and governed it for eight years. They also recalled that as a result of Trujillo's death Dominican policy was decisively influenced by the manipulations of the Department of State through its consular and diplomatic officers. They remembered that what for a time they had believed would be a triumphant civilian–military movement to re-install the deposed President Bosch in office was frustrated by the massive use of U.S. military force and that U.S. troops did not leave the country until they had established a government which could be relied upon to protect and further U.S. interests. A certain political fatalism among Dominicans with respect to U.S. control over their country was confirmed in 1978 when political intervention once again took a direct form. In May, President Carter openly prevented Balaguer from fraudulently continuing in office – a move which would have challenged U.S. human rights policy at the time and the project to democratize the Dominican Republic.

After twelve years of exercising all-encompassing power, Balaguer and his associates refused to accept the results of the elections held 16 May 1978 in which Antonio Guzmán, running on the ticket of the Partido Revolucionario Dominicano, emerged the victor by an overwhelming margin. That night, while the population was watching the general count of votes being broadcast throughout the country on television, military officers who supported the re-election of Balaguer entered the offices of the Junta Central Electoral and interrupted the count, which already showed Guzmán as the certain winner of the election. They immediately began to confiscate and destroy the ballot boxes holding the votes and jailed a large number of representatives of the political parties. The general indignation provoked by this act of force had no parallel in Dominican history. Immediately, organizations throughout the country launched a campaign of peaceful protest and resistance, making it plain that the Dominican nation would not accept a fraudulent prolongation of Balaguer's government. Foreign observers who were in Santo Domingo representing the OAS, the U.S. Democratic Party, the Acción Democrática (AD) of Venezuela, and the Socialist International headed an international movement to repudiate the machinations of Balaguer and his military mafia. On this occasion the United States stood firm in its position of not recognizing any government that had not won the majority of votes. The U.S. position was immediately endorsed by Venezuela and other governments friendly to the Partido Revolucionario Dominicano. Balaguer finally had to give in. He handed over the government to Antonio Guzmán on 16 August 1978 after three months of profound political crisis which demonstrated that Balaguer's government had been in more than one sense a prolongation of the Trujillo era.

Antonio Guzmán took office with more political support than any politician in the Dominican Republic had ever enjoyed. After witnessing the various manoeuvres Balaguer and the military officers had resorted to in their effort to strip the Partido Revolucionario Dominicano of its electoral victory, the majority of the Dominican people had finally turned their backs on him. Guzmán took advantage of the unpopularity of Balaguer and his military chiefs to dismantle the Trujilloist military machine that Balaguer himself had restructured in 1966 and kept in power since then. This machine had become so powerful that it had even forced Balaguer to dismiss his candidate for vice-president during the last weeks of the 1978 electoral campaign. What most offended public opinion, however, were the continuous abuses by the military leaders, who generously doled out contracts for public works among themselves, enjoyed exemptions for the tax-free import of all the consumer goods they desired, and had become rich enough to play the roles of investor and entrepreneur in unfair competition with traditional commercial and industrial groups.

The Dominicans had voted for a change. Guzmán was the candidate of change and his whole electoral campaign was founded on this slogan. Until then, Guzmán had seemed a man obedient to his party's bureaucracy and it was thought that after fifteen years outside the government the party would govern in the manner attempted by Juan Bosch in 1963, that is, by accomplishing fundamental social reforms and accelerating the process of agrarian reform. It soon became apparent, however, that Guzmán intended to install a family-dominated government, betraying the Partido Revolucionario Dominicano. From the first day of his administration Guzmán made it clear that it was his government, not the party's. He appointed his own children, nieces, brothers, cousins and the children of his closest friends to the most important positions, and they governed to their own advantage. Corruption, which had reached scandalous levels in Balaguer's time because of the large number of people involved in it, was now concentrated among one family and its friends.

As a result of this the PRD split into two factions, those who remained outside the government joining the opposition immediately. The rift became much deeper when Guzmán began to work towards his indefinite re-election in the style of Trujillo and Balaguer. Since this operation required a party machine and the PRD had always opposed presidential re-election, Guzmán tried to buy off the middle-level leaders and the party activists by putting them on the government payroll. Guzmán appointed nearly 8,000 new public employees before the end of his first year in office, and within three years he had augmented the state payroll by about 180,000 new public employees.

The government's running expenses soon swallowed up nearly 100 per cent of the national budget. Public works programmes came to a halt for lack of investment resources, as did many other development projects financed with contributions from the Inter-American Development Bank, the Agency for International Development and the World Bank, because the government was left without enough for matching funds. To finance the unprecedented public sector deficit the government was obliged to resort to printing money without the necessary reserves. At first Guzmán and his government tried to justify their economic policy by saying that they were following a neo-Keynesian model of economic growth through the growth of public spending and aggregate demand. Critics of the government pointed out that the Dominican economy was extremely open and that the external sector would not be able to withstand an excessive increase in monetary circulation without incurring large deficits in the balance of payments. Not only were industry and agriculture incapable of supplying the country, but the government itself needed imports in order to assure itself of funds, since 43 per cent of public revenues derived from import taxes. The economic debate was at times conducted with great vehemence, but Guzmán and his government continued to defend their policy of easy indebtedness and subsidized financing of different sectors of the economy, including the public sector.

As the economic distortions became more evident it was recognized that many of them had originated in Balaguer's time, when the rapid growth of import substitution industries was encouraged at the expense of agriculture, and a policy of freezing agricultural prices was pursued to the benefit of urban mass consumers of industrial products whose prices were not subject to control. Guzmán tried to favour agricultural development, which had fallen behind during Balaguer's administration, and he vigorously supported agricultural reform, but in order to finance his rural programs Guzmán also had to resort to printing more paper money, so that the adjustments he made in favor of agricultural products, such as allowing prices to rise, were neutralized by inflation.

The rise in prices also seriously affected public enterprises. The Dominican Republic had one of the largest public-enterprise sectors in Latin America, since Trujillo's entire industrial, commercial, agricultural and livestock holdings were converted into state property in 1961 and 1962 during the confiscations imposed by the Consejo de Estado. The Dominican state found itself the proprietor of 60 per cent of the country's sugar production, the Corporación Dominicana de Electricidad, and nearly fifty commercial and industrial companies which were consolidated in 1966 under the Corporación Dominicana de Empresas Estatales (CORDE). In 1968 the government created a new state corporation, the Instituto de Establización de Precios (INESPRE), whose purpose was to intervene in the whole process of marketing agricultural and agro-industrial products, with the aim of keeping prices stable by subsidizing urban consumers. Over time, because of shortages in agricultural production, INESPRE was transformed into the largest commercial food-importer in the country, with a budget larger than that of the Republic of Haiti. With the increase in dependence on imported food, which resulted from cheap financing under Public Law 480 and the United States Commodity Credit Corporation, Dominican agriculture encountered reduced demand for its products because it was unable to compete with products imported at lower prices and distributed at low cost in the cities by INESPRE.

With the new rise in oil prices in 1979 all these costs began to increase. The internal adjustments in the prices of fuel and oil began to be reflected in the prices of agricultural and industrial products, whether locally produced or imported. With the rising deficit in the balance of payments, Dominican currency was losing its value, so that by 1982 a dollar was worth 1.35 Dominican pesos on the free market despite the government's trying to maintain official parity. Little by little various types of exchange arose which concealed the fact that the government wanted to keep its currency officially overvalued, even at the cost of a reduction in exports. This policy removed the possibility of obtaining foreign currency from outside to pay for imports at a time when the situation of the balance of payments was getting worse because it had to support a type of exchange and a system of import quotas which were favourable to the entry of specific industrial goods.

Eventually, reality caught up with the desires of Guzmán and his economists, the growth of foreign debt and the extraordinary rise in the price of oil leaving the government very little foreign currency with which to pay for other imports. Obliged to incur constant deficits in order to keep the prices of their products down to a politically acceptable level, public enterprises increased their debt and also began to take out foreign loans in strong currencies at high interest rates. Guzmán's government tried in vain to subsidize the central government with resources from the sale of gold from the mining company Rosario Dominicana, which was nationalized at the end of 1979. This did not amount to much, however, and by 1981 it was already evident that the entire public sector was on the edge of bankruptcy.

More than $800 million in foreign loans and grants, which could have been made available to finance the deficit in the balance of payments, went unused by Guzmán because of the lack of matching funds. In spite of the fact that sugar prices had reached their highest level in history, the state sugar mills were afflicted by the highest indebtedness in their history. The Corporación Dominicana de Electricidad continued in its policy of selling cheap energy to the public in order to maintain the government's political popularity. But at the same time it had to purchase expensive foreign oil, and the short-fall in its cash flow was so severe that frequently it found itself unable to pay its suppliers on time, and the country was often left with barely a week's supply of oil reserves. In another effort to conserve his popularity, Guzmán tried to amplify the role of the INESPRE by bringing subsidized food to ever larger numbers of people in the urban areas, consequently aggravating the deficit in the public sector.

In spite of all his efforts, Guzmán's popularity began to evaporate. His government was widely seen as a great political fraud in which the President had exploited the Partido Revolucionario Dominicano to enrich his family and try to keep himself in power indefinitely. Disenchantment became universal. Merchants and industrialists, antagonized from the first day by Guzmán's functionaries, constantly complained about unfair competition from public enterprises and the INESPRE. Landholders protested about the continuous threats levied against them by the government's agrarian officials, who wanted to bring agrarian reform everywhere without complying with the law and without offering compensation to the owners of confiscated land. Labour unions and the poor mass of the population protested constantly against the rise in the cost of living.

As Guzmán's unpopularity grew, the political rehabilitation of Balaguer advanced. His government was increasingly compared favourably with Guzmán's. The policy of freezing the running expenses of the government and the massive public investments which Balaguer had instituted had stimulated the economy, contributed to the broadening of the internal market and enriched many social sectors, principally the urban middle class and industrial and commercial entrepreneurs. Guzmán's most visible achievement had been political: he had dismantled Balaguer's military mafia, he had respected freedom of the press and of speech, and he had also allowed freedom of action on the part of the National Congress, which in Balaguer's time had been a mere extension of the executive branch.

The PRD, meanwhile, which had become divided into two irreconcilable factions and largely a party of opposition, reorganized itself under the leadership of its secretary-general, José Francisco Peña Gómez, and the Senator for the National District, Salvador Jorge Blanco, a well-known lawyer who had run against Guzmán during the first party primaries in 1977. When Guzmán realized that it would no longer be possible to get his party to nominate him for a new term, he tried to have his vice-president, Jacobo Majluta, endorsed. But it was already too late. The party had emancipated itself from the government and chosen as its presidential candidate for 1982 Jorge Blanco, who promised to establish a government of the party and for the party, and who projected an image of irreproachable integrity which was recognized even by his enemies.

Guzmán and his family manoeuvred to prevent Jorge Blanco from being elected president. They even went so far as to make a pact with Joaquín Balaguer and suggested to the military that it might prevent the holding of the elections or see to it that Jorge Blanco not live to take office if he won the election. But the military refused. The composition of the armed forces had been changing thanks to the depoliticization which Guzmán himself had introduced during the first two years of his government and thanks to the insistence by the United States that the Dominican armed forces must be the sustaining power behind the democracy, not a hindrance to it, in order to avoid a cataclysm like the civil war of 1965. As a consequence, Jorge Blanco was elected on 16 May 1982, defeating Joaquín Balaguer, after an impressive electoral campaign in which the most modern marketing techniques were utilized. Guzmán and his family found themselves isolated and disgraced, and some took advantage of the last few months of their term to amass more wealth. In the national banking community, the transfers to banks in Grand Cayman and Panama and the huge quantities of dollars being bought up in the exchange houses of Santo Domingo by some government officials were an open secret. Guzmán himself became acutely depressed and at midnight on 3 July 1982 he committed suicide by shooting himself in the head. Vice President Jacobo Majluta was sworn in immediately as president of the Republic and worked feverishly to get the military officers who had supported Guzmán to accept Jorge Blanco. The latter was finally inaugurated on 16 August 1982, in the middle of a financial crisis which threatened to bring the Dominican Republic to the brink of bankruptcy.

The economic policy of Jorge Blanco's government was designed several months before his election and was prefigured in numerous public discussions in which most of the organized groups of the country participated. During his electoral campaign Jorge Blanco promised to perfect political democracy with an 'economic democracy'. Yet his management of the crisis, like the adjustment plan his government had to carry out in agreement with the International Monetary Fund, buried the dream of building such an economic democracy and led to a process of income concentration more impressive than any that had ever taken place in Dominican history. This took place just as the middle class was suffering from a dramatic fall in its standard of living and the lower classes were burdened by inflation rates never before seen in the Republic.

When he began his term in the mid-1982, Jorge Blanco announced that his government was going to correct the distortions that afflicted the Dominican economy. It was not possible, he said, in a country afflicted by serious problems in the balance of payments, for imports to be protected by an overvalued exchange rate which had nothing to do with the reality of a depreciated currency. Nor was it appropriate in his view for the public sector to continue indebting itself in order to subsidize other economic sectors, particularly import substitution industry. It was unhealthy for the national economy when internal prices did not reflect the structure of prices in the world economy, including interest rates, which in the Dominican Republic were extraordinarily low compared to those in the United States. If in August 1982 there was any consensus about the Dominican crisis, it was that the economy needed to be readjusted. Agriculture was at a standstill for want of incentives. Industry was inefficient because of exaggerated protection and the immense subsidies and incentives offered by the state. Public enterprises were on the edge of bankruptcy because of growing subsidies that the government could no longer afford to pay. The fiscal system had lost its capacity to attract resources to finance the public sector adequately. The deficit in the balance of payments had left the country owing back payments of more than $400 million and with a deficit of more than $700 million in net international reserves.

For a small country with a population of 5.6 million whose exports did not exceed a billion dollars a year and whose budget was only one billion Dominican pesos, this situation was practically insoluble without an extraordinary effort of austerity, limitation of spending and public credit, and a substantial increase in foreign aid, especially emergency aid to attack the problem of the balance of payments. The foreign banks which had so gladly loaned money to Guzmán's government now refused to extend credit to the Dominican Republic unless it came to an agreement with the International Monetary Fund. The negotiations of this agreement were exceedingly stormy because the government tried to take advantage of them to show that austerity, the contraction of credit, the reduction of salaries, the rise of prices and the new restrictions on imports were impositions of the IMF. Jorge Blanco's economists threw themselves into a clumsy campaign of economic adjustments, rejecting the proposals of the IMF but trying to make the public believe that the decisions were imposed by the IMF. Despite the fact that the economic disequilibrium was due to structural imbalances, the Central Bank tried to use force to control the economy. In their determination to reduce the exchange rate with the U.S. dollar to reach a parity lost long ago, the monetary authorities pressured Blanco into sending police and army troops to close the exchange houses so that people would have to buy and sell dollars at the commercial banks. The immediate and predictable result was extraordinary financial disorder, a dizzy flight of capital and wave of speculation which devalued the peso by more than 100 per cent. The government soon had to recognize that these measures had been ill conceived, and finally it chose to legalize the exchange houses in an effort to restore financial equilibrium. But the exchange rate remained at three pesos to the dollar and prices did not stop rising because importers immediately adjusted their domestic prices to reflect the new rate of exchange. In its negotiations with the IMF, Jorge Blanco's government maintained its attitude of denunciation of the conditions the Fund wanted to impose, which were fundamentally the halting of the issue of all unbacked money, the freezing of public spending, the control of the deficits in state enterprises and the public deficit, a rise in direct taxes to increase fiscal revenue, greater control of imports and a rise in interest rates.

All these measures figured in Jorge's program, but the government found in the International Monetary Fund a species of villain to whom it could pass on the political culpability of the adjustment programme. Such a manoeuvre was understandable since a programme of this nature meant adjusting domestic prices to the real rate of exchange with the result that the rise in prices became intolerable for most of the population. The failure of this policy became evident at the end of April 1984 when the government policy-makers attempted to take advantage of the Holy Week vacation to raise the prices of all essential products while the urban middle class was off guard and away from the cities. Their lack of political sensitivity prevented them from seeing that the protest would come from the poor, who had gone neither to the mountains nor to the beaches. On the following Monday the country woke up to a popular uprising which was only quelled three days later when the army killed more than seventy persons staging protests against the government's economic policy.

In spite of the clamour for Jorge Blanco to replace the governor of the Central Bank, the government continued with its policy of conflict with the IMF until December 1984, when it became apparent that the Dominican Republic could not continue without renegotiating its debt with the foreign governments and the commercial banks, not to mention without signing an agreement with the IMF in order to stave off a total collapse in the balance of payments which would have meant the cessation of all foreign credit, the paralysation of the country due to lack of oil, and the cancellation of most imported industrial supplies.

The governor of the Central Bank was finally dismissed, and Jorge Blanco recovered part of his popularity with some industrialists and merchants when on 25 January 1985, a general devaluation was decreed and a new unified exchange rate was created for all the financial operations in the country. When the dollar was allowed to float freely in the markets, the Dominican economy entered thoroughly into a formal process of dollarization similar to the process other Latin American countries had gone through during previous crises. The effects of devaluation were noticeable at once. The imbalances in fiscal budget and in the balance of payments continued, but the new domestic prices and the new official exchange rate served to stimulate the development of a new export sector which had not existed before. By the same token, Dominican agriculture was revived when the prices of its products, previously subject to control, were allowed to float, creating new incentives for the production and export of agro-industrial products.

Meanwhile, the parties began to prepare for the general elections to be held on 16 May 1986. These were the most contentious elections in contemporary Dominican history. Joaquín Balaguer of the Partido Reformista won by a narrow margin of 40,000 votes over Jacobo Majluta, candidate for the PRD. The return of the eighty-year-old ex-president to power for the fifth time in twenty-five years was quite an exceptional event in view of the fact that he lost the presidency in 1978 in the midst of the greatest discredit possible and at a time when glaucoma had already caused the complete loss of his vision. Although blind and ill, Balaguer was able to unify and reorganize his party, assimilating along the way the old Christian Democrat Party, which changed its name to the Partido Reformista Social Cristiano and accepted an ideology and a structure of international relations similar to the social democratic network of contacts of the PRD, which had been associated for years with the Socialist International.

Balaguer's return to power was aided by the constant internal strife in the PRD and its deficient political management of the economic crisis during its eight-year rule. Facing a disorganized and disunited party whose primary convention to nominate presidential candidates in 1986 ended with gunshots and major confusion, Balaguer appeared capable of reorganizing the economy and imposing political authority. Third place in the presidential elections of 1986 went to ex-president Juan Bosch, who in recent years had managed to organize a large ideological party made up of revolutionary cadres, called the Partido de la Liberación Dominicana

(PLD). This party captured almost 20 per cent of the votes in 1986, doubling its performance in the 1982 elections, and signalling the rapid growth of a radical left that proposed to come to power through elections in the Dominican Republic. The growth of Bosch's party can be largely explained by the difference in political style it had brought to the country; while the other large traditional parties had maintained a discourse that expressed their internal strife or the interests of their leaders, Bosch's party, in contrast, consistently maintained a political line of defending the poorest groups in the nation and demonstrated skill in reaping political advantage from the country's deepening economic crisis.

12

HAITI SINCE 1930

During the half century from the 1930s to the 1980s, Haiti, the poorest country of Latin America, experienced a gradual decline in the standard of living, a deterioration in the condition of the land – with an alarming growth of soil erosion throughout the country – and a dramatic growth of its population, from 2.5 to approximately 6 million. Despite occasional efforts by Haitian governments and ambitious schemes sponsored by an endless procession of foreign missions, little was done to halt the country's decline. Indeed, very often the results of these foreign interventions was positively harmful. In most cases the improvements required were not in the individual interests of the peasants and would only work if undertaken as co-operative enterprises among all the landholders in a particular area. Haitian governments were generally unable or unwilling to give the kind of guarantees which would make such projects viable.[1]

Throughout these years Haiti remained a largely agricultural economy, producing food for local consumption together with a few export crops. The principal cash crop was coffee. Efforts to encourage large-scale production of other crops such as sugar, cotton and sisal, met with only limited success. Most manufactured consumer goods were imported, principally from the United States. Attempts to develop copper and bauxite mining achieved no more than modest results. From the late 1960s there was a rapid growth in light manufacturing industries and assembly plants, situated mostly in and around the capital. These accounted for well over half the country's foreign earnings in 1985 when Haiti enjoyed the distinction of being the world's largest producer of baseballs. After the fall of Jean-Claude Duvalier in 1986, however, more than forty of these firms closed.

[1] Mats Lundahl, in a number of his writings, lays considerable emphasis upon these factors as causes of Haitian poverty. See *Peasants and Poverty: A study of Haiti* (London, 1979) and *The Haitian Economy* (London, 1983).

Tourism developed rather unevenly and depended for its prosperity on the fluctuating political and medical reputation of the country. Because of its poverty Haiti remained among the most self-sufficient economies of the Caribbean, having export and import co-efficients significantly lower than other island states of the region.

A notable feature of the period since 1930 was migration, internal and external. As in other parts of Latin America there was a movement of population, mostly women, into the capital, Port-au-Prince, which by the 1980s had a population of well over one million. Equally significant was the migration of Haitian cane-cutters, mostly men, to neighbouring Cuba and the Dominican Republic. Some of these were seasonal migrants, others stayed for several years, while many settled permanently in the host country. Under the Duvaliers the number of migrants to North America escalated into a major population flow.

The power of the predominantly mulatto elite declined during this period, although there is no evidence of major redistribution of wealth among the population. The political strength of the mulattoes waned most notably after the overthrow of President Elie Lescot (1941–6), but even during the darkest days of the Duvalier era they managed to retain a major share of the (declining) national wealth. The black middle sectors of the population, both rural and urban continued to grow in importance. Even at the end of the nineteenth century they were a force to be reckoned with. Under U.S. occupation (1915–34) their social position had been strengthened and the fall of Lescot's government may partly be explained by his failure to understand their power. It is therefore astonishing to find writers on Haiti referring to these groups as politically and socially unimportant. The *noiriste* regimes of Dumarsais Estimé (1946–50) and François Duvalier (1957–71) benefited a favoured sector of the black middle class but usually also secured support from a number of mulatto politicians. During the presidency of Duvalier, Arab merchant families were at last incorporated into the political life of the country. The regime of Jean-Claude Duvalier (1971–86) became increasingly dependent on the good-will of the business community.

The mass of peasants and urban poor exerted a certain influence on political developments in Haiti from the earliest days until the U.S. occupation. Yet this role was sporadic and largely negative in that it usually took the form of removing governments that had become intolerable. The masses rarely had any significant say in the way the country was governed. The overthrow of Jean-Claude Duvalier in 1986 represented, indeed, the revival of a tradition of rural initiative which, despite the populist rhetoric of *noiriste* leaders, declined after the U.S. invasion, with political activity being increasingly centred in the capital.

Despite a deteriorating ecology, a declining economy and a trend – at least up to the mid-sixties – towards an increasingly violent political culture, poetry, novels, visual arts, music and dance flourished during the half century after 1930. The Duvalierist dictatorship, however, drove creative writers into exile and much of the original and significant work came from the Haitian disapora.

The Roman Catholic Church played a central role in the social and political life of the Haitian people, as it had since the Concordat of 1860. The Church suffered a setback with the failure of the 1941 'anti-superstition' campaign, conducted with vigour and sometimes violence against the Voodoo religion. The governments of Estimé and François Duvalier were seen as anti-clerical, using their power, particularly in the field of education, to limit the Church's influence. Indeed, 'Papa Doc' Duvalier dealt a number of severe blows to the political pretentions of the Church. The backing given by churchmen to critics of Duvalierism in the 1980s was a key factor in the overthrow of 'Baby Doc'.

In his 1929 report, the United States High Commissioner in Haiti confidently asserted that the Haitian peasant no longer viewed U.S. occupation with distrust, 'but now rather regards it as a friend'.[2] The United States had been running the affairs of the black republic for fifteen years. The invasion of Haiti in July 1915 was part of a general strategy to control the Caribbean region. With the acquisition of Guantánamo in Cuba, the desire for a naval base in Hispaniola was lessened, but Washington, vitally concerned to prevent European powers from establishing any further positions in the region, was particularly alarmed by the growing power of the German colony in Haiti. By the outbreak of the First World War, Germans controlled most of the foreign commerce of the country and the U.S. State Department was worried that a victorious Germany might try to increase its hold on Haiti. Furthermore, the Americans were keen to establish in the Caribbean regimes favourable to private investment by U.S. nationals. Hence, North American forces occupied Haiti in 1915 with both strategic and economic motives, and in the belief that the United States had a moral obligation to 'assist' these countries of the Caribbean.

[2] *Seventh Annual Report of the American High Commissioner* (3 January 1929), p. 1.

The invasion was welcomed by important sections of the small French-speaking and generally light-skinned elite, and faced only sporadic military resistance. The arrival of the marines was seen by elite groups as a means whereby they might re-establish control over the country, which had been slipping from their hands in the preceding decades. The Americans found an amenable puppet president in the person of Philippe Sudre Dartinguenave (1915–22) and imposed a new constitution that legalized the foreign ownership of land which all constitutions since 1805 (with the exception of Henry Christophe's) had forbidden. Attempts to reintroduce forced labour in the form of the *corvée* were among the reasons for an outbreak, in 1918, of guerrilla resistance to the occupation, led by Charlemagne Péralte. This caused considerable alarm and reinforcements were sent from the United States. After many months of fighting and thousands of casualties Péralte was killed and the revolt was put down.

After 1920, the increasing opposition was generally restricted to the realm of formal politics and journalism. Nevertheless, despite the High Commissioner's optimism in 1929, movements of protest later in the same year resulted in the bombing of Les Cayes by U.S. aircraft and the killing of more than twenty peasants who had been taking part in a peaceful demonstration. President Hoover responded by sending a commission of enquiry headed by an ex-football coach and former governor of the Phillipines, William Cameron Forbes. He arrived in Haiti in February 1930 – accompanied by three elderly journalists and a retired diplomat. None of the commissioners spoke Haitian *Kréyol* and only one spoke French. After two weeks in the country, spent mostly in the capital interviewing disgruntled members of the Haitian elite and U.S. officials, they returned to recommend the rapid Haitianization of the armed forces and the civil service, leading to a withdrawal in 1936. Two commissioners favoured an immediate end to the occupation.[3]

By 1930 the collaborationist regime of Louis Borno (1922–30) had become universally unpopular, and the Forbes Commission recommended fresh elections under a provisional president acceptable to all parties. The elections resulted in victory for Sténio Vincent, a mulatto of the upper middle class, over his principal rivals Seymour Pradel, an elite mulatto, and Jean Price Mars, a black middle-class Haitian from the North. The

---

[3] See Robert Spector, *W. Cameron Forbes and the Hoover Commissions to Haiti (1930)* (Lanham, Md., 1985).

new president soon began to call for the early withdrawal of U.S. troops and reached agreement with Franklin Roosevelt for an end to the occupation in 1934.

In 1930 Haiti was, as it has remained, a predominantly agricultural country, with more than 80 per cent of the population engaged in this sector of the economy. Most of these people lived and worked on small properties owned by themselves or by members of their family, or on land upon which their family had squatted for generations. They produced coffee, which was sold to the *spéculateur* (middleman) and vegetables for local consumption – some retained for family use and the remainder sold at the local market. Women played a key role in the rural economy, not only working in the fields but also dominating the markets. The principal export was coffee, with sugar becoming of increasing importance. Other exports included sisal, timber and bananas. Although much of the land was divided into small plots, there did exist a number of large plantations, owned either by Haitians or by U.S. companies. These companies, such as the Haytian American Sugar Corporation (HASCO), secured concessions of government land, dispossessing small peasants who had for generations been cultivating the land; a potential labour force was thus provided for the newly created estates. Nevertheless, attempts to develop a large-scale agricultural industry, as happened in Cuba, Puerto Rico and the Dominican Republic, failed. One reason for this was the confused state of land ownership and the long and costly legal actions needed to clarify the situation. A cadastral survey was begun under the occupation, but the records were mysteriously destroyed by fire. Most manufactured goods and luxury items were imported from France, from other European countries and, increasingly, from the U.S.A. Small industries producing shoes, soap and other domestic requirements existed in the towns, but wages were very low. The U.S. financial adviser Sidney de la Rue opposed measures to raise them on the ground that capital would cease to be attracted to the country.

The development of sugar industries abroad and dispossessions led to mass emigration from Haiti to work first in Cuba and then in the Dominican Republic. The numbers of Haitians resident in these two countries rose from 5,000 in 1916 to possibly 80,000 by 1930. In 1936–7 alone more than 30,000 Haitians were repatriated from Cuba and in 1937 an unknown number, possibly 15,000–20,000, were massacred in the Dominican Republic as a result of Trujillo's policy of 'deafricanising the border'.[4] The Dominican government accepted responsibility for the slaughter and agreed to pay compensation, little of which appears to have reached the families of the deceased.

The post-occupation years witnessed further U.S. investment in Haiti, and the economy continued to be controlled from Washington since even after the withdrawal of troops a financial officer remained to supervise government policies. President Vincent (1930–41), however, by a skilful combination of patronage and arbitrary imprisonment of opponents, managed to secure a fairly broad basis of support. He introduced a new constitution which gave sweeping powers to the President and paved the way for his re-election. Towards the end of the decade, however, discontent – particularly among some of the black middle class – began to deepen. There were rumours of an army coup, demonstrations among the unemployed took place, and Vincent dismissed a number of senators for encouraging unrest. In 1938 the British consul discouraged the Moyne Commission – which had been appointed to consider the causes of disturbance in the British Caribbean colonies – from visiting Haiti. Such a visit would, in his view, encourage discontent and put the Haitian government in a difficult position. The President's openly expressed belief that democracy was an inappropriate system of government for Haiti and his frank admiration for a number of European fascist leaders became something of an embarassment to the U.S. government. In 1941 he was replaced by Elie Lescot, a former cabinet minister under Borno and Vincent, who had also for some years been on the payroll of Dominican dictator Rafael Trujillo.

The new president was, before his election, Haitian ambassador in Washington and was known to be keenly pro-American. He immediately arranged for huge concessions of land to be made to the U.S.-controlled Société Haïtienne–Américaine de Développement Agricole (SHADA) for the production of rubber and sisal. This involved the expulsion of more than 40,000 peasant families from land they had been working for generations. About 200,000 acres of prime agricultural land were cleared, and by 1943 SHADA was employing more than 90,000 workers. Like almost all large-scale agricultural schemes since independence, the rubber project failed disastrously; traditional agriculture was disrupted for years, many

---

[4] See José I. Cuello, H., (ed.) *Documentos del conflicto dominico–haitiano de 1937* (Santo Domingo, 1985); also Juan Manuel García, *La matanza de los haitianos: genocio de Trujillo, 1937* (Santo Domingo, 1983).

thousands remained homeless and millions of dollars were lost. When the United States entered the Second World War, Lescot lost no time in declaring war on the Axis, taking the opportunity to confiscate property owned by Germans and Italians. Unlike Vincent, Lescot made little effort to keep something of a balance between blacks and mulattoes. Blacks found themselves systematically excluded from positions of profit and influence in public life and members of Lescot's family were appointed to government posts. As discontent increased, so oppression intensified. With the victory of the Allies in 1945, however, a new spirit of optimism was abroad. In France, to which many Haitian intellectuals still looked for inspiration, a left-wing alliance of Socialists, Communists, and Christian Democrats seemed to be emerging. Radical social change was the order of the day. This mood reinforced a growing discontent with the repressive policies of Lescot's government. The visit to Haiti, in December 1945, of André Breton, the French surrealist author, was the spark which ignited the revolutionary compound. A special number of *La Ruche,* edited by a group of young intellectuals including Jacques Stéphen Alexis and René Depestre, was published in honour of Breton and included the text of his speeches. The journal was seized by the police. Student protests ensued, and soon workers from a number of industries joined the demonstrations. In January 1946 an army junta of three took over the government, politely escorting the president to the airport. The people sang:

> Lescot ou allé, ou allé, ou allé
> Lescot ou allé, et ou pas di'm ain.
> (Lescot, you left . . . without a word)

The departure of Lescot marked the beginning of a period of intense political activity. Parties formed and split; alliances and 'fronts' were established and dissolved. Not merely in the capital but throughout the country, aspiring politicians emerged. Journalistic activity was unprecedented; more than sixty daily and weekly newspapers were being printed in 1946–7. Most journals were based in the capital, but many appeared in the provinces. In Gonaïves alone at least four journals were published: *La Cité, Le Populaire, L'Artibonite Journal* and *Lumière.*

The early weeks of the 1946 presidential campaign were dominated by ideological and class issues, but as the campaign became more intense the ever-present colour question emerged as a decisive factor determining alliances. The most influential party of the left was the largely Marxist Parti Socialiste Populaire (PSP), dominated by mulattoes from elite families, but supporting a liberal black candidate from the South, Edgard Nere Numa. The leading ideologies of this group were Etienne Charlier and Anthony Lespès. The small Parti Communiste d'Haïti (PCH) was a predominantly black group, led by an Anglican priest, Félix Dorleans Juste Constant, who was also supported as candidate by a group of young radicals – the Parti Démocratique Populaire de la Jeunesse Haïtienne (PDPJH), associated with the Journal *La Ruche*.

Among *noiristes*, the Mouvement Ouvrier Paysan (MOP) was headed by Daniel Fignolé – a charismatic mathematics teacher who was the idol of the Port-au-Prince poor. This movement, whose secretary was the enigmatic Dr François Duvalier, was vocal in its protests against the power of the elite. Its political arm was the Parti Populaire Nationale headed by Fignolé, Emile St Lot and Clovis Désinor. Since Fignolé was too young to run for president the MOP promoted the candidature of D. P. Calixte, a former head of the Garde d'Haïti who had been dismissed by President Vincent and was described by the *noiriste* journal *Flambeau* as one of the first victims of the bourgeois reaction and of the politics of 'mulatrification'. A wide range of more conservative *noiristes*, particularly strong in many of the rural areas, favoured Dumarsais Estimé, a schoolteacher from Verrettes in the Artibonite. These black groups, together with the PCH and the PDPJH, formed a loose federation called the Front Revolution-naire Haïtien.

Conservative forces were divided into a large number of political group-ings, determined largely by personal and family allegiances. The Parti Démocratique de l'Evolution Nationale controlled the journal *L'Observa-teur*, the Parti Nationale Intransigeant published *La Verité*, and the weekly *La Fronde* was effectively an 'in-house' journal of the Brutus family. Most conservatives gave support to Bignon Pierre-Louis, though with little hope of victory in the face of the radical temper of the time. Significantly, all the leading candidates for the presidency were black. Colour was manifestly the most salient factor in the political struggles of 1946.

The general election for the Senate and the Legislative Assembly took place in May 1946 and the president was to be chosen by a joint session of the two houses. 'Vote black to win the revolution', cried *L'Action Na-tionale*. While it was clear that the new president would be black, the *noiristes* denounced Pierre-Louis and Nere Numa as puppets of the elite. The mulatto-dominated groups generally avoided explicit references to colour, speaking of the need for economic development and social reform, but the *noiristes* were less inhibited. They demanded the election of an 'authentic' representative of the black masses and berated the exclusivism and arrogance of the mulatto elite.

When Estimé was elected in the second ballot his principal opponents rallied to his support. Calixte announced he was withdrawing from public life; Fignolé of the MOP and George Rigaud of the PSP agreed to join his first cabinet; the PCH and the majority of the PDPJH also declared their support. René Depestre saw the new government as the avant-garde of the proletariat and peasants, preparing the way for 'a total transformation of the conditions of life'. The general accord was, however, short-lived and these groups soon went into opposition. Mulattoes of the PSP attacked the government for colour prejudice while the MOP claimed that nothing was being done for the black masses. In an article published in November 1946, under the title 'Les mulâtres sont mauvais', the MOP journal *Chantiers* proclaimed: 'History proves that despite the good will of the black towards the mulatto, he is always the victim of mulatto hypocrisy and cynicism'. Throughout the presidency of Estimé the military triumvirate of Franck Lavaud, Antoine Levelt and Paul Magloire remained in the background. With their coup of January 1946 an old tradition of militarism had re-emerged. The U.S. occupation had manifestly failed in its attempt to form a professional and non-political military.

The government took increasingly repressive measures against opponents and attempted to ban some trade unions. The most vocal of the union groupings was the MOP – operating in the docks, the water company, the Bata shoe factory, and sugar production. The Marxist-dominated Fédération des Travailleurs Haïtiens represented workers in electricity, railways, printing and copper mining. A third group, L'Union Nationale, affiliated to the American AFL-CIO, had members in tobacco, tanning, customs and bakeries. There were also some independent unions, including chauffeur-guides and construction workers. The unions were concentrated in the capital and therefore had an influence out of proportion to their small membership. The quiet and unobtrusive François Duvalier, for some time Secretary of State for Labour and Public Health, took a particular interest in these labour movements. During the Estimé regime Duvalier, in collaboration with Lorimer Denis, also used his influence to promote the 'folklorique' movement and to cultivate a more sympathetic approach to the Voodoo religion. This led to conflicts with the Roman Catholic Church, represented by such men as Père Foisset and Bishop Paul Robert.

The years following the end of the war saw high prices for coffee on the world market and this meant a certain prosperity for key sectors of the

Haitian population. Estimé broke up the banana-export monopoly of Standard Fruit and gave concessions to his supporters, but the industry declined dramatically. He encouraged tourism and organized an ambitious celebration of the bicentenary of Port-au-Prince. He managed to spread some state patronage beyond the small elite, modestly improving the position of the black middle class in his home department of the Artibonite and in Port-au-Prince. It has been estimated that by 1950 this class numbered almost 40,000 in the capital, or a quarter of its population. Estimé had, however, antagonized important groups; exiles began to organize in the Dominican Republic with support from Trujillo and when Estimé attempt to change the constitution so as to allow a second term of office, he provoked a military coup by the same triumvirate – Lavaud, Levelt and Magloire – who had despatched Lescot.

This coup and its sequel represent a desperate attempt by the elite to reassert its hegemony. Magloire (1950–6) was effectively the sole candidate for the presidency in 1950 and his election was hailed by the business community and the Church as a victory for sanity and civilization. Though coming from a black family, Magloire presented himself as the apostle of national unity, and was seen as spokesman of the mulatto elite. From his newly built three-storey palace, Bishop Robert of Gonaïves referred to him as 'a saviour' who had come to bring 'a new liberation' to the country. Intellectuals like Dantès Bellegarde and Luc Fouché joined in the chorus of praise. Magloire maintained good relations with both the United States and Trujillo, and spent lavishly on presidential functions in the capital. His government made a few improvements in roads and wharfs, but some of his major projects, like the Péligre dam, were unrealized. In the early years economic conditions were favourable to the government. World coffee prices continued to rise until the mid-1950s and production remained fairly stable. Tourism developed rapidly during the Magloire years, with the number of visitors to Haiti quadrupling.

As Magloire's term of office drew to an end discontent grew. In October 1954 a hurricane had devastated much of the South, not only destroying towns but uprooting coffee and cacao trees. Governmental corruption became more blatant and the President began to make arrangements to continue in office. As groups which had been excluded from power protested, acts of terrorism increased. The outbreak of popular demonstrations in the capital further signalled the weakness of the regime and prompted the high command to remove their colleague and escort him to the airport.

The departure of Magloire was the signal for a period of open political competition between nine leading contenders for presidential office. A series of short-lived provisional regimes attempted to maintain control and to make arrangements for an election on terms they believed would be favourable to their candidate. The army played a key role in these manoevers, but the officer corps was scarcely less divided than the civilian politicians. Elections were planned for September 1957, by which time only two effective candidates remained in the field. Some had found the going too rough and dropped out; Fignolé was sent into exile; Clément Jumelle had been closely associated with Magloire and was feared by the army. François Duvalier, the mild-mannered black country doctor and amateur ethnologist, was opposed by Louis Déjoie, a suave mulatto businessman from the south. Antonio Kébreau, who had emerged as victor in the struggle for powers within the army, favoured the former, whom he believed could be manipulated. The elite, the church hierarchy and the U.S. embassy favoured Déjoie. The U.S. ambassador had, however, been persuaded by the bishop of the Eglise Episcopal (Anglican Church) that Duvalier was an acceptable candidate.

The election resulted in a clear victory for Duvalier, who polled particularly strongly in the North and Artibonite and in most of the cities. Only in parts of his native South and around the capital did Déjoie secure a majority. No doubt malpractices occurred on both sides, but it is likely that the result generally reflected popular sentiment at the time.

Voodoo remained the religion practiced by the great majority of the Haitian population although most would have claimed also to be Catholics. Voodoo had developed among the slaves of colonial Saint-Domingue as an amalgam of African religions which gradually incorporated elements of Christianity. Essentially it is concerned with a worship of God (*Granmet* or *Bondié*) and the spirits, or *lwa* as they are called. The cult involves prayers and the singing of hymns, accompanied by drums and the drinking of white rum (*clairin*), with the offering of sacrifices and the phenomenon of 'possession', as it is misleadingly described by anthropologists. Haitian devotees themselves speak, rather, of becoming horses (*chewal*) and being 'ridden' (*monté*) by the *lwa,* which has a somewhat different connotation.

Throughout the nineteenth century educated and literate Haitians tended to play down the importance of Voodoo and even denied its existence as anything more than a popular dance. For them Europe provided the pattern of culture to be followed; such institutions as Voodoo were a distinct embarrassment. However, following the ethnological movement of the 1920s, associated with J. C. Dorsainvil and Jean Price Mars, many Haitians began to accept and to value these African elements in popular culture. This movement was closely associated with the nationalist demand for an end to the occupation, but after 1934 it became more radical in its racial theories.

Under the inspiration of the ethnological movement and particularly of the esoteric theories of Arthur Holly, some younger men, like François Duvalier and his literary associate Lorimer Denis, began to insist that Haitians, being biologically of the African or black race, were psychologically different from whites and should not try to follow European patterns of culture, education and social structure. Some of these men formed the *Griots* group, named after the wise old man in the African village who passes on folk wisdom to the younger generation. For them, Voodoo was not magic or superstition but 'the work of a spirituality returning to a legendary past . . . the transcendent expression of the consciousness of a race before the enigmas of this world'.[5] The group was composed mostly of young blacks from the rising middle class, but it also included the remarkable mulatto poet Carl Brouard, whose father – a businessman – was for some time mayor of Port-au-Prince. At this time Brouard composed Voodoo hymns, and verses which romanticized the poor peasant with callused feet who descends from the mountain with his produce.

Like many in this group, Brouard admired European fascism and defended an authoritarian politics based upon a populist ideology. Mussolini became something of a model of political leadership for such men, until he invaded Ethiopia. This was the moment of truth for these Haitian intellectuals, who became fiercely critical of the Italians and of the inaction of other European nations. Some of the mulatto Catholic writers, however, continued to speak well of Italian as well as of Spanish and Portuguese fascism, while Action Française found a spokesman in Gérard de Catalogne. Even Hitler had his Haitian apologists. President Vincent received support from these mulattoes and blacks who admired his authoritarian pose, although he was himself critical of the *noiriste* emphasis upon the African heritage of Haiti, seeing this as a divisive tendency.

A number of Haitian poets, including Roussan Camille, Jean F. Brierre and Régnor Bernard, achieved international reputation in the francophone

---

[5] F. Duvalier and L. Denis, 'Psychologie ethnique et historique', *Les Griots* 4 (1939): 500–1.

world as prophets of the *négritude* movement, while in the 1940s other writers were strongly influenced by European surrealism. The two leading representatives of this movement were René Belance and Clément Magloire Saint-Aude. The latter's volume *Dialogues de mes lampes* (1941) is perhaps the most radical expression of this tendency. Jacques Roumain described it as 'an infernal machine: anti-bourgeois but negative and anarchist'. The year 1946 witnessed an explosion of literary talent among the younger generation, particularly those associated with *La Ruche*. Perhaps most notable was the strident voice of the twenty-year-old René Depestre, whose volume of poems *Etincelles* reflects the optimistic mood of the time.

The so-called anti-superstition campaign conducted in 1941 by the Roman Catholic Church with full support from the Lescot government marked a decisive stage in the struggle for supremacy in the cultural sphere. It can be seen as a determined attempt by the mulatto elite to maintain its hegemony, by suppressing or at least containing the revival of interest in folklore and particularly in the Voodoo religion. Mission services were held throughout the country in which the faithful were urged to take an 'anti-superstition' oath and to destroy their Voodoo sacred objects *(wangas)*. Voodoo temples were broken up and their contents burned. Leading figures in the campaign included the bishop of Gonaïves, Paul Robert, and a young Haitian priest, Rémy Augustin, who composed a book of hymns for the occasion; these figures will reappear in the account of Duvalier's conflict with the Church in the 1960s. The campaign roused such fierce opposition that after several months it was brought to an abrupt close, when shots were fired in a church where a mission service was taking place.

A leading critic of the campaign was Jacques Roumain, the director of the Bureau d'Ethnologie, who denounced the government and the church hierarchy. The Haitian people, he argued, are no more superstitious than others; Voodoo should be regarded as a religion and, like all religions, was a product of alienation and destined to pass away when its social and economic basis was removed. In the post-occupation years Roumain had emerged as the commanding intellectual figure on the left. Born in 1907 of an elite mulatto family, he was educated mostly in Europe, returning to Haiti in 1927 and immediately joining the literary circle which centred on the journals *La Trouée* and *La Revue Indigène*. While he defended the nationalist movement demanding an end to the U.S. occupation, Roumain claimed that bourgeois nationalists were using the movement to strengthen their hold over the masses. Colour prejudice, too, was a mask behind which unscrupulous politicians of all colours juggled with class conflicts for their own ends. In the early thirties Roumain had founded the Communist Party, but was soon sent into exile by Vincent.

Largely under the influence of Price Mars and the ethnological movement Roumain wrote poems and novels about rural Haiti, with its African traditions, as well as stories depicting the shallowness of bourgeois life in the capital. His most celebrated work, *Gouverneurs de la rosée,* published in 1944 (the year of his death), is about a cane-cutter who returns from Cuba to his native village, where he challenges the fatalistic attitudes of the people. The message of the novel is that by a knowledge of reality and by co-operative action, men and women can determine their future, irrigate their land and become 'masters of the dew'. Roumain insisted that art must be seen as an important weapon in the service of the revolution.[6]

Other socialists of the period emphasized the need for the technocratic management of social and political life. Such men as Jules Blanchet wrote of the importance of experts and envisaged a bureaucratic Utopia, where social scientists planned an ever brighter future. Socialism in general and Marxism in particular was very much an elite phenomenon and little effort was made to solicit the interest or support of peasants or of the small urban proletariat until the mid-forties.

François Duvalier came to power in 1957 with support from key groups of mostly black middle-class politicians and local leaders. In the countryside these were owners of medium-sized properties, able to provide occasional employment for their poorer neighbours and to make them loans for seed, fertiliser and other needs. Some of them were *spéculateurs,* buying coffee from the small peasant and selling to the export houses in the ports, thus constituting an important link between town and countryside. They included a number of *houngans* (Voodoo priests), who played an influential role in village life. It was from these middle sectors of the rural population that the *caco* and *piquet* (guerrilla) leaders had come in the previous century, and it was they who had led the armed struggle against the U.S. occupation. Duvalier also had backing from middle-class groups in the capital and in the provincial towns. He was supported by the Parti Unité National, founded in February 1957, with its journal *Panorama.* This group included Jules Blanchet, who had been associated with the old PSP, and his brother Paul; also Michel Aubourg,

[6] Jacques Roumain, 'Préjugé de couleur et lutte de classe', in *Analyse Schématique, 32–34* (Port-au-Prince, 1934).

Joseph Baguidy and other *noiriste* ideologists. These people represented the 'left wing' of Duvalierism – nationalist in rhetoric, anti-American and thus dubbed by the U.S. embassy as 'crypto-Communist'. Duvalier was also supported by a number of disaffected mulatto politicians, including Frédéric Duvigneaud and Victor Nevers Constant, businessman Ernest Bennett and ex-Nazi-sympathizer Jean Magloire. The last two were associated with the Eglise Episcopale, whose bishop played a key role in securing U.S. support for Duvalier in the early days.

Cleverly reassuring the bishops by appointing, for the first time in Haitian history, a priest as Minister of Education, Duvalier announced that he was inviting a mission of U.S. Marines to help train the armed forces. These steps effectively tied the hands of two powerful elements in the country – the Church and the U.S. embassy – and enabled the new president to deal with more pressing matters.

Duvalier's first moves were directed against his political opponents and against the army leadership. With help from his civilian militia, known as *cagoulards* (hooded men), organized and led by Clément Barbot, he terrorized opposition leaders and dealt ruthlessly with their inept attempts to overthrow his government. He transferred a number of senior army officers to rural areas and was then able to remove the isolated Kébreau from his post. In his early years Duvalier frequently changed the military leadership, removing politically ambitious officers and promoting younger black soldiers loyal to himself. The militia was reorganized into the Volontaires de la Securité Nationale, the Duvalieristes Intégrales and other smaller agencies. These groups were known as *tontons macoutes,* after the figure in folklore who carries off naughty children in his knapsack. Although the *macoutes* were primarily an instrument of terror and vigilance, they also performed the vital function of recruiting support for the regime throughout the country and encouraging ordinary Haitians to feel that they were playing an important role in the political life of the nation. Scraps of financial patronage were also funnelled through these groups.

Having removed the most pressing threats to his regime, Duvalier turned on a number of priests, particularly those engaged in schoolteaching. The head of the Holy Ghost Fathers, Père Etienne Grienenberger, formerly a close friend of President Magloire, was an early victim. Together with another priest, he was expelled from the country in August 1959 for encouraging opposition groups and undermining 'the spiritual unity of the nation', in the words of cabinet minister Paul Blanchet. The archbishop protested and a warrant was issued for his arrest, but was withdrawn. Further conflicts between Church and state ensued when the Catholic daily newspaper *La Phalange* gave moderate support to students who were protesting against the arrest of some of their number.

In late 1960 Archbishop Poirier was expelled on the ground that he had given money to student Communist groups (a bizarre accusation in the light of his authoritarian, right-wing stance). *La Phalange* was closed by the government and dozens of priests and nuns were arrested. Duvalier and all those involved in the expulsion of the archbishop were excommunicated. Further moves against the Roman Catholic Church included the closing of the seminary, the expulsion of the Jesuits, the silencing of church magazines and the banning of Catholic trade unions. Steps were also taken against some members of the Eglise Episcopale, whose bishop was later expelled from the country in 1964. By this time Jean Baptiste Georges, formerly Minister of Education, and another priest were among the principal exile leaders planning invasions from Miami.

During these years Duvalier was also contending with other potential centres of opposition. In mid-1960 he became aware of a conspiracy to assassinate him encouraged by the U.S. embassy and led by Clément Barbot, head of the *tontons macoutes*. Barbot was arrested with a number of his supporters, but some time after he was freed from prison he initiated a campaign of terror against the government which began with an apparent attempt to kidnap the Duvalier children. Barbot and his brother were eventually killed in a shoot-out with government forces in July 1963.

With typical ruthlessness Duvalier rendered ineffective the traditional means by which the business community had been able to bring pressure on governments by closing their shops. Duvalier simply ordered the *macoutes* to open the stores with crowbars, allowing the mob to plunder; proprietors soon returned. Similarly, his response to a student strike was to close the university and to open a new 'state university' under firm government control, into which students were obliged to re-register if they wished to continue with their studies. The trade unions retained their independence rather longer, but in 1964 they too were finally deprived of all autonomy.[7]

One centre of power which proved more troublesome was the United States embassy. Ever since the U.S. invasion of 1915, Washington had assumed some kind of right to determine what happened in Haiti. As

---

[7] A useful summary of the history of trade-unionism in Haiti can be found in J.-J. Doubout and Ulrich Joly, *Notes sur le développement du mouvement syndical en Haïti* (n.p., 1974).

already noted, the United States had been prepared to accept Duvalier as president and it was agreed that a Marine Corps mission should be sent to help train the Haitian forces. This mission, arriving early in 1959, was headed by the flamboyant Robert Debs Heinl, whose understanding of the role which he was playing in the *politique* of Duvalier was manifestly limited.

President John Kennedy found Haiti, with its scant respect for human rights, something of an embarrassment as a member of the 'free world'. The United States protested against the misuse of aid and expressed its displeasure at the 're-election' of Duvalier in 1961, in which the ballot papers for the parliamentary elections were headed 'Dr François Duvalier, President of Haiti'. Voters assumed that this was simply a statement of fact, but afterwards discovered that – unless they had actually crossed it out – they had voted him into a further six-year term of office. However Washington needed Haiti's vote in the Organization of American States, particularly in the meeting of 1962 at Punte del Este, when Cuba was expelled from the OAS. At the last moment Haiti agreed to use its key vote to support the expulsion in exchange for increased U.S. aid. Nevertheless, practically all U.S. aid was suspended later in the same year owing to corruption.

Duvalier's constitutional term of office was due to end in May 1963, but as the time approached it was clear he had no intention of resigning. Opposition groups began a campaign of terror; Duvalier took fierce revenge. His close aide Dr Jacques Fourcand, president of the Haitian Red Cross, declared that there would be a 'himalaya of corpses': 'Blood will flow in Haiti. The land will burn from North to South, from East to West. There will be no sunrise or sunset – just one big flame licking the sky.'[8] Men, women and children were massacred by the *macoutes,* and the embassies were filled with refugees. The Dominican embassy was entered by Duvalier's forces, who took out two refugees, provoking a crisis in relations with the neighbouring republic, where preparations were made for an invasion. The U.S. refused to recognize Duvalier's second term of office and lowered the level of its diplomatic representation. Kennedy intensified the campaign to destabilize the regime by encouraging Haitian exile groups in the United States itself and, with collaboration from President Juan Bosch, in the Dominican Republic. Duvalier spread the rumour that he was planning to flee the country, and preparations on the

[8] *New York Times,* 27 April 1963.

Dominican border for the invasion were halted. Far from leaving, however, Duvalier increased his repression of supposed dissidents and began planning his inauguration as president-for-life – an office which went back to Haiti's early days.

The campaign leading to the referendum which confirmed Duvalier as president-for-life witnessed a growing appeal to religious symbolism on the part of his propagandists. Posters appeared of Jesus with his arm round Duvalier and the words 'I have chosen him'. Jean M. Fourcand published a *Catéchisme de la révolution* which included hymns and various prayers adapted to the cause. Duvalier was proclaimed the greatest patriot of all times, emancipator of the masses and renovator of the country in whom the great leaders of the past – Toussaint, Dessalines, Christophe, Pétion and Estimé – were reincarnated. The booklet includes acts of faith, hope and charity, confessions and a 'Lord's Prayer' addressed to Duvalier. The 'Apostles' Creed' begins:

I believe in Our Doc, our all-powerful chief, builder of the new Haiti, and in his patriotism. Our Saviour who was elected President in 1957 who suffered for his people and for his country, who was re-elected in 1961 and proclaimed President-for-Life. . . .

One of the most remarkable episodes in the early years of the regime was the President's determination to change the Haitian flag from the blue and red, horizontally placed, to the black and red vertically placed with the black to the mast. The former had been the flag at independence (though Duvalier refused to accept this), but had been changed to black and red by Dessalines in the Constitution of 1805. When Haiti was divided in 1806, Christophe retained the black and red flag, while Pétion returned to the blue and red. The latter, which remained the official flag until Duvalier's day, was said to symbolize the sharing of power by blacks (blue) and mulattoes (red), with both colours reaching the mast. The black and red, with black to the mast, symbolized the fact that blacks should control power. Other esoteric interpretations of the flag were put forward by Arthur Holly, a *noiriste* writer of the U.S. occupation period, who insisted that the flag should be changed to black and red.[9] Duvalier attempted to make the change in 1957, but there was so much opposition that he dropped the project. By 1964, however, he was in a strong enough position to introduce the black and red flag. (The reappearance of the blue

---

[9] Arthur Holly, ('Her-Ra-Me-El') *Dra-po: étude ésoterique de egrégore africain, traditionnel, social et national* (Port-au-Prince, 1928).

and red flag was a notable feature of the demonstrations in January and February 1986, which led to the fall of Jean-Claude Duvalier.)

The suspension of most foreign aid in the early 1960s produced a serious financial crisis. Almost no money was available to pay regular government employees let alone the *macoutes;* civil servants received copies of the president's *Œuvres essentielles* in lieu of cash. Nevertheless, Duvalier's supporters, calculating that they were unlikely to do any better under another government, remained faithful and hoped for better days. With the flight of many Haitian businessmen to the United States and elsewhere the field was wide open to the influx of an extraordinary succession of suspect financiers including the Egyptian Mohammed Fayed, Prince Azod of Iran and George Mohrenschild from the United States. Largely in collaboration with Haitian banker Clémard Joseph Charles, these men were given various commercial concessions in the hope that they would bring much-needed foreign exchange into the country. After some months, Fayed managed to transfer a considerable sum of public money to his own account and then promptly disappeared.

In certain respects 1965 may be seen as the turning point of the regime of François Duvalier. By this time he had removed major threats to his government from within and outside the country. He had come to an understanding with the United States, arrived at an implicit agreement with what was left of the business community, eliminated independent trade unions and brought the army leadership to heel. It only remained for him to reach an accommodation with the Roman Catholic Church. In 1966 he turned his attention to this matter. The Vatican agreed to the appointment of a new indigenous hierarchy, with the generally pliant François Wolf Ligondé as archbishop. The aged Bishop Cousineau was the sole remaining white bishop. At the ceremony the President declared that it was a great comfort to know that he could now count on 'the support of the highest moral authority in the world'. The church hierarchy was thereby shorn of political power for almost two decades. Duvalier later took further action against the Holy Ghost Fathers, who controlled one of the principal high schools in the capital, on the ground that they were a subversive influence.[10]

The economy of the countryside, where 80 per cent of Haitians worked,

[10] For further details on Church–State relations at this time, see David Nicholls, 'Politics and Religion in Haiti', *Canadian Journal of Political Science* 3, no. 3 (1970); also 'Documents: The Catholic Church in Haiti', *IDOC International,* North American edition, 6 (27 June 1970): 6–7. Duvalier's own account of these events can be found in *Mémoires d'un leader du tiers monde* (Paris, 1969).

continued to be plagued with problems. Besides the occasional hurricane and drought, soil erosion had become chronic. Lack of effective incentives for the small farmer, and the difficulty of obtaining credit, prevented progress in the rural sector. In the early 1960s world coffee prices fell and output per acre remained below most countries of Latin America. There was, however, a slow growth in rural co-operatives, which by 1963 numbered more than two hundred. In the late fifties and early sixties first bauxite and then copper became significant exports, and in the late sixties U.S. firms began to exploit the very low wages in Haiti by opening labour-intensive light manufacturing and assembly plants. These grew steadily in the following decade, and by 1974 these had been a substantial jump in foreign earnings from factories using local components.

François Duvalier died in April 1971 after some months of illness. The Constitution of 1964 had been modified to give him power to nominate his successor as president-for-life, and just before his death he named his teenage son, Jean-Claude. This step led to something of a crisis in the presidential family, with ambitious sisters and their husbands competing for power. It was generally predicted by foreign journalists that the regime could not last more than a few months. Yet Papa Doc had built up a formidable structure of power, with key sectors of the population supporting the government and the potential centres of opposition largely disabled. Furthermore, the U.S. government believed that some form of continuity was preferable to an open conflict in which radical forces might come to power. In the days following the death of Duvalier the U.S. Navy patrolled the island to discourage invasions by exiles and a smooth transfer of power was effected.

Jean-Claude embarked on his political career under the wary eye of his mother. He managed to balance one interest against another, changing his cabinets frequently and keeping watch on the army leadership. The regime announced that, as Papa Doc had achieved the political revolution, so his son would devote himself to the economic revolution. After the poor coffee crop of 1970, there was a significant growth in the following years and sugar production expanded. The early 1970s also witnessed a recovery in tourism. Increased emphasis was placed on foreign investment, with the light manufacturing sector further expanding. The government also had considerable success in attracting development assistance, with foreign aid advancing from $9 million in 1970 to $106 million in 1980. Roads were vastly improved with French and U.S. aid. To secure these developments, however, the government had to relax the system of terror and put forward a favourable image to the various international agencies and donor governments. Under Jean-Claude the activities of the *macoutes* and the power of the old Duvalierists were therefore restricted and a feature of the seventies was the growing influence of a group of younger 'technocrats', many from elite mulatto families.

The president's marriage in 1980 to Michele, daughter of a mulatto businessman, Ernest Bennett, effectively checked the influence of his mother and strengthened his links with sections of the business community. At the same time, the regime lost much support from the black middle class, which had been François Duvalier's mainstay. Local *chefs de section* and rural *macoute* leaders saw little patronage coming their way and viewed with dismay the extravagant expenditure and blatant corruption of the President and his wife. The increasingly powerful role played by Ernest Bennett was also cause for unease among these groups. The regime made efforts to strengthen its connection with the masses by appealing over the heads of local officials. Radio programmes were designed to allow ordinary Haitians to complain about local corruption and inefficiency. 'Community councils' were set up and the Comité National d'Action Jeanclaudiste (CONAJEC), vainly endeavoured to strengthen popular support for the regime and to portray it – in contrast to the older Duvalierism – as youthful, vigorous and progressive.

Although the 1970s were years of modest economic growth, Haiti was hit by the rise in world oil prices of 1979–80 and by a hurricane. Three government-backed industrial projects, in sugar, essential oils and fishing, proved financially disastrous. Although the International Monetary Fund advanced $20 million to keep Haiti out of the red, a similar sum was almost immediately transferred from the exchequer to the presidential palace. Desperate attempts were made by the government to find further financial aid, but it was not until the appointment in March 1982 of Marc Bazin, a former World Bank official, as Finance Minister that these met with success. Bazin announced that he would undertake major fiscal reforms and would ensure that all sums received were properly accounted for. It was not long before he was relieved of his post and five of his assistants were gaoled. Nevertheless U.S. aid continued and Haiti was able to gain some benefits from President Reagan's Caribbean Basin Initiative.[11]

[11] On U.S. relations with Haiti since 1971, see Ernest H. Preeg, *Haiti and the CBI: A Time of Change and Opportunity* (Miami, 1985).

In the late seventies President Carter's emphasis on human rights led to U.S. pressure on Duvalier to permit an open opposition. Although the terror was relaxed somewhat, government critics were frequently arrested and tortured and a number of arbitrary beatings of opponents took place. Two parties, of a liberal Christian Democrat flavour, were formed under Sylvio Claude and Grégoire Eugène; an organization for the defence of human rights was founded and pamphlets and manifestos were published. But these movements had little influence beyond a small circle of intellectuals in the capital. Although generally critical of the government, they hardly attacked the president himself. Having a much wider appeal – in a country with over 80 per cent illiteracy – were radio commentators, whose broadcasts in the *Kréyol* language reached the furthest corners of the land. Small groups would gather around a transistor radio and listen to the witty and penetrating observations on political issues of the day by Compère Filo, Jean Dominique and others. Occupying a more ambivalent position were Dieudonné Fardin and his associates, who published the weekly journal *Le Petit Samedi Soir*. Although making outspoken criticisms of the administration, this group clearly had close contacts with the presidential palace, possible through the Bennett family. Even after the clampdown on opposition groups which occurred in November 1980, this journal continued to appear; it represented a cautiously independent voice and had considerable influence among young people.

A few exile attacks took place during the regime of Jean-Claude Duvalier, but these had no prospect of success. In 1972 a dozen or so men landed on the isle of La Tortue and held off the government forces for some time, but were ultimately defeated. The Hector Riobé brigade, based in Miami, also organized some hit-and-run attacks. After one of these a number of young men of Arab descent were arrested in the belief that they were internal sympathizers of the brigade. They were eventually released, but told that if they did not leave the country they would suffer.

Nonetheless, the total silencing of critics, practiced by Jean-Clande's father was now impossible. The regime had become increasingly dependent on the mulatto elite who were much more responsive to U.S. pressure than were the black middle classes. Anything likely to threaten their commercial enterprises and high living standard was anathema, and this meant maintaining good relations with Washington. This elite was also more responsive to the voice of the Catholic hierarchy than were the black middle classes. Thus the major shift in the regime's basis of support had important effects and made it increasingly susceptible to U.S. pressure or to any large protest movements from within, especially if backed by the Church.

Migration – internal and external – was a significant factor throughout the period of the Duvaliers. A major movement from the countryside, particularly from the South, into the capital occurred. This consisted mostly of women, who were better able than men to find jobs in Port-au-Prince, being primarily employed in domestic work and the new light-manufacturing industries. As a result the population of the capital had grown to about one million by the mid-eighties.

The flow of Haitian cane-cutters into the Dominican Republic continued, and considerable controversy centred on the system of 'indentured' seasonal labour operated by the two governments. In the seventies and eighties up to 18,000 were recruited, with the Haitian government being paid a fee for each worker. The conditions in which they lived were so appalling that they became the subject of investigation by international agencies, including the Anti-Slavery Society. Nevertheless, the fact remains that Haitians have been keen to enlist, despite the conditions of which they must be aware. By the 1980s there were perhaps as many as 200,000 Haitians living in the neighbouring republic.[12]

In the early years of the Duvalier regime significant numbers of political exiles went to New York, Chicago, Montreal and other North American cities. Many of these were skilled workers, including medical doctors, agronomists and other professionals. They were followed by friends and relations throughout the sixties and seventies so that by 1980 there were almost half a million Haitians resident – legally and illegally – in the United States and about 40,000 in the Bahamas. Significant numbers were also to be found in France, in the Francophone countries of Africa, in Puerto Rico and Mexico. The late seventies witnessed a new wave of migration to the United States. Thousands of Haitians secured passages on small boats which set sail for the Florida coast. In 1980–1 an average of 1,500 per month landed in the state. Others were lost at sea. The flow of migrants stopped only when agreement between the two governments permitted U.S. naval ships to patrol the north coast of Haiti and turn back

---

[12] On this migration, see Maurice Lemoine, *Bitter Sugar* (London, 1985); Ramón Antonio Veras, *Inmigración, Haitianos, Esclavitud* (Santo Domingo, 1983). See also *Estudios Sociales* (Santo Domingo), 59 (January 1985), a special number devoted to 'Haitianos en la República Dominicana'.

departing migrants. Some Haitian politicians objected to this indignity, but continued aid was made conditional on such an arrangement.[13]

External migration had certain important consequences. In the first place, large numbers of migrants sent back remittances to family and friends in Haiti; according to one estimate this amounted to as much as $100 million per annum by the 1980s. This could be the most effective form of foreign aid from which Haiti has benefited. Returning migrants also brought back money with them, boosting the local economy. Secondly, migration deprived Haiti of many technically qualified, imaginative and vigorous elements of the population. Although the migrant communities themselves developed a lively cultural tradition – producing journals, plays, novels and poetry – their attempts to influence political events in Haiti were ineffective. Exile invasions invariably proved a fiasco and the fall of the Duvalier regime eventually occurred as a result of movements from within the country.

The Duvalier years in Haiti were not notable for a flowering of culture, and yet a few important developments took place. In the sphere of imaginative literature the early years saw an active group of playwrights, poets and novelists including René Depestre and Jacques Stéphen Alexis. These men, passionately interested in politics and committed to varieties of Marxism, soon fell out with each other and with the government. Alexis had in fact been closely associated with Déjoie in the election campaign of 1957. Born at Gonaïves in 1922, he was the son of a distinguished writer and, as we have seen was one of the group which produced the journal *La Ruche* in 1945–6. His most celebrated novels were *Compère Général Soleil* (1955), *Les arbres musiciens* (1957), *L'espace d'un cillement* (1959) and *Romancero aux étoiles* (1960). In developing the idea of the 'marvellous realism' of Haitian literature Alexis criticized the belief in a monolithic black or African culture that was characteristic of some of the *négritude* writers of an earlier generation. He maintained that national and regional influences had led to a peculiarly Haitian literary tradition. After visiting the Soviet Union, Alexis returned to Haiti in 1961 by boat from Cuba in an attempt

---

[13] There is a considerable literature on this migration, including G. Loescher and J. Scanlan, 'Human Rights, U.S. Foreign Policy, and Haitian Refugees', *Journal of Interamerican Studies and World Affairs* 26, no. 3 (1984); and A. Stepick, *Haitian Refugees in the United States* (London, 1982). For the Bahamian migration, see Dawn Marshall, *'The Haitian Problem': Illegal Migration to the Bahamas* (Kingston, Jamaica, 1979).

to lead a revolt against the Duvalier government. He was arrested, tortured and executed.[14]

René Depestre's most significant poetry dates from the mid-1940s but he continued to publish novels, verses and works of literary and political criticism. Like Alexis he saw himself as continuing the work begun in Haiti by Jacques Roumain. In 1957, Depestre generally supported Duvalier, but he soon went abroad and became a vocal critic of the regime from his base in Cuba. In a controversy with Aimé Césaire in 1955 he had assailed the *négritude* dogma which he later blamed for providing Duvalierism with ideological backing, as exemplified in the writings of Jean Price Mars.[15] A number of other Haitians have been writing from exile, including Jean F. Brierre, Anthony Phelps and Paul Laraque.

Within the country itself René Philoctète, Frank Etienne and Jean-Claude Fignolé have published significant works, many written in *Kréyol*. These have necessarily avoided explicit reference to Haitian politics, though indirect allusions became more common in the late seventies. Frank Etienne's *Ultravocal* (1972) is the clearest example of *spiralisme,* a style developed by these Haitian writers under the influence of French structuralism. In the final years of the Jean-Claude Duvalier regime, small street-theatre groups performed thinly disguised attacks on the regime, and the film, *Pélin Tèt* – on a similar theme – was immensely popular.

Although French remained the official language of Haiti, fewer than ten per cent of the population spoke it fluently. The French-based *Kréyol* was spoken by the whole population, including the francophone minority. The elite and even the black middle classes valued their ability to speak both languages since this reinforced their control of the instruments of power. Many of those influenced by the ethnological movement of the thirties argued that *Kréyol* should be recognized as at least on a par with French as one of the official languages of the country and that school-teaching at the lower levels and legal proceedings should be conducted in the popular language of Haiti.

François Duvalier's government made halfhearted moves in this direction, but it was not until Joseph Bernard became Minister of Education in

---

[14] See M. Laroche, *Le romancero aux étoiles: et l'oeuvre romanesque de Jacques-Stéphen Alexis* (Paris, 1978); J. Michael Dash, *Jacques Stéphen Alexis* (Toronto, 1975), and Dash, *Literature and Ideology in Haiti, 1915–1961* (London, 1981), chap. 7.

[15] René Depestre, *Bonjour et adieu à la négritude* (Paris, 1980).

1979 that a more determined attempt was made to modify the school syllabus, allowing teaching in the early years to take place in *Kréyol*. This proposal, part of a larger educational reform, led to an outcry on the part of many of the elite. Even some of the poorer Haitians saw it as a conspiracy to keep their children from acquiring fluency in French, which is one of the passports out of rural poverty. Because insufficient preparation for the change was made by the government, teachers had not properly been trained and few textbooks were available, opponents were given the chance to force Bernard out of office and to check the reform. While the French embassy, particularly through the Institut Français, was keen to maintain the position of the French language, many North Americans – particularly Protestant missionaries and others living in the countryside – spoke only *Kréyol*. It is significant to note that the educational reform was strongly backed by the U.S. embassy and financed by the World Bank. With the migrations to the United States and the Bahamas, however, and with continued American commercial involvement in the country, Haitians were beginning to see English as more useful than French. Also many families, even those of the old francophile elite, were now sending their children to study in the United States.

Duvalier, particularly during his battle with the bishops welcomed the presence of many Protestant groups in Haiti. In the early years, he had close connections with some of the leading Episcopalians, but by 1963 this relationship had become strained. The more evangelical groups, however, tended to avoid explicit political involvement, giving tacit support to 'the powers that be'. They were granted the utmost freedom to preach, convert, open schools and run rural development projects of various kinds. So numerous were these groups by the 1970s that any white man travelling in the countryside would automatically be called 'pastor' by the local people. In 1976 one government minister, Aurélien Jeanty, denounced these Protestants as an instrument in foreign hands and 'the skeleton of an illegal ecclesiastical empire'. It is likely that by the mid-1980s as many as 20 per cent of Haitians would have called themselves Protestant, but this does not necessarily mean that they would have broken definitively with Voodoo or with Catholicism.

The growth of Protestant sects clearly alarmed the Roman Catholic Church. From the late seventies the bishops were careful not to be too closely identified either with the regime or with the elite. In public pronouncements they condemned government corruption and contraventions of human rights; they also supported the claims to the poor. The arrest of a prominent Catholic layman in late 1982 provoked a strongly worded statement from the bishops. During his visit to Haiti in the following March, Pope John Paul II insisted that 'things must change' in Haiti. At the parochial level the Church began to sponsor a considerable number of development projects, including agricultural co-operatives and irrigation, drainage, terracing and handicraft projects. Although many of these – like the large venture run for many years by Père Ryo in Laborde or the integrated project sponsored by the Oblates of Mary, and supported by such voluntary agencies as OXFAM, in the region of Les Anglais in the South – were somewhat paternalistic, they increased the confidence of peasants and led them to question local structures of power.

In February 1986, President Jean-Claude Duvalier took the familiar presidential path into exile. The scenario was in certain ways a replay of the events forty years earlier which had led to the political demise of President Lescot. A government which came increasingly under the control of a small sector of the elite had forfeited any basis of support among the mass of the people and among key middle sectors. Student protests were, in both cases, followed by more general demonstrations and the government lost command of the situation. The army took over and a period of political uncertainty followed.

There were, however, significant differences between the two movements. In the first place church leaders and the Catholic Radio Soleil cautiously but positively, supported the recent protests, having helped to stimulate them through their sponsorship of development projects throughout the country. Second, the revolution of 1946 began in the capital and all activity appears to have centred there, whereas the movement of 1985–6 began in Gonaïves, spreading to Petit Goâve, Cap Haïtien and other provincial towns before manifesting itself in Port-au-Prince. It was, in fact, the first time that such a movement had begun outside the capital since the days of U.S. occupation. It may be that the recruitment of the rural masses in the Volontaires de la Securité Nationale (VSN) (*macoutes*) and the popularist rhetoric of François Duvalier had more radical consequences than had been intended.

The Church was undoubtedly one of the major actors in the drama of Duvalier's downfall. The arrest late in 1982 of a Catholic layman, the broadcaster Gérard Duclerville, marked an important stage in the growth of church power since he was released soon after his detention was denounced from pupits throughout the country. The pope's visit to

Haiti had strengthened the hand of the bishops; they became more outspoken in their denunciation of human-rights violations and of the desperate state of poverty in Haiti. The Catholic Radio Soleil became a principal channel for criticism of the government. Having become increasingly dependent on support from the business community and the elite, Baby Doc was unable to ignore or to suppress clerical criticisms as his father had done, for the bourgeoisie tended to associate itself, at least in political terms, with the Church. Bishops condemned the shooting of students in the Gonaïves demonstration of November 1985, the requiem held for the victims being seen as an important gesture of support for the protest movement. In this period Radio Soleil was the most important means by which news of provincial demonstrations became known throughout the country. Duvalier attempted to close the station, but episcopal pressure soon forced him to retract.

The influence of the Roman Catholic Church and of some Protestant churches was significant at another level. As we have seen, for many years local parishes had been sponsoring, often with aid from international agencies, various development projects and co-operative enterprises that enabled small groups of peasants to discuss local problems and to organize social action. The intention of the organizers of these projects was not usually political in the immediate sense, and indeed these developments were attacked by radical exiles as conservative in that they encouraged peasants to put up with a situation which would otherwise be intolerable. Yet it was precisely from these groups that leaders emerged who were to challenge the regime in 1985–6. *Le Petit Samedi Soir* referred to the Church, in the middle of the crisis, as 'ce leader politique qui ne dit pas son nom'. 'Are we in the midst of a Christian revolution?', asked the editors.

It would be unduly cynical to view the role of the Church in the last few years merely as a revenge for the humiliation suffered under François Duvalier or as part of an attempt to re-establish its former role as a major political force in Haiti by siding with the growing opposition movement. Although these considerations may have carried some weight, many parish priests and some of the bishops have genuinely and sincerely identified themselves with the cause of the poor and oppressed people of the country. The Church constituted one of the few Haitian institutions to have retained sufficient credibility to act effectively in the situation.

A major factor in the social and cultural life of ordinary Haitians throughout this period, in the countryside and in the poorer parts of the towns, was the Voodoo religion. Like all religions, Voodoo is generally conservative in its social consequences. There were, nevertheless, occasions when it played a more radical role. One of the important contributions of Voodoo was to perpetuate the consciousness of an African identity on the part of the masses. François Duvalier was able to exploit this fact and secure support from a number of *houngans* for his *noiriste* ideology. Jean-Claude seems to have been less interested in Voodoo than his father was and made no claims to supernatural powers, yet his fall was marked by violent attacks on many *houngans*. Estimates of the numbers killed in early 1986 vary greatly from around one hundred to more than a thousand. It should, however, be emphasized that not all Voodooisants supported the regime.

As a result of the carefully arranged structure bequeathed him by his father, Jean-Claude had been able to forestall any possibility of a military coup. Nevertheless he gradually lost the support of many *macoute* leaders who by the early eighties were evidently unwilling to defend the regime. By November 1985 there was considerable disillusionment and confusion in their ranks. The dismissal of Minister of the Interior, Roger Lafontant, a few weeks earlier was strongly resented by some of his *macoute* supporters, and one of the notable features of the events culminating in the flight of Duvalier was the relatively insignificant role played by the VSN. Only in the final days did some of them rally to the President and violently attempt to suppress the opposition.

Despite the drift towards disorder in January 1986, the army leaders were clearly unwilling to act independently to take over the country. During the twenty-nine years of Duvalier dictatorship, a new generation of officers had grown up for whom the notion of an army coup was practically inconceivable. François Duvalier had been able to claim by 1964 – with some justification – that he had removed the army from its role of arbiter of political events. It appears that General Henri Namphy's eventual agreement to head a junta after Jean-Claude Duvalier's departure was the result of persuasion by the U.S. embassy, by some Haitian politicians and by Duvalier himself. The United States had played an important part in maintaining Jean-Claude Duvalier in power, and it was not until the final days that Washington decided to cut its losses and use its influence to secure the departure of the President. Even then U.S. opinion was divided and it is widely believed that the advice being given by former ambassador Ernest Preeg was that Washington should persuade Duvalier to remain and should help shore up his government.

One factor which weakened the regime of Baby Doc was the worsening condition of the economy in the eighties that left him with diminished sources of patronage as increasing hardship was felt by the mass of rural Haitians. The problems were greatly exacerbated by the plague of swine fever which spread from the Dominican Republic. Under pressure from the Organization of American States, the Haitian government decreed the destruction of the whole population of hardy black pigs which represented for many Haitians their only capital investment. Arrangements were made for compensation, but inevitably most of the money went elsewhere. Various agencies supplied imported pink pigs, but generally on condition that they were guaranteed imported pig-feed and housed in sties with concrete floors. Since poor peasants could not afford these luxuries the beneficiaries were the richer farmers. Army generals, including Namphy, took advantage of the offers. (One encouraging aspect of the situation was that those people who took the pigs and ignored the guarantees, feeding them with the same diet of garbage which the black pigs had received, found that their pink pigs thrived.) Another cause of hardship in the mid-eighties was the ending of the migration of 'boat people' to the United States when under pressure from Washington the Duvalier government agreed that U.S. naval vessels should patrol the Haitian coasts turning back migrant boats.

With the departure of Jean-Claude Duvalier on 7 February 1986, a military-dominated Conseil National de Gouvernement (CNG) was left in control. In the early months the junta, headed by General Henri Namphy, generally restricted itself to maintaining some degree of order rather than embarking on major policy changes. Namphy himself was thought to be an honest man without political ambitions who wished to allow a maximum of freedom for different tendencies to be heard. Pushed by public opinion, manifested in demonstrations and strikes, the junta rid themselves of some notorious Duvalierists and, as a gesture of support for 'dechoukaj' (the uprooting of Duvalierism), brought to trial a few *macoutes*. Also in a symbolic renunciation of the old regime they changed the Haitian flag back to the blue and red of pre-1964 days. The reputed 'strong man' of the junta was Colonel Williams Régala, who headed the Ministry of the Interior. He and Finance Minister Leslie Delatour were widely denounced as politically conservative and as agents of the United States. The junta set out a timetable for the formulation of a new constitution and for the eventual election of a new president in November 1987.

The disturbances that began in November 1985 and culminated in the downfall of Duvalier had deepened Haiti's economic problems. Some firms in the assembly and light-manufacturing sector closed down, leading to a loss of 12,000 jobs. This was partly due to political uncertainty, as well as to the fear of wage demands, resulting from the creation of free trade unions, and to new U.S. restrictions on textile imports. Again, U.S. health regulations led to problems with the importing of Haitian fruits. Tourism also declined, leaving hotels deserted. The cutting of the U.S. quota of sugar imports from the Dominican Republic left a huge sugar surplus, much of which found its way into Haiti, undermining the market for locally produced sugar and leading to the closure of sugar factories. Thousands of employees, and many more small cane-farmers, were put out of work. Contraband of all kinds flooded into Haiti under the provisional government, much of it controlled by high-ranking military officers. For example, rice from the United States and elsewhere lowered the price below that at which local farmers could survive. Cement, wheat, cars and other manufactured goods also entered illegally. Corruption under the CNG exceeded even that of the Duvaliers.

The churches remained divided. Returned exile priests called for the resignation of Archbishop Ligondé owing to his past associations with the Duvaliers. Some younger priests, notably Jean-Bertrand Aristide, a Salesian, organized the poor into action groups and called for profound social changes. Bishop Willy Romulus of Jérémie, the only bishop with radical tendencies, gave cautious support to these movements, but others, led by Bishop Gayot of Cap Haïtien, favoured the old Christian Democrat theories of post-1945 Europe and were suspicious of the base communities (known as 'ti legliz'), which had sprung up throughout Haiti.

With Duvalier's fall many exiles returned home to found political movements: Leslie Manigat and Marc Bazin, both regarded as 'moderates', Serge Gilles, heading a party with links to the Socialist International, and René Théodore, Communist Party leader. Political leaders who remained in the country included Sylvio Claude and Grégoire Eugène, with their rival Christian Democratic parties, and Hubert de Ronceray, a cabinet minister under Jean-Claude Duvalier.

Three distinct trade union groups emerged. One had close links with the International Confederation of Free Trade Unions (and thus with the American AFL/CIO), the others were politically more left wing. The Confederation Autonome des Travailleurs Haitiens (CATH), whose leaders were forced into exile under the previous regime, split into two, one being associated with the Latin American labour movement (CTAL). Although numerically weak, the unions exercised some influence on political developments because their membership was centred in Port-au-Prince.

Although there was little popular interest in the election of the constitutional commission, the new constitution was approved almost unanimously by the 50 per cent or so of the population who voted. The Constitution stipulated that serving military personnel could not stand for public office and included a ten-year ban on those closely associated with the Duvalier dictatorship. It set up an autonomous Electoral Council, with nine members nominated by various social groups, to supervise elections. For the first time *Kréyol* was recognized as an official language of Haiti and legislation against the Voodoo religion was rescinded.

General elections were planned for 29 November 1987 and the Electoral Council resisted attempts by the CNG to take over the running of the poll. Twelve presidential candidates were disqualified for their involvement in the Duvalier regime, though at least five others had also been involved at some stage. Of the remaining twenty-three candidates, four emerged as leading contenders: Sylvio Claude, a populist pastor who had actively opposed the regime of Baby Doc; Marc Bazin, a former World Bank official who had been Finance Minister under Jean-Claude Duvalier for a few months; Gérard Gourgue, an educationalist and human-rights activist; and Louis Déjoie II, the only mulatto, son of François Duvalier's principal opponent in 1957. Bazin, Déjoie and Gourgue represented – each in his own way – an alliance between elements in the commercial elite and a mass movement among the poor. The elite, which continued to live in considerable luxury and enjoy a high standard of living, manifestly thought their privileged position would best be secured by such an alliance. This was most evident in the case of Gourgue, who was backed by many grass-roots organizations throughout the countryside. Crucial in the forging of this front was former Roman Catholic priest Jean-Claude Bajeaux. This alliance between elite and masses was directed largely against the black middle classes, many of whom had been associated with the Duvalier regime and held key positions in the rural areas as *chefs de section, spéculateurs* or peasants with middle-sized properties, and in the towns as civil servants, teachers and agronomists, and – most importantly – in the army. These black middle classes feared that any president who emerged from such an election would be likely to challenge the gains they had made under the Duvaliers.

Groups of gunmen, in the pay of some of the disqualified Duvalierists and under the protection of the army, roamed the streets causing terror and prevented voting materials from reaching their destination in the North and Artibonite. The election was called off after the slaughter of dozens of voters and the CNG stated that elections would be held in January 1988 under a new electoral council appointed by itself. The four leading candidates refused to take part, leaving as viable candidates only those of whom the army approved. Voting took place quietly on 17 January 1988, with a very low turn-out and many irregularities. Leslie Manigat, the candidate favoured by most of the army, was declared victor and inaugurated on 7 February. As a young foreign ministry official, he had been associated with François Duvalier's regime, and had adopted a *noiriste* position in his numerous writings on Haitian history. Manigat broke with Duvalier in the early 1960s and spent twenty-five years in exile, as a teacher of political science and international relations in Paris, Trinidad and Caracas and at Yale. His tenure of power lasted just four months. In June a conflict with the army leadership led to his removal by the same officers who had secured his election. A period of direct army rule followed.

Haiti has often been called the poorest country of Latin America, and from the material standpoint this is probably the case. Nevertheless, with respect to human resources and cultural traditions, Haiti is one of the richest countries of the hemisphere. Haitians have frequently shown an extraordinary resourcefulness in dealing with the problems which face them, particularly in the rural areas. The protest movements which began in November 1985 demonstrated that the Haitian peasant was not as 'apathetic' as was often suggested. Among the large number of colourful murals appearing throughout the capital after the flight of Jean-Claude Duvalier was one which well encapsulated the optimistic mood of the time. It pictured the guinea fowl, a national symbol, on whose breast was inscribed the phrase 'Fok nou volé piwo' (we must fly higher).

13

PUERTO RICO SINCE 1940

After four hundred years of Spanish colonial rule Puerto Rico fell under the direct control of the United States in 1898. It has remained so ever since. Its status within the U.S. political system has always been uncertain and anomalous. Unlike Hawaii and Alaska – considered territories 'incorporated' into the United States and thereby candidates for future inclusion in the federal system as states of the Union – Puerto Rico was placed in the novel judicial category of an 'unincorporated territory'. No one in political authority in the United States ever accepted that Puerto Rico, unlike Cuba and the Philippines, should be directed towards even nominal independence.

The island's colonial dependency continued, therefore, into the twentieth century under a new and culturally alien power. Indeed, as the century draws to a close dependency is still in issue. After ninety years under the U.S. flag, of participation of its youth in U.S. wars in Europe and Asia, large migrations to and from the northern metropolis, complete economic integration, and subjection to U.S. sponsored 'modernization' in all its forms – Puerto Rico remains a fundamentally Spanish-speaking 'Latin American' country with a clear sense of cultural and political seperateness from the system of which it is, for better or worse, part.

In 1940 on the eve of U.S entry into the Second World War the executive power on the island was still exercised by presidentially appointed governors; the educational system remained firmly committed to the imperial idea of 'Americanization'; the major industry, sugar, hard-hit by the world depression of the 1930s, was in clear decline; unemployment, poverty and discontent were rampant; political violence was increasing; and a wave of nationalism and aggressive movements for Hispanic cultural affirmation were gathering force and influence. Forty years of direct colonial rule –

albeit often more bumbling than brutal – seemed to have reached a crisis point.

The political regime on the island had always been a peculiar mixture. After two years of direct U.S. military rule a civilian government structure was created by the U.S. Congress. Federal authority was directly exercised through an appointed governor and an array of important federally-appointed functionaries in the Puerto Rican government such as the Justices of the Supreme Court, the Auditor and the Commissioner of Education. There was a popularly elected lower legislative chamber and, as of 1917, a directly-elected Senate as well. Local party politics, with roots dating well back into the Spanish regime, coexisted, often very uncomfortably, with the alien executive power – and the local leaders were unhappy with the institutional arrangement. Whether they believed in eventual statehood, national independence, or something in between, they were all opposed to the political inferiority imposed by the North Americans.

The economy of the island was transformed even more profoundly under U.S. control. Sugar rapidly replaced coffee and tobacco as the principal export crop, and much of the economy was turned into a large-scale corporate agricultural factory system under mainly absentee ownership and with an increasing proletarianization, displacement and alienation of the agrarian population – and all this took place in the context of rapid demographic growth. Class divisions began to affect party politics; the Socialist Party was founded at the time of the First World War. The world depression of the 1930s and especially its impact on the sugar industry exacerbated the social ferment and contributed to the rumblings of a renewed nationalism which did not take long to erupt. The Partido Nacionalista led by Pedro Albizu Campos, numerically small but influential as a catalyst for discontent and of national affirmation, failed, however, effectively to capitalize upon wide-spread labour unrest, particularly among sugar-cane workers.

It is in the local context of economic depression and the decline of sugar, the experimentation of Roosevelt's New Deal and its interesting permutations in Puerto Rico, the resurgence of nationalism on the island and the feeling of helplessness and irrelevance of the political system that the important events beginning in 1940 must be understood. That year marked the initiation of a new political epoch on the island in which the terms of the colonial relations between the United States and Puerto Rico came to be redefined, if not completely resolved.

POLITICS AND STATUS

The year 1940 ushered in a quarter of a century of one party domination which was to shape Puerto Rico's development and to define many of its later problems and challenges. The Popular Democratic Party (Partido Popular Democrático, or PPD) was created in 1938 and, under the leadership of Luis Muñoz Marín, quickly became the driving force of Puerto Rico's development in the 1940s and 1950s. The party's creation and initial successes can be understood in terms of the convergence of several factors emanating from the problems of the 1930s. The first of these was the disruption and decline of the existing political parties. Local government had been controlled since 1932 by a coalition of the Republican Party and the Socialist Party, both vaguely in favour of eventual statehood for Puerto Rico, inheritors of originally incompatible ideologies, but long since resigned to the politics of patronage. The electoral system was generally perceived as unreliable and corrupt, and was the source of widespread cynicism. Another factor was the political influence exercised on the island by the federal government's programs for relief and rehabilitation, and the interplay between the Roosevelt administration's colonial administrators of those programs and the local political elite. Much of the political history of the 1930s can be explained in terms of the manoeuvrings of local politicians to control, or at least to glean political credit for, the aid and economic reconstruction programs which the New Deal exported to Puerto Rico. Until 1936 Muñoz Marín had held the advantage in this process since his ability to cultivate contacts in Washington, his colloquial English, his eloquence and his New Dealish sympathies stood him in good stead with the Roosevelt administration.

Finally, there was the matter of the ideological setting and class base on which the PPD was to emerge as a mass party. In his early political career Muñoz had been associated with the Socialist Party of Santiago Iglesias Pantín. This had been a true labour party, pragmatic, non-Marxist and, significantly, pro-United States. Since its inception it had possessed a pro-independence faction, but under Iglesias' strong leadership it was officially uninterested in the 'status' problem, which it saw as irrelevant to the tasks of bettering the workingman's plight. As the Socialist Party became increasingly conservative and pro-American, Muñoz in the late 1920s moved to the Liberal Party. He was elected to the Senate in 1932 and became its president. In early 1936 political violence on the island had resulted in the assassination of police chief Francis Riggs, as a result of which Muñoz's career took a new turn when he refused a request from Ernest Gruening, head of the Puerto Rico Reconstruction Administration, to condemn the police chief murder unless the North Americans also condemned the lynching, in police headquarters, of the assassins. In the complex backwash of these emotional events, Muñoz lost his almost automatic entrée into the circles of power emanating from Washington. He also broke with the leader of the Liberal Party, and in an attempt to take over the reins of that party he was in effect expelled, being blamed in the process for the party's failure in the elections of 1936.

There were at least three basic elements in the initial ideological posture of the PPD. The first was its moderate independentism. It was no secret that the principal leaders of the new party were believers in independence as the eventual solution to the island's perennial status problem. The pro-statehood political coalition was identified with the largely absentee-owned corporate interests dominating the sugar economy and thus a target of popular discontent during the difficult depression years. This discontent had been largely expressed in terms of intensification of nationalist feeling and the Popular Party reflected this mood.

However, the party's independentism never took the form of a hard-and-fast official commitment. Muñoz Marín, for example, had always tempered his independentism with the overriding priority of dealing directly with the problems of economic growth and social justice within the realm of political possibilities. Thus the new party sought the elimination of electoral corruption and special privileges and the creation of an administrative infrastructure that would permit a more coherent direction for economic activity. These goals were to be achieved by the political means available through the electoral system and in subsequent negotiation with the federal authorities. Pragmatism was stronger than independentism in the ideological armory of the PPD, which was closer to the New Dealism of Roosevelt than to the nationalism of Albizu Campos or even the socialism of the younger Santiago Iglesias.

The PPD's ideology also derived from the nature of the party's leadership and its relations with the rank and file and with the electorate at large. At the start the PPD was a thoroughly populist party although it did not possess that streak of anti-intellectualism which has often characterized other populist movements. These was an almost total identification of the movement with the personality of its leader and founder. At a time ripe for populist mobilization the PPD was able to exploit a remarkable combination of charismatic appeal, mass receptivity and the collapse into near insignificance of other political groupings. Under Muñoz the party was dominated by the 'mandate theory' of politics, whereby mass approval was to be registered (and renewed) every four years at election time, after which the party was to have free rein in the management of public affairs.

After a remarkable campaign the PPD garnered some 38 per cent of the total vote in the elections of November 1940. This was not enough to elect the Resident Commissioner in Washington (the non-voting member of the federal House of Representatives to which Puerto Rico has been entitled since 1904), but the party achieved a clear majority in the Senate, and Muñoz was chosen as its president. The PPD was also able to control the House for most of the four-year term through the cooperation of sympathetic members of the old Liberal Party.

The electoral success of the PPD was followed by the appointment in 1941 of Rexford Guy Tugwell as governor. The coincidence of an experienced New Deal 'brain-truster', pledged to the principles of rational planning and the active role of public authority in economic and social development, and an activist party leader who could claim public support for his programmes for change, resulted in a period of intense activity and cooperation that was certainly not always comfortable but was unusual in the history of relations between the colonial administrators and the local political elite. Finding a receptive attitude on the part of Governor Tugwell, the PPD-led legislature pressed ahead with a series of important measures designed to strengthen and centralize the administrative infrastructure of the island government. A Planning Board and a Budget Bureau were created in 1942. The problem of land distribution and agrarian reform was addressed in a controversial piece of legislation passed in 1941 creating the Land Authority and providing for a new system of farm ownership and management known as the 'proportional benefit' farm. Following legal procedures begun in the late 1930s, the administration moved to enforce the restrictions on corporate-held land to 500 acres. These controls had been incorporated into both the organic acts setting up civil government in Puerto Rico, but had never been enforced in the face of unbridled corporate expansion of the sugar industry.

The advent of the Second World War produced a number of problems. In the economic sphere it meant increasing shortages of certain basic supplies and goods on the island and the need to impose a degree of centralized regulation which was, in general, consonant with the activist ideologies of both the colonial governor and the emerging political leader. On the other hand, the war brought a special boon to the Puerto Rican economy through enhanced revenues flowing to the island's treasury from the growing sales of Puerto Rican rum products on the mainland. (By virtue of administrative and legal interpretations of the Organic Laws of 1900 and 1917, all taxes levied on Puerto Rican products sold in the States reverted to the treasury of Puerto Rico.) The war also served to sanction a postponement of any direct attack upon the status question. Albizu Campos had been imprisoned in Atlanta since 1938 as a result of his conviction in a federal court on the island for conspiracy to overthrow the government by force. Muñoz and the PPD had conducted the campaign of 1940 with the slogan that the political status of the island was not an issue in those elections and that the party if victorious would devote itself exclusively to the problem of economic and social justice. During the period between 1941 and 1944 the independentist leanings of the *popular* leadership were kept firmly, though conspicuously, in the background.

By 1944 the political base of the PPD had been solidly established. The elections in November of that year (Puerto Rican elections being held on the same day as the federal elections in which the U.S. presidential electors are chosen) saw a sweeping PPD victory and established a pattern which was to continue with only minor variations until 1968. The party won 64.7 per cent of the popular vote and all but two seats in the House and the Senate. The democratic mandate requested by Muñoz was granted; the task now was to solve the fundamental problems of poverty, the search for social equity and, in democratic fashion, the colonial problem itself. Muñoz and the PPD leadership had always assumed that these two problems were separate. Their strategy was to tackle the problem of economic development with the resources which the existing relations with the United States provided, while dealing with the issue of political status and the elimination of colonialism in a gradual, piecemeal manner. This pragmatic strategy was a reflection of what the PPD leadership reasonably assumed could be expected from the United States as the hegemonic power in the anti-communist world, willing to liquidate the harsher manifestations of colonialism as long as its national interests were adequately protected. The unfolding of this strategy provides the framework of Puerto Rico's political history in the post-war period.

The economic strategy of the PPD was clearly marked out from the beginning. The Industrial Development Company (*Fomento*) and the Government Development Bank were created in 1942 as mechanisms to stimulate industrial development on the island. At first there was disagreement over whether *Fomento*'s policy was to play a direct role in financing and managing industrial plants, either as pilot projects or models for stimulation and emulation for the private sector, or as a conduit for the encouragement and initial subsidization for new industries to be brought in from outside (North American) investors. Tugwell himself was cautious about the latter, but the policy struggle was to be won by those in the PPD government who unambiguously favoured industrial initiatives to attract outside investors. Tugwell left the governorship in 1946, and by that time the policy of industrial incentives – tax exemption for new industries, the provision of government-built plants, government-subsidized worker training and general orientation and assistance to the potential investor – was already under way.

Although the agricultural reform programs initiated in the early 1940s resulted in a moderate redistribution of land through the proportional benefit farm arrangements stemming from the Land Authority Act and in the reduction of some the larger corporate sugar holdings, they also tended to languish in contrast to the vigorous pursuance of the policy of industrialization. As the overriding enthusiasm for industrial development eclipsed agriculture in the policy orientations of the new regime, agrarian reform became less and less significant.

While these developments in economic policy were taking place, the status problem was being attended to in similar pragmatic fashion. The second PPD campaign was again waged with no formal commitment as to the proper solution to the colonial problem. Although some prominent members of the party leadership were anxious for it to take a more open stance in favour of eventual independence, the official position upheld by Muñoz was that the status question could not be faced until after the war. It was increasingly clear that for Muñoz economic realities and the need for development dictated the continuance of Puerto Rico's 'special relation' with the United States through free market access, common currency and financial system, and U.S. citizenship; the problem of political dependency would have to be solved within the confines of economic reality. Colonialism was defined by the populist leaders of the time as a legal issue of status rather than as a political problem of breaking with the habits and institutions of colonialism.

By 1946 it was clear that Muñoz had abandoned whatever independence leanings he might once have had. In a series of public statements and party manoeuvrings he forced a showdown with the hard core *independentistas* in the party. A group of them left in that year and founded the Partido Independentista Puertorriqueño (PIP), which was to participate in the upcoming elections of 1948. Meanwhile, and as the culmination of a process which had begun with a series of communications between former Governor Tugwell, Muñoz Marín as president of the Senate, and President Truman, Congress passed Public Law 362 authorizing the direct election of the governor of Puerto Rico.[1] The stage was set for the elections of 1948 and the second overwhelming victory of the PPD, whose leader now assumed the formal position of governor. The policy of industrial development was to enter its most intensive phase, and the problem of constitutional reform – the long-awaited solution to the status problem – was finally to be tackled under the aegis of popular support from the Puerto Rican masses and official blessing from Washington.

Immediately after the victory of 1948 moves were made toward the establishment of what was to be known in English as the Commonwealth of Puerto Rico and in Spanish as the Estado Libre Asociado. This was to be the culmination of the ideal of autonomy for the island – home-rule, self-government, control of local affairs within the framework of association with the metropolitan power – which had been an important ideological current throughout much of Puerto Rico's history. After the usual negotiations and exchange of letters with President Truman, Congress passed Public Law 600, which authorized the writing of a constitution for Puerto Rico by a constituent assembly on the island, subject to ultimate approval by the U.S. Congress, and maintaining the basic framework of federal relations with the island as determined by the former Jones Act of 1917. The Constitutional Convention met in San Juan between November 1951 and January 1952. The vast majority of its members were *populares,* but these were minority delegations from the Partido Estadista Republicano and the Socialist Party (which was to disappear as a legal entity after the elections of 1952.) The PIP refused to participate. The Constitution was finally approved by Congress, after two significant modifications were accepted by the Puerto Rican convention. It was ratified in a popular referendum by the Puerto Rico electorate, and came into effect 25 July 1952.

From the beginning the Commonwealth arrangement was a bone of legal and political contention, and reams of paper have been used to prove

[1] A description of the process leading up to the passage of this law can be found in Surendra Bhana, *The United States and the Development of the Puerto Rican Status Question, 1936–1948* (Lawrence, Kans., 1975), pp. 92–103.

that it is or is not, can be or cannot be, the solution to the colonial problem of the island. It established the basis for a local constitutional jurisprudence under the overriding prior jurisdiction of the federal system. It provided for internal self-government, but federal administrative and military agencies continued to operate fully on the island; the appointive powers of the elected governor of Puerto Rico over the Comissioner of Education and the Supreme Court justices had already been conferred by Congress in the Elective Governor Act of 1947. (The Constitution of 1952 did at last transfer to the Governor the appointment of the State Auditor–Controller.)

Independentists condemned the Constitution from the beginning as a fraud and a delusion; statehooders saw it as a transitional status leading to full incorporation into the federal union. Its defenders and principal architects in the PPD, while admitting its open-ended nature, tended to look upon it as a permanent solution, a creative and unique way of solving the colonial dilemma while preserving the conditions for economic sustenance and progress. At best, it would need to be adjusted from time to time, in consultation with Congress. For the *populares* the fundamental dimensions of the colonial problem of Puerto Rico were solved in 1952. What remained was to be an on-going process of political consultation with the U.S. authorities to assure continued autonomy for Puerto Rico and the reasonable elimination of whatever colonial vestiges or inequalities might still remain.

But the attempts to improve or culminate the commonwealth failed. The U.S. Congress proved intransigent or apathetic; the shifts in the composition and alignment of the political parties in Puerto Rico prevented the massive mobilization necessary for 'solving' the colonial problem within the framework of autonomy. The transformations in Puerto Rico's society under the populist tutelage gave rise to a new politics, which reflected, in a way reminiscent of the politics of the 1930s, the contradictions of a class-riven society moored to the treadmill of colonial dependency.

The decline of the one-party populist period in Puerto Rico's political history began in 1964. In that year Muñoz Marín decided to retire from the governorship and to relinquish the post to his long-time confidant and trouble-shooter, Roberto Sánchez Vilella. At this time the position of the PPD seemed secure enough. The only opposition parties were the PIP, which had achieved its best result in 1952 with 19 per cent of the vote, but had since declined steadily in electoral strength; and the old Republican Party, now called the Partido Estadista Republicano (PER), the only party of the 1930s to have survived more or less intact. Congress had rejected through inaction a proposal for amending the Federal Relations Act in the form of the "Fernós–Murray Bill" of 1950.[2] A new attempt to culminate the constitutional situation was being undertaken; the economic development program was continuing in high gear; and the time seemed ripe for institutionalizing the party.

However, continuing congressional intransigence and the new political facts of Puerto Rican life were to frustrate these intentions. Tensions between the new governor and both Muñoz and important elements in the party organization contributed to the end of the PPD's hegemony. Before Sánchez's term was over, a plebiscite on Puerto Rico's political future was held, the governor of Puerto Rico had been in effect expelled from his own party, a new statehood party was to emerge as a major political force, and the PPD was finally to lose an election.

In 1962 the *popular* government approached Congress for the second time with a formal request to modify the Federal Relations Act. Rather than accede to the original request, Congress in 1964 created a special commission to study the matter of Puerto Rico's future status, explore all the possible alternatives openly and thoroughly, and provide Congress with responsible guidelines for future action. The commission, composed of seven U.S. and six Puerto Rican members, published its lengthy report in 1966, indicating that all three alternatives (the classical trio of statehood, commonwealth/autonomy, and independence) were equally worthy, and suggesting a clear declaration by the Puerto Rican people of their preference. Although the report was non-committal and anything but radical in its conclusions, it did permit the PPD government to champion commonwealth status and to proceed to the holding of a plebiscite over the three status alternatives.

The plebiscite was held 23 July 1967. The independence movement boycotted the elections, and the *populares,* after a strenuous campaign led personally by Muñoz, gathered a 60.5 per cent majority in favour of the commonwealth. But the remaining 39 per cent for the statehood alternative was hardly a negligible figure. The principal campaigner for the statehood symbol was Luis A. Ferré, an industrialist who for many years

---

[2] The fate of the Fernós–Murray Bill, as well as that of the second attempt to modify the commonwealth compact, mentioned in the next paragraph, are described in Henry Wells, *The Modernization of Puerto Rico* (Cambridge, Mass, 1969), pp. 250–8. See also José Trías Monge, *Historia constitucional de Puerto Rico,* vol. 4 (Río Piedras, 1980).

had been a co-leader of the Partido Estadista Republicano. Ferré had defied the party, which had officially decided not to participate in the plebiscite. He now found himself with the enthusiastic nucleus of a new political grouping which was transformed into the Partido Nuevo Progresista (PNP) in the same year.

In the elections of 1968 the new party, aided by the defection from the PPD of Sánchez Vilella, who formed his own party and gained some 11 per cent of the total vote, Ferré was elected governor, and the PPD was cast in the role of opposition despite winning a one-seat majority in the Senate. The PPD recaptured the governorship and a simple majority in 1972, but the PNP went on to elect its candidate for governor in 1976 and again, though with a razor-thin plurality, in 1980. In the elections of 1984 it lost the governor's race by only about 3 per cent – the same as its winning margin had been in 1976.

Thus, in the mid-1980s, the forces of the 'autonomist' PPD and the 'statehood' PNP were, in electoral terms, quite evenly balanced. No governor since 1968 had achieved an absolute majority of the total vote; there was a split legislature between 1969 and 1973; and an executive controlled by one party and the two houses of the legislature controlled by the other between 1981 and 1984. This emerging 'two-party system' reflected a complex process of social realignments and class conflict that was distorted by the parties' ideologies and procedures for electoral mobilization around the status question.

The strategy of the PPD, as sanctioned by the Status Commission Report, was to proceed with the formation, in co-operation with the U.S. Congress, of special 'ad hoc committees', which were to devise mutually acceptable modifications of commonwealth status in order to broaden Puerto Rico's areas of autonomy and contribution to the federal system. These modifications were then to be accepted respectively by the Congress and the Puerto Rican electorate in referendum. The break between the party and Governor Sánchez prevented the naming of such a group during his term, and the PNP victory of 1968 stifled these plans until the *populares* took over again in 1973. Governor Ferré did form an ad hoc committee during his term, but it was charged only with reporting on the viability of extending to the people of Puerto Rico the right to vote in the U.S. presidential elections. The committee submitted a report in 1971 which was favourable to the presidential vote, but the PPD victory of 1972 put a stop to any further action, and the subsequent alternation in power of the two parties prevented any concerted attempt to resolve the issue.

During the first PPD administration of Governor Rafael Hernández Colón (1973–6) the most serious effort thus far to modify commonwealth status suffered a significant, and probably final, defeat. After long months of preparation, an ad hoc committee submitted its project for what the *populares* called the 'New Pact'. It met with considerable apathy on the part of the U.S. administration, caught up in the aftermath of the Watergate affair and controlled by a Republican Party which had no natural sympathies with the *populares,* who had traditionally been loosely allied with the Democrats. At the end of his term in office President Ford in effect rejected the committee's report and issued a proclamation indicating it was time to proceed with arrangements for making Puerto Rico a state of the federal Union.

The second victory of the PNP, in 1976, combined with the Ford Declaration, and the capture, by 1978, of the federal Democratic Party in Puerto Rico by a group of young politicians allied to the PNP and committed to statehood, seemed to indicate that Puerto Rico had arrived at a new crossroads in its agonizing status battles. As the elections of 1980 approached, the incumbent PNP governor, Carlos Romero Barceló (who had taken over the party after Ferré's defeat in 1972), attempted to prepare public opinion for a confrontation over status after his presumed re-election in 1980 by planning a new plebiscite which would include only the alternatives of statehood and commonwealth. However, the extreme narrowness of his victory that year – it was virtually a tied election – effectively put an end to that possibility.

The independence movement was unable to make much headway within the context of electoral politics, rapid industrialization, and the absorption of Puerto Rican cultural affirmation in the autonomist ideology of the PPD in the post-1940 period. Economic and social changes increased assimilationist rather than separatist tendencies. Nonetheless, the uncertainties of political status, the difficulties in the path to statehood, the facts of colonial dependence – however they are perceived – made the independence movement a major factor in Puerto Rican politics. Although there existed a multitude of independence groups with widely differing ideologies and tactics, the principal organizations in the independence movement in the mid-1980s were the Partido Independentista Puertorriqueño (PIP) and the Socialist Party (PSP). (The latter should not be confused with the old Socialist Party which had disappeared by the mid-1950s.) Since its foundation in 1946 the PIP had occupied an institutionalized position within the

party system. As the principal electoral organization espousing independence it constituted the nucleus of an electoral satellite to the two-party
constellation. It attempted to project a middle-of-the-road ideology, and in
recent years it advocated a loose commitment to 'democratic socialism',
pointedly avoiding identification with the 'Marxist-Leninist' PSP to its left
and affiliating itself with the Socialist International organization of democratic socialist parties in Europe and Latin America.

The PSP was created as the Movimiento Pro-Independencia de Puerto
Rico (MPI) in 1961 by disaffected former members of the PIP, assuming
its new name and a formal commitment to Marxism–Leninism in 1970. A
tiny party in electoral terms, polling less than 1 per cent of the vote in
1976 and even a smaller number in 1980; it did not run candidates in
1984. However, it had a certain presence in the island's political structure
through the circulation of a weekly newspaper and various other publications which analyzed Puerto Rican political matters from a Marxist perspective, its relations with some sectors of the labour movement and its
carefully cultivated, if not always comfortable, ties with socialist regimes
abroad, particularly Cuba.

ECONOMIC AND SOCIAL CHANGE: THE DEEPENING OF THE DILEMMA.

The 'modernization' of Puerto Rico has been in many ways impressive and
precipitous. As early as 1956 manufacturing activities were contributing
more to the national product than agriculture, and by 1964 manufacturing had overtaken agriculture as the principal source of net income for
Puerto Rican workers.[3] The decline in agriculture in relation to other
economic sectors has been rapid and continuous throughout the post-war
years. By 1980 only 4 per cent of the island's net income was from
agriculture; in 1940 it had been over 31 per cent. The decline of the sugar
industry, already evident in the late 1930s, continued apace as the amount
of acreage in cane cultivation was reduced from almost 400,000 *cuerdas* in
1950 to 85,000 in 1980.[4]

The rush to industrialization, through the attraction of external invest-

---

[3] Wells, *Modernization of Puerto Rico,* p. 153.
[4] Puerto Rico Planning Board, *Economic Report to the Governor, 1980.* Angel L. Ruiz, 'Costo e impacto
socio-económico de la industria azucarera en Puerto Rico', *Revista de Administración Pública,* 16, no.
2 (March 1984): 113. A *cuerda* is 4,000 square metres – almost an acre.

ment under direct government stimulus and incentives, led to the establishment of some 170 factories by 1952 and 2,246 by 1963.[5] Most of these were small 'labour-intensive' subsidiaries of U.S. firms. By the mid-1960s the *Fomento* program began to direct its energies to the attraction of heavier, more capital-intensive industries, particularly petro-chemicals and oil refineries. The crisis in petroleum prices of the early 1970s severely affected the industry, and as a result there were large cut-backs, plant shutdowns and bankruptcy proceedings. The conversion of the petro-chemical industry into the nucleus of multiplying downstream, adjacent and dependent industries never materialized. The economic recession of the mid-1970s slowed the general rate of economic growth significantly, and industrial growth even more sharply.

The most recent chapter in the development of manufacturing on the island has been the establishment and proliferation of branch plants of the U.S. pharmaceutical industry and other high technology industries such as electronics and electrical products. In the 1980s pharmaceutical companies constituted the largest group within what were known as 'possessions corporations', which, due to Section 936 of the federal Tax Reform Act of 1976, were exempt from federal income taxes on business and passive investment income from operations in Puerto Rico and 'other U.S. possessions'. These '936 Corporations' (as they were called in Puerto Rico) accounted for some 70,000 jobs in 1982, about 10 per cent of all employment on the island and over half of the employment in the manufacturing sector. In the period 1976–1982 there were between 400 and 500 of these factories in Puerto Rico, the pharmaceutical firms accounting for almost 46 per cent of total net assets, followed by electric and electronic equipment companies with 19.5 per cent. Between 1970 and 1983 the chemical industry's proportion of the island's total income from manufacturing rose from 11 per cent to 37 per cent.[6] It is not surprising that much of the energies of the Hernández Colón administration, elected in 1984, were expended on efforts to prevent the U.S. Congress from reducing or otherwise tampering with the tax advantages sanctioned by 'Section 936', in the name of tax reform, budget balancing and the closing of tax 'loopholes'. Perhaps nothing illustrates better the economic advantages and the political vulnerability of Puerto Rico's special brand of dependence on the United States.

[5] Wells, *Modernization of Puerto Rico*, p. 152.

[6] U.S. Department of the Treasury, 'The Operation and Effect of the Possessions Corporations System of Taxation: Fifth Report' (Washington; D.C., May 1985): 1–2, 31–38.

The shifts in the occupational structure in Puerto Rico in the post-war period reflect the movement away from the rural areas and the absolute decline in agriculture, the importance of the construction and manufacturing sectors, and the steady rise of public and service sectors as principal sources of employment. Public employment has accounted for about a quarter of the employed work force and of the salaries paid since the mid-1970s. The respective figures for 1985 were 23.7 per cent and 25.1 per cent.[7] The economic development programme did not succeed in reducing substantially the unemployment rates. Official unemployment figures hovered around a rate of 12 per cent in the early 1960s and began to rise in the 1970s. By 1983 unemployment had reached a record 23.4 per cent, with unofficial estimates a good deal higher.[8] A striking characteristic of the Puerto Rican economy's utilization of human resources is the very low proportion of the population over fourteen years of age which is in the active labour force. The figure, already low at 44.5 per cent in the early 1970s, had fallen to 41 per cent in 1983. (The comparable figure for the continental United States in 1976 was 62 per cent.)[9]

Nevertheless, it was the 'escape valve' of worker migration to the continental United States which kept the unemployment rate from rising even higher. The story of the Puerto Rican diaspora is an extraordinary drama. The enormous exodus of Puerto Ricans by air to the eastern United States began in the 1950s. During the first four years of the decade net emigration averaged close to 50,000 annually. It declined to about 20,000 yearly during the 1960s, and even further thereafter. It is still a significant factor, however; there was a net emigration of some 35,000 people in the fiscal year 1982–83.[10]

This massive migration of Puerto Rican workers was but the latest in a series of population displacements which had begun even before the turn of the century. It has meant that a large sector of the island's proletariat has been 'relocated', through the operation of economic pressures and easy access as United States citizens, in the urban heart of the metropolitan power. Because of the unresolved constitutional status, easy and continued movement of information and people back and forth between the main-

---

[7] Puerto Rico Planning Board, *Informe económico al Gobernador, 1985.*

[8] *Informe económico al Gobernador, 1984.* Official unemployment rates for 1974 and 1975 were 12.0 per cent and 15.4 per cent respectively. *Informe económico al Gobernador, 1976.*

[9] *Informe económico al Gobernador, 1976.* U.S. Department of the Treasury, 'Operations' p. 23.

[10] José L. Vázquez Calzada, *La población de Puerto Rico y su trayectoria histórica* (San Juan, Universidad de Puerto Rico, Recinto de Ciencias Médicas, July 1978). U.S. Department of the Treasury, 'Operations', p. 18.

land and the island, and the attendant continuing resistance to assimila-
tion into mainstream North America, Puerto Rico has, like many others,
become a divided nation, almost half of whose population are located off
the island. To complicate the picture further, in recent years there has
been a visible pattern of reverse migration of Puerto Ricans returning to
the island after relatively prolonged residence on the mainland, including
many young 'ethnic' Puerto Ricans (in U.S. terminology) born and reared
in the United States. On the island itself the migration to the mainland
was accompanied by rapid relative depopulation of the rural areas, particularly in the central mountain region, and the enormous growth in the
metropolitan areas, especially San Juan and its environs. In 1980 almost
two-thirds of the population lived in urban areas, and almost a third lived
in the seven municipalities which make up the metropolitan area of San
Juan.

By the time the PPD achieved its dominance in the early 1940s the
organized labour movement had already been drastically weakened and
divided.[11] One of the cornerstones of the industrialization program was
the attraction for imported capital in labour-intensive industries of a
relatively inexpensive labour supply and a 'co-operative' labour movement. Puerto Rico's constitutional status meant that federal minimum
wages did not necessarily apply to the island, and for many years it was the
policy of the government to deal with minimum wages on an ad hoc basis,
permitting local adjustments below the federal minimums. This policy
was abandoned in the 1970s, and the pertinent federal minimums now
apply in Puerto Rico. Real wage differentials still exist between Puerto
Rico and the mainland, but the distance has been slowly but significantly
shrinking.

By the 1980s organized labour still comprised substantially less than 15
per cent of the employed labour force. There were virtually no organized
labour unions in the crucially important pharmaceutical industry, but the
organization of public sector employees had accelerated and by the end of
the 1970s some of the most militant unions were to be found among
public workers – in spite of the fact that there was no overall legislation
on the island level recognizing or regulating the matter of union organization, collective bargaining or the right to strike in the public sector. This
unresolved problem is potentially serious, given the increasing importance
of public employment in Puerto Rico.

[11] See Angel Quintero Rivera, 'La clase obrera y el proceso político en Puerto Rico', *Revista de Ciencias
Sociales* 20 (1976); 3–48.

The quantitative successes of modernization during the post-war period have not been achieved exclusively through the processes of autonomous economic growth or industrial development. A prominent portion of Puerto Rico's income originates directly in transfers from the federal government in the form of direct subsidies or grants to government programmes and, perhaps more importantly, through direct payments to citizens in the form of veterans' benefits, social security pensions, unemployment insurance, and, from 1974, the food stamp programme (which was converted to a system of direct cash payments in 1982.)

In 1976 federal transfers to individuals amounted to $1,493.3 million, equivalent to 19.8 per cent of the Gross National Product (GNP) and representing a 43.7 per cent increase over the preceding year. The food stamp programme alone accounted for $806 million. (It had been estimated in 1975 that almost 74 per cent of the population were eligible for participation in that programme and that 55.5 per cent were already receiving its benefits.) In 1980 direct net federal transfers to individuals accounted for almost 23 per cent of the island's total GNP; when net transfers to government are included the proportion of the GNP is almost a third. As a result of federal budget cutbacks, the termination of public service jobs programmes and the imposition of a statutory ceiling on federal nutrition assistance to Puerto Rico, these amounts had declined slightly by 1985, but they still amounted to $3,183.8 million in transfers to individuals, equivalent to 21.5 per cent of the GNP.[12]

Like the federal relief agencies of the 1930s, these programmes of federal assistance are of central importance for the maintenance of the Puerto Rican economy and, probably, of its relative social and political stability. They are also seen by many as fortifying dependence and as basic shapers of long-term political attitudes.

RESISTANCE AND ACCOMMODATION.

Modernization came to Puerto Rico in the undisguised and direct form of 'Americanization'. Yet there was near consensus among the island's elite that Puerto Rico's culture should not be assimilated into that of the mainstream United States. Advocates of statehood based their arguments

---

[12] Figures are taken from the "Economic Reports to the Governor" for 1976 and 1985; Angel L. Ruiz and Parimal Choudhury, 'The Impact of the Food Stamp Program on the Puerto Rican Economy: an Input-Output Approach', (Rio Piedras: University of Puerto Rico, Department of Economics, Serie de Ensayos y Monografías No. 7 (September, 1978): 5; and U.S. Department of the Treasury, 'Operations', pp. 24–5.

on the concept of equal political rights for all American citizens and on the economic and social security that statehood would allegedly guarantee, rather than on any perceived notion that Puerto Ricans were effectively turning into North Americans. Commonwealth and independence advocates began, of course, with the premise of national separateness and identity. The difference between the supporters of statehood and their opponents was not one of varying degrees of 'American-ness' or 'Puerto Rican-ness', but was over whether or not that status would signify or confirm the effective end of Puerto Rican identity.

The problems of Puerto Rico as it entered the last decade of the twentieth century continued to be 'political' in the broadest sense of the term. Basic and emotionally charged questions regarding the proper dimensions and definitions of the political community itself remained unanswered and unsettled. The interplay of resistances and accommodations to the facts of the United States economic, political and cultural domination had, if anything, become more complex since 1940.

Military service in the U.S. armed forces (more than 250,000 Puerto Ricans had served in the army since 1940), return migration from the United States (in the late 1970s there were some 25,000 pupils in public schools listed as primarily English-speaking and in need of bilingual instruction), and the American origin of virtually all news about the outside world carried in the mass media, were all important factors in 'integrating' Puerto Rico into its American connection.[13]

One of the most controversial and sensitive areas in which public policies and attitudes towards Americanization were thrashed out was that of language and educational policy. Language had been a major political and social issue in Puerto Rico since the arrival of the North Americans. Before the Elective Governor Act, which went into effect in 1948, American officials on the island were still insisting on the necessary primacy of English. Once the Popular Party was entrenched in power and the Commissioner of Education appointed directly by the Governor, instruction in Spanish was set at all levels of public education, with English taught as a

---

[13] The figure on army service was supplied by the Public Affairs Office, Fort Buchanan, San Juan. For a review of the language problem and bilingual education in New York and Puerto Rico, see Language Policy Task Force, 'Language Policy and the Puerto Rican Community', *The Bilingual Review/La Revista Bilingüe* (Department of Foreign Languages, CUNY), 5, nos. 1 and 2 (January-August 1978); reprinted as Centro de Estudios Puertorriqueños, CUNY Working Papers no. 1 (1978). For a study of the written daily press in Puerto Rico, see Robert W. Anderson, *La prensa en Puerto Rico* (San Juan: Comisión de Derechos Civiles, Informe 1977-CDC-006E, July 13, 1977.)

second language compulsorily from the first primary grades on through to the second year of university. Spanish was the language of the masses, the medium of instruction in public education, and the vehicle for mass communication and artistic expression through the written and spoken word. But English continued to hold a privileged place, and its inroads into the linguistic reality of Puerto Rico were increasing, to the dismay of some and the approval of others.[14] In 1976 some 17 per cent of the total school-age population were enroled in private schools, the language of instruction in many of which, both parochial and lay, was English.[15] Social stratification according to English-language ability was a distinct possibility, although no studies designed to discover its degree had been carried out as yet among the island population.

Progress in the levels of schooling and formal education had been one of the prominent watchwords of Puerto Rico's development since 1940. In 1980 it was estimated that some 80 per cent of the population between six and eighteen years of age were attending schools.[16] The island boasted one of the highest proportions in the world (40 per cent in 1977) of college-age population attending institutions of higher learning. Throughout the 1940s and into the early 1970s the universities, and most prominently the main campus of the State University of Puerto Rico at Río Piedras (with an enrolment of some 25,000 in 1975), were important and highly visible centers of anti-imperialist and pro-independence student movements, usually closely attuned to political groups outside the university and almost always arrayed against a university administration allied to and economically dependent on the government. With the proliferation of campuses within the state university system, the rapid growth of private colleges and universities and the growing emphasis on technological curricula, the political and cultural centrality of the main University of Puerto Rico campus as an arena for the resistance to 'Americanization' had diminished somewhat. In 1976, for the first time, there were more students enroled in private colleges and universities than in the public system (58,625 to 52,686). By 1984–5 almost 63 per cent of all college students on the island were attending

[14] See, for example, Germán de Granda, *Transculturación e interferencia lingüística en el Puerto Rico contemporáneo, 1898–1968* (Río Piedras, 1972.)

[15] Language Policy Task Force, 'Language Policy and the Puerto Rican Community', p. 10.

[16] The figures are from Estado Libre Asociado de Puerto Rico, Comisión sobre Reforma Educativa, *Informe final* (Hato Rey, June 20, 1977): 51–3, 202; and from information supplied directly by the Department of Education.

private post-secondary institutions (97,549 out of a total college enrol-ment of 155,726.)[17] The educational system in Puerto Rico, committed to quantity and divided among complex tiers of public and private, parochial and secular, technological institutes and traditional liberal arts, was probably more a reflection of the dilemmas and contradictions of 'Americanization' rather than a source of possible resistance to it.

Puerto Rico approached the last years of the century with both its colonial dilemmas and its puzzling status intact. Its place in the interna-tional community was uncertain. The United Nations, through its Com-mittee on Decolonization, had expressed its continuing interest in the unsettled status problem, even though in 1953 the General Assembly absolved the United States from the obligation to report on Puerto Rico annually as a 'non-self-governing territory'.[18] Independence advocates were active in eliciting international moral support for the cause. During the 1950s commonwealth governments attempted to increase Puerto Rico's role in the Caribbean as an autonomous entity – attempts which were not to go very far because of difficulties inherent in the restrictions of commonwealth status itself and the opposition to such an autonomous role by large sectors of local public opinion. Defenders of commonwealth insist, nevertheless, on the expanded international role which an autono-mous Puerto Rico could undertake within the commonwealth structure.[19]

From 1985 the PPD administration under Hernández Colón had tried to encourage the expansion of Puerto Rico's industrial and commercial role in the Caribbean. Its strategy was to stimulate the 'possessions corpora-tions', create 'twin plant' factories, and invest in co-operative ventures in other countries of the area in order to link the activities of those corpora-tions with the Reagan administration's 'Caribbean Basin Initiative' plan. At the same time, the Puerto Rican administration sought to ensure the permanence of the beneficial '936' tax concessions, which were clearly only possible under the 'fiscal autonomy' implicit in the present status. This strategy was, then, directed towards the strengthening of the common-wealth status quo and not towards any legal or formal tampering with it.

[17] Consejo de Educación Superior, Río Piedras, Puerto Rico, 'Estadísticas sobre instituciones de educacion superior en Puerto Rico, año académico 1984–85' (March, 1985), table 1.

[18] For a documented chronicle of the case of Puerto Rico in the United Nations, see Carmen Gautier Mayoral and María del Pilar Argüellos (eds.), *Puerto Rico y la ONU* (Río Piedras, 1978).

[19] See, for example, W. M. Reisman, *Puerto Rico and the International Process: New Roles in Association*, The American Society of International Law, Studies in Transnational Legal Policy, No. 6 (Washing-ton, D.C., 1975). Herbert Corkran, Jr., *Patterns of International Cooperation in the Caribbean* (Dallas; 1970) describes inter alia the Commonwealth's role in the Caribbean under the PPD governments.

The enhancement of autonomy continued to exist as a kind of abstract and repeatedly postponed goal of the PPD.

It is possible that the dilemmas and contradictions in Puerto Rico's tortuous version of the problem of decolonization will continue indefinitely. Whatever its very special circumstances, the disappearance of Puerto Rico as a Latin American country does not, in any case, seem imminent.

Part Four

PANAMA

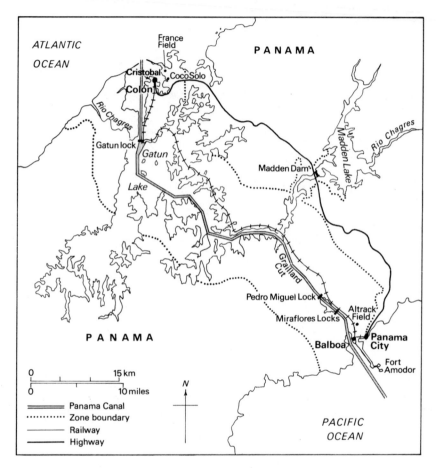

The Panama Canal Zone

14

PANAMA SINCE 1903

Since its 'discovery' in 1501, the Isthmus of Panama has been a crossroads. During the Spanish colonial era mule trains carried cargo across the isthmus, connecting Spain with the Pacific. Annual fairs in the town of Portobelo on the Caribbean coast attracted agents from great merchant houses, as tons of Peruvian silver were traded for European goods. Even after the eclipse of the fairs Panama continued to thrive on commerce and shipping, in the eighteenth century still under Spanish rule and in the nineteenth century as a province of the independent republic of Colombia.

People of different backgrounds settled in Panama. The first Spaniards founded a handful of towns, divided Indians into *encomiendas* and farmed the best lands along the Pacific watershed. Several hundred of these families formed a rural oligarchy that was not particularly wealthy but controlled both land and people. In addition, the Spanish government designated Panama City as a key commercial and defence site in the Pacific, which it regarded as its private sea. Bureaucrats, military officers, merchants, seamen, artisans and African slaves dominated its population. Later, agents of Caribbean merchants also settled in Panama.

The colonial and nineteenth-century experience of Panama affected its history as a nation after 1903. There was an enduring tension between two elites, one rural and descended from the early settlers, often called *interiorano;* and another cosmopolitan, racially and culturally mixed, and based in Panama City and the northern transit port of Colón. Panama's multiple connections with the outside world brought people, capital and other benefits, yet also tied its fortunes to international economic cycles. Moreover, the province's strategic location and narrowness (called its greatest natural resource) induced world powers to vie for influence there. And finally, Panama's maritime and commercial vocation weakened its geopolitical identification with its neighbours.

Panama's history in the twentieth century has also been profoundly affected by the nature of its independence. Panamanian leaders declared their separation from Spain in 1821 but decided to join the newly formed Republic of Gran Colombia. Several times during the course of the nineteenth century, however, they broke away from Colombia, usually because of conservative policies adopted in Bogotá. Colombia put down these separatist movements militarily. In addition, the United States (under the 1846 Bidlack–Mallarino Treaty with Colombia) guaranteed Colombian sovereignty in Panama, especially after the construction by a New York firm of the Panama Railroad (inaugurated in 1855). Thus, resentment of outside control shifted from Spain to Colombia and the United States.

Hopes of recommencing canal work on a trans-isthsmus canal across Panama (abandoned since the ill-fated French project of the 1880s), combined with fears that the site might be moved to Nicaragua, re-ignited separatist sentiments and, supported by the United States, led to independence from Colombia in 1903. Late independence, however, left Panama relatively ill-prepared for self-government, and the Panamanians (like the Cubans) had to accommodate to U.S. interests as they set out to build their nation. One authority has noted that Panama's 'marriage of convenience' with the United States resulted in a 'hybrid nation with a compromised sovereignty'.[1]

Until about 1930 the United States exercised ultimate authority in Panama, which became a U.S. protectorate in all but name. Later, when the United States renounced overt intervention, U.S. influence continued in myriad ways. The United States guaranteed law and order for the purpose of operating the canal; protected the transit zone from external threats; monitored politics; and fed the local economy with canal wages and purchases. U.S. officials wished foremost to move ships through the canal and to protect U.S. interests in the isthmus, and they expected Panamanians to embrace these goals. The Panamanian elite, on the other hand, wanted to make money from the canal and ancillary services, to raise their standard of living and build their nation. This difference in objectives generated mountains of correspondence between the two countries, eight treaties (1903, 1909, 1926, 1936, 1947, 1955, 1967, 1977 – the third, fifth and seventh unperfected) two agreements (the Taft Agreement of 1904 and the Bases Agreement of 1942), several confrontations and generally troubled relations.

[1] Gustavo Adolfo Mellander, *The United States in Panamanian Politics* (Danville, Ill., 1971), pp. 189–90.

The heterogeneity of Panama's society increased after independence because of the influx of people from all corners of the globe. Between 1896 and 1930, total population rose from 316,000 to 512,000. Immigration enriched the country's skills yet inhibited the process of nation-building. Ethnic, religious, racial and cultural diversity divided Panamanians, especially in the political arena. One writer called Panama a 'rachitic nation'[2] because of this diversity.

After 1904 Panama's leaders pursued a number of national strategies. The most important was the struggle to modify and eventually abrogate the hated Treaty of 1903, by which the United States gained the Canal Zone and quasi-sovereign rights to build and operate the canal. Another was to denounce the United States in the international arena (for example, before the League of Nations in 1927, the ILO and the United Nations in 1944–6, the UN in 1973), bringing world opinion to bear on the country's particular problems. Third, Panamanian opinion was united against the Colossus of the North, making coexistence unpleasant for Zone employees and military personnel. Finally, after the Second World War Panama attempted to diversify her economy, to reduce her reliance on canal transfers, wages and purchases.

Despite frequently confrontational strategies, Panama's elites usually collaborated with the United States. Political, economic and social accommodation was reached between U.S. and Panamanian officials in the early days of the republic and constituted an informal alliance. This allowed both countries to pursue their separate goals without disrupting canal operations. This underlying co-operation was obscured by the strident speeches, denunciations, riots and angry headlines which dominate Panama's history. Moreover, it helped the local elites to remain in power and control the masses.

INDEPENDENCE AND THE TREATY OF 1903

Panama's independence on 3 November 1903 is usually seen as a prelude to the drama of building the Panama Canal. A group of powerful men representing financial and political interests on two continents conspired to separate the province of Panama from Colombia for the purpose of re-initiating work on a canal across Panama. U.S. President Theodore Roosevelt became committed to the project, supported the conspirators

[2] Eric de León, *Ensayo sobre la naturaliza psico-social del hombre panameño y otros problemas sociales* (Panama, 1970), p. 22.

and dictated an advantageous treaty that the Panamanians had to accept.

Panama's independence movement began among officials of the Panama Railroad, prominent and mostly elderly men who had a close relationship with both their firm's New York headquarters and the French holding company that owned the railroad and canal excavations. Their major fear was that the United States, committed to building an inter-oceanic canal, might select Nicaragua rather than Panama as the site for the canal. Panama had never been closely integrated into Colombia, and Panamanians believed that Colombia wished to extract financial profit from the isthmus rather than promote its development. Panamanians were also out of step ideologically with the Colombians. They tended to be anti-clerical, laissez-faire capitalists, with an international orientation, whereas Colombians were generally conservative, Catholic and parochial. Finally, the Panamanians wanted peace in order to pursue their business interests, and Colombia seemed destined to suffer perpetual civil war, the latest example of which was the War of a Thousand Days (1899–1902), which devastated many regions of the country, including Panama.

U.S. and French interests supported a Panamanian conspiracy. Roosevelt, angry with the Colombians for rejecting the recently negotiated Hay–Herrán treaty, preferred to get authorization for a canal without their participation. He was also anxious to proceed with construction, hoping to tout the canal in his 1904 election campaign. Philippe Bunau-Varilla, a French engineer associated with the canal operation since the 1880s, provided liaison between U.S. officials and the Panamanian conspirators. He stood to profit from the sale of the French company's rights to the U.S. government and also wished to vindicate French pride by arranging for the completion of the Panama work. Bunau received advice from the Panama Railroad's lawyer in New York, William Nelson Cromwell, who promoted the interests of stockholders holding a substantial portion of the French company's shares.

In August 1903 one of the principal plotters, former governor and army physician Manuel Amador Guerrero (1833–1909), travelled to New York to meet Cromwell and to learn of prospects for U.S. backing for the revolt. After several meetings, Cromwell broke off contacts due to a warning from the Colombian minister. Amador then met with Bunau, who gave him assurances, based upon conversations with Roosevelt and Secretary of State John Hay, that they would recognize Panama's independence and protect the revolutionaries. Bunau even furnished an 'independence kit' containing a flag, a declaration, military plans and a promise of $100,000. In exchange, he obliged the Panamanians to name him minister plenipotentiary in Washington.

Amador returned to Panama encouraged but still indecisive about the plot. He held meetings to bolster the conspirators' enthusiasm because most were reluctant to risk their fortunes, careers and even lives on the assurances of the Frenchman. One decisive convert, however, was General Esteban Huertas, a young military hero whose troops would secure independence. On the day designated for the revolt, 3 November 1903, Amador, his wife Doña Maria, General Huertas and a few others (including the U.S. superintendent of the Panama Railroad) managed to suborn the local garrison, imprison visiting Colombian generals and neutralize their troops, and proclaim Panama's independence. The entire episode resulted in only one death. That evening the Panama City council ratified the act and sued for recognition by the United States. This was granted three days later, U.S. warships off Panama and Colón guaranteeing the safety of the new republic.

The first independent government was a Junta composed of early stalwarts of the revolt, José Agustín Arango, Tomás Arias and Federico Boyd, heading a cabinet composed of men from both the Liberal and Conservative parties who represented the local elite and the Panama Railroad. Amador and Boyd were empowered to negotiate a canal agreement with the United States. Simultaneously, Bunau, recently appointed Panamanian minister in Washington, began talks with Hay, intending to sign a treaty before the Panamanians arrived. Hay agreed, knowing that Bunau would have to accept whatever he demanded. He drafted a much less generous treaty than that already rejected by the Colombians. The treaty, under which Panama conceded rights of sovereignity, in perpetuity, over a ten-mile-wide Canal Zone through the centre of the republic (some 500 square miles) to the United States in return for a lump sum of $10 million and an annuity of $250,000, making Panama virtually a U.S. protectorate (the United States acquired the right to intervene in Panama City and Colón to maintain public order), was signed on 18 November, just hours before Amador and Boyd arrived in Washington to present their credentials.

The Panamanian Junta ratified the treaty despite great displeasure with its terms, since Bunau and Hay intimated that delay might lead to new negotiations with Colombia. Thus, Panama's independence was tied inextricably to the signature of the canal treaty. The treaty of 1903 became an original sin that poisoned relations between the two countries for generations.

THE FORMATIVE YEARS: 1903–30

The Panamanian Junta called elections for late December 1903 to select thirty-two delegates to a Constitutional Assembly that would convene the following month. The elections drew a small turn-out and were dominated by pro-independence municipal leaders in the provinces. On paper, the Conservative and Liberal parties were equally represented, but in fact the Conservatives prevailed in both the Junta and the Assembly. Within a month they had produced a constitution that centralized the executive (provincial governors were appointed) but balanced it with a unicameral legislature and a judiciary. Passage of Article 136 provoked a partisan split in the assembly. Tomás Arias, inspired by the Platt Amendment imposed on Cuba, proposed that the United States should have the right to intervene anywhere in Panama to maintain peace and constitutional order. This measure was passed against the opposition of Liberal delegates, who argued that it violated the nation's sovereignty. At the conclusion of its duties the Assembly selected Amador for a four-year term as president and then converted itself into a National Assembly. It disbanded in June 1904.

Amador appointed more Conservatives to his cabinet, undermining its bipartisan character and provoking a crisis. When Amador sought to gain greater authority over the 250-man army the Liberal General Huertas demanded that he revoke the new cabinet appointments. The crisis came to a head in November, Amador requesting U.S. intervention to prevent a coup by Huertas. The U.S. ambassador warned Huertas that any unconstitutional act by him would cause the United States to send in the marines. Huertas had no alternative but to resign and withdraw from politics.

Amador took advantage of Huertas's resignation to disband the army altogether, an idea that had been broached in discussions with U.S. envoys, who agreed that canal troops could protect Panama from external as well as internal threats. Moreover, an army consumed a great deal of money and tended to destabilize politics. In its stead, Amador created the National Police, which guaranteed the Conservatives in power but also made Panama more dependent upon the United States.

In the first months after independence Amador and the revolutionaries played down their Conservative Party identity by calling themselves Constitutionalists. Once the new government had consolidated its authority, however, partisanship resurfaced. Panama's parties had their roots in Colombia's Liberal and Conservative parties, yet differences existed. First, the more pragmatic and business-oriented Panamanian elite avoided the rivalries that had led to civil war in Colombia. Fewer insoluble conflicts existed in Panama, and religion barely mattered. Personalities and family ties weighed more heavily than ideology. Nevertheless, Panamanian Conservatives tended to be racially white and to belong to the *interiorano* elite. One of their few strongly held beliefs was preference for private contracting of public works. Liberal leaders, on the other hand, often had black or Indian heritage, came from the ranks of artisans, small ranchers and the 'newer Negroes', and were more successful in securing the support of the non-white masses.

The U.S. government favoured the Conservatives, and after 1903 a tacit alliance existed between them. In response the Liberal Party approached the U.S. minister with a proposal for office-sharing between the two parties, but this was rejected. Such favoritism towards the Conservatives became less tenable, however, after the Liberals won overwhelming majorities in the December 1904 municipal elections. Henceforth, U.S. officials meddled in a more guarded fashion.

President Amador spent much of his time holding the Liberals at bay. In mid-1905 he hit upon a scheme to disenfranchise Belisario Porras (1856–1942), the hero of the War of a Thousand Days who had emerged as the foremost Liberal leader. In 1905 the Supreme Court revoked his citizenship on the grounds that he had not embraced the independence of Panama in 1903, but the National Assembly soon restored it. The midterm elections of June 1906 also revealed the Conservatives' desperation. With U.S. acquiescence, the National Police used all manner of fraud to ensure that they won the assembly and municipal elections.

By 1908, Amador could look back upon a number of accomplishments in his four-year term. He had consolidated the country's independence, supervised the writing of a constitution and codification of the laws inherited from Colombia, established the rudiments of a bureaucracy, wrested Canal Zone concessions from the United States (in the Taft Agreement on trade between Panama and the Zone), and had given the country a monetary system based on the U.S. dollar.

The 1908, presidential succession remained in doubt until four days before the July election. The choice had settled on two candidates, the elderly José Domingo de Obaldía, a Liberal, and Ricardo Arias, a Conservative who enjoyed the backing of Amador and other prominent administration figures. Ironically, each received support from the other nominal party. The Roosevelt cabinet, probably fearing a crisis like that in Cuba in 1906, early decided to help Obaldía covertly. Secretary of War William

H. Taft, Republican candidate in the U.S. elections, travelled to Panama
in May and was briefed. Believing that Obaldía and the Liberals would
win a fair election and thus be mollified, Taft met with Amador and
dictated specific measures to guarantee free suffrage, including U.S. supervision of the balloting. Amador complied, Arias withdrew from the contest, Obaldía was elected unopposed, and the United States began a new
phase of tutelage, that of supervisor of elections.

Obaldia died in March 1910. The vice-president was Carlos A. Mendoza (1856–1916), who had emerged as one of the country's most popular
figures. Descended from a family of soldiers and politicians, he had been
active in government since his youth, joining the revolutionaries of 1903
and writing the Declaration of Independence. Tall, articulate, bold and
possessing handsome negroid features, Mendoza had a large following
among the non-white population of the Santa Ana district, which, with its
plaza a focal point of the *arrabal* or zone outside the walled perimeter of
the old city, had become the scene for demonstrations and political meetings. Mendoza has been described as the prototype of the *lider metropolitano*
for his influence among the urban lower classes.[3] According to the constitution the assembly would choose a president to finish the remainder of
Obaldía's term. Mendoza was the favourite, but his succession was
blocked by the U.S. director of the canal project, Colonel George
Goethals, and the U.S. chargé in Panama, Richard O. Marsh. Goethals
and Marsh disliked the Liberals, whom they judged unfriendly to the
United States and irresponsible in their arousal of the lower classes. They
also disliked Mendoza's dark skin, which they considered an affront to
Panama's mostly white elite. Marsh campaigned to force Mendoza to
withdraw his name and even threatened occupation should he resist. In
the end, Mendoza accepted the post of Minister of Finance, while seventy-
five-year-old Pablo Arosemena gained the presidency with bipartisan support. A British diplomat commented, 'It is really farcical to talk of Panama as an independent state. It is really simply an annex of the Canal
Zone'.[4] Mendoza, widely praised by other U.S. and British officials, was a
victim of what William Franklin Sands, the diplomatic trouble-shooter,
later called in his book published in 1944, 'jungle diplomacy'. Goethals,
meanwhile, disassociated himself from Marsh's interventionism, and the
State Department called Marsh home in disgrace.

[3] J. Conte Porras, *Arnulfo Arias Madrid* (Panama, 1980), p. 46.
[4] Mallet to Grey, 22 August 1910, FO (Foreign Office) 371/944/33140, Public Record Office,
London.

Another victim of the coup was Belisario Porras. Porras, who hailed from the province of Las Tablas, had studied law in Bogotá and became a militant in the Liberal party while still a teenager. In Panama, he worked with the Liberal *caudillo* Buenaventura Correoso and as a reward received a three-year fellowship to study law in Paris, returning to work in the legal department of the French canal company. Exiled to Central America after 1895, Porras conspired against the Conservatives in Colombia and eventually commanded Panamanian troops during the War of a Thousand Days. From exile in Nicaragua, Porras criticized the 1903 revolt which he considered a Conservative take-over and the subsequent surrender of sovereignty to the United States. A man of strong convictions, he never changed this view, which led to the revocation of his citizenship in 1905– 6. With the approach of the 1912 elections, however, Porras became the logical Liberal candidate, Mendoza lending his support in exchange for a promise of the nomination in 1916. Although U.S. representatives monitored the election, the Conservative opposition withdrew, enabling Porras to impose a Liberal hegemony for almost two decades.

Porras's first administration (1912–16) brought considerable stability and progress to the country. Partisan fighting ended. The canal, completed in 1914, was celebrated with an International Exposition the following year. Projects initiated by his predecessors – law codes, telegraph lines, modernization of Panama City, and schools – were completed. Porras created civil and land registry offices, and also authorized a railroad in the western province of Chiriquí in order to encourage banana cultivation.

The end of canal construction and the onset of the First World War had a depressing effect on Panama's economy. Canal officials laid off thousands of West Indian labourers and reduced wages to a minimum. Since canal paychecks represented the largest single source of national income, the entire economy suffered. The government pressured canal authorities to repatriate West Indians and to provide relief by purchasing local products, but little was done. Relations between Porras and the United States were further soured when in 1914, Secretary of State William Jennings Bryan forced Panama to concede a monopoly on radio to canal authorities for the purpose of monitoring shipping and naval traffic. Then in mid-1916 the U.S. Navy confiscated high-powered rifles belonging to the National Police, on the grounds that they were too dangerous for the excitable constabulary to handle. Many Panamanians regarded the move as a national humiliation and later believed it gave Costa Rican troops an advantage when they invaded disputed territory in 1921.

In 1916, Porras reneged on his promise to endorse Mendoza for the presidency, and the latter died in February. He favoured instead the Liberal Ramón M. Valdés. Porras went to Washington as ambassador, his prestige much enhanced, but Valdés died after only two years in office, and wartime exigencies prevented him from accomplishing much. Upon Valdés's death, Liberals split over the presidential succession, supporters of the ideologue Eusebio Morales attempting to delete the constitutional rule that only native-born Panamanians were eligible to hold the office. They failed, however, and Belisario Porras returned to the presidency.

Porras served out Valdés's unexpired term and was subsequently re-elected for the period 1920–4, pursuing throughout these years the constructive policies he had begun in 1912. He inaugurated the country's first university, the School of Law and Political Science, in 1918. He created the Fiscal Agency (to improve tax collection); the National Press; a teacher-training college; the National Lottery; the National Archives; and Coiba Penitentiary in addition to building two hundred new schools and a number of roads. He also founded the Santo Tomás and Panama hospitals, the country's first modern facilities.

Porras's record in foreign affairs proved less successful. In 1914, Panama had rejected an arbitration decision on her border with Costa Rica, and in February 1921 Costa Rican troops seized the disputed territory. Crowds in Panama City protested and demanded a military expedition. The National Police had few rifles but Porras mobilized volunteers, and for a fortnight there was desultory fighting, which spread to the Bocas region on the Atlantic. The United States, meanwhile, pressured him to accept the 1914 arbitration. Early in the conflict, Porras announced that 'War between Panama and Costa Rica . . . would be an absurdity. . . . I have decided that this is a matter for diplomatic solution'. Upon hearing Porras's statement, a mob that had gathered at Santa Ana Plaza marched to the presidential palace to depose him, but a detachment of U.S. Army troops finally broke up the demonstration. Several months later Costa Rica received U.S. permission to occupy the disputed lands. Porras threatened to send his volunteers again but was prevented by a U.S. Marine battalion. It was a bitter pill for Panamanians to swallow, and Porras's opponents used the loss of territory to brand him a traitor. The border dispute was ultimately settled in Costa Rica's favour in 1941.

Canal issues challenged Porras on several occasions. In 1920 a strike broke out among non-U.S. employees, who demanded wage increases, collective bargaining and job security. Most strikers were West Indians, but a significant number of Panamanians were involved and public opinion favoured them. Porras's stand-in president, Ernesto Lefevre, resisted demands by the canal management to break up strike meetings in Panama City and Colón. He gave in, however, when threatened with military occupation. The strike eventually failed, and the so-called 'Silver Rate' (non-U.S.) workers were kept in an inferior position.

Porras chose Rodolfo Chiari, a wealthy sugar and cattle baron, to succeed him in the presidency. The son of an Italian immigrant and a relative newcomer to isthmian politics, Chiari was beholden to Porras, who had appointed him in an effort to extend his own influence. Chiari's term saw the extension of the Chiriqui railroad to the Pacific port of Armuelles, of great importance to the banana industry. He also continued Porras's road and public works projects which were financed with easy U.S. bank loans and bond issues. However, by 1928 Chiari had captured control of the Liberal Party, replacing the ex-president's middle-class lawyers and intellectuals with businessmen and technocrats. As a result, he was able to block a re-election bid by Porras, choosing instead Florencio Harmodio Arosemena (1872–1945).

An engineer who had campaigned unopposed on the platform of 'Order, work and frugality', Arosemena did Chiari's bidding until he was overthrown on 2 January 1931. Contemporaries regarded his administration as unusually corrupt because of the many construction contracts he awarded to friends and associates, but he was personally honest. Among his major accomplishments were completion of the Santiago–David highway, a hospital in David and the Paitilla airport outside Panama City.

By the 1920s Panama's leaders had come to accept what one historian called 'protective paternalism', whereby U.S. authorities set limits on the issues politicians could raise and the methods they could employ.[5] Panama's leaders recognized that they could never jeopardize the construction, operation, maintenance and defence of the canal. Equally, they allowed U.S. diplomats the right of consultation, and occasionally of veto, regarding the selection of presidents and cabinet secretaries. As a result, some experience of working with U.S. citizens was necessary. Porras went so far as to say that the embassy in Washington was the 'stage upon which Panama's presidents were made'. Panamanians learned that U.S. officials preferred to deal with white, upper-class Panamanians, and in English.

---

[5] Mellander, *The United States in Panamanian Politics*, p. 193.

Finally, they tried to comply with the U.S. desire that politics be reasonably democratic, constitutional, peaceful and predictable.

This modus vivendi remained informal and succeeded due to the intermingling of the elites of the canal and the country through marriages, club memberships, employment of well-to-do Panamanians by the canal, education of elite youths in the Canal Zone high school, business dealings and social affairs. In this way U.S. impositions seemed less onerous and in fact benefited a number of prominent families.

Within these parameters, the political elite of Panama created a system of government which, if not entirely constitutional, had rules, sanctions and rewards. Government provided patronage (sinecures, contracts, concessions, privileges and honorary titles) for persons of rank and merit, and through election the politician won the right to distribute such favours. One observer even spoke of Panamanians' 'oriental conception of government'.[6] Personalism and family-based activities permeated government practice. Political groups with little ideological content were often given nicknames indicating who led them, for example, 'Porrismo' and 'Chiarismo'. Family ties (both positive and negative) usually proved more influential than ideas. Power tended to be concentrated in as few hands as possible. The president appointed governors, who in turn appointed mayors. City councils and the National Assembly rarely influenced the executive officers with whom they theoretically shared authority.

Given the scarce amounts of power, money and status available to them, politicians tried to limit access to their ranks. The old elite families tried to monopolize office-holding, but they could not prevent talented and ambitious men from breaking into public life. Elite leaders then seduced the newcomers with advantageous marriages, business partnerships, money, partisan favours and honorary status. The symbol of arrival was membership of the exclusive Union Club, whose luxurious building near Cathedral Plaza overlooked the bay.

The populace enjoyed some influence in public life since the political superstructure rested on a foundation of *gamonalismo,* or local bossism. In the major cities and towns, each neighbourhood had a long-time leader who arranged favours, solved problems, distributed jobs and generally provided liaison between the citizenry and the government. He kept voters registered and delivered them to the polls at election time. The *gamonal* did not bother to consult his constituents regarding larger issues

[6] Davis to Secretary of State, 719.00/8–2950, State Department, U.S. National Archives, RG 59.

of policy, but he assured minimal levels of citizen satisfaction. Demonstrations which did not threaten U.S. interests could have considerable impact on events. These politics gave rise to the figure known as the *líder metropolitano,* a species of populist orator exemplified by Domingo Turner and Demetrio Porras (Belisario's socialist son). One of the easiest ways to stir up a crowd was to attack the United States, the perfect scapegoat.

The local elites were deeply disappointed that the terms of the 1903 treaty failed to guarantee them lucrative roles in construction and services. Rather, scores of U.S. contractors and businessmen set up operations inside the Canal Zone, contributing little to Panama's economy. Moreover, the financial arrangements proved miserly: Panama received the same annuity that Colombia had for the Railroad, $250,000. Canal officials did, however, designate sixty middle-management positions for prominent Panamanians, who were on the coveted Gold Roll. Equally, the arrival of tens of thousands of West Indian and other labourers, most of whom had to live in Panama City or Colón, provided a clientele for Panama's business class. Investors who owned land near the canal built roominghouses, stores, saloons, brothels and other establishments. Many also joined forces with U.S. investors in utilities, banks, streetcars, breweries and factories. Finally, a great many expanded their law practices to represent persons who lost assets when the Canal Zone was created. The U.S. representatives, in the canal and diplomatic missions, recognized both the legitimacy and the practicality of providing adequate income to Panama's well-to-do families.

During and after the First World War, canal purchasing agents began contracting with Panamanian suppliers for staples consumed in the Zone. Wartime shortages also protected domestic markets for these suppliers. Generally speaking, coffee came from mountainous Chiriquí province; cattle from the Azuero Peninsula; sugar from Coclé; and rum from Herrera. (Most of the bananas from Chiriquí and Bocas went to the United States.) As long as Panamanian suppliers delivered acceptable goods at reasonable prices, the Canal Zone bought them in order to help the local economy. The relationship gave canal authorities considerable leverage with local authorities.

Panama's half-million inhabitants in the 1920s resembled not so much a melting pot as a stew, containing numerous clumps of people unwilling to blend with the rest. The West Indians, the largest group, had settled permanently after the construction of the canal. About half lived in the Canal Zone and half in Panama City and Colón. Despite the varied origins and cultures of the West Indians (Barbadians, Jamaicans, Martiniquans, etc.), Panamanians lumped them all together with the pejorative term *chombos*. They in turn created a protective subculture with their own churches, schools, brotherhoods, sports clubs and labour unions.

Other ethnic groups retained their separate identities without suffering as much discrimination as the West Indians, although a 1923 manifesto decried 'the diversity of races here that confront and mix with one another'.[7] The Chinese were active in retail commerce, laundries and restaurants. The Jewish community had long been a powerful force in commerce and banking. A sizeable group of Lebanese operated stores while little knots of British, French, Italian, Spanish and German residents lived in Panama City.

The only case of violent ethnic conflict occurred in 1925, the so-called Tule revolution among the Kuna Indians of the San Blas Islands. A fiercely independent people, the Kuna had resisted effective Panamanian control until 1915, when one of two tribal confederations allowed Panama to establish an administrative headquarters and a special police force. The ensuing government programme aimed at eradicating Kuna culture led to numerous confrontations and scattered violence, and eventually to the organized rebellion of 1925, in which some police were killed and others fled the region.

The rebellion was abetted by the former U.S. chargé Richard Marsh, who had taken a Kuna delegation to Washington in 1924 and composed a lengthy declaration proclaiming an independent republic. U.S. Minister J. G. South conveyed a party of U.S. and Panamanian officials to San Blas aboard the cruiser *Cleveland* and mediated an agreement whereby the Indians laid down their arms in exchange for guarantees of better treatment. Because Kuna leaders denied Marsh's role in the affair, South arranged for him to be expelled from the country without punishment. After that time the Kuna renegotiated their relationship to Panama several times, leaving them firmly incorporated into the nation but with a significant measure of autonomy.

Other forms of resistance and protest occurred during the 1920s. Labour unions organized during the war became militant during the postwar recession. Banana-workers in Bocas went on strike in 1919 in protest against the closure of plantations there. Silver-workers in the Canal Zone staged a major strike in 1920, as we have seen. Panamanian union leaders,

---

[7] Conte Porras, *Arnulfo Arias Madrid,* p. 62.

led by Spanish anarchist José María Blásquez de Pedro, formed the Labour Federation of Panama in 1921. Shortly afterward labour militants created a Communist cell within the federation, the forerunner of the Communist Party (1930). Several other unions and federations emerged in the 1920s. Strikes did not usually succeed, and unions remained weak for the next fifty years, but their appearance did have an unsettling effect on political and economic life. Equally, frustration with U.S. abuses and Panamanian surrenders caused a number of protests in the 1920s. In 1920 demonstrators picketed General Pershing when he visited Panama in an effort to incorporate Taboga Island into the Canal Zone. The rent strike of 1925 against slum landlords was fuelled in part by the fact that the U.S. government held title to much of the real estate in Colón. And early in 1927 protests and demonstrations helped convince the National Assembly to reject a treaty on the Canal Zone (to replace the Taft Agreement) recently negotiated with the United States.

By the end of the 1920s Panama had achieved a degree of stability and constitutional government, but it was not by any means a sovereign nation. U.S. tutelage and interventions (the last of which occurred during the rent strike), ethnic diversity and the disorganized economy all prevented Panamanians from taking full control of their destiny.

FORGING THE NATION-STATE: 1931−59

On the morning of 2 January 1931, conspirators belonging to the secret organization Acción Communal (AC) captured police headquarters and the presidential palace, deposing President Arosemena. This coup began a new phase in Panama's history, one marked by a struggle to strengthen the country internally. The United States continued to be the principal foil of the nationalists, but domestic reconstruction emerged as a compelling theme. The depression did not cause the coup, but the hardships of the early 1930s galvanized the rebels, few of whom had participated in the independence movement.

The 1931 coup marked the passing of a political generation and brought two extraordinary brothers to the centre of national life: Harmodio and Arnulfo Arias Madrid. Harmodio Arias (1886−62) dominated politics during the 1930s, and Arnulfo Arias (1901−88) had been in and out of the limelight since his first presidency in 1940−1. The Arias brothers were born in the province of Coclé, where their father had settled after immigrating from Costa Rica in the mid-nineteenth century. They belonged to the rural middle class and were unrelated to the oligarchic Arias clan. Both sons studied in Panama City and then went abroad for professional degrees, Harmodio to Cambridge for law and Arnulfo (some years later) to Harvard for medicine. Upon his return from England, Harmodio became a lawyer and began to dabble in politics, though displaying little ability to sway the masses. A loner who listened more than he spoke, Harmodio possessed a great capacity for personal manipulation, which, in combination with his professional reputation, led the British minister to describe him as Panama's only statesman.

Harmodio's debut in politics was sponsored by the AC, which was formed in 1923 by young well-to-do professionals opposed to the way the country was governed. They stressed nationalism and strengthening the country's institutions. They wished to reassert traditional Panamanian values and culture, including the Spanish language. Most of all, they sought to end U.S. tutelage, and in this spirit flayed President Chiari for requesting U.S. police action during the 1925 rent strike.

Harmodio shared the AC members' anger with the Porras administration and in 1924 ran for deputy on an opposition ticket. He denounced a recent presidential statement that 'Panama exists because of and for the canal'. Rather, Harmodio said, 'Panama exists because of and for the Panamanians'. As an unofficial AC spokesman in the assembly, Harmodio sponsored nationalistic bills, such as that which created the flag of convenience to encourage shipping companies to register their vessels in Panama. His greatest triumph was to block the 1926 canal treaty, publishing a copy of the secret document along with a manifesto calling it a violation of Panama's sovereignty. His campaign caught on in the press, embarrassed the Chiari government and led the National Assembly to reject the treaty early in 1927. In 1928, Harmodio committed himself further to politics by purchasing the *Panama-American,* a sensationalist bilingual daily.

Arnulfo, a very different personality, actually led the AC coup of 2 January 1931. Only two years old when Harmodio left home, Arnulfo had an unusual relationship with an older brother whom his mother lauded to the skies. Later in life he alternated between emulating and rejecting Harmodio's career in a kind of unresolved sibling rivalry. Harmodio, for his part, usually protected his impulsive younger brother, even when opposed to him. Upon his return from studies abroad, Arnulfo had begun treating patients in Santo Tomás hospital, but as one observer noted, 'politics were in his blood'.[8] Articulate, handsome and intrepid, he was anxious to make a name for himself, and joined AC in 1930 when the coup against Arosemena was being planned.

Once the AC conspirators learned, on the night of 1 January 1931, that their plot had been revealed to the authorities, they proceeded immediately to capture the police headquarters, disable the telephones at the presidential palace, and overpower the palace guard. Arnulfo emerged as the hero during the final operations. The revolutionaries held President Arosemena and his family prisoner, installing Harmodio Arias as provisional president. However, a constitutional sleight-of-hand produced an interim administration under Ricardo Alfaro (1882–1971), the negotiator of the 1926 treaty. Harmodio played a moderating role among the AC militants, and when he stood as candidate in the 1932 presidential election the United States declined to intervene against him.

The Chiaristas, victims of the coup, attempted a comeback by nominating Francisco Arias Paredes ('Don Pancho') to oppose Harmodio. Don Pancho, one of Panama's wealthiest ranchers, was known as the 'gentleman politician' because of his expensive suits and automobiles, but he was an effective public speaker and appealed to leftist groups despite the fact that the U.S. embassy considered him pro-American. Harmodio's greatest asset was his identification with the nationalists of AC, who promised to strengthen the country and bolster its collective self-esteem. Presenting himself as 'el cholito de Rio Grande' and 'candidate of the poor', he promised to shield the West Indian community from deportation and chauvinistic legislation in exchange for their electoral support. After winning a reasonably honest election, Harmodio appointed Arnulfo (who had received a gun wound in the neck during the campaign) minister of health and many other AC stalwarts to government posts. Colonel Manuel Pino was appointed commander of the National Police, protecting the Arias brothers and their allies.

The Arias administration introduced programmes to overcome the effects of the depression, negotiated a new treaty with the United States, and founded the University of Panama. Unemployment, largely due to canal lay-offs, threatened the political stability of the country; a new rent strike in 1932 led to violence; and demonstrations demanding the deporta-

[8] John Gunther, *Inside Latin America* (New York, 1941), p. 147, cited in Larray LaRae Pippin, *The Remón Era* (Stanford, 1964), p. 22, n2.

tion of West Indians (a majority of the unemployed) took a sharply racist character. Harmodio attempted to aid agriculture by creating a workers' and farmers' fund, the Fondo Obrero y Campesino, and distributing some government land. He carried out several programmes for the poor and homeless in the cities, including the establishment of a Popular Savings Bank, the Caja de Ahorro.

Harmodio avoided a debt moratorium until 1933 but then suspended debt payments and made a direct appeal to Washington for relief. U.S. President Franklin Roosevelt, receiving Harmodio in October 1933, promised to modify the 1903 treaty in order to improve Panama's profits from trade. Subsequent negotiations produced a new treaty in March 1936 (which was not, however, ratified by the United States until July 1939). The main elements were a renunciation of the U.S. right to intervene in Panamanian affairs and thus an end to protectorate status; a declaration that future acquisitions of land by the Canal Zone would require Panama's consent; and measures to reduce Zone commissary sales to Panamanian citizens. Further reforms made in the spirit of the Good Neighbor policy included repatriation and/or stipends for retired 'Silver' employees, to ease the burden of the unemployed. Finally, agreement was reached on construction of the trans-isthmian highway.

One of Harmodio's most important achievements was the creation of the National University in 1935. Although some college courses had been offered previously, proposals for a university had languished for almost two decades. Harmodio pushed legislation through the assembly and then appointed the distinguished writer Octavio Méndez Pereira as rector. Until the inauguration of its own campus in 1952, the university functioned in the law school and National Institute. By the mid-1930s a new generation of intellectuals had supplanted that of the independence era, and the university became their home. Called Neo-Liberals, they rejected laissez-faire policies and embraced Comte's positivism and Durkheim's organicism. They favoured centralized, interventionist government; national integration through universal education; class harmony achieved by state intervention; social justice; and limited property rights. This highly nationalistic generation saw the United States as an obstacle to Panama's national consolidation and progress. The students took up these banners and began to play a major role in political life.

In 1935, Harmodio Arias tried to amend the constitution to allow re-election, but this initiative split his party and eventually failed. He then decided to back his weak foreign minister, Juan Demóstenes ('J.D.')

Arosemena (1879–1939), Arnulfo organizing a new coalition, the Partido National Revolucionario (PNR), to manage Arosemena's election. Insiders knew that the price was support for Arnulfo in 1940. The 1936 election saw high levels of fraud and violence, which tarnished Harmodio's reputation for fair play but secured the presidency for Arosemena. Arnulfo's PNR collaborators, who called themselves Panameñistas, dominated Arosemena's cabinet and provincial appointments, effectively isolating the Chiaristas and laying the basis for the younger Arias's victory in 1940.

Arnulfo Arias had carefully groomed himself to take over from his older brother. In 1935, Harmodio had given him the ministry of agriculture and public works to collect money from contractors while Arnulfo continued to work at the Santo Tomás Hospital, where he acquired a reputation as a caring doctor. After the 1936 election, Arnulfo held several diplomatic posts in Europe, including minister to Germany and Italy. Critics later detected elements of Hitler's racism and Mussolini's demagoguery in Arnulfo and called him a creole führer. Whatever the case, Arias proved to be an exceptional political leader, personally courageous and a brilliant though not always grammatical public speaker whose rhetoric held crowds in his thrall. At his best while on the attack, Arnulfo displayed a genius in playing the righteous reformer whilst Harmodio provided organizational support, lining up business support and conducting the campaign from his offices in the *Panama-American*. Ricardo Alfaro believed the United States would support him in the following election and returned to Panama in January 1940 to confront the Arias juggernaut. However, the virulence of the attacks against him forced his withdrawal from the race in May, Arnulfo easily winning the July elections, which were the most violent and corrupt yet witnessed in the country.

Arnulfo Arias's accession to the presidency in October 1940 opened a remarkable career in which he ran for the presidency five times, won three times, and was deposed by the National Police or National Guard three times. Over the following years Arnulfo spent two and a half years as president, two years in jail, and fifteen years in exile. The most successful vote winner in Panama over several decades, he was a genuine populist in the mould of Perón, Haya de la Torre and Velasco Ibarra.

Arias's inaugural address in 1940 proclaimed a new era in which native values and traditions would supplant foreign ways under the slogan 'Panama for the Panamanians'. A committee was convened to draft a new constitution which would reflect the intellectual currents of the 1930s, particularly the writings of José Moscote, which stressed nationalism, racial purity and the social responsibility of the state. Arnulfo impatiently suspended the Constitution of 1904, held a plebiscite in December and promulgated the new charter on 2 January 1941, the tenth anniversary of the 1931 coup. The Constitution strengthened the president's office vis-à-vis the assembly, extended his term to six years and contained social policies similar to those of the 1917 Mexican constitution. Women gained the right to vote and hold public office. Most controversially, it defined citizenship so strictly that tens of thousands of immigrants and their children lost rights they had acquired under previous legislation. The principal targets of these clauses were non-whites from the West Indies, Asia and the Middle East. These racist overtones led critics to call the constitution fascist. Other nationalist measures limited foreign ownership of retail commerce and required that a majority of the employees of certain establishments be native Panamanians. The President also hinted that he wished to nationalize utilities, like the U.S.-owned Power and Light Company. On several occasions he forced growers to sell their cattle, rice and sugar to the state. These measures had an unsettling effect on the country, especially in the context of the war, although this was qualified to some degree by the establishment of a social security system, a public savings bank, a land-reform law, community property rights, the Agricultural and Livestock Bank and the Central Bank. Even critics admitted that his nationalism seemed to foster a sense of pride and citizenship.

The autocratic and disciplinarian style of the President provoked criticism of a 'storm of petty rules' that were unenforceable. Schoolchildren and teachers had to wear uniforms. The speaking of Spanish was enforced in public places and bars were fined for playing too much foreign music. A Civic Guard of PNR supporters upheld such regulations and political orthodoxy while Arnulfo opened several official newspapers, censoring those not under his control. He also attempted to gain control of Harmodio's *Panama-American,* which he had been unable to silence. He legalized gambling, which provided considerable graft money, and began deducting PNR dues from government workers' pay. In sum, arbitrary regimentation replaced the toleration and compromise which had prevailed before 1930. One biographer called Arnulfo a 'popular tyrant'.[9]

Arias also created difficulties for the U.S. government. Believing that Germany would win the war, he kept Panama neutral for as long as possible, befriended diplomats from the Axis countries, and made it

---

[9] Conte Porras, *Arnulfo Arias Madrid,* p. 8.

clear that Panama would no longer be the pawn of the Colossus of the North. The police tolerated activity by Axis agents and propagandists while the President declined a public invitation to join the Society of Friends of the United States. He protested against the importation of Jamaican labourers for new canal work and refused to arm vessels flying the Panama flag, despite nearby submarine activity. Finally, he imposed difficult conditions for U.S. leases of defence sites outside the Canal Zone. Although this brash political style and Yankee-baiting met with working-class approval, the middle and upper classes became disturbed, especially since Arnulfo gave every appearance of being mentally unstable. As charges of megalomania and paranoia built up against his brother, Harmodio broke with him and warned U.S. officials that Arnulfistas might endanger canal security.

Arnulfo governed alone and avoided close collaborators. Nevertheless, he depended on justice Minister Ricardo Adolfo de La Guardia (1899–1969) to manage domestic politics and supervise the police. Whether or not de la Guardia was involved in any conspiracy, he must have known of plans for a coup by mid-1941. In October he executed one himself. Arnulfo had flown incognito to Cuba to visit a mistress, and canal officials informed de la Guardia. The unauthorized trip violated Arnulfo's own constitution, so de la Guardia had cause to remove him. He consulted with the chief of civil intelligence in the Canal Zone, confirmed that U.S. authorities would welcome the removal of Arnulfo, and then declared himself president. Arnulfo returned to Panama and was jailed for a week, then flew to Managua and eventually into exile for the duration of the war in Buenos Aires.

De la Guardia immediately improved relations with the United States and declared support for the Allies. The defence-sites agreement was hammered out, and in 1942 the United States signed another accepting a twelve-point Panamanian list of demands as a quid pro quo. Police and intelligence services rounded up some twelve hundred suspected spies, mostly Germans, Japanese and Italians, and sent five hundred to camps in the United States.

De la Guardia co-operated closely with Washington but had no popular support. He was therefore obliged to form a coalition government of the major parties in addition to suspending enforcement of the most illiberal parts of the constitution, but the administration was widely viewed as inept and corrupt. As the war drew to a close, some government and business circles sought to rekindle nationalism while avoiding the chauvinism of the Arnulfistas. The recently formed Asociación de Comerciantes e Industrialistas wished to limit the extent of foreign ownership in the economy. The foreign minister wished to gain control over civil aviation, previously a Canal Zone monopoly, and to eliminate commissary and PX sales to Panamanians. Public pressure arose to reduce the U.S. military presence in Panama and to protect her sovereignty. Cultural leaders began promoting *hispanidad,* or Hispanic values, while the government pushed for implementation of the twelve-point agreement signed in 1942. Although they still tried to maximize the cash flow from the canal, Panamanians increasingly argued in favour of diversifying the economy and industrialization to reduce dependence on the canal.

President de la Guardia faced a difficult transition in late 1944 because the approach of peacetime raised expectations of democratic, constitutional government. Moreover, enough of the quasi-fascist constitution remained in effect to discredit the president. Faced with rising opposition in December, he disbanded the Assembly and suspended the constitution. By shifting power to his cabinet he managed to hang on until June 1945, when he agreed to let the Constituent Assembly elected the previous month appoint a replacement. Don Pancho Arias Paredes, who ran for president in 1932, had seemed the most likely person to replace de la Guardia. During the war he had organized opposition groups into a coalition with his own Partido Renovador, he remained popular and had won the support of the West Indian descendants, now called *criollos.* However, for tactical reasons, Don Pancho and his party supported Enrique A. Jiménez (1888–1970) for interim president in June 1945. Jiménez, nicknamed '*el submarino*' for his ability to torpedo opponents and surface at the right moment, ended up serving until October 1948 since Don Pancho died before elections could be scheduled.

One of Jiménez's first problems was Arnulfo Arias, who had turned his exile to advantage and had grown more popular. In order to undercut this, Jiménez authorized his return from Buenos Aires in October 1945, but Arnulfo immediately took the offensive, claiming to be the rightful president and conspiring to overthrow Jiménez. Such a response proved misguided: an uprising in December 1945 collapsed and as a result of the death of a policeman in it Arnulfo was imprisoned for most of 1946. Meanwhile, the constitutional convention produced a new charter that included progressive social and labour provisions, banned discrimination of all kinds and limited the presidential term to four years (as it had been before the Constitution of 1941).

Relations with the United States became acrimonious after 1945. In 1947 the Jiménez administration negotiated an agreement for the maintenance of the remaining U.S. bases in Panama, but the assembly, responding to demonstrations in the streets, rejected it. There were further difficult exchanges over the construction of Tocumen international airport, the building of highways to Colombia and Costa Rica, and labour relations in the Zone. All these factors contributed to making the rejection of the 1947 treaty a decidedly low point in Panama–United States relations. Internally, however, Jiménez reaped benefit from the establishment of a free trade zone in Colón and efforts to diversify the economy.

The 1940s saw students gain a greater voice in educational policy and national affairs. The Federación de Estudiantes Panameños (FEP) organized congresses and demonstrations and soon formed a network linking secondary and college students. FEP played a major part in the campaign against the 1947 treaty and became a potent element in later foreign-policy disputes. Labour federations also tried to intervene in the post-war dialogue. The Federación Sindical de Trabajadores (FST) was founded in 1946, as was Local 713 by the Canal Zone employees, in an effort to protect workers from the economic dislocations caused by the end of the war. The canal, for example, reduced its payroll sharply and curtailed construction, especially after 1947.

The National Police consolidated its role as arbiter of civilian politics in the 1940s, and its chief – José Antonio Remón – grew wealthy through dealings with politicians and businessmen. The force had fewer than two thousand men, but its cavalry, motorized divisions and modern crowd-control techniques made it efficient in most situations. Since 1941 Remón had recruited middle-class officers like himself, and in 1948 he created a training school with the aim of giving the police a true military capability without posing a threat to the Canal Zone. The force was deployed in the 1948 presidential elections – the first since 1940 – to great political effect. Arnulfo Arias, who had begun campaigning as soon as he was released from jail, made nationalism the central plank in his platform. His opposition to the 1947 defence agreement with Washington boosted his popularity despite the autocratic and racist image of his 1940–1 administration. Jiménez, meanwhile, designated Domingo Díaz Arosemena (1875–1949) as official candidate. Government intervention in the campaign created a climate as tense as that of 1940, the police, in particular, becoming increasingly unpopular. Off-duty officers and hired toughs formed pro-Díaz gangs called *pie de guerra* (war-footing) to intimidate the opposition. The National

Assembly tried to remove Jiménez, who only stayed in office due to
Remón's support, and when the government-controlled election board declared Domingo Díaz the winner, the discontent, fanned by Panameñista
newspapers, erupted in the streets. Arias himself moved to Costa Rica to
organize a revolution. The political elite, traditionally able to do business
without violence, had become badly divided.

Díaz served only ten months before being killed by a heart attack. His
major accomplishment was an air transport convention with the United
States, whereby commercial flights would use the new Tocumen airport
instead of Zone fields. The agreement temporarily improved relations
with the United States but provided more ammunition for government
opponents. Protests and police repression became endemic, and the Arias
brothers attempted yet another coup. From late July to November 1949
the country experienced great instability under interim presidents Daniel
Chanis (who failed to force Remón's resignation) and Roberto Chiari,
Remón's cousin and son of the former president, who was installed by
Remón and removed after a week by the Supreme Court. Remón, indisput-
able king-maker but a villain in the eyes of most of the public and
politicians, then surprised the nation by installing Arnulfo Arias in the
presidency. Remón and the Arias brothers had been enemies since the
mid-1930s, but the police chief realized that public opinion would not be
satisfied until Arnulfo got a chance to prove – or disgrace – himself in the
presidency. He therefore had the electoral board reverse its findings and
declare Arnulfo president. In return, Arias agreed to retain Remón and
augment his budget.

Arnulfo Arias's second presidency was characterized as one of 'irresponsi-
bility, pillage, and privilege'.[10] Nepotism flourished as the President
appointed relatives to government positions. Having no children of his
own, he showed favouritism towards Harmodio's sons while party bosses
were rewarded with contracts and cash, and associates' smuggling operations, worth millions of dollars in narcotics and gold, were given protection. Determined to make up for lost time, he barely tried to disguise
these activities, obliging bank managers to approve his personal loans and
forcing his political enemies to sell property at prices below market. He
himself took over Arco Iris, the country's largest coffee plantation. Graft
among officials reached unprecedented levels, while public finances became chaotic. Arias's relationship with Remón remained unstable, and

---

[10] Pippin, *The Remón Era*, p. 64.

although he was careful not to offend the chief nor to threaten him openly, he made the two-hundred-man Secret Police answerable to himself.

The U.S. government withheld recognition from Arias for several weeks to signal displeasure with his accession. No substantial aid programmes were signed during his term. The worst blow was the canal reorganization of 1951, when, after several years of close scrutiny of the operation of the canal, the U.S. government decided to cut costs, which in turn meant fewer expenditures in Panama. The consequences of the changes were that Panama faced rising unemployment and severe financial problems, which only exacerbated political troubles.

In early 1951 Arnulfo became increasingly isolated and autocratic, confirming the view of his critics that he was unsuited to democratic politics. His arbitrary acts, confiscation of property, partisanship and censorship eroded his popularity. After a bid for support from the West Indian community in 1948, he reinstituted measures that threatened their citizenship. A collaborator believed he had a mental illness which caused him to alternate between reasonable behaviour and violent paranoia. Harmodio and his son, newspaper editor Roberto ('Tito'), had long since turned against Arnulfo. In May 1951, Arias told the cabinet that he would resurrect the 1941 constitution and, if necessary, disband the National Assembly. These announcements provoked wide-spread protest, to which Arnulfo responded that he needed more time and authority to combat communism. Remón began to think about running for president, spurred by his talented and ambitious wife, Cecilia, and by pressure to 'do something' about Arnulfo. On 10 May 1951, following a congressional impeachment of Arnulfo, the police recognized Alcibíades Arosemena (1883–1958) as president in line with the constitutional stipulations for succession. Arnulfo and about five hundred supporters refused to leave the palace, and two officers who tried to approach Arias were killed by point-blank pistol fire. Police then attacked the palace, resulting in nine dead and scores wounded. Arnulfo was stripped of his political rights by the Assembly and spent a year in jail awaiting trial for the murder of the commander of the palace guard.

Arosemena depended entirely upon Remón, who made decisions and appointments behind the scenes in the midst of an economic recession that left businesses ruined and thousands unemployed. The State Department granted some aid to alleviate conditions, but it did not off-set the impact of the canal reorganization. Political strikes and demonstrations occurred almost weekly.

Remón, perhaps the only person capable of maintaining order and extracting more money from the United States, had become the sole viable candidate for president, despite the fact no police commandant had previously run for office. Remón's forebears had settled in rural Panama in the early nineteenth century. In 1914 his father died of alcoholism (an affliction he himself would suffer), his mother making financial sacrifices to send him to the National Institute in Panama City and later to the Military Academy of Mexico. There he graduated third in his class in 1931 and returned home as a lieutenant to run foul of the AC leaders, who forced his resignation in 1935. He only got his commission back under de la Guardia. His marriage to Cecilia ('Ceci') Pinel did not initially prove fruitful as they were unhappy and childless, but later her ambition fuelled his political career.

The strongest opposition to Remón's 1952 election bid came from Harmodio Arias and the students, while the police provided his most valuable support. Remón was unpopular because of his repression of students and torture of prisoners since becoming police chief in 1947. He had little personal charm and was physically unattractive. The police were known to skim millions of dollars from deals while he himself had financial interests in cattle, the abattoir, bus lines, gasoline wholesaling, a construction company, narcotics and the daily *La Nación*. He was connected through family or business with about a quarter of Panama's elite. Doña Cecilia emulated Evita Perón and tried to give Remón some of Perón's appeal. An energetic campaigner, she travelled throughout the country by jeep distributing pots and pans and medical supplies under her social-assistance programme. She became known as the *dama de la bondad,* or Lady Bountiful, and deserved much credit for Remón's election.

Remón struck deals with leaders of five parties to create the Coalición Nacional Patriótica (CPN). Resigning as chief of police so as to be eligible for election, he established good relations with leaders of the West Indian community. Coached by his wife, he travelled through the country conducting a diligent campaign on a platform that promised restoration of internal order, economic development, better relations with the United States and access by all citizens, especially in rural areas, to government services. His slogan was 'peace, work and bread'. The opposition to Remón did not stand much of a chance in the 1952 election. Arnulfo tried to gain some leverage but overreached himself and eventually ordered his followers to boycott the contest. The opposition gravitated to Roberto Chiari, who had been briefly installed as president by Remón in 1949.

Underfinanced and running a negative campaign, Chiari merely legitimized Remón's victory. Following a quiet election, the electoral board
awarded Remón 63 per cent of the votes.

Remón led a vigorous administration, helped by the fact that his
brother presided over a pro-government majority in the assembly. Economic reforms were introduced to reduce Panama's dependence on the
canal and traditional lines of commerce, and the tax system was reorganized to reduce the budget deficit. Commercial agriculture flourished as a
result of increased purchases by the Zone while the president's ambitious
highway and public-works programme absorbed some of the canal's unemployed. Remón reduced the fragmentation of parties by requiring 45,000
signatures for legal recognition. His own CPN was the principal beneficiary while many splinter groups and even Arnulfo's party were disqualified. He effectively prohibited strikes, outlawed radical groups, jailed
Communists and imposed a 'voluntary' censorship on the press. At the
same time, the judiciary was weakened through political appointments
and intimidation. These changes created a quasi-dictatorship not unlike
that of Remón's fellow strongman Anastasio Somoza in Nicaragua. In
1953 Remón converted the police into the National Guard, a change he
had long advocated. Still less than a regular army, the Guard now gained
long-coveted paramilitary responsibilities and benefits. Its repressive powers and prestige abroad were enhanced as Panama now qualified for military aid from the United States and could participate in joint manoeuvres
with neighbouring countries. Remón recruited lower-middle-class blacks
and mestizos to the officer corps in a policy that would bear fruit years
later.

Remón was quick to press for a review of U.S.-Panamanian relations
and succeeded in getting an audience with President Eisenhower in September 1953. After sixteen months of negotiations, accompanied by public demonstrations in Panama, a new treaty was signed in January 1955.
The principal concessions secured were an increase in the canal annuity to
$1.93 million, the restriction of commissary sales to U.S. canal and
service personnel, the transfer to Panama of sales to ships and equal pay for
employees in the same grade regardless of nationality. The major beneficiaries of these new terms were the Panamanian treasury and local entrepeneurs. Remón's technique of pressuring the United States was just as
important as the treaty itself. On 15 March the president began a speech
calling for deep changes in canal operations with the ringing slogan 'Neither charity nor millions: we want justice'! And on 27 August he

convoked the citizenry to a huge rally called an 'appointment with the fatherland'. Nevertheless, veteran statesmen like Harmodio Arias, Octavio Fábrega and Ricardo Alfaro were hostile to Remón's willingness to come to terms with Washington and accept much less than they proposed.

Remón was assassinated on 2 January 1955, only weeks before the treaty was signed. His shocking gangland-style execution has yet to be clarified fully, but subsequent investigations revealed a bizzare and sordid story involving the President, his wife, political associates and rivals, international drug-smugglers and hired gunmen. It tarnished the generally favourable image Remón had achieved and ended CPN leaders' plans to remain in power indefinitely. If, as a historian of this era concludes, Remón was 'in part, responsible for own his untimely death', he still deserved credit for many accomplishments in his unfinished presidential term.[11]

After Remón's death the CPN managed to elect businessman Ernesto de la Guardia for the 1956–60 term. However, the scandals aired in the assassination trials so damaged the coalition that it broke up before the 1960 election. Moreover, Egyptian nationalization of the Suez Canal in 1956 made the concessions just won from the United States seem paltry, public disappointment being inflamed by politicians. As one U.S. official wrote, 'high Panamanian officials were stating publicly that the agreements did not satisfy Panama's aspirations and a deliberate campaign was launched to expand, by unilateral interpretation, many of the concessions'.[12]

De la Guardia's election campaign featured the slogan 'Bread and liberty'! but proved uninspiring, and his administration began with unpopular attempts to increases tax revenue. Plagued with numerous strikes and demonstrations, de la Guardia tried to alleviate social tensions with the appointment of Doña Ceci as Minister of Labour, Health and Welfare. He undertook a school-construction programme to keep up with Panama's exploding population, which passed the million mark in 1960, and created the Instituto de Vivienda y Urbanismo to resettle thousands of families forced to leave the Zone. De la Guardia attempted to promote industrialization, but foreign investors remained shy; the only major new project was a Standard Oil refinery at Colón.

Aquilino Boyd, the Foreign Minister, meanwhile demanded from the

[11] *The Remón Era*, p. 161.
[12] November 1956 report in Eisenhower Library, document 1984–1865, *Declassified Documents Quarterly Catalogue* (Washington, D.C., 1975).

United States a percentage of canal tolls to replace the annuity, as well as reversion of mineral rights, territorial waters of twelve miles, and display of the Panamanian flag in the Zone. Although this led to his removal, public sentiment was now clearly in favour of demands for Panama to receive greater benefits from the canal.

Panama had apparently become a nation-state in the period since 1930. Its territory was now secure from encroachments by neighbours and the Zone. Since the United States no longer sent troops into the country the National Guard held a monopoly on the means of physical coercion. The great majority of Panamanians shared a common language and culture, and recognized their government as the legitimate authority, which upheld a uniform set of laws throughout the territory. The major question remaining with regard to nationhood was the Panamanians' belief in it. As long as the Canal Zone existed, they did not feel sovereign. Panamanians viewed it as a violation of their territory. Despite the perpetuity enshrined in the Convention of 1903 they regarded the Zone as theirs and only assigned temporarily to the United States. The fourteen military bases intimidated as well as ultimately defended them. The descendants of West Indians and other immigrant groups living in the Canal Zone were not wholly incorporated into society since many spoke English, worshipped in Protestant churches, and were believed to owe more loyalty to the United States than to Panama.

COMING TO TERMS WITH THE UNITED STATES, 1959–81

The year 1959 marked a turning point in the history of Panama. There were three insurgencies, including an unsuccessful invasion by Tito Arias, Harmodio's son, with Cuban support; the poor and unemployed of Colón staged a hunger march to dramatize depressed conditions in the nation's second city; and in November student protesters twice surged into the Zone to raise a Panamanian flag as a symbol of their country's sovereignty and there followed one of the worst explosions of anti-American violence in Panama's history. Henceforth, Panama's leaders could no longer take civil obedience for granted.

The Eisenhower admininstration attempted to improve U.S.–Panamanian relations in 1960 by announcing a nine-point program to benefit employees of the canal, appointing new officials, placing responsibility for U.S. policy clearly in the hands of the ambassador, and permitting the display of a Panamanian flag in the Zone. Washington approved grants and loans to Panama of some $11 million for road construction and budget support while the National Security Council recommended the construction within twenty years of a sea-level canal which would require the government 'to maintain our interests in the Canal Zone and . . . prepare Panama for responsible cooperation in preparation for and subsequent operation of a sea-level canal'. The stage was set for a new era of Panamanian politics and relations with the United States.

In the elections of 1960, which were boycotted by the Arnulfistas, the opposition candidate Roberto Chiari won the presidency with a promise to carry out social and economic reforms that would forestall revolution. Chiari's slogan, 'It's time for a change', suggested that the oligarchy was sufficiently worried about civil unrest to make economic overtures to the middle and lower classes. Anti-American riots in 1958 and 1959, though less serious than those to come in 1964, hurt business and threatened general insurgency. Chiari's goals, therefore, closely paralleled those of the Alliance for Progress, unveiled in 1961.

With aid from the United States, Chiari began a major construction programme. He completed a modern hospital for the Social Security Administration, inaugurated the Bridge of the Americas across the canal, and created a short-wave communications system for rural towns. Nevertheless, tension mounted, as banana-workers went on strike, students closed the university and peasant leagues began to form. In June 1962, Chiari met President Kennedy to request further concessions. Kennedy appointed a new Zone governor, accelerated studies for a sea-level canal, and made various changes not requiring treaty action. A high-level U.S. task force fed suggestions to a binational commission established to improve relations. However, a revision of the treaties was postponed until after presidential elections in both countries and in mid-1963 relations soured due to slow progress and Chiari's belief that the test-ban treaty of that year would prevent excavation of a sea-level canal by nuclear blasts. Chiari called home his negotiators, and the discouraged U.S. ambassador resigned.

On 9 January 1964 violent riots broke out, lasting several days and costing at least twenty-two lives. President Chiari protested at the fighting, which began when Zone students raised the U.S. flag in an unauthorized site and prevented Panamanians from raising theirs, and broke relations with Washington. This was the first foreign crisis to confront U.S. President Lyndon Johnson, who did not even have an ambassador in

Panama. After an OAS investigation and some posturing by leaders in both countries, Chiari and Johnson restored relations and agreed to negotiate every aspect of the canal, a tacit commitment to replace the 1903 treaty.

Chiari backed his long-time associate and relative Marco Robles in the 1964 presidential elections. A middle-class figure with a tough reputation, Robles promised 'Reforms now,' criticized the United States, and pledged himself to negotiate the replacement of the 1903 treaty. Arnulfo Arias, meanwhile, campaigned under his customary nationalist banner but now assumed a more conciliatory stance towards the United States, concentrating attacks on the oligarchy. Many West Indian descendants whom he had disfranchised in 1941 now voted for Arnulfo to prove their patriotism. As a result, he probably won the election, but the official tally gave Robles victory by ten thousand votes.

Robles renewed treaty talks with the U.S. government, which disbursed unprecedented amounts of aid, increasing the level after the June 1966 riots in Colón in protest at the killing of a student leader. A wide range of public works projects kept employment up and provided schools and housing for the poor. Although Robles inaugurated a new highway from the capital to the Costa Rican border and a hydroelectric dam in Veraguas, land and tax reform never got off the ground because the president remained beholden to the wealthy families that would be most affected.

The canal negotiations from late 1964 produced in June 1967 three interlinked treaties to replace the 1903 convention. The first, covering the lock canal, recognized Panama's sovereignty in the territory but extended U.S. operation until 1999. Management would be provided by a binational commission, and Panama would share directly in toll revenues. Most services in the canal area would be administered jointly by the two countries. The second treaty gave the United States the option to build and jointly operate a sea-level canal, whereupon the lock canal would pass to Panamanian ownership. The third authorized the continuation of U.S. bases in Panama.

The approach of presidential elections in both countries politicized the ratification and caused the treaties to be shelved. Robles's foreign minister, Fernando Eleta, had run negotiations in a closed fashion that aroused popular suspicions. Leaders of Panamanian unions in the canal feared that their wages and working conditions would deteriorate under the co-management scheme. Nationalists and students wanted an immediate end to U.S. occupation. Arnulfo Arias questioned the value of the treaties without, however, criticizing the United States. When, in late 1967, Robles realized he did not have enough votes to ratify the treaties, he informed the State Department, which then withdrew them from consideration and shut down most aid programmes. The tabled treaties were not a major issue in the 1968 election, since neither candidate embraced them.

Robles' coalition split over the succession, and he immediately became a lame duck. He had announced in September that he would back his finance minister, David Samudio, for president. Samudio, a technocrat trained in the United States, did not belong to the old families, and his tax proposals brought instant opposition from Chiari and most of the oligarchy. Moreover, the president could give Samudio little support since he himself was impeached by the assembly in February 1968 and was only saved from deposition by National Guard commander Bolívar Vallarino.

The older families (Arias, Guardia, de la Guardia, Arosemena, Chiari, Boyd, Vallarino) had made their money in oligopolistic industries like publishing, sugar-refining, cattle, cement, brewing and staple commodities, as well as from law, importing and wholesaling firms. They had protected their interests through government contacts and friendly ties with Canal Zone officials. Now faced with an untrustworthy group in power and great insecurity regarding future arrangements with the United States, they decided to drop their traditional opposition to Arias on the assumption that, mellowed by his sixty-seven years and by denial of public office, he could readily be controlled and used. Moreover, Arnulfo commanded the single largest party in the country, as a result of the reverence in which he was held by the masses. Mounting a wide coalition that included many Chiaristas, the West Indian community, elements of the National Guard and most of the assembly deputies, Arias received 55 percent of the vote in the 1968 election.

The unusual electoral coalitions of 1968 revealed a certain desperation in the struggle for power. If the pre-1931 period saw rivalries among the major families, and the 1931–59 era witnessed incursions by newcomers (the Arias brothers and Remón), the 1968 election contained even more complex equations. The Guard remained a principal arbiter yet no longer acted with a single will. The bureaucracy was in the hands of figures like Robles, Samudio and Eleta, who had arrived recently on the political scene and whose fortunes came from management of public moneys. If they had been able to hold on to power, they could have pushed through the treaties and reaped vast financial rewards. The reforms they promoted in line with the Alliance for Progress suggested that they did not respect the interests of the old families and their businesses. The reformist elements of Samudio's 1968 platform convinced the oligarchy that he was not to be trusted with power.

The election did not settle the political climate, however, provoking accusations of fraud, fights in the streets and conspiracies in barracks. The most ominous development was the politicization of Guard officers. Although Vallarino had declined an invitation from Chiari to run for president and had done his best to stay out of the contest, he had not been able to prevent junior officers from election activity. Initially primed to support Robles's candidate, many were angered when asked to remain neutral or shift to Arnulfo, their traditional enemy. Remón had always kept political activity to a few top colleagues, but in the 1960s it had spread through the middle ranks, a result of growing professionalization, according to one analyst. In September top officers struck a deal with Arnulfo. The president-elect demanded that Vallarino retire after the 1 October inaugural, and the latter agreed on the condition that his deputy, José Manuel Pinilla Fábrega, assume command and that the hierarchy remain intact. Vallarino, who could receive a civilian post in the government, hoped that this deal would deter politicization of the Guard, which could then protect him and the oligarchy. However, Arnulfo decided that an unreconstructed hierarchy would not allow him to govern, and on 4 October he announced the removal of both Vallarino and Pinilla. Many senior officers were to be moved out of the capital or sent to foreign posts, because of their pro-Samudio activities during and after the election. This caused the Guard to depose Arnulfo on 11 October, the coup leaders first asking the vice-president to assume office, and then, when he refused, establishing a junta headed by Colonel Pinilla (Vallarino had withdrawn from service several days before). U.S. authorities immediately voiced their opposition to the coup; they gave Arias and his cabinet temporary asylum in the Zone and later arranged for exile in Florida. The United States only recognized the Junta in November.

The Junta appointed a youthful but conservative cabinet that had ties with many political camps and issued a very bland statement of goals, although officials who had supported Arnulfo were retired. Yet, within several days, two forceful officers who had risked the most in the coup, Lieutenant Colonel Omar Torrijos and Major Boris Martínez, emerged as true leaders of the new government. Torrijos had seniority, having joined the Guard in 1952, and more experience in civilian affairs than most officers. He assumed leadership naturally because of the roles he had played from the 1950s in the commandant's office, civic action programme and counter-insurgency operations. He was well known, popular for his easy, flexible manner and regarded as the 'least military' among top officials. Seeing that it would be difficult to win the support of the oligarchs, Torrijos began contacting non-elite civic groups that might lend their support to the military. Martínez was a more forceful, daring figure who had captured the city of David during the coup, but his scanty political skills relegated him to second spot. By December 1968, Torrijos had consolidated his position as commander-in-chief of the Guard, and two months later he sent Martínez into exile.

Born in the province of Veraguas in 1929, Torrijos belonged to a generation of Panamanian leaders that had experienced neither independence or the 1931 coup. His father was a teacher, and he himself had attended the Santiago Normal School, the most important centre of student nationalism in the interior. When he was a boy of ten, accompanying his mother to Panama City, he saw her pushed around by U.S. policemen while crossing the Zone by bus. He later said that convinced him Panama had to take back the Zone. In 1947 he won a scholarship to attend the military academy in El Salvador, where he graduated in 1952. As an officer he was once turned away from the Union Club in Panama City, and afterwards he refused to set foot in it, ordering his officers to do the same; beneath the easygoing, small-town demeanour lay strong anti-American and anti-oligarchic sentiments.

Torrijos' drive to consolidate power relied on several strategies. Foremost was the use of force against opponents. A number of people were imprisoned and tortured and several died from mistreatment. Unwanted public demonstrations were forcibly dispersed, such terror making it easier to intimidate and exile opponents. Torrijos also utilized modern intelligence techniques to keep track of opponents. Through much of this period his spy unit, G-2, was under the command of Manuel Antonio Noriega, who would eventually succeed him as commander-in-chief. Torrijos also used civic action programmes to create a favourable image of himself, stressing his support for construction projects and concern for the poor with the use of techniques acquired during training tours at Fort Sherman and in a fashion similar to that employed by General Velasco Alvarado in Peru. Torrijos encouraged Guard officers to profit from their positions in government, a tradition started by Remón that lessened the chance of disloyalty within the ranks, over which he kept firm control. Finally, Torrijos expanded the size of the Guard and promoted officers frequently.

The first civilians Torrijos tried to recruit to his side were students, but they rejected his overtures and he closed the university for several months. He then formed a Movimiento Nuevo Panamá, which also failed to catch on. Similarly, his proposal for a single labour federation to support the regime never coalesced. Torrijos did, however, expand his influence over the working class by enacting a highly favourable labor code. (The code was softened in 1976 because of the depressing effect it had on business.) Torrijos's most successful initiative came in rural areas, where he had conducted civic action programmes and could speak to farmers and peasants in familiar terms. There he enjoyed the image of the popular *caudillo,* flying around the country by helicopter to help rural townships and villages. He founded co-operatives, rural schools, clinics and marketing centres as well as releasing public lands for colonization. One of his goals was to stem the tide of migrants to the cities, since by the 1970s over half the country's population lived in Panama and Colón provinces. All the same, his work in rural areas earned him the respect of those who had already settled in urban shanty-towns and a surprising amount of support from rural teachers, who often emerged as local leaders after 1968. By the mid-1970s, Torrijos, familiarly known as 'Omar' or 'El General', enjoyed a charismatic popularity among the rural masses. His friendship with Fidel Castro, Graham Greene and García Márquez added to the mystique.

Torrijos orchestrated a constituent assembly in 1972 by holding elections for representatives from the *corregimientos,* or municipalities. The assembly confirmed Torrijos as head of state, ratifying his appointed figurehead president, Demetrio ('Jimmy') Lakas, and a centrist charter with autocratic overtones. Virtually all delegates were newcomers and in no sense represented the oligarchy, which remained on the margins of power. Parties, disbanded in 1968, remained illegal.

Torrijos's major accomplishment was the signing of two treaties with the United States in September 1977 (finally ratified in April 1978). Based on two of the three 1967 treaty drafts – those relating to the existing canal and defence (the U.S. had dropped the sea-level canal project) – the 1977 treaties recognized full Panamanian sovereignty over the Canal Zone (which therefore ceased to exist) and allowed for joint operation of the canal until 1999, when it would come under exclusive Panamanian control, and joint defence of the canal, with the U.S. retaining primary responsibility until 1999. In the meantime, payments to Panama from tolls and from the annuity were considerably increased.

Another accomplishment of the Torrijos years was diversification of the economy. In 1970 he issued legislation to encourage the establishment of international banks in Panama, with the guarantee of complete secrecy of operations. Panama soon experienced a boom in off-shore banking, which increased capital investment, white-collar employment, and high-rise construction in Panama City. A share of the money flowing through the banks came from South American drug exports to the United States, but Torrijos and his successors protected secret accounts from investigators. The banking industry gave Panama an economic shot in the arm and lessened the country's dependence on the canal.

Other schemes were adopted to diversify the economy and to make Panama an exporter of international services rather than simply a shipping route. The registration of ships under her flag and provision of insurance and other facilities was by now traditional. A petroleum pipeline was laid across western Panama since supertankers carrying Alaskan crude to the East Coast were too big to transit the canal, yet could save money by pumping their cargoes across the isthmus into smaller tankers. The emphasis on services was due in part to the difficulty of expanding commodities exports. Bananas were no longer a growth industry and once-rich fishing grounds had been exhausted. Panama's labour costs were too high to permit marketing tropical products abroad. A promising plan to refine copper at Cerro Colorado in northwestern Panama was abandoned, a victim of falling world prices in the late-1970s. Nevertheless, the diversification was generally successful, Panama dramatically reducing the share of national income derived from the Panama Canal. Services to the Canal Zone as a share of GDP fell from 8.6 per cent in 1950 to 5.8 per cent in 1975. The price, however, was the highest per capita external indebtedness in the world.

After the new canal treaties were signed in 1977 and before the critical debate over U.S. ratification, Torrijos began to withdraw from the front line of politics. He was tired of running the country and managing canal negotiations, and he was drinking too much. Moreover, U.S. negotiators feared that his image as a left-of-centre dictator might hurt their chances of winning Senate ratification. Torrijos therefore created the Partido Democrático Revolucionarió (PRD) to coordinate the various groups and sectors he had co-opted. The party overlapped closely with the bureaucracy and enjoyed generous official sponsorship. Torrijos also designated as new civilian president Aristides Royo, one of his treaty negotiators and a trusted associate. Royo, a debonair former university professor, was fashionably leftist but his authority depended entirely on the personal confidence he enjoyed with Torrijos. The 1979 Panama Canal Act (PL 9670) to implement the canal treaties, known to Panamanians as the Murphy Law after its sponsor, Representative John Murphy, turned out to be a bitter pill to swallow, since it undermined the objective of the negotiators to create a semi-autonomous canal administration independent of the Pentagon and of Congress and left open for negotiation the question of U.S. forces in Panama after 1999. Hence, while the Panamanians had to live with it, they continued to draw attention to the inconsistencies between the treaties and the act.

Torrijo's semi-retirement ended tragically in August 1981, when the small plane in which he was travelling crashed and exploded. Charges of sabotage were not satisfactorily answered. There was no doubt, however, that Panama had lost one of its most forceful and colourful leaders, and that his death brought to a close a critical era in the country's history.

PANAMA SINCE TORRIJOS

With the implementation of the 1977 treaties the canal became much less of a major issue in Panamanian politics. From 1979 it was administered as a bilateral commission, and as the century drew to a close Panama gained increased operational control. Beginning in 1990, the chief executive officer of the canal, called the Administrator, was to be a Panamanian.

After 1981 politics drifted without clear direction. General Noriega, however, soon managed to shoulder aside rivals and gain control of the Guard, called the Panamanian Defence Force after 1983. He made the important decisions and appointments behind the facade of civilian governments. Being president was neither comfortable nor secure. Royo, forced to resign, was substituted by Ricardo de la Espriella, who was in turn driven from office in 1984. While graft continued to enrich the officer corps and undermine public administration Noriega seemed to have no particular programme in mind.

The U.S. government cooled toward Noriega, especially when it was revealed that he was profiting from drug-money laundering, arms sales and intelligence brokering. The State Department went to some lengths to help President Nicolás Ardito Barletta, elected fraudulently over Arnulfo Arias in 1984, pull Panama out of its economic stagnation and thereby win more authority for civilian government. Foreign aid was pumped in and Barletta won applause as a good technocrat, yet his political inability to win over either the oligarchy or PRD elements facilitated his removal after only a year in office when he authorized an investigation of Noriega's role in the brutal killing of Hugo Spadafora, a popular critic of the regime.

In mid-1987, Noriega's imposed peace collapsed, as a series of civilian protests provoked the most serious political crisis in decades. When he tried to retire his second-in-command, Roberto Díaz Herrera, the latter objected and publicly accused Noriega of major crimes, including the execution of Spadafora and rigging the 1984 election. Civilian groups – students, the Chamber of Commerce, the Lions' Club – coalesced around Díaz in a broad opposition movement called the Cruzada Civilista Nacional to force Noriega's removal. For several months they conducted protests and demonstrations, to which Noriega responded with unusual violence. Civil disobedience united the bulk of the population behind the middle-class opposition. The crisis of 1987 revealed the dictatorial nature of the regime and led to a U.S. Senate censure of Noriega, yet the Defence Force remained loyal to its chief. This created an exceptionally awkward situation for the U.S. government, which had to collaborate with Panamanian representatives in managing the canal yet by early 1988 was conducting an open campaign to overthrow the country's government.

After six months of tense stalemate Washington resorted to imposing tight external restrictions on an economy that was peculiarly vulnerable to foreign interference. The seizure of Panamanian assets by the U.S., withholding of canal payments, and refusal to supply dollar notes, upon which the economy is based since the country has no paper currency of its own, immediately closed the strategic banking system and produced a severe crisis. As a result of the government's inability to cover state obligations or pay its employees on a regular basis, opposition spread to the lower classes. However, U.S. expectations of a rapid retreat on Noriega's part proved misguided when he easily overcame a coup attempt and imposed a new puppet president. The U.S. garrison in the Zone was augmented with hundreds of extra troops and fears were expressed for the security of the canal after an alleged invasion by Panamanian forces.

On the other side, Noriega and his supporters denounced U.S. plans for a direct military intervention in the country, which had been requested by the Cruzada Civilista once it became evident that its own protest campaign would not remove the dictator. Its reputation already thoroughly tarnished, the regime had little option but to resort to increasing repression and nationalist rhetoric. The generation of patriotic fervour was certainly predictable and attracted much less authentic popular support than Noriega expected since his removal was now widely viewed as the only means by which a modicum of normality might be restored. However, the government's campaign led to declarations by almost all Latin American governments against U.S. military intervention. It also provided a clear expression of the historic contradiction at the heart of Panamanian national identity engendered by North American control of the canal. Even the most unsavoury and disgraced regime could extract political capital from defending national sovereignty.

When George Bush was elected president in November 1988, Noriega believed his problems with the United States would subside, for he regarded the new president as his ally. As Director of the CIA in the 1970s, Bush had supervised Noriega's intelligence gathering and had met with him again in 1985, apparently in connection with the Iran–Contra dealings. If revealed, these contacts could embarrass the new president. Equally, Noriega could stir up more trouble at the military bases, and U.S. residents constituted a potential hostage population.

Noriega, however, overestimated his power. In Panama's presidential elections of May 1989, Bush supported the opposition candidate Guillermo Endara with some $10 million and teams of observers. When the polling swung in favor of Endara, Noriega had the contest annulled, provoking condemnation from the OAS and the international press. Four months later, when Noriega installed a crony as puppet president, Bush refused to recognize the new regime. (A key element in this decision was the fact that under the 1977 treaty a Panamanian would become Administrator of the canal in January 1990, and Noriega's nominee was unacceptable to the United States.)

Noriega now faced a unified U.S. administration that was committed to remove him by any means available. Emissaries tried to persuade him to step down, but they also encouraged conspiracies among Defence Force commanders and spoke of lifting the ban on assassinating foreign leaders. After a U.S.-sanctioned coup by dissident officers failed in October 1989, the White House ordered plans for a military take-over. Noriega finally provoked the invasion by declaring that a state of war existed with the United States. Some 14,000 assault troops landed in Panama on 20 December 1989 and, in combination with forces stationed there, established military control within days. It was the first uninvited intervention since Panama's independence and the largest U.S. military operation since Vietnam.

After first taking refuge in the Vatican embassy, Noriega finally surrendered to U.S. authorities for arraignment on charges of drug-smuggling, money-laundering and other crimes. The United States installed Endara as president and helped him to re-establish order and restore economic activity. The Endara administration, however, had little legitimacy, and stood to pay a high price in the future for dependence on Washington. Panamanian nationhood remained exceptionally fragile. Indeed, Panama's future as a sovereign nation was left in some doubt.

15

THE PANAMA CANAL ZONE, 1904–79

In the history of twentieth-century Latin America, the Panama Canal – and the Canal Zone – have always possessed a great emblematic significance. The canal runs through the territory of a tiny Hispanic republic dependent from birth on the patronage of the United States, and for seventy-five years its operation was under exclusive U.S. control. Throughout the century the canal has been an outstanding symbol of Washington's power to dominate the weaker states of the hemisphere.

U.S. determination to control the transit across the isthmus of Central America dates from the 1840s, when the Union reached the North American Pacific seaboard. In 1846 a treaty with New Granada (Colombia) gave Washington a right of way across Panama, then a province of Colombia, in exchange for a U.S. guarantee of Colombian sovereignty over the province, and by 1855 the American-owned Panama Railroad was in business. The railway was seen by some as the forerunner of a U.S.-controlled canal, but by the Clayton–Bulwer Treaty of 1850 Britain had insisted on an equal share in any future canal project, and the attractiveness of trans-continental railroads further reduced North American canal promotion. In the event, it was the French who began work on a Panama seaway in the 1880s under de Lesseps, architect of the Suez Canal, although the venture collapsed well short of completion.

In spite of the French débâcle, U.S. pressure for a canal was sustained, most notably by advocates of naval power such as Captain Alfred Mahan and his admirer Theodore Roosevelt, and it was given a huge stimulus by the war with Spain in 1898, when the battleship *Oregon* had to steam from Seattle to Cuba via Cape Horn. Once the war was won, a canal seemed indispensable to link Washington with its newly acquired Pacific dependencies in Hawaii and the Philippines. The United States moved rapidly, first to negotiate the abrogation of the 1850 treaty with Britain and remove the barrier to unilateral American control of the canal, then to decide on Panama rather than Nicaragua as the route to develop. In January 1903 the Roosevelt administration proceeded to sign the Hay–Herrán treaty with Colombia, which granted the United States extensive rights to build and operate a canal through Panama.

When the Colombian Senate held out for better terms and refused to ratify the treaty Roosevelt committed one of the most dubious acts of his presidency, abetting the secession of Panama from Colombia. The Panamanians were fearful that Roosevelt would turn instead to Nicaragua, as was the French canal company, which stood to make $40 million from the sale of its assets. The two came together in a plot to break away from Bogotá, using as their Washington agent Philippe Bunau-Varilla, a former de Lesseps's aide. Bunau-Varilla was given to understand that the United States would back a separatist movement. And U.S. Navy vessels were positioned at the terminal ports of Panama and Colón to prevent Colombian forces from landing to reassert Bogotá's authority after the separatist coup of 3 November 1903 – this in spite of the commitment of 1846 to defend Colombian sovereignty. U.S. intervention made the rebellion irreversible, and Colombia was despoiled of a potentially invaluable possession. 'I took the Isthmus', Roosevelt later boasted; or, in the enigmatic bon mot of Professor Samuel Hayakawa: 'We stole it fair and square.'

Within a fortnight of Panama's declaration of independence, Secretary of State John Hay and Bunau-Varilla signed a new canal convention, which gave the United States even more than the earlier agreement reached with Colombia. In his memoirs Bunau-Varilla claimed responsibility for writing the entire document, though the bulk of the treaty was in fact drafted in the State Department. To make certain of U.S. Senate approval, enormous concessions were stipulated, which placed the United States in charge of everything to do with the canal and which correspondingly shut out Panama from even the semblance of participation previously bestowed on Colombia.

Washington gave a great deal less than it got from the Hay–Bunau-Varilla convention. Panama was to be paid a lump sum of $10 million and an annuity of $250,000 for the rights it conferred, but it surrendered reversionary title to both the canal and the railway, the railway annuity of $250,000 and the right to a percentage of the canal's gross revenues. Nor was it to acquire any land owned by the canal or the railway in the terminal cities. At the same time, Panamanian sovereignty was nowhere acknowledged in the treaty, whereas Colombian sovereignty had been explicitly recognized in the Hay–Herrán accord. The most Hay was prepared to concede was to make Panama an American protectorate through a guarantee of its independence, but even this was intended only as a deterrent to Colombian reconquest.

Panama in return alienated its heartland, and more. A zone ten miles wide running through the centre of the republic was granted in perpetuity for canal purposes, and Bunau-Varilla went still further. Although he succeeded in having the terminal cities taken out of the zone, where Hay had placed them, he made a quite extraordinary donation on Panama's behalf. By Article 3 the United States was to possess nothing less than the rights of sovereignty within the zone and over whatever land outside the zone it requisitioned for the canal. This was to be the bedrock of the U.S. position on the isthmus throughout its tenure. In addition, under Article 7, Bunau-Varilla gave the United States authority to intervene in Panama City and Colón to enforce sanitation measures and to maintain public order. The consequence of Panama's emancipation from Bogotá was, therefore, its vassalage to Washington: meaningful independence did not lie in the foreseeable future.

THE FIRST GENERATION, 1904–29

The Canal Zone which came into being in 1904 was modelled on the complex of concessions, spheres and settlements imposed on China in the nineteenth century. It was a state within a state, and an enclave with only one raison d'être, the efficient working of the waterway which opened to shipping in 1914. As such, it was answerable only to the president of the United States through an administrator who from 1907 was always a senior officer of the U.S. Army Corps of Engineers. This structure prevailed over two alternatives: a civilian authority which would have given a continuous lesson in government to a supposedly benighted hemisphere; and a military command headed by the general of the Zone garrison.

The Zone regime was shot through with paradox. What was in many ways an army reservation was dedicated to the canal as a civil enterprise that served mercantile interests and was highly resistant to the idea that its primary function was strategic. At the same time it stood in stark contrast to the ideals of American capitalist democracy, since no U.S. resident was allowed to vote or own real property under a system powerfully reminiscent of welfare socialism. By the 1920s the Zone had developed into a formidable micro-state, dealing with Panama via a governor who acted like a potentate in his own right, and effectively beyond the reach of his nominal masters in Washington. When the Harding administration sent out a board of enquiry in 1921, most of the reforms it urged were soon shelved and the Zone continued to be managed as before, in the belief that the rule of the Engineers, like the very U.S. presence on the isthmus, was meant to be unending and untrammelled by outside interference.

In one important area the canal authorities were forced to curb their drive for omnipotence. Soon after the treaty went into effect in 1904 the Zone was sealed off from Panama by a high tariff wall, while imports from the United States were let in duty-free. This move stood to devastate the economy of a country heavily dependent for its national revenue on customs receipts, and it was countermanded by Roosevelt, who feared it would engender serious political instability just as canal construction got under way. A compromise arrangement, the so-called Taft Agreement, produced a modus vivendi until the canal opened whereby Panama was to levy duties on certain goods entering the Zone and the tariff barrier was eliminated.

Shortly afterwards, however, the bid to make the Zone commercially self-sufficient was given a sharp boost by the failure of Panamanian merchants to supply food for the canal work force at competitive prices. Within a few years the Railroad Commissary was shipping in not only necessities for canal personnel but also an increasing range of luxury goods, as well as operating a whole cluster of installations inside the zone to meet consumer demand. Panamanian protests were rejected with the blunt response that such measures were justified by the treaty, which did indeed contain language broad enough to let the canal directorate do very much as they pleased.

Nonetheless, the U.S. authorities, above all General Goethals, chairman of the Canal Commission and first governor in 1914, chafed under the Taft Agreement. Goethals was determined to see the agreement abrogated to clear the way for the large-scale development of bonded warehouses at the Atlantic terminal, which would make the canal a magnet for international trade. With the agreement gone, the Zone administration also believed they would be entitled to sell whatever they chose to an unrestricted clientele of Panamanians and tourists as well as employees on the U.S. government payroll. On both counts they ran up against the State Department, anxious for diplomatic reasons to moderate what it saw as the overbearing arrogance of the canal leadership. Although the Taft

Agreement was cancelled in 1924, the purpose was to open negotiations with Panama for a supplementary treaty, not to hand carte blanche to the Zone. Throughout the talks there were repeated clashes with a governor whom the State Department believed despised the Panamanians as 'an inferior race who should be kicked about and told what to do'. Moreover, the State Department upheld Roosevelt's line that the Zone had never been intended as a commercial entrepôt.

The treaty signed in July 1926 reflected a partial retreat. Bonded warehouses were sanctioned and Panama ceded the New Cristóbal quarter of Colón to the Zone, but the canal was forced to accept permanent limitations on its market: in future it could sell only to customers officially connected with the zone. Moreover, a ban was placed on any further private business operations on Zone territory. Although the treaty became a dead letter when Panama refused to ratify it early in 1927, the canal was still not a free agent. The Taft Agreement was maintained informally and Panama thereby protected against the full force of zonal competition.

The social impact of the Zone on the country was no less far-reaching than its commercial influence. The canal introduced an entire new community into Panamanian life in the shape of the work force brought in to build the waterway and operate it once completed. From the outset the force was stratified on two separate levels. Skilled men, paid in gold dollars, fell into the select minority of the Gold Roll, while the semi-skilled and unskilled labourers were assigned to the Silver Roll and waged in silver coin. Virtually all Golds were white North Americans, enjoying a markedly superior standard of living, with tax-free salaries 25 per cent higher than those of their counterparts in the continental United States, holidays with pay, free accommodation, health care and schooling for their children, and access to low-priced merchandise in the Railroad's stores. Few North Americans, white or black, featured among the Silvers, who were predominantly blacks from the British West Indies, mostly from Barbados. The railway engineers who began canal construction would very much have preferred the Chinese coolies they had hired back home, but both the American unions and Panamanian public opinion blocked that option. The West Indians came in in droves and unlike their predecessors who had laboured for the French, they came to stay, settling in enormous ghettos in the terminal cities of Panama and Colón.

The native Panamanians, equipped with neither the skill for Gold status nor the brawn for Silver work, stood outside these categories. A small number were taken on to the Gold Roll as a goodwill gesture and

Panamanians were given nominal equality with North Americans in selection for Gold posts, but while Panamanian governments were no doubt aware of the token nature of this promise, they did not press the point. Panamanians thus remained on the fringe of the conflicts within the labour force which emerged after the canal went into operation.

The Zone administration found itself under constant pressure from its Gold men to maximize their privileges and minimize the opportunities for West Indians to move into positions classifiable as skilled. Thanks to their affiliation to the American Federation of Labor and to the AFL's close liaison with Congress, they had their way. In 1915, for example, an executive order charging rent to the Gold elite was suspended and then revoked the following year. The West Indians, on the other hand, were given short shrift. The canal had not urged their repatriation because it was well aware of the advantages of having a large pool of unemployed on tap in case of need. Black labour was cheap and plentiful, and West Indians lived in appallingly poor circumstances. To add to their problems, local organization was practically non-existent; the large-scale strike eventually mounted in February 1920 was promoted by a black railwaymen's union based in Detroit. It folded within a week, after all strikers resident in the Zone were summarily evicted and decanted into Panama. There was to be no further serious attempt to unionize the West Indian work force for nearly twenty years.

In the wake of the strike fiasco the West Indians suffered yet another set-back. In 1921 a federal board of inquiry into canal operations recommended drastic cost-cutting by an extensive 'silverization' of the work force, that is, the replacement of Golds by Silvers wherever possible. Backed energetically by the boss of the AFL, Samuel Gompers, the Gold lobby easily resisted this proposition. The West Indians were reduced to petitioning the canal authorities for improved pay and conditions and better schooling, but to little effect. In 1927 up to one hundred were permitted to be hired at Gold rates, but nothing was done to tackle their basic grievances. They remained a submerged mass, penalized by hostile Panamanian legislation and utterly reliant on the goodwill of a paternalistic canal regime; at the close of the 1920s they seemed to have no other future.

The third main field where the Zone made its presence unmistakably felt was Panamanian politics. Washington's interest here, of course, was to see Panama provide a stable environment in which the canal could function undisturbed. The new republic, in other words, should forswear the

Latin American tradition of coup and counter-coup and settle down to a life of well-ordered constitutional propriety. To this end overt U.S. pressure in 1904 compelled the resignation of the would-be *caudillo* General Esteban Huertas and the disbandment of the minuscule Panamanian army. Henceforth Panama retained no more than a police force, but as the United States rapidly discovered, this was a doubtful improvement, and it was periodically moved to intervene in Panama's internal affairs throughout the early years of the republic.

The tendency to intervention was greatly heightened by the fact that Panama City and Colón, the chief breeding-grounds of trouble, were geographically if not administratively embedded in the zone, and an upsurge there could have damaging repercussions for the canal. Moreover, whereas the 1846 treaty had never been interpreted as a directive for the United States to arbitrate isthmian political disputes, Washington was now too closely involved with Panama to make a hands-off policy feasible. While the United States successfully ignored the occasional pleas of some Panamanian conservatives for outright U.S. annexation, the Panamanian constitution sanctioned North American intervention throughout the country, and this, together with Article 7 of the canal treaty (allowing U.S. policing of the terminal cities in an emergency) provided justification enough for a protectorate if Washington wished to enforce it.

During the construction decade American guardianship was most obviously on display when it came to elections. But the State Department also kept a tutelary eye on Panamanian public spending. Reports of prodigality by successive presidents led to a deep reluctance to allow Panama to use any of the monies paid out for the canal as collateral for loans, and a veto was clamped on any Panamanian bid to amend the constitution to make this possible. However, attempts to control the national police were a good deal less successful. The terminal cities, the U.S. minister remarked in 1909, reminded him of nothing so much as Deadwood in the saturnalian days of the Black Hills gold rush, and the police reacted violently to North Americans out on the town. After the killing of several U.S. citizens, a U.S. police instructor was appointed, only to be ignored by a police chief given to late-night orgies with local whores. Interventionism, it seemed, would have to move into a higher gear if any lasting impression were to be made on Panama's political establishment.

During the first few years of canal operation, that is to say, immediately after 1914, this always seemed likely. American exasperation mounted fast, and the Zone hierarchy increasingly looked to a military occupation as the only real answer to the spread of corruption and endemic chaos in Panama. But Washington stopped short of imposing its own candidate in the presidential election of 1916 – as the young John Foster Dulles, then assistant to Panama's New York agent, proposed. The man believed more likely to introduce reforms was given tacit approval, but when the expected house-cleaning failed to materialize, the Zone authorities took matters into their own hands. The garrison commander, General Richard Blatchford, was a man with a mission. The United States had brought sanitation to Panama; he would give it moral hygiene. He opened his crusade in May 1918 with an order limiting all off-duty servicemen to the wholesome confines of the Zone. A month later, countering a government bid to postpone the forth-coming National Assembly elections, Article 7 of the 1903 treaty was invoked, triggering a U.S. Army takeover of the terminal cities, which Blatchford was publicly to compare – unfavourably – with Sodom and Go-morrah. The occupation was short-lived, but more fundamental measures were applied to keep Panama on the straight-and-narrow path. At the end of the year the U.S. police instructor appointed in 1917 was given decisive powers, and, following a pattern already set in Washington's other Latin American dependencies, a fiscal adviser was installed to keep tight hold of the Panamanian national purse-strings.

Intervention in the 1920s did not come up to expectations, however. Twice it was provided on Panamanian request: in 1921 to rescue President Porras from a hostile mob; and in 1925 to save President Chiari from the wrath of the tenants of the urban slums. U.S. officials on the spot were intensely interventionist: the governor of the canal did not hesitate to brandish the threat of Article 7 in 1921, and in 1925 the commanding general drafted an elaborate plan for military control. But the State Depart-ment held back, refusing to supervise any more presidential elections and throwing no weight behind either the police instructor or the fiscal ad-viser. The reason often given for this forbearance was the need to keep Panama sweet throughout the treaty negotiations which took up so much of the decade. The result was American impotence to determine the course of events in the republic. Two large loans – $4.5 million in 1923 and $12 million in 1928 – went through unopposed. There were no illusions in Washington as to the use the Panamanian ruling class would make of this bounty, but it was apparently decided to leave them to their own devices.

All involvement in Panamanian affairs was, of course, ancillary to the central purpose of the canal, namely, to move ships, especially the vessels of the U.S. Navy, efficiently across the isthmian divide. The canal gave what was a one-ocean fleet something approaching a two-ocean capability by allowing it to concentrate relatively quickly wherever it might be most needed. As such, it was a national asset of pivotal strategic importance, and although there was a vocal school of thought which argued for the neutralization of the canal in the 1900s, Washington was determined it should be a defended waterway and that its defence should rest exclusively in North American hands.

Defence was to be the task of the army, not the navy. Roosevelt had no wish to see the navy tied down to the chore of coastal protection. Powerful fortifications at the canal terminals would release it for its prime duty: to engage an enemy fleet. They would hold a naval bombardment force at bay, oppose a landing on the isthmus, and cover U.S. warships as they moved through from sea to sea. By 1914, when the canal opened, the batteries were in place, although the garrison to man them was decidedly under strength – an economy measure imposed by Taft on the assumption that reinforcements could be rushed out in an emergency.

Within the scheme of defence worked out as the canal approached completion Panama was expected to be no more than an obedient subordinate. The navy, in control of wireless traffic to and from the Zone, demanded absolute authority over radio in the republic itself, and got it soon after the outbreak of the First World War. At the same time Washington decreed that all Panamanian railway projects must conform to the requirements of canal security. Panama was understandably unhappy about these further inroads on its sovereignty, but it had no choice except to bow to the will of its effective overlord.

The first great test of the canal as a strategic highway arrived with the world war of 1914–18. It did not come through with flying colours. Earth slides in the central cut had been a continual worry, and in the autumn of 1915 they closed the canal for a full year. At a time when war with Japan as well as Germany seemed a distinct possibility, Wilson turned to the alternative of a two-ocean navy which the canal had been designed to make unnecessary. Moreover, as Washington geared itself to enter the war early in 1917, it was evident that the fortress guns so recently installed were already out-ranged by the latest naval armament and that the canal works were highly vulnerable to shelling from the sea.

Within the Zone, meanwhile, a bitter argument raged between the governor, General Goethals, and the garrison commander, General Edwards. Edwards proposed an ambitious road-building programme in Panama to provide long-range ground defence beyond the zonal boundary.

He also envisaged raising two militias, one to consist of the canal work force, the other to be recruited in Panama. Goethals opposed these schemes; he had formulated the existing close-in defence of the canal installations and saw no good reason to scrap it. He was determined that his men not be diverted from the job of canal operation by part-time guard duty, and he refused to put weapons in the hands of West Indian labourers, let alone the excitable Panamanians (whose police he had only just succeeded in disarming). With the departure of Edwards in the spring of 1917 the debate came to nothing, however, and in the short span of U.S. belligerency the canal enjoyed a quiet war. In view of the deficiencies evident since 1914, this was just as well, but the post-war decade brought no improvement. The batteries presented no serious problem: although they were undoubtedly obsolete, a fleet bombardment was seen as an increasingly remote contingency. But another threat at once moved in to replace it. Three fleet exercises in the 1920s showed how easily carrier planes could penetrate rudimentary anti-aircraft defences, and air attack became the Zone's first preoccupation. Another defect lay in the width of the locks. Although Germany had widened the lock chambers of the Kiel Canal to 147 feet before the war, the locks at Panama were only 110 feet across, and by 1919 the beam of new battleships and carriers had to be narrowed in consequence. The ten-year suspension of capital-ship construction under the Washington naval disarmament treaty of 1922 postponed the need for a decision on bigger lock capacity but did not eliminate it, and the canal had reached the limit of its potential to carry the largest warships afloat.

The eclipse of the waterway by the speed of technological innovation made remarkably little impact in some quarters. In November 1918 four-fifths of the island of Taboga was demanded for fortifications to repel the seaborne onslaught that now appeared so unlikely. In the treaty negotiations with Panama, the army and navy insisted on a degree of control over civil aviation and radio broadcasting in the republic, which was completely at odds with the rapid developments taking place in both fields. In short, Panama was still being ordered about in the manner of the era of the big-stick, and it compounded its own subjection by volunteering to place its territory unreservedly at Washington's disposal in wartime. Even the seemingly all-embracing stipulations of 1903 had been surpassed. But the treaty was rejected by Panama, on this and other grounds. As the first generation of the U.S.-Panama relationship drew to a close, it was a portent of changes to come in the second.

THE SECOND GENERATION, 1930–55

In a period dominated by the onset of the Second World War and the prospect of a third, the defence of the canal stood even higher in the Zone's order of priorities. During the 1930s concern over security mounted in direct ratio to the rising challenge of Germany and Japan. In the spring of 1934, army intelligence reports of a Japanese plot to sabotage the canal after the transfer of the fleet into the Atlantic led to a plan for elaborate counter-measures, including ship inspection and transit guards. Japan's denunciation of the naval disarmament treaties in December 1934 prompted legislation for a third, bigger set of locks to be placed at the exclusive disposal of the navy. An air-defence network starved of funds for most of the decade finally received vital support with Roosevelt's expansion of the army air corps in the wake of Hitler's triumph at Munich in September 1938.

Defence issues were also at the heart of renewed negotiations for a treaty, in which the service departments became convinced that Roosevelt and Under Secretary of State Sumner Welles were betraying American interests in the name of appeasement. Under Article 2 of the final draft signed in March 1936, Washington surrendered the right to take land outside the Zone on demand; under Article 10, the United States was bound to consult Panama in the event of an international crisis touching the waterway. Inroads were made into the navy's hitherto absolute control of Panamanian radio and there was no formal agreement to allow army manoeuvres on Panama's territory. As a result the treaty was delayed in the Senate for more than three years until satisfactory assurances were extracted from Panama on the consultation clause and manoeuvres. The treaty then went through in July 1939, just weeks before the outbreak of war in Europe.

The canal entered the war in a vulnerable state. The anti-sabotage scheme went into immediate effect but there was no tightly meshed air-defence screen. Moreover, Panama was not the co-operative partner Roosevelt had expected it to be. When talks opened for the acquisition of bases in the republic, the regime of President Arnulfo Arias proved a singularly hard bargainer on the salient issues of tenure, payment and jurisdiction. Even after his sudden removal in October 1941, Arias' successors showed themselves almost equally determined to extract expensive concessions from Uncle Sam. The bases agreement of May 1942 was accompanied by a package of largesse which Welles had earlier denounced as blackmail but which he now accepted as the necessary price of a deal. It was clinched at a time when U.S. fears for the canal's safety were at their peak. However, the anticipated Japanese carrier strike did not materialize, and with the navy's triumph at Midway soon afterwards the nightmare of a second Pearl Harbor faded from view.

During the war the canal's continuous availability as a short-cut between Atlantic and Pacific was a priceless benefit. Yet the war also threw its long-term strategic significance into question. In the summer of 1940 Congress funded a two-ocean navy which, once built, was bound to diminish the old importance of the canal as an instrument for making the most of a one-ocean fleet. There was a further ominous development in May 1942 when work on the third locks was halted for the duration because of the decision to suspend construction of the 60,000-ton *Montana*-class leviathans for which they had been designed. Thereafter, the re-fit of battleships with anti-torpedo blisters made it impossible for them to pass through the existing lock chambers, and even the third locks could not have accommodated the *Midway*-class fleet carriers now on the stocks.

The advent of the atomic bomb in 1945 destroyed the standing of the canal as a national asset of the first rank. So, too, did the change in Washington's international circumstances. The United States now held world responsibilities, and the shift in the main focus of its attention to Europe and the Middle East placed the canal in a radically altered perspective. It had been built to serve the purposes of a regional power with relatively limited military resources. Those days were done, and the waterway increasingly began to seem the relic of a bygone age.

There were some who believed the canal could recapture its cardinal role, provided it were modernized. Three options lay open: an enlarged version of the third-locks development; a symmetrical revision of the lock canal with a triple lift and a terminal lake at either end; and a sea-level canal which dispensed with lift locks altogether. The second of these alternatives was the brain-child of Captain Miles DuVal, USN, while Governor Joseph Mehaffey was committed to the seaway, largely on the grounds of its superior capacity to withstand nuclear attack. In the summer of 1947 the Governor reported in favour of a sea-level project and his findings were endorsed by a majority of the General Board of the Navy.

The sea-level scheme was torpedoed, however, partly by Panama's refusal in December 1947 to lease bases in the republic for long-range canal defence. A wrangle over the future of the wartime bases in Panama had been in process since late 1945, with Panama calling for U.S. evacuation one year after the Japanese surrender, that is, by September 1946. The commanding general in the Zone was at first insistent that the entire wartime defence network be retained even though no Russian penetration was reckoned possible before 1957. He then came round to the view that a more modest set of installations would be acceptable if a sea-level canal were built, since this would have inherent passive defence qualities. Although Panama eventually accepted these reduced demands, the Panamanian National Assembly voted unanimously to reject them and U.S. forces withdrew into the Zone. The Pentagon, although publicly regretful, privately welcomed the defeat of the bases agreement as a blessing in disguise. The protection of the canal, once considered paramount, had by this time dropped well down America's scale of priorities, and during negotiations for a new treaty with Panama in 1953 and 1954 defence issues were marginal. The canal was certainly a valuable logistical artery in any crisis – as the Korean War proved – but it could no longer be seen as the crux of American national security.

Washington kept its involvement in Panamanian politics to a minimum throughout most of this period from the 1930s to the mid-1950s. When the Acción Comunal movement toppled President Florencio Arosemena in January 1931 the Zone authorities sat tight. Once Franklin Roosevelt had abrogated the Platt Amendment in 1934, the formal protectorate of Panama under the 1903 convention became untenable. It was ended by the new treaty signed in 1936 under the Good Neighbor policy whereby Roosevelt dropped his namesake's claim to act as patrolman of the hemisphere and preached instead an inter-American system based on fellow-feeling and mutual trust. The U.S. Army, however, had other ideas on how best to preserve political stability on the isthmus. Highly alarmed by what it saw as the commander-in-chief's loss of grip, it drafted its own secret plan for a military occupation of Panama.[1] Periodically updated, this lay in reserve for future use, an abiding refutation of good neighbourliness and everything it stood for.

The kind of emergency envisaged by the army began to brew from October 1940 on, with the inauguration of the nationalist president Arnulfo Arias, who was tempted into cumulative defiance of U.S. wishes by the expectation of an Axis victory after the spectacular German successes of 1940–1. Washington was, of course, suspected of mastermind-

---

[1] U.S. National Archives (USNA), Washington, D.C. Record Group 407, Adjutant General's Office, Registered Documents, 309 F. The Panama Plan, edition of 7 July 1947.

ing the coup which deposed him in October 1941. There is no evidence to support the charge, but the chief of Zone intelligence, Captain Leo McIntire, was apparently in close touch with the conspirators throughout, and certainly dissuaded Arias from attempting a comeback. For the remainder of the war the United States was guaranteed a docile ally in President Ricardo Adolfo de la Guardia. The Panamanian police, for their part, were now the decisive force in the country's politics, a commanding position which they were henceforth to retain and which suited Washington well enough. Thereafter whenever a crisis erupted the United States preserved a strict non-interventionism. In 1948, for example, it maintained a studied neutrality as the government rigged the election to make certain of Arnulfo Arias' defeat. In November 1949 it stood back while José Remón, the chief of police, first dismissed President Daniel Chanis and then installed Arias. Eighteen months later it watched from the sidelines as Arias revoked the constitution and then resigned in the face of a general strike and the siege of the presidential palace.

There was a consistency in U.S. policy which was presented for public consumption as exemplary self-restraint when in truth it amounted to a willingness to live with any Panamanian leader – even the bête noire Arnulfo Arias – provided he did not attack U.S. interests and cracked down hard on any hint of communism. After the fall of the undoubtedly anti-communist Arias in 1951 the U.S. embassy detected pro-communist sympathies among associates of the successor regime and drew nervous parallels with Guatemala, where the reformist Jacobo Arbenz had recently been elected. When, therefore, Remón became a presidential nominee, Ambassador John Wiley urged a $2 million aid programme to boost his prospects. Remón won the election in 1952 without this gratuity, but the incoming Eisenhower administration stood ready to pay a considerable price to damp down the fires of nationalism. In this way Panama might be steered off the path taken not only by Guatemala but by Iran, where foreign-owned oil companies had been expropriated, and most ominously of all by Egypt, whose new revolutionary government seemed set to challenge Anglo-French control of the Suez Canal.

From the Panamanian viewpoint the most desirable form of aid was admission to the business opportunities generated by the canal. This had been Panama's prime objective since its birth and it was to remain central throughout this period. Since Washington had always seen the political benefits of taking the edge off the Panamanian appetite, there was room to strike a bargain.

The first serious move in this direction during the period after 1930 came in October 1933 when President Harmodio Arias visited Roosevelt in the White House in a renewal of the effort to conclude a new treaty which had foundered with Panama's rejection of the accord reached in 1926. The commercial clauses of the document eventually signed in March 1936 substantially echoed the corresponding articles of the 1926 agreement. The concessions, however, had to be fought through in the teeth of revived opposition from the canal hierarchy, even though it had already accepted them a decade earlier. To the Governor this element of the treaty still marked a capitulation: the surrender of Washington's sovereign right under Article 3 of the 1903 convention to sell anything to anybody, regardless of Panama.

Worse was to come, from the point of view of the Zone authorities. Although a Panamanian call for a share in toll revenues was abruptly turned down, several additional concessions were made. The annuity was raised to $430,000 compensating for the 1934 devaluation of the dollar and the Zone's demand for the incorporation of New Cristóbal was dropped. To soothe Panamanian anxiety over the repeal of prohibition the Zone was pledged to buy all but light wines and beer from Panama's liquor merchants. All this amounted to a package significantly more generous than the 1926 treaty, and Panama owed a great deal of it to Roosevelt himself.

Yet the treaty did not end the commercial colonialism of the Zone. The commissary's outlets and the army's post exchanges ignored its provisions in practice, and even before the wartime boom of 1939–43 began to subside, they once again became the targets of Panamanian protest. U.S. observers in their turn accused Panama of failing to compete with the Zone by reducing its tariffs and of lacking the political courage to use the obvious alternative source of revenue, an income tax, for fear of a furious backlash from the men of property who had dominated the country since its inception. After the war, commentators on the isthmian scene continually pointed to its overwhelming dependence on the service sector, and its unwillingness to diversify and raise more income from agricultural production. Remón certainly made a start towards diversification. But the Panamanian fixation on the canal as the fount of all affluence was still predominant and in 1952 the Remón administration, like all its predecessors, saw economic salvation primarily in terms of tapping as much of this liquidity as the United States could be prevailed on to part with.

In the negotiations for a third treaty in the autumn of 1953, therefore, the Panamanian government linked all its demands to the canal: better job opportunities; reinforcement of the commercial concessions of 1936; a share in toll revenues; and an increased annuity. Washington put up resistance on almost every front. The army's objections were unambiguously materialistic. Southern Command, with its headquarters in the Zone, was not known as 'Southern Comfort' for nothing and it refused to give up any of its manifold perquisites to please Panama. In the event, the treaty did meet Panama half way on this score, but whether its provisions would be more strictly enforced than those of 1936 was highly questionable.

Opposition to a Panamanian tolls dividend and to a raised annuity had another dimension. Though Egypt received 7 per cent of gross tolls income from the Suez Canal, Panamanian participation in tolls profits was ruled out of court on the grounds that this could give Panama a voice in the canal administration. Secretary of State John Foster Dulles was prepared to increase the annuity by $1.5 million, but wanted this tied to an explicit admission by Panama that nothing in the new agreement gave it any right to revise existing treaties. No such statement was in fact inserted, although the treaty was signed in January 1955 on the understanding that the fundamentals of the U.S. position in the Zone stood unchanged.

The Panamanian treaty demand regarding employment reflected the importance which labour issues had assumed over the previous twenty years. In the depression decade of the 1930s, when jobs were at a premium, both North Americans and Panamanians had been avid to replace the 7,000 or so West Indians of the Silver Roll. The canal authorities resisted the pressure from both quarters. Although the West Indians were offered assisted passages back to their islands, there were few takers and they continued to make up the bulk of the unskilled and semi-skilled work force suffering the many disabilities of Silver Roll status. Panama was placated with a note attached to the 1936 treaty, promising maintenance of the supposed equality over employment established during the construction era. This was, however, made subject to the future requirements of the canal, a proviso which rendered the pledge meaningless for practical purposes.

The Second World War, coming only weeks after the 1936 treaty went into force, made labour relations in the Canal Zone a major bone of contention. Trouble did not stem from the West Indians. An early attempt at unionization was soon aborted, the one and only strike in 1940 was answered by deportations, and the many thousands of labourers imported for wartime construction work were all repatriated by the end of the war. The Americans on the Gold Roll were likewise held in check. Their annual amendment to canal legislation, calling for an exclusive American title to skilled and semi-skilled posts, was ritually met with a presidential suspension. But Roosevelt had termed the war a crusade for human rights and when in 1944 Panama indicted Gold–Silver discrimination before the International Labour Organization, the Zone was immediately placed on the defensive. Thus, despite the fact that the Governor rejected the abolition of the Gold and Silver rosters as a recipe for chaos and, although Roosevelt discarded his professed liberalism to back him up, the topic remained high on Panama's agenda.

In the post-war decade the movement for change gathered pace with the West Indians' acquisition of Panamanian citizenship under the Constitution of 1946. The Zone administration now faced a united Silver front of Caribbean and Hispanic Panamanian workers, organized by the United Public Workers of America (UPWA), itself affiliated to the Congress of Industrial Organizations (CIO). Although the local branch of the union could not lobby as effectively as the Gold Men's Metal Trades Council, it pressed hard for the reform of employment practices and even after the expulsion of the UPWA from the CIO early in 1950, its more moderate successor pursued much the same objectives. Their cause was buttressed, moreover, by developments in Washington. In 1947, Panamanians were allowed to take the civil service examinations, while a government report urged that labour policy be taken out of the Zone's hands and given over to an inter-departmental committee sitting in the capital. As a first step the Gold and Silver designations should be scrapped. Segregation in the Zone should then be gradually phased out until it became a showcase for the freedoms the United States claimed to champion in the emergent Cold War with the Soviet Union.

This was anathema to an unreconstructed canal directorate, which had so far been answerable to no one but the President and it fought a successful rear-guard action. The controversial Gold and Silver nomenclatures were dropped but their colourless replacements, 'U.S.-rate' and 'local-rate', meant practically the same things. In 1951, however, the old administration was wound up and superseded by a new Panama Canal Company much more responsive to federal government thinking. One of the main reasons for establishing the company had been to trim canal expenditure, and it was advised to stop paying the 25 per cent differential to its American employees and to substitute as many of them as possible with

Panamanians. The first of these propositions was not acted upon since it would almost certainly have produced mass resignations and shut down the canal altogether. The second was feasible, though still deeply unpopular with the Zonians.

What was not acceptable was the Panamanian call in the treaty talks which opened in 1953 for a single wage-scale based on U.S. rates alone. This would have taken the parity affirmed in 1936 to the point of bankrupting the company with a ruinous salary bill. The final compromise was to place the existing two scales end to end to form what looked like a single ladder. Whichever rate was assigned to a particular job would apply to Americans and Panamanians alike, regardless of nationality. This preserved the American hold on skilled jobs virtually intact, but it also acknowledged the principle of equal pay for equal work, and in the light of fifty years of systematic inequity this was a remarkable concession on Washington's part.

The restructuring of the canal administration in 1951 was a clear sign that times were beginning to change. The impetus came from the fiscal watchdog of the White House, the Bureau of the Budget. In the spring of 1947 two Bureau officials returned from an inspection tour of the Zone to report that it was 'a museum of administrative antiquities', hidebound by the inertia and traditionalism of its high command. 'Social evolution stopped in 1908, if not earlier, for most of these gentlemen', a State Department observer later declared.[2] When the Governor failed to put his own house in order Truman accepted the Bureau's blueprint for reorganization. Management of the canal was now divided between a Panama Canal Company responsible for the waterway's operation, and an agency entitled the Canal Zone Government, in charge of municipal functions. Though there was still a governor, he was now no more than a subordinate of the Secretary of the Army, as Assistant Secretary Karl Bendetsen made unmistakably clear when the Governor questioned the new order.

A key object of the reformation was to put the canal on a business footing and bring an end to the fringe benefits of the work force funded by generous subsidies taken out of toll revenues. Early in 1952 the General Accounting Office called for wide-ranging price rises to make government employees bear a greater percentage of costs and so avoid stepping up tolls. The Governor was enraged, but his term was running out and his successor was appointed in the firm expectation that he would wield the

---

[2] USNA, Record Group 59. 8IIF. 43/9–1751.

axe. Governor John Seybold did just that. A steep rent increase was followed by the introduction of commercial rates for a host of services and drastic cuts in an expensive housing programme for West Indian workers. Close on the heels of this trauma came the concessions made in the new treaty of January 1955. The Zone had undergone some radical changes, but no one could have dreamed that its third quarter-century would see its extinction.

THE THIRD GENERATION, 1955–79

In the 1955 treaty with Panama, the United States emphatically reasserted its perpetual title to sovereign rights over the Canal Zone. In the treaty of 1977 (which came into force in 1979) it accepted the immediate liquidation of the Zone and the transfer of the canal itself to Panama in 1999. How did this revolution in U.S. canal policy come about?

Without doubt the ball was set rolling by Egypt's nationalization of the Suez Canal in July 1956. Panama's attempt to exploit the crisis by bidding for a seat on the canal company board was brushed aside, but Egypt's ultimate success in holding on to Suez helped generate a nationalist protest movement more militant than anything Panama had experienced in the past. In May 1958, Panamanian students asserted the country's claim to sovereignty in the Zone by planting the national flag on Zone territory. In November 1959 a second incursion led to angry confrontations with American troops and outbreaks of rioting. Eisenhower was disposed to be conciliatory. In 1958 his brother Milton had called on him to allow the Panamanian *bandera* to be flown in the zone and to offer Panama a large package of economic aid. In April 1960 the aid programme went through and the following September orders were given for one Panamanian flag to be raised inside the Zone.

Both actions roused fierce congressional opposition. Representative Daniel Flood predicted that the day the flag of Panama was formally hoisted would mark the beginning of the end of U.S. dominion over the canal. The high feeling in Congress was doubtless a key influence in shaping the firm approach to Panama taken by the Kennedy administration from 1961 to 1963. Panama was now seeking nothing less than the return of the Zone to its jurisdiction and a thoroughgoing revision of all existing treaties with the United States. The State Department was reportedly in favour of coming to terms, but Kennedy insisted on a delay until he was given a feasibility report on excavating a sea-level canal with thermonuclear devices. When in August 1963 American signature of the test-ban treaty all but ruled out the use of hydrogen bombs for blasting open an isthmian seaway, the Panamanians felt deceived. The likely bearing of the test-ban on the sea-level scheme had not been made clear to them, and relations with Washington were instantly soured.

Progress towards a new treaty was thus at a standstill when the worst crisis yet between the United States and Panama exploded in January 1964. It was touched off by North American pupils of the Balboa High School who flouted an official instruction by raising the Stars and Stripes outside the school building. Within hours the Zone border with the terminal cities was the scene of rioting which left at least twenty-two dead, three of them North Americans, and was to prove a watershed in the history of the canal.

The Panamanian government was not slow to capitalize on the situation in calling for fundamental treaty revision, but for President Lyndon Johnson any such concession would have spelled political suicide in an election year. Very few North Americans were in the mood to listen to Senator William Fulbright when he asked the country to disabuse itself of the myth that there was 'something morally sacred' about the Convention of 1903. Nor would many have accepted the verdict of army counsel Joseph Califano that the root cause of the upsurge was the juxtaposition of the Zonians' affluent suburban life-style with the glaring poverty of Panama. Tension could only be reduced if Washington were ready to make some basic adjustments, but it was not until after he was safely confirmed as president in November that Johnson could publicly state his willingness to accept a new treaty with a fixed time-limit. It would recognize Panamanian sovereignty over the Zone and the area would revert to Panama when the treaty expired. The abandonment of the Zone, however, was subject to the consummation of the sea-level canal project, which was resurrected to provide Washington with extra bargaining power in the forthcoming negotiations.

Panama was further hamstrung by Washington's 'three or none' negotiating strategy, that is, the insistence on an inseparable trio of agreements covering the existing canal, a sea-level waterway and U.S. bases, to be accepted or rejected en bloc. Even so, the treaties were initialled in June 1967. Canal operation and jurisdiction in the canal area were to be shared until 1999, when control would pass to Panama alone; Panama would also draw an annuity of up to $25 million from tolls. Defence would rest largely in American hands, although here, too, there was provision for a degree of joint responsibility. A hundred-year U.S. option would be retained on a seaway. But there were immediate objections in Congress, notably from the arch-conservative senator Strom Thurmond, and the package was shelved until after the 1968 elections in both countries. By the close of 1968, however, the military regime of Colonel Omar Torrijos ruled Panama, and in September 1970 it rejected the treaty settlement. It was, said Torrijos, much too reminiscent of the old status quo and it gave Panama far too little in both material and juridical terms.

If Torrijos believed he could prise more out of President Richard Nixon, he was mistaken. In 1964 Nixon had stated that Washington should bargain over 'the little irritating things' but not over the vital issue of U.S. control. This was the line taken by his spokesman, Robert Anderson, when talks reopened in June 1971 and it had already been foreshadowed in a study on the sea-level project produced by Anderson six months earlier. The duration of the treaty was extended to fifty years and exclusive American jurisdiction in some spheres was to last for that entire period. The United States was also to keep a full two-thirds of the Zone for canal purposes and Panama was cut out of any meaningful part in canal administration or defence. Faced with this staggering retreat from the terms offered in 1967, Torrijos understandably broke off negotiations in December 1972.

Washington was evidently still treating Panama as a country of little consequence. In 1927 a Panamanian diplomat had taken a fatalistic view of the republic's predicament: 'When you hit a rock with an egg, the egg breaks. Or when you hit an egg with a rock, the egg breaks. The United States is the rock. Panama is the egg. In either case, the egg breaks'.[3] By the early 1970s, however, the attitude of the Panamanian leadership was altogether different. In October 1971, Torrijos declared that if Panama could not reach its objectives at the negotiating table the time would have come 'for one generation to offer its lives so that another generation can live in a free country'. The model Torrijos no doubt had in mind was North Vietnam, then fighting the United States to a standstill in its bid for national unification. But Panama was no North Vietnam, as Torrijos almost certainly knew, and he had to turn to another option to make up for its intrinsic weakness. This was to internationalize the issue of the canal by taking it to the United Nations. In March 1973 the UN Security Council met in Panama City to debate a Panamanian resolution calling for

[3] *The New York Times*, 2 October 1927.

'a just and fair treaty' to fulfil Panama's legitimate aspirations. When the United States vetoed the resolution it placed itself in a minority of one, and Panama had swung the weight of world opinion behind its case.

The U.S. response was to abandon its extremist stance and return roughly to the line set by the 1967 drafts. This signified the resurgence of the State Department, which had been shut out of the second phase of discussions, and the corresponding decline of the Pentagon, whose influence was clearly discernible in the uncompromising demands made in round two. The change was embodied in Anderson's replacement by the veteran diplomatist Ellsworth Bunker, who took over in the summer of 1973. Bunker not only accepted the negotiating principles drawn up by the Panamanian foreign minister, Juan Antonio Tack, but improved on them substantially from Panama's point of view. Panama, as in 1967, was to be allotted a positive role in canal management and protection. At the same time the sea-level plan, which a former U.S. ambassador believed the military had injected into the bargaining process primarily to make mischief, was finally dropped. When Secretary of State Henry Kissinger set his seal on Bunker's work in February 1974 the way to a treaty appeared open.

Yet negotiations went forward against a background rumble of die-hard fury in the United States. After the fall of South Vietnam in the spring of 1975 the Pentagon was reported to feel that President Gerald Ford should 'stand up if tested and be firm' on Panama. Thurmond could garner thirty-five votes in the Senate for a resolution affirming 'undiluted United States sovereignty over the Canal Zone', one more than enough to deny consent to a treaty. In 1976 the aspiring Republican nominee Ronald Reagan won fervent applause (but not the nomination) with his simplistic battle-cry, 'We bought it, we paid for it, it's ours!' All this, it should be noted, was in aid of preserving a national asset whose value was now far more symbolic than real. In the fiscal year 1972–3 the canal had suffered the first of a series of operating deficits, and on the Governor's admission it handled less than 1 per cent of the U.S. gross national product. On its sixtieth birthday in 1974 it was said to be showing signs of 'technological arteriosclerosis'. In 1957 the defence correspondent of the *New York Times*, Hanson Baldwin, had written that it would 'probably never again occupy the same permanent strategic position it did in the days of the nineteen-thirties and in World War II'. The military establishment was no doubt much more concerned to preserve its large vested interest in Southern Command, but as several commentators, including Torrijos, pointed out, that elaborate structure bore little relation to the security of the canal and hence had no justification whatever in the 1903 convention.

The line taken by the Nixon and Ford administrations after 1973 was clearly based on the premise that the canal was a growing liability, and it was reinforced by an awareness that it would be extremely difficult to defend against a belligerent Panama. This sense of vulnerability was shared by the Carter administration, which took office in January 1977. Jimmy Carter's Secretary of State, Cyrus Vance, who had witnessed the backwash of the 1964 riots, had come to believe that 'sooner or later Panama would resort to major violence, even to the point of destroying the canal'. The army's chief of staff, General George Brown, declared that even with 100,000 men he could not guarantee the canal against a hostile population, and the spectre of a second Vietnam was raised when the journalist Tom Wicker wrote of the possibility of 'lingering and unwinnable guerrilla war'. These may have been scare tactics designed to promote support for a treaty, and Torrijos certainly did not go out of his way to offer reassurance, but it would have been unreasonably optimistic of Washington to have gone ahead on the assumption that the worst would never happen.

Carter moved rapidly to clinch an agreement with Panama and two treaties were signed in Washington in September 1977. The canal treaty stipulated full Panamanian sovereignty over the Zone as soon as it entered into force, and the progressive involvement of Panama in the new operating agency, the Panama Canal Commission, until 31 December 1999, when the waterway would come under exclusive Panamanian management. In the interim Panama would receive some $53 million a year from tolls, an annuity of $10 million for services and $10 million more if canal income allowed it. The defence of the canal against 'armed attack or other actions' was to be a joint concern, with the United States retaining primary responsibility up to 1999. By the terms of the neutrality treaty only Panama would station troops on the military bases in the republic after 1999, but the United States would still be bound to uphold the canal's neutrality for the indefinite future. This pledge, which applied to the entire country, was said to be designed to prevent the transit from becoming a military objective in any armed conflict fought out between other states.

The U.S. role under the neutrality treaty came close to destroying the chances of ratification. At the signing ceremony Torrijos warned that the treaty 'if not administered judiciously by future generations, could become an instrument of permanent intervention'. To remove Panamanian suspicions Carter joined Torrijos in a public statement proclaiming that U.S. action would 'never be directed against the territorial integrity or political independence of Panama'. Early in 1978, as the Senate reached the climax of its debate on the treaty, the statement was adopted as a substantive amendment sponsored by the Senate leaders Robert Byrd and Howard Baker.

There were, however, still those in Washington who found non-intervention an offensive denial of U.S. power. When asked by congressional visitors what would happen if after 1999 Panama said it was closing the canal for 'repairs', national security adviser Zbigniew Brzezinski replied that the United States would 'move in and close down the Panamanian government for repairs'. Desperate to win the necessary two-thirds Senate majority, Carter accepted a condition which pandered to this chauvinism. Entered by Senator Dennis DeConcini, it gave the United States the right to take whatever measures it chose – even against Panama – to keep the canal open. Although the condition did not have the binding force of the Byrd–Baker amendment, it was seen in Panama as a licence for a perpetual American inspectorate. It bought DeConcini's vote, however, and the treaty scraped through on 16 March by a breathtaking 68 to 32, just one more than the necessary two-thirds majority. The canal treaty was approved a month later by the same narrow margin, together with a reassuring leadership reservation on the lines of the Byrd–Baker proviso.

The passage of the treaties was inevitably condemned by Carter's enemies as a sell-out, and he was given a cool reception by several of his fellow-citizens when he went to Panama in June to exchange ratifications with Torrijos. Yet the losers got even to some degree in the implementing legislation enacted in 1979. The government's bill was defeated in the House and Carter had to accept a Panama Canal Act which was largely the handiwork of Representative John Murphy, a long-standing opponent of any compromise with Panama. The canal was to be operated not by a semi-official corporation as Carter had wanted, but by a commission answerable to the Pentagon and dependent on Congress for its appropriations. Stringent controls were imposed on the terms governing treaty payments to Panama, and in an additional challenge to Torrijos, the President was authorized to negotiate with Panama to keep U.S. forces in the canal area after 1999. When he signed the act on 27 September 1979, Carter felt obliged to state that nothing in it would make him or his successors do anything inconsistent with the letter or the spirit of the treaties.

Four days later, on 1 October 1979, the settlement came into force and the Canal Zone ceased to exist. As Panama redeemed the territory most Americans had thought of as their own domain, the U.S. community was heavy with the sense of bereavement. 'The past is dead', lamented one inconsolable Zonian. 'Teddy Roosevelt is in the ground'.[4]

In January 1904 that same Teddy Roosevelt told Congress: 'If ever a Government could be said to have received a mandate from civilization to effect an object the accomplishment of which was demanded in the interest of mankind, the United States holds that position with regard to the interoceanic canal'. In 1912 Roosevelt's idol, Admiral Alfred Thayer Mahan, was to write that 'the Isthmus of Panama, because of its inter-oceanic possibilities, was and is a world concern. . . . If the United States do not give good administration and security she will hear from the world, though she be a strong state'.

The history of Washington's seventy-five-year tenure of the canal, however, demonstrates just how hypocritical this internationalism really was. U.S. canal policy was rooted in the conviction that the waterway was a vital national interest, to be insulated from foreign interference by every possible means. To Mahan and his disciples unilateral U.S. control was as sacrosanct as diplomatic isolation, the Monroe Doctrine and the ban on Asiatic immigration. When the idea of a multilateral agreement to secure the canal's neutrality was floated in the late 1900s, Mahan turned it down flat. To ask for guarantees of neutrality from other states, in his view, was 'to constitute over ourselves a kind of protectorate'. Roosevelt was similarly dismissive of the suggestion that the issue of the canal's fortification be submitted to the Permanent Court of Arbitration at The Hague.

A particularly telling indication of Washington's nationalistic attitude to the waterway was provided by the Panama Canal Act of 1912, which exempted American coastwise shipping from tolls. The United States, claimed President Taft, enjoyed 'absolute rights of ownership and control, including the right to allow its own commerce the use of the canal upon such terms as it sees fit'. In the Anglo-American canal treaty of 1901 Washington had subscribed to a version of the rules set by the Constantino-

---

[4] *The New York Times*, 1 October 1979.

ple Convention of 1888 to direct the international use of the Suez Canal, of which Rule 1 ordained equal treatment to ships of all countries. This Washington had flouted, and although the exemption was repealed in the face of a strong British protest, the canal regulations adopted in July 1914 maintained that transit was a privilege, not a right.

Having made their point the British were ready to accept an American monopoly over Panama, on the tacit assumption that as a fellow-member of the imperialist brotherhood the United States would in turn acknowledge Britain's paramounty over Suez. Thus at the Paris Peace Conference in 1919 the two stood shoulder to shoulder to rebuff the Bolshevik proposal for the internationalization of both canals, and the United States ignored the call by the Panamanian Eusebio Morales for the League of Nations to operate the Panama Canal and to take over the guarantee of Panama's independence.

Between the wars Washington consistently brushed aside every Panamanian attempt to seek an international counterweight to offset the massive influence it exerted on the tiny republic through mastery over the canal. In 1921 the State Department denied the competence of the League to act in Panama's border dispute with Costa Rica and then blocked successive Panamanian efforts to obtain arbitration of the running battle over the extent of U.S. sovereign rights under the convention of 1903. In 1932 the Senate disembowelled an inter-American arbitration treaty for fear it could be used to cast doubt on U.S. sovereign powers in the Zone. During the negotiations for the new treaty eventually signed in 1936, Panama complained there was no provision for the arbitration of several key articles. The reply of Under Secretary Sumner Welles was that critical U.S. interests such as the canal were not open to the arbitration process. In 1934 President Franklin D. Roosevelt had described the United States as 'a trustee for all the world' in respect of the canal. With Franklin, as with Theodore, however, the rhetoric concealed a very different reality.

In the Second World War the United States embraced internationalism in a decisive move away from the isolation of the past. With respect to the Panama Canal, however, that internationalism had distinctly narrow limits. Sitting on a post-war planning committee in 1942, Welles urged international control for the British base at Singapore but would not contemplate it for the Canal Zone. When the International Labour Organization (ILO) took up the question of the zone's discriminatory employment policies, the Governor put up impenetrable resistance to an 'inquisitorial super-state'. When the United Nations asked for information on the Zone as a dependent territory, the Zone's allies in the State Department joined forces with Panama to make certain the initiative was never repeated.

The canal could not, however, be divorced from outside developments, especially the post-war conflict between Britain and Egypt over the destiny of the Suez Canal. When the Egyptian revolutionary regime of Nasser nationalized the canal in July 1956, Washington was deeply embarrased by the parallels Panama drew between the two instances. The legalistic way out of this uncomfortable fix was to assert their differences. Suez could be internationalized, but not Panama, declared Secretary Dulles, since Panama's status derived from the bilateral treaties of 1901 and 1903, whereas Suez was governed by the multilateral Constantinople Convention. Long before, during the tolls controversy with Britain, the young Dulles had argued that the Panama waterway was 'affected with an international use'. To have taken that line in 1956 would have been to give Panama the opening for a frontal assault on American prerogatives, and the old Dulles was not about to do that. The citadel built by Hay and Bunau-Varilla stood unshaken.

Five years after Suez the Kennedy administration went so far as to toy with the notion of inter-American control of a future sea-level canal, no doubt on the assumption that it would still be under tight U.S. supervision. In the subsequent crisis with Panama early in 1964, however, Washington reverted to form, minimizing the involvement of the Organization of American States and excluding the United Nations altogether. But Panama could not be stopped from rallying the UN to its side when the Security Council met in Panama City in 1973 and voted overwhelmingly to support the Panamanian cause. The ensuing American willingness to negotiate a relatively conciliatory agreement was perhaps born at least partly out of the determination to nip any further international intervention sharply in the bud. The canal treaty incorporated an arbitration clause and the neutrality treaty invited adherence by every state in the world. The heads of all Latin American governments were summoned to witness the signing ceremony. Yet the settlement reached in 1977 was strictly between the two interested parties, as had been every previous accord between the United States and Panama. At its core was the provision for an everlasting U.S. watch on the isthmus, beyond the moment of withdrawal. The price of Panamanian liberty remained, as it was after 1903, eternal North American vigilance. Although in the late 1980s General Manuel Noriega threw a serious question mark over Washington's ability to control events in Panama, there was no doubt that the will to dominate was still as strong as ever (as was demonstrated in the eventual overthrow of Noriega in December 1989). The 1977 treaties had shown, wrote one of their most enthusiastic partisans, 'that we are sincere in our desire to relegate hemispheric paternalism and hegemony to the history books'.[5] The century to come will put that claim to the test, in Panama and in the Americas at large.

[5] Gale McGee, 'After Panama: Some Lessons and Opportunities in the Aftermath of the Canal Treaties Debate', *South Atlantic Quarterly* 78 (1979): 7.

1. MEXICO, c. 1930–46

The best guide to Mexican history in the period is the multi-volume, multi-authored *Historia de la revolución mexicana* published by the Colegio de México, ten volumes of which cover the period 1928–52. The first two, written by Lorenzo Meyer, Rafael Segovia and Alejandra Lajous, entitled *Los inicios de la institucionalización* (Mexico, 1978) and *El conflicto social y los gobiernos del maximato* (Mexico, 1978), deal respectively with the political and social history of the Calles *maximato*. Four successive volumes cover the Cárdenas presidency: Luis González, *Los artífices del Cardenismo* (Mexico, 1979), sets the scene; the same author's *Los días del presidente Cárdenas* (Mexico, 1979) deftly captures both the key events and the President's character; Alicia Hernández Chávez, *La mecánica cardenista* (Mexico, 1979) offers acute analysis and original research; Victoria Lerner, *La educación socialista* (Mexico, 1979), deals with education policy in the 1930s. Historical research on the 1940s – a crucial but relatively little-studied decade – has been pioneered by Luis Medina, *Del cardenismo al avilacamachismo* (Mexico, 1978); Blanca Torres Ramírez, *México en la segunda guerra mundial* (Mexico, 1979); Luis Medina, *Civilismo y modernización del autoritarismo* (Mexico, 1979); and Blanca Torres Ramírez, *Hacia la utopía industrial* (Mexico, 1984).

The Colegio series, however, offers no broad interpretations of Cardenismo. These can be found in Fernando Benítez, *Lázaro Cárdenas y la revolución mexicana*, vol. 3: *El cardenismo* (Mexico, 1978), which is persuasively sympathetic; Tzvi Medin, *Ideología y praxis política de Lázaro Cárdenas* (Mexico, 1972), a sound, balanced analysis; Anatoli Shulgovski, *México en la encrucijada de su historia* (Mexico, 1968), an unusually good piece of Soviet historiography; and Nora Hamilton, *The Limits of State Autonomy:*

Post-Revolutionary Mexico (Princeton, 1982), which places Cardenismo within an accessible theoretical context. Some sense of contrasting interpretations of Cardenismo is provided by: Octavio Ianni, *El estado capitalista en la época de Cárdenas* (Mexico, 1977); Arnaldo Córdova, *La política de masas del cardenismo* (Mexico, 1974); Romana Falcón, 'El surgimiento del agrarismo cardenista – Una revisión de las tesis populistas', *Historia Mexicana* 27, no. 3 (1978): 333–86; Liisa North and David Raby, 'The Dynamics of Revolution and Counter-revolution: Mexico Under Cárdenas, 1934–40', *Latin American Research Unit Studies* (Toronto), 2, no. 1 (October 1977). The place of Cardenismo within the broad revolutionary process is discussed by Donald Hodges and Ross Gandy, *Mexico 1910–1982: Reform or Revolution* (London, 1983); Juan Felipe Leal, 'The Mexican State, 1915–1973: A Historical Interpretation', *Latin American Perspectives* 2, no. 2 (1975): 48–63; and Alan Knight, 'The Mexican Revolution: Bourgeois, Nationalist, or Just a "Great Rebellion"?,' *Bulletin of Latin American Research* 4, no. 2 (1985): 1–37.

More personalist in approach are Nathaniel and Sylvia Weyl, *The Reconquest of Mexico: The Years of Lázaro Cárdenas* (London, 1939), and William Cameron Townsend, *Lázaro Cárdenas, Mexican Democrat* (Ann Arbor, Mich., 1952), both somewhat hagiographic; they can be contrasted with Victoriano Anguiano Equihua's critical *Lázaro Cárdenas, su feudo y la política nacional* (Mexico, 1951), which has in turn influenced Enrique Krauze, *General misionero, Lázaro Cárdenas* (Mexico, 1987). In contrast to these analytical and judgemental sources, John W. F. Dulles, *Yesterday in Mexico: A Chronicle of the Revolution, 1919–1936* (Austin, Tex., 1961), offers a straightforward, detailed narrative of the early 1930s.

On the crucial agrarian question, Eyler B. Simpson, *The Ejido, Mexico's Way Out* (Chapel Hill, N.C., 1937) is a compendious classic, but its analysis stops c. 1934; Nathan L. Whetten, *Rural Mexico* (Chicago, 1948), covers the whole period. Many excellent local studies shed light on the agrarian reform (as well as on local politics, *caciquismo,* and state–federal relations): Dudley Ankerson, *Agrarian Warlord, Saturnino Cedillo and the Mexican Revolution in San Luis Potosi* (De Kalb, Ill., 1984); Raymond Buve, 'State governors and peasant mobilisation in Tlaxcala', in D. A. Brading (ed.), *Caudillo and Peasant in the Mexican Revolution* (Cambridge, 1980); Ann L. Craig, *The First Agraristas: An Oral History of a Mexican Agrarian Reform Movement* (Berkeley, 1983), which deals with los Altos de Jalisco; Romana Falcón, *Revolución y caciquismo. San Luis Potosí, 1910–1938* (Mexico, 1984); Romana Falcón and Soledad García Morales,

La semilla en el surco, Adalberto Tejeda y el radicalismo en Veracruz, 1883–1960 (Mexico, 1986), whose subject has also been tackled by Heather Fowler Salamini, *Agrarian Radicalism in Veracruz, 1920–1938* (Lincoln, Neb., 1971); Paul Friedrich, *The Princes of Naranja: An Essay in Anthrohistorical Method* (Austin, Tex., 1986), which deepens and extends the author's earlier study of the radical Michoacan community of Naranja, *Agrarian Revolt in a Mexican Village* (Chicago, 1970). Geographically close but politically distant stands San José de Gracia, the subject of Luis González, *Pueblo en vilo: microhistoria de San José de Gracia* (Mexico, 1968; English trans., 1974), a classic study of a Michoacan community through the *longue durée* from the Conquest down to the 1960s. Less evocative but more analytical is Tomás Martínez Saldana and Leticia Gándara Mendoza, *Política y sociedad en México: el caso de los Altos de Jalisco* (Mexico, 1976), which ranges from the Revolution to the 1970s. David Ronfeldt, *Atencingo: The Politics of Agrarian Struggle in a Mexican Ejido* (Stanford, 1973) describes agrarian activism and politicking in Puebla during the same period; Frans J. Schryer, *The Rancheros of Pisaflores: The History of a Peasant Bourgeoisie in Twentieth-Century Mexico* (Toronto, 1980), is a perceptive study of highland Hidalgo; Arturo Warman, . . . *Y venimos a contradecir: los campesinos de Morelos y el estado* (Mexico, 1976; Eng. trans., 1980), and Guillermo de la Peña, *A Legacy of Promises: Agriculture, Politics and Ritual in the Morelos Highlands of Mexico* (Manchester, 1982), analyse the post-revolutionary experience of Zapata's fellow-Morelenses.

The important Laguna conflict and expropriation have been analysed in Clarence Senior, *Land Reform and Democracy* (Gainesville, Fla., 1958); Joe C. Ashby, *Organized Labor and the Mexican Revolution under Lázaro Cárdenas* (Chapel Hill, N.C., 1963); Iván Restrepo and Salomón Eckstein, *La agricultura colectiva en México: La experiencia de la Laguna* (Mexico, 1975); and Barry Carr, 'The Mexican Communist Party and Agrarian Mobilization in the Laguna, 1920–40: A Worker-Peasant Alliance', *Hispanic American Historical Review* 62, no. 3 (1987): 371–404. The rise and fall of collective *ejidos* outside the Laguna are recounted by Fernando Benítez, *Ki: El drama de un pueblo y de una planta* (Mexico, 1962), which deals with Yucatán; Susan Glantz, *El ejido colectivo de Nueva Italia* (Mexico, 1974), on Michoacán; and Ronfeldt, *Atencingo*. Moisés González Navarro, *La Confederación Nacional Campesina: un grupo de presión en la reforma agraria mexicana* (Mexico, 1968), tackles the official *campesino* movement.

Studies on the labour movement include Ashby, *Organized Labor;* Arturo Anguiano, *El estado y la política obrera del cardenismo* (Mexico, 1975), a leftist critique of Cardenismo; Victor Manuel Durand, *La ruptura de la nación: Historia del Movimiento Obrero Mexicano desde 1938 hasta 1952* (Mexico, 1986); and the valuable series edited by Pablo González Casanova, *La clase obrera en la historia de México,* the relevant volumes of which are: Arnaldo Córdova, *En una época de crisis (1928–1934)* (Mexico, 1980); Samuel León and Ignacio Marván, *En el cardenismo (1934–1940)* (Mexico, 1985); and Jorge Basurto, *Del avilacamachismo al alemanismo (1940–1952)* (Mexico, 1984).

The petroleum-workers' movement and the expropriation of 1938 are best covered by Lorenzo Meyer, *México y los Estados Unidos en el conflicto petrolero (1917–42)* (Mexico, 1968). E. David Cronon, *Josephus Daniels in Mexico* (Madison, Wis., 1960), analyses the important role of the U.S. ambassador, whose own memoirs appeared as *Shirt-Sleeve Diplomat* (Chapel Hill, N.C., 1947). General overviews of U.S.–Mexican relations are provided by Howard Cline, *The United States and Mexico* (New York, 1963), and Karl M. Schmitt, *Mexico and the United States, 1821–1973: Conflict and Co-existence* (New York, 1974); while Mexican economic nationalism – the nub of several U.S.–Mexican disputes in the inter-war period – is discussed by Alan Knight, 'The political economy of revolutionary Mexico, 1900–1940', in Christopher Abel and Colin M. Lewis (eds.), *Latin America: Economic Imperialism and the State* (London, 1985).

On the politics of the left during the period, see Manuel Márquez Fuentes and Octavio Rodríguez Araujo, *El partido comunista mexicano (en el periodo de la Internacional Comunista, 1919–1943)* (Mexico, 1973); Karl M. Schmitt, *Communism in Mexico, A Study in Political Frustration* (Austin, Tex., 1965); and Arturo Anguiano, Guadalupe Pacheco and Rogelio Viscaíno, *Cárdenas y la izquierda mexicana* (Mexico, 1975). The key figure of Vicente Lombardo Toledano is described by Robert Paul Millon, *Mexican Marxist – Vicente Lombardo Toledano* (Chapel Hill, N.C. 1966). For the development of the official party, first PNR then PRM, see the meticulous study of Luis Javier Garrido, *El partido de la Revolución institucionalizada: La formación del nuevo Estado en México (1928–1945)* (Mexico, 1986). Data on the political elite are analysed in Peter H. Smith, *Labyrinths of Power: Political Recruitment in Twentieth-Century Mexico* (Princeton, 1979).

Education has been well-researched by Lerner, *La educación socialista;* John A. Britton, *Educación y radicalismo en México,* 2 vols. (Mexico, 1976); Josefina Vázquez de Knauth, 'La educación socialista de los años treinta', *Historia Mexicana* 18, no. 3 (January–March, 1969): 408–23; and David L. Raby, *Educación y revolución social en México, 1921–1940* (Mexico, 1974).

On anti-clericalism, see the final section of Jean Meyer, *La Cristiada, I, La guerra de los cristeros* (Mexico, 1973); and, for an important case study, Carlos Martínez Assad, *El laboratorio de la revolución: El Tabasco garridista* (Mexico, 1979). The resurgent Catholic radical right of the 1930s has been researched by Jean Meyer, *El sinarquismo, un fascismo mexicano?* (Mexico, 1979); for older, more hostile analyses, see Whetten, *Rural Mexico,* chap. 20, and Mario Gill, *El sinarquismo: Su origen, su esencia, su misión* (Mexico, 1944). Hugh G. Campbell, *La derecha radical en México, 1929–49* (Mexico, 1976), analyses both the Catholic and the secular radical right. T. G. Powell, *Mexico and the Spanish Civil War* (Albuquerque, 1981), discusses the foreign-policy issue which most agitated domestic politics. These several currents fed into the contentious 1940 presidential election discussed by José Ariel Contreras, *Mexico 1940: industrialización y crisis política* (Mexico 1977), and Albert L. Michaels, 'The Crisis of Cardenismo', *Journal of Latin American Studies* 2 (May 1970): 51–79.

The broad patterns of government policy and budgeting during the 1930s and 1940s are charted in James W. Wilkie, *The Mexican Revolution: Federal Expenditure and Social Change since 1910* (Berkeley, 1970). Economic trends can be followed in Clark W. Reynolds, *The Mexican Economy: Twentieth-Century Structure and Growth* (New Haven, 1970), and Leopoldo Solís, *La realidad económica mexicana: retrovisión y perspectivas* (Mexico, 1970). Trade is discussed by Timothy King, *Mexico: Industrialization and Trade Policies since 1940* (London, 1970); mining, by Marvin D. Bernstein, *The Mexican Mining Industry 1890–1950* (New York, 1964); agriculture, by Cynthia Hewitt de Alcántara, *La modernización de la agricultura mexicana, 1940–1970* (Mexico, 1978), and Steven E. Sanderson, *Agrarian Populism and the Mexican State: The Struggle for Land in Sonora* (Berkeley, 1981), both of which combine general analysis with case studies of the state of Sonora; on the process of import substitution stimulated by the depression, see Enrique Cardenas, 'The Great Depression and Industrialization: The case of Mexico', in Rosemary Thorp, (ed.), *Latin America in the 1930s: The Role of the Periphery in World Crisis* (London, 1984), pp. 222–41. Sanford A. Mosk, *Industrial Revolution in Mexico* (Berkeley, 1954) focusses on wartime industrialization.

Finally, foreign eye-witness accounts of the 1930s and early 1940s include: Graham Greene, *The Lawless Roads* (London, 1939), an anti-anticlerical tract; Frank L. Kluckhohn, *The Mexican Challenge* (New York, 1939), by a journalistic critic of Cardenista policy; R. H. K. Marett, *An Eye-witness of Mexico* (London, 1939), and Virginia Prewett, *Reportage on*

Mexico (New York, 1941), which are rather more neutral; and Betty Kirk, *Covering the Mexican Front* (Norman, Okla., 1942), which emphasizes the Axis threat. Partisan and often unreliable as these are, they at least engage with current political and social issues. In contrast, the eye-witness accounts of the later 1940s and 1950s tend towards bland travelogues: proof that Mexico was seen no longer as a troublesome nest of banditry and Bolshevism, but rather as a safe haven of tourism and tequila.

2. MEXICO SINCE 1946

There is not yet an extensive historiographical literature on Mexico in the period after 1946 because of both its proximity to the present day and the absence of epic events. Nor is there a long-standing tradition of political or public memoirs, although this may now be in an incipient phase. For a general overview, see Michael C. Meyer and William L. Sherman, *The Course of Mexican History* 3d ed. (New York, 1987). Interpretive studies of Mexican politics include Daniel Levy and Gabriel Székely, *Mexico: Paradoxes of Stability and Change* (Boulder, Colo., 1983; rev. ed., 1987); Roberto Newell, G. and Luis Rubio F., *Mexico's Dilemma: The Political Origins of Economic Crisis* (Boulder, Colo., 1984); and Roderic A. Camp (ed.), *Mexico's Political Stability: The Next Five Years* (Boulder, Colo., 1986); Judith Gentleman (ed.), *Mexican Politics in Transition* (Boulder, Colo., 1987). Earlier analyses include José Luis Reyna and Richard S. Weinert (eds.), *Authoritarianism in Mexico* (Philadelphia, 1977), and Miguel Basáñez, *La lucha por la hegemonía en México, 1968–1980* (Mexico, 1981).

Standard works on the Mexican political system by North Americans include Robert E. Scott, *Mexican Government in Transition* (Urbana, Ill., 1958; 2d ed., 1964); Frank R. Brandenburg, *The Making of Modern Mexico* (Englewood Cliffs, N.J., 1964); L. Vincent Padgett, *The Mexican Political System* (Boston, 1966; rev. ed., 1976); and Kenneth F. Johnson, *Mexican Democracy: A Critical View* (Boston, 1971; 3d rev. ed., 1984). Studies of political economy include Raymond Vernon, *The Dilemma of Mexico's Development: The Roles of the Private and Public Sectors* (Cambridge, 1963), and Roger D. Hansen, *The Politics of Mexican Development* (Baltimore, 1971). A classic Mexican interpretation of the regime is Pablo González Casanova, *Democracy in Mexico* (New York, 1970). On the formation of political elites, see Peter H. Smith, *Labyrinths of Power: Political Recruitment in Twentieth-Century Mexico* (Princeton, 1979), and the many works of Roderic A. Camp, especially *Mexico's Leaders: Their Education and Recruit-*

ment (Tucson, 1980). What little we know about the contemporary army is contained in David Ronfeldt (ed.), *The Modern Mexican Military: A Reassessment* (La Jolla, Calif., 1984). Essential research tools are provided in Roderic A. Camp, *Mexican Political Biographies, 1935–1975* (Tucson, 1976), and Presidencia de la República, *Diccionario biográfico del gobierno mexicano* (Mexico, 1984).

For speculation and analysis on the presidential succession, see Roderic A. Camp, 'Mexican Presidential Candidates: Changes and Portents for the Future', *Polity*, 16, no. 4 (1984), Daniel Cosío Villegas, *La sucesión presidencial* (Mexico, 1975), and Francisco José Paoli, *El cambio de presidente* (Mexico, 1981). On elections, see Arturo Alvarado (ed.), *Electoral Patterns and Perspectives in Mexico* (La Jolla, Calif., 1987), and essays by Kevin J. Middlebrook, Juan Molinar Horcasitas and Wayne A. Cornelius in Paul W. Drake and Eduardo Silva (eds.), *Elections and Democratization in Latin America, 1980–1985* (La Jolla, Calif., 1986). A broad analysis of political forces and prospects appears in Wayne A. Cornelius, Judith Gentleman and Peter H. Smith (eds.), *Mexico's Alternative Political Futures* (La Jolla, Calif., 1989).

Path-breaking work on the period from the Second World War to 1960 appears in a series of studies on the *Historia de la Revolución Mexicana* carried out by a team at El Colegio de México. These include, on 1940–52, Luis Medina, *Civilismo y modernización del autoritarismo* (Mexico, 1979), and on 1952–60, Olga Pellicer and José Luis Reyna, *El afianzamiento de la estabilidad política* (Mexico, 1978), and Olga Pellicer de Brody and Esteban L. Mancilla, *El entendimiento con los Estados Unidos y la gestación del desarrollo estabilizador* (Mexico, 1978). Other treatments of this period include James W. Wilkie, *The Mexican Revolution: Federal Expenditure and Social Change Since 1910* (Berkeley and Los Angeles, 1967). An illustrative case study from the López Mateos era can be found in Susan Kaufman Purcell, *The Mexican Profit-Sharing Decision: Politics in an Authoritarian Regime* (Berkeley and Los Angeles, 1975). On the López Portillo *sexenio*, see Gabriel Székeley, *La economía política del petróleo en México, 1976–1982* (Mexico, 1983), and Carlos Tello, *La nacionalización de la banca* (Mexico, 1984). A unique source on the de la Madrid presidency is the annual publication of the Unidad de la Crónica Presidencial, Presidencia de la República, *Crónica del sexenio. Las razones y las obras: Gobierno de Miguel de la Madrid*. A compelling description of the 1982 crisis appears in Joseph Kraft, *The Mexican Rescue* (New York, 1984); for a broad perspective, see William R. Cline (ed.), *International Debt and the Stability of the World Economy* (Washington, D.C., 1983). An important recent contribution is Rosario Green, *La deuda externa de México de 1973 a 1988: de la abundancia a la escasez de crédito* (Mexico, 1989).

Important studies of economic policy include Clark W. Reynolds, *The Mexican Economy: Twentieth-Century Structure and Growth* (New Haven, 1970) and his well-known interpretive article 'Why Mexico's "Stabilizing Development" Was Actually Destabilizing (With Some Implications for the Future)', *World Development* 6, nos. 7–8 (July-August 1978): See also Leopoldo Solís, *Economic Policy Reform in Mexico: A Case Study for Developing Countries* (New York, 1981). On foreign investment, see Bernardo Sepúlveda and Antonio Chumacero, *La inversión extranjera en México* (Mexico, 1973); Gary Gereffi, *The Pharmaceutical Industry and Dependency in the Third World* (Princeton, 1983); Douglas C. Bennett and Kenneth E. Sharpe, *Transnational Corporation versus the State: The Political Economy of the Mexican Automobile Industry* (Princeton, 1985); and Harley Shaiken and Stephen Herzenberg, *Automobile and Global Production: Automobile Engine Production in Mexico, the United States, and Canada* (La Jolla, Calif., 1987). For broad treatments of Mexican agriculture, see Gustavo Esteva, *La batalla en el México rural* (Mexico, 1980), Paul Lamartine-Yates, *Mexico's Agricultural Dilemma* (Tucson, 1981), and Susan W. Sanderson, *Land Reform in Mexico: 1910–1980* (Orlando, Fla., 1984). Merilee Serrill Grindle provides an valuable analysis of Echeverría's 'integrated' development plan in *Bureaucrats, Politicians, and Peasants in Mexico: A Case Study in Public Policy* (Berkeley and Los Angeles, 1977). On the policies of the López Portillo administration, see Cassio Luiselli Fernández, *The Route to Food Self-Sufficiency in Mexico: Interactions with the U.S. Food System* (La Jolla, Calif., 1985), and Jonathan Fox, "The Political Dynamics of Reform: The Case of the Mexican Food System, 1980–1982," (unpublished Ph.D. dissertation, Massachusetts Institute of Technology, 1986). On the official *campesino* movement, see Moisés González Navarro, *La Confederación Nacional Campesina: un grupo de presión en la reforma agraria mexicana* (Mexico, 1968). On political attitudes in the countryside, see Carlos Salinas de Gortari, *Political Participation, Public Investment, and Support for the System: A Comparative Study of Rural Communities in Mexico* (La Jolla, Calif., 1982).

The political outlook and resources of migrant slum dwellers form the subject of Wayne A. Cornelius, *Politics and the Migrant Poor in Mexico City* (Stanford, 1975), and Susan Eckstein, *The Poverty of Revolution: The State and the Urban Poor in Mexico* (Princeton, 1977). Among the remarkably scarce studies of organized labour are Kevin Jay Middlebrook, 'The Political Economy of Mexican Organized Labor, 1940–1978,' (unpublished Ph.D. dissertation, Harvard University, 1982), and César Zarzueta and Ricardo de la Peña, *La estructura del Congreso del Trabajo. Estado, Trabajo y capital en Mexico: Un acercamiento al tema* (Mexico, 1984). A welcome addition to this field is Ian Roxborough, *Unions and Politics in Mexico: The Case of the Automobile Industry* (Cambridge, 1984).

Donald J. Mabry offers a sweeping historical interpretation of campus politics in *The Mexican University and the State: Student Conflicts, 1910–1971* (College Station, Tex., 1982). Daniel C. Levy analyses the contemporary scene in *University and Government in Mexico: Autonomy in an Authoritarian System* (New York, 1980). For compelling material on the student movement of 1968 and the Tlatelolco massacre, see Ramón Ramírez, *El movimiento estudiantil de México: julio-diciembre de 1968,* 2 vols. (Mexico, 1969), and Elena Poniatowska, *La noche de Tlatelolco* (Mexico, 1971).

Standard sources on Mexican foreign policy are the masterful studies by Mario Ojeda, *Alcances y límites de la política exterior de México* (Mexico, 1976), and *México: El surgimiento de una política exterior activa* (Mexico, 1986). On relations with the United States, see Joséfina Zoraida Vázquez and Lorenzo Meyer, *The United States and Mexico* (Chicago, 1986); Carlos Vásquez and Manuel García y Griego (eds.), *Mexican-U.S. Relations: Conflict and Convergence* (Los Angeles, 1983); Clark Reynolds and Carlos Tello (eds.), *U.S.-Mexican Relations: Social and Economic Aspects* (Stanford, 1983); and George W. Grayson, *The United States and Mexico: Patterns of Influence* (New York, 1984). A subsequent flurry of books around the time of the presidential succession of 1988 included Robert A. Pastor and Jorge Castañeda, *Limits to Friendship: The United States and Mexico* (New York, 1988); George W. Grayson (ed.), *Prospects for Mexico* (Washington, D.C., 1988); Susan Kaufman Purcell (ed.), *Mexico in Transition: Implications for U.S. Policy* (New York, 1988); and the report of the Bilateral Commission on the Future of United States–Mexican Relations, *The Challenge of Interdependence: Mexico and the United States* (Lanham, Md., 1988), an effort that also led to the publication of Rosario Green and Peter H. Smith (eds.), *Dimensions of United States–Mexican Relations,* 5 vols. (La Jolla, Calif., 1989).

3. CENTRAL AMERICA SINCE 1930

There is abundant literature on Central America since 1930. See Edelberto Torres Rivas and Maria Eugenia Gallardo, *Para entender Centroámerica: resumen bibliográfico* (San José, 1985), and Kenneth Grieb, *Central America in the Nineteenth and Twentieth Centuries: An Annotated Bibliography* (Boston, 1988). An analysis of what has been written in the last twenty-five years, however, reveals that 80 per cent of all Spanish texts about Central America in general or any of the countries in particular have been written since 1979. Similarly what has been written in English consists, in essence, of a literature of 'the crisis'. Nevertheless, both before and after 1979, important works were published which are fundamental to an understanding of Central American history.

There are few works which treat the Central American region as a whole and which at the same time respect national features and local peculiarities. Franklin Parker, *The Central American Republics* (London, 1964), contains an analysis of and useful information about the economy, society and institutions of each country, covering the period up to 1960. More comprehensive and underlining regional homogeneity is Ralph L. Woodward, *Central America: A Nation Divided* (2d ed., New York, 1985), which also contains an exhaustive Selective Guide to the Literature on Central America. The two-volume text by Mario Monteforte Toledo, *Centro América: subdesarrollo y dependencia* (Mexico, 1972) is important for the quantitative information it contains. Also important because they contain interpretive propositions for the entire region are Edelberto Torres-Rivas, *Interpretación del desarrollo social centroamericano* (San José, 1971), one of the first works to treat the region as a whole; and Héctor Pérez Brignoli, *Breve historia de Centroamérica* (Madrid, 1986). The most detailed and comprehensive political history of Central America in the twentieth century is James Dunkerley, *Power in the Isthmus: A Political History of Modern Central America* (London, 1988).

Several other works also address themselves to Central America as a whole but concentrate on specific aspects or specific periods. Rodolfo Cerdas Cruz, *La hoz e el machete* (San José, 1986) examines the role of the Third International in Central America. For the period of the Second World War and its immediate aftermath, see Thomas M. Leonard, *The United States and Central America 1944–1949* (University, Ala., 1984); Andres Opazo, *Estructura agraria, dinámico de población y desarrollo capitalista en Centroamérica* (San José, 1978), is a detailed analysis of changes in agriculture and population movements. In *The Religious Roots of Rebellion: Christians in Central American Revolution* (New York, 1984), Phillip Berryman explains the changes experienced by the Central American Church and the role of the clergy in political struggle. Of the many works written on the political crisis that developed at the end of the 1970s, three contain particularly well-articulated analytical propositions: Donald E. Schulz and Douglas H. Graham (eds.), *Revolution and Counterrevolution in Central America and the Caribbean* (Boulder, Colo., 1984), a collection of historical and theoretical essays; Walter LaFeber, *Inevitable Revolution: The United States in Central America* (New York, 1984), an examination of U.S. policy in the region; and Morris Blachman et al., *Confronting Revolution: Security Through Diplomacy in Central America* (New York, 1986), a collection of essays on international relations in the Central American crisis.

On the Central American economy several books are indispensable. First is the result of an ambitious research project carried out by SIECA (Secretaria de Integración Económica Centroamericana), also called the Rosenthal report, after the economist who headed the project: *El desarrollo integrado de Centroamérica en la presente década: bases y propuestas para el perfeccionamiento y la reestructuración del Mercado Común* (Buenos Aires, 1973) comprises thirteen volumes of the most complete review of the regional economy ever undertaken. Two recent studies with a regional perspective by North American economists are John Weeks, *The Economies of Central America* (New York, 1985), a general analysis concentrating on the period since 1950; and Robert C. Williams, *Export Agriculture and the Crisis in Central America* (Chapel Hill, N.C., 1986), an extraordinary and well-documented look at the effects of the regional economic 'boom' of the sixties and seventies and, in particular, the social – and ecological – impact of the introduction into Central America of the export production of cotton and cattle. W. A. Durham, *Scarcity and Survival in Central America: Ecological Origins of the Soccer War* (Stanford, 1979), contains a rigorous quantitative analysis of population problems in El Salvador and an interpretation of the so-called 'useless war' of 1969. Also important is Richard Fagen (ed.), *Transition and Development: Problems of Third World Socialism* (New York, 1986), which brings together various analyses of economic policy in revolutionary Nicaragua and offers a theoretical discussion on the viability of socialist change in the Central American 'periphery'.

Finally, mention should be made of Victor Bulmer-Thomas, *The Political Economy of Central America Since 1920* (Cambridge, 1987) which is without any doubt the best work published to date on Central America. It contains not only an economic history of the last sixty years but also an outstanding analysis of the region's political and social life.

4. GUATEMALA SINCE 1930

Despite its age and limited attention to historical developments, Richard N. Adams, *Crucifixion by Power: Essays on Guatemalan Social Structure, 1944–1966* (Austin, Tex., 1970) continues to occupy a central place in the literature on Guatemala in the twentieth century. A more recent narrative account of republican history is Jim Handy, *Gift of the Devil: A History of Guatemala* (Toronto, 1984), popular in style but with a full scholarly apparatus. The period up to the mid-1930s is covered in the engaging study by Chester Lloyd Jones, *Guatemala Past and Present* (Minneapolis, 1940). Providing full statistical material supported by a rather uneven text on the following two decades is Mario Monteforte Toledo, *Guatemala: monografía sociológica* (Mexico, 1959), while Carlos Guzmán-Böckler and Jean-Loup Herbert, *Guatemala: una interpretación histórico-social* (Mexico, 1970) is overwhelmingly analytical in perspective. Alfonso Bauer Paiz, *Como opera el capital Yanqui en Centroamérica: el caso de Guatemala* (Mexico, 1956), and Thomas and Marjorie Melville, *Guatemala: The Politics of Land Ownership* (New York, 1971), are both polemical in style and secondary studies but do give cogent overviews of two important factors in twentieth-century society and economy.

General economic developments in the post-war period are treated in more technical fashion in World Bank, *The Economic Development of Guatemala* (Baltimore, 1951), and Lehman B. Fletcher et al., *Guatemala's Economic Development: the Role of Agriculture* (Ames, Iowa 1970). The complexities of peasant agriculture are treated in many studies, among the most suggestive of which are Lester Schmid, 'The Role of Migratory Labor in the Economic Development of Guatemala', Research Paper, Land Tenure Center, University of Wisconsin (Madison, 1967); Manuel Gollas, 'Surplus Labor and Economic Efficiency in the Traditional Sector of a Dual Economy: the Guatemalan Case', *Journal of Development Studies* 8, no. 4 (1972); Ivon Lebot, 'Tenencia de la Tierra en el Altiplano Occidental de Guatemala', *Estudios Sociales Centroamericanos,* no. 13 (1976); Thomas J. Maloney, 'El Impacto Social del Esquema de Desarrollo de la Franja Transversal del Norte sobre los Maya-Kekchi en Guatemala', *Estudios Sociales Centroamericanos,* no. 29 (1981), and Carol A. Smith, 'Local History in Global Context: Social and Economic Transition in Western Guatemala', *Comparative Studies in Society and History* 26, no. 2, (1984). Smith's long article on the urban sector, 'El Desarrollo de la primacia urbana', *Mesoamérica,* no. 8 (1984), is one of the very few studies to follow the pioneering work in this field by Bryan Roberts, *Organizing Strangers* (Austin, Tex., 1973), although it takes a more structural and historical perspective.

Much of the extensive work undertaken in the field of anthropology subordinates historical approaches, but some studies in this discipline have greatly advanced historical knowledge and thrown light on contemporary socio-political developments: Eric Wolf, *Sons of the Shaking Earth* (Chicago, 1959); Ruth Bunzel, *Chichicastenango. A Guatemalan Village* (Seattle, 1952); Ricardo Falla, *Quiché Rebelde* (Guatemala, 1979); John D. Early, 'The Changing Proportion of Maya Indian and Ladino in the Population of Guatemala, in 1954–1969', *American Ethnologist*, 2, no. 2 (1975); Paul Diener, 'The Tears of St Anthony: Ritual and Revolution in Eastern Guatemala', *Latin American Perspectives* 5, no. 3 (1978); Robert M. Carmack, 'Spanish-Indian Relations in Highland Guatemala, 1800–1944', in Murdo J. Macleod and Robert Wasserstrom (eds.), *Spaniards and Indians in South Eastern Mesoamerica: Essays in the History of Ethnic Relations* (Lincoln, Neb., 1983); 'Death and Disorder in Guatemala', *Cultural Survival Quarterly* 7, no. 1, Special issue (1983); and *Panzós: testimonio* (Guatemala, 1979). A magisterial but highly controversial survey of the history of the 'Indian question' is given in Severo Martínez Peláez, *La patria del criollo* (Guatemala, 1973), to which a vivid and powerful autobiographical counterpoint may be found in Elizabeth Burgos Debray (ed.), *I . . . Rigoberta Menchú* (London, 1983). Both works are placed in a general contemporary context in Carol A. Smith, 'Indian Class and Class Consciousness in Pre-revolutionary Guatemala', Working Paper no. 162, Latin American Program Woodrow Wilson Center (Washington, D.C., 1984).

Consolidated studies of developments in the formal and national circles of power and politics are much thinner on the ground. Other than the contemporary hagiographies, Kenneth J. Grieb, *Guatemalan Caudillo: The Regime of Jorge Ubico* (Athens, Ohio, 1979), is a solitary study and remains the principal consolidated source on politics during the 1930s. The final section of David McCreery, 'Debt Servitude in Rural Guatemala, 1876–1936', *Hispanic American Historical Review* 63, no. 4 (1983), provides a somewhat more sober view of the impact of Ubico's policies in one important area. The relevant chapters of Handy's *Gift of the Devil* are the best substitute for the startling lack of a comprehensive survey of the reform between 1944 and 1954. However, certain aspects of this period are covered in Ronald M. Schneider, *Communism in Guatemala, 1944–1954* (New York, 1958); Leo A. Suslow, *Aspects of Social Reform in Guatemala,*

1944–1949 (New York, 1950); Neale J. Pearson, 'Guatemala: The Peasant Union Movement, 1944–1954', in Henry A. Landsberger (ed.), *Latin American Peasant Movements* (Ithaca, N.Y., 1969); and Robert Wasserstrom, 'Revolution in Guatemala: Peasants and Politics under the Arbenz Government', *Comparative Studies in Society and History* 17, no. 4 (1975); Luis Cardoza y Aragón, *La Revolución Guatemaltica* (Guatemala City, 1955); Manuel Galich, *Por Que Lucha Guatemala. Arévalo y Arbenz. Dos hombres contra un Imperio* (Bueno Aires, 1956). Far greater attention has been paid to the intervention and counter-revolution of 1954, but the leading studies of that crisis do consider its local background to varying degree: Stephen Schlesinger and Stephen Kinzer, *Bitter Fruit. The Untold Story of the American Coup in Guatemala* (New York, 1982); Richard H. Immerman, *The CIA in Guatemala: The Foreign Policy of Intervention* (Austin, Tex., 1982); José M. Aybar de Soto, *Dependency and Intervention: The Case of Guatemala in 1954* (Boulder, Colo., 1978). A wider range of Guatemalan and U.S. literature on the intervention and its background is noted in Julio Adolfo Rey, 'Revolution and Liberation: A Review of Recent Literature on the Guatemalan Situation', *Hispanic American Historical Review* 38, no. 2 (1958).

From 1954 the government of Guatemala rested largely with the military and proved resistant to detailed monographic treatment. Differing views on the electoral process can be found in Kenneth F. Johnson, 'The Guatemalan Presidential Election of March 16, 1966: An Analysis' (Institute for the Comparative Study of Politics, Washington, D.C., 1967), and John W. Sloan, 'Electoral Frauds and Social Change: The Guatemalan Example', *Science and Society* 34, no. 3 (1970). A polemical, pro-guerrilla perspective is taken in Eduardo Galeano, *Guatemala: Occupied Country* (New York, 1969), and views from within the guerrilla provided in Ricardo Ramírez, *Lettres du Front Guatemaltèque* (Paris, 1970), and Orlando Fernández, *Turcios Lima* (Havana, 1968), themselves subjected to unsympathetic analysis in David A. Crain, 'Guatemalan Revolutionaries and Havana's Ideological Offensive of 1966–1968', *Journal of Inter-American Studies* 17, no. 2 (1975). Mario Payeras, *Days of the Jungle: The Testimony of a Guatemalan Guerrillero, 1972–76* (New York, 1983), is an insider's account of the emergence of the second generation of rebels against a military order described in great detail and with minimal sympathy in Michael McClintock, *The American Connection: State Terror and Popular Resistance in Guatemala* (London, 1985). Both sides are depicted in the polemical study of contemporary politics by George Black, *Garrison Guate-*

mala (London, 1984), which is more up-to-date but less sober and interested in socio-economic developments than Roger Plant, *Guatemala: Unnatural Disaster* (London, 1978), while a wider variety of sources is provided in Jonathan Fried et al. (eds.), *Guatemala in Rebellion: Unfinished History* (New York, 1983), which shares the radical tone of the other two texts.

5. EL SALVADOR SINCE 1930

Despite a significant increase in the number of studies – largely of a secondary character – since 1980, the scholarly literature on El Salvador in the twentieth century remains thin. Although they were written before the political developments that prompted the 'new wave' of books, two English language texts remain indispensable as general surveys: David Browning, *El Salvador: Landscape and Society* (Oxford, 1971), which adopts a predominantly geographical approach to socio-economic development, and Alastair White, *El Salvador* (London, 1973), which devotes more space to history and politics. Mario Flores Macal, *Origen, desarrollo y crisis de las formas de dominación en El Salvador* (San José, 1983), and Rafael Guidos Vejar, *Ascenso del militarismo en El Salvador* (San José, 1982) provide general overviews of political history, while the work of Rafael Menjivar links politics more closely to developments in political economy: see *Crisis del desarrollismo: caso El Salvador* (San José, 1977); *El Salvador: el eslabón mas pequeño* (San José, 1981); and *Formación y lucha del proletariado* (San José, 1982). Menjivar also contributes a chapter to *Centroamérica hoy* (Mexico, 1976), an important collection of comparative essays that situates the country within a regional framework. W. H. Durham, *Scarcity and Survival in Central America: ecological origins of the Soccer Wars* (Stanford, 1979) also takes a comparative approach, contrasting the rural subsistence economy of the country with that in Honduras, a counterpoint being given by Eduardo Colindres, *Fundamentos económicos de la burgesía salvadoreña* (San José, 1977), which was the basis for the author's many articles on the landlord class and direction of the modern coffee and cotton sectors. Other useful economic surveys include T. J. Downing, 'Agricultural Modernization in El Salvador' (Occasional Paper, Centre for Latin American Studies, University of Cambridge, 1978), and Hector Dada, *La economía de El Salvador y la integración social, 1954–1960* (San José, 1983).

Segundo Montes, *El compadrazgo: una estructura de poder en El Salvador* (San Salvador, 1979), and Carlos Cabarrús, *Génesis de una revolución* (Mexico, 1983), are rare studies of social structure, the first concentrating on aspects of Indian society and the second focussed on the north of the country and the origins of the contemporary peasant rebellion. There is still no adequate study of the 1932 revolt from the perspective of the peasantry, but the general origins and political course of the uprising are covered in some detail by Thomas P. Anderson, *Matanza: El Salvador's Communist Revolt of 1932* (Lincoln, Nebr., 1971). Roque Dalton, *Miguel Marmol* (New York, 1987) is an outstanding biographical account of a radical activist that covers the first four decades of the twentieth century. A modest biography of the Communist leader of the 1932 rising is provided by Jorge Arias Gómez, *Farabundo Martí* (San José, 1972), but none yet exists for General Martínez. Aspects of Martínez's government are, however, covered in Kenneth J. Grieb, 'The United States and the Rise of General Maximiliano Hernández Martínez', *Journal of Latin American Studies*, 3, no. 2 (1970); Everett Wilson, 'The Crisis of National Integration in El Salvador, 1919–1935', unpublished Ph.D. thesis, Stanford, 1970, and Robert E. Elam, 'Appeal to Arms: The Army and Politics in El Salvador, 1931–1964, unpublished Ph.D. thesis, University of New Mexico, 1968), which remains the best resource on modern military history. The 1969 war with Honduras is treated in general terms by Thomas P. Anderson, *The War of the Dispossessed: Honduras and El Salvador, 1969* (Lincoln, Neb., 1981), and within a socio-economic framework in Marco Carías and Daniel Slutsky (eds.), *La guerra inutil* (San José, 1971), and Vincent Cable, 'The "Football War" and the Central American Common Market', *International Affairs* 45 (1969). Material on modern political parties is scarce, the only monograph being Stephen Webre, *José Napoleón Duarte and the Christian Democratic Party in Salvadoran Politics, 1960–1978* (Baton Rouge, 1979), written before Duarte became president but valuable for its treatment of political life in the 1960s. A good example of orthodox political science that reflects the expectations of some democratic progress during that decade is Ronald H. McDonald, 'Electoral Behaviour and Political Development in Salvador', *Journal of Politics*, 31, no. 2 (1969).

Material on the 1970s and 1980s is much more extensive and frequently contains useful and original treatment of the previous period even though many contemporary books adopt a generally polemical tone. Latin America Bureau, *El Salvador Under General Romero* (London, 1979), contains a detailed analysis of the military regime of 1977 to 1979, and James Brockman, *The Word Remains: A Life of Oscar Romero* (New York, 1982), provides an interesting survey of local ecclesiastical life as well as a biography of the archbishop who opposed his namesake in the presidential palace. Jenny Pearce, *Promised Land: Peasant Rebellion in Chalatenango, El Salvador* (London, 1985) develops some of the themes of Cabarrús's text and is one of a growing caucus of books containing oral testimonies. Michael McClintock, *The American Connection: State Terror and Popular Resistance in El Salvador* (London, 1985) is no less unsympathetic to U.S. policies but provides considerable detailed information on the military and paramilitary forces, while Morton Halperin (ed.), *Report on Human Rights in El Salvador* (Washington, D.C., 1982) is one of the most lucid examples of the burgeoning oeuvre that itemizes the results of their activity. General studies of political developments since the early 1970s include: Enrique Baloyra, *El Salvador in Transition* (Chapel Hill, N.C., 1982); Robert Armstrong and Janet Shenk, *El Salvador: The Face of Revolution* (London, 1982); James Dunkerley, *The Long War: Dictatorship and Revolution in El Salvador,* 2d. ed. (London, 1985); Tommy Sue Montgomery, *Revolution in El Salvador: Origins and Evolution* (Boulder, Colo., 1982). Tomás Guerra (ed.), *Octubre Sangriento* (San José, 1980), and Dermot Keogh, 'The Myth of the Liberal Coup: The United States and the 15th October 1979 Coup in El Salvador', *Millennium* 13, no. 2 (1984) concentrate on the important final months of 1979. Mario Menéndez, *El Salvador: una auténtica guerra civil* (San José, 1980) is a highly partisan but vivid account of the guerrilla war. Adolfo Gilly, *Guerra y política en El Salvador* (Mexico, 1981), contains suggestive political essays from the left on the first phase on the conflict. And Raymond Bonner, *Weakness and Deceit: U.S. Policy and El Salvador* (New York, 1985), is a detailed account of the following years from a journalist's perspective as well as a strong attack on U.S. policy.

6. HONDURAS SINCE 1930

The social and economic backwardness of Honduras in the period since 1930 is reflected in the shortage of good general works and specialized monographs. Only in the last few years, as Honduras has become a focus of international attention, has the situation begun to change, although few works on Honduras in this recent period cannot be regarded as scholarly.

One of the more satisfactory general studies of Honduras is Mario Posas and Rafael Del Cid, *La construción del sector público y del estado nacional en Honduras 1870–1979* (Tegucigalpa, 1981), which is broader in coverage than its title implies and particularly strong in its interpretation of the period up to 1972. The standard text on Honduras in English is William S. Stokes, *Honduras: An Area Study of Government* (Madison, Wisc., 1950), a remarkably detailed picture of Honduras up to the close of the Cariato, but weak on economics. James Morris, *Honduras; Caudillo Politics and Military Rulers* (Boulder, Colo., 1984), tries to pick up the story where Stokes left it but lacks Stokes' insights and is rather descriptive. As a solid introduction to Honduras, although very heavy on factual information, Howard Blutstein et al., *Area Handbook for Honduras* (Washington, D.C., 1970) still has value.

No history of Honduras in the twentieth century can ignore the fruit companies. On the earlier period, there is a wealth of information in Charles Kepner and Jay Soothill, *The Banana Empire: A Case Study in Economic Imperialism* (New York, 1935). The Standard Fruit and Steamship Company has found a competent biographer in Thomas Karnes, *Tropical Enterprise* (Baton Rouge, 1978), but the United Fruit Company has still not spawned a satisfactory monograph; Stacy May and Galo Plazo, *The United Fruit Company in Latin America* (New York, 1958) is a eulogistic account. There is, however, a good study of the Honduran banana industry from its origins in V. Lainez and V. Meza, 'El enclave bananero en la historia de Honduras' in *Estudios Sociales Centroamericanos* (May, 1973). A similar, slightly more detailed study is Daniel Slutzky and Esther Alonso, *Empresas transnacionales y agricultura: el caso del enclave bananero en Honduras* (Tegucigalpa, 1982). The dispute between rival banana companies, which nearly provoked a war between Honduras and Guatemala, is described in Virgilio Rodríguez Beteta, *No es guerra de hermanos sino de bananos* (Guatemala, 1980).

The Cariato (1933–48) remains one of the most barren periods in Honduran historiography. There is a most unflattering portrait of the dictator in Filánder Díaz Chávez, *Carias – el ultimo caudillo frutero* (Tegucigalpa, 1982), and an interesting study of the problems facing the Liberal Party at this time in Carlos A. Contreras, *Entre el marasmo: analisis de la crisis del Partido Liberal de Honduras 1933–1970* (Tegucigalpa, 1970). There is also an account of Honduras in this and later periods in Guillermo Molina Chocano, 'Honduras: de la Guerra Civil al Reformismo Militar', in Pablo Gonzalez Casanova (ed.), *América Latina: historia de medio siglo,* vol 2 (Mexico, 1978). The last years of the Cariato and the relationship between Honduras and the United States during that period are covered in Thomas Leonard, *The United States and Central America, 1944–49* (Birmingham,

Ala., 1984). For the economic history of Honduras in these years there is much of interest in the Comisión Económica para América Latina (CEPAL), *El desarrollo económico de Honduras* (Santiago, 1960).

The banana strike of 1954 deserves a monograph in its own right but has not yet received one. One of the best discussions of the strike is to be found in Mario Posas, *El Movimiento Campesino Hondureño* (Tegucigalpa, 1981). A study that compares the strike with the peasant uprising in El Salvador in 1932 is Vinicio González, 'La Insurrección Salvadoreña de 1932 y la Gran Huelga Hondureña de 1954', *Revista Mexicana de Sociología* (April 1978). Other competent works on the Honduran labour movement are Victor Meza, *Historia del Movimiento Obrero Hondureño* (Tegucigalpa, 1980), and Mario Posas, *Lucha ideológica y organización sindical en Honduras* (Tegucigalpa, 1980). There is also an interesting anthology for the 1970s by Victor Meza, *Antología del Movimiento Obrero Hondureño* (Tegucigalpa, 1980).

The social reforms begun under President Ramón Villeda Morales are studied in several works. There is a good biography of Villeda Morales, which discusses his social programme in detail, by Stefania Natalini de Castro, María de los Angeles Mendoza Saborio and Joaquín Pagan Solorzano, *Significado histórico del gobierno del Dr. Ramón Villeda Morales* (Tegucigalpa, 1985). The agrarian reform is usefully discussed in R. Robleda, 'Latifundio, Reforma Agraria y Modernización', *Economía Política* (January 1982). This journal, published by the Instituto de Investigaciones Económicas y Sociales at the Universidad Nacional Autónoma de Honduras, has done much to stimulate research and writing on twentieth century Honduran social science. A recent study of agrarian reform, bringing the story up to the mid-1980s, is Charles Brockett, 'Public Policy, Peasants and Rural Development in Honduras', *Journal of Latin American Studies* 19/1 (1987).

The war with El Salvador in 1969 is discussed thoroughly in Thomas Anderson, *The War of the Dispossessed* (Lincoln, Neb., 1981). Another study, which concentrates much more on the international law aspects of the dispute, is James Rowles, *El conflicto Honduras–El Salvador* (San José, 1980). However, William Durham's study of the ecological origins of the war remains by far the most satisfactory; *Scarcity and Survival in Central America* (Stanford, 1979). This was the first work to draw proper attention to the land shortage created by Honduran geography on the one hand and demographic pressure on the other. It finally dispelled the notion that Honduras was a land-surplus country. There is also an interesting series of essays in Marco Carías and Daniel Slutzky (eds.), *La Guerra Inutil: Análisis socioeconómico del conflicto entre Honduras y El Salvador* (San José, 1971).

Several works cover Honduran economic development in recent decades. In INFORPRESS, *El Futuro del Mercado Comun Centroamericano* (Guatemala, 1983), there is an illuminating discussion of the reasons for Honduras' departure from the Central American Common Market. A fine, detailed study of the emergence of the beef industry is Daniel Slutzky, 'La agroindustria de la carne en Honduras', *Economía Política* (July 1977). On Honduran industrialization see Rafael Del Cid, 'Honduras: industrialización, empleo y explotación de la fuerza de trabajo', *Economía Política, no.* 13 (1977). An overview of Honduran economic development can be found in Benjamín Villanueva, 'Institutional Innovation and Economic Development, Honduras: A Case Study', unpublished Ph.D. thesis, University of Wisconsin, 1968. Surprisingly, there is still no major work on the Honduran coffee sector.

There have been remarkably few studies on the military as an institution in Honduras. An early effort is Steve Ropp, 'The Honduran Army in the Sociopolitical Evolution of the Honduran State', *The Americas* 30 (April 1974). Ropp, with James Morris, has attempted to build a corporate model to explain Honduran development, but the result is not wholly convincing: 'Corporatism and Dependent Development: A Honduran Case Study', *Latin American Research Review* 12 (Summer 1977). There are also few works on the Catholic Church as an institution in Honduras, although several books describe the growing political involvement of individuals within the Church. See, for example, Father James Guadalupe Carney, *To Be a Revolutionary* (San Francisco, 1987), the posthumously published autobiography of a Catholic priest killed in eastern Honduras.

The growing U.S. involvement in Honduras in the 1980s and the repercussions of the regional crisis on Honduras have produced a huge literature of uneven quality. One of the better efforts is Mark Rosenberg and Philip Shepherd (eds.), *Honduras Confronts Its Future* (Boulder, Colo., 1986), which presents a series of essays by leading Hondurans on the political economy of the 1980s. A perceptive account of the recent period can be found in Guillermo Molina Chocano, 'Honduras: la situación política y económica reciente', in Donaldo Castillo Rivas, *Centroamérica — más allá de la crisis* (Mexico, 1983). Finally, mention should be made of a book by Gautama Fonseca, a Honduran journalist who has written a number of reflective essays on the Honduran political system: *Cuatro ensayos sobre la realidad política de Honduras* (Tegucigalpa, 1982).

7. NICARAGUA SINCE 1930

Nicaraguan historiography is extremely uneven in both quality and quantity. Although there is still no satisfactory general work on the years since independence, certain events in Nicaraguan history have attracted enormous attention, notably the proposed inter-oceanic canal in the nineteenth century; the U.S. occupation in the first third of the twentieth century; the Sandino episode; and, more recently, the Sandinista revolution.

The international attention devoted to Nicaragua since the collapse of the Somoza dynasty in 1979 has created a demand for comprehensive bibliographies, previously a neglected area. The most impressive is the three-volume *Nicaraguan National Bibliography, 1800–1978,* produced by the Latin American Bibliographic Foundation (Redlands, Calif., 1986–7), with more than twenty thousand entries. A more modest, but useful, bibliography is in the Clio Press series: Ralph Lee Woodward, Jr., *Nicaragua* (Oxford and Santa Barbara, 1983). For the post-1979 period, there is such a rapid increase in publications every year that any bibliography runs the risk of being out-of-date as soon as it is published. Hans Aalborg, however, has compiled a helpful work for the first five years of the revolution: *The Nicaraguan Development Process* (Centre for Development Research, Copenhagen, 1984).

Of several good works on the U.S. occupation of Nicaragua, which ended in 1933, the best is William Kamman, *A Search for Stability: United States Diplomacy Towards Nicaragua, 1925–1933* (Notre Dame, Ind., 1968), although this focusses almost exclusively on the period after the marines returned to Nicaragua in 1926. Roscoe Hill, *Fiscal Intervention in Nicaragua* (New York, 1933), is an excellent study dealing with the non-military side of U.S. intervention. For a dry, but very thorough, account of the intervention years, see Department of State, *The United States and Nicaragua: A Survey of the Relations from 1909 to 1932* (Washington, D.C., 1932). A more interesting account, written by a U.S. journalist, is Harold Denny, *Dollars for Bullets: The Story of American Rule in Nicaragua* (New York, 1929). This book was deservedly reprinted by Greenwood Press in 1980.

The Sandino episode has generated two waves of publications. The first, written by contemporaries, ended with the publication of Anastasio Somoza, *El verdadero Sandino, o el Calvario de las Segovias* (Managua, 1936). The second wave began with the Nicaraguan revolution and has been spearheaded by the Instituto de Estudio del Sandinismo in Managua.

During both these periods, writings on Sandino and Sandinismo have suffered from a lack of scholarly detachment. Fortunately, a small number of works were produced on Sandino between the two waves, which are exemplary in their attention to detail; these include Neill Macaulay, *The Sandino Affair* (Chicago, 1967), and Gregorio Selser, *Sandino: General de Hombres Libres,* 2 vols. (Buenos Aires, 1959), although the latter is at times somewhat uncritical. Mention should also be made of Donald Hodges, *Intellectual Foundations of the Nicaraguan Revolution* (Austin, Tex., 1986); although Hodges does not succeed in his ambition to establish Sandino as a consistent and original political thinker, he does provide a wealth of new material and gives due attention to the intellectual climate in which the Sandino episode evolved. Another excellent book, drawing attention to the international and regional situation at the start of the 1930s, is Rodolfo Cerdas Cruz, *La hoz y el Machete* (San José, 1986), which, while focussing on the role of the Communist International throughout Central America, devotes a great deal of research to Nicaragua during the Sandino episode.

A number of general works on the history of Nicaragua during the years of the Somoza dynasty include Richard Millett, *Guardians of the Dynasty* (New York, 1977), concerned mainly with the National Guard from its formation at the end of the 1920s but with much of interest on other aspects of Nicaraguan society. Both Bernard Diederich, *Somoza* (London, 1982), and Eduardo Crawley, *Dictators Never Die* (London, 1979), are primarily concerned with the Somoza family but also furnish useful accounts of the general political background. Claribel Alegría and D. J. Flakoll, *Nicaragua: la revolución Sandinista: una crónica política 1855–1979* (Mexico, 1982), is a good account of the rebirth of the Sandinista movement after the assassination of Sandino in 1934; despite the title, however, it has little to say on the period before Sandino's death. Another useful book focussing on the revival of Sandinismo is Hugo Cancino Troncoso, *Las raíces históricas e ideológicas del movimiento Sandinista: antecedentes de la revolución nacional y popular Nicaragüense, 1927–1979* (Odense University Press, 1984). Finally, mention should be made of Humberto Ortega's *50 años de lucha Sandinista,* which, published in 1976 in 'algún lugar de Nicaragua', provides the Frente Sandinista de Liberación Nacional account of how the Sandinista struggles of the 1960s and 1970s were linked to the much earlier Sandino episode.

The economic history of Nicaragua has attracted growing interest since the publication of Jaime Wheelock's influential *Imperialismo y dictadura:*

crisis de una formación social (Mexico, 1975). Jaime Biderman, 'Class Structure, The State and Capitalist Development in Nicaraguan Agriculture' (unpublished Ph.D. dissertation, University of California, 1982), is an excellent study highlighting the rise of the cotton industry after the 1940s. Earlier works which still have much to offer include International Bank for Reconstruction and Development, *The Economic Development of Nicaragua* (Washington, D.C., 1953); Comisión Económica para América Latina, *El desarrollo económico de Nicaragua,* (New York, 1966), and Luis Cantarero, 'The Economic Development of Nicaragua, 1920–47' (unpublished Ph.D. dissertation, University of Iowa, 1948).

The labour movement under the Somoza dynasty, neglected for years, has recently received some attention. A good study of the 1940s is Jeffrey Gould, ' "For an Organised Nicaragua": Somoza and the Labour Movement, 1944–1948', *Journal of Latin American Studies* 19, no. 2 (1987). A more general work is Carlos Pérez Bermúdez and Onofre Guevara, *El Movimiento Obrero en Nicaragua* (Managua, 1985). This controversial work seeks to justify the role played by the Partido Socialista Nicaragüense under Somoza but nevertheless is an unrivalled source of information on many aspects of the labour movement's history.

The Nicaraguan revolution leading to the overthrow of Somoza has produced many books and articles, of which the best are John Booth, *The End and the Beginning: the Nicaraguan Revolution* (Boulder, Colo., 1982), and George Black, *Triumph of the People: The Sandinista Revolution in Nicaragua* (London, 1981). Anastasio Somoza's own version of the events leading to his overthrow, *Nicaragua Betrayed* (Boston, 1980), gives a very partial, but fascinating, description of his relationship with the Carter administration. This same question is taken up by Robert Pastor in *Condemned to Repetition: the United States and Nicaragua* (Princeton, 1987), where the author makes a courageous effort to explore what went wrong in a relationship in which he himself played a minor part as President Carter's Latin American specialist on the National Security Council.

The period since the revolution has seen an explosion in writings on Nicaragua. The best of these tend to be sympathetic to the revolution, but fall short of the highest standards of scholarship; examples are Thomas Walker (ed.), *Nicaragua: The First Five Years* (New York, 1985); Carlos Vilas, *The Sandinista Revolution* (New York, 1986); and Richard Harris and Carlos Vilas (eds.), *Nicaragua: A Revolution Under Siege* (London, 1985). A less committed but still sympathetic treatment of the revolutionary period can be found in David Close, *Nicaragua: Politics, Economics and Society*

(London, 1988). Works critical of the revolutionary period tend to be written by exiles or foreigners without access to primary sources; among the better examples is Xavier Zavala et al., *1984 Nicaragua* (San José, 1985).

Economic development, including agrarian reform, under the Sandinista regime has begun to receive the attention it deserves. A good example, bringing together many of the best scholars in the field, is Rose Spalding (ed.), *The Political Economy of Revolutionary Nicaragua* (Boston, 1987). Specialist works on agriculture include Forrest Colburn, *Post-Revolutionary Nicaragua: State Class and the Dilemmas of Agrarian Policy* (Berkeley, 1986), although this study was subsequently overtaken by changes in Nicaraguan agrarian reform. The latter is studied in a large number of articles, including I. Luciak, 'National Unity and Popular Hegemony: The Dialectics of Sandinista Agrarian Reform Policies, 1979–86', *Journal of Latin American Studies* 19 (1987), and Carmen Diana Deere, Peter Marchetti and Nola Reinhardt, 'The Peasantry and the Development of Sandinista Agrarian Policy, 1979–84', *Latin American Research Review* 20 (1985).

Sandinista foreign policy, a major source of friction in U.S.–Nicaraguan relations, is discussed in Mary Vanderlaan, *Revolution and Foreign Policy in Nicaragua* (Boulder, Colo., 1986). The Catholic Church in Nicaragua has received a great deal of attention in recent years, both because of the friction between the hierarchy and the Sandinista government and because of the growth of a 'popular' church. A thoughtful study which reflects both sides of the question is Laura O'Shaugnessy and Luis Serra, *The Church and Revolution in Nicaragua* (Athens, Ohio, 1986). Another work along similar lines is Rosa Maria Pochet and Abelino Martinez, *Iglesia: manipulación o profecía?* (San José, 1987).

The Atlantic coast region and its ethnic minorities have not yet received proper attention. Craig Dozier, *Nicaragua's Mosquito Shore: The Years of British and American Experience* (Birmingham, Ala., 1986), gives an excellent account of the coast in the nineteenth century, but offers only a sketchy treatment of the more recent period. It is to be hoped, however, that the new Centro de Investigación y Documentación de la Costa Atlántica, which has begun the difficult task of assembling in Nicaragua the relevant documents, will stimulate research in this area. A special issue of the Nicaraguan journal *Encuentro* was devoted to the Atlantic coast in 1985 and deals with both the past and present; see 'La Costa Atlántica: Pasado y Presente', *Encuentro* (April-September, 1985).

8. COSTA RICA SINCE 1930

A pioneering general interpretation of Costa Rica that considers the country's development from a variety of perspectives is Samuel Stone, *La dinastía de los Conquistadores* (San José, 1975). The same broad approach is also adopted in the excellent studies written by Carolyn Hall: *El café y el desarrollo histórico-geográfico de Costa Rica* (San José, 1976) and *Costa Rica: una interpretación geográfica con perspectiva histórica* (San José, 1984). Other general interpretative surveys include José L. Vega, *Poder político y democracia en Costa Rica* (San José, 1982), and *Orden y progreso: la formación del estado nacional en Costa Rica* (San José, 1975); Carlos Meléndez's more dated *Costa Rica: evolución de sus problemas más destacados* (San José, 1953); Wilburg Jiménez, *Génesis del gobierno de Costa Rica, 1821–1981* (San José, 1986), which concentrates upon administrative issues; and the collection of provocative essays edited by Chester Zelaya, *Costa Rica contemporánea* (San José, 1979). The perspective of the Partido Liberación Nacional (PLN) is reflected in Carlos Monge, *Historia de Costa Rica* (San José, 1962); Eugenio Rodríguez, *Apuntes para una sociología costarricense* (San José, 1953) and Hugo Navarro, *La generación del 48. Juicio histórico sobre la democracia costarricense* (Mexico, 1957). For a rigorously Marxist interpretation, see Reinaldo Carcanholo, *Desarrollo del capitalismo en Costa Rica* (San José, 1981).

Studies of social groups and the development of the labour force include: Lowell Gudmundson, *Hacendados políticos y precaristas: la ganadería y el latifundismo guanacasteco, 1800–1950* (San José, 1983); Mitchell Seligson, *Peasants of Costa Rica and the Development of Agrarian Capitalism* (Madison, Wisc., 1980); Roger Churnside, *Formación de la Fuerza Laboral Costarricense* (San José, 1985). Raimundo Santos and Liliana Herrera, *Del artesano al obrero fabril* (San José, 1979) is strongly syndicalist in its approach but contains useful information. Important studies of other sectors include: Víctor H. Acuña, 'La ideología de los pequeños y medianos productores cafetaleros costarricenses', and Alfonso González, 'El discurso oficial de los pequeños y medianos cafetaleros (1920–1940; 1950–1961)' in *Revista de Historia,* Universidad Nacional, Heredia, no. 16 (1987); and Manuel Rojas, 'El Movimiento Obrero en Costa Rica', in P. González Casanova (ed.), *Historia del movimiento obrero en América Latina* (Mexico, 1984). The debate over the nature of social and political power in the country is engaged from an entirely different perspective in the two volumes written by Oscar Arias: *Grupos de presión en Costa Rica* (San José,

1971), and *Quién gobierna en Costa Rica?* (San José, 1977). A number of studies analyse the role of elites from different sectors of the economy. For the cattle ranchers, see Irene Aguilar and Manuel Solís, *La elite ganadera en Costa Rica* (San José, 1988). For sugar, see Mayra Achio and Ana C. Escalante, *Azúcar y política en Costa Rica* (San José, 1985). For the banana industry, Chester Lloyd Jones, *Costa Rica and Civilization in the Caribbean* (Madison, Wisc., 1935) remains useful for the background; Frank Ellis, *Las transnacionales del banano en Centroamerica* (San José, 1983), covers the more modern period from an economist's perspective; and Jeffrey Casey Gaspar, *Limón: 1880–1940. Un estudio de la industria bananera en Costa Rica* (San José, 1979), provides an excellent case study.

The question of land tenure, which acquired particular importance in the post-war era, is treated in CEPAL, *Costa Rica: características de uso y distribución de la tierra* (San José, 1972), and critically analysed in two suggestive essays: Mario Fernández, 'Dinámica de capital, evolución de la estructura de la tenencia de la tierra y paisaje rural en Costa Rica', *Revista de Estudios Centroamericanos,* no. 36 (1983), and Edelberto Torres Rivas, 'Elementos para la caracterización de la estructura agraria de Costa Rica', *Avances de Investigación,* Instituto de Investigaciones Sociales, Universidad de Costa Rica (San José, 1978). The role of the state in economic development became the subject of increasing debate with the onset of economic crisis at the end of the 1970s. Rodolfo Cerdas provided an early contibution in 'Del estado intervencionista al estado empresario. Notas para el estudio del estado en Costa Rica', *Anuario de Estudios Centroamericanos,* no. 5 (1979), and 'La crisis política nacional: origen y perspectivas', in Armando Vargas (ed.), *La crisis de democracia en Costa Rica* (San José, 1981). Other works that consider this subject in the light of modern developments in the country's political economy include: Ana Sojo, *Estado empresario y lucha política en Costa Rica* (San José, 1984); Mylena Vega, *El estado costarricense de 1974 a 1978. CODESA y la fracción industrial* (San José, 1982); Helio Fallas, *Crisis económica en Costa Rica* (San José, 1980); and Juan M. Villasuso (ed.), *El sector productivo: crisis y perspectivas* (San José 1984). The liberal approach to this issue is represented in Víctor H. Cespedes, Alberto Dimare and Ronulfo Jiménez, *Costa Rica: recuperación sin reactivación* (San José, 1985), and in the publications of the Academia de Centroamérica, such as *Problemas Económicos de la Década de los 80* (San José 1982) and *Costa Rica: estabilidad sin crecimiento* (San José, 1984).

Among general surveys of the evolution of political thought, two in particular stand out: Constantino Láscaris, *Desarrollo de las ideas filosóficas en Costa Rica* (San José, 1983), and Luis Barahona, *Las ideas políticas en Costa Rica* (San José, 1977). Those who are particularly interested in the philosophical influences on the 'Generation of '48' who dominated the country's politics after the civil war of that year should also consult Roberto Brenes, *El político* (San José, 1942).

The literature on modern history is notably uneven in terms of its concentration on certain periods, particular attention being paid to the late 1940s. However, a number of valuable studies consider the social and political background to the crisis of the 1930s that decisively influenced subsequent developments. For an excellent appraisal of a leading political figure of the 'Olympian' epoch, see Eugenio Rodríquez, *Ricardo Jiménez Oreamuno: su pensamiento* (San José, 1980), which is usefully complemented by Joaquín Vargas Coto, *Crónicas de la epoca y vida de Don Ricardo* (San José, 1986). Marina Volio, *Jorge Volio y el Partido Reformista* (San José, 1972), and Miguel Acuña, *Jorge Volio, el Tribuno de la Plebe* (San José, 1972) give good accounts of the career and ideas of the leading oppositionist of the 1920s, whose influence is discernable in later decades. More general surveys of this period include Cleto González, *El sufragio en Costa Rica ante la historia y la legislación* (San José, 1978), and Tomás Soley, *Historia Económica de Costa Rica* (San José, 1949). International relations are treated in Richard Salisbury, *Costa Rica y el Istmo, 1900–1934* (San José, 1984). The development of the labour movement, which exercised growing influence from the early 1930s, is presented in Vladimir de la Cruz, *Las luchas sociales en Costa Rica (1870–1930)* (San José, 1983).

The birth of the Communist Party is set in its socio-economic context in Ana María Botey and Rodolfo Cisneros, *La crisis de 1929 y la fundación del Partido Comunista de Costa Rica* (San José, 1984), and analysed in terms of external influences in Rodolfo Cerdas, *La Hoz y el Machete. La Internacional Comunista en América Latina y la Revolución en Centro América* (San José, 1986). The speeches and activities of its principal leaders provide a vital source for understanding the party's subsequent development: Gilberto Calvo and Francisco Zúñiga (eds.), *Manuel Mora: discursos (1934–1979)* (San José, 1980); Arnoldo Ferreto, *Vida militante* (San José, 1984); and Marielos Aguilar, *Carlos Luis Fallas: su época y sus luchas* (San José, 1983).

One of the very few studies of the administration of León Cortés (1936–40) is Theodore A. Creedman, 'León Cortés y su tiempo', *Anales de la Academia de Geografía e Historia de Costa Rica*, (1967–9). Carlos Calvo,

Costa Rica en la Segunda Guerra Mundial (1939–45) (San José, 1985), provides an extensive analysis of the war years, and relations with the United States up to the Cold War are treated in some detail in Jacobo Schifter, *Las alianzas conflictivas: las relaciones de Estados Unidos y Costa Rica desde la segunda guerra mundial a la guerra fría* (San José, 1986). Another work by this author, *La fase oculta de la guerra civil en Costa Rica* (San José, 1981), provides a complementary analysis of developments within the country during the civil conflict of 1948.

The civil war and its origins are the subjects of an extensive literature. Oscar Aguilar, *Costa Rica y sus hechos políticos de 1948: problemática de una década* (San José, 1969), contains a very useful selection of documents and interviews, as does Guillermo Villegas, *Testimonios del 48* (San José, 1977). The same author's *El otro Calderón Guardia* (San José, 1985) provides important insights on the leader of the defeated forces, and another text, *El Cardonazo* (San José, 1986), considers an important event in the immediate aftermath of the fighting. From the point of view of the victorious rebels, Alberto Cañas, *Los ocho años* (San José, 1955), continues to be a classic text, as is *El espíritu del 48* (San José, 1987), by their leader, José Figueres. Roberto Fernández, *La huelga de Brazos Caidos* (San José, 1953), gives a good depiction of the political atmosphere on the eve of the conflict. The perspective of the Communist Party is presented in Partido Vanguardia Popular, *Como y por qué cayó la democracia en Costa Rica* (Guatemala, 1948), and Manuel Mora, *Dos discursos en defensa de Vanguardia Popular* (San José, 1959). Later, and more sophisticated, interpretations made from the same political perspective include Manuel Rojas, *Lucha social y guerra civil en Costa Rica* (San José, 1980), and Gerardo Contreras and José Manuel Cerdas, *Los años 40: historia de una política de alianzas* (San José, 1988). The record of the defeated Picado regime is defended in Enrique Guier, *Defensa de los Señores Licenciados Teodoro Picado y Vicente Urcuyo* (San José, 1950), and by Picado himself in *El pacto de la embajada de México; su incumplimiento* (Managua, n.d.). Another attack on Figueres, this time for his failure to honour pledges to the Caribbean Legion, is made in Rosendo Argüello, *Quienes y como nos traicionaron* (Mexico, 1954). John Patrick Bell, *Crisis in Costa Rica: The 1948 Revolution* (Austin, Tex., 1971) remains one of the best sources on the civil war and its immediate background.

For studies of Archbishop Victor Sanabria, who played a major role in the political events of the 1940s, see Ricardo Blanco, *Monseñor Sanabria* (San José, 1962); Santiago Arrieta, *El pensamiento político-social de Monseñor*

Sanabria (San José, 1977); and James Baker, *La iglesia y el sindicalismo en Costa Rica* (San José, 1978). Rafael Calderón Guardia is the subject of a number of studies in addition to that by Villegas just noted. Among the most useful are: Carlos Fernández, *Calderón Guardia: líder y caudillo* (San José, 1939); the compilation edited by Mario Hidalgo, *Dr Calderón Guardia: reformador social de Costa Rica* (San José, 1983); and Jorge M. Salazar, *Calderón Guardia* (San José, 1985). The literature on Figueres is more extensive and includes a number of eulogistic or uncritical works, such as Hugo Navarro, *José Figueres en la evolución de Costa Rica* (Mexico, 1953); Arturo Castro, *José Figueres: el hombre y su obra. Ensayo de una biografía* (San José, 1955); and Charles Ameringer, *Don Pepe: A Political Biography of José Figueres of Costa Rica* (Albuquerque, 1978). A useful bibliography is Harry Kantor, *Bibliography of José Figueres* (Tempe, Ariz., 1972); the same author's *The Costa Rican Election of 1953: A Case Study* (Gainesville, Fla., 1958) is also valuable to students of Figueres' role in national politics. The Constitutent Assembly of 1949 is described from a journalistic perspective in Rubén Hernández, *Desde la barra: como se discutió la Constitución de 1949* (San José, 1953) while the Charter itself is analysed in the excellent work by Oscar Aguilar, *La Contitución Política de 1949: Antecedentes y Proyecciones* (San José, 1975). For broader consideration of constitutional issues, see Hernán G. Peralta, *Las Constituciones de Costa Rica* (Madrid, 1962), and Jorge Saénz, *El despertar constitucional de Costa Rica* (San José, 1985). The fullest survey of the nationalization of the banks undertaken during this period is Rufino Gil, *La nacionalización bancaria* (San José, 1962), which complements the same author's *Ciento cinco años de vida bancaria en Costa Rica* (San José, 1974). For the post-civil war administration of Otilio Ulate, José Luis Torres, *Otilio Ulate: su partido y sus luchas* (San José, 1986), stands alone in its field. It is usefully supplemented by Ulate's own writings, collected in *A la luz de la moral política* (San José, 1976). Further information on this period may be gleaned from the relevant chapters of two general studies: Joaquín Garro, *Veinte años de historia chica: notas para una historia costarricense* (San José, 1967), and Jorge Rovira, *Estado y política económica en Costa Rica, 1948–1970* (San José, 1983).

The presidency of Mario Echandi still awaits a detailed historical assessment. However, some interesting material is available in María Gamboa (ed.), *Los vetos del Presidente Echandi: sus razones y justificación: 1958–1962* (San José, 1962), and Mark Rosenberg, *Las luchas por el seguro social en Costa Rica* (San José, 1980). The literature on the Trejos Fernández administration is similarly thin, but important documentation is given in José J. Trejos Fernández, *Ocho años en la política costarricense* (San José, 1973), and a number of useful insights may be derived from Oscar Aguilar, *Democracia y partidos políticos en Costa Rica (1950–60)* (San José, 1977), and Jorge E. Romero, *Partidos, poder y derecho* (San José, 1979).

By contrast, the history of the PLN is covered by numerous works. For the party's background, see Carlos Araya, *Historia de los partidos políticos de Costa Rica: liberación nacional* (San José, 1968), which provides a most useful analysis despite the partisan position of the author. A key programmatic statement from the early years is *Ideario costarricense: resultado de una encuesta nacional* (San José, 1943), important documentation of subsequent developments being contained in two anthologies: Alfonso Carro (ed.), *El Pensamiento Socialdemócrata. Antología* (San José, 1986), and Carlos José Gutiérrez (ed.), *El pensamiento político costarricense: la socialdemocracia* (San José, 1986), which is more extensive and systematic in its coverage. The leaders of the PLN have themselves produced a number of important works. Daniel Oduber, *Raíces del Partido Liberación Nacional: Notas para una evaluación histórica* (San José, 1985), is extremely useful on the origins of the party, and Figueres' writings provide abundant material on the development of the PLN's ideology and outlook. *Cartas a un ciudadano* (San José, 1956); *Los deberes de mi destino* (San José, 1957); *Estos diez años* (San José, 1958); and *La pobreza de las naciones* (San José, 1973), are broadly representative of the ex-president's output, although it should be noted that his views did not always enjoy a consensus within the party. Moreover, an understanding of the early approach adopted by currents which were later to form the PLN cannot be gained without reference to the work of Rodrigo Facio, particularly *Estudio sobre economía costarricense* (San José, 1942); *El centro ante las garantías sociales* (San José, 1943); and *La moneda y la Banca Central en Costa Rica* (Mexico, 1947). For independent treatments of the party, see Burt H. English, *Liberación nacional in Costa Rica: The Development of a Political Party in a Transitional Society* (Gainesville, Fla., 1971), and James L. Busey, *Notes on Costa Rican Democracy* (Boulder, Colo., 1962). A critical analysis is given in Susanne Jonas Bodenheimer, *La ideología socialdemócrata en Costa Rica* (San José, 1984). Analysis of elections constitutes an important feature of the literature on Costa Rican politics. Among the best work containing both data and interpretation, see Eduardo Oconitrillo, *Un siglo de política costarricense* (San José, 1981), and Wilburg Jiménez, *Análisis electoral de una democracia* (San José, 1977). Other studies in this area include Olda M. Acuña and Carlos F. Denton,

La elección de un presidente: Costa Rica 1982 (San José, 1984); Mario Sánchez, *Las bases sociales del voto en Costa Rica (1974–78)* (San José, 1985); and C. Granados and A. Ohlsson, 'Organización del Territorio y Resultados Electorales en Costa Rica, 1953–1982', *Estudios Sociales Centroamericanos*, no. 36 (1983).

The general survey of the post-war economy provided in Carlos Araya's *Historia económica de Costa Rica, 1950–1970* (San José, 1975) is complemented for the more recent period by Jorge Rovira, *Costa Rica en los años 80* (San José, 1987). The nature of industrialization in the post-war epoch is considered in Leonardo Garnier and Fernando Herrero, *El desarrollo de la industria en Costa Rica* (Heredia, 1982), and Garnier's 'Industria, Estado y Desarrollo en Costa Rica: Perspectivas y Propuestas', *Revista de Estudios Centroamericanos*, no. 37 (1984). The Escuela de Ciencias Económicas y Sociales of the Universidad de Costa Rica produced a number of publications concerning important economic developments from the late 1950s under the general title of *El desarrollo económico de Costa Rica: estudio del sector externo de la economía costarricense* (San José, 1958); *Estudio del sector industrial* (San José, 1959); and *Estudio del sector público* (San José, 1962). For an analysis of the country's economy in the immediate postwar period from a North American perspective, see Stacey May (ed.), *Costa Rica. A Study in Economic Development* (New York, 1952). Two quite different interpretations of developments in the modern era may be found in Rodolfo Cerdas, *Crisis de la democracia liberal en Costa Rica* (San José, 1972), and Sergio Reuben, *Capitalismo y crisis económica en Costa Rica* (San José, 1982).

9. CUBA *c.* 1930–59

Valuable chapters on Cuba during the period from the *machadato* to the Revolution can be found in the following general studies: Hugh Thomas, *Cuba, The Pursuit of Freedom* (New York, 1971); Jaime Suchlicki, *Cuba: From Columbus to Castro* (New York, 1974); Jorge Domínguez, *Cuba: Order and Revolution* (Cambridge, Mass. 1978); Louis A. Pérez, Jr., *Cuba: Between Reform and Revolution* (New York, 1988). See also Ramón Ruiz, *Cuba: The Making of a Revolution* (Amherst, Mass., 1968). Among the better recent general historical surveys published in Cuba are Julio E. Le Reverend, *Historia de Cuba* (Havana, 1973); Ministerio de Fuerzas Armadas Revolucionarias, *Historia militar de Cuba* (Havana, n.d.). A complete history of Cuba is in the ten-volume collaborative work supervised by Ramiro Guerra y Sánchez, *Historia de la nación cubana* (Havana, 1952). Also of some use is the three-volume work by Emeterio S. Santovenia and Raúl M. Shelton, *Cuba y su historia,* 3d ed. (Miami, 1966) and the five-volume work by José Duarte Oropesa, *Historiología cubana* (n.p., 1969–70). The two-volume anthology published under the auspices of the Grupo de Estudios Cubanos of the University of Havana, *La república neocolonial* (Havana, 1975–1979), deals expertly with a variety of topics including labour, economic history, the armed forces and the ABC. Wyatt MacGaffey and Clifford R. Barnett, *Twentieth Century Cuba* (New York, 1965), an invaluable reference work, contains much data on social, economic, political and cultural developments on the island. A similar format was used in the volume published by the Foreign Area Studies of American University, *Cuba, A Country Study,* 2d ed. (Washington, D.C., 1985). Another useful reference work, particularly for its wealth of statistical data, is José Alvarez Díaz et al., *A Study on Cuba* (Coral Gables, Fla., 1965). The most useful statistical compilation available is Susan Schroeder, *Cuba: A Handbook of Historical Statistics* (Boston, 1982).

Luis E. Aguilar, *Cuba 1933: Prologue to Revolution* (Ithaca, N.Y., 1972), remains one of the most balanced and judicious accounts of the *machadato* and the revolutionary tumult of the 1930s; see also Louis A. Pérez, Jr., *Cuba Under the Platt Amendment, 1902–34* (Pittsburgh, 1986). The most complete study of the events of 1933, including an extensive treatment of the 1920s, is the three-volume work of Lionel Soto, *La revolución del 33* (Havana, 1977). An excellent study of the eclipse of the revolutionary movement of the 1930s is found in José A. Tabares del Real, *La revolución del 30: sus dos últimos años,* 3d ed. (Havana, 1975). Some of the older accounts of the events of 1933 are still of considerable value: Ricardo Adam y Silva, *La gran mentira. 4 de septiembre de 1933* (Havana, 1947); M. Franco Varona, *La revolución del 4 de septiembre* (Havana, 1934); and Alberto Lamar Schweyer, *Como cayó el presidente Machado* (Madrid, 1941). Raymond Leslie Buell et al., *Problems of the New Cuba* (New York, 1935), remains as a landmark study of Cuba during the 1930s, dealing with virtually every aspect of Cuban national, provincial and municipal life. The International Bank for Reconstruction and Development, *Report on Cuba* (Baltimore, 1951) is similar in approach and scope. Together these two studies are indispensable reference works for the period. An excellent monograph which concludes with a treatment of the 1920s and 1930s is Jules R. Benjamin, *The United States and Cuba: Hegemony and Dependent Development, 1880–1934* (Pittsburgh, 1977). Samuel Farber, *Revolution and Reaction in Cuba, 1933–1960* (Middletown, Conn., 1976), is an excellent study

tion, employment, social welfare and international economic factors. Jorge Domínguez, *Cuba Order and Revolution* (Cambridge, Mass., 1978), focusses on politics and government. Some update is provided in Domínguez, (ed.), *Cuba: Internal and International Affairs* (Beverly Hills, Calif., 1982). Good, short, general summaries on many topics are in Sandor Halebsky and John M. Kirk (eds.), *Cuba: Twenty-Five Years of Revolution: 1959 to 1984* (New York, 1985).

Other useful books on the economy are: Archibald Ritter, *The Economic Development of Revolutionary Cuba: Strategy and Performance* (New York, 1974), which gives a good coverage of the 1960s; Claes Brundenius, *Revolutionary Cuba: The Challenge of Economic Growth with Equity* (Boulder, Colo., 1984), and Alberto Recarte's *Cuba: economía y poder (1959–1980)* (Madrid, 1980), which cover the 1970s as well. Interesting discussion of the Cuban economy cast in a wider social and political context from a Marxist perspective is to be found in James O'Connor, *The Origins of Socialism in Cuba* (Ithaca, N.Y., 1970), for the earlier years, and Arthur MacEwan, *Revolution and Economic Development in Cuba* (New York, 1981), for a later period. Cuba's leading academic economist, José Luis Rodríguez, publishes mostly through the CIEM. A bibliographical and technical overview of the problems of estimating Cuba's economic growth rates is available from Carmelo Mesa-Lago and Jorge Pérez-López, 'A Study of Cuba's Material Product System, Its Conversion to the System of National Accounts, and Estimation of Gross Domestic Product Per Capita and Growth Rates', *World Bank Staff Working Papers,* no. 770 (Washington, D.C., 1985). A somewhat bitter but occasionally enlightening debate on this topic, between Mesa-Lago and Pérez-López versus Claes Brundenius and Andrew Zimbalist, appeared in *Comparative Economic Studies* in 1985 and 1986. See also Jorge F. Pérez-López, *Measuring Cuban Economic Performance* (Austin, Tex., 1987).

Four books have been published from the research project led by Oscar Lewis in Cuba in 1969–70, the only major field research conducted by outside scholars in revolutionary Cuba. The project ended when the Cuban government confiscated many of its tapes and notes and forced the Lewis group to leave. Their books provide much information on the lives of ordinary Cubans. Oscar Lewis, Ruth M. Lewis and Susan M. Rigdon are responsible for *Four Men* (Urbana, Ill., 1977); *Four Women* (Urbana, Ill., 1977); and *Neighbors* (Urbana, Ill., 1978), while Douglas Butterworth is responsible for *The People of Buena Ventura: Relocation of Slum Dwellers in Postrevolutionary Cuba* (Urbana, Ill., 1980).

Several books have captured important facets of Cuban politics and government policy in the 1960s. A superb discussion of the personal role and style of Fidel Castro is Edward Gonzalez, *Cuba Under Castro: The Limits of Charisma* (Boston, 1974). The best extended interview with Fidel Castro was published (along with excellent photographs) by Lee Lockwood in *Castro's Cuba, Cuba's Fidel* (New York, 1969). A thorough discussion of the factional politics of early revolutionary rule is provided by Andrés Suaréz in *Cuba: Castroism and Communism* (Cambridge, Mass., 1967). A discussion of the radical politics of the 1960s appears in K. S. Karol, *Guerrillas in Power* (New York, 1970), and in René Dumont, *Cuba: Est-il socialiste?* (Paris, 1970), both rather critical; a more sympathetic approach to the regime's goals is given in Richard Fagen, *The Transformation of Political Culture in Cuba* (Stanford, 1969). Valuable collections, covering several topics mostly dealing with Cuba in the 1960s, have been edited by Rolando Bonachea and Nelson P. Valdés, *Cuba in Revolution* (Garden City, N.Y., 1972); by Jaime Suchlicki, *Castro, Cuba and Revolution* (Coral Gables, Fla., 1972); and by Carmelo Mesa-Lago, *Revolutionary Change in Cuba* (Pittsburgh, 1971).

Other work on internal Cuban politics and political economy since the 1970s is, surprisingly, not very extensive. Special attention should be paid to the studies of Susan Eckstein, William LeoGrande and Nelson P. Valdéz, some of which have appeared in *Cuban Studies*. A good, general collection on the 1980s is the seventh edition of Irving L. Horowitz's *Cuban Communism* (New Brunswick, N.J., 1989). On human rights and internal security, see the seven reports on Cuba issued by the Inter-American Commission on Human Rights of the Organization of American States (Washington, D.C.), various years, most recently 1983. See also Luis Salas, *Social Control and Deviance in Cuba* (New York, 1979). There is little work on the Cuban armed forces. A useful manual is the U.S. Department of Defense, Directorate for Intelligence Research, Defense Intelligence Agency, *Handbook on the Cuban Armed Forces* (Washington, D.C., 1979), which is not classified.

There has been an increase in publications concerning the international relations of the Cuban revolution. Four edited collections gather much good work. They are Carmelo Mesa-Lago and Cole Blasier, *Cuba in the World* (Pittsburgh, 1979); Martin Weinstein; *Revolutionary Cuba in the World Arena* (Philadelphia, 1979); Carmelo Mesa-Lago and June Belkins, *Cuba in Africa* (Pittsburgh, 1982); and Barry Levine, *The New Cuban Presence in the Caribbean* (Boulder, Colo., 1983). See also: Carla A. Robbins, *The Cuban Threat* (New York, 1983); Lynn D. Bender, *Cuba vs. United States: The Politics of Hostility,* 2d rev. ed. (San Juan, 1981); W. Raymond Duncan, *The Soviet Union and Cuba* (New York, 1985); Pamela Falk, *Cuban Foreign Policy: Caribbean Tempest* (Lexington, Mass., 1985); H. Michael Erisman, *Cuba's International Relations: The Anatomy of a Nationalistic Foreign Policy* (Boulder, Colo., 1985); Wayne E. Smith, *The Closest of Enemies* (New York, 1987); and Peter Shearman, *The Soviet Union and Cuba* (London, 1987). A recent study of U.S.-Cuban relations since the 1950s is Morris H. Morley, *Imperial State and Revolution: The United States and Cuba, 1952–1986)* (Cambridge, 1988).

An important source, monitoring U.S.-Cuban relations over time, and generating a great deal of information for primary research on this topic, has been the U.S. House of Representatives, Committee on Foreign Affairs, Subcommittee on Inter-American Affairs, through its published hearings records. The series of documents occasionally published by the Central Intelligence Agency, National Foreign Assessment Center, entitled *Communist Aid to Less Developed Countries of the Free World,* provides a useful, though at times controversial and incomplete, listing of the Cuban overseas presence. This organization also published two valuable reference aids in the late 1970s and early 1980s, namely, the *Directory of Officials of the Republic of Cuba,* and the *Chronology,* various years. All are unclassified.

There are some excellent sources on certain specialized topics. Seymour Menton's *Prose Fiction of the Cuban Revolution* (Austin, Tex., 1975) discusses literature and its social and political setting. On labour, see Maurice Zeitlin's *Revolutionary Politics and the Cuban Working Class* (New York, 1970) and Carmelo Mesa-Lago, *The Labor Sector and Socialist Distribution in Cuba* (New York, 1968). Juan and Verena Martínez Alier, in their *Cuba: economía y sociedad* (Paris, 1972), are especially helpful on the early social, political and economic background of agrarian questions, and on gender and colour.

11. THE DOMINICAN REPUBLIC SINCE 1930

There are few academic studies of the changes which have taken place in the Dominican Republic during the last sixty years, and these generally devote more attention to the political process than to the evolution of economy and society.

On the antecedents and origins of the Trujillo era there are two important political histories: Luis Felipe Mejia, *¡De Lilís a Trujillo Historia* *contemporánea de la República Dominicana* (Caracas, 1944), and Víctor Medina Benet, *Los responsables* (Santo Domingo, 1976). Both excellent monographs are based partially on the documented memoirs of the authors, who were witnesses to the fall of President Horacio Vásquez and were present when Trujillo conspired to seize power and establish his dictatorship. The outstanding book on the Trujillo regime is Jesús de Galíndez, *La era de Trujillo. Un estudio casuístico de una dictadura hispanoamericana* (Santiago de Chile, 1956), which began as a doctoral dissertation at Columbia University and is full of accurate documentation, mostly official publications and newspapers. More revealing of the intimate life of the regime is Gregorio Bustamante, *Una satrapía en el Caribe* (Mexico, 1950). Bustamante is the pseudonym of José Almoina, who had earlier been Trujillo's secretary. Both Galíndez and Almoina were Spanish exiles from the Civil War, and both were assassinated on Trujillo's orders for having written these books. A useful text on the mechanisms used by the dictator to build his economic empire is German E. Ornes, *Trujillo: Little Caesar of the Caribbean* (New York, 1958). Also interesting for its psychological interpretation of the dictator is Juan Bosch, *Trujillo: causas de una tiranía sin ejemplo* (Caracas, 1959). Both authors partially rely on Albert Hicks, *Blood in the Streets: The Life and Rule of Trujillo* (New York, 1946), an important but sensationalist journalistic version that seems to have been based on an article by C. A. Thompson, 'Dictatorship in the Dominican Republic', *Foreign Policy Reports* 12 (15 April 1936), the first study of Trujillo's commercial and financial manipulations and the establishment of his monopolies. For a critical biography and history of his regime, the best book published to date is Robert D. Crassweller, *Trujillo: The Life and Times of a Caribbean Dictator* (New York, 1966). It is exciting reading and its documentation is impeccable. Howard Wiarda, *Dictatorship and Development: The Methods of Control in Trujillo's Dominican Republic* (Gainesville, Fla., 1968), is based on interviews and newspaper sources; its content is principally political. Two Marxist interpretations of the Trujillo era are Roberto Cassá, *Capitalismo y dictadura* (Santo Domingo, 1982), and Luis Gómez, *Las relaciones de producción predominantes en la República Dominicana, 1875–1975* (Santo Domingo, 1977), which share grandiloquent theorizing and a commitment to ideological speculation. Both try to interpret the figures of the statistical series annually published by the Dominican government in the *Anuario estadístico de la República Dominicana* (Ciudad, Trujillo, 1936–1956, a task in which Gómez fails lamentably and Cassá struggles with better luck while arriving at some farfetched conclusions.

The pro-Trujillo bibliography is extraordinarily abundant, as can be verified from Emilio Rodríguez Demorizi, *Bibliografía de Trujillo* (Ciudad Trujillo, 1955), which contains more than five thousand citations of articles, books and pamphlets published in praise of the dictator and his work during the first twenty-five years of his regime. In this mountain of publications very few, if any, academic works stand out. That most resembling an academic study is Joaquín Balaguer, *La realidad dominicana: semblanza de un país y de su régimen* (Buenos Aires, 1947), although it is in reality a tendentious apology for Trujillo in the context of a pessimistic and extreme racist interpretation of Dominican history. This book was written as part of the propaganda campaign launched to justify the murder of the Haitians in 1937 and to explain the Dominicanization of the frontier. It reviews a large part of the ideology of Trujillo's regime and condenses the official vision of the economic and social problems of the 1940s. It would have remained almost forgotten had not Balaguer reedited and published it again under the new title *La isla al revés* (Santo Domingo, 1985). Another book by Balaguer on Trujillo is *La palabra encadenada* (Mexico, 1975), which is important as a psychological portrait of Trujillo despite its tendentious, falsifying and self-justificatory contents. The third volume of Ramón Marrero Aristy, *La República Dominicana: origen y destino del pueblo cristiano más antiguo de América* (Ciudad Trujillo, 1958), the conclusion to an official history of the country, outlines the dictatorship's ideology and explains the providential presence of Trujillo as the 'saviour' of Dominican nationality. Trujillo himself tried to provide a systematic ideological justification for his regime in *Fundamentos y política de un régimen* (Ciudad Trujillo, 1959).

Relations between Trujillo and the United States are described in Pope Atkins and Larman Wilson, *The United States and the Trujillo Regime* (New Brunswick, N.J., 1972), although the authors could have taken more advantage of the voluminous documentation they handled in the National Archives of the United States in Washington, D.C. Bernardo Vega, *Los Estados Unidos y Trujillo; colección de documentos del Departamento de Estado y las Fuerzas Armadas Norteamericanas* (Santo Domingo, 1982–6), has started the publication of a series of volumes which attempt to gather the Dominican-American diplomatic documentation between 1930 and 1961. A Trujilloist and anti–North American interpretation of relations at the end of dictatorship is given in Arturo Espaillat, *Trujillo: The Last Caesar* (Chicago, 1964). Marlin D. Clausner, *The Dominican Republic: Settled, Unsettled, Resettled* (Philadelphia, 1973), also mentions aspects of

Dominican-American relations before and after Trujillo, with special emphasis on the development of education and agriculture. José Israel Cuello, *Documentos del conflicto Dominico-Haitiano de 1937* (Santo Domingo, 1985), has published the diplomatic and confidential correspondence of the Dominican government produced by the Ministry of Foreign Relations as a result of the genocide of the Haitians in 1937, on which see also Juan Manuel García, *La matanza de los haitianos: genocidio de Trujillo, 1937* (Santo Domingo, 1983).

The transition of dictatorship to a new, more democratic political order has been studied in exacting detail by Howard Wiarda, *Dictatorship, Development and Disintegration: Politics and Social Changes in the Dominican Republic,* 3 vols. (Ann Arbor, Mich., 1975). Another of Wiarda's works, which records the efforts at building a democratic order after Trujillo's death in 1961, is *The Dominican Republic: A Nation in Transition* (New York, 1969). Most books on the twenty-five years or so since the end of the dictatorship deal mainly with political changes and the struggles between parties or civil–military relations. Some have as their principal setting the civil war of 1965. Important among these are John Bartlow Martin, *Overtaken by Events: The Dominican Crisis from the Fall of Trujillo to the Civil War* (Garden City, N.Y., 1966), the memoirs of a special ambassador of the United States to the Dominican Republic; Juan Bosch, *The Unfinished Experiment: Democracy in the Dominican Republic* (New York, 1964); Abraham F. Lowenthal, *The Dominican Intervention* (Cambridge, Mass., 1971), which presents a detailed account of decision-making in the United States; Jerome Slater, *Intervention and Negotiation* (New York, 1970); Piero Gleijeses, *The Dominican Crisis: The 1965 Constitutionalist Revolt and the American Intervention* (Baltimore, 1978), which offers an excellent interpretation and an extraordinary mass of new details on the civil war not covered by other authors. Gleijeses' view of the military intervention is radical and close to the Dominican nationalist position. A nationalist interpretation is Eduardo Latorre, *Política Dominicana contemporánea* (Santo Domingo, 1975), which tends to see the Dominican political process as the result of tension between the traditional forces embodied in *caudillismo* and modernizing forces represented by liberal and democratic populism. Another useful work which presents the view of the anti-Trujilloist exiles is Nicolás Silfa, *Guerra, traición y exilio,* (Barcelona, 1980, 1981). The inner conflicts and the social organization of the constitutionalist forces during the civil war are described in José A. Moreno, *Barrios in Arms* (Pittsburgh, 1970).

On the events following the civil war of 1965, several works deserve to be mentioned: José Israel Cuello, *Siete años de reformismo* (Santo Domingo, 1973), written to oppose the regime of Joaquín Balaguer; Pope Atkins, *Arms and Politics in the Dominican Republic* (Boulder, Colo., 1981), a revealing study of the relations between President Balaguer and the military between 1966 and 1978, based on primary and private sources; Roberto Cassá, *Los doce años* (Santo Domingo, 1986), a Marxist study of Balaguer much inclined to interpretive theorizing; Ian Bell, *The Dominican Republic* (Boulder, Colo., 1981), a general history written by a former British ambassador; Howard Wiarda and Michael Kryzanek, *The Dominican Republic: A Caribbean Crucible* (Boulder, Colo., 1982), which introduces the reader to contemporary party politics.

On the Dominican economy after 1961, Julio César Estrella, *La moneda, la banca y las finanzas de la Republica Dominicana* (Santo Domingo, 1971), still stands out as a general but rather unbalanced monetary history. A useful although apologetic study on the earlier part of the Balaguer regime is the little book by Eduardo Tejera, *Una década de desarrollo económico dominicano 1963–1973* (Santo Domingo, 1975). An equally useful interpretation of the impact of recent economic policy-making is Miguel Ceara Hatton, *Tendencias estructurales y coyunturales de la economía dominicana 1968–1983* (Santo Domingo, 1985), which has a structuralist slant. A Marxist study from the *'dependentista'* school is provided in Wilfredo Lozano, *El reformismo dependiente* (Santo Domingo, 1985), which contains a rich mixture of speculation with some statistical data. Also important are the serial publications produced by the Oficina Nacional de Planificación, the Banco Central de la República Dominicana, and the Oficina Nacional de Estadística. Complementing those sources are the three volumes published in the mid-1970s by the Comisión de Economía de la Academia de Ciencias de la República Dominicana, *Economía Dominicana* (Santo Domingo, 1975, 1976 and 1977). As part of a series of thirty volumes containing studies on contemporary socio-economic and political issues published between 1982 and 1988, Frank Moya Pons (ed.), *Los problemas del sector externo en la República Dominicana* (Santo Domingo, 1982), *El régimen de incentivos en la economía Dominicana* (Santo Domingo, 1983), *La situación cambiaria en la República Dominicana* (Santo Domingo, 1984) and *Causas y manejo de la crisis económica Dominicana* (Santo Domingo, 1986), brings together up-to-date studies and discussions about the origins and management of the Dominican economic crisis, external debt and the economic policies of the governments of Balaguer, Guzmán and Jorge Blanco.

Other recent studies of the structural socio-economic and political changes after Trujillo include: Isis Duarte, *Capitalismo y superpoblación en Santo Domingo* (Santo Domingo, 1980), which treats the demographic implications of underdevelopment, urbanization and migration from a Marxist perspective; José Luis Alemán, *27 ensayos sobre economía y sociedad dominicana* (Santiago de los Caballeros, 1982); Frank Moya Pons, *El pasado Dominicano* (Santo Domingo, 1986), which contains several historical studies on the problems of modernization in the Dominican Republic in the twentieth century; and Rosario Espinal, *Autoritarismo y democracia en la política Dominicana* (San José, 1987), which deals with the evolution of the Dominican political system between 1930 and 1986 from the perspective of the dynamics of the political parties.

Several important unpublished doctoral dissertations deserve mention: Gustavo Segundo Volmar, 'The Impact of the Foreign Sector on the Domestic Economic Activity of the Dominican Republic from 1950 to 1967', (Columbia University, 1971); Howard Wiarda, 'The Aftermath of Trujillo Dictatorship: The Emergence of a Pluralistic Political System in the Dominican Republic' (University of Florida, 1965); Rosario Espinal, 'Classes, Power and Political Change in the Dominican Republic' (Washington University, Mo., 1985); Rafael Francisco de Moya Pons, 'Industrial Incentives in the Dominican Republic 1880–1983', (Columbia University, 1987). Bibliographical works include: Howard Wiarda, *Materiales para el Estudio de la Política y el Gobierno de la Republica Dominicana, 1930– 1966* (Santiago de los Caballeros, 1966); Deborah Hitt and Larman Wilson, *A Selected Bibliography of the Dominican Republic: A Century after the Restoration of Independence* (Washington, D.C., 1968); and Wolff Grabendorff, *Bibliographie zu Politik und Gelellschaft der Dominikanischen Republik: Neuere Studien 1961–1971* (Munich, 1973). A recent and very useful economic bibliography is Banco Central de la República Dominicana, *Biblografía Económica de la República Dominicana* (Santo Domingo, 1984). Frank Moya Pons has compiled a *Bibliografía nacional dominicana* (forthcoming) with more than sixteen thousand items which amount to nearly all books and pamphlets published on the Dominican Republic up to 1985.

12. HAITI SINCE 1930

In 1973 the Scarecrow Press published an appendix to Max Bissainthe's *Dictionnaire de bibliographie haïtienne* (Washington, D.C., 1951); together they still represent the best bibliography of works on Haiti and by Haitians. Kraus International has recently published *The Complete Haitiana 1900–1980* (New York, 1982), edited by Michel Laguerre. Mention should also be made of Max Manigat, *Haitiana, 1971–1975* (LaSalle, Quebec, 1980), and vol. 39 in the World Bibliographical Series, compiled by Frances Chambers, *Haiti* (Oxford, 1983). There is, in addition, a useful bibliography of works on Haiti in English and *Kréyol* by Robert Lawless, 'Bibliography on Haiti', published as Occasional Paper No. 6 of the Center for Latin American Studies, University of Florida (Gainesville, 1985).

General works dealing with the period from 1930 to the present include David Nicholls, *From Dessalines to Duvalier: Race, Colour and National Independence in Haiti* (Cambridge, 1979), and especially the last four chapters, which looks particularly at the social and political thought of the period; Lyonel Paquin, *The Haitians: Class and Color in Politics* (New York, 1983), which is primarily concerned with the period since 1930. A popular and somewhat journalistic account of the Haitian past is given in Robert Rotberg, *Haiti: The Politics of Squalor* (Boston, 1971). Robert Debs Heinl, who was in charge of the U.S. Marines' mission to Haiti in the early years of the Duvalier regime, has written, with Nancy Heinl, a highly ethnocentric and anecdotal history of Haiti: *Written in Blood: The Story of the Haitian People* (Boston, 1978).

Rayford Logan's *Haiti and the Dominican Republic* (London, 1968) is a useful volume and specially strong on relations of Haiti with the United States. Other works concentrating on Haiti's foreign relations include Leslie F. Manigat, *Haiti of the Sixties: Object of International Concern* (Washington, D.C., 1964), and Robert Tomasek, 'The Haitian-Dominican Republic Controversy of 1963 and the Organisation of American States', *Orbis* 12 (1968).

Dealing particularly with literary and cultural developments in the period are J. Michael Dash, *Literature and Ideology in Haiti, 1915–1961* (London, 1981), and *Haiti and the United States: National Stereotypes and the Literary Imagination* (New York, 1988). See also Ulrich Fleischmann, *Ideologie und Wirklichkeit in der Literatur Haitis* (Berlin, 1969); *Kréyol* trans., *Ideyoloji ak reyalite nan literati ayisyen* (Geneva, 1981). René Depestre, *Bonjour et adieu à la négritude* (Paris, 1980), and Laënnec Hurbon, *Culture et dictature en Haïti* (Paris, 1979), consider Haitian culture from a historical standpoint. Frère Raphael Berrou and Pradel Pompilus have produced a revised and enlarged edition of their *Histoire de la littérature Haïtienne* (Port-au-Prince, 1975), which is a somewhat uncritical and didactic but nevertheless useful manual. Léon François Hoffmann, in *Le nègre romantique* (Paris, 1973), more recently in *Le roman haïtien* (Princeton, 1982) and in a number of articles in *Caribbean Review* and elsewhere, has greatly added to our knowledge and appreciation of the Haitian literature of this period. Two short monographs on J. S. Alexis have appeared in recent years: Michael Dash, *Jacques Stéphen Alexis* (Toronto, 1975) and Maximilien Laroche, *Le romancero aux étoiles* (Paris, 1978). Claude Souffrant deals with Jacques Roumain and J. S. Alexis, together with the U.S. poet Langston Hughes, in *Une négritude socialiste* (Paris, 1978).

Robert Spector, *W. Cameron Forbes and the Hoover Commissions to Haiti (1930)* (Lanham, Md., 1985), contains some useful information, but lacks sophisticated analysis. The best book on the U.S. occupation remains Hans Schmidt, *The United States Occupation of Haiti, 1915–1934* (New Brunswick, N.J. 1971), a superb critical study of U.S. policies in Haiti. Schmidt, however, deals only incidentally and somewhat inadequately with Haitian reactions to the occupation. Kern Délince, *Armée et politique en Haiti* (Paris, 1979), contains useful historical information.

Works on the Duvalier period range from the lurid account of Bernard Diederich and Al Burt, *Papa Doc: Haiti and Its Dictator* (London, 1970), to the rather dull collection edited by Charles Foster and Albert Valdman, *Haiti – Today and Tomorrow* (Lanham, Md., 1984). More recently the Latin America Bureau has published *Haiti: Family Business* (London, 1985). See also James Ferguson *Papa Doc, Baby Doc* (London, 1987), both of which provide useful accounts of the Duvalier dictatorship. More analytical is Michel-Rolph Trouillot, *Les racines historiques de l'état duvaliérien* (Port-au-Prince, 1986). Some chapters in David Nicholls, *Haiti in Caribbean Context* (London, 1985), also deal with the modern period.

Roger Dorsinville, *Marche arrière* (Outremont, Quebec, 1986), takes the form of extended interviews with the veteran intellectual, who recalls and comments on the post-1930 years. Also in the biographical mode is Patrick Bellegarde-Smith's study of his grandfather Dantès Bellegarde, a major figure in the cultural and political life of Haiti during this period: *In the Shadow of Powers: Dantès Bellegarde in Haitian Social Thought* (Atlantic Highlands, N.J., 1985). Other biographical studies include two books by Carlo A. Désinor, *L'affaire Jumelle* (Port-au-Prince, 1987), and *Daniel* (Port-au-Prince, 1986), on populist leader Daniel Fignolé.

Although there is still no good economic history of Haiti, a number of works approach the Haitian economy from an historical perspective. These include Mats Lundahl's two books, *Peasants and Poverty: A Study of Haiti* (London, 1979), and *The Haitian Economy: Man, Land and Markets* (London, 1983), as well as Christian Girault, *Le commerce du café en Haïti: habitants, spéculateurs et exportateurs* (Paris, 1981). The growth of the small trade-union movement is outlined in Jean-Jacques Doubout and Ulrich Joly, *Notes sur le développement du mouvement syndical en Haïti* (n.p., 1974).

Several works have recently appeared on Haitian migration. Maurice Lemoine deals with the migration of Haitian cane-cutters to the Dominican Republic in *Sucre amer: esclaves aujourd'hui dans les Caraïbes* (Paris, 1981; English trans., London, 1985), as does Ramón Antonio Veras in *Inmigración, Haitianos, Esclavitud* (Santo Domingo, 1983). The massacre of Haitians by Trujillo is the subject of Juan Manuel García, *La matanza de los haitianos: genocidio de Trujillo, 1937* (Santo Domingo, 1983); Jose I. Cuello has edited *Documentos del conflicto dominicano–haitiano de 1937* (Santo Domingo, 1984). Another important migration is considered in Dawn Marshall, *'The Haitian Problem': Illegal Migration to the Bahamas* (Kingston, Jamaica, 1979). There are numerous articles on Haitian migration to North America; these are reviewed by Robert Lawless, 'Haitian Migrants and Haitian Americans: From Invisibility into the Spotlight', *Journal of Ethnic Studies* 14, no. 2 (1986).

13. PUERTO RICO SINCE 1940

Much of the raw material for the history of Puerto Rico since 1940 is buried in the statistics gathered by various agencies of the commonwealth government. Puerto Rico is probably one of the most 'measured' societies in Latin America. The statistics are generally reliable, if copious and not always easily available. The yearly Economic Reports to the Governor, published by the Planning Board, are a useful source of basic information on the economy, as are the monthly reports on employment and unemployment put out by the Department of Labor and Human Resources. The Division of Social Planning of the Planning Board has published a number of special reports and studies; an example is its 1974 study 'Informe Recursos Humanos: Puerto Rican Migrants, a Socio-economic Study'. The annual reports of the important government agencies, such as the Departments of Public Education, Commerce, Agriculture, Labor and Human Resources, and Fomento and the Electoral Commission, are sources of useful, though undigested, data. The *Report of the United States–Puerto Rico*

Commission on the Status of Puerto Rico (August, 1966), with its supplementary background papers, is a major source of information on Puerto Rico as well as a crucial document in itself.

Gordon K. Lewis, *Puerto Rico: Freedom and Power in the Caribbean* (New York, 1963), is a standard work on modern Puerto Rico. A supplement and update to that book are the author's *Notes on the Puerto Rican Revolution* (New York, 1975). An important recent general work on Puerto Rico, from a 'neutral', European point of view, is Raymond Carr, *Puerto Rico: A Colonial Experiment* (New York, 1984).

The story of the New Deal in Puerto Rico and the political events of the 1930s are chronicled in Thomas Mathews, *Puerto Rican Politics and the New Deal* (Gainesville, Fla., 1960). For the origins of the PPD, its ideological orientations and its early history, see Robert W. Anderson, *Party Politics in Puerto Rico* (Stanford, 1965). For the war years (1940–5), R. G. Tugwell, *The Stricken Land* (New York, 1947) is essential reading. A good description of Governor Tugwell's administration is to be found in Charles Goodsell, *The Administration of a Revolution: Executive Reform in Puerto Rico Under Governor Tugwell, 1941–1946* (Cambridge, Mass., 1965). The history of the policy of industrial incentives under the Tugwell administration during the Second World War is described in detail in David Ross, *The Long Uphill Path* (San Juan, 1976). On the process leading up to the passage of the law authorizing direct elections for governor of Puerto Rico in 1948, see Surenda Bhana, *The United States and the Development of the Puerto Rican Status Question, 1936–1948* (Lawrence, Kans., 1975). And on constitutional and economic developments generally in the post-war period, see Henry Wells, *The Modernization of Puerto Rico* (Cambridge, Mass., 1969).

On economic and development policy in the contemporary period an interesting and critical view is Richard Weisskoff, *Factories and Food Stamps: The Puerto Rican Model of Development* (Baltimore, 1985). On party politics, Kenneth Farr, *Personalism and Party Politics: Institutionalization of the Popular Democratic Party of Puerto Rico* (Hato Rey, 1973), contains mainly descriptive material. Volume 2 of Bolívar Pagán's *Historia de los partidos políticos puertorriqueños* (San Juan, 1972) contains some information on the post-1940 period, but largely anecdotal and quite unsystematic. A view of local party structure is given in Angel Quintero Rivera, *El liderato local de los partidos políticos en el estudio de la política puertorriqueña* (Río Piedras, 1970) and Rafael Ramírez, *El arrabal y la política* (Rio Píedras,

(Panama, 1975). Among the best biographies are Manuel Octavio Sisnett, *Belisario Porras o la vocación de la nacionalidad* (Panama, 1959); Carlos Manuel Gasteazoro, *El pensamiento de Ricardo J. Alfaro* (Panama, 1981); Baltasar Isaza Calderón, *Carlos A. Mendoza y su generación* (Panama, 1982); and Gil Blas Tejeira, *Biografía de Ricardo Adolfo de la Guardia* (Panama, 1971). The brief *Florencio Harmodio Arosemena, 1872–1945* by Bey Mário Arosemena (Panama, 1982), is also useful.

The Arias Madrid brothers have received much biographical attention. The best is J. Conte Porras, *Arnulfo Arias Madrid* (Panama, 1980), a careful study which gives much valuable information in the appendices. Felipe J. Escobar, *Arnulfo Arias o el credo panameñista: ensayos psico-patológicos de la política panameña* (Panama, 1946) is a remarkable text by a participant-observer. Mélida Ruth Sepúlveda, *Harmodio Arias Madrid: El hombre, el estadista y el periodista* (Panama, 1983), is based on interviews with family members and personal papers. A memoir critical of the Arias brothers' administrations is Demetrio Porras, *Veinte años de luchas y experiencias* (Buenos Aires, 1947).

More general studies that cast light on Panama's social history are John and Mavis Biesanz's excellent *The People of Panama* (New York, 1955); Daniel Goldrich, *Sons of the Establishment* (Chicago, 1966); and Omar Jaén Suárez, *La población del Istmo de Panamá del siglo XVI al siglo XX* (Panama, 1978). Michael Conniff, *Black Labor on a White Canal: Panama, 1904–81* (Pittsburgh, 1985), details the experience of the West Indian immigrant community and its descendants. A thoughtful assessment of social integration appears in Alfredo Castillero Calvo, *La sociedad panameña: historia de su formación e integración* (Panama, 1970). The story of the Kuna rebellion is told by James Howe in 'Native Rebellion and U.S. Intervention in Central America: The Implications of the Kuna Case for the Miskito', *Cultural Survival Quarterly 10, no. 1* (1986): 59–65. Donald Lee DeWitt, 'Social and Educational Thought in the Development of the Republic of Panama, 1903–1946', (unpublished Ph.D. dissertation, University of Arizona, 1972), provides a good intellectual history of Panama. Finally, Nestor Porcell's survey research is presented in *El panameño actual y otros ensayos* (Panama, 1986).

The Torrijos era has been the object of many analyses. Rómulo Escobar Bethancourt, *Torrijos: Colonia americana, no!* (Bogotá, 1981) is based on a great deal of first-hand information but the most authoritative treatment is given in Steve C. Ropp, *Panamanian Politics: From Guarded Nation to National Guard* (New York, 1982). Renato Pereira, *Panamá: fuerzas arma-*

das y política (Panama, 1979), based upon the author's doctoral thesis at the Sorbonne, contains much information and fresh interpretation. On civil rights violations under Torrijos, see the Inter-American Human Rights Commission report *Informe sobre la situación de los derechos humanos en Panamá* (Washington D.C., 1978). George Priestly, *Military Government and Popular Participation in Panama: The Torrijos Regime, 1968–1975* (Boulder, Colo., 1986), attempts to build a theory of military populism.

Panama's recent economic experience is explored in World Bank, *Panama: Structural Change and Growth Prospects* (Washington, D.C., 1985), and in Robert E. Looney, *The Economic Development of Panama* (New York, 1976). Historical material on the banana industry is found in *Revista Lotería* 242 (1976), and in Humberto E. Ricord et al., *Panamá y la frutera* (Panama, 1974). A great deal of economic information is also contained in Omar Jaén Suárez, *Geografía de Panamá* (Panama, 1985).

First attempts to analyse the crisis of the late 1980s can be found in John Weeks, 'Panama: The Roots of Current Political Instability', *Third World Quarterly*, no. 9 (1987): 763–87, and John Weeks and Andrew Zimbalist, 'The Failure of Intervention in Panama: Humiliation in the Backyard', *Third World Quarterly*, no. 11 (1989): 1–27.

15. THE PANAMA CANAL ZONE, 1904–79

The best existing bibliography on the subject is Wayne Bray, *The Controversy over a New Canal Treaty Between the United States and Panama: A Selective Annotated Bibliography of United States, Panamanian, Colombian, French, and International Organization Sources* (Washington, D.C., 1976). Another extremely useful work of reference is the third volume of Marjorie Whiteman (ed.), *Digest of International Law* (Washington, D.C., 1964). The most comprehensive collection of documentary material is Library of Congress, Congressional Research Service, *Background Documents Relating to the Panama Canal* (Washington, D.C., 1977). An indispensable primary source is the series edited in the Department of State since 1861 and successively entitled *Papers Relating to the Foreign Relations of the United States*, *Foreign Relations of the United States: Diplomatic Papers* and *Foreign Relations of the United States*. See also the *Annual Report* of the chairman of the Isthmian Canal Commission for the years 1904 to 1914, of the governor of the Panama Canal for the years 1914 to 1951, and of the president of the Panama Canal Company for the years 1951 to 1979 (Washington, D.C., 1904–79).

General secondary works include Alfred Richard, 'The Panama Canal in American National Consciousness, 1870–1922, (unpublished Ph.D. dissertation, Boston University, 1969); William McCain, *The United States and the Republic of Panama* (Durham, N.C., 1937), valuable though dated; and, more recently, Walter LaFeber, *The Panama Canal: The Crisis in Historical Perspective* (New York, 1978), and David Farnsworth and James McKenny, *U.S.-Panama Relations, 1903–1978: A Study in Linkage Politics* (Boulder, Colo., 1983). See also Herbert Knapp and Mary Knapp, *Red, White and Blue Paradise: The American Canal Zone in Panama* (San Diego, 1985). Ronald Landa, 'U.S. Policy Toward Panama, 1903–present. Questions of Recognition and Diplomatic Relations and Instances of U.S. Intervention: A Tabular Summary', *Department of State Bulletin* 70 (22 April 1974), offers a succinct résumé. The view from Panama may be sampled in two books: Ricardo Alfaro, *Medio siglo de relaciones entre Panamá y los Estados Unidos* (Panama, 1959); and Ernesto Castillero Pimentel, *Panamá y los Estados Unidos* (Panama, 1953). On the canal itself, see Richard Baxter, *The Law of International Waterways with Particular Regard to Interoceanic Canals* (Cambridge, Mass., 1964), and the standard work by Norman Padelford, *The Panama Canal in Peace and War* (New York, 1942). The legal status of the Canal Zone is well treated by Martha Shay, 'The Panama Canal Zone: In Search of a Juridical Identity', *New York University Journal of International Law and Politics* 9 (1976): 15–60; also useful is Edwin Hoyt, *National Policy and International Law: Case Studies from American Canal Policy* (Denver, Colo., 1967). On engineering problems, see Miles DuVal, 'Isthmian Canal Policy–An Evaluation', *U.S. Naval Institute Proceedings* 81(1955): 263–75.

On social relations between Zone and republic, three publications are particularly worthy of note: John and Mavis Biesanz, *The People of Panama* (New York, 1955); Michael Conniff, *Black Labor on a White Canal: Panama, 1904–1981* (Pittsburgh, 1985); and Ramón Carillo and Richard Boyd, 'Some Aspects of Social Relations between Latin and Anglo Americans on the Isthmus of Panama', *Boletín de la Universidad Interamericana de Panamá* 2 (1945): 703–84.

On relations between the United States and Colombia before 1903, see the history of isthmian interventions recorded by Colby Chester, 'Diplomacy of the Quarterdeck', *American Journal of International Law* 8 (1914): 443–76. Miles DuVal, *Cadiz to Cathay: The Story of the Long Diplomatic Struggle for the Panama Canal* (Stanford, 1947), and Gerstle Mack, *The Land Divided: A History of the Panama Canal and Other Isthmian Canal*

Projects (New York, 1944), both retain their value. Another graphic account of nineteenth-century canal development may be found in David McCullough, *The Path Between the Seas: The Creation of the Panama Canal 1870–1914* (New York, 1977). More specific is Dwight Miner, *The Fight for the Panama Route: The Story of the Spooner Act and the Hay–Herrán treaty* (New York, 1940). One of the best insights into the mind of Theodore Roosevelt may be found in the first seven volumes of Elting Morison (ed.), *The Letters of Theodore Roosevelt* (Cambridge, Mass, 1951–54); see also Frederick Marks, 'Morality as a Drive Wheel in the Diplomacy of Theodore Roosevelt', *Diplomatic History* 2 (1978): 43–62. Relations from the Colombian point of view are extensively treated in Eduardo Lemaitre, *Panamá y su separación de Colombia* (Bogotá, 1971).

The Panamanian revolution of November 1903 and the consequent canal treaty with Washington are considered in the following: Bernard Weisberger, 'The Strange Affair of the Taking of the Panama Canal Zone', *American Heritage* 27 (October 1976): 6–11, 68–77, a good, popular account; Richard Turk, 'The United States Navy and the 'Taking' of Panama, 1901–1903', *Military Affairs* 38 (1974): 92–8, and John Nikol and Francis Xavier Holbrook, 'Naval Operations in the Panamanian Revolution of 1903', *American Neptune,* 37 (1977): 253–61; both of which examine the U.S. Navy's role. See also Richard Lael, *Arrogant Diplomacy: U.S. Policy Toward Colombia, 1903–1922* (Wilmington, Del., 1987). Philippe Bunau-Varilla, *Panama: The Creation, the Destruction, and Resurrection* (London, 1913), a long self-justification, is to be taken with a great deal of salt, as is Theodore Roosevelt, 'How the United States Acquired the Right to Dig the Panama Canal', *Outlook* 99 (September-December 1911): 314–18. See also the supremely self-righteous speech by Elihu Root, 'The Ethics of the Panama Question', in *Addresses on International Subjects* (Cambridge, Mass., 1916). For a more balanced view, see Charles Ameringer, 'Philippe Bunau-Varilla: New Light on the Panama Canal Treaty', *Hispanic American Historical Review* 46 (1966): 28–52 and John Major, 'Who Wrote the Hay-Bunau-Varilla Convention?', *Diplomatic History* 8 (1984): 115–23. On the response of American public opinion, see Terence Graham, *The "Interests of Civilization"? Reaction in the United States Against the "Seizure" of the Panama Canal Zone, 1903–1904* (Lund, Sweden, 1983).

The first generation of U.S. tenure, from 1904 to 1929, is unevenly covered. The most intensive treatment is reserved for the construction era, for which see the works previously cited by Mack, *The Land Divided,* and McCullough, *The Path Between the Seas*. Also important as a history of canal building is Miles DuVal, *And the Mountains Will Move: The Story of the Building of the Panama Canal* (Stanford, 1947). And see Jerome Laval, *Panama and the Building of the Canal: Photographs from the Keystone–Mast Stereograph Collection* (Fresno, Calif., 1978).

On the canal in U.S. strategy, William Adams, 'Strategy, Diplomacy and Isthmian Canal Security, 1890–1917', (unpublished Ph.D. dissertation, Florida State University, 1974); Richard Challener, *Admirals, Generals and American Foreign Policy, 1898–1914* (Princeton, 1973); and Robert Seager, *Alfred Thayer Mahan: The Man and His Letters* (Annapolis, 1977). The issue of canal administration is dealt with by George Washington Goethals, *Government of the Canal Zone* (Princeton, 1915), a candid apologia, and by Alfred Chandler, 'Theodore Roosevelt and the Panama Canal: A Study in Administration', in Elting Morison (ed.), *The Letters of Theodore Roosevelt*, vol. 6 (Cambridge, Mass., 1952): 1547–57. The involvement of the United States in Panamanian politics is treated by Ralph Minger, *William Howard Taft and United States Foreign Policy: The Apprenticeship Years, 1900–1908* (Urbana, Ill., 1975) and by Gustavo Mellander, *The United States in Panamanian Politics: The Intriguing Formative Years* (Danville, Ill., 1971).

There is so far little of substance on the years 1914 to 1929, but the following are useful: George Baker, 'The Wilson Administration and Panama, 1913–1921', *Journal of Inter-American Studies* 8 (1966): 279–93; Thomas Leonard, 'The United States and Panama: Negotiating the Aborted 1926 Treaty', *Mid-America* 61 (1979): 189–203; and Hugh Gordon Miller, *The Isthmian Highway: A Review of the Problems of the Caribbean* (New York, 1929).

On the period 1930 to 1955, one of the best studies is unpublished: Almon R. Wright, 'The United States and Panama, 1933–1949', Department of State, Bureau of Public Affairs, Research Project No. 499 (August 1952). The question of the 1936 treaty and its aftermath is fully covered in Lester Langley, 'The United States and Panama, 1933–1941: A Study in Strategy and Diplomacy', (unpublished Ph.D. dissertation, University of Kansas, 1965), and the impact of Franklin Roosevelt in John Major, 'F.D.R. and Panama', *Historical Journal* 28 (1985): 357–77. Military matters are handled in Stetson Conn and Byron Fairchild, *Guarding the United States and Its Outposts. {The U.S. Army in World War II: The Western Hemisphere}* (Washington, D.C., 1964) and in two unpublished works, U.S. Army, Caribbean Defense Command, Historical Section, *History of the Panama Canal Department*, 4 vols. (Quarry Heights, CZ,

1947), and Kathleen Williams, *Air Defense of the Panama Canal, 1 January 1939–7 December 1941*, Army Air Forces Historical Studies No. 42 (Washington, D.C., 1946). See also on this theme Almon Wright, 'Defense Site Negotiations Between the United States and Panama, 1936–1948', *Department of State Bulletin* 27 (11 August 1952): 212–19.

For the post-war years the following are valuable: John Major, 'Wasting Asset: The U.S. Re-assessment of the Panama Canal, 1945–1949', *Journal of Strategic Studies* 3 (1980): 123–46, and ' "Pro mundi beneficio"? The Panama Canal as an International Issue, 1943–8', *Review of International Studies* 9 (1983): 17–34; and Charles Fenwick, 'Treaty of 1955 Between the United States and Panama', *American Journal of International Law* 49 (1955): 543–7.

On the final years of the Canal Zone, Margaret Scranton, 'Changing United States Foreign Policy: Negotiating new Panama Canal Treaties, 1958–1978', (unpublished Ph.D. dissertation, University of Pittsburgh, 1980), is valuable. In the wake of the 1964 riots two interesting symposia were published: Lyman Tondel (ed.), *The Panama Canal. Background Papers and Proceedings of the Sixth Hammarskjöld Forum* (Dobbs Ferry, N.Y., 1965), and Georgetown University, Center for Strategic Studies, *Panama Canal: Issues and Treaty Talks* (Washington, D.C., 1967). A first-hand account of the treaty-making process in the 1970s is provided by William Jorden, *Panama Odyssey* (Austin, Texas, 1984). Two detailed studies of the U.S. debate over the treaties have recently appeared: George Moffett, *The Limits of Victory: The Ratification of the Panama Canal Treaties, 1977–1978* (Ithaca, N.Y., 1985), and J. Michael Hogan, *The Panama Canal in American Politics: Domestic Advocacy and the Evolution of Policy* (Carbondale, Ill., 1986). See also William Furlong and Margaret Scranton, *The Dynamics of Foreign Policymaking: The President, the Congress and the 1977 Panama Canal Treaties* (Boulder, Colo., 1984), and G. Harvey Summ and Tom Kelly (eds.), *The Good Neighbors: America, Panama and the 1977 Canal Treaties* (Athens, Ohio, 1988). Perhaps the most reasoned case against the treaties has been put by Paul Ryan, *The Panama Canal Controversy: United States Diplomatic and Defense Interests* (Stanford, 1977), and for the Carter administration the best vindication is Cyrus Vance, *Hard Choices: Four Critical Years in Managing America's Foreign Policy* (New York, 1983). See also Sol Linowitz, *The Making of a Public Man: A memoir* (Boston, 1985). The texts of the treaties have been published by the Department of State, Bureau of Public Affairs, Office of Media Services, *Texts of Treaties Relating to the Panama Canal* [Selected Documents No. 6A] (Washington, D.C., 1977). The debate in the Senate and the various amendments to the treaties are available in the three volumes of U.S. Congress, Senate, Committee on the Judiciary, Subcommittee on the Separation of Powers, *Panama Canal Treaties {United States Senate debate}* 1977–78 (Washington, D.C., 1978). The Panama Canal Act of 1979 can be found in full in U.S. Statutes at Large, *Public Law 96–70 of 27 September 1979: The Panama Canal Act of 1979* [93 Stat. 452] (Washington, D.C., 1979). The legislative history of the act is in volume 2 of U.S. Code, *Congressional and Administrative News: 96th Cong., 1st Sess., 1979* (Washington, D.C., 1980).

INDEX